The Politics of Making Kinship

The Politics of Making Kinship

Historical and Anthropological Perspectives

Edited by Erdmute Alber, David Warren Sabean, Simon Teuscher, and Tatjana Thelen

NEW YORK · OXFORD
www.berghahnbooks.com

First published in 2023 by
Berghahn Books
www.berghahnbooks.com

© 2023, 2025 Erdmute Alber, David Warren Sabean, Simon Teuscher,
and Tatjana Thelen
First paperback edition published in 2025

All rights reserved. Except for the quotation of short passages
for the purposes of criticism and review, no part of this book
may be reproduced in any form or by any means, electronic or
mechanical, including photocopying, recording, or any information
storage and retrieval system now known or to be invented,
without written permission of the publisher.

Library of Congress Cataloging-in-Publication Data
Names: Alber, Erdmute, editor. | Sabean, David Warren, editor. | Teuscher, Simon, editor. | Thelen, Tatjana, editor.
Title: The politics of making kinship : historical and anthropological perspectives / edited by Erdmute Alber, David Warren Sabean, Simon Teuscher, and Tatjana Thelen.
Description: First Edition. | New York : Berghahn Books, 2023. | Includes bibliographical references and index.
Identifiers: LCCN 2022028514 (print) | LCCN 2022028515 (ebook) | ISBN 9781800738003 (Hardback) | ISBN 9781800737853 (eBook)
Subjects: LCSH: Political science--Anthropological aspects. | Kinship--Political aspects. | Political anthropology.
Classification: LCC GN492 .P664 2023 (print) | LCC GN492 (ebook) | DDC 306.83--dc23/eng/20220816
LC record available at https://lccn.loc.gov/2022028514
LC ebook record available at https://lccn.loc.gov/2022028515

British Library Cataloguing in Publication Data
A catalogue record for this book is available from the British Library

EU GPSR Authorized Representative
LOGOS EUROPE, 9 rue Nicolas Poussin, 17000, LA ROCHELLE, France
Email: Contact@logoseurope.eu

ISBN 978-1-80073-800-3 hardback
ISBN 978-1-83695-076-9 paperback
ISBN 978-1-83695-214-5 epub
ISBN 978-1-80073-785-3 web pdf

https://doi.org/10.3167/9781800738003

Contents

List of Illustrations	viii
Acknowledgments	x
Introduction. Politics of Making Kinship Erdmute Alber, David Warren Sabean, Simon Teuscher, Tatjana Thelen	1
Part I. Epistemologies	23
Chapter 1. Quantifying Generation: Peter Damian Develops a New System of Kinship Calculation *Simon Teuscher*	29
Chapter 2. Kinship Matters: Genealogical and Historiographical Practices between 1750 and 1850 *Michaela Hohkamp*	53
Chapter 3. Race and Kinship: Anthropology and the "Genealogical Method" *Staffan Müller-Wille*	79
Chapter 4. Kinship Meets Corporation: Perspectives on Kinship and Politics in the Formative Moment of Social Anthropology *Thomas Zitelmann*	114

Chapter 5.
German Kinship: Forming a Political Unit and an Epistemic Void   144
Tatjana Thelen

Part II. Projects   167

Chapter 6.
Making Family and Kinship: Reflections on Hegel and Parsons   172
David Warren Sabean

Chapter 7.
Conceptualizing Kinship in Sixteenth-Century Political Theories:
Bodin's and Hotman's Ideas of Monarchy   204
Julia Heinemann

Chapter 8.
Commonwealths of Affection: Kinship, Marriage, and Polity in
Eighteenth- and Nineteenth-Century America   235
Susan McKinnon

Chapter 9.
Toward a Political Economy of the Maternal Body: Claiming
Maternal Filiation in Nineteenth-Century French Feminism   262
Caroline Arni

Part III. Deployments   291

Chapter 10.
Inventing the Extended Family in Colonial Dahomey/Benin   296
Erdmute Alber

Chapter 11.
"As If Begotten and Born of Freeborn Parents": Indicators and
Considerations on Parentalization of Emancipated Slaves in the
Post-Roman Occident   324
Ludolf Kuchenbuch

Chapter 12.
From Natural Difference to Equal Value: The Case of Egg Donation
in Norway   354
Marit Melhuus

Chapter 13.
Family and Kinship in Early Modern Contractarian State Theories   377
Jon Mathieu

Chapter 14.
Translating the Family   398
Claudia Derichs

Index   417

Illustrations

Figures

Figure 1.1. Two different methods of counting degrees. Created by Simon Teuscher.   34

Figure 1.2. Legendre's reconstruction of the diagram used by Peter Damian. Cf. Legendre, *Dossier*, 135. Pierre Legendre, *Leçons IV, suite: Le Dossier occidental de la parenté; Textes juridiques indésirables sur la généalogie*, in collaboration with Anton Schütz, Marc Smith, and Yan Thomas. Paris: Fayard, 1988. Used with permission.   39

Figure 3.1. Pedigree forming part of a series covering the genealogy of the "Western Tribe of Torres Straits." The pedigree contains cross-references ("see 3," etc.) to the other pedigrees in the series, the whole series thus constituting one continuous genealogy. Source: A. C. Haddon et al., *Sociology, Magic and Religion of the Western Islanders*, table 1A.   84

Figure 3.2. Part of Lewis Henry Morgan's "schedule" inquiring for kinship terms in a foreign language and their English translation. Source: Lewis Henry Morgan, *Circular in Reference to the Degrees of Relationship among Different Nations*, Smithsonian Miscellaneous Collections (Washington, DC: Smithsonian Institute, 1860).   86

Figure 3.3. Diagram illustrating a notation system that Francis Galton used to compile pedigrees of "eminent" individuals. Source: Francis Galton, *Hereditary Genius: An Inquiry into Its Laws and Consequences* (London: Macmillan, 1869), 52.   89

Table

Table 13.1. Haller's 1816 Sample of Contractarian State Theories.   380

Acknowledgments

The idea for this book first emerged through the lively discussions within the interdisciplinary research group 'Kinship and Politics: Rethinking a Conceptual Split and Its Epistemic Implications in the Social Sciences' at the Center for Interdisciplinary Research (ZIF) in Bielefeld (https://www.uni-bielefeld.de/(en)/ZiF/FG/2016Kinship). We thank all the fellows and guests of the research group who shared their insights with us during ten months in Bielefeld. Our thanks go to the ZIF, which made it possible and financed two workshops in which we discussed the chapters of the book. Thanks also to Jennifer Rasell for coordinating and helping us in Bielefeld in the preparation for this volume; Daniel Flaumenhaft for copy editing; Nadja Bscherer, Radoslaw Kawalek, Julia Malik, and Hanna Vietze for their support with formatting and preparing the final manuscript and Nathalie Büsser for arranging the index. We also thank the Universities of Bayreuth, Vienna, Zürich, and UCLA for financial support.

The editors

Introduction
Politics of Making Kinship

Erdmute Alber, David Warren Sabean, Simon Teuscher, and Tatjana Thelen

To Western observers, kinship and politics, seemingly not distinguished in "underdeveloped" or "premodern" societies, are and ought to be kept separate from each other in modern states. Development specialists, economists, bureaucrats, and social scientists widely endorse this view. But this is not the whole story. Kinship has neither completely disappeared from the political cultures of the West nor played the determining social and political role elsewhere that has been ascribed to it. This volume explores political and academic issues that arise once the sharp divide between kinship and politics is no longer taken for granted. Its aim is to demonstrate how political processes have shaped concepts of kinship over time and, conversely, how political projects have been shaped by specific understandings, idioms, and uses of kinship.

Under the particular historical conditions of modern Western states, kinship came to be conceptualized by anthropologists and historians as a form of archaic social and political organization no longer necessary or even present in modern public life. Kinship was thought by its very nature to have always supported particularized interests, inimical to the generalized and rational aims of bureaucratic states. For modern societies, the "public" came to designate the space where politics was enacted, laws were made for everyone, and general interests prevailed.[1] In contrast, the "private" constituted a sphere of special interests, the place where families pursued their concerns without giving heed to the good of the whole.

Social scientists, colonial administrators, missionaries, and other observers developed the thesis that "primitive" or "premodern" societies were based on kinship, an idea that became part of the nineteenth- and twentieth-century colonial imaginary that justified domination by more "advanced" societies and underscored the idea that a central feature of modernization was severing the connection between obligations to kin and economic and political participation. From the Enlightenment onward, kinship within Europe was privatized and relegated to the sphere of domestic relations and became associated with ever-more-articulated distinctions of gender in which it was coded "female." Its projection outward associated masculinity with conquest over feminized colonial subjects, while internally it became an instrument to stem the tide of women's demands for political participation.

In the social and political sciences, modern political life has been articulated within the public sphere and analyzed through its institutions: modern bureaucracies, parliaments, courts, civil society, and journalism and other forms of mass communication. Politics and kinship have come to be thought of as separate domains, each with its own principles of operation. While states may, for example, intervene in definitions of property and play a role in how wealth and property are distributed, the transmission of property between generations itself has been relegated to the private sphere, although Thomas Piketty and Melinda Cooper among others have recently brought such issues into clearer focus.[2]

However, the issue of how to articulate the interplay of kinship and politics in Western states or in states outside the West then becomes a central conceptual problem. We cannot brush it off with simplistic notions of "corruption," the illegitimate incursion of family interests into government, or "kinship in the wrong place."[3] It is time for kinship and family to be reintegrated into political theory, as they were in the early modern West. The erasure of kinship from politics is clearly superficial, an ideological pretension with far-reaching epistemological implications. It may be true that political offices less often follow lines of descent or alliance, but wealth certainly continues to and is therefore at the heart of the political order.[4] As the *New York Times* put it a decade ago: "The vast expansion of the government over past century has embedded marriage into all areas where the state and the individual intersect, from tax obligations to disability benefits to health care decisions to family law."[5] All of this suggests a project: how to reconceptualize kinship(s) and political orders.

Kinship, as it emerged as a scientific concept toward the end of the nineteenth century and was elaborated during the next half century by anthropologists and historians, was decisively tied to an exercise of mapping that concerned terminologies of relations of descent and alliance and their visual representation. This often had a jural cast, tracing a set of rights and duties determined by the circumstances of birth. The networks of kinship were conceptualized as offering the possibility of social regulation, even when no state in the modern sense was present. Indeed, it was assumed that no state was needed to carry on political life where kinship embraced all aspects of society. Social scientists and historians often worked with the hypothesis, whether explicit or implicit, that "pre-state" societies were regulated by ties of kinship, which was given precedence over voluntary, friendship, neighborhood, or even household ties.[6]

In this set of assumptions, premodern or "developing" societies were opposed to modern, developed ones—that is, small polities with large kinship groups to large states with small family units. Once the family was relegated to the private field of particular interests with specific claims on privatized property, and its small size gave it no weight in political life, kinship was no longer seen as playing a role in the modern, rational polity or having any legitimate claim to its public goods. The spatial distinction between private and public translated into a temporal succession: kinship was conceptualized as always coming "before" and as linked to "traditional" or "past" societies. As a few necessary functions and hazy claims remained, the West adopted the word "family" to designate its own institutions and to differentiate them from its own past and from other societies where the claims of kin prevailed.

After sociologists came to be seen as specialists of modernization and concerned themselves with the (primarily Western) kind of family characterized from the 1940s as the "nuclear family," historians turned their interests toward issues of social change; whether they took on kinship or family depended on whether they studied premodern or modern societies. Anthropology continued to deal with stateless forms of political organization or with polities defined by hereditary power. With kinship, as a characteristic of the "savage" other, outsourced to anthropology or relegated to the premodern in historiography, the two disciplines came to face similar problems of rethinking the political and reassessing kinship.

Toward the end of the twentieth century, the construction of kinship and the (modern) state as inherently independent units of analysis was increasingly challenged within anthropology and history, both theoretically and empirically. Historians have looked at long-term processes in Western state development and reconfigurations of structural features in Western kinship.[7] Meanwhile anthropologists have critiqued the conceptual separation between kinship and the state and started to examine their coevolution in significant new contexts, ranging from new forms of reproduction to issues of care, citizenship, and transnational migration.[8] These shifts in thinking are already underway in efforts to overcome the polarity between kinship, with its prerational or irrational or particularistic attributes, and what counts for political life in modern states. This volume addresses the problem of how to reconceptualize kinship and politics by examining some ways in which their interaction led to them mutually constituting each other. Since historians and anthropologists are both in the process of overcoming the constricting paradigms of traditional-society-with-kinship and modern-society-without-kinship, it goes without saying that an exchange of conceptual shifts and empirical findings can help break down obsolete assumptions in both disciplines and open up significant new territories for investigation. In the following, we trace some lines of discussion in both disciplines. We do not intend to give a comprehensive history of kinship debates in anthropology and history; instead, we concentrate on issues that have proved to be central in fueling debates and embed them in the political contexts of their emergence.

Categories, Comparison, Change: Debating Kinship in Anthropology

Kinship has been a fundamental topic in anthropology. In the formative period of the discipline during the second half of the nineteenth century, some key categories were framed that continued to mark scholarship for the following century and a half. Sexual reproduction was a core concern, along with questions of historical evolution and societal reproduction. How had kinship been implicated in the evolution of politics, and how had the modern state evolved out of earlier forms of political organization? Asking these questions implied an understanding of kinship as preceding state politics and entailed searching for forms of organization without central rule. Unarticulated political interests underlay the scientific interests of nineteenth-century European and American scholars. Audra Simpson has diagnosed an anthropological desire at that time "for order, for purity, for fixity and cultural perfection," which became translated into practices of documentation and theorization.[9] She demonstrates that processes of authenticating the Iroquois contributed to the making of the new category of "Indian" in the emergent nation of the United States of America. She argues that this internal other was needed to shape the political self-understanding as a settler nation. In particular, Simpson emphasizes the role of one of the founders of the academic discipline of anthropology, the lawyer turned anthropologist

Lewis Henry Morgan (1818–81). Morgan's anthropological career began with a specific interest in the political and kinship organization of the Iroquois. This work mirrored, as she argues, the desire to construct a stable and coherent tradition of a society seen as non-Western, as part of making a unit comparable through difference.[10] While Morgan's large-scale comparative work *Systems of Consanguinity and Affinity of the Human Family* (1870) assumed a universal principle of procreation, it also needed to identify differences so readers could understand the particular set of principles behind each cultural form, classify their structures, and study them in relation to each other. This agenda contributed to the shaping of a research methodology that ignored history as well as contemporary political processes.

Morgan established two of the central topics for subsequent research regarding politics and kinship. In *Systems*, he devised a set of protocols for comparing kinship throughout the world; in *Ancient Society* (1877), published seven years later, he arranged these systems in an evolutionary schema with the Western form of kinship representing the highest, most rational stage so far.[11] Adopting an evolutionary perspective allowed Western observers to differentiate themselves from societies organized without state institutions and for which kinship seemed to be the necessary mechanism.[12]

This tension between stability, change, and difference would constitute a recurrent topic of anthropological debates. During the 1930s and 1940s, many British anthropologists studying Africa, culminating with E. E. Evans-Pritchard and Meyer Fortes's *African Political Systems* (1940), tried to identify a range of societies that could be understood as kinship-based and to which the term *politics* in the modern Western sense did not apply. Certainly, their vision was continually questioned by other anthropologists, notably the "Manchester School" founded by Max Gluckman in 1947 in a string of important ethnographies.[13] Nonetheless, Evans-Pritchard and Fortes's synthesis led for some time to a trend within social and cultural anthropology of specializing either in political or kinship anthropology and more or less separating the two from one another.[14]

Evans-Pritchard's most prominent study on Nuer politics, conducted only twenty years before much of Africa became independent, was firmly embedded within the British colonial endeavor that sought to "pacify" the region. Perhaps that is why he presented Nuer as without political leadership, downplaying recent changes brought about by (among others) spiritual leaders. In this respect, it is interesting that German, French, and Italian anthropologists each highlighted different aspects of the region's political organization. Not only would the variety of diagnoses attest to different theoretical understandings but the diversity would also reflect the political needs of their home countries. Subsequently, central debates in anthropology have circled around how to approach comparison, the questionable neutrality of its methods, the intellectual origins of its instruments, and the ways classification schemes have been and can be used in colonial contexts, nation building, and political conflict. A good example is the "genealogical method" formalized by W. H. R. Rivers (1864–1922), which generations of ethnographers used as a research tool in their fieldwork.[15] In 1984, the American cultural anthropologist David Schneider attacked this method's claims for neutrality by insisting that Rivers had confused social and physical relationships and finally imposed English kin terminologies on all societies.[16] Schneider argued that kinship studies assumed notions of biological reproduction that were by no means universal.

Meanwhile, Rodney Needham, in his introduction to the edited volume *Rethinking Kinship and Marriage* (1971), had already asked whether there was a separate field of human action or universally shared form that could be called kinship.[17] This critique was extended by Mary Bouquet, who in 1993 insisted that kinship theory, especially as it had developed among British anthropologists, depended on the genealogical method formulated by Rivers, which she considered bound up by British middle-class assumptions about pedigree. According to her, kinship studies in essence imposed provincial categories elaborated in British universities on the rest of the world.[18]

Following the fundamental critique of earlier kinship studies, large-scale comparisons and classification became increasingly questioned in anthropology. One author who still held to them in the second half of the twentieth century was Jack Goody, whose wide-ranging comparative project later influenced historical research. Goody distinguished Eurasian and African types of societies and related differences of property and marriage systems to ecological differences. This became the basis for his reflections on marriage prohibitions in medieval Europe (see below).

A further way of looking at kinship as a means of constructing difference was developed by French structuralism. In dialogue with structural linguistics, Claude Lévi-Strauss (1908–2009) looked for a formal grammar of kinship and enduring mental structures as the shared basis of humanity, upon which differences among human societies rested. The political context influenced a nostalgic undertone of regret for the loss of cultural diversity through processes of modernization and change.[19]

Diachronic traces in the work of Claude Lévi-Strauss became most apparent in his category of *société à maison* (house society), introduced subsequent to his great 1949 work on the elementary structures of kinship.[20] As earlier anthropologists, he developed this concept around property, which he proposed instead of biology as the organizing principle of human sociality. House societies were interpreted as an intermediary form between simple societies organized by kinship and complex ones organized by class and contract. As such, medieval European dynasties and the local perpetual establishments (houses) of the native Kwakiutl of Vancouver Island were understood as jural entities (*personnes morales*) lasting for several generations and holding duties and rights of both material and symbolic value. To Lévi-Strauss, houses were both institutions and fetishizations of relationships. Although house societies might use the language of kinship to express forms of social organization, such forms followed a different logic: perpetuating the internal hierarchies of local domination.

The concept of house societies allowed phenomena of transition to be addressed but was fundamentally understood as a step in the long story of kinship's decline in the West and reinstated the presumption, otherwise largely discarded, of a uniform, unidirectional development path all societies and polities must take. Later anthropologists took up the topic of "house societies" and used it to overcome the stalemate Schneider's critique of kinship had produced. In this literature, modeling flexible domestic relationships provided an alternative to the idea of societies organized through descent (lineages). For example, Susan McKinnon used it to rethink Evans-Pritchard's model of the patrilineal Sudanese Nuer society, asking what would happen if the complexities he described in his empirical work that contrasted with his somewhat static theoretical model were seen not through the lens of lineage but as a house society.[21]

The concepts of the house and house societies were seen, in anthropology, as a closer understanding of lived, flexible relationships and, later, as a paradigmatic example of the entanglements between persons, places, and biographies.[22] For a while, taking the house as an appropriate unit of analysis seemed to offer an alternative to the dead end of kinship research in anthropology. With an empirical focus on immediate, tangible interactions and material dimensions that mediate relationships, the concept contributed to increasing presentism within anthropology at the expense of long-term perspectives. However, in the meantime, new political agendas related to changing family configurations in the West again led to a renewed interest in kinship. From the late 1980s, reproductive technologies, transnational and queer families, and (transnational) adoption increased awareness of the political constitution and implications of kinship. Ethnographic studies of these configurations put more explicit emphasis on the political.[23] In addition, focusing on shifting configurations in the West has been one step toward challenging naturalizing assumptions of a preexisting kinship that was always already there.

In sum, tracing some anthropological paths of thinking about kinship reveals the concept's political implications. The development of categories of analysis and attempts to compare societal formations often served as a means for self-reassurance and political engineering. Though framed as neutral, categorizing kinship established its anteriority to politics and had long-lasting epistemological implications. It also contributed to constructions of difference and the reproduction of political hierarchies, as in the case of Iroquois and other colonial settings or when degrees of kinship are deployed to measure racial and national purity.[24] In the next section, turning to the use of these kinship categories and concepts in historical research, we can see similar topics and discussions around difference and change, the universal and particular, and the development of adequate tools and epistemological approaches reappearing.

Decline, Denial, and Reconsiderations of the Modern: Kinship in History

It may seem ironic that the topic of kinship began to preoccupy historians of the West just as kinship studies in anthropology had come under fundamental critique. But in many ways these moves were complementary. Since the 1970s, anthropologists had become hesitant to examine kinship—at least by using the old methods and categories—both because of the category's inherent Westernism and the methodological shortfalls, for example, of the genealogical method. During the 1960s and 1970s, historians discovered the need to take kinship into account as a crucial aspect of modern Western societies, from the analysis of which kinship had long been excluded systematically. These turns in each discipline worked toward overcoming a divide between societies with kinship and societies with state politics.

In general, historians have long been hesitant to address kinship as a concept that was made and changed over time, spaces, and disciplines. Some historians agreed explicitly with the older anthropological assumption that kinship structures in non-Western societies around the world were a basic part of those cultures that had always been there, and many more agreed implicitly. Regardless of the period in question, they tended to assume that whenever their research begins, kinship was just about to lose its former importance or strength. The pattern of placing kinship in a position of anteriority was particularly marked among historians relying on theories of modernization. Treating kinship as quintessentially traditional—as the other of modernity—they followed sociological and modernization theories, as well as a related disciplinary distribution of labor that attributed kinship to those dealing with traditional societies: thus, anthropology. Wherever kinship mattered in the past or still matters in the present, this was read as an indicator that modernity and the related process of political democratization had not yet (at least fully) set in.

Assumptions about the anteriority of kinship were common even in the least theoretical historical literature. We have read time and again that associations, insurance schemes, childrens' and old age care, and many other phenomena of the West in the nineteenth and twentieth centuries had become necessary to replace practices of social security that had previously been assured by the solidarity and cohesion among kin. Historians have argued that political institutional processes such as the formation of guilds or city councils had already become necessary in the Middle Ages because kin groups had lost their former sway over local societies. With the transition to the early modern period, the emergence of the state was explained by societies no longer being able to rely on structures of kinship to meet their needs. And this again resonated with the assumptions of anthropologists who saw societies organized in states as those in which kinship tended to fade out. For the longest time, no attempt at examining the long-term development had exposed the inconsistency of a historiography, in which assumed decline seems to recur in period after period, and each time explaining presumed change.

The temporality ascribed to kinship blocked research from asking about its making. History, as it had emerged as an academic discipline in the nineteenth century, had a bias for objects that evolved over time. Unlike archaeologists, anthropologists, and folklorists, historians felt no particular impetus to examine what had been left behind in the process. Accordingly, they had long been more inclined to dwell on the history of the family with a teleological perspective that saw the modern nuclear family or the loving couple at the end. The assumption went that the nuclear family, with an emphasis on emotional bonds, had been formed in the process of modernization. Ideas about the dominance of kin groups, including residential patterns involving several generations of a patriline in premodern Europe, had already been developed by the pioneers of empirical-historical social research, including Frédéric le Play in France and Wilhlem Riehl in Germany.[25] For many historians, small families were an intermediary phase on the path toward a full-fledged individualism. And for most of them, these emerged as older structures built around more extended kin disintegrated.

Although Jack Goody's hypotheses followed the same pattern in many ways, they triggered the first major debate about how systems of kinship are created, shaped, and made rather than simply handed down. Goody examined the rapid extension of ecclesiastic marriage prohibitions in Europe during the Central Middle Ages. Put very simply, he argued that the Catholic Church pushed these prohibitions ever further in order to undermine the marriage and inheritance strategies of noble kin groups. By reshaping kinship around radical prescribing of exogamous marriage, the argument went, the church aimed at diverting the flow of property away from the next generation and to itself. In the course of the last decades, critics have whittled away most elements of Goody's arguments one by one. But in the process, productive debates emerged about the ways in which different actors, including local noblemen, their dependent monasteries, and royal administrations, competed for the authority to define, shape, license, and sanction kin relations. These discussions opened eyes to the possibility of change in kinship structures rather than pure decline; to political debates, contentions, and manipulations these could give rise to; and, last but not least, to how kinship itself, as a way of seeing, naming, and doing relationships, was made and transformed.

The most prominent early attempts at examining transformations in rather than a decline of kinship are associated with Karl Schmid and Georges Duby, both historians of the nobility in the Western Middle Ages.[26] Whereas Goody pointed to interferences between political interests and kinship at the level of large institutions ("the Church") and broad social groups ("the nobility"), Duby and Schmitt related transformations to forms of domination on the ground, on the local level. This was the level that had become relevant after the large realms of the heirs of Charlemagne had been fragmented—the Western embodiment of segmentary societies?

Schmid took the naming practices of the early medieval nobility—in particular a shift from the sole use of first names to a combination of first and last names that persisted over generations—as a point of departure to explore the formation of dynastic kin organization. His efforts were continued by Duby, and can be summarized as follows: during the Carolingian period (late eighth to ninth centuries), noble kin groups were primarily constructed through in-law and cousin relationships and formed extended, overlapping groups constituted by relations among living people. Such groups are sometimes described as horizontal because they were formed from genealogical ties among contemporaries, not through common ancestors.

Generational depth, in contrast, characterized the newer pattern of organization that emerged from the eleventh century onward. Here, kin organized themselves along lines of paternal descent into what could be classified as houses or dynasties. This was accompanied by a new tendency to pass on property in a direct line of successions from fathers to sons, often excluding daughters, who upon marriage joined their husband's dynasty. Only now, and as an expression of male succession, did family names begin to stabilize themselves, along with coats of arms and a notion of ancestral lands or castles. Variations of this form of kin organization, including Lévi-Strauss's *sociétés à maison*, would characterize large sections of European elites until the eighteenth century. Some historians, especially in France, followed Lévi-Strauss in understanding such house societies as signs of a transition toward more complex organization.[27]

From the perspective of our volume, questions about the Schmid-Duby thesis's soundness matter less than its status as a model case for relating transitions of the political order and kinship. For Duby and Schmid it was clear that the transition they had detected was integral to a groundbreaking political change. They related the older form of kinship to the Carolingian Empire and its successor organizations with their large-scale power structures and a comparably high degree of institutionalization. Here, some kind of relation to the emperor and his leading officers (whether through cousins or in-laws) was key to being appointed to profitable offices.

The newer form of organizing kinship was an answer to the subsequent fragmentation of large empires in the Central Middle Ages and the emergence of smaller seigneuries, often organized around castles and including landed possessions and jurisdictional and fiscal claims, as the decisive political entities. Such political units needed to be passed on undivided in order to maintain their political effectiveness. Usually, they passed from fathers to sons. They stood at the center of what was passed on from generations but could also constitute entities such as the *Geschlecht*, the *maison*, or the house. There have been many objections to the so-called Schmid-Duby transition, but to our knowledge none have fallen back on claiming kinship's anteriority to the political order. All have maintained the perspective that kin organization is integral to modes of domination and their transformation. Dynastic and house organizations came to play an important role in many regional elites in Europe up to the eighteenth century.

The extent to which the new dynastic forms were kinship in the strict sense has been disputed. Joseph Morsel, for example, has referred to Lévi-Strauss's idea of European house societies in suggesting that dynastic forms were instead an expression of power relations veiled by the language of kinship during a period characterized by a general "deparentalization"—a decreasing structuring effect of kinship on social organization.[28] However if kinship in house societies was no longer any more than a means of expressing relations determined by factors other than kinship, at what point in the history of the West had kinship been anything more than that? And how would we know? Even during the so-called Dark Ages around the year 1000, scholars in jurisprudence and theology continued to conceptualize kinship in the tradition of ancient law and philosophy, in which kinship appeared less as a domain on its own than as an aspect of the legal or political order. The question points to the broader problem of treating kinship as an autonomous domain, separate from (or prior to) politics, the law, the economy, or the distribution of power.

From the 1970s, when anthropological research on kinship had already started to be problematized and had rejected the idea of kinship and politics as separate fields of human action (see above), historians of the early modern and modern periods began to examine kin relations more broadly and to connect them with political and economic transformations. Attention to kinship became an important ingredient in many microhistories, and more generally in attempts to expand social history beyond a concern with class and conflict, to include solidarities, bonds, and emotions in political change. Detailed investigations, such as those of Christiane Klapisch, Gerard Delille, or David Sabean, were strongly inspired by anthropological kinship studies.[29] They examined the importance of kinship in local land markets, in economic production, in support of orphans and the poor, and in communal politics.

When this tradition of research began, it seemed likely that kinship mattered in premodern European societies in the past for the same reasons that it was assumed to matter in non-Western societies in the present: where formal markets, bureaucracies, and state institutions were poorly developed, kinship could be expected to assume important roles in providing local societies with coherence, solidarity, and conflict management and in organizing cooperation and structuring power relations. Empirical-historical research did indeed confirm all this. But just as anthropological research in the West confirmed the enduring importance of changing formations of kinship, historical research also made clear that kinship did anything but vanish as one moved forward on the timeline. Many historians with an interest in kinship focused on the *Sattelzeit* (1770–1830), presumably bridging the division between premodern and modern. They found that kinship was heavily implicated in developments usually associated with modernization, such as state building or class formation. David Sabean has described how kin relations up to the early eighteenth century that had been organized vertically and that connected people from different points in hierarchies began to be reoriented toward relations between people of similar status. At the same time, kin endogamous marriages became more frequent. Women's historians of the nineteenth and twentieth centuries turned to kinship to reveal areas where women exercised power and influenced politics despite their exclusion from the formal institutions of parliamentary democracies.[30] And business historians found an explanation in kinship for how early industrialism and global trade pooled capital before the emergence of investment banking.[31]

Historical approaches to kinship produced a great variety of results but little support for notions of a general decline. Most of these studies looked at small segments of society (villages, noble groups, urban patricians, or individual families), and many were committed to microhistory. Authors were more eager to challenge existing generalizations than to offer new ones. Despite a growing number of specialized investigations that pointed to the contrary, narratives of the decline of kinship remained a central element in historical explanations of modernity, the great divergence, and the societal foundations of democracy. It took much pleading to get authors of specialized studies to make an effort to examine major trends in the development of kinship that could challenge received ideas. One attempt at this was the volume *Kinship in Europe*, which suggested that the development of kinship in Western Europe between 1300 and 1900 followed two major transformations, each of which made kinship formative in new areas of interaction.[32] The first, connecting the Central Middle Ages to the early modern period, was characterized by verticality, emphasizing the perpetuation of kin groups and lineages through descent beyond the lifespan of individuals, their endowment with jural rights and duties through the devolution of property, and their power to define hierarchies through persistent practices of patronage. The other, extending from the late eighteenth century into the early twentieth, emphasized horizontal relationships, class and kin endogamous marriages, the pooling of capital over continuous successions within one line, and the provision of networks of support in partly meritocractic systems.

Common Questions

Abandoning the idea of the decline of kinship not only offers the possibility of looking at the many modifications of kinship relations connected to and sometimes caused by political change, it also opens a path to studying how kinship itself as a way of seeing, naming, and doing relationships contributes to political transformation. Asking how forms of kinship emerge and are made provides new insights into the history of state building, class formation, biopolitics, citizenship, and migration—to mention just a few examples. In this volume, we take three specific routes, asking about the development of epistemologies of kinship and their political implications, about kinship as an element in political projects, and about the deployment of kinship in political, legal, and administrative systems. These questions are deeply interrelated around issues of how to conceive of social change and difference, as the chapters in the book will show.

The chapters of the first section address the tools that support the epistemologies and conceptualizations of kinship, including diagrams, visualizations, and quantification in the form of degrees. Such devices of kinship reckoning had until recently been taken for granted and seen as neutral and thus were rarely made subjects of research. These initial examinations show us the implications that changes and continuities in their configuration and application had for politics of kinship. Furthermore, specific conceptualizations of kinship reveal some aspects of it and conceal others, with tremendous consequences for both political visions of the world and scientific epistemologies.

The chapters of the second section, on "projects," concern the use of families, households, and kinship structures to examine the workings of political and social orders and to frame cultural values and legal prescriptions. In many instances, the family has been regarded as the foundation of the state, but political theorists, social scientists, and moral philosophers also consider how the state ought to mold, shape, and regulate familial relationships. Politics and kinship are articulated at many levels, including those relating to issues of nurture, succession, hierarchies, marriage, authority, sexuality, and the distribution of wealth.

A relatively recent field of research looks at the conceptualizations of kinship in the administrative, academic, and legal venues involved in implementing political decisions. These are discussed in the third section, dealing with "deployments." As long as kinship was seen as anterior to the development of states and administrative systems, attempts by lawyers, scientists, translators, and administrators to define it received little research attention—possibly because they appeared to merely reiterate something that already existed. Once we acknowledge the dynamism of kinship, we can see such efforts as contributions to making and remaking concepts, laws, languages, and systems of kinship. Twenty-first-century legislators are still busy changing all kinds of laws; regulating surnames, adoption, and surrogacy; or adapting inheritance law to the children of same-sex couples. Although ancient concepts of marriage and filiation are far from disappearing, they can receive new meanings in the process. No modern state can leave kinship behind.

Historically, the vision of a unified kinship founded in nature itself is anything but universal. Before the eighteenth century, no one would have associated similarities and differences between species with processes of descent or kinship. When exactly this need to unify visions of kinship and descent arose in different fields and why it did still remain to be explored. Our book attempts to contribute to this by following the politics of specific epistemologies, projects, and deployments of kinship.

Erdmute Alber is professor of social anthropology at the University of Bayreuth. She co-led the research group on kinship and politics at ZIF in Bielefeld. Her books include *Transfers of Belonging* (Brill 2018) and (with Tatjana Thelen) *Reconnecting State and Kinship* (2017).

David Warren Sabean is Henry J. Bruman endowed professor of German history Emeritus and distinguished research professor of European history at the University of California, Los Angeles. He co-led the research group on kinship and politics at ZIF in Bielefeld. His books include *Kinship in Neckarhausen* (1998).

Simon Teuscher is professor of medieval history at the University of Zurich. He co-led the group on kinship and politics at ZIF in Bielefeld. His books include *Lords' Rights and Peasant Stories* (2012) and (with David Sabean and Jon Mathieu) *Kinship in Europe: Approaches to Long-Term Developments (1300–1900)* (2007).

Tatjana Thelen is professor at the Department for Social and Cultural Anthropology, University of Vienna. She co-led the group on kinship and politics at ZIF in Bielefeld. She coedited *Stategraphy: Toward a Relational Anthropology of the State* (2017) and (with Erdmute Alber) *Reconnecting State and Kinship* (2017).

Notes

1. Jürgen Habermas, *The Structural Transformation of the Public Sphere: An Inquiry into a Category of Bourgeois Society*, trans. Thomas Burger with the assistance of Frederick Lawrence (Cambridge, MA, 1989 [1962]).
2. Thomas Piketty, *Capital and Ideology*, trans. Arthur Goldhammer (Cambridge, MA: Harvard University Press, 2020); Melinda Cooper, *Family Values: Between Neoliberalism and the New Social Conservatism* (Brooklyn, NY: Zone Books, 2017).
3. Michael Herzfeld, "Corruption as Political Incest: Temporalities of Sin and Redemption," in *Reconnecting State and Kinship*, ed. Tatjana Thelen and Erdmute Alber (Philadelphia: University of Pensylvania Press, 2018), 39–60.
4. Cooper, *Family Values*, 123: "The empirical data on wealth distribution suggests that inheritance is almost as decisive at the beginning of the twenty-first century as it was in the nineteenth. This phenomenon also and inevitably entails the reassertion of the private family as a critical economic institution and a portal to social legitimacy. The fact that marriage and family formation have become the overriding concern of queer politics; the claim, axiomatic among American social policy theorists, that marriage is now a marker of class and a means to social mobility; the fact that the recreation of the private family unit has become a key ambition of welfare policy—all of these trends point to the resurgence of the family as the essential vector for the distribution of wealth and status."
5. "The Wrong Reasons for Same-Sex Marriage," op-ed, *New York Times*, 15 May 2011.
6. This singled-out status of kinship has been itself shaped in the process of knowledge production. Mainly referring to how kinship became the dominant concept at the expense of friendship and others, Marilyn Strathern, *Relations: An Anthropological Account* (Durham, NC: Duke University Press, 2020), 29ff., has argued that this shift happened in the course of the seventeenth century, when scholars like John Locke conceptualized kinship as natural relations. In consequence, friendship and civil organization emerged as contrastive concepts in the West.
7. For example: David Warren Sabean, Simon Teuscher, and Jon Mathieu, eds., *Kinship in Europe: Approaches to Long-Term Developments (1300–1900)* (New York: Berghahn Books, 2007); Christopher H. Johnson, et al., eds., *Transregional and Transnational Families in Europe and Beyond* (New York, 2011).
8. For example, Sarah Franklin and Susan McKinnon, eds., *Relative Values: Reconfiguring Kinship Studies* (Durham NC: Duke University Press 2001); Susan McKinnon and Fenella Cannell, eds., *Vital Relations: Modernity and the Persistent Life of Kinship* (Santa Fe: SAR Press, 2013); Tatjana Thelen and Erdmute Alber, eds., *Reconnecting State and Kinship* (Philadelphia: University of Pennsylvania Press, 2018); Erdmute Alber and Tatjana Thelen, eds., *Politics and Kinship: A Reader* (New York: Routledge, 2022); On the state, see Michel-Rolph Trouillot. "Anthropology of the State in the Age of Globalization," *Current Anthropology* 42, no. 1 (2001): 125–38; Akhil Gupta, "Blurred Boundaries: The Discourse of Corruption, the Culture of Politics, and the Imagined State," *American Ethnologist* 22, no. 2 (1995): 375–402; Tatjana Thelen, Larissa Vetters, and Keebet von Benda-Beckmann, *Stategraphy: Toward a Relational Anthropology of the State* (New York: Berghahn, 2018).
9. Audra Simpson, *Mohawk Interruptions: Political Life across the Borders of Settler States* (Durham, NC: Duke University Press, 2014), 69.
10. Simpson, *Mohawk Interruptions*, 69.
11. Lewis Henry Morgan, *Ancient Society (1877)* (OCR reproduction of the original by General Books LLC) (Memphis, TN, 2009): 337. "Like the successive geological formations, the tribes of mankind may be arranged according to their relative conditions,

into successive strata. When thus arranged, they reveal with some degree of certainty the entire range of human progress from savagery to civilization."
12. Among others, Friedrich Engels based his history of property and family forms directly on the work of Henry Lewis Morgan. Friedrich Engels, *The Origins of the Family, Property, and the State* (Chicago: CH Kerr & Co, 1902). German original: *Der Ursprung der Familie, des Privateigentums und des Staates*, Im Anschluss an Lewis H. Morgans Forschungen (Hottingen-Zürich, Verlag der Schweizerischen Volksbuchhandlung, 1884).
13. On the Manchester School, see Richard Werbner, *Anthropology after Gluckman: The Manchester School, Colonial and Postcolonial Transformations* (Manchester: Manchester University Press, 2020): 3. He claimed that given its high heterogeneity, its character of a "school" could only be confirmed from an outsider's perspective.
14. Edmund Leach, *Pul Eliya, A Village in Modern Ceylon: A Study in Land Tenure and Kinship* (Cambridge: Cambridge University Press, 1961). But see Maurice Godelier, *The Metamorphoses of Kinship*, trans. Nora Scott (London: Verso, 2011 [2004]), 484. "It is no longer possible to assert, as so many anthropologists did for over a century, that so-called 'primitive societies,' that is, societies without castes or classes and without a state, were 'kin based.' There has never been any such thing as 'kin-based' societies, except in the anthropology and sociology textbooks. But to affirm this is not to claim, as Leach did, that kinship is merely a language or veil, or worse an invention on the part of anthropologists and therefore of the West."
15. William H. R. Rivers, "The Genealogical Method of Anthropological Inquiry," *Sociological Review* 3 (1910): 1–12. Some of these instruments and their visualizations still remain popular, as we can see in the activities of the amateur genealogists analyzed by Elisabeth Timm. See Elisabeth Timm, "Ich bin Glied einer Kette": Entgrenzung, Personalisierung und Gouvernementalität von Verwandtschaft am Beispiel der populären Genealogie," in *Verwandtschaft heute*, ed. Erdmute Alber, Bettina Beer, Julia Pauli, and Michael Schnegg (Berlin: Reimer 2010): 47–71. They also remain in use in biomedical environments such as genetic counseling. See Anna Jabloner, "Relative Risks: Measuring Kiship for Future Health," *Social Analysis* 65, no. 4 (2021).
16. David M. Schneider, *A Critique of the Study of Kinship* (Ann Arbor: University of Michigan Press, 1984): 107.
17. Rodney Needham, ed., *Rethinking Kinship and Marriage* (London: Tavistock, 1971): 3–4.
18. Mary Bouquet, *Reclaiming English Kinship: Portugese Refractions of British Kinship Theory* (Manchester: Manchester University Press, 1993): 16–17. See also Mary Bouquet, "Family Trees and their Affinities: The Visual Imperative of the Genealogical Diagram," *Journal of the Royal Anthropological Institute* 2 (1996): 43–66. Later writers inevitably had considerable reservations about Schneider's and Bouquet's critiques. One example was Maurice Godelier, who insisted that the numerous genealogies that he collected from the Baruya of New Guinea were not at all a "matter of projecting our vision of consanguinity, our notions of fatherhood and motherhood. ... The notions of father, mother and siblings ... cannot mean the same thing for a Baruya as for a Western European born into a kinship system centred on the nuclear family. ... It is impossible to project one's own concept of consanguinity onto their way of thinking and living." Maurice Godelier, *Metamorphoses of Kinship* (London: Verso, 2011): 68f.
19. Lévi-Strauss was well aware of social change, but unlike the evolutionary and developmental theorists he saw it largely as a process of homogenization and a global loss of the cultural richness and diversity of non-European populations. Rejecting the colonial politics of the French state as well as the Western universalist humanism of many of his French colleagues such as Sartre, he sought to preserve human difference. See also Stefanos Geroulanos, *Transparency in Postwar France: A Critical History of the Present* (Stanford: Stanford University Press, 2017).

20. See the definition in Claude *Lévi-Strauss, The Way of the Masks (Seattle: University of Washington Press, 1982):* 194. "A corporate body holding an estate made up of both material and immaterial wealth, which perpetuates itself through the transmission of its name, its goods and its titles down a real or imaginary line considered legitimate as long as this continuity can express itself in the language of kinship or of affinity and, most often, of both."
21. Susan McKinnon, "Domestic Exceptions: Evans-Pritchard and the Creation of Nuer Patrilineality and Equality," *Cultural Anthropology* 15, no. 1 (2000): 35–83.
22. See Janet Carsten and Stephen Hugh-Jones, eds., *About the House: Lévi-Strauss and Beyond* (Cambridge: Cambridge University Press, 1995); Janet Carsten, "House-Lives as Ethnography/Biography," *Social Anthropology* 26, no. 1(2018): 103–16.
23. See, among many others, Kath Weston, *Families We Choose: Lesbians, Gays, Kinship* (New York: Columbia University Press, 1997); Susan Kahn, *Reproducing Jews: A Cultural Account of Assisted Conception in Israel* (Durham, NC: Duke University Press, 2000); Signe Howell, *The Kinning of Strangers* (New York: Berghahn Books, 2006); Deborah Brycson and Ulla Vuorela, *Transnational Families in the Twenty-First Century* (Oxford: Berg, 2002).
24. See, among others, Ann Laura Stoler, "Rethinking Colonial Categories: European Communities and the Boundaries of Rule," *Comparative Studies in Society and History* 31 (1989): 134–61; Kim TallBear, *Native American DNA: Tribal Belonging and the False Promise of Genetic Science* (Minneapolis: University of Minneapolis Press, 2013); Susan McKinnon, "The Work of the American Eugenics Record Office: Technologies for Terminating 'Degenerate' Family Lines and Purifying the Nation," *Social Analysis* 65, no. 4 (2021).
25. Frédéric Le Play, *L'Organisation de la famille selon le vrai modèle signalé par l'histoire de toutes les races et de tous les temps* (Paris, 1871); Wilhelm H. Riehl, *Die Naturgeschichte des Volkes als Grundlage einer deutschen Socialpolitik*, 2nd ed., vol. 3: *Die Familie* (Stuttgart und Augsburg, 1855).
26. Georges Duby, "Structures familiales aristocratiques en France du XIe siècle en rapport avec les structures de l'État," in *L'Europe aux IXe et XIe siècles: Aux origines des Etats nationaux*, ed. T. Manteuffel and A. Gieysztor (Warsaw: Naukowe, 1968); Georges Duby, "Lignage, noblesse et chevalerie au XIIe siècle dans la région mâconnaise: Une révision," in *Annales ESC* 27 (1972); Karl Schmid, "Zur Problematik von Familie, Sippe und Geschlecht, Haus und Dynastie beim mittelalterlichen Adel: Vorfragen zum Thema 'Adel und Herrschaft im Mittelalter,'" *Zeitschrift für Geschichte des Oberrheins* 105 (1957).
27. Elie Haddad, "Qu'est-ce qu'une 'maison'? De Lévi-Strauss aux recherches anthropologiques et historiques récentes," in *L'Homme* 212 (2014).
28. Joseph Morsel and Christine Ducourtieux, "L'histoire (du Moyen Âge) est un sport de combat ... Réflexions sur les finalités de l'Histoire du Moyen Âge destinées à une société dans laquelle même les étudiants d'Histoire s'interrogent," LAMOP/Joseph Morsel (Paris: LAMOP, 2007): 196.
29. David Sabean, "Verwandtschaft und Familie in einem württembergischen Dorf 1500 bis 1870: Einige methodische Überlegungen," in *Sozialgeschichte der Familie in der Neuzeit Europas*, ed. W. Conze (Stuttgart: E. Klett, 1976); Gérard Delille, *Famille et propriété dans le royaume de Naples (XVe – XIXe siècle)* (Rome: Ecole française de Rome 1985); Christiane Klapisch-Zuber, *La maison et le nom: Stratégies et rituels dans l'Italie de la Renaissance* (Paris: Éd. de l'École des Hautes Études en Sciences Sociales, 1990).
30. Elisabeth Joris, *Liberal und eigensinnig: Die Pädagogin Josephine Stadlin – die Homöopathin Emilie Paravicini-Blumer; Handlungsspielräume von Bildungsbürgerinnen im 19. Jahrhundert* (Zürich: Chronos, 2010); Leonore Davidoff and Cathrine Hall, *Family Fortunes: Men and Women of the English Middle Class 1780–1850* (London, Routledge, 1987).

31. See Francesca Trivellato, *The Familiarity of Strangers: The Sephardic Diaspora, Livorno, and Cross-Cultural Trade in the Early Modern Period* (New Haven, CT: Yale University Press, 2009); Simone Derix, *Die Thyssens: Familie und Vermögen*, Familie—Unternehmen—Öffentlichkeit: Thyssen im 20. Jahrhundert, Bd. 4 (Paderborn, Ferdinand Schöningh, 2016).
32. David Warren Sabean, Simon Teuscher and Jon Mathieu, ed., *Kinship in Europe: Approaches to Long-Term Development (1300–1900)* (New York: Berghahn Books, 2007). With the follow-up volumes: Christopher H. Johnson, David Warren Sabean, Simon Teuscher and Francesca Trivellato, ed., *Transregional and Transnational Families in Europe and Beyond: Experiences since the Middle Ages* (New York: Berghahn Books, 2011); Christopher H. Johnson and David Warren Sabean, eds., *Sibling Relations and the Transformations of European Kinship 1300–1900* (New York: Berghahn Books, 2011); Christopher H. Johnson, Bernhard Jussen, David Warren Sabean and Simon Teuscher, ed., *Blood and Kinship: Matter for Metaphor from Ancient Rome to the Present* (New York: Berghahn Books, 2012).

Bibliography

Alber, Erdmute, and Tatjana Thelen, eds. *Politics and Kinship: A Reader*. New York: Routledge, 2022.

Anon., "The Wrong Reasons for Same-Sex Marriage." *New York Times*, 15 May 2011.

Bouquet, Mary. *Reclaiming English Kinship: Portugese Refractions of British Kinship Theory*. Manchester: Manchester University Press, 1993.

―――. "Family Trees and Their Affinities: The Visual Imperative of the Genealogical Diagram." *Journal of the Royal Anthropological Institute* 2 (1996): 43–66.

Browner, Carole, and Carolyn Sargent, eds. *Reproduction, Globalization, and the State*. Durham, NC: Duke University Press, 2011.

Brycson, Deborah, and Ulla Vuorela. *Transnational Families in the Twenty-First Century*. Oxford: Berg, 2002.

Carsten, Janet. "House-Lives as Ethnography/Biography." *Social Anthropology* 26, no. 1 (2018): 103–16.

Carsten, Janet, and Stephen Hugh-Jones, eds. *About the House: Lévi-Strauss and Beyond*. Cambridge: Cambridge University Press, 1995.

Cooper, Melinda. *Family Values: Between Neoliberalism and the New Social Conservatism*. Brooklyn, NY: Zone Books, 2017.

Davidoff, Leonore, and Cathrine Hall. *Family Fortunes: Men and Women of the English Middle Class 1780–1850*. London: Routledge, 1987.

Delille, Gérard. *Famille et propriété dans le royaume de Naples (XVe–XIXe siècle)*. Rome: Ecole française de Rome, 1985.

Deomampo, Daisy. "Defining Parents, Making Citizens: Nationality and Citizenship in Transnational Surrogacy." *Medical Anthropology* 34, no. 3 (2015): 210–25.

Derix, Simone. *Die Thyssens: Familie und Vermögen*. Familie—Unternehmen—Öffentlichkeit: Thyssen im 20. Jahrhundert, Bd. 4. Paderborn: Ferdinand Schöningh, 2016.

Duby, Georges. "Structures familiales aristocratiques en France du XIe siècle en rapport avec les structures de l'État." In *L'Europe aux IXe et XIe siècles: Aux origines des Etats nationaux*, edited by T. Manteuffel and A. Gieysztor, 57–62. Warsaw: Naukowe, 1968.

———. "Lignage, noblesse et chevalerie au XIIe siècle dans la région mâconnaise: Une révision." *Annales ESC*, 27 (1972): 803–23.

Edwards, Jeanette, and Charles Salazar, eds. *European Kinship in the Age of Biotechnology*. New York: Berghahn Books, 2009.

Engels, Friedrich. *The Origins of the Family, Property, and the State*. Chicago: Charles H. Kerr & Co., 1902.

Franklin, Sarah, and Susan McKinnon, eds. *Relative Values: Reconfiguring Kinship Studies*. Durham, NC: Duke University Press, 2001.

Franklin, Sarah, and Helena Ragoné eds. *Reproducing Reproduction: Kinship, Power and Technological Innovation*. Philadelphia: University of Pennsylvania Press, 1998.

Geroulanos, Stefanos. *Transparency in Postwar France: A Critical History of the Present*. Stanford, CA: Stanford University Press, 2017.

Godelier, Maurice. *The Metamorphoses of Kinship*. Translated by Nora Scott. London: Verso, 2011 [2004].

Gupta, Akhil. "Blurred Boundaries: The Discourse of Corruption, the Culture of Politics, and the Imagined State." *American Ethnologist* 22, no. 2 (1995): 375–402.

Habermas, Jürgen. *The Structural Transformation of the Public Sphere: An Inquiry into a Category of Bourgeois Society*. Translated by Thomas Burger with assistance from Frederick Lawrence. Cambridge, MA: MIT Press, 1989 [1962].

Haddad, Elie. "Qu'est-ce qu'une 'maison'? De Lévi-Strauss aux recherches anthropologiques et historiques récentes." *L'Homme*, 212 (2014): 109–38.

Herzfeld, Michael. "Corruption as Political Incest: Temporalities of Sin and Redemption." In *Reconnecting State and Kinship*, edited by Tatjana Thelen and Erdmute Alber, 39–30. Philadelphia: University of Pennsylvania Press, 2018.

Howell, Signe. *The Kinning of Strangers*. New York: Berghahn Books, 2006.

Jabloner, Anna. "Relative Risks: Measuring Kinship for Future Health." In "Measuring Kinship," edited by Tatjana Thelen and Christof Lammer. Special issue, *Social Analysis* 65, no. 4 (2021).

Johnson, Christopher H., Bernhard Jussen, David Warren Sabean, and Simon Teuscher, eds. *Blood and Kinship: Matter for Metaphor from Ancient Rome to the Present*. New York: Berghahn Books, 2012.

Johnson, Christopher H., David Warren Sabean, Simon Teuscher, and Francesca Trivellato, eds. *Transregional and Transnational Families in Europe and Beyond: Experiences since the Middle Ages*. New York: Berhahn Books, 2011.

Joris, Elisabeth. *Liberal und eigensinnig: Die Pädagogin Josephine Stadlin — die Homöopathin Emilie Paravicini-Blumer; Handlungsspielräume von Bildungsbürgerinnen im 19. Jahrhundert*. Zürich: Chronos, 2010.

Kahn, Susan. *Reproducing Jews: A Cultural Account of Assisted Conception in Israel*. Durham, NC: Duke University Press, 2000.

Klapisch-Zuber, Christiane. *La maison et le nom: Stratégies et rituels dans l'Italie de la Renaissance*. Paris: Éd. de l'École des Hautes Études en Sciences Sociales, 1990.

Leach, Edmund. *Pul Eliya, a Village in Modern Ceylon: A Study in Land Tenure and Kinship*. Cambridge: Cambridge University Press, 1961.
Le Play, Frédéric. *L'Organisation de la famille selon le vrai modèle signalé par l'histoire de toutes les races et de tous les temps*. Libraire: Paris, 1871.
Lévi-Strauss, Claude. *The Way of the Masks*. Seattle: University of Washington Press, 1982.
Lammer, Christof, and Tatjana Thelen, eds. "Measuring Kinship—Negotiating Belonging." Special issue, *Social Analysis* 65, no. 4 (2021).
McKinnon, Susan, and Fenella Cannell eds. *Vital Relations: Modernity and the Persistent Life of Kinship*. Santa Fe: SAR Press, 2013.
———. "Domestic Exceptions: Evans-Pritchard and the Creation of Nuer Patrilineality and Equality." *Cultural Anthropology* 15, 1 (2000): 35–83.
———. "The Work of the American Eugenics Record Office: Technologies for Terminating 'Degenerate' Family Lines and Purifying the Nation." In "Measuring Kinship," edited by Tatjana Thelen and Christof Lammer. Special issue, *Social Analysis* 65, no. 4 (2021).
Morgan, Lewis Henry. *Ancient Society (1877)*. Memphis, TN: General Books LLC, 2009 (OCR reproduction).
Morsel, Joseph, and Christine Ducourtieux. *L'histoire (du Moyen Âge) est un sport de combat ... Réflexions sur les finalités de l'Histoire du Moyen Âge destinées à une société dans laquelle même les étudiants d'Histoire s'interrogent*. Paris: LAMOP, 2007.
Needham, Rodney, ed. *Rethinking Kinship and Marriage*. London: Travistock, 1971.
Piketty, Thomas. *Capital and Ideology*. Translated by Arthur Goldhammer. Cambridge, MA: Harvard University Press, 2020.
Riehl, Wilhelm H. *Die Naturgeschichte des Volkes als Grundlage einer deutschen Socialpolitik*. Stuttgart, Augsburg: Cotta, 1855.
Rivers, William H. R. *Kinship and Social Organisation*. London: Constable, 1914.
Rivers, William H. R. "The Genealogical Method of Anthropological Inquiry." *Sociological Review* 3 (1910): 1–12.
Sabean, David Warren. "Verwandtschaft und Familie in einem württembergischen Dorf 1500 bis 1870: Einige methodische Überlegungen." In *Sozialgeschichte der Familie in der Neuzeit Europas*, edited by W. Conze, 231–46. Stuttgart: Ernst Klett Verlag, 1976.
Sabean, David Warren, Simon Teuscher, and Jon Mathieu, eds. *Kinship in Europe: Approaches to Long-Term Developments (1300–1900)*. New York: Berghahn Books, 2007.
Schmid, Karl. "Zur Problematik von Familie, Sippe und Geschlecht, Haus und Dynastie beim mittelalterlichen Adel: Vorfragen zum Thema 'Adel und Herrschaft im Mittelalter.'" *Zeitschrift für Geschichte des Oberrheins*, 105 (1957).
Schneider, David M. *A Critique of the Study of Kinship*. Ann Arbor: University of Michigan Press, 1984.
Simpson, Audra. *Mohawk Interruptions: Political Life Across the Borders of Settler States*. Durham, NC: Duke University Press, 2014.
Stoler, Ann Laura. "Rethinking Colonial Categories: European Communities and the Boundaries of Rule." *Comparative Studies in Society and History*, 31 (1989): 134–61.

Strathern, Marilyn, *After Nature*. Cambridge: Cambridge University Press, 1992.
———. *Relations: An Anthropological Account*. Durham, NC: Duke University Press, 2020.
TallBear, Kim. *Native American DNA: Tribal Belonging and the False Promise of Genetic Science*. Minneapolis: University of Minneapolis Press, 2013.
Timm, Elisabeth. "'Ich bin Glied einer Kette': Entgrenzung, Personalisierungund Gouvernementalität von Verwandtschaft am Beispiel der populären Genealogie." In *Verwandtschaft heute: Positionen, Ergebnisse, Perspektiven*, edited by Erdmute Alber, Bettina Beer, Julia Pauli, and Michael Schnegg, 47–71. Berlin: Reimer Verlag, 2010.
Trouillot, Michel-Rolph. "Anthropology of the State in the Age of Globalization." *Current Anthropology* 42, 1 (2001): 125–38.
Tremayne, Soraya, ed. *Managing Reproductive Life*. New York: Berghahn Books, 2001.
Trivellato, Francesca. *The Familiarity of Strangers: The Sephardic Diaspora, Livorno, and Cross-Cultural Trade in the Early Modern Period*. New Haven, CT: Yale University Press, 2009.
Werbner, Richard. *Anthropology after Gluckman: The Manchester School, Colonial and Postcolonial Transformations*. Manchester: University of Manchester Press, 2020.
Weston, Kath. *Families We Choose: Lesbians, Gays, Kinship*. New York: Columbia University Press, 1991.

Part I

Epistemologies

Efforts to detect, quantify, classify, visualize, and map kin relations are the subject of the first part of this book. The chapters explore some of the political struggles, ambitions, and plain misunderstandings involved in attempts to understand kinship and to keep track of the many relations included in the concept. Few things seem to have had as great an impact on ideas of what constitutes kinship and why and where it matters as attempts to depict and define it and its use in law, administration, and science.

In some cases, such attempts consisted largely in transferring a system of categorization from one field to another. One early example involves methods Roman inheritance law deployed to measure the closeness of kin, a system consolidated by the sixth century CE. In the course of the Early and Central Middle Ages, the Catholic Church developed ever more rigid incest prohibitions, and specialists in church law found it necessary to reconfigure how they were to be applied. In the process, they developed methods of measuring kinship that not only concerned dyadic relationships but also could delineate groups as well. Staffan Müller-Wille and Jörg Rheinberger have demonstrated how heredity studies in biology have, since their beginnings in the nineteenth-century, relied on transfers of concepts of relatedness and transmission between generations from early modern inheritance law, which in turn had been influenced by the canon law on marriage prohibitions. In other words, a basic element of current scientific understandings of life depends on conceptualizations of kinship as they have developed in Western jurisprudence since late antiquity.[1]

Attempts at detecting, visualizing, and mapping kinship are usually not ends in themselves and are often linked to political goals: the implementation of ecclesiastic marriage prohibitions, the necessity to regulate the succession to a throne or to settle disputes among claimants, or the desire to define citizenship. Today, kinship is often examined as a genetic link in attempts to determine fatherhood through DNA testing or to assign individuals to ethnic origins using genetic ancestry testing; both are linked to claims on citizenship or access to resources such as inheritance or material and emotional care.[2] In scientific contexts, they are used to find out which species are "closest" to humans. Each of these individual or scientific purposes affects how kinship is politically conceptualized and reconceptualized.

Chapters in this part are concerned with epistemological efforts to map, visualize, and order kinship relations. They trace consequences that were often unforeseen in the original attempts at drawing up models. By no means were any of the technologies of representation uncontested: alternative schemas always offered different epistemological assumptions. Examining purposes, strategies, and attempts to figure out how people are related to each other and what the consequences might be for this or that connection has come to undermine the idea that kinship can be seen as its own domain: it has always been immanent in struggles for power, marking boundaries, constituting groups, and supporting or denying rights and claims. By opening up the history of depicting and defining kinship, we are able to stress that kinship has always been in the making and has depended on regulations and conventions that, however "scientific," always have political implications.

Epistemological histories of kinship confront us with unfamiliar temporalities. With a few modifications, methods of quantification that originated in ancient Rome still remain in use in present-day genetics, and diagrams of descent developed by specialists of canon law in the twelfth century were reused by biologists in the nineteenth.[3] There is no way to harmonize such observations with a rupture between traditional and modern worlds or with the idea of steady linear developments since the Middle Ages. Instead, we get loops back and forth across centuries, old techniques reused for new purposes and old framings into which new insights are fitted. In models of kinship, we find strange and as yet untangled combinations of familiarities and differences between examples from different time periods.

The contributions to this part strengthen our awareness of the significant political, social, and epistemological productiveness of methods of mapping, detecting, and defining kin relations. These methods' role in shaping kinship becomes apparent as soon as we give up ideas about its age-old character. And they are representative of the many fields in which kinship is bound up with politics.

Simon Teuscher examines two highly technical but nonetheless furious letters by Peter Damian, a theologian of the eleventh century. These letters introduced the method of calculating kinship degrees that is today often called the "Germanic method," summoning up ideas about tribal and ancient origins. Yet throughout the letters, the method emerged in the context of very specific political intentions and configurations. Peter Damian wrote as an advocate of the reform of the Catholic Church, of its emancipation from secular power and law and a severe implementation of rules for laypeople, including marriage prohibitions. In the process, Peter analyzed genealogical accounts in the Bible and relied on his own ideas of the physiology of kinship. Although his proposal might have followed the tactical considerations of the moment, it had groundbreaking implications in the long run. While kinship degrees had previously been used to measure the closeness of kinship between two people, Peter's method and new visualizations allowed for their use in delimiting groups. It thus laid the foundation for the much later use of kinship and descent to determine noble status or racial affiliation, issues that would become prominent during the fifteenth century and preoccupy scientists and scholars for centuries after.

Michaela Hohkamp raises epistemological problems related less to kinship as such than to genealogy, the central method of its description, visualization, and communication. In recent years, a growing body of work has examined how genealogy contributed to the formation of modern biology and anthropology, shaping their basic concepts, premises, and questions.[4] Hohkamp points to the—perhaps less obvious but all the more powerful—effects genealogy had on the formation of history as a modern academic discipline between the mid-eighteenth and mid-nineteenth centuries. By the second half of the eighteenth century, genealogy had become an established method of communicating, organizing, and substantiating information about the past and had high standards for providing and investigating evidence. Hohkamp presents the results of a close reading of methodological and historiographic texts by, in particular, Johann Christoph Gatterer (1727–99) and Johann Daniel Schöpflin (1694–1771). She demonstrates how their reliance on genealogy shaped the unspoken premises of a nascent discipline that sought for "true" representation and consequently reduced earlier, highly ornamented, and organic images of transmission of status and wealth in noble families and genealogies to bare diagrams lacking the earlier legal and political sidebars with extensive commentaries and explanations. By the turn of the nineteenth century, genealogy had begun to be intertwined with historiography in the form of "genealogical history." Genealogy was thought to contribute academic rigor and self-evidence to mechanisms of inclusion and exclusion in history writing: in particular, it provided a mechanism for excluding some actors based on their gender, ethnicity, or nationality and for claiming the self-evidence of territorial framings.

The contribution of Staffan Müller-Wille also emphasizes the epistemic impact of genealogy and more specifically the way in which the genealogical method emerged from classic works in anthropology. He examines Francis Galton's *Hereditary Genius* (1869), Lewis H. Morgan's *Systems of Consanguinity and Affinity* (1871), W. H. R. Rivers's "Genealogical Method of Anthropological Inquiry" (1910), and Franz Boas's *The Mind of Primitive Man* (1911). He shows that two of the discipline's central research domains were heavily shaped by genealogy: racial anthropology and social anthropology with its focus on systems of kinship. Although the two fields are profoundly different in both their objects of study and their ideological implications, they appear as two sides of the same coin in their dependence on genealogical method and metaphors of shared blood. Staffan Müller-Wille contests David Schneider's claim that classic kinship studies in anthropology necessarily naturalized relationships. Instead, he emphasizes the method's great capacity as a tool for detecting difference in order to individualize, distribute, and interrelate, operations that owe more to geometry than to biology. Throughout the discipline's history, the genealogical method has proven its exceptional versatility and been applied to the most different ideologies.

The chapter by Thomas Zitelmann examines the epistemological consequences of working with alternative concepts of kinship linked to the political order. Following the intellectual genealogies and applications of an important concept, "corporatism," from the first half of the nineteenth century, he shows how it took different ethnographic, cultural, and localized shapes among different national versions of and political ambitions linked to anthropology. Nevertheless, it remained associated with methodological collectivism, based on assumptions about collective mentalities of social groupings analogous to the physical body, or *corpus*. Particularly, within British social anthropology from the 1930s, corporatism became fundamental for imagining a unity between kinship and politics in so-called segmentary societies. British anthropologists merged the concepts of kinship and corporate groups through that of lineages. Their German colleagues who were conducting research in the same regions worked with a broader concept of community that embraced relations of blood and place as counterimages to modernity. The Romantic European legacy of the corporate group has been linked to the assumption of a third space between the family and the state that influenced not only liberal ideas but also fascist social imaginations of authoritarian rule and family life. Although apparently developing these concepts from fieldwork, here anthropologists were actually standing on the shoulders of Hegel, Maine, and Gierke, for whom that space was held by ancient and medieval corporations. Zitelmann works out the implications of the long history of collectivism for the apparatus anthropologists developed to understand the societies they visited, paying close attention to different national traditions of research and their political/colonial implications.

In the last chapter of this part, Tatjana Thelen demonstrates the long-term epistemic consequences of the conceptual split between kinship and politics with the example of Germany before and after unification. Rather than looking at how specific conceptual tools made kinship visible, she examines the role of concepts in making them undetectable. Her chapter deals with how and why the social sciences have, for the most part, ignored the extensive kinship ties across the German-German border during the Cold War, ties that were economically important, were emotionally significant, and received strong political support. The reason for this analytical blindness, she argues, lies in the understanding of modernity as characterized by the conjugal family. While in the following chapter in part 2 Sabean traces these ideas back to Hegel and Parsons, this chapter points to the consequences of this epistemological void not only for our understanding of the role of kinship in contemporary societies but also for the possibilities of social scientific critique. Building upon assumptions about modern families, scholarly discourses contrasted socialist kinship practices as "unmodern," goal-oriented, strategic behavior from "modern," emotionally structured families in the capitalist world, thereby considerably limiting the analysis. Besides being embedded in political structures, this case makes it evident how ideas and descriptions of kinship produce political classification and othering.

Notes

1. Staffan Müller-Wille and Hans-Jörg Rheinberger, "Heredity—The Production of an Epistemic Space," *Max Planck Institute for the History of Science*, preprint 276 (2004): 1–26. Staffan Müller-Wille, and Hans-Jörg Rheinberger, eds., *Heredity Produced: At the Crossroads of Biology, Politics, and Culture, 1500–1870* (Cambridge, MA: The MIT Press, 2007).
2. Katharina Schramm, "Genomics en Route: Ancestry, Heritage and the Politics of Identity across the Black Atlantic," in *Identity Politics and the New Genetics: Re/Creating Categories of Difference and Belonging*, ed. Katharina Schramm, David Skinner, and Richard Rottenburg (New York: Berghahn Books, 2012), 167–92.

3. Anna Jabloner, "Kinship, Risk, Race: Scales of Belonging in US Genetic Counseling," in "Measuring Kinship," ed. Tatjana Thelen and Christof Lammer, Special Issue, *Social Analysis* 65, no. 4 (2021): 111–30, Catherine Nash, "Genetic Kinship," *Cultural Studies* 18, no. 1 (2004): 1–33.
4. Nils Petter Hellström, "Darwin and the Tree of Life: The Roots of the Evolutionary Tree," *Archives of Natural History* 39, no. 2 (2012): 234–52; Marianne Sommer, "Population-Genetic Trees, Maps and Narratives of the Great Human Diasporas," *History of the Human Sciences* 28, no 5 (2015): 108–45; Marianne Sommer and Veronika Lipphardt, eds., "Visibility Matters: Diagrammatic Renderings of Human Evolution and Diversity in Physical, Serological and Molecular Anthropology," special issue, *History of the Human Sciences* 28, no. 5 (2015).

Bibliography

Hellström, Nils Petter. "Darwin and the Tree of Life: The Roots of the Evolutionary Tree." *Archives of Natural History* 39, no. 2 (2012): 234–52.
Jabloner, Anna. "Relative Risk: Measuring Kinship for Future Health in US Genetic Counseling." In "Measuring Kinship," edited by Tatjana Thelen and Christof Lammer. Special issue, *Social Analysis* 65, no. 4 (2021): 111–30.
Müller-Wille, Staffan, and Hans-Jörg Rheinberger. "Heredity—The Production of an Epistemic Space." *Max Planck Institute for the History of Science*, preprint 276 (2004): 1–26.
_____, eds. *Heredity Produced: At the Crossroads of Biology, Politics, and Culture, 1500–1870*. Cambridge, MA: The MIT Press, 2007.
Nash, Catherine. "Genetic Kinship." *Cultural Studies* 18, no. 1 (2004): 1–33.
Schramm, Katharina. "Genomics en Route: Ancestry, Heritage and the Politics of Identity across the Black Atlantic." In *Identity Politics and the New Genetics: Re/Creating Categories of Difference and Belonging*, edited by Katharina Schramm, David Skinner, and Richard Rottenburg, 167–92. New York: Berghahn Books, 2012.
Sommer, Marianne. "Population-Genetic Trees, Maps and Narratives of the Great Human Diasporas." *History of the Human Sciences* 28, no. 5 (2015): 108–45.
Sommer, Marianne, and Veronika Lipphardt, eds. "Visibility Matters: Diagrammatic Renderings of Human Evolution and Diversity in Physical, Serological and Molecular Anthropology." Special issue, *History of the Human Sciences* 28, no. 5 (2015).

Chapter 1

Quantifying Generation
Peter Damian Develops a New System of Kinship Calculation

Simon Teuscher

Peter Damian was only interested in kinship insofar as it helped him pursue his real preoccupation: to rationalize the allocation of love throughout the world. Nevertheless, this eleventh-century Italian monk and papal adviser must not be omitted from a history of kinship or even from a broader history of social categorization.[1] The new method of measuring the closeness of kin relations that he developed came to play a prominent role in later conceptualizations of race, ethnicity, and hereditary status and remains productive in genetics and other fields to this day. This chapter tries to understand Peter Damian's work in the context of contemporary politics and from the perspective of a history of kinship in Europe over the long term.

In current debates about kinship in both anthropology and history, a new interest in the tools and techniques of representing, mapping, testing, and measuring kin relations is emerging. This is also related to a growing skepticism as to the master narrative about the decline of kinship.[2] Accounts of modernization have long offered little room for doubt that systems of kinship originated in traditional stages of society. Changes kinship had undergone in the process of modernization, in particular in the West, tended to be categorized as a form of decline or dissolution. Based on the premise that kinship had always already existed, scholarly work on kinship appeared as mere ex post facto rationalization of ideas that were about to lose their sway anyway. Once we are open to the possibility that kinship not only is transmitted from the past but can also be crafted and transformed to some extent at any given moment, the work put into shaping understandings of kinship becomes more interesting.

While administrators and scholars are far from the only ones who have engaged in conceptualizing and reconceptualizing kinship, their work had and continues to have considerable impact and can thus be traced most easily.

The quantification of kinship in the form of degrees, a technique that would later be referred to as *computus*, is a particularly interesting case. Peter Damian systematized a new variation of computus in the midst of a struggle to emancipate the Catholic Church from secular powers and ecclesiastic norms from secular law.[3] This project included a call for rigid prohibitions of marriage between close kin.[4] The basic idea that prohibitions against marrying kin were needed to optimize the distribution of love can be traced at least back to Saint Augustine in the fourth century CE.[5] Throughout the Early Middle Ages, clerics had debated where to draw the line prohibiting marriage between consanguineous kin and in-laws. The limits were moved back and forth by leaps and bounds, most of which depended on political considerations of the moment. But seen over the long term, synods and popes ended up extending marriage prohibitions ever further.[6] By the eleventh century, most prelates agreed that these should extend as far as the seventh degree of consanguinity. But at about the same time, a fierce debate broke out on how to count these degrees and how to define the first degree—that is the zero point of kinship quantification.[7] The responses to these questions affected the range of kin that would fall within the prohibited seventh degree. And the methods of counting were tied to ideas about what kinship was and how it mattered to politics.

Peter Damian has the reputation of having promoted an unrealistically radical solution that would soon turn out to be impossible to implement.[8] Although he may simply have intended to make incest legislation as strict as possible,[9] we should not reduce his innovation to a mere extension of the range of prohibited kin. We will miss some of the most important opportunities his texts offer if we assume that the kinship he measured in a new way was exactly the same thing it had been before him or that it still continues to be the same thing today. The tools used for measuring and mapping an object affect how it is constituted. Peter Damian's revision of the measuring technique had implications both for the epistemology and the ontology of kinship.

The particular appeal of examining Peter Damian's eleventh-century texts is that they can shed a critical light on assumptions that to this day tend to remain unquestioned. These include the notion that the closeness of kinship can be quantified—measured in degrees calibrated according to acts of reproduction and infinitely traceable through both the male and female lines. These ideas seem so obvious today that we tend to ascribe them to the nature of reproduction or the logic of genes themselves. But none of these assumptions were a given or a result solely of close observation of nature. They alle were products of theological reflection and consciously developed—*made*, so to speak—at particular points in time and under particular circumstances. At first, Peter Damian's proposals met with much opposition since they clashed with other understandings of kinship. Exposing the rather tacit reconstitutions of kinship implicit in Peter Damian's work can give us some distance from our own concepts and help raise questions where we expect certainty.

The significance of Peter Damian's writings cannot be measured in terms of their immediate "impact." Although there is reason to believe that his proposal on how to quantify kinship was fairly influential during his lifetime,[10] it is perhaps more important that the ideas he developed under very specific circumstances continued to be resorted to much later, and in entirely different and no less particular circumstances. Around 1500, for instance, collegiate chapters used them as means of determining whether prospective members were of true noble descent or had "pure Christian blood." In the early modern period, colonial officers drew on them when seeking criteria for assigning individuals to racial groups.[11] And in the nineteenth century, biologists took them up to develop models of heredity. One way to grasp how old modes of thought weigh on contemporary ones is to borrow Hans-Jörg Rheinberger and Staffan Müller-Wille's notion of a history of *régimes de savoir*. With this term, they describe something that is less a concept than a way of thinking about a matter. Such regimes can emerge at a remote point in history in one field of practice (for example, marriage prohibitions) and centuries later begin to matter in a completely different one (for example, in modern concepts of heredity in the natural sciences).[12]

I shall analyze two letters Peter Damian addressed to fellow clerics. In the first, probably written around the year 1046, he followed up on some oral debates in which he had participated in Ravenna. He wrote the second several years later and dedicated it to a more specific aspect of his measuring method.[13] A third text I will quote contains a decree by Pope Alexander II (reigned 1061–73) endorsing the method of measuring kinship that Peter Damian had advocated. This decree is supported by a selection of Peter's arguments in a condensed form that is perhaps more compelling but also less exploratory than his own letters. Although the controversies among theologians and jurists about just how to measure kinship were not definitively resolved by this decree, in the twelfth century it was included in Gratian's compendium of canon law that was to become the basis of all later church law through the early twentieth century.[14]

In what follows, I shall begin by explaining the debate in which Peter Damian intervened and then present his case for defining kinship in a way that extended beyond the relations people were conscious of. Next I shall ask how Peter extracted methodological principles from authoritative texts, and finally examine the understanding of kinship implied in Peter's method and why this has affected conceptualizations of kinship up to our time.

A Vitriolic Debate

Peter wrote his first letter at the beginning of a controversy about how to measure the closeness of kin relations. On one side, jurists who had participated in the so-called rediscovery of Roman law centered in Bologna and Ravenna wanted to follow the precise prescriptions they found in Roman law as codified under Justinian in late antiquity. On the other side, a school of church reformers led by Pope Alexander II and Peter Damian argued for a system that they claimed Catholic authorities had already been applying for some time. Peter Damian's sulfurous letter hardly contributed to calming this controversy.

The dispute was fierce. At its height, Pope Alexander denounced the "perverse shrewdness"[15] of clerics from Naples, who taught the opposite method. He denounced them as "ignorant professors" who clung to their "pestilential chairs and lessons worse than stinking belches."[16] Peter Damian reported that when discussing the methods of measuring kinship in Ravenna he too experienced an "angry quarrel." He felt he was engaged in a constant war, and he mobilized metaphors of venom and disease to describe the ideas of his opponents.[17] He deplored how they continued to spread their "poison of dogmatic perversion."[18] He appealed to his readers to help stop an error that he characterized as a "pestilential cancer extending through the bowels of the church."[19] And he even hoped "that the snake of Moses would return to devour the vipers that were in the process of bewitching people."[20]

As vitriolic as this dispute was, it seems to have been confined to a narrow circle and barely extended beyond the close advisors of the pope and legal scholars. The whole debate stood out by the level of erudition displayed by participants and their subtly crafted arguments. Damian described the marriage law as a "masterly art in the church discipline," complained about the canniness with which his opponents "engaged in reasoning, in speculating, in drawing conclusions, in composing a great many jeering arguments," and promised that he himself would reciprocate with "the refined spirit (*faceta urbanitas*) of a lawyer."[21] And so he did.

If Peter's letter is to be believed, the whole debate had been triggered by a very precise, almost technical question. A messenger from the city of Florence had arrived in Ravenna to ask the city's leading jurists whether the Florentine interpretation of the prohibition of marriage up to the seventh degree was correct: there, according to the messenger, they counted four degrees up to a common ancestor along one line of descent and then three down along the other, for a total of seven. Peter was there when the jurists of Ravenna assembled to discuss how to answer the question.[22] Some supported the Florentine position by quoting the *Institutiones*, the civil law collection compiled under the Roman emperor Justinian in the sixth century: "No one can marry his brother's or his sister's granddaughter either, although she is in the fourth degree."[23] Peter was appalled to hear some of the jurists of Ravenna use this quote to support what he considered a spurious argument: "If the granddaughter of my brother is already separated from myself in the fourth degree, accordingly my son is in the fifth [from her], my grandson in the sixth and my great-grandson in the seventh degree."[24]

Both sides agreed on the text since ancient authorities unequivocally designated the seventh degree of kin as the distance within which marriage was prohibited. The disagreement concerned the method of measuring this distance: how to count those seven degrees between two people. According to both sides, one began by finding the closest common ancestor to the people in question. The Roman law method counted from Person A, adding her parent, then grandparent, and so on until reaching a common ancestor. From this person, one counted descendants down to Person B. For example, the children of two siblings were in the fourth degree: one step from the first sibling up to her parent, a second for that up to her grandparent (their common ancestor); then a third step down to the latter's child (the second person's parent) and then a fourth down to the second person. In contrast, Peter Damian counted the number of generations that separated each of the potential spouses A and B from their closest common ancestor and used the smaller number. According to this method, the children of two siblings were only in the second degree (see figure 1).

According to Roman civil law, the seventh degree was just beyond second cousins. For Peter Damien, the seventh degree included a vast range of kin: every descendant of as distant a common ancestor as a fifth great-grandparent (the parent of a great-grandparent's great-grandparent). In principle, this reckoning would mean identifying a generation of 128 ancestors who lived almost two hundred years ago and whose descendants would be practically impossible to determine (see figure 2).

New and old stood in a complicated relationship in this quarrel that had everything to do with a reemerging interest in classic texts of Roman law in Italian cities, especially Ravenna.[25] Lawyers who scrutinized the original wording of these texts must have become aware that the methods of measuring the closeness of kinship employed in ecclesiastical courts at that time differed considerably from calculations in the Roman law that had originally been their model. Peter Damian was probably not entirely wrong when he denounced the ideas of his opponents as novelties even though they had found them in very old texts. In their own time, this methodology of calculating kinship was probably unknown, while most of the principles Peter Damian insisted on had been expressed in one or another text on church law in previous centuries.[26] But Peter was the only one who emphasized the difference between these principles and those established in Roman law and thus elevated them to the status of an alternative system.

At that time, Roman law still provided by far the most systematic authoritative conceptualization of kinship available and the most potent method for measuring its closeness. It had originally been devised by Varo in the first century BCE, specifically to determine the closest heir of a deceased person, and further developed in the third century CE by Paulus Prudentissimus, but neither related it to the problem of incest.[27] Of course, the ancient Romans had incest prohibitions too, but determining whether a relationship was incestuous was then, as Philippe Moreau has underlined, usually a matter of assigning it to classes or types of relationships (such as agnates). Only very exceptionally were such prohibitions expressed in terms of the closeness of relationships.[28] When clerics and

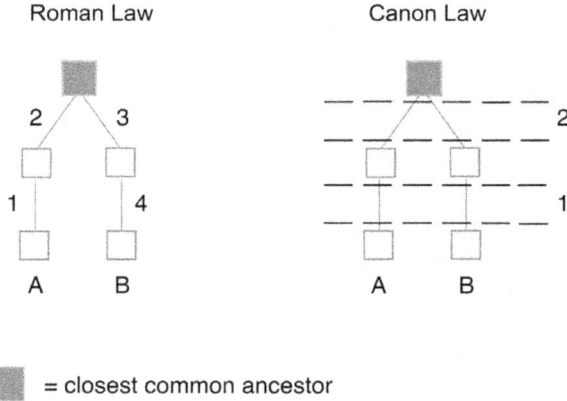

Figure 1.1. Two different methods of counting degrees.
Created by Simon Teuscher.

canon lawyers began applying Roman civil law in their definitions of Catholic marriage prohibitions during the first centuries of the Middle Ages, they relied on this almost mathematical, systematizing idiom that had been developed to regulate the devolution of property and now turned out to be helpful in making extended relationships comprehensible that were hardly ever mentioned in everyday communication.

Although it may look like begging the question, I would here like to depart from the hypothesis that it was Peter Damian and his contemporaries alone who developed a radically new and equally elaborate way of thinking about kinship, one that included very extended forms. A contrary hypothesis is more common, but it is also just a hypothesis: that this system was an immediate reflection of or adaptation to the period's popular perceptions of kinship that some historians refer to as the "Germanic" system. Some quote the early twentieth-century legal historian Champeaux, who surmised that the new ecclesiastical method of counting generations was based on popular ideas according to which kinship was constituted by shared blood that was passed on from one generation to the next.[29] Each ancestor, along with his direct descendants, then constituted a group with common blood, and the canon law method of gradation then attributed one degree to this group of people who share the same substance. Recent research has cast doubt on the idea that there ever was such a thing as a Germanic kinship system. Karl Ubl considers the notion a fantasy of nineteenth-century legal historians, German ones in particular.[30] And there is not the least mention of blood in the arguments of Peter Damian. All of this fully accords with Anita Guerreau-Jalabert's finding that blood only became a prominent theme in debates about kinship toward the end of the Middle Ages.[31]

It is true that Peter Damian's system was not new in every respect. In Roman times, incest prohibitions also applied to relationships outside kinship as conceptualized by Roman civil law, which emphasized *agnatio* and defined paternity based on recognition as well as conception. Early Roman incest rules already included the physiological *genitor* in addition to the legal *pater* and under the late Empire were extended symmetrically to bilateral kin.[32] But significantly, there seems to have been no need to systematically describe a kinship that was conceived of in this way. As late as 868, the Synod of Worms had still ruled that in matters of marriage prohibitions kinship could not be defined by a specific number of generations.[33]

Even without a full review of recent research on kinship in the Early Middle Ages, a great deal of evidence indicates that the erudite theological debate was as much aimed at overcoming popular understandings as it was nourished and driven by them. While theologians like Peter Damian quarreled about how far beyond the great-grandparents one should look to determine who was kin, everyday concepts of relatedness seem to have put more weight on cousin and in-law relationships than on remote common ancestors. And while radical reformers such as Pope Alexander II and Peter Damian wanted the Church to detach its definition of kinship from the transmission of property, the few aristocrats who could trace kinship back several generations did so by following the transmission of castles, property, titles, and coats of arms—which could sometimes also be passed down to in-laws or non-kin—rather than filiation in the strict sense. This has led Anita Guerreau-Jalabert to describe such aristocratic concepts as *topolignées*, a term she uses to describe something very similar to Lévi-Strauss's *société à maison* (house society) that could not serve as a model for the conception of kinship Peter advocated.[34]

Most probably, the intensifying confrontation with the sophistication of the Roman law model and method made it necessary to elaborate on ways of applying the ecclesiastical prohibitions. This would also explain why Peter's letters dealt almost exclusively with consanguinity, although Peter made it very clear that he, like most of his contemporaries, found marriage prohibitions of affinal kin no less important: affinity played a very minor role in Roman inheritance law, and the methods of measuring its closeness in the Catholic Church depended on the calculations used for consanguineous kin.

A Scholastic Position: Kinship beyond Consciousness

With "naked words," Peter wrote, he had been fighting an "emerging heresy" in that assembly in Ravenna.[35] He felt nothing needed to be added to his oral explanations there except what had come down from the ancients. Careful quotations from authorities and their exegesis distinguished Peter's letter from the "naked words" of his oral intervention. His writing seems to have been all about reading—and about conveying what he had found in the texts of the authorities to a broader audience.[36]

Peter approached the problem as a scholar. He faced the difficulty that the body of authoritative texts contained no explicit norms on how exactly to measure kinship as he defined it. Instead, he had to look for clues. He contrasted his own investigation with the polemics of such lawyers as those he had clashed with in Ravenna. They had, he complained, thrown opinions at him like rocks.[37] Instead of responding in kind, he said, he would pick up some of those rocks and rub them against each other to strike a spark and give light to his cloudy-eyed opponents.[38] To him, kinship was something that could become the object of systematic elucidation. It would be naïve to believe that Peter was unbiased, but his text abounds with the rhetoric of open-ended exploration and an engagement with ascertaining a truth that would be convincing to both parties.

What textual authorities did Peter resort to? He did quote rules issued by popes and church councils (*canones*). However, the most trenchant parts of his letter are concerned with the Old and the New Testaments — in particular passages from Job, Leviticus, and the epistles of St. Paul. From references to generation in biblical passages, Peter tried to infer principles of quantifying descent. He looked closely at the passages about inheritance in Roman civil law on which his opponents relied and took particular interest in a kinship diagram shaped like a human body that was apparently found in some manuscripts. This also led him to reflect on the corporeal aspects of kinship. But in this respect, Peter's method differed fundamentally from modern science: for Peter, the human body, the physical world, and nature did not represent the last resort of truth. Instead, he saw them as resources in his quest to understand venerable texts whose authority he held to be indubitable. This is also probably why none of the participants in this dispute about the range of prohibited kin questioned the specific number of *seven* prohibited degrees. The number was mentioned in authoritative *canones*, but the meaning of the numbered steps was not.

Peter introduced the problem by quoting a passage from Justinian's *Institutes* that equated the fourth degree with a sibling's granddaughter — the sentence that had caused such discord in Ravenna. Peter countered by invoking a definition of kinship contained in Burchard of Worms's (d. 1025) collection of *canones*: "Eos autem consanguinei dicimus, quos divinae et saeculi leges consanguinei appellant et in haereditatem suscipiunt et non repelli possunt" (we understand by kin those whom secular and divine law call kin and admit to and cannot exclude from inheritance).[39] Throughout his treatise Peter used this sentence as a kind of minimal standard in the strictest sense: whenever we realize we can name people by a kinship term or have the slightest chance to become their legal heirs, they certainly belong to our kin and need to be subject to marriage prohibitions. (We will return to the kinship terminology used in this discussion). Peter Damian further developed this thought by subsuming the reach of terminology and of legitimate inheritance claims under the term *memoria*, with its broad range of meanings that included knowledge or consciousness as well as memory. Marriage prohibitions, he asserted, should extend beyond the range of people with whom a common filiation was retained in memory.[40] Pope Alexander II made this principle even more prominent in the decree that built on Peter's arguments.[41] For Peter and Alexander the limits of kinship had to be located beyond the consciousness of those who were concerned. This brought into play knowledge of a new kind, not anchored in the day-to-day awareness or the deeds of the concerned ones but in chains of filiations that needed to be probed by experts.

Once the limits of kinship lay beyond memory or consciousness, defining them became a fairly abstract, not to say academic, endeavor: hence the importance of a quantitative measure of kinship and of a reliable definition of the measuring unit, the degree. Kinship, as Peter understood it, included but was not limited to the related groups and persons one interacted with in everyday life. Perhaps it was the artificiality of Peter's conceptualization of kinship that made him designate it by constantly changing terms. Burchard's definition used *consanguinei*, which corresponds to what today we would call consanguineous kin or blood relations. But Peter seems to have meant the same set of people when he wrote about *parentela, genus, genus cognationis*, those with whom we share an *affinitas generis*, and those who simply belong to our *affinitas* (which would from at least the twelfth century on become the name for kin by marriage only—that is, expressly nonconsanguineous kin).[42] There appears to have been no single term current for the kind of kinship Peter struggled to define.

The principle that one should not marry anyone of whom there was any *"memoria"* of being related was not entirely new, but Peter subjected it to systematic elaboration. A couple of older *canones* had stated this principle before but can be read as referring to subjective memories: as prohibiting any kin of whom an individual was conscious.[43] Peter set himself a more ambitious goal: he wanted to establish a generalized system that comprised all relations anybody could *possibly* have memories about or be conscious of. Here, Peter relied on the rules of Roman inheritance law as a generalized expression of who in principle people could be consciously related to. "How can you possibly choose to marry a person as a stranger, while being admitted by the law of kinship to inherit from her or him?" he asked.[44]

At this point, Peter delved into the kinship diagram that was shaped like a human body and found in many law collections at the time. This showed six degrees in the ascendant, the descendant, and the collateral lines. Why, Peter asked, would there be so many more persons in the diagram if the seventh and last degree of kinship could be reached by counting four persons along one branch descending from a common ancestor and three along the other?[45] This would result in the paradox of a diagram of kin relations that contained non-kin! No diagram that accords fully with Peter's description is extant, but an attempt at reconstructing it by Pierre Legendre is shown in figure 1.2.[46] The squares below the genitals of the schematic male figure represent descendants; the ones above represent ancestors in the direct and collateral lines. The latter descend parallel to the line of direct ancestors in the middle and fill the space between the open arms and fingers.

At this point Peter invokes an analogy between how each degree in the body-shaped diagram is situated on a joint and the human body itself. Whoever saw the great-granddaughter of a great-grandchild of one branch descending from a common ancestor and the great-grandson

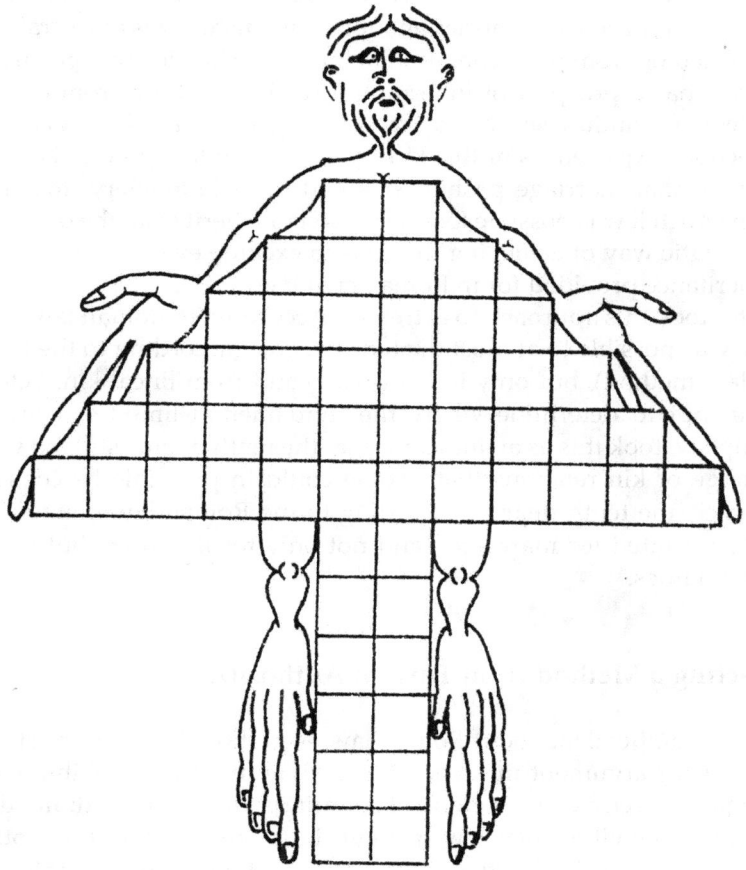

Figure 1.2. Legendre's reconstruction of the diagram used by Peter Damian. Cf. Legendre, *Dossier*, 135. Pierre Legendre, *Leçons IV, suite: Le Dossier occidental de la parenté; Textes juridiques indésirables sur la généalogie*, in collaboration with Anton Schütz, Marc Smith, and Yan Thomas. Paris: Fayard, 1988. Used with permission.

of a great-grandchild of the other branch as entirely free from any bond of kinship (*affinitatis vincula*) would also have to pretend that the limbs on the left side of a human body were unrelated to the limbs on the right side. Or, as he adds, to "express this in even brighter light," he, Peter, might as well pretend that the fingers of his own left hand were unrelated to the hand that was writing these words.[47] We will return later to these comparisons between kinship and the human body.

Peter partly did use Roman inheritance law because at that time no more elaborate systematization of kinship was available, but probably also because it concerned property. He was very aware that one of the strongest supports of memories about ties of kinship was ancestral property passed on from one generation to the next. The idea was persuasive: whoever has a prospect of inheriting a castle or a farm from even the remotest of granduncles would scarcely forget about that particular kin connection. Experiences of this kind probably underlay Peter Damian's argument that marriage prohibitions had to include every imaginable pair in which it was possible for one person to inherit from the other. And a systematic way of achieving this was to exclude every theoretical pair of inheritance provided for in Roman civil law.

Peter took this approach to extremes. According to Roman law, inheritance was possible to at most the tenth degree (according to the Roman civil law method), but only in the *agnatio* and from lineal kin. Peter, in his attempt to determine where the fundamental limits of conscious kinship lay, took this as an indicator that the tenth degree still fell within the range of kin relations that people could in principle be conscious of. Hence, the tenth degree (according to the Roman law method) had to be prohibited for marriage—and not only for the direct but also for collateral lines.[48]

Extracting a Method from Textual Authorities

Peter was ambivalent about Roman law even though it was the starting point for his argument in favor of extending marriage prohibitions: he subsequently rejected its method of counting. Although he admitted that according to civil Roman law it might be correct to count a brother's granddaughter as the fourth degree, such a method would contradict the Bible—where he claimed generations or degrees were only counted once for both lines.[49] He demonstrated this by a series of examples, of which several were taken from the books of Moses, whom he characterized as great legal specialist. Moses had not only decided many cases as a judge but also promulgated laws himself.

One example Peter took from Moses occurs in Genesis. Joseph, who lived one hundred years (Gen. 50:22–23), saw not only Ephraim's (his younger son's) children *to the third generation* but also the sons of Mahir (the son of Joseph's older son Manasseh), who "were brought up upon Joseph's knees." Had Moses used the Roman law method, Peter explained, the distance between the grandchildren of each of Joseph's two sons should have added up to six generations. However, the Bible did not count the two lines twice but only once. He offered a few more examples of this kind and asserted that he could add so many more that the sun would set before he finished.[50]

A distinctive feature of Peter Damian's method was that the first degree of consanguinity—the basic unit of his calculation system—included a parent along with all of his or her children. While the older civil law method had treated each relationship between individuals as one degree, his method implied a collective core. Contemporaries saw this as a radical departure from tradition, as witnessed by the decree Pope Alexander II issued in 1068 that imposed the method on all ecclesiastic courts. Roman law, the pope wrote, counted the degrees from one person to another person because its calculation was about property, which could only be passed on from one person to the next, so each transmission or potential transmission corresponded to one degree. But concerning marriage the matter at stake was the unity of groups, and such a unity never started with one but with several.[51]

The collective character of the first degree also implied that when measuring the closeness of a kin relation across several filiations one would always reach a number of degrees that was lower than the number of persons involved in the filiation. This was a point that seems to have been rather unintuitive for contemporaries and became the topic of an additional controversy to which Peter Damian dedicated most of his second letter. Here, he investigated, among other passages in the Bible, those concerning the genealogy of Christ and the statement in Matthew 1:17 that there had been fourteen generations each between Abraham and David, between David and the Babylonian captivity, and between the Babylonian captivity and Christ. The last of these three genealogical segments raised the problem that the Bible only mentions thirteen names. Peter Damian discussed how St. Jerome and St. Augustine had dealt with this problem before him, but he finally came up with a solution of his own: Joseph and the Virgin Mary had to be counted as a generation each. As the two had never become one flesh (which would make them one generation), the "line of descent in some sense makes an angle," with the relation between Joseph and Mary representing a "spiritual generation." (He then characterized the one between Mary and the Christ as a "singular generation").⁵² Such were the challenges ambitious scholarship had to overcome to deduce our still-common method of measuring kinship from Scripture.

Peter Damian ended his first letter by praising quantification. Despite mainly rejecting Roman law in this matter, he returned to Justinian's great compendium for a quote on how much easier it was to express kin relations in numbers than by naming relationships: "facilius respondere quo quisque gradu sit, quam propria cognationis appellatione quemdam denotare" (it is easier to say who is in which degree than to indicate the relation by an exact kinship term).⁵³ This was responding to defenders of the old Roman law method, who accused Peter Damian and Alexander of "weaving genealogies so far apart" that there were no longer any words (kinship terms) to describe the relationships they wanted to include within the limits of prohibited kin. They said: "When you say that there is consanguinity between the *trinepos* (the great-grandson of great-grandchild) and the *trineptis* (the great-granddaughter of a great-grandchild) descending in the direct line, what would you call their relationship? If there is no word (*nomen*) for their relationship, what kind of consanguinity is this?"⁵⁴ For the reformers, the notion that kinship had to go beyond memory also implied that it went beyond what could be precisely expressed in kinship terminology.

It is worth noticing that kinship was among the first abstract phenomena to have been quantified. Kinship was expressed in degrees already in Roman times, long before it became usual to either measure temperatures or densities in constant units and still longer before today's great wave in which the intensity of pain, the prevalence of crime, and the quality of universities are all being quantified.⁵⁵ Even so, quantifying kinship remained unintuitive for many centuries: as late as the thirteenth century, Thomas Aquinas still felt compelled to defend it. Some said that it was ridiculous that relationships as different as a nephew's to an uncle and an uncle's to a nephew should fall under the same degree. Others found it absurd to describe kinship, which after all was a form of personal closeness, with degrees of distance.⁵⁶ Thomas did not agree with such critics and could have referred to Peter Damian's justification. He had taken quantification to a new level by pushing the limits of kinship so far that they could no longer be measured by other than quantitative means.

The Nature of Kinship

We need to address why Peter Damian did not try to reject his opponents' method entirely but instead suggested that the two different methods of counting kinship ought to exist side by side. This was perhaps the boldest move in his argument. It risked not only degrading ancient textual authorities such as Justinian but also undermining the very idea that a conclusive method of measuring existed at all. Peter's stance on measuring the closeness of kinship was indicative of his understanding of the nature, or more precisely the ontology, of kinship.

Peter Damian's solution was to inscribe the two systems into the medieval duality of the sacred and the profane, which was of course a way of hierarchizing them.[57] He acknowledged the usefulness of the Roman law method for the very limited profane purpose of determining the right heir. But beyond that, he did not hold this system in high esteem. After his reductio ad absurdum of Justinian's method of counting, he asked: how should we interpret Justinian's description of how to measure? "Nihil nostra interest," he answers his own question: "We couldn't care less."[58] Specialists in secular law should be left to deal with their own questions, he continued, reminding his readers that lower things do not always match higher ones, nor do mundane affairs accord with sacred, nor human ones with divine.[59]

Peter Damian made his claim for the superiority of his own method credible by establishing it as the more general one and relegating the Roman law method to the very limited domain of inheritance questions. Part of this argument was implicit and relied on his choice of passages from the Bible: not a single one concerned inheritance, the issue for which the Roman law counting method had originally been developed. Most were not about marriage either, despite the fact that this was the subject of Peter Damian's letter. Instead, his biblical examples suggested that his way of measuring the closeness of kinship came up in the most diverse contexts or that it was inherent to kinship as such. Pope Alexander II's decree made this even more explicit: it dismissed the Roman law method as narrow since it could only solve mundane inheritance problems and was unable to describe the extension of kinship as such.[60] In contrast to what we would expect today, for Peter Damian and Pope Alexander II, kinship as such (that is, beyond inheritance questions) was not kinship according to nature but according to Scripture. Peter had begun his investigation by opposing his own approach to those found in authoritative texts and those of the jurists. And he ended by similarly opposing his own conceptualization of kinship to those of the jurists. Separating the sacred from the profane and emancipating the Catholic Church from secular authorities were general concerns of the Gregorian reforms that Alexander and Peter Damian pioneered.

As far as kinship was concerned, the separation of the secular and the sacred had very particular implications. First among them was that kinship as Peter Damian conceived of it was entirely purged from concern for property, which had probably been involved in most previously available conceptualizations of family relations across more than two or three generations. Of course, debates about marriage prohibitions before Peter Damian had already been about something distinct from property devolution. But as long as Roman law provided the most elaborate model of kinship and the most sophisticated method of measuring its closeness, even attempts to reject an account of relatedness based on the history of property transmission depended on an idiom that was all about property and its transmission.

In Roman civil law, kinship was a system that related humans—provided they were free Roman citizens—through the intermediary of property. Its use in the context of Catholic marriage prohibitions had frequently led to confusion, as for example with the status of male offspring of a *genitor* who did not acknowledge them as sons in the legal sense. In Roman law, such children were not called sons but *spurii* and were excluded from inheriting. In contrast, the ecclesiastical law unequivocally treated them as sons and as such included them in the range of kin that were forbidden for marriage. Isidor of Seville, the seventh-century encyclopedist who tried to reconcile ancient learning with Christian faith, had already been led into major contradictions in his discussion of how *spurii* were related to their parents.[61]

According to a strict reading, kinship in the sense of Roman inheritance law applied neither to slaves nor unfree people.[62] We should at least ask whether all social groups in the Central Middle Ages felt that Roman law conceptions of kinship concerned them. Although only later texts in canon law began to address this explicitly, Peter Damian cannot have entirely overlooked the issue, obsessed as he was with regulating the marriages of all Christians regardless of their status in the secular sphere. [63] In the Central Middle Ages, a large portion of the population—and even of the political elite—were neither free nor property owners in the Roman sense of the word. Not only peasants but also the lower ranks of nobility stood in some or other form of subordination to a lord who entrusted them with fiefs. At death, fiefs returned to the lord, who in turn often reinvested the holder's children with them. But this was not the kind of direct transmission that Roman inheritance law regulated. A distinctive aspect of the kinship system advocated by Peter Damian and Pope Alexander II was that it related Christians as Christians, regardless of status and without the intermediary of property.

Peter Damian's particular method of measuring kinship implied a specific understanding of what was being measured, but since his treatise was concerned with methodological rather than theoretical or ontological questions, his idea of the core nature of kinship remained largely implicit. Interestingly, the one moment when Peter Damian hinted at it was when he referred to the body-shaped kinship diagram. As mentioned before, Peter argued that denying kinship between the different lines of descendants in the diagram was like denying that different parts of one human body belonged together. To support this statement, he quoted St. Paul (1 Cor. 12:12): "For as the body is one, and hath many members, and all the members of that one body, being many, are one body." In its original context, this quote referred to the unity of the church, but Peter was quick to transfer this idea to the descendants of one ancestor (*progenitor*) who also constitute a unity of kin (*genus*).[64]

Peter borrowed boldly from St. Paul's language on the coherence and unity of the church to describe the coherence and unity of kin. At one point, he talked about the body of kin (*corpus parentele*) that needed to be traced to its full extent on all sides before new marriages could be concluded.[65] The prerequisite for this harmonious image of kinship, of course, was Peter Damian's own conceptualization of kinship—from which he had expelled property and all the conflict that came with its distribution. He turned an understanding of kinship that had been about transmission into one that could give a systematic account of proximity.

One thing that is entirely missing from the arguments of both Peter Damian and his adversaries is the idea that kinship was constituted by blood and that the church had to adapt to such an idea. As I noted earlier, such an idea has been ascribed to Germanic culture by some scholars. Peter Damian had quite a lot to say about physiological aspects of kinship, which would be worth a closer examination. For instance, he asserted that the bowels of kin produced the same odor.[66] But he never mentioned blood. Quite likely, the development was the reverse: it was not ideas about blood that called for the new method of counting, but the new type of quantification prepared the ground on which new ideas of kinship as shared blood or as portions and mixtures of other substances could emerge. However, this did not happen with much consistency before the end of the Middle Ages.

Epilogue

Peter developed a systematized conception of kinship that was emancipated from property transmission and sufficiently abstract to apply to all humans and potentially to all beings that reproduce sexually (although Peter and his contemporaries did not do this yet). This allowed for its use in entirely new domains—in Peter's case, more coherent and less ambiguous marriage prohibitions that applied to all Catholics regardless of status and property.

The new measuring method and the imagery of kinship as a body lend themselves to drawing sharp delimitations between groups, as when Peter Damian set the outer limits of the body of kinship at the seventh degree. However, he did not himself exploit this possibility to define mutually exclusive groups as he was probably too captivated by kinship's potential role as a multiplier in the project of generalizing the ties of love throughout the community of the faithful.

From the fifteenth century on, Damian's measuring technique became a precondition for a series of attempts at using kinship as an instrument of inclusion and exclusion. Now, indeed, kinship was regularly associated with shared and mixed blood that could be divided (into halves, quarters, eighths, etc.) according to the succession of generations. This was the systematization on which tests of the *limpieza de sangre* (purity or cleanliness of blood) in Spain beginning in the fifteenth century depended (after a short initial phase during which they had relied more on paternal than maternal descent). These tests excluded Christians with impure blood, containing Jewish or Muslim "portions," from many offices and privileges that required proof of pure Christian descent, and they are often seen as an important foundation of modern racism.

Iberian colonists exported the testing procedure method to India and the Americas, where it was a major influence on the development of an elaborate *casta* system in which someone's classification depended on that of several generations of ancestors. It thus can be seen as one of the origins of modern conceptions of race. A similar procedure of measuring according to generations and portions was used beginning in the fifteenth century in German *Ahnenproben* in order to prove the pure noble descent of men who wanted to enter chapters of collegiate churches or tournament societies.[67] And much later, the pioneers of genetics resorted to this logic to describe descent. Peter Damian remains with us, and recalling his work also reminds us of the historicity of such an account of relatedness.

Simon Teuscher is professor of medieval history at the University of Zurich. His research interests include kinship and other personal relationships, rural society, and administrative culture during the Late Middle Ages in Western and Northern Europe. He was a coeditor of *Kinship in Europe: Approaches to Long-Term Development (1300–1900)* (2007). His publications also include *Lords' Rights and Peasant Stories: Writing and the Formation of Tradition in the Later Middle Ages* (2012). He codirected the interdisciplinary research group on kinship and politics at the Center for Interdisciplinary Research in Bielefeld.

Notes

1. I would like to thank Erdmute Alber, David Sabean, Tatjana Thelen, Ludolf Kuchenbuch, Susan McKinnon, and all the participants and visitors in our ZiF research group who commented on previous versions of this chapter. Thanks also to ZiF for allowing me to ponder medieval theories of kinship.
2. For this paragraph, cf. David Warren Sabean and Simon Teuscher, "Kinship in Europe: A New Approach to Long-Term Development," in *Kinship in Europe: Approaches to the Long-Term Development (1300–1900)*, ed. David Warren Sabean, Simon Teuscher, and Jon Mathieu (New York: Berghahn Books, 2007); Simon Teuscher, "Problems of Scale and Mediation in Studies of Kinship in the Past," in *Reframing the History of Family and Kinship: From the Alps towards Europe*, ed. Dionigi Albera, Luigi Lorenzetti, and Jon Mathieu (Bern: Peter Lang, 2016).
3. Johannes Laudage, *Gregorianische Reform und Investiturstreit* (Darmstadt: Wissenschaftliche Buchgesellschaft, 1993); Werner Goez, *Kirchenreform und Investiturstreit 910–1122* (Stuttgart: Kohlhammer, 2000); Harald J. Bermann, *Law and Revolution: The Formation of Western Legal Tradition* (Cambridge, MA: Harvard University Press, 1983), 94–113.
4. David L. D'Avray, "Peter Damian, Consanguinity, and Church Property," in *Intellectual Life in the Middle Ages: Essays Presented to Margaret Gibson*, ed. Benedicta Ward and Lesley Smith (London: Hambledon Press, 1992); Owen J. Blum, "The Monitor of the Popes, St. Peter Damian," *Studi Gregoriani*, no. 2 (1947).
5. Augustine, *De Civitate Dei*, book 15, chaps. 15 and 16. For English and Latin texts side-by-side, see Saint Augustine, *The City of God against the Pagans* (Cambridge, MA: Harvard University Press, 1966), vol. 4, book 15, chaps. 15 and 16, pp. 492–511; Enric Porqueres i Gené, *Individu, personne et parenté en Europe* (Paris: Éditions de la Maison des sciences de l'homme, 2015), 42–54.
6. Karl Ubl, *Inzestverbot und Gesetzgebung: Die Konstruktion eines Verbrechens (300–1100)* (Berlin: De Gruyter, 2008).
7. Laurent Barry, *La Parenté* (Paris: Gallimard, 2008), 541; Anton Schütz, "Les données immédiates de la parenté: L'Église, la filiation, le marriage, le droit canonique," in *Leçons IV, suite: Le Dossier occidental de la parenté; Textes juridiques indésirables sur la généalogie*, ed. Pierre Legendre (Paris: Fayard, 1988), 210–12; Patrick Corbet, *Autour de Burchard de Worms: L'église allemande et les interdits de parenté (IXèeme–XIème siècle)* (Frankfurt a. M.: Vittorio Klostermann, 2001).
8. Barry, *Parenté*, 572.
9. This is the interpretation of Ubl, *Inzestverbot*, 457.
10. Ubl, *Inzestverbot*, 459.
11. Maria Elena Martinez, Genealogical Fictions, Limpieza de Sangre, Religion, and Gender in Colonial Mexico (Stanford, CA: Stanford University Press, 2008), chaps. 1–2, 26–60; Angela Barreto Xavier, "Languages of Difference in the Portuguese Empire: The Spread of 'Caste' in the Indian World," Anuario Colombiano de Historia Social y de la Cultura 43, no. 2 (2016).
12. Staffan Müller-Wille and Hans-Jürgen Rheinberger, "De la génération à l'hérédité: Continuités médiévales et conjonctures historiques modernes," in *L'hérédité entre Moyen Âge et Époque Moderne: Perspectives historiques*, ed. Charles de Miramon and Maaike van der Lugt (Florence: SISMEL, 2008).
13. Both letters are included in the monumental German edition *Monumenta Germaniae Historica* (MGH). Petrus Damianus, "Briefe der deutschen Kaiserzeit 4,1," in *Monumenta Germaniae Historica*, 179–99 (Letter 19) and 339–45 (Letter 36).
14. *Decretum magistri Gratiani*, ed. Lipsiensis secunda post Aemilii Ludovici Richteri curas ad librorum manu scriptorum et editionis Romanae fidem recognovit et adnotatione

critica instruxit Aemilius Friedberg (Leipzig 1879; reprint: Graz, 1959), (Corpus iuris canonici 1), Decreti pars secunda, causa 35, questio 2, canon 2, 1264. On the surprisingly rapid acceptance of Peter Damian's ideas, see Corbet, *Burchard*, 290–92.

15. Pierre Legendre, ed., *Leçons IV, suite: Le Dossier occidental de la parenté; Textes juridiques indésirables sur la généalogie* (Paris: Fayard, 1988), 178: "perversa quadam calliditate." Ed. in Hermann Hüffer, *Beiträge zur Geschichte der Quellen des Kirchenrechts und des römischen Rechts im Mittelalter* (Münster, 1862), 119–20.
16. Legendre, *Leçons*, 178.
17. MGH, "Briefe 4,1," 341.
18. MGH, "Briefe 4,1," 199.
19. MGH, "Briefe 4,1," 198.
20. MGH, "Briefe 4,1," 198.
21. MGH, "Briefe 4,1," 187–88.
22. MGH, "Briefe 4,1," 180–81. Possibly the question had come up due to the marriage between Henry III and Agnèse of Poitou. Ubl, *Inzestverbot*, 452.
23. "Sed nec neptem ... fratris vel sororis ducere quis potest, quamvis quarto gradu sit." MGH, "Briefe 4,1," 180; cf. Justinianus, *Institutiones*, vol. 1, 4 (10, 3).
24. MGH, "Briefe 4,1," 180–81.
25. Manlio Bellomo, *The Common Legal Past of Europe* (Washington, DC: The Catholic University of America Press, 1995. [Italian Original: *L'Europa del diritto commune* (Rome: Il Cigno Galileo Galilei, 1988), 58–65.]
26. Just how new Peter Damian's method of kinship computation really was has been controversial among specialists. Its novelty is emphasized by Christopher Brooke, *The Medieval Idea of Marriage* (Oxford: Oxford University Press, 1989), 135, but is questioned by, among others, Constance B. Bouchard, "Consanguinity and Noble Marriages in the Tenth and Eleventh Centuries," *Speculum*, no. 56 (1981). I agree with the intermediate position that Peter Damian provided an already existing computation with a "firm definition in face of a challenge," as stated by D'Avray, "Peter Damian," 71n5.
27. Legendre, *Dossier*, 27–120.
28. Philippe Moreau, *Incestus et prohibitae nuptiae: L'inceste à Rome* (Paris: Les Belles Lettres, 2002), 181–86.
29. Ernest Champeaux, "Jus sanguinis," *Revue historique de droit français et étranger* 12, no. 2 (1933). His idea of a continuity of ideas about mixed blood since the early Middle Ages has been repeated many places, including Schütz, "Données," 206; Maurice Godelier, *The Metamorphoses of Kinship* (London: Verso, 2011), 329, and, most recently, Porqueres i Gené, *Individu*.
30. Ubl, *Inzestverbot*, 8–9, 18–25. Corbet (*Burchard*, 102) also rejects the idea of an underlying popular system of reckoning kinship.
31. Anita Guerreau-Jalabert, "Flesh and Blood in Medieval Language about Kinship," in *Blood and Kinship: Matter for Metaphor from Ancient Rome to the Present*, ed. C. H. Johnson, B. Jussen, D. W. Sabean, and S. Teuscher (New York: Berghahn Books, 2012).
32. Barry, *Parenté*, 483-84.
33. Corbet, *Burchard*, 94–95.
34. Anita Guerreau-Jalabert, "Sur les structures de parenté dans l'Europe médiévale (Note critique)," *Annales ESC*, no. 36 (1981); Elie Haddad, "Qu'est-ce qu'une maison? De Lévi Strauss aux recherches anthropologiques et historiques récentes," *L'homme*, no. 212 (2014).
35. MGH, "Briefe 4,1," 181.
36. MGH, "Briefe 4,1," 181.
37. MGH, "Briefe 4,1," 190.
38. MGH, "Briefe 4,1," 190.

39. MGH, "Briefe 4,1," 181.
40. MGH, "Briefe 4,1," 152.
41. Friedberg, *Decretum magistri gratiani*, cols. 1273–74; Legendre, *Dossier*, 184.
42. MGH, "Briefe 4,1," 183; Legendre, *Dossier*, 136.
43. Ubl, *Inzestverbot*, 362–63.
44. MGH, "Briefe 4,1," 181.
45. That is, the method in which the brother's granddaughter is in the fourth degree—one on one side of the common ancestor and three on the other.
46. Legendre, *Dossier*, 135.
47. MGH, "Briefe 4,1," 182–83.
48. Cf. Ubl, *Inzestverbot*, 455.
49. There "offspring that come from the same common ancestor (generis auctor) in different lines" are never counted twice but must be seen as one generation. MGH, "Briefe 4,1," 188.
50. MGH, "Briefe 4,1," 189.
51. "Quia uero nuptiae sine duabus non ualent fieri personis, ideo sacri canones duas in uno gradu constituere personas." Text edited in Friedberg, *Decretum magistri gratiani*, col. 1272; Legendre, *Dossier*, 180.
52. MGH, "Briefe 4,1," 344–45.
53. MGH, "Briefe 4,1," 197. Cf. *Justinian*, vol. 3, titulus 6.5: "*D. Justiniani Institutionum libri quatuor: The Four Books of Justinian's Institutions*, translated into English, with notes, by George Harris, 3rd ed. (Oxford, 1811; reprint, 2010), 210.
54. MGH, "Briefe 4,1," 196.
55. On the epistemic potentials of quantification, see Wendy Nelson Espeland and Mitchell L. Steven, "A Sociology of Quantification," *European Journal of Sociology* 49, no. 3 (2008).
56. *Tertia Pars Summae Theologiae*, in *Sancti Thomae Aquinatis Opera Omnia*, vol. 12, q. LIV, art. 2, 104 (Rome, 1906).
57. Jérôme Baschet, *Corps et âmes: Une histoire de la personne au Moyen Âge* (Paris: Flammarion, 2016).
58. MGH, "Briefe 4,1," 192.
59. MGH, "Briefe, 4,1," 192.
60. Friedberg, *Decretum magistri gratiani*, Sp. 1272; Legendre, *Dossier*, 180.
61. Cf. Thomas Laqueur, *Making Sex: Body and Gender from the Greeks to Freud* (Cambridge, MA: Harvard UP, 1990), 25–63, quoting Isidore of Seville.
62. Moreau, *Incestus*, 278. Cf. Justinian, vol. 3, titulus 6.10.
63. MGH, "Briefe 4,1," 183.
64. "Sicut ergo multa membra per participationem sui totius simul coeunt, ut unum dicantur irreprehsibiiter corpus, ita nimirum diversae personae, quae ab uno progenitore communiter prodeunt, unum sunt proculdubio genus." MGH, "Briefe 4,1," 183.
65. MGH, "Briefe 4,1," 194.
66. MGH, "Briefe 4,1," 184–85.
67. Ute Küppers-Braun, "'Allermassen der teutsche Adel allzeit auf das mütterliche Geschlecht fürnemlich ... gesehen': Ahnenproben des hohen Adels in Dom. und kaiserlich-freiweltlichen Damenstiften," in *Die Ahnenprobe in der Vormoderne: Selektion—Initation—Repräsentation*, ed. Elisabeth Harding and Michael Hecht (Münster: Rhema, 2011); Martinez, *Genealogical Fictions*, 52; Moritz Trebeljahr, "Adel in vier Vierteln: Die Ahnenprobe im Johanniterorden auf Malta in der Vormoderne," in *Die Ahnenprobe in der Vormoderne. Selektion—Initiation Repräsentation*, ed. Elizabeth Harding and Michael Hecht (Münster: Rhema, 2011).

Bibliography

Augustine. *De Civitate Dei*, book 15, chaps. 15 and 16. For English and Latin texts side-by-side: Saint Augustine. *The City of God against the Pagans*, vol. 4, book 15, chaps. 15 and 16, pp. 492–511. Cambridge, MA: Harvard University Press, 1966.

Barry, Laurent. *La Parenté*. Paris: Gallimard, 2008.

Baschet, Jérôme. *Corps et âmes: Une histoire de la personne au Moyen Âge*. Paris: Flammarion, 2016.

Bellomo, Manlio. *The Common Legal Past of Europe*. Translated by Lydia G. Cochrane. Washington, DC: The Catholic University of America Press, 1995. [Italian original: *L'Europa del diritto commune*. Rome: Il Cigno Galileo Galilei, 1988.]

Bermann, Harald J. *Law and Revolution: The Formation of Western Legal Tradition*. Cambridge, MA: Harvard University Press, 1983.

Blum, Owen J. "The Monitor of the Popes, St. Peter Damian." *Studi Gregoriani*, no. 2 (1947): 459–76.

Bouchard, Constance B. "Consanguinity and Noble Marraiges in the Tenth and Eleventh Centuries." *Speculum* 56 (1981): 268–87.

Brooke, Christopher. *The Medieval Idea of Marriage*. Oxford: Oxford University Press, 1989.

Champeaux, Ernest. "Jus sanguinis: Trois façons de calculer la parenté au moyen âge." *Revue historique de droit français et étranger* 12, no. 2 (1933): 241–90.

Corbet, Patrick. *Autour de Burchard de Worms: L'église allemande et les interdits de parenté (IXèeme–XIème siècle)*. Frankfurt a. M.: Vittorio Klostermann, 2001.

D'Avray, David L. "Peter Damian, Consanguinity, and Church Property." In *Intellectual Life in the Middle Ages: Essays Presented to Margaret Gibson*, edited by Benedicta Ward and Lesley Smith, 71–80. London: Hambledon Press, 1992.

Espeland, Wendy Nelso, and Mitchell L. Steven. "A Sociology of Quantification." *European Journal of Sociology* 49, no. 3 (2008): 401–36.

Godelier, Maurice. *The Metamorphoses of Kinship*. Translated by Nora Scott. London: Verso, 2011.

Goez, Werner. *Kirchenreform und Investiturstreit 910–1122*. Stuttgart: Kohlhammer, 2000.

Gratian = *Decretum magistri Gratiani*, ed. Lipsiensis secunda post Aemilii Ludovici Richteri curas ad librorum manu scriptorum et editionis Romanae fidem recognovit et adnotatione critica instruxit Aemilius Friedberg. Leipzig, 1879. Reprint: Graz, 1959.

Guerreau-Jalabert, Anita. "Flesh and Blood in Medieval Language about Kinship." In *Blood and Kinship: Matter for Metaphor from Ancient Rome to the Present*, edited by C. H. Johnson, B. Jussen, D. W. Sabean, and S. Teuscher, 61–82. New York: Berghahn Books, 2012.

Guerreau-Jalabert, Anita. "Sur les structures de parenté dans l'Europe médiévale (Note critique)." *Annales ESC*, no. 36 (1981): 1028–49.

Haddad, Elie. "Qu'est-ce qu'une maison? De Lévi Strauss aux recherches anthropologiques et historiques récentes." *L'homme*, no. 212 (2014): 109–38.

Hüffer, Hermann. *Beiträge zur Geschichte der Quellen des Kirchenrechts und des römischen Rechts im Mittelalter.* Münster, 1862.
Justinian = D. *Justiniani Institutionum libri quatuor. The Four Books of Justinian's Institutions.* Translated into English, with notes, by George Harris. 3rd ed. Oxford: Collingwood, Newman, and Baxter, 1811. Reprint, 2010.
Küppers-Braun, Ute. "'Allermassen der teutsche Adel allzeit auf das mütterliche Geschlecht fürnemlich ... gesehen': Ahnenproben des hohen Adels in Dom. und kaiserlich-freiweltlichen Damenstiften." In *Die Ahnenprobe in der Vormoderne. Selektion—Initation—Repräsentation,* edited by Elisabeth Harding and Michael Hecht, 175–90. Münster: Rhema, 2011.
Laqueur, Thomas. *Making Sex: Body and Gender from the Greeks to Freud* (Cambridge, MA: Harvard University Press, 1990).
Laudage, Johannes. *Gregorianische Reform und Investiturstreit.* Darmstadt: Wissenschaftliche Buchgesellschaft, 1993.
Legendre, Pierre, ed. *Leçons IV, suite: Le Dossier occidental de la parenté; Textes juridiques indésirables sur la généalogie,* in collaboration with Anton Schütz, Marc Smith, and Yan Thomas. Paris: Fayard, 1988.
Martinez, Maria-Elena. *Genealogical Fictions: Limpieza de Sangre, Religion, and Gender in Colonial Mexico.* Stanford, CA: Stanford University Press, 2008.
Moreau, Philippe. *Incestus et prohibitae nuptiae: L'inceste à Rome.* Paris: Les Belles Lettres, 2002.
Müller-Wille, Staffan, and Hans-Jürgen Rheinberger. "De la génération à l'hérédité: Continutités médiévales et conjonctures historiques modernes." In *L'hérédité entre Moyen Âge et Époque Moderne: Perspectives historiques,* edited by Charles de Miramon and Maaike van der Lugt, 355–90. Florence: SISMEL, 2008.
Petrus Damianus. "Briefe der deutschen Kaiserzeit 4,1." In *Monumenta Germaniae Historica,* 179–99 (Letter 19) and 339–45 (Letter 36). Munich : MGH, 1983.
Porqueres i Gené, Enric. *Individu, personne et parenté en Europe.* Paris: Éditions de la Maison des sciences de l'homme, 2015.
Sabean, David Warren, and Simon Teuscher. "Kinship in Europe: A New Approach to Long-Term Development." In *Kinship in Europe: Approaches to the Long-Term Development (1300–1900),* edited by David Warren Sabean, Simon Teuscher, and Jon Mathieu, 1–32. New York: Berghahn Books, 2007.
Schütz, Anton. "Les données immédiates de la parenté: L'Église, la filiation, le marriage, le droit canonique." In *Leçons IV, suite: Le Dossier occidental de la parenté; Textes juridiques indésirables sur la généalogie,* edited by Pierre Legendre, 189–220. Paris: Fayard, 1988.
Tertia Pars Summae Theologiae. In *Sancti Thomae Aquinatis Opera Omnia,* vol. 12. Rome: Ex Typographia Polyglotta, 1906.
Teuscher, Simon. "Problems of Scale and Mediation in Studies of Kinship in the Past." In *Reframing the History of Family and Kinship: From the Alps towards Europe,* edited by Dionigi Albera, Luigi Lorenzetti, and Jon Mathieu, 33–46. Bern: Peter Lang, 2016.
Trebeljahr, Moritz. "Adel in vier Vierteln: Die Ahnenprobe im Johanniterorden auf Malta in der Vormoderne." In *Die Ahnenprobe in der Vormoderne: Selektion— Initiation Repräsentation,* edited by Elizabeth Harding and Michael Hecht, 333–50. Münster: Rhema, 2011.

Ubl, Karl. *Inzestverbot und Gesetzgebung: Die Konstruktion eines Verbrechens (300–1100)*. Berlin: de Gruyter, 2008.

Xavier, Angela Barreto. "Languages of Difference in the Portuguese Empire: The Spread of 'Caste' in the Indian World." Anuario Colombiano de Historia Social y de la Cultura 43, no. 2 (2016): 89–119.

Chapter 2

Kinship Matters
Genealogical and Historiographical Practices between 1750 and 1850

Michaela Hohkamp

Introductory Remarks

Research on the history of historiography has traditionally emphasized the close connection between genealogical practice and the development of history as a scientific discipline. Historians have regarded the sixteenth and seventeenth centuries as the period during which this relationship was worked out.[1] It was then that scholars began to seek out valid documents, visit archives, search for suitable papers, and try to gain access to the broadest possible range of administrative materials.[2] The authenticity of sources became a particularly important issue for genealogical work.[3] Recent research on kinship has demonstrated a shift during these centuries from displaying genealogies more or less horizontally to displaying them vertically and focused on male lines. Many different works illustrate this shift. However, early modern genealogical artifacts, which took many forms and utilized a variety of materials, have recently been characterized as "genealogies fabuleuses" (fabulous genealogies), raising the question of how credible they were to their intended audiences. Roberto Bizzocchi has found that their claims rested on authority.[4] This finding shifts the research focus from questions of scientific accuracy to practices of acknowledgment and the question of how scholars elicited assent on the part of scholary and lay audiences as well. Seventeenth- and early eighteenth-century scholars were obsessed with sustaining their genealogical work on documents, finding recognition among colleagues, and proving themselves worthy rivals and acknowledged members of the scholarly community—while at the same time serving the political intentions of their noble superiors. The precision of their work appears to have been motivated by their quest to find recognition for their achievements—and vice versa. In the context of seventeenth-century debates, genealogy was thus able to become a laboratory for the elaboration of undeniable facts (*Tatsachen*).[5] By the last decades of the eighteenth century, scholars added the dimension of comprehensibility, which was called *Fasslichkeit* in German methodological texts of the period. In the following exploration, I will capture the salience of this remarkable term by translating it as "graspability."

In this chapter, I intend to investigate the logic underlying the entanglement of genealogical and historiographical writing. I will begin with selected programmatic texts on history and genealogy by Johann Christoph Gatterer (1727–99), professor at the University of Göttingen, director of a research institute, and a respected member of the European republic of letters.[6] I will then turn to two case studies focusing on a politically important scholarly text from this time by Johann Daniel Schöpflin (1694–1771), an eminent scholar and a member of several academies of letters, and on a second text, published in 1769 but less known both now and then, by an anonymous author who applied Gatterer's historiographical methods.[7] Later in the chapter I will discuss two publications written against the backdrop of the political events following the French Revolution that can potentially shed light on the political impact of genealogical history (genea-graphy) during the nineteenth century.[8]

The Order of History (*Eigentliche Geschichte*) and Genealogical Histories (*Genealogische Historien*)

In "On the Historical Plan and the Structure of Its Narratives" (1767), Johann Christoph Gatterer remarked that a nation seeking to improve its taste must study and imitate the models of the ancients before it can embark on bringing forth worthy works of its own.[9] In this essay, the Göttingen scholar tackled the significant question of how to approach the scientific writing of history. Finding an appropriate form in which to depict information was an indispensable desideratum.[10]

> For as long as history has been known to humanity, she has allowed her sister, the art of poetry, to walk before her, but laid claim to the next rank herself. And now, I say, history finds a path lying ahead of her that has been opened up by the poets, an improved and extended language, and a style that follows the models of the ancients. All that is essential now is that the younger sister

should not depart from the path of the elder one, or rather not be seduced away from it, since she herself follows readily in her sister's footsteps when left to her own devices.[11]

Gatterer presented the arts of history and poetry as a sisterly dyad in his text, although the hierarchy that placed poetry as the older and more senior sister and history as the younger still left the status of poetry elevated above that of history.[12] Around the time that Gatterer was writing, scholars were focusing on the problem of how to differentiate disciplines from one another. Lessing's *Laocoon: An Essay on the Limits of Painting and Poetry* (*Laokoon Oder über die Grenzen der Malerei und Poesie*), for example, had appeared only a year before Gatterer's text and was dedicated to an exploration of the similarities and differences that exist between the two art forms. Lessing ultimately concluded that poetry was superior to painting because its narrative form allowed it to capture how events unfolded over time. He also argued that there were paintable and unpaintable facts (*malbare und unmalbare Fakta*) and that the historian could relate the most paintable in just as nonpictorial a manner as the poet could represent the least paintable pictorially.[13] For Lessing and other contemporaries, writing literature and writing history were both based on narration. Writing history was a matter of storytelling like writing literature, so poets were, for an assortment of reasons, seen as more competent in doing so (not least because they used their mother tongue) than historical writers until well into the second half of the eighteenth century.

Like Lessing, Gatterer drew attention to the similarity between poetry and historical writing, explicitly noting that the ancients had distinguished between them regarding form and not content.[14] Over time, poetry had become the more respected art, he thought, and historians still respected it as, so to speak, the older sister, sometimes still neglecting the claims of their own goddess.[15] Even though history had begun to step out of the shadow of literature, it had not fully separated itself from the other art, a step history would have to take in order to fully claim its scientific status.[16] In Gatterer's view, historiography was neither mere narration nor a collection of details but a form of order:

> When the historian has completed the painstaking process of assembling the historical material for a work and selected what is noteworthy from this chaos—for plenty of useless things will be found that need to be discarded, even when one believes that during the gathering of the material he has already paid attention only to significant details meriting people's attention—once this gathering and selection of material has been completed, then, it is time to think about the plan that should be followed, the plan according to which all the great and small components required for the architecture of the work can be brought into the most expedient order, so that it is possible, once

the work has been completed, for it to be effortlessly discerned why each part of the materials had to be placed just where it has been and nowhere else. This is the first task facing the historian after the collection and ordering of the material, whether we call it the arrangement, the ordering, or the structuring of the narratives.[17]

Seen thus, doing history involved recognizing what was noteworthy (*merkwürdig*) and deserving of attention. These noteworthy items (*Merkwürdigkeiten*) formed the raw material, which then had to be ordered in an expedient (*schicklich*) fashion. Whether the material had been ordered well could be determined, Gatterer was convinced, by the ease with which one could discern why one piece of information had been assigned to one place and another to a different place. For Gatterer, historiography meant the creation of perfect order: the successful arrangement of material so that the reader would find everything in just the place where it would be self-explanatory. If the reader was successful in this endeavor, that would prove that this ambition had been achieved.

Genealogical histories (*genealogische Historien*), however, were treated by Gatterer as an exception that was not subject to his usual rules for the ordering of noteworthy items. The arrangement of these special histories was predetermined by their own order.

> The plan [for assembling material in order] here [in genealogical studies] does not require any rules. One follows the order of the genealogical tables, and when a family splits into several branches, as often happens, then one describes the branches one by one. The inclusion of genealogical tables preserves the flow of the narrative and also affords the advantages of a synchronous view with the same ease as is provided by the synchronistic tables in proper history.[18]

Genealogical histories were thus characterized as special cases but not as a discipline of their own: they remained part of proper or grand history (*eigentliche Geschichte*) because the person or the ruler whose genealogical information was presented was considered noteworthy (*merkwürdig*). It followed from this that "genealogical histories" (*genealogische Historien*) formed part of "proper history" (*eigentliche Geschichte*) and provided a suitable mode of organizing a confusing amount of detail.[19] The history of nations was linked through the plan that integrated the genealogical histories of rulers following chronological arrangements.

In Gatterer's *Einleitung in die synchronistische Universalhistorie*, he arranged the chronological development of entire empires and monarchies in tabular form, structuring his material according to sequences of rulers.[20] The genealogical table, with its capacity to simultaneously represent events in both chronological order and according to categories derived from rulers or territories, to place single events (like wars and battles) in the context of the whole by associating them with the person of particular royal figures or other members of elites, and to simultaneously display everything that had happened, proved to be a suitable medium for presenting "proper history." But "genealogical histories" did not merely supply the raw material for generating synchronistic tables as a contribution to "proper history": they were also an integral component of it and could provide an acceptable instrument for establishing a kind of evidence that differed clearly from that brought forth by the fifteenth and sixteenth centuries—which was considered a result of performative practices, representation, and rhetorical art—like the so-called fables.[21]

Fables

Enlightenment scholars were troubled by early modern practices of establishing evidence and the general tendency for history to converge too closely with the art of poetry at the expense of plausibility. At the beginning of the 1760s, for example, the Swiss historian Gottlieb Walther (who has remained a more or less obscure figure) remarked that the genesis of states and the stories of their earliest past generally had been "disfigured with many fables" (*mit vielen Fabeln verunstaltet*). For this reason, it was necessary "for a scholar of both worldly knowledge and a knowledge of history to discover the characteristics by which one might be able to distinguish the fables that darken history from accounts that were true. This desire is justified. Historical truths are buttressed with so many fictions that one must doubt everything and proceed with the greatest mistrust if one wishes to be sure of one's case."[22] In lamenting these tall-tale-laced histories, Gottlieb Walther addressed a problem that was just as relevant to historical works as to genealogical ones, such as early modern derivations of the descent and ancestry of royal and noble houses, families and their members. The heterogeneous manifestations of early modern practices of writing and understanding kinship were passed on to the eighteenth century in painted and printed genealogical works and manuscripts and through a variety of representations and objects, executed in a range of techniques on many different kinds of materials (paper, parchment, woven fabrics, glass, wood, and canvas).[23] The claims to power and dominion presented in these material representations were at times underscored by the use of extravagant substances to add color, such as lapis lazuli, gold, silver, brazilwood, and Tyrian purple (for painting red bloodlines, later replaced by the animal dye cochineal carmine and the vegetable dye madder), on parchment or paper or woven into precious tapestries.[24] In addition to these displays, which made power and claims to dominion visually accessible purely through their costly production methods and special material qualities, the early modern period featured numerous other kinds of genealogical representations that could vary widely in their content and medial presentation, depending on the context in which they arose and the purposes for which they were intended. Family trees of all kinds enjoyed particular interest at the time.

Sets of Information

Among all the ways of representing genealogies, Enlightenment scholars ranked the undocumented family trees as among the most dubious:

> And the so-called family registers, the family trees, and all the other kinds of family information of that nature rank in the very lowest class; they are usually a scant two hundred years old and filled with family legends. … To put it briefly, the historiographers and especially the family registers and so on are to the genealogist what Roman law is to the German jurist. One relies on them only in essential cases, they are subsidiary.[25]

This view was expressed by Gatterer in his 1769 essay "Von der Evidenz in der Genealogie" (On evidence in genealogy),[26] in which he distinguished different groups (four in sum) of genealogical works: unattested genealogical tables (*unbeurkundete Stammtafeln*), attested genealogical tables (*beurkundete Stammtafeln*), dynastic history (*Geschlechtergeschichte*), and genealogical explorations (*genealogische Erörterungen*).[27] The first of these were genealogical tables unsupported by documents: family trees, in other words, where the sets of genealogical information were not supported by any form of document.[28] The second genre of genealogical works were genealogical tables supported by documents.[29] Although this method allowed sets of genealogical information to be confirmed, such tables neither made them sufficiently comprehensible—graspable (*fasslich*)—nor led to evidence as Gatterer understood it.[30] Thus, neither attested nor unattested genealogical tables led to evidence: the unattested lacked veracity in Gatterer's eyes, while the attested were not graspable (*fasslich*) enough.

> The so-called dynastic histories (*Geschlechterhistorien*) can be seen as making up the third genre—a mixed type of work, made up partly of genealogy and partly of history—since they concern themselves not only with the descent of persons belonging to a particular dynasty but also with events in which these were involved. In the best works belonging to this genre, the genealogical

part roughly follows the Du Chesne method,[31] so attempts to attest the genealogical tables have been made, but the true sentences only seldom reach the level of evidence. And as far as the historical part is concerned, the investigation of the evidence of the noteworthy events narrated does not belong here but with the material on the evidence of actual history. Known examples include ... Schöpflin's Historia Zaringo-Badensis. ... Finally, there are also studies that investigate single genealogical topics. I consider these, which I will call genealogical explorations [*genealogische Erörterungen*], to make up the fourth category of genealogical works.[32]

Ultimately Gatterer assigned only the dynastic histories—as one of many possible modes of "genealogical histories"—to the category of texts that could rise to the status of evidence. Only this type of genealogical work merited consideration in relation to the question as to how evidence could be reached. The material helpful for proving particular facts consisted, in Gatterer's view, mainly of *documents*.

But what exactly did the Göttingen scholar mean by "evidence"? Gatterer was concerned with veracity but also with the comprehensibility of the past, with how *graspable* (*fasslich*) it was.[33] In addition, he believed that it must be possible to assimilate attested information quickly (*geschwind*) and easily (*leicht*).[34] For this to succeed, Gatterer explained, it was necessary to establish matches (*Identität*) between sets of genealogical information (*genealogische Sätze*) and the "supporting documents" (*Beweisstellen*) for these sets.[35] Only thus, the Enlightenment historian continued, could genealogists ensure that they did not merely arrive at information that was attested and accurate but also generated information that was comprehensible and could be grasped quickly and easily—information that was, in other words, concise and evident.[36] It was not sufficient for an investigation to be attested and accurate, or for its results to be accepted as valid. It also needed to be communicated in an appropriate way in order to attain the status of evidence.[37] For Gatterer, in short, evidence was produced not by performative skills of any kind (for instance, tapestries, paintings, objects, or even sheer violence) or learned deduction but through sets of attested and quickly and easily understandable genealogical information, for only these could generate graspability and, consequently, evidence. A reasonable form of historiography was one that made history evident.

What counted as sets of genealogical information for Gatterer? He held that these were discovered by sifting through available material in search of the following pieces of information:

> 1) descent, 2) time and place of birth, 3) social status, offices, titles, etc., 4) time and place of death, 5) marriage, and then the descent, birth, offices, title, death,

etc., also of the spouse, 6) children, for people of the male sex always, and for women only when one intends to show a person's maternal lineage.[38]

And, Gatterer continued, "once this has been established as far as possible for each person whose genealogy is to be derived, then the sets of genealogical information drawn from the sources are used to assemble one or more genealogical tables in the usual manner."[39] To avoid mixing genealogy and history inappropriately,[40] Gatterer advised minimizing the information in the genealogical tables attested by documents and including only those details necessary to demonstrate the ancestry of a person and distinguish them clearly from one another. All other essential genealogical information—items of note (*Merkwürdigkeiten*) about a person, for example—ought to be incorporated into the running text.[41]

Genealogy and history were related to each other in Gatterer's thinking in a distinctly ambivalent fashion: pieces of information about a person that were "noteworthy" also belonged to proper history (*eigentliche Geschichte*). In this sense, genealogy and history were intertwined. To avoid their intermingling at the wrong moment, however, he advised withholding information on such indispensable matters, even when it constituted a form of proof that was essential for demonstrating the validity of the attested genealogical tables. Genealogical tables and information on persons and events together formed the dynastic history that—unlike the other three types of genealogical work—Gatterer saw as capable of being raised to the level of evidence.

Deeds versus Blood

In his text "Von der Evidenz," Gatterer had cited the seven-volume *Historia Zaringo-Badensis*, written in Latin by the Baden court historiographer and Strasbourg rhetoric professor Johann Daniel Schöpflin, as a fine example of a dynastic history that expressly connected history and genealogy in the right manner.[42] This investigation was commissioned by the margraves of Baden at a time when the reunification of two confessionally different parts of the country needed to be managed and political claims to power legitimized. With his principal's intention in mind, Schöpflin traced the descent of the margraves of Baden back to the dukes of Zähringen. He assembled all the documents pertaining to the history of the rulers of the margraviate that he could gain access to and then ordered them according to the sequence and circumstances in which they had been produced. Family trees, supported by documents and interspersed with the text, repeatedly illustrated this chronologically structured account and also displayed the side branches and minor lines of the margravial house. With his work on the kinship ties between the margraves of Baden and the Zähringer, Schöpflin had addressed a sensitive political issue of the time. Amid intense jostling for position and power, a diverse assortment of narratives had emerged on this topic.[43] The rulers of Bern, for instance, from the late medieval period on, favored a story that depicted their city-state as having stepped into a power vacuum created by the extinction of the Zähringer in 1218. The Habsburgs, meanwhile, asserted their position as the traditional lords of the southwest of the Holy Roman Empire and portrayed themselves as ancestors (or, alternately, as descendants) of the Zähringer.[44] Against this background, Schöpflin published his work declaring that the documents presented demonstrated that the Zähringer and the margraves of Baden were undeniably connected via a male bloodline.[45]

If this was correct, then the House of Zähringen had never become extinct, and neither the Habsburgs nor the city-state of Bern (nor any other political player) could be its rightful successor in the southwestern territories of the Holy Roman Empire. Schöpflin's genealogical tables, supported by attested tables (*beurkundete Stammtafeln*) and items of note pertaining to individuals, demonstrated that the dukes of Zähringen and the margraves of Baden shared a common male ancestry: a single progenitor whose blood could be traced through a continuous line of male relatives down to Charles Frederick, margrave of Baden, in the eighteenth century. According to Daniel Schöpflin's reasoning, the margravial house of Baden was thus the main Zähringer line at the time. When Charles Frederick was granted the status of elector in 1805, he duly incorporated this information into his new title, styling himself Duke of Zähringen: in full, Charles Frederick, by the grace of God Margrave of Baden and Hochberg, Duke of Zähringen, Sovereign Elector of the Holy Roman Empire, Count Palatine of the Rhine, Landgrave of Breisgrau, of Sausenberg, and in the Ortenau, etc.[46] The grand ducal title he subsequently adopted in August 1808 was rather more concise: Charles Frederick, Grand Duke of Baden, Duke of Zähringen. The new grand duke was not simply descended from the Zähringer: he *was* the Duke of Zähringen because the margrave of Baden and the duke of Zähringen had shared parentage in the past and thus had the same (male) bloodline. The blood of his Zähringer forebears flowed in the veins of the margrave of Baden. Passed down through generations, it had not lost its effectiveness as the legitimizing basis for political power over the centuries, and it was Schöpflin who had attested this.[47]

Another contemporary writer, the anonymous author of the study on Gatterer's methods—"Beyspiel zur Erläuterung der Gattererschen

Methode in der Genealogie" — took up the problem of the Zähringer kinship by looking at what he called the "proper documents of the factual kinship" (*durch gehörige Beweise die wirkliche Anverwandtschaft*). The main question here was whether the last duke of Zähringen, Berthold V (died 1218), only had one sister, Agnes, or if he also had a second one called Anna. This question was significant because — as Schöpflin reported — this Anna was thought to have married a nobleman from the house of Kyburg and borne him a daughter, Helwig, who later married a Habsburg count. If Rudolf of Habsburg, the first king from the House of Habsburg, had been the issue of this marriage, the Habsburgs would indeed have been kinsmen of the Zähringer but would not have been linked to them through a male bloodline, which had been shown to be the case for the margraves of Baden. Keeping this in mind, the anonymous author of the "Beyspiel" decided to approach the question cautiously during his chronological and systematic ordering of the documents he selected as evidence, opting to neither deny Anna's existence nor acknowledge it as proven[48] and advancing only a twelfth-century chronicle that mentioned two sisters of Berthold V. But as the sisters (*sorores*) in this document were not mentioned by name and only Agnes, the presumed second sister, was named in other documents, the author could not quite bring himself to see Anna's existence as having been conclusively attested. Nevertheless, he offered some evidence of his own. He argued, that the sister of the last Duke of Zähringen was married to a Count of Kyburg and that this is proven by part of the Zähringen lands in the hands of the counts of Kiburg.[49]

In the absence of documents naming Anna as the sister of the last Duke of Zähringen, the anonymous eighteenth-century author was prepared to see the mere transfer of possessions through a female line — which he suggested must have occurred after the death of Berthold — as a record of the existence of a sister in this example of genealogical work. In early modern kinship practice, such a "full" sister was in fact entitled to inherit even though she could not continue the (male) bloodline.[50] In the context of a practice of writing kinship that increasingly placed emphasis on patrilineal descent by male blood, Anna (and many other sisters or daughters of rulers with her) had to be rendered invisible for epistemic reasons. Trawling male bloodlines for ancestors, as scholars did hundreds of times in the seventeenth and eighteenth centuries in the service of the European nobility, put them at odds with their own research. The persistent attempts of Gottfried Wilhelm Leibniz to trace the descent of the Brunswick-Lüneburg to the most remote forebear possible without any gaps are a case in point and illustrate the dilemmas in which all scholars could find themselves stuck in this period. Leibniz was working in the service of the electors of Hanover, who had claims to the English throne as well as various other ties and titles, and his research in this matter lasted some thirty years. Learned rivalries and controversies developed, and it frequently seemed as if Leibniz might lose not only his scientific reputation but also the favor of his principal. His investigation into the ancestors of the presumptive future king of England never did find a suitable form. During his search for a pure male bloodline, he had to face the fact that the documents he discovered in the archives demonstrated the important role of female kin in the transfer of territorial property.[51] It was possible, therefore, that pure male blood might not serve to legitimize claims to power or territories. This problem of intersecting logics continued until the end of the eighteenth century. As was already clear above, even the anonymous author who set out to illustrate Gatterer's methods was still confronted with it.

Genealogical History: Origins and Trees

In 1794, Johann Justus Herwig (1736–1810) published a "genealogical history" of the House of Hohenlohe, which he served as an archivist and administrator from 1763 to 1801.

> Just as shedding more light on the history of states, principally to prove that states are inherently founded on the rights of humanity, has become a significant demand of our times—so equally as much does the history of the origins and fortunes of the House of Hohenlohe, already a most noteworthy house in the mists of ancient times, merit closer elucidation and discerning criticism. Only in this present century have historians become accustomed to ceasing to rely on conjectures and on murky and inaccurate sources and turned instead to genuine documents and other secure guarantors of truth, especially in their exploration of the history of the Middle Ages, a period that has long been shrouded in the cloak of darkness.[52]

Following these words of introduction, Herwig praised the achievements of those who had concerned themselves with the House of Hohenlohe; he then remarked, at the end of the first section, that "no perceptive and unbiased historian would, in the future, any longer dare to deny the high birth and ancient origins of the House of Hohenlohe."[53] And, continuing, that for the "history of a house—linked to knowledge of its fates and fortunes and of its former and current rulers and their possessions—to be truly pragmatic and generally useful, it had to be written not only for perusal by scholars but so that every citizen could grasp it [*für die Fassung eines jeden Staatsbürgers*]."[54] These few lines reveal some significant connections and references. To begin with, the author references making something "useful," a purpose that had gained considerable impetus during the Enlightenment. But beyond this, arguments pointing directly to the works of Johann Christoph Gatterer are also very discernible. First of all, the author stressed what was noteworthy (*merkwürdig*) and made it possible in the first place to see the history of the house as part of grand or actual history. Herwig also included comprehensibility as a central element in his work. The German word in Herwig's text is *Fassung*, whereas Gatterer used the term *Fasslichkeit*, here translated as "graspability." This notion of comprehensibility/*Fassung* and graspability/*Fasslichkeit* had not the least to do with the language in which a history had been written. Schöpflin's seven-volume *Historia Zaringo-Badensis*, the dynastic history so praised by Gatterer, was in Latin, as was Gatterer's own dynastic history of the Nuremberg patrician family Holzschuher (written beginning in 1755).[55] Only later did Gatterer choose to publish in German as well. So did Herwig. To ensure that his investigation would be easily and quickly understood, he expressly chose to write his genealogical history of the house of Hohenlohe in German. Two years after the German version of his book came out, a French translation was published, also in the Hohenlohe seat of Schillingsfürst.[56] By this point, the author — a convinced royalist who had been a professor of "belles lettres" (*Elegante Literatur*) in Würzburg — was in rather difficult circumstances politically, and his personal situation had also become somewhat precarious.[57] Herwig's decision to publish his work — which continued genealogical and topographical research he had begun in French in 1790 — in German first and then in a French translation, suggests that he had given his possible readership careful consideration, albeit perhaps for entirely political reasons.[58] His work on the Hohenlohe was presented such that its content could be captured by every citizen (*Staatsbürger*) — including both longstanding local residents and émigrés from revolutionary France alike.[59]

In striving for comprehensibility and making his genealogical history — not dynastic history in the sense of Gatterer and Schöpflin — understandable to all readers, whether German or French speaking, Herwig set out not only to provide evidence by using genealogical information for methodological reasons but also to produce a genealogical history that was politically palatable. At that time, the legitimacy of noble rule was very much in doubt, and it was vital to restore it by drawing on the past as a political resource, not least by supplying genealogical and biographical details about ruling houses and in this manner linking current princes to their origins: here, the medieval East Frankish kings. Herwig had already made this connection in a 1793 petition to Emperor Francis II requesting that the title "Serene" (*durchlauchtig*) be granted to the House of Hohenlohe—an application which he had drafted based on his genealogical work and which Charles Albert II, Prince of Hohenlohe-Schillingsfürst had revised.[60] In his genealogical history of the House of Hohenlohe, Herwig established the true and indisputable origin of the ruling family and equipped it with evidence by generating comprehensibility (*Fassung*). While Gatterer's graspability (*Fasslichkeit*) was intended to elevate documented facts to the level of evidence, Herwig's comprehensibility (*Fassung*) set out to create citizens loyal to princely territories. Publishing genealogical history in the vernacular seemed a suitable step in light of this aim.

Political purposes were also pursued in a genealogical history published by Johann Andreas Genßler (1748–1831) in 1801. *The Welfs: A Treatise Proving the Descent of the Royal House of Prussia from the Oldest Still Flourishing Royal Tree in the World*, which contained basic information about the history of the Franconian Hohenzollern territories, was published for the hundredth anniversary of the elevation of the elector of Brandenburg to the status of king in Prussia (initially, not "king of Prussia") and dedicated to his successor, the current king Frederick Wilhelm III (1770–1840). While that event lay in the distant past, the genealogical history it prompted Genßler to write shows clear similarities with Herwig's, which had been initiated by a much more recent event.[61] As Genßler's title indicated, the purpose of his work was to attest a connection between the House of Welf and the Hohenzollern in order to prove that the royal blood of the Hohenzollern preceded the 1701 coronation of the first king in Prussia and to demonstrate continuity in this regard between the Middle Ages and the present.

Herwig and Genßler also resemble each other in several ways that go well beyond the similarities in their works. Like Herwig, Genßler suffered during the revolutionary movements at the end of the eighteenth century. Indeed, in 1796 he published a short text on the destructive appearance of the French in Germany, *Die Vandalen des 18. Jahrhunderts oder Geschichte des französischen Einfalls in einen Landstrich in Franken* (The Vandals of the Eighteenth Century, or the History of the French Invasion of a Stretch of Land in Franconia).[62] And like Herwig, Genßler can be seen as a royalist who loyally served his noble principal. He had taken up a position as tutor to the hereditary prince of Hildburghausen after studying theology in Jena. He worked at the University of Würzburg, among other places, as did Herwig. Genßler's 1802 two-volume history of the Franconian territory of Grabfeld was furnished with genealogical sections and therefore highly graspable, as was his description of the principality of Hildburghausen, published in Weißenburg as volume 7 in a collection of geographical, historical, and statistical treatises.

A number of these works on princely genealogies found recognition with their target audiences in Hildburghausen, where Genßler became court preacher in 1790, a church privy councilor in 1800, and general superintendent in 1819. In the dedication of his genealogical history, he expressed gratitude to the Prussian king for remaining neutral in politically difficult times when he not only had the king to thank for his modest property (*kleine Habe*) but also for guaranteeing that he could "enjoy peace in his little study, work undisturbed in his sphere of activity, remain cheerful and free of anxiety, and enjoy the company of his family without disruption."[63]

As a churchman who "lived bordering the theater of war,"[64] he then described a violent scene. "The invasion of the French in Königsberg hit the clergymen there hard: one was struck down and lost his life, mortal fear took the health of several others, and two of them have passed away by now, one fled into the forest to seek protection in the lairs of the wild animals."[65] Such anti-French tendencies were plain to see and to capture (emotionally) in the work.[66] The intense feelings Genßler infused his text with are palpable in these brief lines: in what was disguised as an expression of Genßler's gratitude for the king's neutrality, Genßler was actually appealing to the Prussian king to take up arms against the forces of revolutionary France.

Other publications by the two authors discussed here include Genßler's "The Vandals" and Johann Justus Herwig's "To German Citizens of all Three Christian Religions on the French Tyranny of Freedom". These, with many similar texts written during this time of fundamental political change at the turn of the nineteenth century, adopted a friend-or-foe rhetoric predicated on a distinction between patriots with roots and attachments and footloose revolutionaries.[67] Written with the events close at hand, they described devastation, death, and horror as everyday experiences. But unlike Gatterer, who discussed territorial entities (such as nations) in the context of historiographic issues, Genßler and Herwig presented politically and topographically determined spaces as physical bodies vulnerable to invasions. The actual history established in Gatterer's methodology (=historiology), which linked nations (as part of actual history) and genealogy and thus supplied the potential for evidence with its inherent (chronological) order, was transformed. The regent, as both political space and person, formed a homogeneous organism in the genealogical history of Herwig or Genßler or any number of other contemporary historical writers and scholars, who likewise formed homogenous organisms whose existence was rooted in the proved (male) origins of the princes and their ruling houses.

In his endeavor to unearth the origins of the kings of Prussia, Genßler carefully compiled and arranged extensive—but almost completely unannotated—genealogical tables. He organized the information chronologically and systematically in a sequence that made the proposed relationship between the House of Welf and the kings of Prussia appear irrefutable. In describing the House of Welf as a flourishing tree, Genßler was presumably alluding to the significant political power the family held. In so doing, he took up the idea of a living plant, entering an epistemic space represented since the turn of the nineteenth century by analogies between people and plants.[68] In the early modern period, tree imagery had largely served to make kinship clear at a glance. Thick books full of foldout family trees (presumably to make them portable) exemplify this practice. But toward 1800, the tree *metaphor* was replaced by an *analogy* between humans and plants, and representational imagery of trees was abandoned. That reference to a tree as an organism revealed an epistemic practice of representing kinship in Genßler's time. He was not trotting out an obsolete image of a flourishing tree here but making use of a contemporary method in which origins dominated the writing of relationships within a network of kin. Herwig, meanwhile, conceived of his writings as political interventions. His history of the House of Hohenlohe, which linked knowledge of its fortunes to its former and current rulers and their possessions, addressed itself to the citizens of the state (*Staatsbürger*) and set out to be truly pragmatic and generally useful (*wahrhaft pragmatisch und allgemein nützlich*). This pragmatic and useful knowledge was drawn from Herwig's long years in the service of the prince of Hohenlohe. He had already drawn upon it in numerous publications and assembled a mass of information for administrative purposes that he was now publishing as part of his genealogical history. Administrative knowledge turned into history. This technique of history writing did not supply new information but provided fatherland and nation with a genealogical history, a history of origins. It is possible to think of this as a history of tribes—with distinct territories that were themselves part of the story of origins—guaranteed by canons of evidence and claims to proof and offering a new sense of identity to citizens. In a much later (1847) history of the House of Saxony, the Saxon judge Christian Ludwig von Stieglitz praised Genßler's genealogical history for attempting to set his entire investigation on firm historical ground by excluding fables or inventions.[69] At the dawn of the nineteenth century, genealogical history, enriched with ideas about origin as a kind of natural identity, could be read as a political guide.

Political Aspects of Writing Genealogical History

In the preface to his history of the Grabfeld district, Genßler linked evidence of kinship by male bloodlines to evidence of origins, referred to the standards in genealogy, and tied genealogies to a variety of identities. Concerning the purpose of studying the earliest origins of the region, he remarked that this work,

> while mainly for the historical researcher, should also be a reading book for people from all walks of life. This is why I have given so many translations of the supporting documents for information; pointers here and there which may prompt thoughts about how to improve the situation of the people—and also about tending to the seed [i.e., the source] of national honor and the courage in war that our nation will perhaps never find dispensable.[70]

The subscriptions listed on the first page of the book show that Duke Friedrich of Saxe-Hildburghausen ordered twelve copies for the court. The hereditary princes of Saxe-Hildburghausen, Joseph and Georg, each had ordered one,[71] as had the court of the Guttenberg estate in Dörflis. The Saxon duchess Anna Amalia had signed up for three, and the princes of Mecklenburg-Schwerin also proved to be interested customers, signing up for seven copies between them. The abbess of Gandersheim, the prince-bishop of Fulda, the landgrave of Hessen-Kassel, the princes of Orange/Nassau(-Dietz), and the Duke of Saxe-Coburg-Saalfeld also expressed interest in the monograph, as did many other districts and individuals. These included officials and other staff in the courts and the administrations of secular and religious rulers and monasteries—schoolteachers, headmasters, tutors of princes, professors, members of the clergy, canons, the court book binder Göhring, an engraver, estate managers, and an "*ObristLieutenant*" von Meiersbach—but also a tanner, a practical doctor, a watchmaker (Weber by name), a master shoemaker, a factory director, a physician in general practice, and a hospital manager.[72] Genßler's work thus sold well, primarily in noble and educated circles, but some tradesmen were clearly also interested. Such an exclusively nationally oriented genealogical history clearly had an audience at the beginning of the nineteenth century.

The significance of the two factors of blood and origin is well illustrated by Genßler's work. Once raised to the status of evidence through processes designed to establish facts as proven beyond doubt, both could be used to generate a homogeneous history that transcended boundaries of class, gender, and social status and could thus become a national history. The translated supporting pieces (*Beweisstellen*) were expected to generate comprehensibility/*Fassung*, the prerequisite for documents and sets of information to attain the status of evidence. But while Gatterer had primarily been concerned with historical methodological problems (historiology), Genßler, Herwig, and all the others after them used document-based genealogical history during the nineteenth century to match blood and territory by linking the person of the ruler and his proven ancestors to the undeniable origins of his territorial possessions displayed as an organic tree with its roots in ancestral soil.

Gatterer had set out to transform the *généalogies fabuleuses* of the early modern period into a scientific discipline based on sets of information and an insistence on evidence. He had set out to order countless pieces of noteworthy information and thus established a synthesized history in which genealogy and history were methodologically intertwined. This methodological interlocking then provided the precondition for the historiographical practice of a genealogical history that emerged at the cusp of the nineteenth century. In the process, comprehensibility/*Fassung*, as a tool of generating evidence, provided the means to address a public that embraced a wide range of social strata and to allow citizens to identify with rulers, whose roots in particular territories were shown as stretching back into the mists of time.

Conclusion

This chapter set out to trace the complex connections between genealogy and historiography between 1750 and 1850. Its close reading of selected texts has shown how a methodological question evolved into a political tool that, during the first half of the nineteenth century, helped create the basis for a politically useful knowledge system that tended to include or exclude members of various groups along national, ethnic, or gender-specific lines, as well as on the basis of religious or cultural attributes. The role of kinship in this process—or, more accurately, the role of communication about kinship in society—was highly significant. The importance of kinship, and highly diverse facets of kinship, has been foregrounded in countless recent studies examining research in the seventeenth and eighteenth centuries, as well as the emergence of new disciplines like biology or anthropology in the eighteenth and nineteenth centuries. This chapter has attempted to connect kinship—or rather the communication of kinship in society, here in the form of genealogical studies—with the establishment of historiography as a discipline between the mid-eighteenth and mid-nineteenth centuries. Since at least the beginning of the nineteenth century, genealogy has traditionally been regarded as more of an auxiliary to historiography than as an integral component of it, so this has in some ways been a challenging endeavor. But reading methodological and historical texts from the second half of the eighteenth century reveals that genealogy—as a mode of communicating about kinship in societies—played a central role in the transformation of history writing into a scientific discipline bound by rigorous standards. In this context, historiography evolved into a form of genealogical history. The political impact of genealogical history, of genea-graphy so to speak, has become clear. It roots itself in the claim to have firmly established indisputable (genealogical) facts. Genealogy, the way society communicates about kinship, turned out to be a decisive factor, one that was in turn linked to specific concepts of graspability/*Fasslichkeit*, comprehensibility/*Fassung*, and evidence. Claims to present the truth through and about history could be advanced on this basis. Only toward the end of the nineteenth century (at the very latest) did this change due to the ideas put forward by Friedrich Nietzsche on genealogy.

Michaela Hohkamp holds the chair for the history of the early modern period (late fifteenth to early nineteenth centuries) in the Department of History at the Leibniz University of Hannover. Her main research interests are political history (power and violence), the history of historiography (from a gender perspective), and kinship.

Notes

1. On the turn of the seventeenth to the eighteenth century, see, for instance, Maciej Dorna, *Mabillon und andere: Die Anfänge der Diplomatik*, trans. Martin Faber (Wiesbaden: Harrasovitz Verlag, 2019); Sven Erdner, "Leibniz und die braunschweig-lüneburgische Hausgeschichte: Leibniz' Suche nach den Vorfahren Azzos II. von Este zwischen 1685 bis 1716 und sein Prioritätsstreit mit Ludovico Antonio Muratori" (PhD diss., Leibniz Universität Hannover, 2019). Martin Gierl, *Geschichte als präzisierte Wissenschaft: Johann Christoph Gatterer und die Historiographie des 18. Jahrhunderts im ganzen Umfang* (Stuttgart: frommann-holzboog, 2012), 103–5, 110, 352 on André Duchesne (1584–1640). On the Holy Roman Empire at the beginning of the sixteenth century, see Alois Schmid, "Von der Reichsgeschichte zur Dynastiegeschichte: Aspekte und Probleme der Hofhistoriografie Maximilians I. von Bayern," in *Späthumanismus: Studien über das Ende einer kulturhistorischen Epoche*, ed. Notker Hammerstein and Gerrit Walther (Göttingen: Wallstein Verlag, 2000); Thomas Maissen, "Ein Mythos wird Realität: Die Bedeutung der französischen Geschichte für das Florenz der Medici," in *Papst Leo X. und Frankreich: Politik, Kultur und Familiengeschäfte in der europäischen Renaissance*, ed. Götz-Rüdiger Tewes and Michael Rohlmann (Tübingen: Mohr Siebeck, 2006).
2. See Jost Eickmeyer, Markus Friedrich, and Volker Brauer, ed., *Genealogical Knowledge in the Making, Tools, Practices, and Evidence in Early Modern Europe* (Berlin: De Gruyter, 2019).
3. See Carlo Ginzburg, *Die Wahrheit der Geschichte: Rhetorik und Beweis* (Berlin: Klaus Wagenbach Verlag, 2001). Especially on the history of historiography, see Anthony

Grafton, *What Was History? The Art of History in Early Modern Europe* (Croydon: Cambridge University Press, 2012).
4. Roberto Bizzocchi, *Généalogies fabuleuses: Inventer et faire croire dans L'Europe moderne* (Paris: Éditions rue d'Ulm, 2010). See (summarizing his book *Genealogie Incredibili: Scritti dei Storia nell`Europa moderna* [Bologna: Il mulino, 1995, and revised 2009]), Roberto Bizzocchi, "Unglaubliche Genealogien: Eine Neubestimmung," *Quellen und Forschungen aus italienischen Archiven und Bibliotheken*, no. 96 (2016): 245, 255. See Markus Völkel in *Francia: Forschungen zur westeuropäischen Geschichte*, no. 4 (2009): https://perspectivia.net/receive/ploneimport2_mods_00006494?q=Bizzocchi.
5. See Lorraine Daston, *Wunder, Beweise und Tatsachen: Zur Geschichte der Rationalität* (Frankfurt a. M.: Fischer, 2001), 120: "Es ist bemerkenswert, daß die Kustoden der Faktensammlungen nicht selbstverständlich Naturwissenschaftler waren, sondern Historiker oder allenfalls Naturhistoriker."
6. See Gierl, *Geschichte als präzisierte Wissenschaft*.
7. Johann Daniel Schöpflin, *Historia Zaringo-Badensis*, 7 vols. (Karlsruhe, 1763–66); Anonymous, "Beyspiel zur Erläuterung der Gattererschen Methode in der Genealogie," in *Allgemeine Historische Bibliothek von Mitgliedern des königlichen Instituts der historischen Wissenschaften zu Göttingen*, ed. Johann Christoph Gatterer, vol. 12, Abschnitt I: *Abhandlungen sonderlich über die historische Kunst* (Göttingen: Gebauer, 1769).
8. Johann Justus Herwig, *Entwurf einer genealogischen Geschichte des Hohen Haußes Hohenlohe* (Schillingsfürst, 1796; 3rd repr., Berlin, 1873); Johann A. Genßler, *Die Welfen: Eine Abhandlung zum Beweis der Abkunft des königlichen Hauses Preussen von dem noch blühenden ältesten Königsstamme der Welt; Mit der Grundlage zu einer künftigen Geschichte des Fränkischen Gaues Grabfeld verbunden und entworfen zum achtzehenden Jänner Ein Tausend Acht Hundert und Eins als dem Tage der Sekular Feier der Preussischen Königswürde von I. A. Genßler, Sachsen-hildburghausischem Oberhofprediger, Konsistorialrath und Generalsuperintendur-Vikar mit 7 Stamm- und Ahnen-Tafeln* (Hildburghausen: Witwe, 1801).
9. "Daß eine Nation, die ihren Geschmack verbessern will, die guten Muster der Alten zuerst studieren und nachahmen müsse, alsdann aber erst etwas eigenes mit Zuversicht wagen könne, ist eine alte und bekannte Erfahrung." Johann Christoph Gatterer, "Vom Historischen Plan, und der darauf sich gründenden Zusammenfügung der Erzählungen," in *Theoretiker der deutschen Aufklärungshistorie*, ed. Horst Walter Blanke and Dirk Fleischer, vol. 2, *Elemente der Aufklärungshistorik* (Stuttgart: frommonn-holzboog, 1990), 621.
10. See Martin Gierl, "Plan und Poesie: Erzählte und konstruierte Geschichte bei Johann Christoph Gatterer," in *Die Erzählung der Aufklärung*, ed. Frauke Berndt and Daniel Fulda (Hamburg: Felix Meiner Verlag, 2018).
11. Gatterer, "Vom Historischen Plan," 622: "Die Historie, die, so lang sie unter den Menschen bekant, immer gern ihre Schwester, die Dichtkunst voran gehen lässt, aber auch sogleich nach ihr den Rang zu behaupten pflegt, die Historie, sage ich, findet jetzt unter uns eine durch die Dichter geöfnete Laufbahn vor sich, eine ausgebesserte und erweiterte Sprache, und einen an die Muster der Alten gewöhnten Geschmack. Es kömmt nur darauf an, dass man die jüngere Schwester nicht von dem Wege der älteren abweichen lasse, oder sie vielmehr nur nicht verführe, da sie selbst, wenn es auf sie ankömmt, den Fußstapfen derselben gerne folgt."
12. On siblinghood as the matrix of the modern era, see Stefani Engelstein, "Geschwister und Geschwisterlichkeit in der Epistemologie der Moderne," in "Schwesterfiguren," special issue, *L'Homme; Zeitschrift* für Feministische Geschichtswissenschaft 18, no. 2 (2017). See also Stefani Engelstein, *Sibling Action: The Genealogical Structure of Modernity* (New York: Columbia University Press, 2017).
13. Gotthold Ephraim Lessing, *Laokoon: Oder über die Grenzen der Mahlerey und Poesie (...), Erster Theil* (Berlin, 1766; Stuttgart: Philipp Reclam Junior, 2012), chap. 14, pp. 111–12.

14. On ancient history, see Beate Wagner-Hasel, *Antike Welten: Kultur und Geschichte* (Frankfurt a. M.: Campus, 2017), 60ff., 25–26. See also Hans-Joachim Gehrke, *Geschichte als Element antiker Kultur* (Berlin: De Gruyter, 2004).
15. See Gatterer, "Vom Historischen Plan," 623: "Wir finden anfangs keinen Unterschied zwischen Dichtkunst und Historie" and "allein die Geschichtsschreiber lassen doch noch immer aus einigen Merkmalen die Verschwisterung ihrer Göttin [history] mit der Poesie erkennen."
16. On fables in historiography, see Daniel Fulda, *Wissenschaft aus Kunst: Die Entstehung der modernen Deutschen Geschichtsschreibung 1760–1860* (Berlin: De Gruyter, 1996).
17. See Gatterer, "Vom Historischen Plan," 625: "Wenn der Geschichtsschreiber die mühsame Sammlung des historischen Stoffs zu einem Werke vollendet, und aus diesem Chaos das Merkwürdige ausgelesen hat; denn unnütze Dinge wird man allemal noch wegzuwerfen finden, wenn man gleich schon bey der Samlung des Stoffs nur auf erhebliche und des Andenkens der Menschen würdige Dinge aufmerksam gewesen zu seyn vermeynet; wenn also die Samlung und Auswahl der Materialien geschehen ist, alsdann ist es Zeit an den Plan zu denken, nach welchem alle großen und kleinen Stücke, woraus das Gebäude ausgeführt werden soll, am Schicklichsten in Ordnung gebracht werden können, so dass man, nach der Vollendung des Werks, ohne Mühe begreifen kann, warum ein Stück der Materialien eben hieher, und nicht an einen andern Ort gesetzt worden ist. Dies ist die erste Arbeit des Geschichtsschreibers nach der Samlung und Anordnung des Stoffs, man mag sie nun die Stellung, oder die Anordnung, oder auch die Anlage der Erzählungen heissen."
18. See Gatterer, "Vom Historischen Plan," 631–32: "Man folgt den Reihen der Stammtafeln, und wenn sich eine Familie, wie mehrenteils geschieht, in mehrere Linien theilt, so beschreibt man eine Linie nach der anderen. Die beygefügten Stammtafeln erhalten den Lauf der Erzählung in Ordnung und gewähren zugleich den Vortheil des Gleichzeitigen eben so leicht, als in der eigentlichen Historie die synchronistischen Tabellen."
19. See Gatterer, "Vom Historischen Plan," 633: proper or grand history (*eigentliche[n] oder grosse[n] Historie*), person of the regent (*Person des Regenten*), noteworthy (*Merkwürdigkeit*), genealogical history (*genealogische Historie*), actual history (*eigentliche[n] Geschichte*).
20. See Johann Christoph Gatterer, *Einleitung in die synchronistische Universalhistorie: Zweyter Band, Von Philipp und Alexander M. bis auf unsere Zeit* (n.d., n.p.), Tafel I: Ländereien und Trennung der Persischen Monarchie. On the concept of genealogy pursued in Gatterer's work, see Gierl, *Geschichte als präzisierte Wissenschaft*, 101–22.
21. Evidence had quite a different meaning in the early modern period. See Jan-Dirk Müller, "Evidentia und Medialität: Zur Ausdifferenzierung von Evidenz in der Frühen Neuzeit," in *Evidentia. Reichweiten visueller Wahrnehmung in der Frühen Neuzeit*, ed. Gabriele Wimböck et al. (Berlin: LIT Verlag, 2007).
22. Gottlieb Walther, *Critische Prüfung der Geschichte von der Ausrottung des zähringsichen Stamms durch Vergiftung zweier Söhnen Berchtolds V.* (Bern, 1765): "Dass ein Gelehrter, und in der Weltweisheit so wohl, als in den Geschichten erfahrner Mann in einer mit Fleiss ausgearbeiteten, Abhandlung die Kennzeichen bestimmen möchte, durch welche man die Fabeln, welche die Geschichten verdunkeln, von dem Wahren unterscheiden könnte. Dieser Wunsch ist gerecht. Die historischen Wahrheiten sind mit so vielen Erdichtungen untermauert, dass man allenthalben zweiflen, allenthalben mit vielem Misstrauen fortschreiten muss, wann man vor seinen Fall sicher seyn will."
23. For more on how genealogies were depicted and used, see Natalie Büsser, "Adel in einem Land ohne Adel: Soziale Dominanz, Fürstendienst und Verwandtschaft in der schweizerischen Eidgenossenschaft, 15. bis 18. Jahrhundert" (PhD diss., Universität Zürich, 2016).
24. See Christiane Klapisch-Zuber, *Stammbäume* (München: Knesebeck, 2004).

25. Johann Christoph Gatterer, "Von der Evidenz in der Genealogie," in *Allgemeine Historische Bibliothek von Mitgliedern des königlichen Instituts der historischen Wissenschaften zu Göttingen*, ed. Johann Christoph Gatterer, vol. 12, Abschnitt I: *Abhandlungen sonderlich über die historische Kunst* (Göttingen: Gebauer, 1769), 8: "Aber weit unter sie, oder eigentlich zu reden, in die allertiefste Classe herunter gehören die sogenannten Stammbücher, die Stammbäume und alle übrige Familiennachrichten von gleichem Schlage; denn sie sind meistens kaum 200 Jahre alt, und voll von Familiensagen ... Kurz zu sagen, die Geschichtsscheiber, und noch weit mehr Stammbücher u. d. gl. sind dem Genealogen das, was dem Teutschen Juristen das Römische Recht ist. Man gebraucht sie nur im Nothfalle, im Subsidium."
26. See Gatterer, "Von der Evidenz." This text appeared in the *Allgemeine Historische Bibliothek von Mitgliedern des königlichen Instituts der historischen Wissenschaften zu Göttingen*, a journal he himself had founded.
27. Gatterer, "Von der Evidenz," 4.
28. Gatterer, "Von der Evidenz," 4: "unbeurkundete(n) Stammtafeln, das ist, solche, wo die genealogischen Sätze durch keine Art von Beweis unterstüzet sind."
29. Gatterer, "Von der Evidenz," 4: "beurkundete Stammtafeln."
30. Gatterer, "Von der Evidenz," 4: "fasslich."
31. For an almost paradigmatic example, see André Duchesne, *Histoire généalogique de la Maison de Montmorency et de Level: Justifiée par Chartes Titres, Arrests, et autres bonnes et certaines preuves; Enrichie de plusieurs Figures ... par André Du Chesne, Toyrencay et Géographe du Roy* (Paris, 1624). On Duchesne, see Olivier Poncet, "The Genealogist at Work," in *Genealogical Knowledge in the Making: Tools, Practices, and Evidence in Early Modern Europe*, ed. Jost Eickmeyer, Markus Friedrich, and Volker Bauer (Berlin: De Gruyter, 2019); and also Gierl, *Geschichte als präzisierte Wissenschaft*, 103–5, 110, 352.
32. Gatterer, "Von der Evidenz," 5:

    Die dritte Gattung können die sogenannten Geschlechterhistorien ausmachen: eine vermischte Art von Werken, die aus Genealogie und Historie zusammengesezt sind, denn man beschäftiget sich darin nicht blos allein mit der Abstammung der Personen, die zu einem Geschlechte gehören, sondern zugleich auch mit deren Begebenheiten. In den besten Werken von dieser Gattung ist der genealogische Theil ungefähr nach der Methode de Du Chesne bisher bearbeitet worden, das ist, man hat die Stammtafeln zwar zu beweisen gesucht, aber die Wahrheit der Sätze ist selten bis zur Evidenz erhoben worden. Was den historischen Theil anbelangt, so gehört die Untersuchung über die Evidenz der darin erzählten Merkwürdigkeiten nicht hierher, sondern zur Materie von der Evidenz der eigentlichen Historie. Als Beyspiele sind bekannt ... Schöpflins Historia Zaringo-Badensis, ... Man hat endlich auch Untersuchungen über einzelne genealogische Gegenstände. Ich mache aus ihnen unter dem Namen genealogischer Erörterungen, die vierte Gattung genealogischer Werke.

    On Duchesne und Gatterer, see Gierl, *Geschichte als präzisierte Wissenschaft*, 103–5, 110, 352. Especially on Duchesne, see Poncet, "Genealogist at Work," 199–220.
33. Gatterer, "Von der Evidenz," 3–4.
34. Gatterer, "Von der Evidenz," 4: The evidence of genealogical matters can "alsdann stattfinden, wenn diese Dinge nicht nur als wahr, sondern auch so vorgestellet werden, daß man sich von ihrer Wahrheit geschwind und leicht überzeugen kan."
35. Gatterer, "Von der Evidenz," 11.
36. Gatterer, "Von der Evidenz," 10.
37. Gatterer, "Von der Evidenz," 10: "zum höchstmöglichen Grad der Fasslichkeit gebracht werden" (be made as graspable as possible).
38. Gatterer, "Von der Evidenz," 9: "1) Die Herkunft, 2) Zeit und Ort der Geburt, 3) vom Stand, das Amt, die Würde etc. 4) Zeit und Ort des Todes, 5), die Vermählung, da dann wieder des Gemahls oder der Gemahlin Herkunft, Geburt, Amt Würde, Tod etc.

vorkommen. 6) die Kinder, und zwar bey Personen männlichen Geschlechts allezeit, bey Weibspersonen aber nur alsdann, wenn man vorhat, die mütterliche Abstammung einer Person zu zeigen."

39. Gatterer, "Von der Evidenz," 9: "(w)enn dieses bey allen Personen, die man genealogisch ableiten will, so weit es möglich ist, beobachtet worden; alsdann sezet man nach Anleitung der aus den Quellen gezogenen genealogischen Sätze, Eine oder mehrere Stammtafeln, nach der gewöhnlichen Art zusammen."
40. Gatterer, "Von der Evidenz," 9–10: "wer in Stammtafeln mehr anzeigt, als so eben gemeldet worden, der vermengt zur Unzeit die Genealogie mit der Historie." Deshalb "… thut [man] sehr wol, wenn man in diesem Fall den grösten Theil der in diesen Stammtafeln sonst unentbehrliche genealogischen Sätze auf den Text verspahret, und in die Stammtafeln sonst weiter nichts sezet, als was zur Kenntnis der Abstammung und Unterscheidung einer Person von der anderen nötig ist."
41. Gatterer, "Von der Evidenz," 10.
42. On Johann Daniel Schöpflin, see Jürgen Voss, *Universität, Geschichtswissenschaft und Diplomatie im Zeitalter der Aufklärung: Johann Daniel Schöpflin (1694–1771)* (München: Fink, 1979).
43. See Michaela Hohkamp, *Gemordete Söhne, lebende Schwestern: Herrschaft und Verwandtschaft in historiographischen Texten vom späten Mittelalter bis zum Ende des 18. Jahrhunderts: Ein Beitrag zur Geschichte europäischer Geschichtsschreibung aus verwandtschafts- und geschlechtergeschichtlicher Perspektive* (unpublished manuscript).
44. See Dieter Mertens, "Die Habsburger als Nachfahren und als Vorfahren der Zähringer, mit einem Exkurs zum Grabmal Bertolds V.," in *Die Zähringer: Eine Tradition und ihre Erforschung*, ed. Karl Schmid (Sigmaringen: Jan Thorbecke Verlag, 1986).
45. Johann Daniel Schöpflin, *Historia Zaringo-Badensis*, vol. 1: *Liber Praevius* (Karlsruhe, 1763), unpaginated, 8 pages total: "Per has enim edoctus sum, Zaringiae Ducibus & Marchionibus Badae commune esse sanguinis vinculum & parentem commune."
46. The electoral title held by the Margraves was based on their new acquisitions in the Palatinate, around Heidelberg, while the title Duke of Zähringen was linked to the Landgraviate of Breisgau.
47. See Christopher Johnson et al., eds., *Blood & Kinship: Matter for Metaphor from Ancient Rome to the Present* (New York: Berghahn Books, 2013).
48. See Anonymous, "Beyspiel," 30.
49. Anonymous, "Beyspiel," 31: "So hat des letztern Herzogs von Zähringen Schwester einen Grafen von Kiburg zur Ehe gehabt; dies beweiset auch ein Theil der zähringischen Länder in den Händen der Grafen von Kiburg."
50. See Michaela Hohkamp, "Do Sisters Have Brothers? The Search for the '*rechte Schwester*': Brothers and Sisters in Aristocratic Society at the Turn of the Sixteenth Century," in *Sibling Relations and the Transformation of European Kinship 1300–1900*, ed. Christopher H. Johnson and David W. Sabean (New York: Berghahn Books, 2013).
51. See Erdner, "Leibniz."
52. Herwig, *Entwurf einer genealogischen Geschichte*, 3:

So sehr es in unseren Tagen wesentliches Bedürfniß ist, die Geschichte der Staaten in ein helleres Licht zu setzen, um vornehmlich zu beweisen, dass Staaten überhaupt auf Rechten der Menschheit gegründet sind—so sehr verdient die Geschichte von dem Ursprung und den Schicksalen des bereits in dem grauesten Alterthum sehr merkwürdigen Hauses Hohenlohe eine nähere Erläuterung mit Geschmack und Kritik. Nur erst in dem gegenwärtigen Jahrhunderte gewöhnten sich die Geschichtschreiber nicht mehr nach Konjekturen und trüben unrichtigen Quellen, sondern aus ächten Urkunden und andern gleichzeitig sichern Gewährsmännern die Wahrheit besonders der in so viele Dunkelheiten eingehüllten Geschichte des mittleren Zeitalters zu durchforschen.

53. Herwig, *Entwurf einer genealogischen Geschichte*, 3: "Geschichtforscher von Einsicht und Unbefangenheit (es) mehr wagen wird, dem Hause Hohenlohe die Hoheit und das Alterthum seines Ursprungs zu widersprechen."
54. Herwig, *Entwurf einer genealogischen Geschichte*, 3. To make a history of a house "wahrhaft pragmatisch und allgemein nützlich," it should be written "für die Fassung eines jeden Staatsbürgers."
55. Johann Christoph Gatterer, *Historia Genealogica Dominorum Holzschuherorum ab Aspach et Harlach in Thalheim Cet. Patriciae Gentis tum apud Norimbergenses tum in exteris etiam Regionibus Toga Sagoque Illustris ex incorruptis Rerum Gestarum Monimentis conquisita* (Nürnberg, 1755).
56. Herwig's publication was not universally received enthusiastically by experts; see Landesarchiv Baden-Württemberg, GA 50, Bü. 36. Protest Herwigs gegen eine Rezension seines "Entwurfes einer genealogischen Geschichte" des hohen Hauses Hohenlohe in der Allgemeinen Literaturzeitung.
57. Herwig's documents and official papers are held by the Landesarchiv Baden-Württemberg. GA 50, Bü. 19 (Dienst), Bü. 20 (zur Person, Konversion und Ehescheidung).
58. Landesarchiv Baden-Württemberg, GA 50, Bü. 32.
59. The Royalist army of the Prince of Condé was headquartered in the Hohenlohe Residence at Schillingsfürst, where Louis XVI's former confessor also resided during the 1790s. Many other émigrés from revolutionary France were also welcomed there.
60. Landesarchiv Baden-Württemberg, GA 50, Bü. 34. On history and histories as a historiographical concept, see Reinhart Koselleck, *Vergangene Zukunft* (Frankfurt a. M.: Suhrkamp, 1984), 50.
61. At this point, in 1801, Frederick Wilhelm III of Prussia was still attempting to maintain a generally neutral foreign policy. He only joined the anti-French coalition shortly before the Battle of Jena und Auerstedt (1806).
62. *Die Vandalen des 18. Jahrhunderts oder Geschichte des französischen Einfalls in einen Landstrich in Franken* appeared in Hildburghausen in 1796.
63. "[R]uhige Plätzchen auf meiner Studirstube, meinen ungestörten Wirkungskreis, meine sorgenfreie Heiterkeit, das ungeschränkte Zusammenseyn meiner Familie," in *Die Welfen*, Vorrede, unpaginated.
64. "[A]n den Grenzen des Kriegsschauplazzes wohne," in *Die Welfen*, Vorrede, unpaginated.
65. "[D]er Einfall der Franzosen ins Amt Königsberg kam den dasigen Geistlichen theuer zu stehen. Einem raubte ein Schlag das Leben, mehrern die ausgepresste Todesangst die Gesundheit, von welchen auch schon zwei entschlafen sind, einer entfloh in den Wald, um einen Schuzort auf den Lagerplätzen der wilden Thiere zu suchen," Genßler, *Die Welfen*, Vorrede, unpaginated.
66. Elisabetta Lupi, "Eine Nation 'una di memorie, di sangue e di cor'? Das antike Sizilien und die Magna Graecia in der italienischen Altertumsforschung des 19. Jahrhunderts." *Historische Zeitschrift*, forthcoming.
67. "An Teutschlands Bürger von allen drei christlichen Religionen über die französische Freyheitstyrannei (1793)."
68. See Sophie Ruppel, *Von Pflanzen und Menschen: Botanophilie in der aufklärerisch-bürgerlichen Gesellschaft um 1800* (Köln: Böhlau, 2019).
69. Christian Ludwig von Stieglitz, *Das Haus Sachsen* (Dresden: Weinhold und Söhne, 1847), 29.
70. Johann Andreas Genßler, *Geschichte des Fränkischen Gaues Grabfeld* (Schleusingen, 1802), vi: "Mein Buch, wenn es gleichwohl vorzüglich nur dem Geschichtsforscher angehört, sollte doch auch Lesebuch für allerlei Stände werden. Daher nun so viele Übersezzungen der Beweisstellen; darum hie und da Winke, um Anlass zu geben, über die verbesserte Lage des Volks nachzudenken — auch den Keim der Nazionalehre

zu pflegen und den kriegerischen Muth, der unserer Nazion vielleicht nie entbehrlich sein dürfte." (Underlines in the original.)
71. Genßler, *Geschichte des Fränkischen Gaues Grabfeld*, ix.
72. Genßler, *Geschichte des Fränkischen Gaues Grabfeld*, ix–xiv. This list is not necessarily complete.

Bibliography

Anonymous. "Beyspiel zur Erläuterung der Gattererschen Methode in der Genealogie." In *Allgemeine Historische Bibliothek von Mitgliedern des königlichen Instituts der historischen Wissenschaften zu* Göttingen. Vol. 12, Abschnitt I: *Abhandlungen sonderlich* über *die historische Kunst*, edited by Johann Christoph Gatterer, chap. 18. Göttingen: Gebauer, 1769.

Bizzocchi, Roberto. *Genealogie Incredibili: Scritti di Storia nell'Europa moderna*. Bologna: Il mulino, 1995.

———. *Généalogies fabuleuses: Inventer et faire croire dans L'Europe moderne*. Paris: Éditions rue d'Ulm, 2010.

———. "Unglaubliche Genealogien: Eine Neubestimmung." *Quellen und Forschungen aus italienischen Archiven und Bibliotheken*, no. 96 (2016): 245–63.

Büsser, Natalie. "Adel in einem Land ohne Adel: Soziale Dominanz, Fürstendienst und Verwandtschaft in der schweizerischen Eidgenossenschaft, 15. bis 18. Jahrhundert." PhD diss., Universität Zürich, 2016.

Daston, Lorraine. *Wunder, Beweise und Tatsachen: Zur Geschichte der Rationalität*. Frankfurt a. M.: Fischer, 2001.

Dorna, Maciej. *Mabillon und andere: Die Anfänge der Diplomatik*. Translated by Martin Faber. Wiesbaden: Harrassovitz Verlag, 2019.

Duchesne, André. *Histoire généalogique de la Maison de Montmorency et de Level: Justifiée par Chartes Tiltlres, Arrests, et autres bonnes et certaines preuves; Enrichie de plusieurs Figures ... par André Du Chesne, Toyrencay et Géographe du Roy*. Paris, 1624.

Eickmeyer, Jost, Markus Friedrich, and Volker Brauer, ed. *Genealogical Knowledge in the Making, Tools, Practices, and Evidence in Early Modern Europe*. Berlin: De Gruyter, 2019.

Engelstein, Stefani. "Geschwister und Geschwisterlichkeit in der Epistemologie der Moderne." In "Schwesterfiguren," edited by Almut Höfert, Michaela Hohkamp, and Claudia Ulbrich. Special issue, *L'Homme: Zeitschrift für Feministische Geschichtswissenschaft* 18, no. 2 (2017): 49–68.

———. *Sibling Action: The Genealogical Structure of Modernity*. New York: Columbia University Press, 2017.

Erdner, Sven. "Leibniz und die braunschweig-lüneburgische Hausgeschichte: Leibniz' Suche nach den Vorfahren Azzos II. von Este zwischen 1685 bis 1716 und sein Prioritätsstreit mit Ludovico Antonio Muratori." PhD diss., Leibniz University Hanover, 2019.

Fulda, Daniel. *Wissenschaft aus Kunst: Die Entstehung der modernen Deutschen Geschichtsschreibung 1760–1860*. Berlin: De Gruyter, 1996.

Gatterer, Johann Christoph. *Einleitung in die synchronistische Universalhistorie: Zweyter Band, Von Philipp und Alexander M. bis auf unsere Zeit*. N.p., n.d.

———. *Historia Genealogica Dominorum Holzschuherorum ab Aspach et Harlach in Thalheim Cet. Patriciae Gentis tum apud Norimbergenses tum in exteris etiam Regionibus Toga Sagoque Illustris ex incorruptis Rerum Gestarum Monimentis conquisita*. Nürnberg, 1755.

———. "Von der Evidenz in der Genealogie." In *Allgemeine Historische Bibliothek von Mitgliedern des königlichen Instituts der historischen Wissenschaften zu* Göttingen. Vol. 12, Abschnitt I: *Abhandlungen sonderlich über die historische Kunst*. Edited by Johann Christoph Gatterer, 1–17. Göttingen: Gebauer, 1769.

———. "Vom Historischen Plan, und der darauf sich gründenden Zusammenfügung der Erzählungen." In *Theoretiker der deutschen Aufklärungshistorie*. Vol. 2: *Elemente der Aufklärungshistorik*, edited by Horst Walter Blanke and Dirk Fleischer, 621–62. Stuttgart: frommann-holzboog, 1990.

Gehrke, Hans-Joachim. *Geschichte als Element antiker Kultur*. Berlin: De Gruyter, 2004.

Genßler, Johann Andreas. *Die Welfen: Eine Abhandlung zum Beweis der Abkunft des königlichen Hauses Preussen von dem noch blühenden ältesten Königsstamme der Welt ... und entworfen zum achtzehenden Jänner Ein Tausend Acht Hundert und Eins als dem Tage der Sekular Feier der Preussischen Königswürde von I. A. Genßler, Sachsenhildburghausischem Oberhofprediger, Konsistorialrath und Generalsuperintendur-Vikar mit 7 Stamm- und Ahnen-Tafeln*. Hildburghausen: Witwe, 1801.

———. *Geschichte des Fränkischen Gaues Grabfeld*. Schleusingen, 1802.

Gierl, Martin. *Geschichte als präzisierte Wissenschaft: Johann Christoph Gatterer und die Historiographie des 18. Jahrhunderts im ganzen Umfang*. Stuttgart: frommann-holzboog, 2012.

———. "Plan und Poesie: Erzählte und konstruierte Geschichte bei Johann Christoph Gatterer." In *Die Erzählung der Aufklärung*, edited by Frauke Berndt and Daniel Fulda, 599–607. Hamburg: Felix Meiner Verlag, 2018.

Ginzburg, Carlo. *Die Wahrheit der Geschichte: Rhetorik und Beweis*. Berlin: Klaus Wagenbach Verlag, 2001.

Grafton, Anthony. *What Was History? The Art of History in Early Modern Europe*. Croydon: Cambridge University Press, 2012.

Herwig, Johann Justus. *Entwurf einer genealogischen Geschichte des Hohen Haußes Hohenlohe*. Schillingsfürst, 1796. 3rd reprint. Berlin, 1873.

Hohkamp, Michaela. "Do Sisters Have Brothers? The Search for the *'rechte Schwester'*: Brothers and Sisters in Aristocratic Society at the Turn of the Sixteenth Century." In *Sibling Relations and the Transformation of European Kinship 1300–1900*, edited by Christopher H. Johnson and David W. Sabean, 65–83. New York: Berghahn Books, 2013.

———. *Gemordete Söhne, lebende Schwestern: Herrschaft und Verwandtschaft in historiographischen Texten vom späten Mittelalter bis zum Ende des 18. Jahrhunderts; Ein Beitrag zur Geschichte europäischer Geschichtsschreibung aus verwandtschafts- und geschlechtergeschichtlicher Perspektive* (unpublished manuscript).

Johnson, Christopher, Bernhard Jussen, David W. Sabean, and Simon Teuscher, eds. *Blood & Kinship: Matter for Metaphor from Ancient Rome to the Present*. New York: Berghahn Books, 2013.

Klapisch-Zuber, Christiane. *Stammbäume*. München: Knesebeck, 2004.

Koselleck, Reinhart. *Vergangene Zukunft*. Frankfurt a. M.: Suhrkamp, 1984.

Lupi, Elisabetta. "Eine Nation 'una di memorie, di sangue e di cor'? Das antike Sizilien und die Magna Graecia in der italienischen Altertumsforschung des 19. Jahrhunderts." *Historische Zeitschrift* 314 (2022), 283–311.

Lessing, Gotthold Ephraim. *Laokoon: Oder über die Grenzen der Mahlerey und Poesie (…), Erster Theil*, chap. 14. Stuttgart: Philipp Reclam Junior. First published 1766 in Berlin.

Maissen, Thomas. "Ein Mythos wird Realität: Die Bedeutung der französischen Geschichte für das Florenz der Medici." In *Papst Leo X. und Frankreich: Politik, Kultur und Familiengeschäfte in der europäischen Renaissance*, edited by Götz-Rüdiger Tewes and Michael Rohlmann, 117–36. Tübingen: Mohr Siebeck, 2002.

Mertens, Dieter. "Die Habsburger als Nachfahren und als Vorfahren der Zähringer, mit einem Exkurs zum Grabmal Bertolds V." In *Die Zähringer: Eine Tradition und ihre Erforschung*, edited by Karl Schmid, 151–74. Sigmaringen: Jan Thorbecke Verlag, 1986.

Müller, Jan-Dirk. "Evidentia und Medialität. Zur Ausdifferenzierung von Evidenz in der Frühen Neuzeit." In *Evidentia: Reichweiten visueller Wahrnehmung in der Frühen Neuzeit*, edited by Gabriele Wimböck, Karin Leonhard, Markus Friedrich, and Frank Büttner, 57–81. Berlin: LIT Verlag, 2007.

Poncet, Olivier. "The Genealogist at Work." In *Genealogical Knowledge in the Making: Tools, Practices, and Evidence in Early Modern Europe*, edited by Jost Eickmeyer, Markus Friedrich, and Volker Bauer, 199–220. Berlin: De Gruyter, 2019.

Ruppel, Sophie. *Von Pflanzen und Menschen: Botanophilie in der aufklärerisch-bürgerlichen Gesellschaft um 1800*. Köln: Böhlau, 2019.

Schmid, Alois. "Von der Reichsgeschichte zur Dynastiegeschichte: Aspekte und Probleme der Hofhistoriografie Maximilians I. von Bayern." In *Späthumanismus: Studien über das Ende einer kulturhistorischen Epoche*, edited by Notker Hammerstein and Gerrit Walther, 84–112. Göttingen: Wallstein Verlag, 2000.

Schöpflin, Daniel. *Historia Zaringo-Badensis*. Vol. 1: *Liber Praevius*. Unpaginated, 8 pages in total. Karlsruhe, 1763.

Stieglitz, Christian Ludwig von. *Ueber den ältesten Ursprung des durchlauchtigsten Hauses zu Sachsen*. Dresden: Weinhold und Söhne, 1847.

Völkel, Markus. "Review." *Francia: Forschungen zur westeuropäischen Geschichte*, no. 4 (2009). Retrieved 26 August 2020 from https://perspectivia.net/receive/ploneimport2_mods_00006494?q=Bizzocchi.

Voss, Jürgen. *Universität, Geschichtswissenschaft und Diplomatie im Zeitalter der Aufklärung: Johann Daniel Schöpflin (1694–1771)*. München: Fink, 1979.

Wagner-Hasel, Beate. *Antike Welten: Kultur und Geschichte*. Historische Einführungen 8. Frankfurt a. M.: Campus, 2017.

Walther, Gottlieb. *Critische Prüfung der Geschichte von der Ausrottung des zähringsichen Stamms durch Vergiftung zweier Söhnen Berchtolds V.* Bern, 1765.

Chapter 3

Race and Kinship
Anthropology and the "Genealogical Method"

Staffan Müller-Wille

> Hier wie dort geht es um Verwandtschaft, nicht um Verbrüderung.
> (Here as there, it is affinity that matters, not fraternization.)
>
> —Marcel Beyer on ornithology and poetry in *Putins Briefkasten*
> (Frankfurt/M.: Suhrkamp, 2016), 117, my translation

Introduction

Late nineteenth-century anthropological research was to a large extent preoccupied with questions of inheritance, but with regard to two disparate sets of phenomena. On the one hand, anthropologists subjected physical, psychological, linguistic, and cultural differences to taxonomic description and comparison. Inheritance was of interest here insofar as the contemporary distribution of "races" and "tribes" was interpreted as bearing some relation to the stages and divisions through which humanity had evolved. On the other hand, societies outside of Europe began to be scrutinized for the institutions that enabled their reproduction. In this respect, kinship systems and the associated organization of societies into clans, moieties, or castes—in other words, the structures along which names, status, and property were passed on—attracted attention because social and economic order seemed to be perpetuated along these lines. While contemporary anthropology, and the historiography it has generated, largely considers the former, evolutionist, approach as outdated—and as intimately related to ideologies of progress, white supremacy and racism that justified the imperial and colonial ambitions of European nation-states—the latter, structural-functionalist approach has kept a hold on the discipline despite fundamental criticisms from within that have emphasized the fluidity of kinship as a matter of practice and negotiation. A whole wave of anthropological studies of kin relations in contemporary societies, and the metamorphoses they have undergone in the context of new genetic and reproductive technologies, has born witness to this over the past three decades.[1]

The much-lamented divide between biological and sociological approaches to human inheritance thus seems to be firmly rooted in the nineteenth century: to put it bluntly, Darwin with his *Descent of Man* (1871) and Engels with his *Ursprung der Familie* ("Origin of the Family," 1891) provided two radically different departure points for what was to follow. But was there really no common ground between the two? Notions of descent, genealogy, consanguinity, affinity, and above all, the metaphor of "shared blood," seem to afford a common conceptual framework for both domains. As George Stocking has pointed out, up to the end of the nineteenth century, "'blood'—and by extension 'race'—included numerous elements that we would today call cultural; there was not a clear line between cultural and physical elements or between social and biological heredity."[2] Modern European racial discourse, as argued by Renato Mazzolini, had itself grown out of the extension of a caste system of European making with corresponding interdictions and regulations regarding marriage and inheritance.[3] Eugenicists and racial hygienists relied on what clearly can be, and indeed were, addressed as rules of exogamy (avoidance of incest) and endogamy (exclusion of the "unfit") in their programs for social reform.[4] The bonds created by race and kin therefore appear as two sides of the same coin, a coin that was kept in circulation as an object of scientific scrutiny by fears that promiscuity and incest endangered natural and social order, and by corresponding desires to control and direct human procreation.

This entanglement of kinship and race through the metaphor of blood has provided a strong motive for the influential critique of kinship studies that David Schneider put forward in 1984. The object of this critique was what Schneider called the "genealogical grid" or "method" that analyzes kin relations "in terms of the relations arising out of the processes of sexual reproduction." Rather than being a universally applicable tool, Schneider argued, European "folk conceptions, categories and ideology in general are carried over into [this] analytic scheme, the etic grid, with but minor modifications." In particular it was the assumption that "Blood Is Thicker than Water" that made "kinship or genealogical relations unlike any other social bonds, for they have especially strong binding force and are directly constituted by, grounded in, determined by, formed by, the imperatives of the biological nature of human nature." The genealogical method was just another expression of the "ethnoepistemology of European culture," or "what might be called 'biologistic' ways of constituting and conceiving human character, human nature and human behavior."[5]

In this chapter, I want to problematize yet at the same time specify and reinforce Schneider's critique. My reason for this revisionist exercise is that the precise relationship between kinship and race becomes curiously unclear as soon as one ceases to take the meaning of the metaphor of "shared blood" for granted.[6] The categories that are used to analyze kin and race relations, respectively, simply do not map onto each other. Racial categories obey the logic of the Linnaean hierarchy, constituting a system of mutually exclusive classes contained within more extensive and again mutually exclusive classes. Ideally, therefore, an evolutionary explanation of the formation of races would trace them back to a single point of origin. The history of racial descent, and the bonds or "blood relations" that descent presumably produces, is one of progressive differentiation, usually compared with a growing tree. Categories describing kin relations, on the other hand, overlap systematically—an individual can be a daughter, a mother, a wife, a sister-in-law, a cousin, an aunt, and a niece at one and the same time. And the bonds resulting from these relations do not derive from singular origins but from sexual unions that produce new relations of affinity and consanguinity with each generation. Kin relations, therefore, do not unfold like a growing tree. They constitute a network or a structure reminiscent of "a trellis—a figure made up of lines crossing as often as they divide," as Claude Lévi-Strauss formulated it long ago. The corresponding image that comes to mind for the historical process that reproduces these relations is therefore not that of a growing tree but of the weaving of a continuous piece of cloth.[7]

To get a clearer understanding of the genealogical method, its epistemological grounding, and its biopolitical constitution, I am going to shift emphasis in this chapter from the ideological content of the genealogical method to its use as an analytic instrument. In the first section, I will describe Rivers's genealogical method and then turn to two earlier attempts in the second half of the nineteenth century, by Francis Galton (1822–1911) and Lewis Henry Morgan (1818–81), to provide rigidly analytical "grids" or schemata describing kin relations. I will make two points regarding these schemata: first, that they were explicitly introduced to overcome perceived shortcomings of "Western" vernacular kin terminologies; and, second, that their authors' primary aim was to make kin relations commensurable and calculable and to map them out as completely and consistently as possible.

In the second section, I will then proceed to place Galton's and Morgan's "inventions" in the context of a much broader history of genealogical analysis. My point there will be that the genealogical method was specifically informed by methods for measuring kinship and defining racial status that emerged in the early modern period. The third section will then turn to a case study and look in detail at the role that kinship and race played in the anthropometric work of Franz Boas (1858–1942). What a close look at his research practices reveals is that he used genealogical analysis to deconstruct assumptions about the inheritance of racial traits. This did not supplant race as an empirical category, however. Quite on the contrary, Boas's anthropometric studies relied on the ability of both observers and observed to determine a person's racial ancestry.

In short, while being "biologized" in a certain limited but important sense, namely in the sense of universalizing filiation, kinship was also, and probably more importantly, politicized by the genealogical method, emerging from the process as a powerful biopolitical instrument that shaped populations and subjectivities. Rivers's genealogical method simply emulated, on the smaller scale of anthropological surveys and fieldwork, the methods of registering and classifying kin that had grown from the efforts of national and colonial administrations to impose categories of inclusion and exclusion onto heterogenous and dynamic populations. Its universal applicability was therefore not predicated on some shared understanding of kinship but rather on the shared presumption that, ultimately, filiation provided the analytic lens under which kin relations, and the language that was used to engage with them, revealed their true meaning.

Analyzing Kinship

The invention of the "genealogical method" is conventionally ascribed to an article that the British anthropologist William Halse Rivers Rivers (1864–1922) published in the *Sociological Review* in 1910.[8] The method itself, as described by Rivers, is deceptively simple. In essence, it consists in constructing complete genealogies of an observed "community" from interviews that employ "as few terms denoting kinship as possible." Thus, in an example from the Eastern Solomon Islands that Rivers presented to illustrate the method, a genealogy or "pedigree" comprising four generations and twenty-four related individuals was generated by posing questions to a single "informant" — "Kurka or Arthur," as he was named in the article[9] — using only the terms "father, mother, child, husband and wife." Making sure that these terms were understood in their "proper" or "real" sense and cross-examining several informants from the same community supposedly enabled the anthropologist to obtain "complete" and "accurate" genealogies of a community with great geographical spread and historical depth.[10] Rivers published the genealogies he and others had constructed on this basis during the Torres Straits expedition in seventeen page-filling "tables" that were included in volume 5 of the *Reports of the Cambridge Anthropological Expedition to Torres Straits* (1904; see figure 3.1). In his words, they "furnish[ed] a fairly complete register of births, deaths and marriages extending back for about a hundred years" for inhabitants of the islands of Mabuiag and Badu.[11]

It is important to note that Rivers did *not* suppose that the drawing up of such pedigrees alone would provide any deeper anthropological insights. Rather, the genealogical method consisted in collating these pedigrees with *other* information relevant to a given anthropological subject. Thus, for the study of kinship systems (or "systems of relationship" as Rivers also called them), one had to proceed by asking an informant "the terms which he would apply to the different members of his pedigree; and reciprocally the terms which they would apply to him."[12] This was "the first and most obvious use" of the genealogical method according to Rivers, but certainly not the only one; in an analogous manner, he insisted, other subjects of interest to the anthropologist—like "the regulation of marriage," "the laws regulating descent and the inheritance of property," "migrations," "magic and religion," "various demographic problems," and "problems of heredity"—could be fruitfully studied by employing the genealogical method.[13]

If the core of the genealogical method consisted of mapping all kinds of social and biological relationships and processes onto an abstract genealogical grid, two features of the method stand out: first, the *analytical* reduction of the genealogical grid to a minimal set of elementary kin relations—"father, mother, child, husband and wife"—that immediately issue from filiation and, notably, include both cognate (parent-child) and affinal relations (husband-wife);[14] and second, the construction of supposedly *complete* pedigrees of entire populations based on a meticulous concatenation of these elementary relations alone. Both analyticity and completeness may appear as goals that any genealogical representation would self-evidently strive for. But they had in fact enjoyed a fairly recent history when Rivers proposed his method. In the following, I will complement my description of Rivers's method by looking in some detail at two earlier proposals for an analysis of kinship that may well have influenced his own.

The first proposal I want to turn to stems from Morgan, whose distinction of descriptive and classificatory kinship terminologies in *Systems*

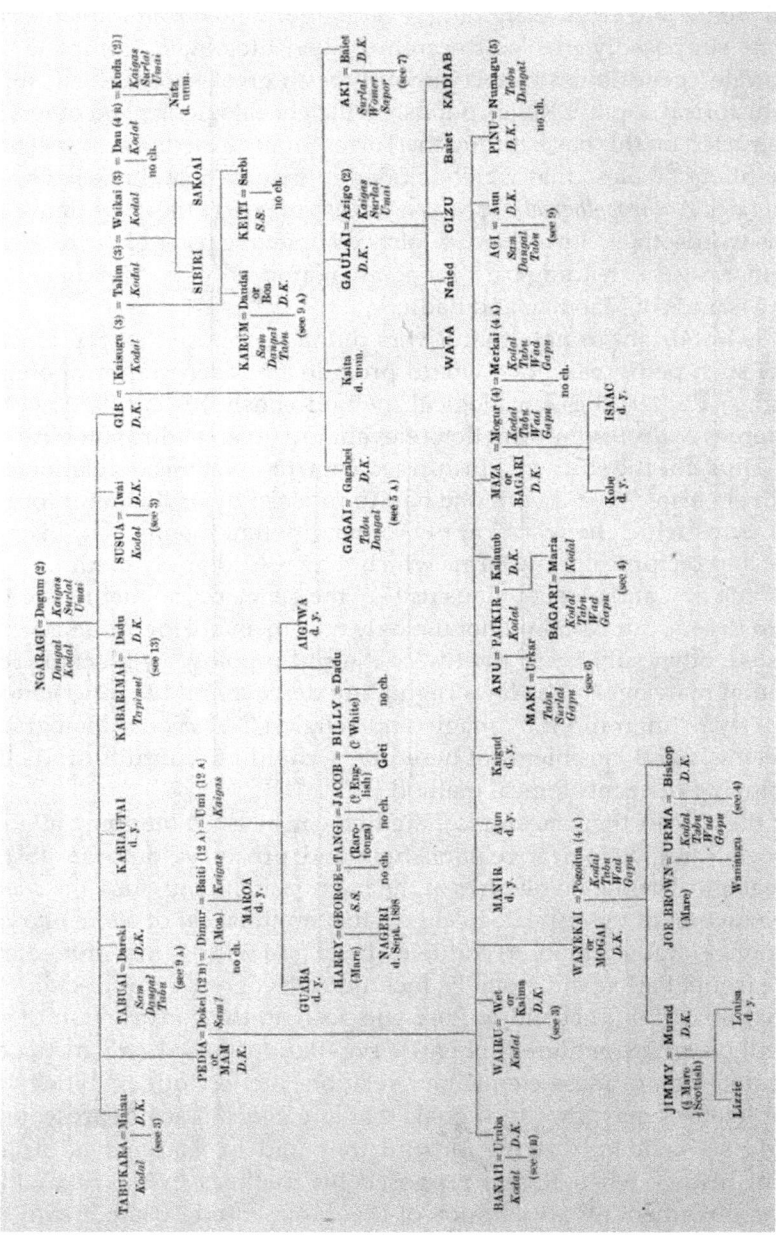

Figure 3.1. Pedigree forming part of a series covering the genealogy of the "Western Tribe of Torres Straits." The pedigree contains cross-references ("see 3," etc.) to the other pedigrees in the series, the whole series thus constituting one continuous genealogy. Source: A. C. Haddon et al., *Sociology, Magic and Religion of the Western Islanders*, table 1A.

of Consanguinity and Affinity (1871) formed one of the chief theoretical problems that Rivers addressed on the basis of the genealogies he had collected in the Torres Straits.[15] Morgan's initial motivation for studying kinship was a curious one. When he carried out his first investigations of Iroquois society in New York State in 1844, he wanted to understand the organization of their social life in order to emulate it in a fraternal organization, the Grand Order of Iroquois, which he had joined after completing his legal studies and being admitted to the bar in 1842.[16] After the renewal of his ethnographic interests in 1857, he began to collect data on kinship terminologies more extensively and systematically, first within North America and then for other countries as well, especially in Asia.

Morgan conducted this research by circulating questionnaires or "schedules" containing questions regarding tribal organization and kinship terminology. According to the introductory chapter of *Systems of Consanguinity and Affinity of the Human Family*, Morgan first sent out printed schedules to "the several Indian missions in the United States, to the commanders of the several military posts in the Indian country, and to the government Indian agents." Unsatisfied with the answers he received, Morgan took it upon himself to carry out "annual explorations among the Indian nations" to gather kinship terms. To get at similar information outside of North America, he asked both the Smithsonian Institution and the US government for assistance. This was granted, and another version of the schedule was printed, adding up to 218 kin terms (see figure 3.2), which was then sent out to a worldwide network of diplomatic staff, missionaries, and traveling naturalists to procure the relevant data from interviews with native speakers of various languages.[17]

Initially, Morgan's schedules were modeled on lexical lists used by other American ethnographers for linguistic studies and hence simply asked for a translation of a number of English kin terms, resulting in two-columned tables. He soon, however, expanded his kin vocabulary to encompass kin terms that spanned several generations and covered relatives up to the fifth collateral degree. Many of these had no clear equivalent in the English vernacular but could be constructed from available terms designating simpler relations. As he later recalled, compiling these kin terms implied "considerable labor," as they had to be "sufficiently full to describe every known relationship, and yet arranged upon such a method as to be simple and intelligible."[18] More importantly, however, it resulted in a tripartition of the lists: foreign terms and their English equivalents were now tabulated together against an additional column headed "Description of Relationship." In the words of Morgan's biographer Thomas R. Trautmann, this indicated a "departure from the philological model" by employing "semantic rather than lexical means." The table did

DEGREES OF RELATIONSHIP—Continued.

Description of Relationship.	Name, or Native Word, in English Letters.	Translation of the same into English.
26. My Father's Sister's Husband		
27. " Mother's Brother		
28. " " Brother's Wife		
29. " " Sister		
30. " " Elder Sister		
31. " " Younger Sister		
32. " " Sister's Husband		
33. My (a Man's) Brother's Son		
34. " " Son's Wife		
35. " " Daughter		
36. " " Daughter's Husband		
37. " " Grand-Son		
38. " " Daughter		

Figure 3.2. Part of Lewis Henry Morgan's "schedule" inquiring for kinship terms in a foreign language and their English translation. Source: Lewis Henry Morgan, *Circular in Reference to the Degrees of Relationship among Different Nations*, Smithsonian Miscellaneous Collections (Washington, DC: Smithsonian Institute, 1860).

not simply record words in two different languages that were deemed to be synonymous but rather compiled the ways in which these words were used in two different languages in relation to the same domain of objects. What became visible in the second and third column of the table was thus not simply different terminologies but also differences in the way in which each of these terminologies systematized kin relations by means of classification, combination, and augmentation.[19] A good example is provided by the table comparing data from the "Seneca-Iroquois" and the "Tamil People of South Asia" that Morgan published in *Systems*. By tabulating both Iroquois and Tamil terms, together with their respective English translations, against a column now headed "Description of persons," patterns emerge in the arrangement of words, roots, prefixes, and suffixes that reveal how both terminologies are representative of what Morgan called "classificatory systems of relationship": systems that classify collateral cousins of various degrees with siblings.[20]

What Morgan's schedule shares with Rivers's genealogical method is the reduction of kinship to filiation, which allowed for the construction of more complex relations from a few, elementary relations. The "description" of kin expressed each possible relation between an assumed "ego" (indicated by the first-person pronoun "my") and another person by a combination of primitive terms—"mother," "father," "son," "daughter," "sister," "brother," and, for affine relatives, "husband" and "wife." The list of terms thus constructed extended from simple terms like "my son" to composite ones like "my father's brother's son's wife" or "my mother's mother's mother's brother's son's son's son." Morgan himself called this "a natural system, numerical in character ... resting upon an ordinance of nature," referring to the fact that, thus constructed, the overall grid of relations could be used to quantify degrees of relationship. "All of the descendants of an original pair, through intermediate pairs," he stated, "stand to each other in fixed degrees of proximity, the nearness or remoteness of which is a mere matter of computation."[21]

Morgan called his schedule a "new instrument in ethnology," and it did make its way, list of kin terms included, into the first edition of *Notes and Queries on Anthropology* that was issued in 1874 by the British Association for the Advancement of Science.[22] But unlike Rivers—as far as I could see from the secondary literature—he never used it to chart concrete pedigrees or genealogies. Instead, his interest was restricted to the comparison of kinship systems as they emerged from the tabulation of kinship terminologies against his "schedule." Morgan believed that this would furnish "the most simple as well as compendious method for the classification of nations on the basis of affinity of blood"—similarity in kinship systems indicated proximity in evolutionary descent.[23]

Searching for predecessors of the "genealogical method" as a device to draw up "complete registers" of actual populations takes one in a different direction that was still evident from the title of Rivers's first publication on the subject. Discussing his method for the first time in an article published in the *Journal of the Anthropological Institute of Great Britain and Ireland* in 1900, he referred to it as a method for "Collecting Social and Vital Statistics."[24] As Henrika Kuklick has suggested, this firmly places his genealogical method—as an "instrument of survey research"—in the British tradition of medical, psychological, and sociological statistics rather than making him an heir of Morgan's comparative methods.[25] And as indicated above, problems of demography and heredity, that is, essentially statistical problems, remained high on the agenda for Rivers in his 1910 article as well.

This brings me to the second proposal for an analysis of kinship that may have formed the background for Rivers's genealogical method but is rarely discussed in this context. Two years before Morgan's *Systems*, in 1869, Francis Galton published *Hereditary Genius*, a book that tried to demonstrate statistically that "man's natural abilities are derived by inheritance."[26] A whole chapter, titled "Notation," was dedicated to the question of how to extract and document genealogical information from the biographical literature Galton perused in order to support his hypothesis that particular talents were more frequent within certain families than one would expect from their random distribution. Like Morgan, Galton found vernacular English unsuited for the purpose; "our ordinary nomenclature," he claimed, "I found far too ambiguous as well as cumbrous for employment in this book." In order to get "rid of all [the] confused ... language," Galton introduced a notation system that symbolized seven fundamental kinds of male kin by single letters: father, grandfather, uncle, nephew, brother, son, and grandson. In addition, typography was used to indicate the gender of a relative and whether he or she was related on the maternal or paternal side: italics indicated female gender, whereas capital letters referred to paternal and lowercase letters to maternal kin. Thus, although the abbreviation "*u*" was derived from "uncle," it denoted a maternal aunt, or one's mother's sister. "The notation I employ," Galton claimed, "disentangles relationships in a marvellously complete and satisfactory manner, and enables us to methodise, compare, and analyse them in any way we like."[27] Decisively, as with Morgan, it allowed Galton to count and determine degrees of relationship, which was essential to his argument since it consisted in showing that the frequency of talented individuals diminished the more distant their relation was to a particularly talented person.[28]

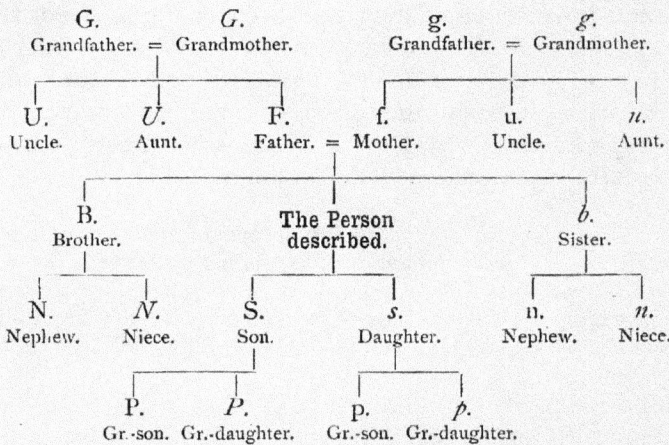

Figure 3.3. Diagram illustrating a notation system that Francis Galton used to compile pedigrees of "eminent" individuals. Source: Francis Galton, *Hereditary Genius: An Inquiry into Its Laws and Consequences* (London: Macmillan, 1869), 52.

A diagram that Galton added to illustrate his notation system can bring to the fore further peculiarities of his, as well as Morgan's, analytic kin terminologies (see figure 3.3). Two features of the diagram are striking. First, it strictly structures kinship by generational cohorts; two or more persons are aligned within the same generation solely based on their ancestry, and irrespective of their age. Second, the diagram is strictly symmetrical because it includes both maternal and paternal kin. In an article published in *Nature* in 1883, Galton used both features to suggest that the "binary system of arithmetic" was not only a sufficient but actually a far superior means to express relations of ancestry. "If we were familiar with [binary] notation," he maintained,

> we should long since have described each form of ancestry by it. Instead of saying that "B was a grandmother, namely a father's mother, of A," we should have said "B was 101 of A." Or again, instead of saying that "C was first cousin once removed to D, the father's father's parents of C being the mother's parents of D," we should have said "the 1000-1 of C are the 110-1 of D."[29]

Galton here exhibits an unlimited (and hilarious) trust in the power of mathematics to replace the vernacular with a language of precision and clarity. The ambition is clear: to document the "kindred," as Galton called it, surrounding a given person as unambiguously and completely as feasible.[30] *Hereditary Genius* was filled with genealogical diagrams that tried to do so for "eminent persons" in order to convince the reader that a surprisingly high number of equally "eminent" persons were to be found in their vicinity, measured by kinship in the first, second, and third degree. Galton's later suggestion of using binary numbers for the notation of kin relations, moreover, clearly shows that he believed that such a system could be expanded to uniquely identify any conceivable cognate relation. "This notation," he explained, "has the advantage of an index, and of showing very compendiously how much has been done, and how much remains to do."[31]

Elements of "Western" Kinship

Both Morgan and Galton thought of their analytic kinship schemata as innovations, emphasizing their instrumental nature in gaining new insights into the evolution of kinship systems and the inheritance of "talent," respectively. They were not theories themselves but tools designed to generate new insights. This is also the reason why both schemata were introduced without any elaborate theoretical justification or discussion of sources. As tools or instruments, Morgan's "schedule" and

Galton's "notation" had to prove themselves by offering answers to specific questions. This, of course, is not to say that their "invention" came out of the blue. But in order to see exactly where it came from, one has to cast the net wider and look at a range of heterogenous concepts and practices, old and new, mundane and specialized, that were mobilized by nineteenth-century scholars and scientists to forge new understandings of kinship.

The first thing to note in this respect is that some of the concepts that we consider to be of obvious relevance for understanding kinship today, both in its social and biological senses, such as generation, reproduction, or heredity, were either undergoing radical change in the nineteenth century or were else in the process of being articulated for the first time. Generation, which since antiquity had been used to designate individual acts of procreation, was given the additional meaning of a cohort of "people born in about the same time" by a whole range of biological and political thinkers in Europe and North America in the early nineteenth century. Reproduction came to mean production of offspring, the re-generation (and renewal) of populations in analogy to the capitalist production of wealth. And heredity, finally, entered the biological lexicon—from the fringes of breeders' lore and physicians' knowledge of family diseases—only around the time of Darwin's publication of *Origin of Species* (1859), with Galton being one of the first to call for its theoretical articulation. Underlying these developments was an abstraction from the physiology of procreation, pregnancy, and birth to gain a perspective on the interconnected and communal life of populations.[32]

The fluidity of concepts of inheritance and reproduction, and the fact that the very object of their theoretical endeavors was still under construction, imply that neither Morgan nor Galton could presuppose a theory that would have allowed them to draw any concrete conclusions about the biological or cultural significance of specific kin relations. In consequence, the assumptions they built on were extremely thin abstractions. These assumptions included, first, that all kinship relations can be reduced to filiation, that is, to the set of elementary relations resulting among two individuals producing a third through sexual intercourse; second, that these elementary relations are additive and commensurable, so that kinship degrees could be expressed in quantitative terms; and third, that these relations are universal and hence can be used to assign to each and every individual a unique position within a web of kin relations potentially spanning the whole of humanity. "Biological" knowledge enters these assumptions only to the degree that they build on the conviction that sexual reproduction is universal in humans: to put it simply, that every individual, without exception, is born from one (and only one) mother and sired by one (and only one) father.

Even if Morgan's and Galton's kinship schemata were not derived from already articulated theories of human reproduction, it is nevertheless possible to relate them to similar schemata that played an important role in the articulation of such theories. The first of these takes us immediately into the tangled history of race and kinship. It was epitomized by a visual genre, titled *Las Castas*, in eighteenth-century Mexico. Often arranged as a grid, these paintings showed mixed couples and their children and were often inscribed with short sentences assigning the two parents to their respective *castas* and naming the *casta* of their child as the product of their "mixture" (*mestizaje*). An *Español* and a *Negra*, for example, produced a *Mulato*, an *Español* and an *India* a *Mestizo*. The offspring from mixed marriages could themselves enter unions again, thus leading to a further proliferation of *casta* categories.[33]

These paintings, it should be noted, were largely produced for the Iberian market, and how far they reflect realities of a strict racial stratification of early modern colonial societies remains a matter of scholarly debate. There is little doubt, however, that they document a fascination with the underlying logic of race mixture among European audiences and Creole elites.[34] This fascination became even more pronounced once the visual genre was translated into scholarly texts. Often presented in tabular form, the mixture of races appeared as a phenomenon of strict regularity that could also be mathematically expressed.[35] On the ad hoc assumption that both parents contributed equally to the generation of a child, the mixed child was assigned certain proportions of "blood." Thus the French naturalist Georges-Louis Leclerc, Comte de Buffon (1707–88), explained in 1777 in one of the founding texts of the natural history of man that a *quarteron*, issuing from a *mulâtre* and a *négresse*, "has three quarters of black and one quarter of white" (*a trois quarts de noir & un quart de blanc*).[36] And Alexander von Humboldt (1769–1859), in his *Essai politique sur le royaume de la Nouvelle-Espagne* (1811), presented the following table to illustrate the system of defining *castas* terms by the "mixture of blood" (*mélange du sang*), which in his view built on "principles ... sanctioned by custom" (*principes sanctionnés par l'usage*):

Castes.	Mélange du sang.
Quarterons,	¼ nègre ¾ blanc.
Quinterons,	⅛ nègre ⅞ blanc.
Zambo,	¾ nègre ¼ blanc.
Zambo Prieto,	⅞ nègre ⅛ blanc.[37]

What is striking about the *casta* system, and in part may explain its attraction for eighteenth- and nineteenth-century scholars, is the way in which it functions as both a taxonomic and an analytic scheme. Reducing social reproduction to filiation, it allows to assign every individual unambiguously to its *casta* simply by taking into account its parents' *casta*, while a person's *casta* provides information not only about the *casta* its immediate parents belonged to but also, through decomposition, about the *casta* of more distant ancestors as well. While theories of generation up until the mid-nineteenth century usually assumed that male and female contributions to the constitution of the offspring were unequal, the *casta* system gave both contributions equal weight and assumed that portions of ancestral "blood" simply combined additively in offspring.[38] The Oxford English Dictionary documents that terms like "quarteron" (or more often "quadroon"), "octeroon," and even "quinteron" (or "quintroon") became part of vernacular English in the course of the eighteenth century, and Galton used the terminology when illustrating his conception of the "stirps"—the generative substance that gives rise to both parents and offspring and receives discrete contributions from each generation of ancestors—with reference to the inheritance of human skin color.[39] Morgan, a monogenist and abolitionist, was less concerned with physical race, but an inventory of his library shows that he possessed Josiah C. Nott and George R. Gliddon's *Types of Mankind* (1855), which contained a detailed table of *casta* terms.[40]

Galton, but especially Morgan, would also have been very familiar with another scheme that has a longer history than the *casta* system. In canon law, diagrams exploring consanguine and affine kinship relations respectively—so-called *arbores consanguinitatis* and *affinitatis*—had been in use since the High Middle Ages in order to determine which kin would fall under incest prohibitions, and similar diagrams were used in civil law, whose roots reached all the way back to Roman law, to regulate inheritance and succession, especially in the absence of a will or, as in the Napoleonic Code, in cases where the law stipulated inheritance portions that were due to certain kin.[41] The relations issuing from filiation were central for this scheme as well, but it used these to introduce a systematic measure for the closeness of kin. Degrees of kinship were defined by the number of generations that separated two given individuals from their last common ancestor, or alternatively, but more rarely, by counting the number of filiations that connected two individuals with each other. With the dawn of the early modern period, the metaphor of blood began to be used increasingly to emphasize the importance of relations of lineage and descent, at once "facilitat[ing] processes of mixing and diluting … [and] … paving the way for very exclusive conceptions of belonging."[42]

Morgan, like many other early social anthropologists, was a lawyer and very familiar with the long-standing tradition of such diagrams. He annotated the section of his own copy of William Blackstone's (1723–80) *Commentaries on the Laws of England* (originally published in 1765–70) that explained "the true notion of ... kindred or alliance in blood" with the help of a diagram. Morgan also included a table titled "Diagram of Consanguinity: English" in his *Systems*, which he explicitly modeled on Blackstone's.[43] I have not been able to ascertain any explicit references to legal accounts of kinship by Galton, but in his statistical work on the inheritance of "talent," as we saw above, he heavily relied on measuring kinship by "degrees." It is also notable that his central theoretical concept, the already mentioned *stirps*, directly reflects the terminology of the legal tradition, where *stirps* (meaning trunk, stock, or root) designates the filial line from which collaterals of various degrees descend.[44]

Speaking of the juridical tradition of tables of consanguinity and affinity, it is tempting to add a final element to the mix from which Morgan's and Galton's "inventions" emerged. In a now classic article, Mary Bouquet argues "that the neglected *visual force* of the genealogical diagram derives from ... scientific and Biblical precedents, as well as secular family trees." To make this point, she surveys late eighteenth-century Dutch family trees and Tree of Jesse depictions, as well as Ernst Haeckel's (1834–1919) evolutionary "Pedigree of Man" (*Stammbaum des Menschen*, 1874), which she suggests to consider as "formidable precedents for Rivers's visualization of kinship in the genealogical diagram."[45] The trouble with this interpretation, is that the reduction to (male or masculinely connotated) lineages, shared by all the examples that Bouquet surveys, constitutes a limitation that genealogical analysis, as conceived by Morgan, Galton, and eventually Rivers, was explicitly designed to transcend. In fact, Galton's own diagram (see figure 3.3)—with its symmetrical treatment of paternal and maternal, lineal and collateral, cognate and affine, ascendent and descendent kin—barely resembles a tree, unless one considers "The Person described" in the middle as the trunk of the tree and all of their relatives, ancestors as well as descendants, as so many branches growing out of it, which barely makes sense. The same urge to map out kin in all possible directions without privileging any one specific relationship is at work, as we saw in the previous section, in Morgan's "schedule" (see figure 3.2) and in the pedigrees that Rivers drew up of the "Western Tribe of Torres Straits" (see figure 3.1).

If any "precedents" come to mind, they are again from the legal sphere, with another diagram in Blackstone's *Commentaries*: the "Table of Descents," a foldout displaying the "Paternal" and "Maternal Line" of one "John Stiles" in symmetrical fashion and symbolizing cognate relationships with stylized ropes and marriage bonds with a handshake. Strikingly different in visual appearance from the traditional *arbores consanguinitatis* and *affinitatis*, this "table" was used by Blackstone to illustrate "the manner in which we must search for the heir of a person." And indeed, although rules of succession stipulated a strong preference for the paternal line, in the absence of any surviving agnates, relatives in the maternal line might ultimately be entitled to an inheritance too. Blackstone chose the symmetric layout, that is, for the systematic reason that it could capture even the unlikely case that no male heir was available to accept an inheritance.[46]

Diagrams like Blackstone's, or Galton's almost a century later, remain a rarity in print until the very end of the nineteenth century, despite the fact that such visual representations seem to chime well with the interests of what David Sabean and Simon Teuscher have called "a 'kinship-hot' society, one where enormous energy was invested in maintaining and developing extensive, reliable, and well-articulated structures of exchange among connected families over many generations."[47] A context for which these evolving interests have been particularly well-documented is psychiatry. Attempting to uncover causes for "familial degeneration," psychiatrists began to include information about the incidence of mental diseases, mental retardation, suicides, and alcoholism among relatives in their case histories of individual patients from the early nineteenth century onward, and on this basis distinguished between patients with "directly," "indirectly," "atavistically," or "collaterally" inherited mental diseases depending on which kind of relatives in networks of extended kin were afflicted by the same diseases. Yet, even in this context, it was only in the 1890s that physicians and psychiatrists started to include family pedigrees in their publications, resulting in a veritable explosion of genealogical diagrams that tried to capture the complete network of kin surrounding a person of interest—or even entire populations, as in the case of Rivers—in order to discern and study patterns of inheritance.[48]

Reducing kinship to elementary relations of filiation—and turning these into an analytical instrument that could serve to chart out any number of relations among individuals across entire populations—was thus not the consequence of an ancient "visual imperative" for the family tree, even if this may have lent rhetorical power to the pedigrees published by the likes of Rivers. On the contrary, genealogical analysis provided the condition for establishing an entirely *new* regime of visibility. This new regime, moreover, was not established at a stroke but had to prevail over considerable epistemological and technological obstacles: it is actually not at all obvious how comprehensive "pedigrees" of entire populations can be constructed let alone made to fit within the confines of paper space, and what they might be able to reveal about reproductive processes is far from evident. To appreciate this in more detail, I want to turn to a case study in the next section that shows how something approaching the genealogical method was deployed in the decades before Rivers eventually formalized it.

Constructing Populations

Franz Boas is usually not included in critical studies of the anthropology of kinship, despite the fact that his formative influence on twentieth-century anthropology is beyond doubt. The reason may be that Boas's persistent criticism of the evolutionist and typological assumptions underwriting most anthropological work at his time make him an unlikely suspect in endorsing the kind of biologism that allegedly is built into the genealogical method. Yet, as I will try to show in this section, Boas's criticism in part built on what can be considered an early, and probably inadvertent, application of the genealogical method.

In 1891, Boas was commissioned by Frederic Ward Putnam, head of the Department of Ethnology and Archaeology of the World's Columbian Exposition that was to be staged in Chicago in 1893, to prepare an exhibition on physical anthropology. Boas seized this opportunity to demonstrate his prowess in advanced methods of anthropometry, and he organized field surveys during the summers of 1891 and 1892 that sent about seventy trained volunteer assistants swarming out all over the United States "to measure native peoples of America." In the end, about twelve thousand individuals had been measured, and the results were presented to visitors of the World's Fair in an exhibition consisting of "charts, diagrams, photographs, scientific instruments used in the work, and collections of skulls and skeletons of the native peoples."[49]

From the anthropometric surveys Boas organized, many original data sheets have been preserved in the archives of the American Museum for Natural History in New York and the American Philosophical Society in Philadelphia. I have argued elsewhere that the way in which Boas's assistants recorded geographical and genealogical data on these sheets resulted in an astonishing potential for re-analysis of the material collected—in fact, as recently as 2003, physical anthropologist Richard L. Jantz praised Boas's data as "a resource with many as yet unexploited research possibilities."[50] Here, I want to focus on the way in which genealogical information was recorded and later exploited by Boas in order to draw and present conclusions from his anthropometric campaigns.

For his anthropometric surveys, Boas used printed forms that his assistants had to fill out, thus leaving little room for initiative by the latter and ensuring that information was collected in a standardized manner. At the top of the form, Boas asked his field observers to "[n]umber each record in order used and write your name after number." A subset of datasheets that I have studied in detail and that pertain to Chickasaw individuals living in Stonewall and Tishomingo in the Indian Territory, now Oklahoma, shows that these instructions were indeed heeded: the data for Chickasaw was collected by one "Richard T. Buchanan," who entered a consecutive serial number for each record of anthropometric variables produced from a particular individual.[51] In addition, the "place" and the "date of observation" was dutifully noted by Buchanan.

Boas did not stop at isolated observations, however. By asking his assistants to also record genealogical relationships between the study subjects, he rather created sets of data sheets that were structured by genealogical relations. The Chickasaw, who had been forced to settle near a closely related tribe, the Choctaw, in the Indian Territory in 1832 and who successfully resisted subsequent attempts to merge them with the Choctaw, provide a particularly intriguing example of the complexity of the resulting connections.[52]

A first way in which the data sheets established genealogical connections was by asking individuals to specify kin relations directly. In this, however, field assistants were offered a very limited range of options. The printed observation sheets were differentiated by sex, and for female study participants the observer had to fill in fields entitled "Mother of No.," "Daughter of No.," and "Sister of No.," and for male ones the corresponding fields "Father of No.," "Son of No.," and "Brother of No." In the sheets on the Chickasaw, I have not come across an example where all of these fields were filled in. Instead, the serial numbers that Buchanan did fill in suggest a pattern according to which he first measured parents, and then their children, possibly moving from household to household, so that the filial relations he captured never extend beyond two generations. But in principle, the questions Boas posed through his questionnaire betray the same ambition that also is at the heart of Rivers's genealogical method: to reduce kinship to elementary relationships in order to be able to construct genealogies across entire populations.

Alongside the fields asking for straightforward parental, filial and sibling relationships, there are two more fields, titled "Tribe of father" and "Tribe of mother," through which genealogical information entered Boas's data in a more indirect but also more intriguing way. As one might expect, each and every individual measured was recorded as belonging to the "Chickasaw" tribe. But answers to the questions relating to the "tribe" of their mother and father reveal very complex, mixed ancestral backgrounds. On one sheet for a female study subject, for example,

"Half-breed" is entered for "Tribe of father," while her mother is stated to have been "Chickasaw." If one looks at the records of the same woman's children, one finds "¾ Chickasaw ¼ white" recorded as the tribe of their mother. "Half-breed" thus reveals itself as referring to individuals with one Chickasaw and one European parent.[53] Many sheets also record mixed Chickasaw and Choctaw, or "Choctaw half-breed" ancestry. The Chickasaw had been a slave-owning tribe, having adopted plantation agriculture, and had intermarried with whites since the late eighteenth century. While they did not adopt their freedmen after emancipation in 1863 (unlike the Choctaw), one does find quite a number of sheets where the tribe of father or mother is stated as "Chickasaw and negro."[54]

The apparent discrepancy between the assignment of "Chickasaw" as the tribe of the persons recorded and the mixed ancestry documented in the tribe of their parents is easily explained. The Chickasaw were organized by exogamous matrilineal clans, and tribal affiliation as well as possessions were passed on along maternal lines.[55] One can therefore safely assume that the persons recorded regarded not only themselves but also their parents as Chickasaw—as long as the parents' mothers were in turn also Chickasaw. This raises the suspicion that the information on mixed ancestry might actually not have been provided by the informants themselves but by the field observer. That this is not the case, however, is evident from occasional notes that the latter jotted down on the data sheets. Thus, Buchanan expressed doubts that a person, whose tribe of father was given as "½ Chickasaw ½ Choctaw" and tribe of mother as "Chickasaw," was really free from admixture: "The gentleman says he has heard two parents say that they had some French blood in them. He shows white blood."[56] In another case, where tribe of both father and mother was stated as "Chickasaw," Buchanan added: "Negro blood appears in complexion ... and in shape of face."[57] Tribal (or racial) affiliation seems to occasionally have been a matter of negotiation between observer and informant, but in the end, the latter seems to have had the last word when it came to filling in the answers for "tribe of father" and "tribe of mother." Another piece of evidence pointing in the same direction is the fact that assessments of mixed ancestry could sometimes acquire a curious form. On one sheet, the tribe of mother was recorded as "⅔ Chickasaw ⅓ white."[58] The only way to make sense of this proportion is to assume that cousin marriage was involved in this case. Since this reduces the number of grandparents to six individuals, an account of blood proportions with reference to grandparental contributions will result in thirds.

The answers given to the questions about parental "tribes" allowed Boas to carry out an analysis of relations that possessed far greater generational depth—in some cases reaching back to the great-grandparental generation—than the ascertainment of direct kin. I have not been able to establish whether Boas had foreseen, or even required, that the language of blood proportions would be used to fill in entries for tribal affiliation or whether the information on racial ancestry emerged spontaneously from the interactions of field observers and their interviewees. In any case, when he summarized results from his anthropometric surveys for the German *Zeitschrift für Ethnologie* (Journal for ethnology) in 1895, he demonstrated considerable virtuosity in handling the information thus obtained. The article focused exclusively on bodily stature and head shape and considered these variables not only among "full blooded" individuals but also among "half-castes (*Mischlinge*) between Indians and other races, especially whites."[59]

Boas proceeded in his analysis by first presenting data for the overall population of tribes and then breaking it down by geographic location, age, gender, and racial descent in ever more complex ways. One feature that particularly fascinated him was that the distribution curves (*Curventafeln*) of "half-blooded Indians" (*Halbblut-Indianer*) did not show simple blending of parental types but usually two maxima indicating a "law of inheritance," according to which a "reversion" (*Rückkehr*) occurs towards either of the parental forms.[60] Moreover, by "classifying mixed-bloods in such a way, that one group includes individuals which have more than half of Indian blood, and the other individuals, which have half or less Indian blood," he tried to demonstrate that the "Indian type" (*Indianertypus*), with regard to certain traits, was characterized by a "stronger hereditary force" (*grössere Vererbungskraft*) than the "white," or more generally, that the "older, black-haired, broad-faced type develops with greater energy than the fair, narrow-faced type that was originally limited to a very small part of inhabited earth." The table to which Boas referred in order to support this remarkable statement compared data for the facial widths of "full-blood" (*Vollblut*), "¾-blood" (¾ *Blut*) and "⅜-blood" (⅜-*Blut*) persons.[61]

In an article published in 1893 under the title "Remarks on the Theory of Anthropometry," Boas discussed the statistical underpinnings of drawing such inferences from variation curves, invoking the authority of Galton but also of lesser-known statisticians like the Baltic-German economist Wilhelm Stieda (1852–1933), who in his view was "the first to express a doubt as to the general applicability of the law chance" to the distribution of anthropometric data.[62] This indicates an interesting context for Boas's anthropometric field studies: according to historian Christine von Oertzen, the Prussian Statistical Office in Berlin played a key role in an "unremarked European revolution in data processing during the 1860s, which in turn yielded a radical transformation of population statistics."⁶³ At the heart of this revolution was the introduction of "counting cards," that is, sheets that contained the complete set of data recorded for an individual, thus creating a "data double" of each individual.⁶⁴ Boas may have well been introduced to these developments when he studied with Rudolf Virchow (1821–1902) in Berlin, but there was also a model to his data sheets closer to his new home. The printed forms Boas used for his anthropometric surveys exhibit some striking similarities to the forms used in the 1890 US Census, which also asked for genealogical ("relationship to head of family") and racial information ("whether white black mulatto, quadroon, octoroon, Chinese, Japanese, or Indian").⁶⁵

After 1900, Boas's interest in the physical anthropology of Native Americans seems to have dwindled. The number of preserved observations abruptly drops to only two in 1901, and then there are none for the remaining years. The reasons for this are very likely political: with the passage of Jim Crow laws and with legislation that increasingly required the allocation of tribal land to individual tribe members who could prove their "purity of blood" (such as the 1898 Curtis Act), having one's ancestry "questioned" was increasingly becoming a highly delicate matter.⁶⁶ The end of his studies on the physical anthropology of Native Americans did not mean the end of Boas's interest in physical anthropology, though. Instead, he changed his subject. In 1910–11, he carried out a large-scale anthropometric survey of some sixteen thousand immigrants of various European populations for the US Immigration Commission to determine whether the physical type of these populations underwent changes as a consequence of their immigration.⁶⁷ The tabulation of raw data, which Boas published in 1928, demonstrates that this study also rested on a meticulous recording of filial relations across the population, using serial numbers to identify individuals and families, as well as abbreviations indicating elementary kin relations: "F means father; M, mother; S, son; D, daughter."⁶⁸

Boas's anthropometric studies did not only provide him with the empirical evidence for the instability of racial types, due to genetic segregation, migration, and environmental plasticity, that underwrote his critique of the race concept. They also motivated a fundamental change in perspective. The populations that physical anthropologists studied as representing different "races" or "physical types," Boas increasingly realized, had to be seen as historically contingent entanglements of a large number of heterogenous "genetic" or "family lines." This change in perspective could have paradoxical effects, as Boas liked to point out to his German colleague Eugen Fischer (1874–1967). In a study of the Rehoboth Basters, a small "mixed" African-European population in South West

Africa, Fischer had shown in 1913 that even "normal" traits like eye color followed Mendelian patterns of inheritance. For Fischer, this constituted a paradigmatic case of race mixture. Boas, in contrast, pointed out that this locally constrained and endogamous population approached "purity of race," since it consisted only of a small number of family lines that intermarried again and again.[69]

While Boas did not employ anything approaching the genealogical method in his ethnographic work on Native Americans, a similar perspective informed this work too. The vocabularies in his first field notebooks from British Columbia, which he had compiled in 1886, do contain kin terms, to be sure, and he also used a diagram in these notes that tried to capture the mechanism by which legends and privileges of a wife's father were acquired by the husband "for the use of his son" — as he would explain in "The Social Organization and the Secret Societies of the Kwakiutl Indians" (1895). But there is no sign that Boas collected this information with systematic reference to individual genealogies. What is evident, however, is that his findings made him skeptical about Morgan's evolutionary scheme of a universal transition from matrilineal to patrilineal societies. Instead, he suggested that the peculiar amalgam of both forms of social organization that he found operating in the Kwakiutl was due to their having "adapted [their] social laws" to the matrilineal "customs" of neighboring tribes to the north.[70] Generalization, for Boas, could not be achieved through global comparisons that "see a proof of dissemination or even blood relationship in each similarity" but through comparisons confined "to contiguous areas in which we know intercourse to have taken place."[71]

Conclusion

Perhaps the most important conclusion from my exercise of recontextualizing the genealogical method is that this method was not just employed for the study of kinship. Rivers, as we saw in the first section, proposed it rather as a method by which problems in the human sciences in general could be attacked, including the anthropological study of kinship but also fields like demography or physical anthropology. There is therefore also no genealogy that connects Morgan in a direct line with Rivers. Rivers's genealogical pedigrees rather resonated with the pedigrees that eugenicists and physical anthropologists constructed in order to reveal laws of heredity. The aim of the method was not to base, or model, kinship on biological assumptions about human reproduction but rather to use the presumed universality of filiation for the construction of complete "registers," as Rivers tellingly put it, that assigned each individual a unique place in relation to all other individuals within a population—precisely as birth and marriage records of modern nation-states do. Such registers could then be used to elucidate the meanings of kinship, among other topics, but were in principle open to semantic plurality, including detection of kin relations that cut across the genealogical grid. Thus, Rivers also advocated his method for identifying usages of kin terms for relationships that were neither by blood nor marriage, but "dependent on membership of a social division."[72]

Applications of the genealogical method therefore do not necessarily result in a naturalization of kinship that goes beyond the claim that each and every human issues from sexual unions, or what Schneider called "The Doctrine of the Genealogical Unity of Mankind."[73] As I stressed in this chapter, the abstractions that this "doctrine" builds upon are very "thin" and in no way rest on the presumption, as claimed by Schneider, that "kinship consists in bonds ... which are compelling and stronger than, and take priority over, other kinds of bonds."[74] Remarkably, this is also true of the clans and moieties of the Iroquois, which first inspired Morgan's investigations.[75] It is therefore doubtful that the metaphor of "naturalization" takes us any further in the critique of the genealogical method. Anthropologists interested in kinship have of course sometimes, if not often, naturalized it in one way or another. But the genealogical method, I claim, is not the chief source for these naturalizations.

A much more apt and interesting metaphor, proposed by Marilyn Strathern, is "literalization."[76] Genealogical analysis, as we saw, explicates kin relations and uses them to construct a relational space in which individuals are each defined by their unique positions in relation to all others, and in which any relationship can literally be "spelled out" in terms of quantifiable degrees. The genealogical method individualizes, distributes, and interrelates. As such, the lines that are drawn in genealogical diagrams are not remarkable so much for the density but rather for the paucity of meaning they carry, and the distance they thus produce between the subject and object of anthropological knowledge.[77] This has little to do with biology but all the more with geometry, or as Bronisław Malinowski polemically put it, "mock-algebra."[78] After all, while genealogical analysis introduces an element of determinism and irreversibility with its emphasis on filial relations, it also acknowledges an irreducible element of contingency, if not choice, by placing equal emphasis on marriage relations. As Strathern emphasizes in *After Nature*, this acknowledgment opens up kinship for plurality and construction rather than mere derivation, whether in culture or nature.[79] It is this openness that explains the versatility with which genealogical analysis has been and continues to be used for the articulation of diverse ideological agendas.[80] But it also explains the otherwise confusing fact that the science of genetics—with its distinction of genotype and phenotype that posits a hidden constitution with visible effects—has led to radical rearticulations, rather than affirmations, of vernacular ways of kinship reckoning, as, for example, when the distribution of genetic risks is seen to depend on a kind of lottery happening among siblings traditionally regarded as "closely" related by virtue of shared parentage.[81]

Does this conclusion exonerate the genealogical method from the charge of introducing a bias into kinship studies? A final remark is in place here. While the assumptions that underwrite genealogical analysis may be biologically "thin," they nonetheless constitute a distinct model of sexual reproduction as a process resulting in the propagation and proliferation of individuals. This aligns the genealogical method, among many other statistical tools, with what Michel Foucault has called the "biopolitical dispositive" and, as we saw with Boas, the biopolitical instruments of modern nation-states: family registers, censuses, surveys.[82] This has two consequences: first, biopolitics reintroduces—through the backdoor, so to speak—the taxonomy of nations, tribes, and races, since one of the chief points of creating genealogical registers is the assignment of citizenship and social identities simply on the basis of who one's parents are. Though race and kinship do not map onto each other, as explained in the beginning of this chapter, it is in this way that they have become permanently entangled in the practices of inclusion and exclusion that constitute nation-states.[83] And secondly—as Helen Gardner has shown in her detailed historical studies of the interaction of anthropologists with their informants—biopolitics creates a common ground, between anthropologists and their informants, for understanding or, rather, "figuring out" the logic that lies behind the genealogical method.[84] The universal applicability of the genealogical method is not so much due to universally shared ideas about the "facts of life." It is simply due to the fact that anthropologists, and their subjects, inhabit the same world of expansive bureaucracies.

Acknowledgments

I am grateful for the opportunity to develop and discuss first ideas for this chapter with members of the research group on kinship and politics at the Center for Interdisciplinary Studies at the University of Bielefeld. Further research enjoyed support from the Swiss National Foundation Sinergia Grant CRSII5_183567, "In the Shadow of the Tree: The Diagrammatics of

Relatedness as Scientific, Scholarly, and Popular Practice." Special thanks are due to Susan McKinnon and her patient insistence that I think again, and to Ludger Müller-Wille, my uncle (or father's younger brother), who allowed me a glimpse at the elaborate genealogical records he produced during fieldwork in late-1960s Utsjoki (Finland).

Staffan Müller-Wille is University Lecturer in the History of Life, Human and Earth Sciences at the University of Cambridge. His research covers the history of the life sciences from the early modern period to the early twentieth century, with a focus on the history of natural history, anthropology, and genetics. Among recent publications is a book coauthored with Hans-Jörg Rheinberger on *The Gene: From Genetics to Postgenomics* (2018) and two coedited collections on *Human Heredity in the Twentieth Century* (2013) and *Heredity Explored: Between Public Domain and Experimental Science, 1850–1930* (2016).

Notes

1. For recent reviews of the state of kinships studies, see Jean-Hugues Déchaux, "Kinship Studies: Neoclassicism and New Wave," *Revue française de sociologie* 49, no. 5 (2008), and Mary Bouquet, "Genealogy in Anthropology," in *International Encyclopedia of the Social and Behavioral Sciences*, 2nd ed., ed. J. D. Wright (Oxford: Elsevier, 2015).
2. George Stocking, "The Turn-of-the-Century Concept of Race," *Modernity/Modernism* 1, no. 1 (1994): 6.
3. Renato Mazzolini, "Colonialism and the Emergence of Racial Theories," in *Reproduction: Antiquity to the Present Day*, ed. N. Hopwood, R. Flemming, and L. Kassell (Cambridge: Cambridge University Press, 2018).
4. While there is extensive literature on eugenics and its concern for the "purity of race," concomitant fears of the consequences of incest are rarely thematized; for intriguing exceptions, see Adam Kuper, "Incest, Cousin Marriage, and the Origin of the Human Sciences in Nineteenth-Century England," *Past & Present*, no. 174 (2002), and Diane B. Paul and G. Spencer Hamish, "Eugenics without Eugenists? Anglo-American Critiques of Cousin Marriage in the Nineteenth and Early Twentieth Centuries," in *Heredity Explored: Between Public Domain and Experimental Science, 1850–1930*, ed. S. Müller-Wille and C. Brandt (Cambridge, MA: MIT Press, 2016). Prominent eugenicists liked to cast the problems of their discipline in terms of endogamy and exogamy, which they explicitly borrowed from anthropology; see, for example, Francis Galton, "Studies in Eugenics," *American Journal of Sociology* 11, no. 1 (1905): 13–15; Edward M. East and Donald F. Jones, *Inbreeding and Outbreeding: Their Genetic and Sociological Significance*, Monographs on Experimental Biology, vol. 4 (Philadelphia: Lippincott, 1919), 13–15.
5. David Murray Schneider, *A Critique of the Study of Kinship* (Ann Arbor: University of Michigan Press, 1984), 174–75.
6. That the metaphor cannot be taken for granted is already apparent from the confusing fact that in English the word "kinship" is ambivalent. On the one hand, the term is commonly understood as blood relationship (consanguinity). The anthropological study of kinship, on the other hand, systematically includes relationships by marriage

(affinity) and other "ritual" relationships (e.g., by adoption) under the term: see *OED Online*, s. v. "kinship, n.," (Oxford, accessed 9 July 2020). In this chapter, I will generally use *kinship* as an actor's term, and the reader should keep in mind that this often preserves the ambivalence. Analytically, however, I sometimes distinguish between relations of consanguinity and affinity and use "kin relations" to designate both in these cases.

7. Claude Lévi-Strauss, "Race and Culture," *International Social Science Journal* 23 (1971): 613; for the cloth metaphor, see Claude Lévi-Strauss, *Le totémisme aujourd'hui* (Paris: Presses Universitaires de France, 1962), 107.
8. Raymond Firth, "Introduction," in W. H. R. Rivers, *Kinship and Social Organization*, comm. R. Firth and D. M. Schneider, LSE Monographs on Social Anthropology, vol. 34 (London: Routledge, 1968), 2; see also Ian Langham, *The Building of British Social Anthropology: W. H. R. Rivers and His Cambridge Disciples in the Development of Kinship Studies, 1898–1931* (Dordrecht: Reidel, 1981); Adam Kuper, *The Invention of Primitive Society: Transformations of an Illusion* (London: Routledge, 1988), 157; Henrika Kuklick, *The Savage Within: The Social History of British Anthropology, 1885–1945* (Cambridge: Cambridge University Press, 1991), 140; Sandra Bamford and James Leach, ed., *Kinship and Beyond: The Genealogical Model Reconsidered* (New York: Berghahn Books, 2009), 2.
9. On Kurka, see Helen Gardner and Patrick McConvell, *Southern Anthropology: A History of Fison and Howitt's Kamilaroi and Kurnai* (New York: Palgrave, 2015), 136.
10. William H. R. Rivers, "The Genealogical Method of Anthropological Inquiry," *The Sociological Review* 3, no. 1 (1910): 1–2.
11. Alfred C. Haddon et al., *Sociology, Magic and Religion of the Western Islanders*, vol. 5 of *Reports of the Cambridge Anthropological Expedition to Torres Straits* (Cambridge: Cambridge University Press, 1904), 122, table 1-18.
12. Rivers, "Genealogical Method," 3–4.
13. Rivers, "Genealogical Method," 6–9.
14. There is no term in English that collectively refers to these relations. In the following, I will use *filiation* metonymically to designate the full set of genealogical relations that spring from the making of a child.
15. Haddon, *Reports*, 129–51; on Rivers "rediscovery" of Morgan, see Meyer Fortes, *Kinship and the Social Order: The Legacy of Lewis Henry Morgan* (London: Routledge & Kegan Paul, 1969), 3.
16. Thomas R. Trautmann, *Lewis Henry Morgan and the Invention of Kinship* (Berkeley: University of California Press, 1987), 40–42.
17. For a detailed account of the evolution of Morgan's schedule, see Trautmann, *Invention of Kinship*, 92–103.
18. Quoted from Elisabeth Tooker, "Lewis H. Morgan and His Contemporaries," *American Anthropologist* 94, no. 2 (1992): 364.
19. Trautmann, *Invention of Kinship*, 95; cf. Tooker, "Lewis H. Morgan," 366–67.
20. Lewis H. Morgan, *Systems of Consanguinity and Affinity of the Human Family* (Washington, DC, 1871), 511.
21. Morgan, *Systems*, 11.
22. British Association for the Advancement of Science, *Notes and Queries on Anthropology, for the Use of Travellers and Residents in Uncivilized Lands* (London: E. Stanford, 1874), 87–91. The entry was authored by John Lubbock (1834–1913) and carried the title "Relationships." Lubbock replaced the list with a general description of ascending, descending and collateral kin in later editions; see John George Garson and John Hercules Read, eds., *Notes and Queries on Anthropology*, 2nd ed. (London: Anthropological Institute, 1892), 203.
23. Morgan, *Systems*, 9. On Morgan's evolutionism, see Gillian Feeley-Harnik, "The Ethnography of Creation: Lewis Henry Morgan and the American Beaver," in *Relative Values: Reconfiguring Kinship Studies*, ed. S. Franklin and S. McKinnon (Durham, NC:

Duke University Press, 2001), 54–84, and Brad D. Hume, "Evolutionisms: Lewis Henry Morgan, Time, and the Question of Sociocultural Evolutionary Theory," *Histories of Anthropology Annual* 7, no. 1 (2011): 91–126.

24. William H. R. Rivers, "A Genealogical Method of Collecting Social and Vital Statistics," *Journal of the Anthropological Institute of Great Britain and Ireland* 30 (1900).
25. Kuklick, *Savage Within*, 141.
26. Francis Galton, *Hereditary Genius: An Inquiry into Its Laws and Consequences* (London: Macmillan, 1869), 1.
27. Galton, *Hereditary Genius*, 50–51.
28. See table II in Galton, *Hereditary Genius*, 50–51, which lists percentage of "eminent men" against "degree of kinship to the most eminent man of the family."
29. Galton, "Arithmetic Notation of Kinship," *Nature* 28, no. 723 (1883): 435.
30. Galton, *Hereditary Genius*, iii.
31. Galton, "Arithmetic Notation," 435.
32. For the concept of generation, see Ohad Parnes, "On the Shoulders of Generations: The Problem of Heredity in 19th Century Science and Culture," in *Heredity Produced: At the Crossroads of Biology, Politics and Culture, 1500 to 1870*, ed. S. Müller-Wille and H.-J. Rheinberger (Cambridge, MA: MIT Press, 2007), 316, and Ohad Parnes, Ulrike Vedder, and Stefan Willer, *Das Konzept der Generation: Eine Wissenschafts- und Kulturgeschichte* (Frankfurt a. M.: Suhrkamp, 2008); on reproduction, see Ludmilla Jordanova, "Interrogating the Concept of Reproduction in the Eighteenth Century," in *Conceiving the New World Order*, ed. Faye D. Ginsburg and Rayana Rapp (Berkeley: University of California Press, 1995); on heredity, Staffan Müller-Wille and Hans-Jörg Rheinberger, *A Cultural History of Heredity* (Chicago: University of Chicago Press, 2012), chap. 4. For a recent critical review of this literature, see Nick Hopwood, "The Keywords 'Generation' and 'Reproduction,'" in *Reproduction: Antiquity to the Present Day*, ed. L. Kassell, N. Hopwood, and R. Flemming (Cambridge: Cambridge University Press, 2018).
33. Ilona Katzew, *Casta Painting: Images of Race in Eighteenth-Century Mexico* (New Haven, CT: Yale University Press, 2004).
34. Rebecca Earle, "The Pleasures of Taxonomy: Casta Paintings, Classification, and Colonialism," *William and Mary Quarterly* 73, no. 3 (2016).
35. On the following, see Renato G. Mazzolini, "Las Castas: Inter-racial Crossing and Social Structure (1770–1835)," in *Heredity Produced: At the Crossroads of Biology, Politics and Culture, 1500–1870*, ed. S. Müller-Wille and H.-J. Rheinberger (Cambridge, MA: MIT Press, 2007).
36. Georges-Louis Leclerc Buffon, *Histoire Naturelle, Générale et Particuliére: Supplément*, vol. 4 (Paris: Imprimerie Royale, 1749), 504; on Buffon's "genealogical style of reasoning," see Claude-Olivier Doron, "Race and Genealogy: Buffon and the Formation of the Concept of 'Race,'" *HUMANA.MENTE Journal of Philosophical Studies* 5, no. 22 (2012).
37. Alexander von Humboldt, *Essai Politique Sur Le Royaume de La Nouvelle-Espagne*, vol. 2 (Paris: F. Schoell, 1811), 52. Humboldt may be misstating the definition for *quinteron*. The usual term for someone one-eighth "Black," which was also used by Buffon, would be *octavon* ("octoroon" in English), while *quinteron* usually refers to persons who are one-sixteenth "Black" (or five generations away from a "Black" ancestor). On the early reception of the castas system by European scholars, see Mazzolini, "Las Castas."
38. Florence Vienne, "Eggs and Sperms as Germ Cells," in *Reproduction: Antiquity to the Present Day*, ed. Lauren Kassell, Nick Hopwood, and Rebecca Flemming (Cambridge: Cambridge University Press, 2018).
39. Francis Galton, "On Blood Relationship," *Proceedings of the Royal Society* 20, no. 136 (1872): 402.

40. Josiah Clark Nott and George Robins Gliddon, *Types of Mankind: Or, Ethnological Researches, Based Upon the Ancient Monuments, Paintings, Sculptures, and Crania of Races, and Upon Their Natural, Geographical, Philological and Biblical History* (Philadelphia: Lippincott, Grambo and Co., 1855), 455. Thomas R. Trautmann and Karl Sanford Kabelac, "The Library of Lewis Henry Morgan and Mary Elizabeth Morgan," *Transactions of the American Philosophical Society* 84, nos. 6–7 (1994): 236, list this book as part of Morgan's library. On Morgan's rejection of American polygenism, see Trautmamn, *Invention of Kinship*, 28.
41. On canon law, see Simon Teuscher, "Flesh and Blood in the Treatises on the Arbor Consanguinitatis (Thirteenth to Sixteenth Centuries)," in *Blood and Kinship: Matter for Metaphor from Ancient Rome to the Present*, ed. Christopher H. Johnson (New York: Berghahn Books, 2013); on civil law, see Karin Gottschalk, "Erbe und Recht: Die Übertragung von Eigentum in der frühen Neuzeit," in *Erbe: Übertragungskonzepte zwischen Natur und Kultur*, ed. Sigrid Weigel, Stefan Willer, and Bernhard Jussen (Berlin: Suhrkamp, 2013), 118–19.
42. Simon Teuscher, "Flesh and Blood," 101; see also Teuscher in this volume.
43. Morgan, *Systems*, 23. On Morgan's copy of Blackstone's commentaries, see Trautmann and Kabelac, "Library," 123. The quote by Blackstone is taken from William Blackstone, *Commentaries on the Laws of England*, ed. George Sweet, vol. 2 (London: Hodges and Smith, 1844), 202.
44. See Blackstone, *Commentaries*, 204. Blackstone, like Galton, had an inclination for mathematics and was also known for work in architectural theory; see Cristina S. Martinez, "Blackstone as Draughtsman: Picturing the Law," in *Re-interpreting Blackstone's Commentaries: A Seminal Text in National and International Contexts*, ed. Wilfrid Prest (Oxford: Hart Publishing, 2014), 33. Galton included Blackstone in the chapter on "The Judges of England" in *Hereditary Genius*, noting that a son and nephew of his were also known jurists; Galton, *Hereditary Genius*, 59.
45. Mary Bouquet, "Family Trees and Their Affinities: The Visual Imperative of the Genealogical Diagram," *Journal of the Royal Anthropological Institute* 2, no. 1 (1996): 62, 59.
46. Blackstone, *Commentaries*, 236–40. The "Table of Descents" uses numbers to indicate a relative's position in succession, and a deceased person's mother has the number thirty-seven—that is, she will be considered an heir only once thirty-six possible agnatic heirs have been excluded. Martinez, "Blackstone as Draughtsman," 48, refers to the table as a manifestation of Blackstone's "creative visual approach."
47. David Warren Sabean and Simon Teuscher, "Kinship in Europe: A New Approach to Long-Term Development," in *Kinship in Europe: Approaches to Long-Term Development (1300–1900)*, ed. David Warren Sabean, Simon Teuscher, and Jon Mathieu (New York: Berghahn Books, 2013), 3.
48. Bernd Gausemeier, "Pedigrees of Madness: The Study of Heredity in Nineteenth and Early Twentieth Century Psychiatry," *History and Philosophy of the Life Sciences* 36, no. 4 (2014); Theodore M. Porter, *Genetics in the Madhouse: The Unknown History of Human Heredity* (Princeton, NJ: Princeton University Press, 2020).
49. Rosemary Lévy Zumwalt, *Franz Boas: The Emergence of the Anthropologist* (Lincoln: University of Nebraska Press, 2019), 164.
50. Richard L. Jantz, "The Anthropometric Legacy of Franz Boas," *Economics and Human Biology* 1, no. 2 (2003), 282. See Staffan Müller-Wille, "Data, Meta Data and Pattern Data: How Franz Boas Mobilized Anthropometric Data, 1890 and Beyond," in *Data Journeys in the Sciences*, ed. S. Leonelli and N. Tempini (Cham: Springer International Publishing, 2020).
51. Franz Boas, "Anthropometric Data Sheets Recorded at Stonewall and Tishomingo, Indian Territory (Oklahoma)," Franz Boas Anthropometric Data and Early Field Notebooks, Mss.B.B61.5, American Philosophical Society.

52. On the history of the Chickasaw, see Wendy St. Jean, *Remaining Chickasaw in Indian Territory, 1830s–1907* (Tuscaloosa: University of Alabama Press, 2011).
53. Franz Boas, "Anthropometric Data," sheets 7–10.
54. Franz Boas, "Anthropometric Data," sheets 2–3 and 18–19. On Chickasaw and slavery, see St. Jean, *Remaining Chickasaw*, 43–44.
55. Duane Champagne, *Social Order and Political Change: Constitutional Governments among the Cherokee, the Choctaw, the Chickasaw and the Creek* (Stanford, CA: Stanford University Press, 1992), 41.
56. Franz Boas, "Anthropometric Data," sheet 26.
57. Franz Boas, "Anthropometric Data," sheet 53.
58. Franz Boas, "Anthropometric Data," sheet 35.
59. Franz Boas, "Zur Anthropologie der nordamerikanischen Indianer," *Zeitschrift Für Ethnologie* 27 (1895): 367.
60. Boas, "Anthropologie," 401.
61. Boas, "Anthropologie," 410–11.
62. Franz Boas, "Remarks on the Theory of Anthropometry," *Publications of the American Statistical Association* 3, no. 24 (1893): 569.
63. Christine von Oertzen, "Machineries of Data Power: Manual versus Mechanical Census Compilation in Nineteenth-Century Europe," *Osiris* 32 (2017): 131.
64. Von Oertzen, "Machineries," 141.
65. The form used in the 1890 US census is available at https://en.wikipedia.org/wiki/1890_United_States_Census#/media/File:1890B.jpg (retrieved 19 July 2022). On the history of racial categories in US censuses between 1850 and 1930, see Jennifer L. Hochschild and Brenna Marea Powell, "Racial Reorganization and the United States Census 1850–1930: Mulattoes, Half-Breeds, Mixed Parentage, Hindoos, and the Mexican Race," *Studies in American Political Development* 22, no. 1 (2008).
66. See St. Jean, *Remaining Chickasaw*, 55.
67. Franz Boas. "Changes in the Bodily Form of Descendants of Immigrants," *American Anthropologist* 14, no. 3 (1912).
68. Franz Boas, *Materials for the Study of Inheritance in Man*, Contributions to Anthropology, vol. 6 (New York: Columbia University Press, 1928), vii.
69. George W. Stocking, "The Critique of Racial Formalism," in *Race, Culture, and Evolution: Essays in the History of Anthropology* (New York: The Free Press, 1968), 161–94; Tracy Teslow, *Constructing Race: The Science of Bodies and Cultures in American Anthropology* (Cambridge: Cambridge University Press, 2014), chap. 2. On Fischer, see Franz Boas, *Race, Language and Culture* (Chicago: University of Chicago Press, 1996), 32.
70. Franz Boas, "The Social Organization and the Secret Societies of the Kwakiutl Indians," in *Report of the National Museum for 1895* (Washington, DC: Government Printing Office, 1897), 334. For the diagram in Boas's field notebook, see Franz Boas, "Field notebook 1886 #1," Franz Boas Anthropometric Data and Early Field Notebooks, Mss.B.B61.5, American Philosophical Society, 44r.
71. Franz Boas, "The Growth of Indian Mythologies. A Study Based upon the Growth of the Mythologies of the North Pacific Coast," *Journal of American Folklore* 9, no. 32 (1896): 6. This paper discussed results from a "statistical inquiry" of myths (Boas, "The Growth," 3), but Boas's historicist method is not reducible to the application of statistics. While he remained committed to an "atomistic" view of culture in his research practice, he also endorsed more holist views of *Volksgeist* in his investigations of cultural production of meaning; see Michel Verdon, "Franz Boas: Cultural History for the Present, or Obsolete Natural History?" *Journal of the Royal Anthropological Institute* 13, no. 2 (2007). For a trenchant analysis of Boas's opposition to Morgan, see Marshall Sahlins, *Culture and Practical Reason* (Chicago: University of Chicago Press, 1976), 57–73.
72. Rivers, "Genealogical Method," 5–6.
73. Schneider, *Critique*, 174.

74. Schneider, *Critique*, 165. See Maurice Godelier, *The Metamorphoses of Kinship* (London, 2011), 19–22, for a forceful critique of Schneider along these lines.
75. Elisabeth Tooker, "Clans and Moieties in North America," *Current Anthropology* 12, no. 3 (1971): 357–76.
76. Marilyn Strathern, *After Nature: English Kinship in the Late Twentieth Century* (Cambridge: Cambridge University Press, 1992), 5.
77. Johannes Fabian, *Time and the Other: How Anthropology Makes Its Object* (New York: Columbia University Press, 2014), 116; Tim Ingold, *Lines: A Brief History* (London: Routledge, 2007), chap. 4.
78. Bronisław Malinowski, "Kinship," *Man* 30 (1930): 20. I thank Helen Gardner for drawing my attention to Malinowski's polemic.
79. Strathern, *After Nature*, 7–9.
80. See Susan McKinnon, "The Economies in Kinship and the Paternity of Culture: Origin Stories in Kinship Theory," in *Relative Values: Reconfiguring Kinship Studies*, ed. Sarah Franklin and Susan McKinnon (Durham, NC: Duke University Press, 2001), 277–301, for a striking analysis of ideological commitments underlying Morgan's and Levi-Strauss's work on kinship.
81. Sarah Franklin, "Biologization Revisited: Kinship Theory in the Context of the New Biologies," in *Relative Values: Reconfiguring Kinship Studies*, ed. Sarah Franklin and Susan McKinnon (Durham, NC: Duke University Press, 2001), 306.
82. Michel Foucault, *The Will to Knowledge* (London: Penguin Books, 1978), 106–7. On the role of "vital records" in the formation of modern states, see Alain Desrosières, *The Politics of Large Numbers: A History of Statistical Reasoning* (Cambridge, MA: Harvard University Press, 1998), and Andrea A. Rusnock, *Vital Accounts: Quantifying Health and Population in Eighteenth-Century England and France* (Cambridge: Cambridge University Press, 2002).
83. Tatjana Thelen and Erdmute Alber, "Reconnecting State and Kinship: Temporalities, Scales, Classifications," in *Reconnecting State and Kinship*, ed. Tatjana Thelen and Erdmute Alber, (Philadelphia: University of Pennsylvania Press, 2018), 14–17.
84. Helen Gardner, "The Genealogy of the Genealogical Method: Discoveries, Disseminations and the Historiography of British Anthropology," *Oceania* 86, no. 3 (2016).

Bibliography

Bamford, Sandra, and James Leach, ed. *Kinship and Beyond: The Genealogical Model Reconsidered*. Repr. ed. New York: Berghahn Books, 2009.

Blackstone, William. *Commentaries on the Laws of England, in Four Books; with an Analysis of the Work*. Edited by George Sweet. London: Hodges and Smith, 1844.

Boas, Franz. "Remarks on the Theory of Anthropometry." *Publications of the American Statistical Association* 3, no. 24 (1893): 569–75.

———. "Zur Anthropologie der Nordamerikanischen Indianer." *Zeitschrift für Ethnologie* 27 (1895): 366–411.

———. "The Growth of Indian Mythologies: A Study Based upon the Growth of the Mythologies of the North Pacific Coast." *Journal of American Folklore* 9, no. 32 (1896): 1–11.

———. "The Social Organization and the Secret Societies of the Kwakiutl Indians." In *Report of the National Museum for 1895*, 313–738. Washington, DC: Government Printing Office, 1897.

———. "Changes in the Bodily Form of Descendants of Immigrants." *American Anthropologist* 14, no. 3 (1912): 530–62.
———. *Materials for the Study of Inheritance in Man*. Contributions to Anthropology, vol. 6. New York: Columbia University Press, 1928.
———. *Race, Language and Culture*. Chicago: University of Chicago Press, 1996.
Bouquet, Mary. "Family Trees and Their Affinities: The Visual Imperative of the Genealogical Diagram." *Journal of the Royal Anthropological Institute* 2, no. 1 (1996): 43–66.
———. "Genealogy in Anthropology." In *International Encyclopedia of the Social and Behavioral Sciences*, edited by J. D. Wright, 806–12. 2nd ed. Oxford: Elsevier, 2015.
British Association for the Advancement of Science. *Notes and Queries on Anthropology, for the Use of Travellers and Residents in Uncivilized Lands*. London: E. Stanford, 1874.
Buffon, Georges-Louis Leclerc. *Histoire Naturelle, Générale et Particuliére: Supplément*. Vol. 4. Paris: Imprimerie Royale, 1777.
Champagne, Duane. *Social Order and Political Change: Constitutional Governments among the Cherokee, the Choctaw, the Chickasaw and the Creek*. Stanford, CA: Stanford University Press, 1992.
Desrosières, Alain. *The Politics of Large Numbers: A History of Statistical Reasoning*. Cambridge, MA: Harvard University Press, 1998.
Déchaux, Jean-Hugues. "Kinship Studies: Neoclassicism and New Wave." *Revue francaise de sociologie* 49, no. 5 (2008): 215–43.
Doron, Claude-Olivier Doron. "Race and Genealogy: Buffon and the Formation of the Concept of 'Race.'" *HUMANA.MENTE Journal of Philosophical Studies* 5, no. 22 (2012): 75–109.
Earle, Rebecca. "The Pleasures of Taxonomy: Casta Paintings, Classification, and Colonialism." *William and Mary Quarterly* 73, no. 3 (2016): 427–466.
East, Edward M., and Donald F. Jones. *Inbreeding and Outbreeding: Their Genetic and Sociological Significance*. Monographs on Experimental Biology, vol. 4. Philadelphia: Lippincott, 1919.
Fabian, Johannes. *Time and the Other: How Anthropology Makes Its Object*. With a new postscript by the author. New York: Columbia University Press, 2014.
Firth, Raymond. "Introduction." In W. H. R. Rivers, *Kinship and Social Organization*, 1–4. Commented by R. Firth and D. M. Schneider. LSE Monographs on Social Anthropology, vol. 34. London: Routledge, 1968.
Fortes, Meyer. *Kinship and the Social Order: The Legacy of Lewis Henry Morgan*. London: Routledge & Kegan Paul, 1969.
Foucault, Michel. *The Will to Knowledge*. London: Penguin Books, 1978.
Franklin, Sarah. "Biologization Revisited: Kinship Theory in the Context of the New Biologies." In *Relative Values: Reconfiguring Kinship Studies*, edited by S. Franklin and S. McKinnon, 302–25. Durham, NC: Duke University Press, 2001.
Galton, Francis. *Hereditary Genius: An Inquiry into Its Laws and Consequences*. London: Macmillan, 1869.
———. "On Blood Relationship." *Proceedings of the Royal Society* 20, no. 136 (1872): 394–402.
———. "Arithmetic Notation of Kinship." *Nature* 28, no. 723 (1883): 435.
———. "Studies in Eugenics." *American Journal of Sociology* 11, no. 1 (1905): 11–25.

Gardner, Helen. "The Genealogy of the Genealogical Method: Discoveries, Disseminations and the Historiography of British Anthropology." *Oceania* 86, no. 3 (2016): 294–319.

Gardner, Helen, and Patrick McConvell. *Southern Anthropology: A History of Fison and Howitt's Kamilaroi and Kurnai.* New York: Palgrave, 2015.

Garson, John George, and John Hercules Read, eds. *Notes and Queries on Anthropology.* 2nd ed. London: Anthropological Institute, 1892.

Gausemeier, Bernd. "Pedigrees of Madness: The Study of Heredity in Nineteenth and Early Twentieth Century Psychiatry." *History and Philosophy of the Life Sciences* 36, no. 4 (2014): 467–83.

Gottschalk, Karin. "Erbe und Recht: Die Übertragung von Eigentum in der frühen Neuzeit." In *Erbe: Übertragungskonzepte zwischen Natur und Kultur*, edited by Sigrid Weigel, Stefan Willer, and Bernhard Jussen, 85–125. Berlin: Suhrkamp, 2013.

Haddon, Alfred C., et al. *Sociology, Magic and Religion of the Western Islanders.* Vol. 5 of *Reports of the Cambridge Anthropological Expedition to Torres Straits.* Cambridge, UK: Cambridge University Press, 1904.

Hochschild, Jennifer L., and Brenna Marea Powell. "Racial Reorganization and the United States Census 1850–1930: Mulattoes, Half-Breeds, Mixed Parentage, Hindoos, and the Mexican Race." *Studies in American Political Development* 22, no. 1 (2008): 59–96.

Hopwood, Nick. "The Keywords 'Generation' and 'Reproduction.'" In *Reproduction: Antiquity to the Present Day*, edited by Lauren Kassell, Nick Hopwood, and Rebecca Flemming, 287–304. Cambridge: Cambridge University Press, 2018.

Humboldt, Alexander von. *Essai politique sur le Royaume de La Nouvelle-Espagne.* 5 vols. Paris: F. Schoell, 1811.

Hume, Brad D. "Evolutionisms: Lewis Henry Morgan, Time, and the Question of Sociocultural Evolutionary Theory," *Histories of Anthropology Annual* 7, no. 1 (2011): 91–126.

Ingold, Tim. *Lines: A Brief History.* London: Routledge, 2007.

Jantz, Richard L. "The Anthropometric Legacy of Franz Boas." *Economics and Human Biology* 1, no. 2 (2003): 277–84.

Jordanova, Ludmilla. "Interrogating the Concept of Reproduction in the Eighteenth Century." In *Conceiving the New World Order: The Global Politics of Reproduction*, edited by F. D. Ginsburg and R. Rapp, 369–86. Berkeley: University of California Press, 1995.

Katzew, Ilona. *Casta Painting: Images of Race in Eighteenth-Century Mexico.* New Haven, CT: Yale University Press, 2004.

Kuklick, Henrika. *The Savage Within: The Social History of British Anthropology, 1885–1945.* Cambridge: Cambridge University Press, 1991.

Kuper, Adam. *The Invention of Primitive Society: Transformations of an Illusion.* 3rd ed. London: Routledge, 1988.

———. "Incest, Cousin Marriage, and the Origin of the Human Sciences in Nineteenth-Century England." *Past & Present* 174 (2002): 158–83.

Langham, Ian. *The Building of British Social Anthropology: W. H. R. Rivers and His Cambridge Disciples in the Development of Kinship Studies, 1898–1931.* Dordrecht: Reidel, 1981.

Lévi-Strauss, Claude. *Le Totémisme aujourd'hui*. Paris: Presses Universitaires de France, 1962.
———. "Race and Culture." *International Social Science Journal* 23 (1971): 608–25.
Malinowski, Bronisław. "Kinship." *Man* 30 (1930): 19–29.
Martinez, Cristina S. "Blackstone as Draughtsman: Picturing the Law." In *Re-interpreting Blackstone's Commentaries: A Seminal Text in National and International Contexts*, edited by W. Prest, 31–58. Oxford: Hart Publishing, 2014.
Mazzolini, Renato G. "Las Castas: Inter-racial Crossing and Social Structure (1770–1835)." In *Heredity Produced: At the Crossroads of Biology, Politics and Culture, 1500–1870*, edited by S. Müller-Wille and H.-J. Rheinberger, 349–73. Cambridge, MA: MIT Press, 2007.
Mazzolini, Renato. "Colonialism and the Emergence of Racial Theories." In *Reproduction: Antiquity to the Present Day*, edited by N. Hopwood, R. Flemming, and L. Kassell, 361–74. Cambridge: Cambridge University Press, 2018.
Morgan, Lewis Henry. *Circular in Reference to the Degrees of Relationship among Different Nations*. Smithsonian Miscellaneous Collections. Washington, DC: Smithsonian Institution, 1860.
Müller-Wille, Staffan. "Data, Meta Data and Pattern Data: How Franz Boas Mobilized Anthropometric Data, 1890 and Beyond." In *Data Journeys in the Sciences*, edited by S. Leonelli and N. Tempini, 265–83. Cham: Springer International Publishing, 2020.
Müller-Wille, Staffan, and Hans-Jörg Rheinberger. *A Cultural History of Heredity*. Chicago: University of Chicago Press, 2012.
Nott, Josiah Clark, and George Robins Gliddon. *Types of Mankind: Or, Ethnological Researches, Based Upon the Ancient Monuments, Paintings, Sculptures, and Crania of Races, and Upon Their Natural, Geographical, Philological and Biblical History*. Philadelphia: Lippincott, Grambo and Co., 1855.
Oertzen, Christine von. "Machineries of Data Power: Manual versus Mechanical Census Compilation in Nineteenth-Century Europe." *Osiris* 32 (2017): 129–50.
Parnes, Ohad. "On the Shoulders of Generations: The Problem of Heredity in 19th Century Science and Culture." In *Heredity Produced: At the Crossroads of Biology, Politics and Culture, 1500 to 1870; A Cultural History of Heredity*, edited by S. Müller-Wille and H.-J. Rheinberger, 315–45. Cambridge, MA: MIT Press, 2007.
Parnes, Ohad, Ulrike Vedder, and Stefan Willer. *Das Konzept der Generation: Eine Wissenschafts- und Kulturgeschichte*. Frankfurt a. M.: Suhrkamp, 2008.
Paul, Diane B., and Hamish G. Spencer. "Eugenics without Eugenists? Anglo-American Critiques of Cousin Marriage in the Nineteenth and Early Twentieth Centuries." In *Heredity Explored: Between Public Domain and Experimental Science, 1850–1930*, edited by Staffan Müller-Wille and Christina Brandt, 49–79. Cambridge, MA: MIT Press, 2016.
Porter, Theodore M. *Genetics in the Madhouse: The Unknown History of Human Heredity*. Princeton, NJ: Princeton University Press, 2020.
Rivers, William H. R. "A Genealogical Method of Collecting Social and Vital Statistics." *Journal of the Anthropological Institute of Great Britain and Ireland* 30 (1900): 74–82.
———. "The Genealogical Method of Anthropological Inquiry." *Sociological Review* 3, no. 1 (1910): 1–12.

Rusnock, Andrea A. *Vital Accounts: Quantifying Health and Population in Eighteenth-Century England and France.* Cambridge: Cambridge University Press, 2002.

Sabean, David Warren, and Simon Teuscher. "Kinship in Europe: A New Approach to Long-Term Development." In *Kinship in Europe: Approaches to Long-Term Development (1300–1900),* edited by David Warren Sabean, Simon Teuscher, and Jon Mathieu, 1–32. New York: Berghahn Books, 2013.

Sahlins, Marshall. *Culture and Practical Reason.* Chicago: University of Chicago Press, 1976.

Schneider, David Murray. *A Critique of the Study of Kinship.* Ann Arbor: University of Michigan Press, 1984.

St. Jean, Wendy. *Remaining Chickasaw in Indian Territory, 1830s–1907.* Tuscaloosa: University of Alabama Press, 2011.

Stocking, George. "The Turn-of-the-Century Concept of Race," *Modernity/Modernism* 1, no. 1 (1994): 4–16.

Stocking, George W. "The Critique of Racial Formalism." In *Race, Culture, and Evolution: Essays in the History of Anthropology,* 161–94. New York: The Free Press, 1968.

Strathern, Marilyn. *After Nature: English Kinship in the Late Twentieth Century.* Cambridge: Cambridge University Press, 1992.

Teslow, Tracy. *Constructing Race: The Science of Bodies and Cultures in American Anthropology.* Cambridge: Cambridge University Press, 2014.

Teuscher, Simon. "Flesh and Blood in the Treatises on the Arbor Consanguinitatis (Thirteenth to Sixteenth Centuries)." In *Blood and Kinship: Matter for Metaphor from Ancient Rome to the Present,* edited by Christopher H. Johnson, 83–104. New York: Berghahn Books, 2013.

Thelen, Tatjana, and Erdmute Alber. "Reconnecting State and Kinship: Temporalities, Scales, Classifications." In *Reconnecting State and Kinship,* edited by T. Thelen and E. Alber, 1–35. Philadelphia: University of Pennsylvania Press, 2018.

Tooker, Elisabeth. "Clans and Moieties in North America." *Current Anthropology* 12, no. 3 (1971): 357–76.

———. "Lewis H. Morgan and His Contemporaries." *American Anthropologist* 94, no. 2 (1992): 357–75.

Trautmann, Thomas R. *Lewis Henry Morgan and the Invention of Kinship.* Berkeley: University of California Press, 1987.

Trautmann, Thomas R., and Karl Sanford Kabelac. "The Library of Lewis Henry Morgan." *Transactions of the American Philosophical Society* 84, nos. 6–7 (1994): I–336.

Verdon, Michel. "Franz Boas: Cultural History for the Present, or Obsolete Natural History?" *Journal of the Royal Anthropological Institute* 13, no. 2 (2007): 433–51.

Vienne, Florence. "Eggs and Sperms as Germ Cells." In *Reproduction: Antiquity to the Present Day,* edited by L. Kassell, N. Hopwood, and R. Flemming, 413–26. Cambridge: Cambridge University Press, 2018.

Zumwalt, Rosemary Lévy. *Franz Boas: The Emergence of the Anthropologist.* Lincoln: University of Nebraska Press, 2019.

Chapter 4

Kinship Meets Corporation
Perspectives on Kinship and Politics in the Formative Moment of Social Anthropology

Thomas Zitelmann

Introduction

The corporate paradigm has had a distinctive history within the intellectual genealogies of Occidental social thought since the first half of the nineteenth century. It has traveled between disciplines, generations, geographical areas, and political outlooks and taken many ethnographic, cultural, and localized shapes. Meanwhile, it has kept a proximity to methodological collectivism as a distinctive structural feature, assuming the unquestioned existence of collective mentalities linked to social groupings imagined in analogy to the unity of a physical body: a *corpus*. Especially in British social anthropology and since the 1930s, it has become a central coupling in an imagined unity between kinship and politics in segmentary societies. This chapter develops questions and arguments about the relationship between practice and theory at the nexus between politics and kinship during the formative moment of social anthropology.

The first section outlines Evans-Pritchard's classic model of the political system of the Nuer, a contribution to the wider perspective on *African Political Systems* (APS), which was edited in 1940 by Edward E. Evans-Pritchard and Meyer Fortes and which introduced a merger of kinship, the corporate paradigm, and politics. Second, I address the "travel" of the corporate paradigm into anthropological discourse and discuss in particular the different and controversial theoretical legacies of Max Weber and Émile Durkheim as well as fascist thought on theory. In the course of its "travels," the paradigm acquired perspectives on legal history, translations, imaginations, and a technical academic language.

The third and fourth sections shift to the intellectual climate and zeitgeist at the International African Institute (IAI) in London, the seedbed in which APS developed and will chronicle the controversy between Bronisław Malinowski and Reginald Radcliffe-Brown about proper approaches to kinship and explore the lesser-known role of the German codirector Dietrich Westermann in the making of APS.

The paradigm of the *corporate group* changed its content in different political and philosophical contexts. In my conclusion, I will present the interface between kinship and corporation as a joint legacy of liberal-conservative and totalitarian tendencies in the perspective on "the family" in "civil society." While social anthropologists claimed that this idea had come from their empirical fieldwork, it clearly was rooted in Romanticism: the Romantics had drawn on Roman and medieval law and sources to elaborate the concept of the corporate group whose early nineteenth-century articulation was most influentially worked out by the German philosopher Georg Friedrich Hegel long before contributors like Henry Maine or Otto Gierke appeared. Hegel identified "civil society" as a space between the family and the state in which the "corporate group" fulfilled a mediating function. In the development of social anthropology, the paradigm took a dogmatic turn, shaping assumptions about relating the individual to collective units and in particular *kinship*, which was thought of as a set of cohesive bonds.

The birth of modern political anthropology, which formulated a nexus between politics and kinship, is generally associated with APS,[1] and the book would become associated with the British social anthropological school. However, its formative academic context more generally was a transnational imperial institution, the London-based International Institute of African Languages and Cultures (IIALC), which was in 1939 renamed as the International African Institute (IAI) and had far-reaching connections to German, French, Italian, American, and other trends in anthropology and African studies.[2]

The introduction to APS by Fortes and Evans-Pritchard established a nexus between kinship and politics. A preface by Radcliffe-Brown claimed that internal law and external war were the political core even of stateless societies, which here were situated within extended patrilineal kinship groups termed "lineages."[3] Within APS, it was Evans-Pritchard's study on kinship and politics among the Nuer of Southern Sudan in particular that linked the ethnographic data to a theoretical model that had its main root in the Romantic reading of ancient Roman sources and the medieval European history of law.[4] The legal fiction of the "corporate group" became a framework for creative adaptation and translation, but the term also obscured the differences embedded in the different conceptual legacies of the corporate.

Evans-Pritchard's Nuer: Politics in the Language of Kinship

The classic study articulating the political nature of stateless society as institutionalized forms of war, feud, and physical force is Evans-Pritchard's on the Southern Sudanese Nuer,[5] which is based on research he directly coordinated with the colonial administration. The chapter in APS introduced the Nuer system as an "extreme political type"[6] and described its basic social structure as an intersection of three demotic and territorial units: the clan (*diel*), the tribe (*cieng*), and the local village community (also *cieng*). The polyvalent term *cieng* implied identificatory shifts within the system of segmentary oppositions between genealogically linked lineages, forming the "tribe." In this system, the "clan" did not act as a political unit but formed "the iron girder upon which the political structure of the tribe is built up."[7] It was described as an agnatic structure, linked genealogically to a mythological ancestor. The clan had no territorial claims, and clan segments were dispersed all over Nuer country. People had to marry outside of their own clans.

Evans-Pritchard considered the actual political unit to be the "tribe" (*cieng*). Beginning with his earliest publications on the Nuer, he adopted Radcliffe-Brown's definition of politics as a matter of keeping internal peace and waging external war. The four necessary characteristics of a political unit, then, were (1) territory, (2) a common name, (3) internal dispute regulation, (4) unity in external war.[8] In the Nuer case, the segmentary structure of a *tribe* included lineages, sublineages, agropastoral village communities, and seasonal cattle camps. The "tribe" had a territorial base, and its agnatic genealogical structure included a memorialized history. The core of each "tribe," which gave particular localities their names, was related to a dominant "clan." Within the framework of the exogamic marriage rule, the dominant group in a place provided wives to members of other clans and to strangers (Dinka, others). "Aggregates of strangers," settling, cooperating, and marrying with the dominant core, accepted the name and the lineage alliance of the core group.[9] However, they maintained separation in terms of clan membership, which was important for exogamic marriages.

The basic residential unit during the rainy season was the village community (*cieng*). During the dry season, men dispersed to cattle camps, where people from different communities met and worked together. In both cases, the needs for cooperation and sharing resources fomented a strong sense of community. This is where we find the intersection between close affinal and consanguineal ties, mutual sentiments, economic cooperation, and political integration, which Evans-Pritchard termed "corporate" in APS.[10] The term *cieng* is a polyvalent. It could be used for every unit—from the level of the village community through the sublineage and lineage to the "tribe"—in which people united in cooperation, sharing resources and applying internal legal concepts like blood money. The meaning of *cieng* in any particular context changed according to the system of segmentary opposition and structured the degrees of cooperation, feuding, and warring.

For Evans-Pritchard, only the village community had a truly corporate character: "except for occasional military ventures, active corporate life is restricted to small tribal segments."[11] Inside village communities, households were related to each other through hypogamic marriage ties to the agnatic core.[12] Members of the agnatic core had firstcomer's rights in the land and were symbolically represented as "bulls." They were "a corner stone in the structure of kinship."[13] Within the village community, eldership and male age-grading existed, but these were not endowed with political or military functions: for Evans-Pritchard: aging represented a natural process.[14] At the tribal level, ritual experts like the Leopard-Skin-Chiefs operated, mediating in intertribal wars, but such positions were not seen as permanent political institutions. Elders, age-sets, and religious experts were considered by Evans-Pritchard to be moral institutions, with some regulatory capacity in "public life." But elders acted through the kin group to which they belonged: in the final instance, the status of a "bull" (an important elder) derived from the linkage with the agnatic core.[15] However, it was not the "bulls" (*tut*) but the village community that as a "democratic society"[16] was the stable political core with a dual organizational task. This unit simultaneously had to keep peace in the inside and to defend its life sustaining resources against the outside. That was the core of the *cieng* (home) and its polyvalent meanings. Within the segmentary structures of the "tribe," different levels of segmentary opposition could develop, uniting people in internal peacemaking and external feuding. The term *cieng* could describe different levels of integration and conflict, and the intersection between *diel* and *cieng* provided the dynamic political structure of the "tribe." The "language of kinship" gave the political structure a "consistent form."[17]

The Contextual Side of Describing *The Nuer*

The specific problem of the colonial administration that induced Evans-Pritchard research was finding persons among mobile pastoralists such as the Nuer who had authority among the people and to whom responsibility and externally imposed tasks could be delegated in accordance with the framework of indirect rule. During the dry season, the eastern Nuer withdrew toward Ethiopian territory to escape from taxation. They then received guns from Ethiopia, which they traded for ivory.[18] Supported by this political-economic relationship with Ethiopia, the Nuer carried out a number of uprisings against the British during the 1920s, which were accompanied by the appearance of "prophets." The colonial administration responded with bloody punishments, including aerial bombing of Nuer cattle herds. As a result of this colonial warfare, British authorities began a serious quest to understand Nuer political structures and locate "responsible" leaders.

The geopolitical context of the situation, which included a constant tension between Ethiopia and the British in the eastern part of colonial Sudan, was excluded by Evans-Pritchard. He represented the spatial movement of Nuer toward Ethiopia as "ecological time"—following conditions of dry and rainy seasons—rather than tax evasion. A more recent anthropological observer has described this as the "the trap of treating the Nuer as if they lived in some timeless anthropological never-never land."[19] Even Evans-Pritchard could not introduce individual agents of responsibility to the colonial administration, and perhaps he did not want to. During 1929–30, before undertaking his 1930–31 fieldwork among the Nuer, Evans-Pritchard negotiated with the colonial administration about research methods and the presentation of data. The administration allowed him to work under the condition that he would present a comprehensive final study. However, they were also eager to get "interim reports."[20]

In a recent publication on administrative representations of the Nuer prior to Evans-Pritchard's research, Douglas Johnson describes a lecture Evans-Pritchard sent to colonial administrators. According to this letter, the colonial conquest of the Nuer was rule by force and for the Nuer it evoked the memory of force.[21] He did not specifically mention "kinship" in his lectures to the administrators but characterized the Nuer as "democratic," with "no political chiefs."[22] His message was that no chief who was administratively installed as an executor of indirect rule would find local support. What we can assume about "kinship" in the case of the Nuer is that it is a part (but not necessarily the only part!) of the moral order in the nexus between people and political institutions—the system of mutual rights and obligations. At the same time, the state administration in the neighboring Empire of Ethiopia did not hesitate to distribute titles, administrative symbols, and obligations to recognized "chiefs" among Nuer segments that had migrated to the Gambella lowland within the borders of Ethiopia. Within the Ethiopian political hierarchy, these shared symbols of political power marked an imperial moral order of rights and obligations.[23] Could one perhaps understand this as a well-placed instrumental exaggeration of artificial kinship by segments of the ruling class in the Ethiopian Empire?

This argument needs some historical and ethnographic elaboration. Some eastern Nuer lineages—among the Gajak-Nuer, in the 1920s and 1930s, in particular—used the unsettled condition of the border between the Ethiopian Empire and Anglo-Egyptian Sudan as an opportunity to create shifting alliances for protest and tax evasion. A number of them settled permanently in the Ethiopian lowlands of Gambella, adjacent to the Upper Nile Province of Sudan. One notable lineage representative, Koryum Tut, was recognized by the imperial Ethiopian institutions as a "chief." During the early 1930s, he was awarded the imperial military-administrative title of *fitawrari* (commander of the vanguard). In early 1935, Koryum Tut visited Emperor Haile Selassie in Addis Ababa, was given robes of honor, and delivered his grievances to the emperor. British colonial sources reported such cases as "unruly border" incidents and examples of the Ethiopian vice of meddling with good British colonial governance.[24] For Evans-Pritchard, the migration of the Nuer between Gambella and Upper Nile was an ecological matter connected to the change between the dry and the wet season. The "regulated anarchy" of the lineage order was mechanical and implied a basic egalitarian sentiment. Following generations of anthropologists introduced "agency" into the segmentary lineage system implying interests, manipulations, and hidden inegalitarian structures.[25] The Nuer migration toward Ethiopian territory demanded multiple perspectives. It contained ecological and social-structural elements linked to kinship, but also Nuer agency (collective, individual) in articulating lineage action and alliances vis-à-vis British colonial and Ethiopian imperial rule. British strategies for "indirect rule" were challenged by imperial Ethiopian strategies and perspectives on kinship, order, and borders.

From the imperial Ethiopian perspective, several issues were salient. Granting military-administrative titles and symbolic paraphernalia of rank to recognized "chiefs" of segmentary systems in borderlands, which was not uncommon, implied the creation of a hierarchical patron-client relationship, veiled in benevolent terms as a patriarchal father-son relationship expressed in affective terms of kinship. The "chief" was seen as the "father" of a "house" society, consisting of kin, retainers, and slaves.[26] Actor-centered strategic decisions about inclusion/exclusion, kin, individual and collective adoptions, close relations and alliances, non-kin, and enemies were common local features in the orbit of the Ethiopian Empire.[27] For the Ethiopian Nuer, the Amharic administrative ascriptive parlance of a "house" (*bet*) literally captured the space of the lineage (*cieng*).[28] From the imperial perspective, "the house" was conceived of as a static hierarchical and inegalitarian order, not as a flexible "regulated anarchy." From an analytical perspective, a recent champion of Ethiopian empire making has mentioned the strategic blurring of hierarchical interactions with kinship terminologies, thus bridging tensions between an imperial hierarchy and more egalitarian local structures.[29] Two examples from classical social anthropology indicate venues for comparison. Max Gluckman found similar tensions for African village headmen sandwiched between the colonial administration and local "corporate-kinship," while Edmund Leach's seminal study of the "Political System of Highland Burma" (1954) described political actors periodically switching between more hierarchical and more egalitarian formations, each implying different kinds of kinship relations.[30] The case of Koryum Tut and its aftermath contained the seeds of conflict, integration, and switching political relations between empire/statehood and segmentary systems.

Looking at the nexus between kinship and politics from Nuer land in the year 1935, a wide spectrum of issues appeared, apart from lineages, corporate groups, administration, and social structure. These touched on foreign policy and boundary making, citizenship and law, defense and empire, actor-centered political strategies, affective relationships, and—ultimately—internal, local, and external academic models of "the house" and "the lineage." This implied many fields of ambiguity and opportunities for political actors to choose among when deciding about kin and non-kin.

Imaginations, Translations, Metamorphosis: The *Corporate Group* Travels

Evans-Pritchard made his ethnographic observations on Nuer segmentary order, kinship, and political system during several periods of fieldwork between 1930 and 1936. His initial ethnographic observations appeared in the flagship publication of the Sudan Colonial Administration, *Sudan Notes and Records*, during the 1930s; however, none of the article referred to the "corporate." However, in his 1940s *The Nuer* and contributions to APS, several references to "corporate action" and "corporate community" appeared.³¹ This suggests that the initial ethnographic observations did not necessarily inspire an immediate imaginative merger of lineage and corporation.

One strong argument about how the two concepts merged relates to Henry Maine's (1822–88) modeling of native Indian village structures as corporations and the transfer of the model from established colonial rule in India to emergent colonial "indirect rule" in Africa.³² While Maine's influence on the anthropological discourse is undeniable, perspectives on the Sudan provide an opportunity to rethink the travel of the corporate model. The concept first appeared in *Sudan Notes and Records* in 1935 in a review by the British-Austrian anthropologist Siegfried Nadel of a popular book by the German Dietrich Westermann, then codirector of the International African Institute (see below). A closer look at Nadel's article and Westermann's book reveals problems of translation between German and British academic styles, paradigms, concepts, and models. The travel of the corporate model either absorbed other concepts or contributed to their metamorphosis under its own hegemony of "the corporate."

The historian Hayden White classified the "corporate" paradigm as part of the metaphysical-Romantic and "organic" thinking that accompanied European nation-building in the nineteenth century.³³ The anthropological concept of the "corporate group" was taken from constitutional and other legal authorities of the nineteenth century. British and German legal historians including Henry Maine and Otto Gierke (1841–1921) contributed centrally to the discourse, as did sociologists like Max Weber (1864–1920) and Émile Durkheim (1858–1917). The terms of the debate were set by early nineteenth-century German discussions.

Hegel's *Grundlinien der Philosophie des Rechts* (*Elements of the Philosophy of Right*), which appeared first in 1821, dealt at length with "corporations," infusing the term with ideas about free communities of interests and fraternal associations (*Genossenschaft*) as intermediaries between family and the state.³⁴ This partly coincided with his notion of civil society in a context that reflected the administrative reforms of the Prussian state under Stein and Hardenberg, including the abolition of merchant and craft guilds following the Napoleonic wars. Hegel disapproved of the abolitions.³⁵ His approach had no direct bearing on anthropological discourse, but it had an extensive indirect influence. Hegel's basic idea, as the editor of one English translation puts it, was that "corporation membership helps individuals to achieve a recognized estate or status (*Stand*)."³⁶ With this comprehensive approach, Hegel composed a melody—fundamentally hierarchical, male centered and gendered—based on which others improvised variations.

When Radcliffe-Brown applied the corporate paradigm to the Australian Kariera people in 1935, he was obviously influenced by—but did not cite—models from Roman Antiquity.[37] The conventional view about his adaptation of the *corporate group* to his version of (structural) functionalism points to his sojourn in Chicago in 1934 and the impact of legal historians at the University of Chicago Law School.[38] From different perspectives, Adam Kuper and Johannes Raum have outlined the historical dimension of political interests linked to sources within British and German legal and constitutional history.[39] Especially important were Maine's works on *Ancient Law* (1861) and Indian village communities (1871) and Gierke's on the history of the German Law of Fraternal Associations (*Genossenschaft*) and Corporations. Gierke contributed to the discourse through his English translator F. W. Maitland: like Gierke, a Romantic nationalist whose thought was rooted in metaphysical-organic assumptions.[40] Radcliffe-Brown was the vehicle for conveying organicist corporate ideas into early social anthropology.[41] Adam Kuper argued that Radcliffe-Brown's corporate model of Australian descent systems directly influenced the formulation on corporate groups, kinship, and politics in Fortes and Evans-Pritchard's introduction to APS:

> We must here distinguish between the set of relationships linking the individual to other persons and to particular social units through the transient, bilateral family, which we shall call the kinship system, and the segmentary system of permanent, unilateral descent groups, which we call the lineage system. Only the latter establishes corporate units with political functions.[42]

Other national anthropologies were influenced by the corporate model as well. Jan Vansina noted that Émile Durkheim's model of the segmentary lineage-cum-corporate idea had by the turn to the twentieth century already been used by Belgian administrators who had studied under Durkheim in the internal administration of the colonial Free State of the Congo.[43] Since the nineteenth century, the historical-juridical school in Italian ethnology had also operated based on the corporate idea.[44] The way the wider contextual discussion had reached into the IAI and the circle of Malinowski's students is exemplified by the political scientist Margery Perham, who in 1934 celebrated the decline of "old liberal individualism" and the rise of corporatism in Europe and Africa. In 1934, in a plea for colonial "indirect rule," she expressed a clear connection between anti-individualistic visions for Europe and reordering African polities:

> Can the co-operative character of African society be transformed in the technical sense, or adopted whole into the new corporative systems which in all the variety they display in Europe to-day show a common tendency to destroy the old liberal individualism?[45]

During the 1930s, fascist and Catholic proposals in Europe, as well as "New Deal" ideas in the United States, used the corporate trope in their propaganda. This belonged to a set of tropes and promises of modernization that constituted a "distant kinship" between fascist and liberal proposals for overcoming crises in capitalist societies.[46] In particular, Italian fascist social ideas and practices had direct consequences for totalitarian imaginations and plans to order social life, especially by influencing family systems. Hegelian ideas about the links between corporations (as guilds), families, paternal authority, and education were turned into instruments of Fascist statehood.[47] During this period, the idea of the *corporate group* was to be found everywhere, taking different shapes and forms and utilized for a variety of social and political interventions.

The corporate model rested on the legal fiction of a supra-individual, enduring organizational entity: group membership gave status. Due to its importance within fascist social theory of the 1920s and 1930s, the corporate model lost some of its glamour: by 1983, the German Social Democrat, refugee from Nazi Germany, and Berkeley economist Carl Landauer (1891–1983) called it a "forgotten idea."[48] Paradoxically, however, it flourished within social anthropology. Anthropologists like Meyer Fortes (1953, 1970) and M. G. Smith (1974) formulated their Africanist examples of corporative models based on segmentary descent and kinship systems against the broader academic trend.[49] Meyer Fortes, for example, introduced Max Weber as an early and politically innocent source in his seminal article "The Structure of Unilineal Descent Groups" (1953) and fused this source with ethnographic data on segmentary systems in sub-Saharan Africa.[50] This synthesis was then taken up by, for instance, Edmund Leach and Lawrence Krader, who extended the corporate idea in social anthropology.[51]

Difficulties in Translating Max Weber

In the early 1970s, the pages of *American Anthropologist* were the scene of a controversial discussion about whether a paradigm developed from the history of European antiquity and the Middle Ages could legitimately be applied to ethnographic data from anywhere else.[52] In particular, James Dow found problems with the reception of Max Weber in Anglophone sociology following the first rendering of Weber into English in 1947 by Talcott Parsons and A. M. Henderson. Here, the "corporate group" rendered the less specific German term *Verband*.[53] The problem Dow outlined was revealed by comparing Weber's original German text *Wirtschaft und Gesellschaft* (1922) with subsequent attempts to render it into English.

Talcott Parsons published an abridged and summarized edition of Weber's original as *The Theory of Social and Economic Organization* in 1947. This was followed three decades later by a full translation edited by Guenther Roth and Claus Wittich, *Economy and Society* (1976).[54] Comparing them reveals that Parsons systematically misrepresented the position that Weber gave to the "corporation" within his analytical universe of basic organizational forms, a misreading that had persisted through decades of Anglophone anthropological discussions.

In Parsons's version of Weber, the term *corporate group* was meant to show how Weber's notion of *Verband* was linked to particular types of authority (*Herrschaft*) intelligible to Anglophone readers.[55] Parsons noted that a simple translation for *Verband* would be "association," but that term carried a notion of equality and did not convey the possibility of "formal differentiation" in a collective body with inherent power structures, such as a distinct "chief" and a top-down flow of authority.[56]

Although Weber's original German version dealt extensively with the "corporate" paradigm, Parsons's translation overemphasized its importance within the overall scheme of Weber's approach. In the German text, *Verband* appeared as an overarching ideal type, embracing three different subtypes of collective legal fictions: the "institution" (*Anstalt*), the "endowment" (*Stiftung*), and the "corporate group" (*Körperschaft*), each with specific but also overlapping properties. For practical and empirical purposes, Weber claimed a "fluidity" of juridical relationships.[57] In Parsons's text the "corporate group" became the overarching ideal type; the second English version of Weber's text changed the translation for *Verband* to "organization."[58]

For his approach to the corporate group, Weber drew heavily—but also critically—on the German legal historian Otto Gierke. Since the middle of the nineteenth century, the latter had written extensively on the legacy of corporate group rights in German and European history. He was a Romantic nationalist with variable national-liberal positions in the discussions on German constitutionalism.[59] For Gierke, corporate groups and corporate law in the German(ic) context were derived from earlier collective popular practices around the organization of local rights and obligations. Through the ages, this had a bearing on legal and social practices in the fields of law, economy, education, and politics, including more recent joint stock companies and trade unions. According to Gierke, the German(ic) collective past of corporative practices was inextricably linked to "fraternal associations" (*Genossenschaft*).[60] However, the fraternal type of association/corporation competed with a contrasting imperial Roman tradition in which corporate units and legal practices were established through public recognition by the state. Weber used many of Gierke's ideas but shunned the dichotomy between Roman and Germanic corporate traditions.[61] After all, in Great Britain the two legal traditions (development of corporate practices from below and imposition of corporative practices from above) had fused to some degree.[62] In France, by contrast, the Revolution of 1789 had ended older corporative rights and practices from the feudal past. However, Weber recognized a resurgence of corporative thought in a France, captivated by new social questions (perhaps a tacit reference to Durkheim's position on the issue that will be discussed below, and that Weber otherwise does not mention in his text).[63]

For Weber, the corporate legacy was clearly a distinctive (Western) European feature.[64] In other geographical areas, such as Russia, China, India, the Islamic World, such collective practices might have existed, but without continuous legal development and practices and hence without consciousness of their own existence.[65] Kinship as such (the German text generally uses *Sippe*, "sib") was not the root of corporate practices of sharing and participating, of rights and obligations, and of rules for inclusion and exclusion. If anything, kinship provided an early kind of legal vocabulary, ordering group relations internally vis-à-vis others. The original blueprint was the ideal type of a localized household economy under a patriarchal head, with dependent family members, retainers and servants, and developing legal practices like endowments (communities of heirs) and corporations.[66] To keep the household unit as a unified entity, regardless of its membership, was in the corporate interest. Kinship, on the other hand, was already an expression of dispersal for Weber: it cut across household units, neighborhoods, and even linguistic units.[67] Kinship provided, to some degree, security and trust in mutual solidarity on a wider scale, but Weber held that kinship units without discernible "chiefs" (*Leiter*) had neither organizational nor corporate character.[68] However, his analytical terminology allowed for wide spaces of fluidity between ideal-types, so an acephalous "ruling organization" (*Herrschaftsverband*) like the Nuer—with more kinship than household and without discrete chiefs—could perhaps have found a corporate niche.

Venues and Limits: Émile Durkheim

As Max Weber observed, corporative issues had a low profile in French academic discussion during the nineteenth century because of their links with the prerevolutionary ancien régime and because the Civil Law of the Code Napoleon had abolished corporate rights and obligations. Nonetheless, Durkheim dealt extensively with the issue of corporative organization of labor relations in his preface to the second edition of *De la Division du Travail Sociale* (1903), which appeared in English translation in 1933.[69]

The French first edition of the book, in 1893, had not yet shown much interest in the corporation. Only a few descriptive and no analytical examples employed corporative topics, although Durkheim's perspective of structuring human development along a transition from a mechanical to an organic division of labor also implied a shift from segmentary, kinship-based relations to modes of organization based on the division of labor.[70] In a final analysis, Durkheim regarded webs of occupational organization that embraced whole populations of industrialized societies as remedies against the anomic trends of industry and capitalism.[71] In the second edition, Durkheim added a new foreword that fell back on traditions to argue for founding a new corporatism. His historical models were Roman corporations—considered cultic-religious associations based on mutual interests in local affairs and labor—which he viewed as functional substitutes for earlier segmentary units of family and kinship. Even though kinship terms (brotherhood, father, and mother) and "artificial kinship" persisted, "the community of interests took the place of the community of blood."[72] Such corporations supported civic morality and ethics in the context of an ever-growing division of labor. In contrast to Weber, Durkheim avoided discussing internal power relations and hierarchies and relationships with wider political orders such as the state.[73]

Although it is likely, there is no explicit evidence that early social anthropologists were directly influenced by Durkheim's approach to corporative groups. The relationship between early ethnographic data and theory indirectly mirrored, as Talal Asad has claimed, the function of corporative examples from sub-Saharan Africa as imagined remedies for a crisis-ridden Europe.[74] However, Durkheim's nephew and intellectual heir Marcel Mauss developed a contrasting position in French anthropology during the 1930s. Although sharing Durkheim's longing for nonrevolutionary social remedies, Mauss was alarmed to see how intellectuals such as Georges Sorel had contributed to the development of fascism by fusing corporative theories with totalitarian state-society models in disregard of individual freedom,[75] and he distanced himself from the zeitgeist of corporative ideas just as they began to flourish in social anthropology.

Two points sum up Weber and Durkheim's views on kinship. One is about the different types of kinship extension they envisioned, the other about the different interests involved in it. For Weber, the significant unit that the "corporate" expressed was not kinship but the household, while for Durkheim, the "corporate" did not signify the "mechanical" and segmentary, kinship-based stage of human development but was already a sign of the "organic" transformations of the division of labor in which it served rather as an organizational tool for enlarging the social order. Both authors had different types of explicit and implicit and public and private interests in mind which were articulated in corporate practices. For Weber, the idea was the protection of an undivided household property under a patriarchal regime expanded by family members and retainers. For Durkheim it was society at large—the order of the social whole—that was integrated through the division of labor that was at stake.

Kinship, Changing Modes of Classificatory Exaggeration, and the Corporate Muddle

In 1929, Bronisław Malinowski denounced speculative modes of kinship research in anthropology, criticizing the older competing schools of evolutionists and diffusionists that were then being challenged by the new school of functionalism.

> We know much more about the so-called anomalous forms of marriage or classificatory exaggerations of kinship than we know about the organization of the family. ... You will find a strange disproportion between the attention given to the everyday facts of life and the singular, between the treatment of the ordinary and the quaint; the family, for instance, and the more abstruse forms of kinship.[76]

The most speculative kinship unit was the "clan," a unit that Malinowski defined as based not on realistic genealogical data and a sound reckoning of descent but on fictive ancestry or totemistic beliefs about kinship rooted in animals, natural phenomena, or spirits. Moreover, the "clan" was connected in particular to "sensational" and "abstruse" speculations about practices and scopes of endogamy and exogamy and to defining incest expansively. This exemplified a type of anthropology that Malinowski shunned.

The article included a further message that combined the attack against old-school kinship studies—for almost a century the central trademark of anthropology—with a promise of collecting sounder data through the methodological instruments of intensive fieldwork and participant observation. Actual families were to be the object of local observation. The intended recipient of this message was the US-based Rockefeller Foundation, already an important source for academic funding and with an interest in expanding the scope of empirical academic research that could be applied to solving social problems. Malinowski offered to shape anthropology into such a science and defined sub-Saharan Africa as the testing ground. More urgently, he warned of the emergence of a specter he called "black bolshevism," the product of underinformed modes of colonial administration, capital flows, and unrecognized side effects of Africans being recruited into the industrial labor force.[77]

The institution Malinowski had in mind to carry out Rockefeller-funded empirical research was the London-based International Institute of African Languages and Cultures (IIALC), founded in 1926 and renamed the International African Institute (IAI) in 1939. Although the IIALC was a transnational institution with a strong missionary background, it was also close to British colonial interests. Its chairman, Lord Lugard, championed "indirect rule" in the British colonies. During its early years, the hallmark of the IIALC changed from research focused on languages, literacy in African languages, and education—topics dear to the missionaries—to social change, Black/white relations, training in field techniques, and the sponsorship of a nonantiquarian anthropology—that is to say, Malinowski-style functionalism. Malinowski joined the board of the IIALC during the late 1920s as an external member: a lecturer in anthropology at the London School of Economics (LSE) and a specialist on Melanesia. His interests in fieldwork and social change dovetailed with the interests of the staff at the IIALC—most notably Joseph Oldham, a missionary and behind-the-scenes founding member, and the two codirectors, the German missionary turned Africanist Dietrich Westermann and the French colonial officer turned Africanist Henri Labouret. A new five-year plan written in 1931 focused on social change, fieldwork, and postgraduate anthropological training and was supported by the Rockefeller Foundation with a generous $250,000 grant.[78]

Although firmly integrated into the British imperial order, the IIALC was a transnational institution with French, German, Italian, and other nationals as collaborators. This fostered the transfer of diverse conceptual frames and translations between national academic styles, which affected how kinship and family studies were carried out. Moreover, the Rockefeller Foundation funding for the IIALC and Malinowski led to two stiff competitions. One of these was between the IIALC and the Oxford University–based Rhodes House, which supported British settler interests in colonial Africa and also sought Rockefeller funding. The other was between Malinowski and the up-and-coming new star of functionalist anthropology Reginald Radcliffe-Brown. Although the latter was more personal and theoretical, it was also enmeshed with desire for funding. The competition between Malinowski and Radcliffe-Brown included theoretical issues connected to the relative positions of the individual and kinship/family and—as Malinowski put it—possible classificatory extensions or exaggerations of kinship. The contributions to APS, except those of Evans-Pritchard, were based on data collected under the IIALC's five-year plan, and thus share a background linked to the competition between Malinowski and Radcliffe-Brown. However, APS was embedded in a colonial framework and was not a simple outcome of this competition.

Evans-Pritchard's research among the Nuer of Southern Sudan during the early 1930s was done outside the scope of the IIALC and sponsored by the Sudanese colonial administration directly. The overarching political structure of colonial Sudan should have been a masterpiece of Lugard-style indirect rule, with political affairs and law delegated to local institutions within tribal limits. In contrast, Rhodes House dealt mainly with colonial settings in East, Central, and South Africa, where white settlers dominated and where Africans were drawn on a large scale into industrial labor and migration. In an academic setting linked to settlers' interests like Rhodes House, promotion of Lugard's "indirect rule" was not favorably received.[79]

The authors of APS are often blamed for excluding the colonial situation in Africa from their models. This is exactly what Malinowski and the Rockefeller Foundation opposed: they were interested in the cultural change resulting from the colonial setting. In a way, APS obstructed Malinowski's research agenda because concentration on "cultural change" contributed to resistance strategies. Radcliffe-Brown and Evans-Pritchard catalyzed the articulation of epistemological and methodological differences with Malinowski.[80] Malinowski-style ethnographic monographs were long and full of ethnographic details. The Rockefeller Foundation had initially funded Malinowski because of his innovative data collection, but cost-intensive, long fieldwork also could produce "bad" data that was apparently useless in solving practical problems. The mood within the foundation regarding financing this type of fieldwork changed,[81] and they came to prefer more elegant and reductive models. In 1937, Fortes and Evans-Pritchard approached Westermann with a request for support for their work on APS and the board of directors agreed.[82]

Westermann not only offered administrative support for APS but also contributed more broadly to its academic ideological message. The Rockefeller Foundation was not particularly interested in kinship/family-related studies as such, only in their relevance to labor relations, migration, and possible local unrest. The most important aspect of Malinowski's innovation involved fieldwork, methods, and data collection. The five-year plan, which was designed by Labouret and

Westermann and written by Malinowski's disciple Audrey Richards, linked kinship/family to the catchword of "social cohesion." "Cohesion," based on the assumption of mutually shared sentiments regulating individual behavior in social groups, was already part of the Durkheimian legacy among early social anthropologists and also a psychological perspective developed by Radcliffe-Brown.[83] However, Westermann used it in the sense of the German *soziale Bindung*, a term drawn from German sociology.[84] The specific German sociological discourse on *Bindung*, as a normative antidote to freedom, expressed "a must, a should-be, a not-to-be-allowed" (Ferdinand Tönnies), and conveyed a materialized and particularly narrow idea of normative rigidity.[85]

In 1934, the IIALC published Dietrich Westermann's *The African Today and Tomorrow: The Study of Change in Africa*.[86] The book became a popular bestseller, with more than seventeen hundred copies sold by the end of 1936.[87] Anthropologist Siegfried Nadel, who reviewed it for the flagship for anthropological articles on the Sudan, *Sudan Notes and Records* (SNR) — where Evans-Pritchard's research on the Nuer had originally appeared — stressed the corporate ideas developed by Westermann. Nadel's review was the first time that the corporate paradigm was used in SNR:

> In the first place the clans or family groups are the bricks of native society. Owing to the fact that they are not, according to our own ideas, an essential feature in administration, they have tended to be overlooked, but they have a very real and corporative existence for the native. Professor Westermann stresses their importance again and again. The individual is a member of his group first and an individual afterwards. His habit of mind is conditioned by his sense of membership of his group which gives him a sense of security and self-assurance, a feeling of being surrounded by friends on whose help he can rely. It is the clan that owns the land, the cattle are marked with the brand of the clan, not of the individual.[88]

What were the roots of this new emphasis on the clan? A comparison between Westermann's English version and the later version in German reveals that Nadel, by his own interpretation, rendered Westermann's use of "community"/*Gemeinschaft* into the "corporate." That term does not appear in any version. However, Nadel, who was initially trained in the German academic system and knew Westermann from Berlin, captured Westermann's intentions and intellectual roots in his review. Westermann's chapter on *Gemeinschaftsformen* (forms of community) refers in theoretical terms to sociologist/anthropologist Alfred Vierkandt and the chapter on the "cooperative social life of primitive people" in his well-established *Handbuch der Soziologie* (1931).[89] Vierkandt was a renowned social scientist, with social-democratic leanings, but in terms of theory was deeply influenced by the several shades of Romantic collectivism.[90]

Vierkandt's contribution to the *Handbuch* was preceded by an article by Ferdinand Tönnies on *"Gemeinschaft und Gesellschaft"* (Community and society),[91] a topic that is the main legacy associated with Tönnies. Vierkandt made no explicit reference to Tönnies in his article, but the implicit relationship between community, the early forms of corporate groups, and cooperative modes of production, consumption, and sharing among the *Naturvölker* were obvious. Two articles on "Familie" (family) by the Viennese cultural-diffusionist anthropologist Wilhelm Koppers ("marriage and family") and Tönnies ("modern family") added to this position.[92] The term "Verwandtschaft" (kinship) was used by Koppers only regarding extensive rules of exogamy.[93] Tönnies offered a very contemporary, sociographic perspective on the modern family. However, he insisted that the modern family, with its patriarchal overtones, derived from the past "extended family" (*Großfamilie*) with the Scottish clan of the eighteenth century brought in as a historical example. In Europe, the continuity of the classical extended family appeared as a privilege of ruling houses and aristocratic classes.[94] A brief reference to "kinship" appears in the statement that in "rural areas" relations by kinship and neighborhood foster the likelihood of marriage.[95] In the articles, "family" appears as the preferred term; however, "kinship" denotes its more extensive aspects, with extensions to a diachronically remote and a synchronically present rural and class other. Koppers's handbook, on the other hand, associated *kinship* with *clans*, and Tönnies associated it with upper-class practices. In the wider discourse, "community" appeared as the term embracing family/kinship. With Nadel's review, the likewise-exaggerated *Gemeinschaft*/community shifted into "corporative existence."

Tönnies regarded *kinship*, alongside neighborhood and friendship, as one possible mode of *community* (of the blood, the place, the mind)[96] and as articulations of social relations outside market relations. A century later, when Meyer Fortes defined his idea of "amity" as a basic altruism related to extended kinship and contrasted with the "market," *kinship* defined as "corporate group" appeared as a colonizing concept in its own right and as a new metamorphosis: it swallowed *community* and neighborhood/friendship, which for Fortes were merely occasional forms of spillover from kinship.[97] The corporate muddle in anthropology continued.

Conclusion

Travel requires space and vehicles. The vehicles of the corporate group were translations, imaginations, and fieldwork. They became used in manifold paths, leading into social-anthropological-style kinship studies. The common freight delivered along the pathways was a concept with historical-legal roots—library- and desk-based knowledge. Along the way, it mutated into an empirical sociological-cum-anthropological tool of analysis for social groups, capable of handling data collection by participating observers. With *fieldwork* as the new mode of knowledge production, the tool became the object of research as anthropologists claimed the *corporate* reflected the native point of view. Evans-Pritchard's study of the Nuer was a case in point. However, the groundwork for the concept was established by library-based knowledge, which, related to several more or less distant pasts, might at one stage also be based on other natives' points of view. Looking at the different pathways or legacies of knowledge provides a perspective into the complexities of thought enmeshed in the *corporative*. The anthropological discourse on corporate groups produced a genre of theoretical hybrids, mixing different legacies of knowledge and practice, which also contributed to the metamorphosis of the object.

During the 1930s, the "corporate group" became an analytical straitjacket for political and colonial observers and administrators. In a posthumously published report on his ethnographic sketch that became known as "The Bridge," Max Gluckman recalled how a dogmatic normative prescription created expectations for presenting ethnographic data.[98] It meant an evaluation of native culture in emotional terms as possessed of intrinsic values that satisfied the deepest aspirations of the Africans, and it produced descriptions of a contented, well-balanced tribal society in which the old, orphaned, indigent, and unfortunate were happily cared for within the motherly, all-embracing kinship system. Trade unionism, for them, threatened tribal solidarity, and social security weakened the strength of kinship ties. They emphasized the disruptive effects on indigenous relationships of "Westernization" and neglected the new forms of social organization emerging in new conditions.[99] From this perspective, the ethnographic focus on extended kinship ties included the danger of creating an ascriptive prison house, denying the wider organizational capacities of African workers and colonial subjects at large. That was not exactly the situation Evans-Pritchard described for the Sudanese Nuer, as they were not yet drawn into industrial labor. However, the introduction and universalization of the corporate paradigm, applied to *kinship*, created a wide range of seemingly comparable African life situations, some with and some without the connection to industrial labor, which mutually supported a conservative, static "evaluation of native culture in emotional terms." That perspective became a generalized mode of "classificatory exaggeration."

Kinship is a polysemous field and should not be confined to the theoretical straitjacket to which Radcliffe-Brown and many early social anthropologists contributed. The roots for that confinement were not only empirical research—the emergent method of fieldwork and participant observation—but also a combination of library-based knowledge and national idiosyncrasies. Malinowski had a more open approach to kinship, putting observable families into the center. However, the basic controversy about families versus the super-organic units called *kinship*, which characterized the final relationship between Malinowski and Radcliffe-Brown, was established before the fieldwork tradition developed.[100] Under new conditions, the early arguments became transformed. They reemerged when flexible *social organization* arose out of the critique of a mechanical *social structure* with a focus on "agency" and "practice." And they reemerged again with "new kinship" and its perspectives on "relations," fusing types of community as kinship/friendship/neighborhood under a new common theme.[101] Decades ago, the "corporate" served a related purpose for Siegfried Nadel.

The polysemous character of kinship has dark, neutral, and bright sides. Critical anthropology recognized this by introducing the idea of "ambivalence" in kinship.[102] The Italian Fascist example highlighted the totalitarian legacy of linking corporatism, kinship, and politics. Meyer Fortes highlighted a bright side by claiming *amity* as an extension of "natural" relations between parent-children and siblings. Nowadays, technical innovations in conception and childbirth and the practices of surrogate parenthood and blended families have bypassed the "natural" dimension of this argument. Other dimensions are still linked to the likewise polysemous meanings of *community*, which Fortes colonized by the means of metaphoric kinship extension. However, as one can learn from Weber and Durkheim, the extension of kinship terms into the complex world of legally framed corporate interests is an ancient and repeating practice, which certainly extends beyond "Western" examples.

What appears to have been salient during the 1930s was the problem of translation, not only between the experiences in the field and ethnographic texts, but between academic traditions. Germans highlighted *community* and British *kinship*. The contents were often similar.[103] Radcliffe-Brown stood for the development of a unified language of technical terms, which contributed foremost to a cohesive body of trained social anthropologists, but without necessarily fully shared terminological meanings.

The Romantic European legacy of the corporate group is linked to the assumption of a third space between the family and the state. Hegel, Maine, and Gierke filled that space with ancient and medieval corporations. Weber highlighted private and Durkheim public aspects and interests. Many social anthropologists were carried on their argumentative shoulders. Corporatism fully entered social anthropology with Meyer Fortes and fused it with the rich ethnographies of segmentary kinship systems. Meyer Fortes stressed the bright, benevolent, and caring side of corporative groups. Earlier, Marcel Mauss had underscored the potential totalitarian aspects of the fascist adaptation of corporate theory and the dangers for individual freedoms. Within social and cultural anthropology, the dialectic of this double legacy continues.

Thomas Zitelmann is a retired senior lecturer at the Institute of Social and Cultural Anthropology, Freie Universität Berlin (Germany). He has conducted academic and applied research in North East Africa (Sudan, Ethiopia, Djibouti, Somalia), the Middle East (Egypt, Israel/Palestine, Lebanon, Syria), and Cambodia. He specializes in the anthropology of nationalism, anthropology of conflict, political anthropology, the ethnohistory of Northeast Africa (with numerous publications on the Oromo), and the history of anthropology. In 2016–17 he participated in the interdisciplinary research group on kinship and politics at the Center for Interdisciplinary Research in Bielefeld.

Notes

1. Meyer Fortes and Edward E. Evans-Pritchard, eds., *African Political Systems* (Oxford: Oxford University Press, 1940); George Balandier, *Political Anthropology* (Harmondsworth: Penguin Books, 1972), 11.
2. Stefan Esselborn, *Die Afrikaexperten: Das Internationale Afrikainstitut und die europäische Afrikanistik, 1926–1976* (Göttingen: Vandenhoeck & Ruprecht, 2018), 11.
3. Alfred R. Radcliffe-Brown, "Preface," in *African Political Systems*, ed. Meyer Fortes and Edward E. Evans-Pritchard (Oxford: Oxford University Press, 1940), xiv.
4. For the early ethnographic application of the "corporate," see Edward E. Evans-Pritchard, "The Nuer of the Southern Sudan," in *African Political Systems*, ed. Meyer Fortes and Edward E. Evans-Pritchard (Oxford: Oxford University Press, 1940). For the early roots of the "corporate" see Lawrence Krader, *Dialectic of Civil Society* (Assen: Van Gorcum, 1976), 40–42.
5. Edward E. Evans-Pritchard, *The Nuer: A Description of the Modes of Livelihood and Political Institutions of a Nilotic People* (Oxford: Oxford University Press, 1940); Evans-Pritchard, "Nuer of the Southern Sudan," passim.
6. Evans-Pritchard, "Nuer of the Southern Sudan," 272
7. Edward E. Evans-Pritchard, "The Nuer: Tribe and Clan (I–III)," *Sudan Notes and Records* 16, part 1 (1933): 24.
8. Evans-Pritchard, "The Nuer: Tribe and Clan (I–III)," 7.

9. Evans-Pritchard, "The Nuer: Tribe and Clan (I–III)," 39.
10. Evans-Pritchard, "Nuer of the Southern Sudan," 274.
11. Evans-Pritchard, "Nuer of the Southern Sudan," 277.
12. Evans-Pritchard, "Nuer of the Southern Sudan," 283.
13. Evans-Pritchard, "The Nuer: Tribe and Clan (IV–continued)," *Sudan Notes and Records* 17, part 1 (1934): 40.
14. Evans-Pritchard, "Nuer of the Southern Sudan," 289.
15. Evans-Pritchard, "The Nuer: Tribe and Clan (IV–continued)," 39–40.
16. Evans-Pritchard, "The Nuer: Tribe and Clan (IV–continued)."
17. Evans-Pritchard, "Nuer of the Southern Sudan," 288.
18. Douglas Johnson, "On the Nilotic Frontier—Imperial Ethiopia in the Southern Sudan," in *The Southern Marches of Imperial Ethiopia—Essays in History and Social Anthropology*, ed. Donald L. Donham and Wendy James (Cambridge: Cambridge University Press, 1986).
19. John A. Barnes, "Edward Evan Evans-Pritchard 1902–1973," *Proceedings of the British Academy*, no. 83 (1987): 464.
20. NRO/Civsec I 112/1/, Hillelson to MacMichael, London 17.6.1929 (NRO Khartoum).
21. Douglas Johnson, "Introduction," in *Empire and the Nuer: Sources on the Pacification of the Southern Sudan, 1898–1930*, ed. Douglas Johnson (Oxford: Oxford University Press, 2016), xxiv.
22. Anonymous, "Epilogue: E. E. Evans-Pritchard Abstract of a Lecture on Administrative Problems in the Southern Sudan (Source: Oxford University Summer School on Colonial Administration. 1938, 75–77)," in *Empire and the Nuer: Sources on the Pacification of the Southern Sudan, 1898–1930*, ed. Douglas Johnson (Oxford: Oxford University Press, 2016), 261–63.
23. Thomas Zitelmann, "Des Teufels Lustgarten: Themen und Tabus der politischen Anthropologie Nordostafrikas" (postdoctoral diss., Freie Universität Berlin, 1999), 227.
24. Bahru Zewde, "Relations between Ethiopia and the Sudan on the Western Ethiopian Frontier 1898–1935" (PhD diss., University of London, 1976), 163; Dereje Feyissa, "Alternative Citizenship: The Nuer between Ethiopia and the Sudan," in *The Borderlands of South Sudan: Authority and Identity in Contemporary and Historical Perspective*, ed. Christopher Vaughan, Mareike Schomerus, and Lotje de Vries (New York: Macmillan, 2013), 113; Christiane Falge, *The Global Nuer: Modes of Transnational Livelihoods* (Köln: Rüdiger Köppe Verlag, 2015), 29; on Koryum Tut's visit to Addis Ababa, Sir Sidney Barton (*Brit.Legation Addis Ababa*) to *Governor General (Khartoum)*, 29.3.35 (Khartoum, NRO: UNP/1/49/353).
25. Evans-Pritchard, *The Nuer*, 51–93; Ladislav Holy, "Nuer Politics," in *Segmentary Lineage Systems Reconsidered*, ed. Ladislav Holy (Belfast: Queen's University, 1979).
26. Tsehai Berhane-Selassie, *Ethiopian Warriorhood: Defence, Land & Society 1800–1941* (Woodbridge: James Curry, 2019), 129–31.
27. Berhane-Selassie, *Ethiopian Warriorhood*, 110–11; Thomas Zitelmann, "Re-examining the Galla/Oromo Relationship: The Stranger as a Structural Topic," in *Being and Becoming Oromo: Historical and Anthropological Enquiries*, ed. P. T. W. Baxter, Jan Hultin, and Alessandro Triulzi (Uppsala: Nordiska Afrikainstitutet, 1996).
28. For the substitution for the Nuer "cieng" of the Amharic "bet(he)," see Falge, "Global Nuer," 66. For comparative perspectives on Nuer lineages and "house societies" on the Ethiopian highlands, see Susan McKinnon, "Domestic Exceptions: Evans-Pritchard and the Creation of Nuer Patrilineality and Equality," *Cultural Anthropology* 15, no. 1 (2000); Michel Verdon, "Where Have All Their Lineages Gone? Cattle and Descent among the Nuer," *American Anthropologist*, no. 84 (1982).
29. Berhane-Selassie, "Ethiopian Warriorhood," 134.
30. Max Gluckman, "The Village Headman in British Central Africa," in *Order and Rebellion in Tribal Africa* (London: The Free Press of Glencoe, 1964); Edmund Leach,

Political Systems of Highland Burma: A Study of Kachin Social Structure (London: G. Bell and Sons, 1954).
31. The index of *The Nuer* does not include any reference to the "corporate."
32. Karuna Mantena, *Alibis of Empire: Henry Maine and the End of Liberal Imperialism* (Princeton, NJ: Princeton University Press, 2010), 148–78.
33. Hayden White, *Metahistory: The Historical Imagination in Nineteenth-Century Europe* (Baltimore: The Johns Hopkins University Press, 1973), 15.
34. Georg W. F. Hegel, *Grundlinien der Philosophie des Rechts* (Leipzig: Felix Meiner, 1911), §250–56 and passim. For the English translation see Georg W. F. Hegel, *Elements of the Philosophy of Right*, ed. Allan Wood, trans. H. B. Nisbet (Cambridge: Cambridge University Press, 1991), 270–72 and passim.
35. Allan Wood, "Editor's Introduction," in *Elements of the Philosophy of Right*, Georg W. F. Hegel, ed. Allan Wood, trans. H. B. Nisbet (Cambridge: Cambridge University Press, 1991), xx.
36. Wood, "Editor's Introduction," xx.
37. Alfred R. Radcliffe-Brown, "Patrilineal and Matrilineal Succession," *Iowa Law Review* 20, no. 2 (1935).
38. George W. Stocking Jr., *After Tylor: British Social Anthropology 1888–1951* (Madison: University of Wisconsin Press, 1995), 357–58; Adam Kuper, "Lineage Theory: A Critical Retrospect," *Annual Review of Anthropology*, no. 11 (1982): 77.
39. Adam Kuper, *The Invention of Primitive Society: Transformations of an Illusion* (London: Routledge, 1988), 190–209; Johannes W. Raum, "Betrachtungen über den Einfluß der Tradition der englischen Rechts- und Verfassungsgeschichte auf die Begriffsbildung in der Deszendenz- und Lineage-Theorie der 'social anthropology,'" in *Die Vielfalt der Kultur: Ethnologische Aspekte von Verwandtschaft, Kunst und Weltauffassung. Ernst Wilhelm Müller zum 65. Geburtstag*, ed. Karl-Heinz Kohl, Heinzarnold Muszinski, and Ivo Strecker (Berlin: Reimer, 1990).
40. Henry S. Maine, *Ancient Law: The Connection with the Early History of Society and Its Relation to Modern Ideas* (London: John Murray, 1861; New York: Henry Holt and Company, 1906); Henry S. Maine, *Village Communities in the East and the West* (London: John Murray, 1871); Otto Gierke, *Political Theories of the Middle Age*, trans. Frederic W. Maitland (1900; repr., Cambridge: Cambridge University Press, 1987). On the relation between Gierke and Maitland, see White, *Metahistory*, 13.
41. Alfred R. Radcliffe-Brown, "The Concept of Function in Social Sciences," *American Anthropologist* 37, no. 3, part 1 (1935): 395.
42. Meyer Fortes and Edward E. Evans-Pritchard, "Introduction," in *African Political Systems*, ed. Meyer Fortes and Edward E. Evans-Pritchard (Oxford: Oxford University Press, 1940), 6.
43. Jan Vansina, "Knowledge and Perception of the African Past," in *African Historiographies: What History for Which Africa?* ed. Bogumil Jewsiewicki and David Newbury (Thousand Oaks, CA: Sage, 1986), 34.
44. Carlo Rossetti, "L'Etnologia Storico-Giuridica Italian nelle Prima Metà del Novecento," in *L'Antropologia Italiana—Un Secolo di Storia*, ed. Pietro Clemente, Alba R. Leone, Sandra Puccini, Carlo Rossetti, and Pier G. Solinas (Bari: Laterza, 1985), 160–61.
45. Margery Perham, "A Re-statement of Indirect Rule," *Africa*, no. 7 (1934): 328.
46. Wolfgang Schivelbusch, *Entfernte Verwandtschaft: Faschismus, Nationalsozialismus, New Deal 1933–1939* (Frankfurt a. M: Fischer, 2005), 23–25; translated into English as *Three New Deals: Reflections on Roosevelt's America, Mussolini's Italy, and Hitler's Germany, 1933–1939* (New York: Metropolitan Books, 2006).
47. Paul Ginsborg, "Family, Civil Society and the State in Contemporary European History: Some Methodological Considerations," *Contemporary European History* 4, no. 3 (1995): 264; Paul Ginsborg, *Die geführte Familie: Das Private in Revolution und Diktatur 1900–1950* (Hamburg: Hoffmann und Campe, 2014), 246–47.

48. Carl Landauer, *Corporate State Ideologies. Historical Roots and Philosophical Origin* (Berkeley: University of California Press, 1983), 1–3.
49. Meyer Fortes, "The Structure of Unilineal Descent Groups," *American Anthropologist* 55, no. 1 (1953): 17–41; Meyer Fortes, *Kinship and the Social Order: The Legacy of Lewis Henry Morgan* (London: Routledge and Kegan Paul, 1969); Michael G. Smith, *Corporations and Society* (London: Duckworth, 1974).
50. Fortes, "Structure of Unilineal," 25.
51. Edmund Leach, "Social 'Structure': The History of the Concept," in *International Encyclopedia of the Social Sciences*, vol. 14, ed. David L. Sills (New York: Macmillan, 1968), 489; Krader, *Dialectic of Civil Society*, 40–41.
52. See Glynn Cochrane, "Use of the Concept of the 'Corporation': A Choice between Colloquialism or Distortion," *American Anthropologist* 73, no. 5 (1971): 1144–50; Ward H. Goodenough, "Corporations: Reply to Cochrane," *American Anthropologist* 73, no. 5 (1971): 1150–52; James Dow, "On the Muddled Concept of Corporation in Anthropology," *American Anthropologist* 75, no. 3 (1973): 904–8.
53. Dow, "On the Muddled Concept," 905.
54. Max Weber, *Wirtschaft und Gesellschaft* (Tübingen: Mohr Siebeck, 1972); Max Weber, *The Theory of Social and Economic Organization*, ed. with an introduction by Talcott Parsons (Glencoe, IL: The Free Press, 1947); Max Weber, *Economy and Society: An Outline of Interpretive Sociology*, ed. Guenther Roth and Claus Wittich (Berkeley: University of California Press, 1978).
55. Talcott Parsons, "Introduction," in *Max Weber: The Theory of Social and Economic Organization*, ed. Talcott Parsons (Glencoe, IL: The Free Press, 1947), 56.
56. See note 76 in Weber, *Theory*, 145.
57. Weber, *Wirtschaft und Gesellschaft*, 425; Weber, *Economy and Society*, 708.
58. Guenther Roth, "Introduction," in *Max Weber: Economy and Society. An Outline of Interpretive Sociology*, ed. Guenther Roth and Claus Wittich (Berkeley: University of California Press, 1978), lxviii.
59. For the wider German nineteenth-century context of the Roman/Germanic binary in legal and constitutional controversies, see James Q. Whitman, *The Legacy of Roman Law in the German Romantic Era: Historical Vision and Legal Change* (Princeton, NJ: Princeton University Press, 1990), 230–31 (with special reference to Otto Gierke).
60. For an overview of Gierke's ideas, see the summary compiled in 1900 by Frederic W. Maitland: Gierke, *Political Theories*, and Gierke, *Community in Historical Perspective*, 1990 (see also endnote 103).
61. Roth, "Introduction," xl.
62. Weber, *Wirtschaft und Gesellschaft*, 436; Weber, *Economy and Society*, 724–25.
63. Weber, *Wirtschaft und Gesellschaft*, 435–36; Weber, *Economy and Society*, 724.
64. Weber, *Wirtschaft und Gesellschaft*, 437–38; Weber, *Economy and Society*, 725–27.
65. Weber, *Wirtschaft und Gesellschaft*, 438–39; Weber, *Economy and Society*, 727–29.
66. Weber, *Wirtschaft und Gesellschaft*, 425; Weber, *Economy and Society*, 708.
67. Weber, *Wirtschaft und Gesellschaft*, 219–21; Weber, *Economy and Society*, 365–66.
68. Weber, *Wirtschaft und Gesellschaft*, 26; Weber, *Economy and Society*, 48.
69. Émile Durkheim, *The Division of Labor in Society*, trans. George Simpson (New York: The Macmillan Company, 1933; Glencoe, IL: The Free Press, 1960).
70. Durkheim, *Division*, 238, 243.
71. Durkheim, *Division*, 402.
72. Durkheim, *Division*, 11–12.
73. Durkheim, *Division*, 19.
74. Talal Asad, "Two European Images of Non-European Rule," in *Anthropology and the Colonial Encounter*, ed. Talal Asad (London: Ithaca Press, 1973), 103–18.
75. Marcel Fournier, *Marcel Mauss: A Biography* (Princeton, NJ: Princeton University Press, 2015), 316–18.

76. Bronisław Malinowski, "Practical Anthropology," *Africa: Journal of the International African Institute* 2, no. 1 (1929): 27.
77. Malinowski, "Practical," 28.
78. For details, see Esselborn, *Die Afrikaexperten*, 176–78; Stocking Jr., *After Tylor*, 398–400; George W. Stocking Jr., "Philanthropoids and Vanishing Cultures: Rockefeller Funding and the End of the Museum Era in Anglo-American Anthropology," in *Objects and Others: Essays on Museums and Material Culture*, ed. George W. Stocking Jr. (Madison: University of Wisconsin Press, 1983), 127–28.
79. Freddy Foks, "Bronisław Malinowski, 'Indirect Rule,' and the Colonial Politics of Functionalist Anthropology, ca. 1925–1940," *Comparative Studies in Society and History* 60, no. 1 (2018): passim.
80. Jack Goody, *The Expansive Moment: Anthropology in Britain and Africa 1918–1970*, (Cambridge: Cambridge University Press, 1995), 55–56.
81. Stocking, "Philanthropoids," 137–38.
82. LSE/IAI 1/23, Documents presented to the seventeenth Meeting of the executive council, Brussels, 8-9.6.1938 (London School of Economics, Archive).
83. Alfred R. Radcliffe-Brown, *The Andaman Islanders: A Study in Social Anthropology* (Cambridge: Cambridge University Press, 1922), 233–34.
84. Esselborn, *Die Afrikaexperten*, 182.
85. "Bindung ist das Gegenteil der Freiheit—jene bedeutet ein Müssen, ein Sollen, ein Nichtdürfen. ..." Ferdinand Tönnies, "Gemeinschaft und Gesellschaft," in *Handwörterbuch der Soziologie*, ed. Alfred Vierkandt (Stuttgart: Ferdinand Enke, 1931), 182.
86. Dietrich Westermann, *The African Today and Tomorrow: The Study of Change in Africa* (London: International African Institute, 1934); Dietrich Westermann, *Der Afrikaner Heute und Morgen* (Essen: Essener Verlagsanstalt, 1937).
87. LSE/IAI/2/16: Minutes of the Twelfth Meeting of the Bureau, 18.12.36.
88. Siegfried F. Nadel, "Reviews: The Study of Change in Africa; 'The African Today' by Prof. Dietrich Westermann," *Sudan Notes and Records* 18 (1935).
89. Alfred Vierkandt, "Das genossenschaftliche Leben der Naturvölker," in *Handwörterbuch der Soziologie*, ed. Alfred Vierkandt (Stuttgart: Ferdinand Enke, 1931).
90. Vierkandt lost his chair at Berlin University under National Socialism. He regained it after the war and taught from 1945 on with Westermann at Humboldt University, East Berlin. Westermann collaborated with National Socialism.
91. Tönnies, "Gemeinschaft und Gesellschaft," 180–91.
92. Wilhelm Koppers, "Familie: I. Ehe und Familie," in *Handwörterbuch der Soziologie*, ed. Alfred Vierkandt (Stuttgart: Ferdinand Enke, 1931), 112–22; Ferdinand Tönnies, "Familie: II. Die moderne Familie," in *Handwörterbuch der Soziologie*, ed. Alfred Vierkandt (Stuttgart: Ferdinand Enke, 1931), 122–31.
93. Koppers, "Familie: I," 119.
94. Tönnies, "Familie: II," 129.
95. Tönnies, "Familie: II," 127.
96. Ferdinand Tönnies, *Gemeinschaft und Gesellschaft: Abhandlung des Communismus und des Socialismus als empirische Culturformen* (Leipzig: Fues's Verlag, 1887), 16–18.
97. Meyer Fortes, "Kinship and the Axiom of Amity," in *Kinship and the Social Order: The Legacy of Lewis Henry Morgan* (London: Routledge and Kegan Paul, 1969), 245.
98. Max Gluckman, "Analysis of a Social Situation in Modern Zululand," *Bantu Studies*, no. 14 (1940): 1–30, 147–74.
99. Robert J. Gordon, "On Burning One's Bridge: The Context of Gluckman's Zulu Fieldwork; With the previously unpublished chapter 'The Research Situation' (circa 1946)," *History in Africa*, no. 41 (2014): 192.
100. Bronisław Malinowski, *The Family among the Australian Aborigines: A Sociological Study* (London: University of London Press, 1913), 168–70.

101. Marilyn Strathern, *Relations: An Anthropological Account* (Durham, NC: Duke University Press, 2020), in particular chapter 6 and passim.
102. Michael G. Peletz, "Ambivalence in Kinship since the 1940s," in *Relative Values: Reconfiguring Kinship Studies*, ed. Sarah Franklin and Susan McKinnon (Durham, NC: Duke University Press, 2001).
103. A further example for the difficulties to translate/render the subtle layers of the German concept of *Gemeinschaft* (community) into English is Anthony Black's "Glossary" for Gierke's approaches to *Gemeinschaft*. "Kinship" is not mentioned by Black, but "kinship" as "corporate group," in the sense outlined by early social anthropologists, contained equivalent layers of social structures. Anthony Black, "Glossary," in *Otto Gierke: Community in Historical Perspective—A Translation of Selections from Das Deutsche Genossenschaftsrecht (The German Law of Fellowship) by Otto von Gierke—principally from Volume I Rechtsgeschichte der deutschen Genossenschaft (The Legal and Moral History of the German Fellowship)* [translated by Mary Fisher; selected and edited by Antony Black] (Cambridge: Cambridge University Press, 1990), xxxi–xxxiii.

Bibliography

Asad, Talal. "Two European Images of Non-European Rule." In *Anthropology and the Colonial Encounter*, edited by Talal Asad, 103–18. London: Ithaca Press, 1973.
Balandier, George. *Political Anthropology*. Harmondsworth: Penguin, 1972.
Barnes, John A. "Edward Evan Evans-Pritchard 1902–1973." *Proceedings of the British Academy*, 83 (1987): 447–90.
Barton, Sir Sidney. British Legation Addis Ababa to Governor General (Khartoum), 29.3.35; UNP/1/49/353, National Records Office (Khartoum).
Berhane-Selassie, Tsehai. *Warriorhood: Defence, Land & Society 1800–1941*. Woodbridge: James Curry, 2019.
Cochrane, Glynn. "Use of the Concept of the 'Corporation': A Choice between Colloquialism or Distortion." *American Anthropologist* 73, no. 5 (1971): 1144–50.
Dow, James. "On the Muddled Concept of Corporation in Anthropology." *American Anthropologist* 75, no. 3 (1973): 904–8.
Durkheim, Émile. *The Division of Labor in Society*. Translated by George Simpson. Glencoe, IL: The Free Press, 1960. First published in English in 1933 by the Macmillan Company (New York).
Esselborn, Stefan. *Die Afrikaexperten: Das Internationale Afrikainstitut und die europäische Afrikanistik, 1926–1976*. Göttingen: Vandenhoeck & Ruprecht, 2018.
Evans-Pritchard, Edward E. "The Nuer: Tribe and Clan (I–III)." *Sudan Notes and Records* 16, part 1 (1933): 1–60.
———. "The Nuer: Tribe and Clan (IV–continued)." *Sudan Notes and Records* 17, part 1 (1934): 1–57.
———. "The Nuer of the Southern Sudan." In *African Political Systems*, edited by Meyer Fortes and Edward E. Evans-Pritchard, 272–96. Oxford: Oxford University Press, 1940.
———. *The Nuer: A Description of the Modes of Livelihood and Political Institutions of a Nilotic People*. Oxford: Oxford University Press, 1940.
———. Letter to C. L. Armstrong; Abwong, 17.07.1940; UNP 1/46/336, National Records Office (Khartoum).

Falge, Christiane. *The Global Nuer: Modes of Transnational Livelihoods*. Köln: Rüdiger Köppe Verlag, 2015.
Feyissa, Dereje. "Alternative Citizenship: The Nuer between Ethiopia and the Sudan." In *The Borderlands of South Sudan: Authority and Identity in Contemporary and Historical Perspective*, edited by Christopher Vaughan, Mareike Schomerus, and Lotje de Vries, 109–31. New York: Macmillan, 2013.
Foks, Freddy. "Bronislaw Malinowski, 'Indirect Rule,' and the Colonial Politics of Functionalist Anthropology, ca. 1925–1940." *Comparative Studies in Society and History* 60, no.1 (2018): 35–57.
Fortes, Meyer. "The Structure of Unilineal Descent Groups." *American Anthropologist* 55, no. 1 (1953): 17–41.
_____. *Kinship and the Social Order: The Legacy of Lewis Henry Morgan*. London: Routledge and Kegan Paul, 1969.
_____. "Kinship and the Axiom of Amity." In *Kinship and the Social Order: The Legacy of Lewis Henry Morgan*, 219–49. London: Routledge and Kegan Paul, 1969.
Fortes, Meyer, and Edward E. Evans-Pritchard, eds. *African Political Systems*. Oxford: Oxford University Press, 1940.
Fournier, Marcel. *Marcel Mauss: A Biography*. Princeton, NJ: Princeton University Press, 2015.
Gierke, Otto. *Political Theories of the Middle Age*. Translated by Frederic W. Maitland. 1900. Repr., Cambridge: Cambridge University Press, 1987.
_____. *Community in Historical Perspective — A Translation of Selections from Das Deutsche Genossenschaftsrecht (The German Law of Fellowship) by Otto von Gierke — Principally from Volume I Rechtsgeschichte der deutschen Genossenschaft (The Legal and Moral History of the German Fellowship)*. Selected and edited by Anthony Black. Translated by Mary Fisher. Cambridge: Cambridge University Press, 1990.
Ginsborg, Paul. "Family, Civil Society and the State in Contemporary European History: Some Methodological Considerations." *Contemporary European History* 4, no. 3 (1995): 249–73.
_____. *Die geführte Familie: Das Private in Revolution und Diktatur 1900–1950*. Hamburg: Hoffmann und Campe, 2014.
Gledhill, John. *Power and Its Disguises: Anthropological Perspectives on Politics*. London: Pluto, 1994.
Gluckman, Max. "Analysis of a Social Situation in Modern Zululand." *Bantu Studies*, no. 14 (1940): 1–30, 147–74.
_____. "The Village Headman in British Central Africa." In *Order and Rebellion in Tribal Africa*, edited by Max Gluckman, 146–70. London: The Free Press of Glencoe, 1963.
Goodenough, Ward H. "Corporations: Reply to Cochrane." *American Anthropologist* 73, no. 5 (1971): 1150–52.
Goody, Jack. *The Expansive Moment: Anthropology in Britain and Africa 1918–1970*. Cambridge: Cambridge University Press, 1995.
Gordon, Robert J. "On Burning One's Bridge: The Context of Gluckman's Zulu Fieldwork. With the Previously Unpublished Chapter 'The Research Situation' (circa 1946)." *History in Africa*, no. 41 (2014): 155–94.

Hegel, Georg W. F. *Grundlinien der Philosophie des Rechts*. Leipzig: Felix Meiner, 1911.

——. *Elements of the Philosophy of Right*. Edited by Allan Wood. Translated by H. B. Nisbet. Cambridge, UK: Cambridge University Press, 1991.

Holy, Ladislav. "Nuer Politics." In *Segmentary Lineage Systems Reconsidered*, edited by Ladislav Holy, 23–48. Belfast: Queen's University, 1979.

Johnson, Douglas, ed. *Empire and the Nuer: Sources on the Pacification of the Southern Sudan, 1898–1930*. Oxford: Oxford University Press, 2016.

——. "Introduction." In *Empire and the Nuer: Sources on the Pacification of the Southern Sudan, 1898–1930*. Oxford: Oxford University Press, 2016.

——. "On the Nilotic Frontier—Imperial Ethiopia in the Southern Sudan." In *The Southern Marches of Imperial Ethiopia—Essays in History and Social Anthropology*, edited by Donald L. Donham and Wendy James, 219–45. Cambridge: Cambridge University Press, 1986.

Koppers, Wilhelm. "Familie: I. Ehe und Familie." In *Handwörterbuch der Soziologie*, edited by Alfred Vierkandt, 112–22. Stuttgart: Ferdinand Enke, 1931.

Krader, Lawrence. *Dialectic of Civil Society*. Assen: Van Gorcum, 1976.

Kuper, Adam. "Lineage Theory: A Critical Retrospect." *Annual Review of Anthropology* 11, no. 1 (1982): 71–95.

——. *The Invention of Primitive Society: Transformations of an Illusion*. London: Routledge, 1988.

Landauer, Carl. *Corporate State Ideologies: Historical Roots and Philosophical Origin*. Berkeley: University of California Press, 1983.

Leach, Edmund. *Political Systems of Highland Burma: A Study of Kachin Social Structure*. London: G. Bell and Sons, 1954.

——. "Social 'Structure': The History of the Concept." In *International Encyclopedia of the Social Sciences*, vol. 14, edited by David L. Sills, 482–89. New York: Macmillan, 1968.

London School of Economics (LSE)/International African Institute (IAI). LSE/IAI/2/4. Minutes of the Second Meeting of the Bureau, 4–5.1.32.

——. LSE/IAI/2/16: Minutes of the Twelfth Meeting of the Bureau, 18.12.36.

——. LSE/ IAI 1/23. Documents presented to the seventeenth Meeting of the executive council, Brussels, 8–9.6.1938.

Maine, Henry S. *Village Communities in the East and the West*. London: John Murray, 1871.

——. *Ancient Law: The Connection with the Early History of Society and Its Relation to Modern Ideas*. New York: Henry Holt and Company, 1906. First published 1861 by John Murray (London).

Malinowski, Bronisław. *The Family among the Australian Aborigines: A Sociological Study*. London: University of London Press, 1913.

——. "Practical Anthropology." *Africa: Journal of the International African Institute* 2, no. 1 (1929): 22–38.

Mantena, Karuna. *Alibis of Empire: Henry Maine and the End of Liberal Imperialism*. Princeton, NJ: Princeton University Press, 2010.

McKinnon, Susan. "Domestic Exceptions: Evans-Pritchard and the Creation of Nuer Patrilineality and Equality." *Cultural Anthropology* 15, no. 1 (2000): 35–83

Nadel, Siegfried F. "Reviews: The Study of Change in Africa. 'The African Today' by Prof. Dietrich Westermann." *Sudan Notes and Records* 18 (1935): 157–65.

Parsons, Talcott. "Introduction." In *Max Weber: The Theory of Social and Economic Organization*, edited by Talcott Parsons, 3–86. Glencoe, IL: The Free Press, 1947.
Peletz, Michael G. "Ambivalence in Kinship since the 1940s." In *Relative Values: Reconfiguring Kinship Studies*, edited by Sarah Franklin and Susan McKinnon, 413–44. Durham, NC: Duke University Press, 2001.
Perham, Margery. "A Re-statement of Indirect Rule." *Africa*, no. 7 (1934): 321–34.
Radcliffe-Brown, Alfred R. *The Andaman Islanders: A Study in Social Anthropology*. Cambridge: Cambridge University Press, 1922.
———. "Patrilineal and Matrilineal Succession." *Iowa Law Review* 20, no. 2 (1935): 286–303.
———. "On the Concept of Function in Social Science." *American Anthropologist* 37, no. 3, part 1 (1935): 394–402.
———. "Preface." In *African Political System*, edited by Meyer Fortes and Edward E. Evans-Pritchard, xi–xxiii. Oxford: Oxford University Press, 1940.
Raum, Johannes W. "Betrachtungen über den Einfluß der Tradition der englischen Rechts- und Verfassungsgeschichte auf die Begriffsbildung in der Deszendenz- und Lineage-Theorie der 'social anthropology.'" In *Die Vielfalt der Kultur: Ethnologische Aspekte von Verwandtschaft, Kunst und Weltauffassung. Ernst Wilhelm Müller zum 65. Geburtstag*, edited by Karl-Heinz Kohl, Heinzarnold Muszinski, and Ivo Strecker, 114–23. Berlin: Reimer, 1990.
Rossetti, Carlo. "L'Etnologia Storico-Giuridica Italian nelle Prima Metà del Novecento." In *L'Antropologia Italiana—Un Secolo di Storia*, edited by Pietro Clemente, Alba R. Leone, Sandra Puccini, Carlo Rossetti, and Pier G. Solinas, 151–203. Bari: Laterza, 1985.
Roth, Guenther. "Introduction." In *Max Weber: Economy and Society. An Outline of Interpretive Sociology*, edited by Guenther Roth and Claus Wittich, 33–110. Berkeley: University of California Press, 1978.
Schivelbusch, Wolfgang. *Entfernte Verwandtschaft: Faschismus, Nationalsozialismus, New Deal 1933–1939*. Frankfurt a. M.: Fischer, 2005.
———. *Three New Deals: Reflections on Roosevelt's America, Mussolini's Italy, and Hitler's Germany, 1933–1939*. New York: Metropolitan Books, 2006.
Smith, Michael G. *Corporations and Society*. London: Duckworth, 1974.
Stocking, George W., Jr. "Philanthropoids and Vanishing Cultures. Rockefeller Funding and the End of the Museum Era in Anglo-American Anthropology." In *Objects and Others: Essays on Museums and Material Culture*, edited by George W. Stocking Jr., 112–45. Madison: University of Wisconsin Press, 1983.
———. *After Tylor: British Social Anthropology 1888–1951*. Madison: University of Wisconsin Press, 1995.
Strathern, Marilyn. *Relations: An Anthropological Account*. Durham, NC: Duke University Press, 2020.
Tönnies, Ferdinand. *Gemeinschaft und Gesellschaft: Abhandlung des Communismus und des Socialismus als empirischer Culturformen*. Leipzig: Fues's Verlag, 1887.
———. "Familie: II. Die moderne Familie." In *Handwörterbuch der Soziologie*, edited by Alfred Vierkandt, 122–31. Stuttgart: Ferdinand Enke, 1931.
———. "Gemeinschaft und Gesellschaft." In *Handwörterbuch der Soziologie*, edited by Alfred Vierkandt, 180–91. Stuttgart: Ferdinand Enke, 1931.

Vansina, Jan. "Knowledge and Perception of the African Past." In *African Historiographies: What History for Which Africa?* edited by Bogumil Jewsiewicki and David Newbury, 28–41. Thousand Oaks, CA: Sage, 1986.

Verdon, Michel. "Where Have All Their Lineages Gone? Cattle and Descent among the Nuer." *American Anthropologist* 84, no. 3 (1982): 566–79.

Vierkandt, Alfred. "Das genossenschaftliche Leben der Naturvölker." In *Handwörterbuch der Soziologie,* edited by Alfred Vierkandt, 191–201. Stuttgart: Ferdinand Enke, 1931.

Weber, Max. *Wirtschaft und Gesellschaft.* 1922. Rev. 5th edition by Johannes Winckelmann. Tübingen: Mohr Siebeck, 1972.

———. *The Theory of Social and Economic Organization.* Edited with an introduction by Talcott Parsons. Glencoe, IL: The Free Press, 1947.

———. *Economy and Society: An Outline of Interpretive Sociology.* Edited by Guenther Roth and Claus Wittich. Berkeley: University of California Press, 1978.

Westermann, Dietrich. *The African Today and Tomorrow: The Study of Change in Africa.* London: International African Institute, 1934.

———. *Der Afrikaner heute und morgen.* Essen: Essener Verlagsanstalt, 1937.

White, Hayden. *Metahistory: The Historical Imagination in Nineteenth-Century Europe.* Baltimore: The Johns Hopkins University Press, 1973.

Whitman, James Q. *The Legacy of Roman Law in the German Romantic Era: Historical Vision and Legal Change.* Princeton, NJ: Princeton University Press, 1990.

Wood, Allan. "Editor's Introduction." In Georg W. F. Hegel, *Elements of the Philosophy of Right.* Edited by Allan Wood. Translated by H. B. Nisbet, vii–xxxii. Cambridge: Cambridge University Press, 1991.

Zitelmann, Thomas. "Re-examining the Galla/Oromo Relationship: The Stranger as a Structural Topic." In *Being and Becoming Oromo: Historical and Anthropological Enquiries,* edited by P. T. W. Baxter, Jan Hultin, and Alessandro Triulzi, 103–13. Uppsala: Nordiska Afrikainstitutet, 1996.

———. "Des Teufels Lustgarten. Themen und Tabus der politischen Anthropologie Nordostafrikas." Postdoctoral diss., Freie Universität Berlin, 1999. https://doi.org/10.13140/RG.2.1.1009.7767.

Zewde, Bahru. "Relations between Ethiopia and the Sudan on the Western Ethiopian Frontier 1898–1935." PhD diss., University of London, 1976.

Chapter 5

German Kinship
Forming a Political Unit and an Epistemic Void

Tatjana Thelen

Introduction

I first presented results from my fieldwork in eastern Germany on dissolution of kinship across the former border at the university in Halle (Saale) in August 2005. That paper described the perspectives of my eastern German interlocutors against the backdrop of German unification. In retrospect, they characterized their western kin as arrogant and materialistic. For example, they recounted receiving parcels containing cheap and unneeded staples, as well as experiencing postunification conflicts over inheritances and political opinions. My presentation and analysis of their narrations was met with indignant—if not aggressive— protest. Specifically, one West German woman in the audience recalled how much effort and money they had put into the packages they sent to the East and the gratitude their care had elicited. As my previous research on postsocialist Hungary had also included stories about family conflicts and had never received such reactions, I was quite shocked at the time. Ever since that first presentation, my findings have evoked similar critical responses. As in the first incident, well-educated West Germans usually emphasized the emotional quality of the relations. This could be expressed either through accounts of lasting relationships or by representing Easterners as having been "appropriately" satisfied by what the Westerners had to give. In this chapter, therefore, I return to my earlier findings and the reactions they provoked in order to trace why it was so important for my audience that I "get things right." This importance belies the reporting of conflicts as purely personal matters in the narrations of my Eastern interlocutors, and hints at the politics of making cross-border kinship, something that has not received enough attention in the social sciences.

In order to make this argument, I need to describe a second line of criticism my work has provoked. Trying to counter the imbalance I presented in my account, better-off West Germans sometimes stressed their joy in receiving goods from the East as well. Usually referring to having received classical music or literature, however, implied that nothing else was available from there, either because of political censorship or a scarcity of other desirable high-quality products. Here, we see again an implicit hierarchy—one that is, curiously enough, mirrored in international scholarly discourse. At my last presentation on the topic in 2017, for example, a colleague from the United States asked about difference in kinship practices, and a Scandinavian scholar wondered if kinship meant something else in the East. After all, both argued that in a situation of shortage, people would use all kinds of relations, including kin, to secure scarce goods. In contrast to the West German claims of emotional closeness and equality despite differential access to resources, international colleagues were, thus, looking for difference. Speculating about diverging practices and interests evokes the supposedly different nature of socialist kinship. In this functionalist interpretation, socialist citizens developed a more strategic investment in kin relations than their capitalist counterparts. Due to the socialist economy failing to provide various goods, Easterners supposedly sought to expand their networks, including extended kin. Instead of emotional closeness, economic inequality became the driving force between essentially different ways of living relatedness. While Germans on both sides leave out any link to the politics involved in making kinship across the border and instead present individual experiences, this second critique excludes politics in favor of economics and represents, at least for anthropology, an unusual veer toward theoretical functionalism and economic determinism.

Rather than lending empirical "proof" to the narratives of my interlocutors, this chapter considers the ideas behind both of these criticisms. Why is it that belonging together appears to be taken for granted on the West German side and cannot (or should not) be questioned by accounts of hierarchy and conflict? What kinds of assumptions about sameness and otherness do the critical utterances imply? Why are the politics of kinship not mentioned? And, most importantly, how could specific interpretations of kinship become pervasive? Ultimately, I argue that an epistemic void has evolved around ideas and practices of German kinship rooted in long-standing Western self-understandings that are characterized by the idea of the decline of kinship and its separation from politics (see the introduction to this volume).

In order to make this argument, I proceed in three steps. First, I summarize and expand my earlier work to outline the politics of making kinship and making politics through kinship against the backdrop of the former German-German border.[1] The political projects of both the socialist East and the capitalist West needed and used kinship in different ways. While the rhetoric of kinship in the West extended to the territory of both states as an expression of the "natural" unity of the German nation, the East tried to restrict kinship. Both sides naturalized kinship as descent, although on different scales, which became a matter of negotiations of international diplomacy around questions of the right to care across the German-German border.

In light of these tensions, the second part of the chapter turns to how the different policies were connected to actual kinship practices. It seems that the high level of political attention on both sides contributed to the expanding of kinship. Having conducted research only in the former socialist parts of Germany, I complement this part with some reflexive remarks on my own kin. The central point is the group of ideas that evolved around these practices of extended kinship. Despite all the politics involved, these networks' evolution and eventual dissolution after unification are framed as personal issues. Even more importantly, this topic has never been taken up in social scientific theories about kinship in contemporary societies. In the third part, therefore, I turn to the scientific production of knowledge about kinship and to why there has apparently been no interest in these economically, politically, and emotionally important practices. I argue that an epistemic void around kinship in a modern society makes it only "detectable" in the socialist East—which is characterized as having deferred a "modern" path. Making extended kinship visible within and across both German states thus offers unique insights into the mechanisms of the coproduction of politics and kinship.

Politics of Making Kinship—Making Politics through Kinship across the Former German-German Border

The critical reactions of the West German audience indicated that they understood my interpretation of East German accounts as affirmation. When I recounted my interlocutors' narratives of inequality and conflict between kin across the former border, this was met with indignation and countered with personal stories of "appropriate" emotional closeness and equality within such relations. In short, I was accused of subscribing to the theories of my interlocutors, as in Fassin's description of reactions to his research on HIV in South Africa.[2] His audience saw connecting the spread of AIDS to power and inequality as unacceptable, similarly to how my audience saw my East German interlocutors' interpretations of hierarchy and conflict. Despite the obvious difference in topics, an otherwise acceptable project of explaining the perspectives of our interlocutors through historical embedding met with a similarly highly emotional response. What was at stake?

This section first sets the scene by delineating how kinship came to play a central role in naturalizing the political unit on both sides of the border. A positive emotional quality—or even equality—of kin relations was (and apparently remains) more important to the Western side, where it demonstrated not only Germany's political unity but also the West's moral superiority: after all, history had proved that they (especially the elite) had been "on the right side." In the East, official policies sought to achieve the reverse—political autonomy—by restricting kinship, which also fed into the increasingly political character and extension of kinship. I will first turn to the rhetoric of and support for kinship across the border in the West, before describing the Eastern response.[3]

Kinship Writ Large: "Natural" Expression of Political Unity in the West

The term "partition" played a central role for West German political self-understanding during the decades of the existence of two German states. Consequently, when the two German states united, this process was termed *reunification (Wiedervereinigung)*. This holds true not only in the national discourse but also internationally. Indeed, some of my language editors regularly try to change my use of "unification" to "reunification." As social scientists, we cannot leave such terminology unquestioned. The term *partition* implies that a preexisting whole had been separated, but explicitly naming that unit would have been problematic in the decades after the atrocities of the Nazi regime. Should it mean Germany within the borders of 1871, 1920, or 1936? Appealing to ethnicity—not to mention race—also seemed out of the question. In contrast, kinship as a "natural expression" of belonging together provided a convenient and seemingly apolitical basis for strengthening the idea of Germany as a political unit.

Neither unity nor kinship as its expression had been high on the agenda immediately after Nazi Germany's defeat. The political situation remained unsettled, and moving between occupation zones was generally easy until 1949, when first the Federal Republic of Germany (FRG) and then the German Democratic Republic (GDR) declared themselves independent states. In the first years after these declarations, West

German political discourse considered promoting the unity of Germany as Communist propaganda because this language was used by the Socialist Unity Party (SED) in the East. But after the building of the Berlin Wall in 1961, an almost complete turn of political interpretation took place, and kinship was a central element.

Now, holding the socialist other responsible for an "artificial" partition required a "natural" alternative symbol of unity. Kinship became, and despite political shifts remained, a central expression of this unit in political discourse before unification. This use was facilitated by the preexisting idea of the German nation being constituted by descent: citizenship was transmitted through blood (jus sanguinis) and also extended to many persons descended from "German" families that had lived for centuries in (for example) Russia, Hungary, or Romania. As kinship apparently constituted belonging together, its terminology was extended to the territory of the GDR. However, the rhetoric such as "our (poor) brothers and sisters in the East" was always ambivalent. While metaphorical references to siblinghood might evoke ideas and sentiments of horizontal equality, siblingship also always entails hierarchies (such as in age or economic inequality).[4] Such a hierarchy was clearly entailed by the ensuing official politics of making kinship, as well as cross-border practices.

During the following decades, repeated campaigns by state and nonstate actors called on West German citizens to send letters and parcels across the border, belying the imagined apolitical nature of spontaneously emerging kin care.[5] Like donations to registered charities, the costs of parcels sent to the GDR could be deducted from taxable income. Appeals to a sense of moral obligation stressed the need and longing of Easterners for the parcels. For example, one postage stamp exhorted, "Your parcel to the other side [drüben]. They wait for it," while a poster asked, "Have you done your share?"[6] Some recommended sending staple foods and secondhand clothing, constantly evoking a sense of urgent material need in the GDR.[7] Additional financial and ideological support came from the so-called Ministry for All-German Affairs (Ministerium für gesamtdeutsche Fragen)—after 1969 the Ministry for Intra-German Relations (Ministerium für innerdeutsche Beziehungen), which, for example, launched school writing and drawing competitions with topics such as "What is the use of your parcel to the zone?" and "The people in the zone need us."[8] The political aim of promoting unity was quite explicitly stated, as in this ministerial memorandum:

> The main idea of this support is, besides material help, a political goal: the parcel as an expression of solidarity should enforce human contact and strengthen the responsibility of the citizens of the FRG for the conservation of a feeling of belonging together.[9]

From the beginning, exchange and care between kin across the border thus had moral overtones and was caught in the tension between equality and hierarchy. The character of West German parcel campaigns—expressed as a call for charitable actions—did not, of course, go unnoticed and was firmly rejected by the consecutive governments in the East.[10]

Restricting Kinship: Building a "Socialist Nation"

Building a "socialist nation" in East Germany entailed the formation of "modern" conjugal families. In contrast to the widening kinship rhetoric of the FRG, consecutive governments of the GDR relied on very narrow definitions of kinship as descent in their policies and generally tried to restrict cross-border kin contact. Contrary to the rhetoric of charity, parcels had to be declared as personal gifts to a specific individual. The so-called *Westpaket* (parcel from the West) became a highly politicized issue, as did having kin in the FRG (for which the term *Westverwandtschaft* was used).[11] After a strict phase in the beginning, policies concerning visits between relatives in later decades shifted toward reluctant acceptance under increasing international pressure that made them somewhat easier.[12] Initially, permission for crossing the border from East to West was granted only to pensioners and disabled persons, who were deemed "unproductive." Other citizens needed to submit travel applications for so-called "urgent family matters." Such matters eventually were extended to potentially include birthdays, marriages, and major wedding anniversaries, as well as serious illnesses and deaths of close consanguineous kin (grandparents, parents, children, and siblings, including half-siblings).

Despite the restrictions and official regulations that generally excluded affinal ties, East German applications for permission to visit West Germany increasingly included extended kin and kin by marriage. An internal police report stated that most applications concerned "more distant relatives" and listed "uncles, aunts, cousins, parents-in-law, brothers- and sisters-in-law, nieces, nephews," and also noted that couples wished to travel together.[13] These documents and legal changes already indicate that more extended relatives beyond the nuclear family were included in kinship practices. International diplomacy also took up the issue in various negotiations, which contributed to an enlargement of the definition of the "significant" kin allowed to take part in mutual exchanges across the German-German border. In the late 1980s, shortly before the Wall fell, the category of significant kin officially broadened to include some affinal ties, such as brothers- and sisters-in-law.

Even though it tried to restrict contact, the socialist state actually contributed as much as the capitalist one to the importance of (extended) kinship as a political symbol. Western state support for the interpretation of separation as "unnatural" was as central as the East's restriction of travel: both policies added to the increasingly politicized character of kinship linked to the understanding of the nation and citizenship. Accordingly, the construction of the German nation as "one people" figured prominently in the East German protests that ended in political unification. Meanwhile, the increasing economic disparity between the two German states contributed to making kinship a humanitarian project of the West. Thus, at the same time that kinship was becoming an expression of political unity, it was increasingly imbued with constructions of East-West difference and hierarchy. The intense political and personal investment in kinship (including its moral overtones) is, I suggest, one reason why—despite a shift from understanding the nation as based in blood to being derived from pride in the constitution and economic achievement—it seems so important for my West German audience that I "get things right." The process of evaluative mirroring did not stop with unification.

The idea of a German unit expressed through kinship became less significant for the unified state, which extended West German political and economic institutions to the former territory of the GDR. It is no coincidence that the first substantial alteration in German citizenship law in place since 1913 occurred after unification. Since 2000, the jus sanguinis has been supplemented by elements of jus soli: citizenship is now granted based on a combination of descent and place of birth, which has also eased the legal acquisition of double citizenship. In addition, the migration of Germans from other former socialist countries (which would now have been possible on a large scale) was restricted and the charitable tone suppressed. Regarding the eastern so-called *Neue Länder* (new states) in unified Germany, which have continued to experience economic inequality relative to the West, it proved increasingly hard to gather political support for monetary transfers, and no new political campaigns were launched to call for individual support. Public discourse shifted from emphasizing sameness to difference, feeding into the new political identifications expressed in my East German interlocutors' accounts of their relations with West German kin—which often ended with de-kinning.[14] These self-identifications built upon the well-established hierarchies and images of East-West that were embodied in practices that had evolved on both sides of the border between extended kin, to which I will turn in the next section. Interestingly enough, these narratives interpreted both extended kinship practices and the dissolution of these relations as personal issues with no link to politics.

Extended Kinship Practices as Symbols of Sameness and Difference

West German politicians and other commentators have often criticized the cross-border restrictions on travel and exchange imposed by the consecutive GDR governments as not only an inhumane practice but also an effective tool to break kinship ties.[15] However, kinship across the border persisted and even expanded during the period of two German states. In this section, I will first outline practices of extended kinship both across the border and within each country before turning to their moral evaluations. As it turns out, both sides accused each other of having a "materialistic attitude" toward kin that failed to live up to an ideal of emotional closeness purified of economic interest. These attitudes were then (and still are) dismissed as a sign of otherness.

Kinning across the Border

During the first decades after the war, exchange and communication across the border often involved persons who had known each other well during the period before the existence of two German states. This was not always true of later generations. Despite the regulations requiring that contacts be personalized, letters and parcels were increasingly not directed to individuals but sent to and received by wider circles of relatives.[16] These included affinal kin like sisters-in-law, as well as distant cousins. Similarly, groups of relatives would often travel together to visit several families on the other side of the border. Gifts were exchanged by the older generation, and in this way these gifts reached the younger as well. Often, women were the main actors in sustaining these interactions.

All of this happened among my own relatives. My mother's oldest sister had the main responsibility for collecting the money from her siblings and organizing the shopping, packing, and sending of parcels to our Eastern relatives. Especially before Christmas and birthdays, goods would be piled in her apartment to be sent. She also received the parcels and letters sent in return. The exchange not only entailed goods but also information: my aunt would read the letters aloud to everybody present at family gatherings, and then they would discuss the details. My aunt also paid regular visits to the East (mainly one small town in Thuringia) along with other relatives (her siblings, husband, son, and/or me, her niece) in a car packed with coffee and other goods. The days we spent on the other side of the border were filled with visits to different households, with a stream of relatives coming to see us where we were staying. At the time, I felt overwhelmed by all the different people we visited or who came to see us, whom we usually just called aunts or uncles. It felt like being related to almost everyone in the town. We also received presents in return. Distributing and accepting gifts often took place at customary gatherings like birthdays, Easter, or Christmas. Thus, the exchange not only bound kin together across the border but also brought together generations and lateral kin within each country to prepare and distribute gifts and to plan and make visits.

Some of the gifts coming from the East were handmade or were industrial goods that had been improved through handicraft. Despite these efforts, many of the GDR goods were seen as undesirable in the West. Sometimes, an embarrassing negotiation process commenced. For example, we were used to disposable paper tissues, and everybody already had plenty of my great-uncle's wife's crocheted handkerchiefs—the next package of them would always be hard to distribute. My cousin and I, as children, were quite unwilling to wear GDR clothing—presumably of inferior quality and style—at home, let alone in public. While feelings of closeness might have been involved in the older generation's acceptance of the gifts, for us it felt like an embarrassing obligation. Although such gifts were clearly out of fashion, rejecting them and thereby initiating a possible long-term de-kinning was not (yet) instantiated, and GDR products were more or less forced on reluctant recipients.

This inability to adequately reciprocate gifts contributed to the ambivalent quality of gifting among kin. It was clear on both sides that Eastern relatives' efforts were judged differently, even if the parcels they sent in return had embodied great effort in obtaining scarce consumer goods or making gifts by hand. In contrast to the personal effort taken in assembling parcels from the East, the contents of *Westpakete* were mostly standardized, even though they were declared as individual gifts. One document listed the following contents for a typical Christmas parcel in 1962:

> 3 kg Nivea-Creme, 2 pounds Rama [margarine], 2 pounds Biskin [shortening], one bottle of oil in a plastic bottle [*sic*], one package of rice, one package of semolina, one package cocoa, 3 chocolate bars, one small sausage, 2 pounds of coffee, 2 packets of cigarettes, dates, figs, one pound of mandarins, 2 lemons, 2 pounds of apples, one package tea, one package custard powder, one soup, 3 sauces, 2 bouillon cubes, 2 packages of salted pretzels.[17]

Such standardized packages could also be ordered at shops, where the employees would assemble and even mail them.[18] As in the list above, specific brands (like Jacobs Krönung coffee or Kinder chocolate) were expected as symbols of Western capitalism. Despite the cost (which my Western kin often complained about at that time), what was thought to count as luxuries in the GDR (like coffee) had already often become staples in the West.

The Western campaigns described above seem to have been generally quite successful in installing or reinforcing the obligation to care for relatives in the East. One of my West German colleagues once recalled how in his childhood his family was desperately looking for someone to send a parcel to and how they felt guilty about not having anyone. In these cases, there were organizations, especially church-related ones, that helped to mediate or create ties to the degree that sometimes persons in the GDR were quite surprised to receive a parcel from an unknown person or even felt humiliated by the gesture.[19] The conscious production of ties—"unnatural" kinship in this case—was clearly rejected. Perhaps the quality of almsgiving simply became too obvious. Beyond kinship, parcels symbolized unequal political systems. Many people in eastern Germany still remember the smell of the *Westpakete* from their childhood and how it symbolized the world of capitalism.[20] In contrast, the Eastern goods smelled of undesired socialism. This inequality reinforced the charitable character of West-to-East transfer and prepared the ground for later dissolution of extended kinship when the border vanished.[21]

(De-)kinning by Devaluing Care: Moral Othering

Due to the humanitarian tone of the campaigns, it was easy for West Germans to overestimate material need in the GDR. This concerned not only care received from strangers but also the embarrassing experience of Easterners who felt like objects of "improper" care by relatives. One of my interlocutors commented on how a cousin of his wife's sent used clothing as if he had been "in Africa." By othering Africans as supposedly in "real need," he expressed offense at their treatment of him as an aid receiver and implicitly constructed himself as the equal of his affinal relatives. As mentioned at the beginning of the chapter, many of the Eastern German accounts about de-kinning after unification contained similar narratives of having received unwanted and unnecessary goods. In retrospect at least, the received care was devalued and interpreted as signs of Western arrogance.

As a child during a visit, I once wanted to show off to a boy of the same age in the GDR by promising to show him how many sweets I could buy with a single West German mark. Back home in the shop, I realized that it actually was not as many as I had imagined and was tempted to cheat a bit. (I don't remember if I actually did.) In any case, no adult stopped me, either during the conversation or later. Showing off the wealth of capitalism was an integral part of kin care. In response, Easterners complained in the accounts of de-kinning I collected after unification about the low monetary value of the staples received, and compared the quality of more durable goods (such as furniture) unfavorably to GDR products. My Eastern interlocutors also said that they understood this only after unification, when the full range of Western products became readily available. They now suspected that their relatives consciously withheld this information from them earlier.[22] Their accounts were met with considerable indignation by my West German audience, as mentioned in the beginning. Why was this the case?

The moral rhetoric of caring constituted a comparatively simple way for West Germans to "do good." It was gratitude rather than material reciprocity that was expected from the recipients, as we still see in the comments made to me. Gifts thereby reproduced the superior status of the West German giver, a dynamic that was in tension with the normative construction of emotional closeness and horizontal equality, as in the rhetoric of siblingship.[23] The positioning of kin in the West as caring for poor relatives in the East influenced constructions of difference that became increasingly acute after unification, when political and economic circumstances changed dramatically. To return to my own experience of visits in the GDR before 1989, my aunts suspected some relatives of coming to see us at the house of another relative we were staying with "only to receive their pack of coffee." The moral undertone suggesting "purely materialistic" interests received yet another twist after unification, when the once regular visits soon stopped entirely. I myself was twenty-one in 1989, and I have not returned there or seen anybody from this large kinship network ever since. Once, when I questioned my aunt about why she stopped visiting, she commented with indignation that "they even had a better car than I did." Not only was there a sudden separation of "them" from "us," the Easterners—always too materially oriented—were now guilty in her eyes of conspicuous consumption. She seemed to imply that, as the once-poor recipients, the relatives did not really deserve the goods they now could afford. Her comment would clearly have confirmed many of the suspicions about West German relatives that I found during research among my East German interlocutors. In addition, the assessments of materialism (as opposed to emotional closeness) echo the second kind of critique mentioned in the beginning of this chapter, which sees socialist kinship as a strategic response to economic shortages. As this critique is mainly advanced by social scientists, I now turn to how extended German-German kinship was (or, rather, was not) theorized. Extended kinship is seen to exist, if at all, only in the socialist East, where it is backed with the construction of a deficient socialist other.

Family Sociology, the Socialist Other, and the Epistemic Void around German Kinship

This part delves into two distinct bodies of scholarship in order to offer a perspective on why the practices across the German-German border that I have described did not feed into a larger theory of kinship. First, I will turn to German family sociology and then link that to the international literature on socialism. This move allows us to see how ideas about "modernity" created a void and, in combination with an ambivalent othering of socialism, led to the idea that socialist citizens must have been not only different from Westerners but also somehow "deficient."

Let me first stress again that it was not only state actors who either supported or hesitantly acknowledged kinship across the border. Distant relatives on each side of the border also would meet to discuss the news and distribute goods received from the other side. Moreover, sending millions of parcels to kin across the border had an immense economic importance that state policies sponsored or learned to rely on.[24] These practices are completely ignored in citizens' self-images, as they also are in studies of the role of kinship in both states. My West German audiences and the East German interlocutors in my research interpreted positive or negative experiences with kin as stories about individuals, not as expressions of politics or as having political ramifications. As such, the Eastern German devaluation of kinship across the border might be dismissed as anecdotal—something that seemed to have taken place in social theory as well. Here, the topic has not emerged at all.

German-German Kinship and Social Scientific Theory

Following the well-known modernization paradigm, the conjugal family was stressed within each of the two states as the only meaningful kinship unit by citizens and scholars alike. Cross-border kin relations and the manifold activities each side engaged in to buy or manufacture, pack, and distribute the things and information given and received have never made it into social scientific analysis. In the case of the socialist GDR, this void might be explained by the weak position of the social sciences: no representative studies of family lives exist that follow comparable standards to those in the West.[25] The only extended study on the everyday life of families in the GDR still paid tribute to Engels's evolutionary model before presenting its own results on what it called "complete" families (that is, the heterosexual conjugal family based on emotional closeness). Its authors even felt the need to "defend" three-generation households at length. The politically sensitive topic of kin relations to West Germany was not mentioned at all.[26] But how, then, was the topic dealt with in Western social sciences with its supposedly greater freedom and importance? As it turns out: not very differently.

An extensive overview of various strands of West German family sociology would be outside the scope of this chapter. Instead, I offer an overview of how the topic is dealt with in several well-known introductory texts, in which I have not found a single mention of extended kinship across the former border. In general, family sociologists have long been preoccupied with an alleged reduced size of and shift to conjugal families due to modernization, which Durkheim called the "law of contraction."[27] These texts usually describe the "modern family" as characterized by individual choice of marriage partners, a loss of economic functions, and a simultaneous increase in the importance of emotional ties.[28] The few specific treatments of either "kinship" or "extended family" in textbooks tend to be brief summaries of mostly outdated anthropological kinship theories and terminologies. The more or less explicit evolutionary and/or cultural-ecological undertone is not that different from that of socialist sociology.[29] Even an author like Franz-Xaver Kaufmann, who mourns the "kinship blindness" of sociology, does not mention the relations across the former border.[30]

In anthropological literature, with its usually greater awareness of kinship, the situation looks surprisingly similar. The only explicit study of letters sent across the border frames them in terms of forming "exchange communities" and not in terms of kinship.[31] Even the most comprehensive ethnographic account of kinship in the two Germanys, by Borneman, emphasizes diverse normative and legal differences between the two countries, but the actual cross-border exchange relations remain almost unnoticed or at least not theoretically central.[32] A few postunification collections give rather anecdotal accounts of the experience of Eastern receivers of the so-called *Westpakete*. I have not yet come across any scientific depictions of the experiences of the West German side, which seems to be unimportant to scholars and for theory.

Comparative quantitative scholarship has analyzed different patterns of birth and marriage rates, as well as the so-called pluralization of family forms in both states, asking the leading question of which pattern points to more or less (achieved) modernization. Thus, authors discuss whether the comparatively young ages of first marriages and births of first child in the GDR indicate a delay in modernization or if, on the contrary, the higher number of births outside wedlock and higher rate of female labor market participation should be seen as an advance. Even if sociological textbooks refer briefly to historical critiques of the idea of the core family as a "modern phenomenon," practices across the former German-German border are not considered.³³

In sum, none of these different approaches mentions, let alone theorizes, the practices of extended kinship within each German state and across the border. The temporal narrative of kinship decline and self-descriptions of modern society as consisting of small, apolitical family units find their "other" in those who supposedly have "not yet" reached modernity and "still" place high importance on kinship.³⁴ Even those anthropologists and sociologists who criticize the narrative as too simplistic and acknowledge the coexistence of several family types in modern societies have either migrant or minority groups in mind.³⁵ Likewise, the extensive literature on transnational kinship networks of migrants from the Global South to the richer countries in the Global North often portrays remittances and other exchanges as an expression of preexisting "traditional" families.³⁶ Being born in a "non-Western" country seems to translate into "having" kinship and following norms of support even after international migration. In the case of the extended German kinship described here, there are no recognized differences in status or ethnic groups involved. Rather than representing mobile "traditional" obligation as in the transnational context, kinship here seems to transcend the border and attest to the indivisibility of the political unit. Being bound to the modernization narrative, the normative sameness and equality of this account does not seem to have lent itself to analysis of the kinship practices across the border. Instead, difference is found in the simultaneous ambivalent construction of the socialist "other." Like kinship support in transnational or minority communities, socialist kin relationships are often understood as functional and oriented toward fulfilling deficiencies in access to goods and services.

Kinship and the Socialist Other

The social scientific interpretation of (post)socialist relationships is not so far from the West German moral evaluations of their relatives' "materialistic attitude" toward kin. In anthropology, the interpretation of difference as based in economy rather than culture has much to do with an atypical hegemony of economic theory in the study of (post)socialist countries. Since Katherine Verdery introduced the writings of Hungarian born economist János Kornai to an anthropological audience as emic knowledge, later ethnographies have taken his analysis of the socialist "economy of shortage" for granted as a "given" context. In Kornai's view, shortages resulted from "improper" property relations and allocations of resources. Despite its assumptions of rational decision-making and of a general scarcity of resources—both of which are otherwise contested in anthropology—this economic analysis has had an enormous impact on anthropological thinking about (post)socialism.

As I described elsewhere, this atypical reliance on economic theory was fostered by an ambivalent othering that shaped the Western view of (European) socialist societies.[37] On the one hand, the socialist state and its institutions were seen through the contrastive lens of difference, while its citizens were deemed to be "the same." The underlying assumption was that because socialist citizens were essentially similar Europeans they acted with the same (rational) motives and attitudes, despite being condemned to live in an inefficient (and irrational) socialist institutional framework. When the outcome of the political and economic reforms after the demise of socialism dashed many hopes of replicating Western European capitalist states, this undermined the conviction of essential sameness, and a new phase of othering began. Now that the institutions were apparently the "same," the people suddenly became different, holding cultural ideas—sometimes even collective socialist ones—that hindered a "normal" economic development.[38]

One remnant of this perspective is a preoccupation with the character of personal relations, which are seen as having developed during socialism in response to its endemic shortages and thus as oriented toward access to resources. This element of functionalist interpretation has remained dominant in many postsocialist ethnographies as the discussions cited in the beginning of this chapter mirror. Most often, however, the formerly socialist part of the now-unified Germany is seen as "too similar" and has vanished almost totally from theoretical interest.[39] If the existence of extended kin is noted at all, it can be interpreted as a kind of leftover socialist "abnormality": with unification, East Germany is seen as having "returned" to modern normality.

Conclusion

This chapter started with two typical types of reaction to my analysis of eastern German accounts of de-kinning across the former border as symptoms of the centrality of certain interpretations of kinship. Although the accounts of kinship and critical reactions were obviously highly politicized, the politics of making kinship vanished behind personalized interpretations. In order to explore the implicit ideas behind the critical appraisal of my interpretations, I first outlined the contrasting politics of making kinship as expressions of the respective political visions in both German states and as part of the making of politics across the border, which both had repercussions on vernacular as well as on scientific perspectives.

One type of critique is found in the personal accounts of well-educated West Germans who react against Eastern stories about paternalism and conflict, recounting close emotional relations with Eastern kin and their "appropriate" levels of gratitude for the care they received. The stress on emotional quality causes the politics implicit in the making of ties to fade out of sight. Although aimed at contesting my interpretation, these reactions in effect support it—or rather support the narratives of my eastern German interlocutors of Western paternalism. Actual experiences of kin relations surely varied, but the Western voice has become authoritative in defining the nature of German-German kinship. Such interpretations play an important part in political self-understanding, not only in the construction of Germany as a political unit but also in that of West Germany as its better part both in the past and in the unified present. Some of these elements also show up outside vernacular discourse in the social scientific type of critique that places West Germany as the more "modern" element of the Cold War binary. This second type of critique starts not with equality and mutuality in emotional closeness but with difference and materialist functionality. Economic deficiencies of the socialist state are stressed and are interpreted as having led to an essentially different form of kinship in the East. This argument maps the political binary onto kinship with the socialist form based less on emotions and more on materialistic interest.

Both variants can be linked to ideas about modernization, though in different ways. These elements of interpretation have reached a state of "naturalness" and dominance that goes unquestioned and has therefore left these kinship relations in an epistemic void. As argued in the introduction to this book, classical twentieth-century modernization theories, broadly speaking, posit a separation of politics and kinship. Parallel to this separation they attest to a decreasing importance of extended kin and a simultaneous emotionalization of close relations. Both elements are essential to understanding the politics of making kinship across the former German-German border, as well as that topic's neglect in social theory. At the same time, both assumptions are also challenged by kinship practices in the two German states and later in the unified Germany. The development of extended kinship ties across the German-German border, as well as within each country, defies ideas about the decreased role of kinship in modern societies. Similarly, the importance of kinship for the formation of states questions its apolitical nature.

Besides representing affection between relatives, kinship across the border was important for naturalizing the construction of the German nation as a political unit. The siblingship metaphor of poor brothers and sisters in the East expressed the tension present in normatively equal relations early on. Unity ideally was expressed in practices of kin care across the German-German border. When this support did not evolve "naturally," repeated state campaigns highlighted the need and longing for support of East Germans. Moral emphasis on suffering Easterners also allowed Westerners to position themselves on the "right" side in international politics and reified Western supremacy. This humanitarian framing was not welcome on the other side, although its restrictive policies nevertheless contributed to the importance of kinship. The politics of making kinship entailed the making of politics through kinship.

These political representations had ambivalent repercussions in daily practice. Sending and receiving letters, parcels, and visitors involved extended kin on both sides of the border. Not only would one receive goods from a distant relative but distribution also took place among kin gatherings where letters were read aloud. Political pressure and economic hierarchies supported these investments in extended kinship and simultaneously heightened its emotional ambivalence. Parceling up mundane, quotidian goods and everyday staples in the West to be sent to relatives reinforced the idea of Eastern families who were seen as in need and, if not actually suffering, at least deprived. On the other side this construction of kin care induced feelings of humiliation. On both sides, exchange involved embarrassment, and when the Wall came down many relatives broke off ties across the former border.

Although politically advocated, economically important, and emotionally significant, extended kinship, as well as the mutual constituency of state/s and kinship before and after unification, are largely ignored by the social sciences. The question arises as to why. The reason for this analytical blindness, I argue, lies in each country's respective self-understanding as "modern" so that kinship ties beyond the conjugal family cannot even be seen by scientists. Its neglect testifies to the epistemological void created by the focus on the "nuclear family"—an epistemic consequence of the idea that kinship is not something that exists for individuals in "modern" states. This void is not merely a negligible if deplorable omission. It has serious consequences not only for our understanding of contemporary societies but also for the policies devised to encourage or restrict one or the other form of kinship. Paying attention to the practices of extended German-German kinship does not just provide an interesting exception to classical ideas of modernization. Instead of relegating it to a distant nebulous past or reducing it to a functional response to economic conditions, moving it to the center of attention can offer general insights into the phenomenon of political and everyday production of kinship within so-called modern societies.

From the example of German kinship ties, we can see how much they are entangled in state and even international politics. The politics of making kinship reflects back on state ideas of belonging and ideas of otherness. As such, they are crucial elements and product of all so-called modern societies.

Tatjana Thelen is a professor at the Department for Social and Cultural Anthropology, University of Vienna, Austria. Her research interests include kinship, state, care, and property. Recently, she has been a fellow at the Institute for Advanced Study in Paris and in 2023 will hold the Austrian Chair at Stanford University. She coedited *Reconnecting State and Kinship* (2018), *Measuring Kinship* (2021), and *Politics and Kinship: A Reader* (2022). She codirected the interdisciplinary research group on kinship and politics at the Center for Interdisciplinary Research in Bielefeld.

Notes

I would like to thank my coeditors for their comments of an earlier version as well as Jeannette Edwards and Christof Lammer for extremely helpful suggestions on how to develop the argument further.

1. Tatjana Thelen, "Partition and Partings: The Paradox of German Kinship Ties," in *The Partition Motif in Contemporary Conflicts*, ed. Smita Tewari Jassal and Eyal Ben-Ari (Thousand Oaks, CA: Sage, 2007); Tatjana Thelen, *Care/Sorge: Konstruktion, Reproduktion und Auflösung bedeutsamer Bindungen* (Bielefeld: transcript, 2014); Tatjana Thelen, "Wege einer relationalen Anthropologie: Ethnographische Einblicke in Verwandtschaft und Staat," *Vienna Working Papers in Ethnography*, no. 4 (2015). Retrieved 8 July 2022 from https://ksa.univie.ac.at/en/research/publications/vienna-working-papers-in-ethnography/details/#c245589.
2. Didier Fassin, "The Endurance of Critique," *Anthropological Theory* 17, no. 1 (2017).
3. There is a great deal of historical work on the ethnic understanding of the German nation rooted in ideas of common descent, language, and cultural heritage. Some authors see the sources of this development within fragmented small states and the comparatively late first creation of a unified nation-state in 1871; others point to little influence from colonization, which would have made an integration of persons with a background in other regions of the world necessary. See Rogers Brubaker, *Citizenship and Nationhood in France and Germany* (Cambridge, MA: Harvard University Press, 1992); Marc Alan Howard, "Die Ostdeutschen als ethnische Gruppe? Zum Verständnis der neuen Teilung des geeinten Deutschlands," *Berliner Debatte Initial*, no. 4 (1995): 123; Andreas Staab, *National Identity in Eastern Germany: Inner Unificiation or Continued Separation?* (Westport, CT: Praeger, 1998), 127–28.
4. On different ways to establish siblingship, see Tatjana Thelen, Cati Coe, and Erdmute Alber, "The Anthropology of Sibling Relations: Explorations in Shared Parentage, Experience, and Exchange," in *The Anthropology of Sibling Relations: Shared Parentage,*

Experience, and Exchange, ed. Erdmute Alber, Cati Coe, and Tatjana Thelen (New York: Palgrave Macmillan, 2013).
5. Neither exchanging letters nor sending parcels was necessarily a new or singular innovation. The parcel campaigns built upon the example of earlier American "CARE Packages," while various initiatives to instigate letter exchanges were used more widely as means of establishing new peaceful cross-border relations after the war. See Eckart Klaus Roloff, "'Lasst sie nicht allein!' Paketkampagnen zwischen menschlicher Hilfe und politischen Zielen," *DAS ARCHIV*, no. 3 (2009).
6. Kabus, Petra. "Liebesgaben für die Zone: Paketkampagnen und Kalter Krieg." In *Das Westpaket: Geschenksendung, keine Handelsware*, edited by Christian Härtel and Petra Kabus, 121–39. Berlin: Links, 2000, 129–30. More also in Roloff, "'Lasst sie nicht allein!'"; Volker Ilgen, *CARE-Paket & Co. Von der Liebesgabe zum Westpaket* (Darmstadt: Primus, 2008).
7. With the advent of the politics of detente (*Entspannungspolitik*), these campaigns no longer seemed politically appropriate. In addition, citizens of the FRG slowly began to define themselves more in terms of economic success or pride in their constitution (see Staab, *National Identity*, 15–16). Border crossings decreased in the 1970s and 1980s.
8. Petra Kabus, "Liebesgaben für die Zone: Paketkampagnen und Kalter Krieg," in *Das Westpaket: Geschenksendung, keine Handelsware*, ed. Christian *Härtel and* Petra Kabus (Berlin: Links, 2000), 126–28. The term *Zone* derives from the occupational zones after the war but was still used in West Germany as an indicator for the GDR long after the latter had declared itself an independent state.
9. Cited in Kabus "Liebesgaben für die Zone," 127 (my translation).
10. Kabus, "Liebesgaben für die Zone," 129.
11. The terms *kinship* (*Verwandtschaft*) and *kin* (*Verwandte*) are more commonly used in everyday speech in German than in most contemporary variants of English. However, no parallel term to *Westverwandtschaft* was used to denote kin in the East, hinting at its even more politicized role in the everyday life of the GDR.
12. In 1967, compulsory currency exchange policies forced travelers to the GDR to purchase a certain amount of East German marks (and spend them while there). West German parcels sent to citizens of the GDR were relied on to make up for certain shortages. See Bernd Lindner, "'Dein Päckchen nach drüben': Der deutsch-deutsche Paketversand und seine Rahmenbedingungen," in *Das Westpaket: Geschenksendung, keine Handelsware*, ed. Christian Härtel and Petra Kabus (Berlin: Links, 2000), 36–37.
13. Landesarchiv Magdeburg –LHA–, Rep. M24, BDVP Magdeburg 1975–1990, Abteilung PM, Nr. 17105; printed in Jutta Gladen, *"Man lebt sich auseinander": Von der Schwierigkeit, Verwandte drüben zu besuchen*, Sachbeiträge, no. 19 (Magdeburg: Die Landesbeauftragte für die Unterlagen des Staatssicherheitsdienstes der ehemaligen DDR in Sachsen-Anhalt, 2001), 23.
14. As Staab phrases it, "East Germans soon began to establish their own excluding boundaries which marked their identities off from that of Western Germany." See Staab, *National Identity*, 159.
15. One example of this view is provided by Edda Ahrberg, the Commissioner for Former Secret Service Documents in Saxony-Anhalt (*Landesbeauftragte für die Unterlagen der Staatssicherheit der ehemaligen DDR*), who states that employees in state agencies processing travel applications were responsible for families slowly drifting apart: in Gladen, "Man lebt sich auseinander," 2.
16. Ina Dietzsch, "Geschenkpakete—ein fundamentales Missverständnis: Zur Bedeutung des Paketaustausches in persönlichen Briefwechseln," in *Das Westpaket: Geschenksendung, keine Handelsware*, ed. Christian Härtel and Petra Kabus (Berlin: Links, 2000); Ina Dietzsch, *Grenzen überschreiben? Deutsch-deutsche Briefwechsel 1948–1989* (Köln: Böhlau, 2004).

17. Astrid Segert and Irene Zierke, "Gesellschaft der DDR: Klassen—Schichten—Kollektive, G23," in *DDR-Geschichte in Dokumenten*, ed. Matthias Judt (Bonn: Bundeszentrale für politische Bildung, 1998), 194–95 (my translation).
18. Larger gifts (like cars and houses) could be made through the special gift transfer service Genex, see Franka Schneider, "Ein Loch im Zaun: Schenken über die Genex Geschenkdienst GmbH," in *Das Westpaket: Geschenksendung, keine Handelsware*, ed. Christian Härtel and Petra Kabus (Berlin: Links, 2000).
19. Kabus, "Liebesgaben für die Zone," 121.
20. See various descriptions in Härtel and Kabus, *Das Westpaket*.
21. Thelen, *Care/Sorge*; Thelen, "Partition and Partings." In one of my research projects, I explicitly asked a random sample of twenty-four informants in a large formerly socialist enterprise whether they had relatives in the West and what had happened to these relations in recent times. Sixteen had relatives in the West; in one case there was no contact during partition. In another three cases, the relation had ended due to death or divorce before unification. I never came across a case in which the relationship had become more intense. Instead, most individual stories were about decline. In a few cases, people stated that the relationship had remained more or less the same. In general, they gave three main categories of conflict between relatives after unification: inheritance, reinterpretation of help formerly received, and political disagreements.
22. Thelen, "Partition and Partings," 233–34.
23. On the expectations of gratitude and hierarchy embedded in East and West German relations, see John Borneman, *Belonging in the Two Berlins: Kin, State, Nation* (Cambridge: Cambridge University Press, 2000), 145; Dietzsch, *Grenzen überschreiben?* 204–13; Ina Merkel, *Utopie und Bedürfnis: Die Geschichte der Konsumkultur in der DDR* (Köln: Böhlau, 1999), 289.
24. No exact statistics exist, but it is estimated that the annual number of parcels sent from West to East was around forty-five million in 1960 and declined to about twenty-five million in the 1980s (Andre and Nagengast cited in Roloff, "'Lasst sie nicht allein!'"; see also Härtel and Kabus, *Das Westpaket*.
25. Norbert F. Schneider, "Familienforschung in der ehemaligen DDR," in *Familie: Soziologie familialer Lebenswelten*, ed. Laszlo A. Vaskovics (München: Oldenbourg, 1994).
26. Jutta Gysi, ed., *Familienleben in der DDR: Zum Alltag von Familien mit Kindern* (Berlin: Akademie-Verlag, 1989).
27. Michael Mitterauer, *Familie und Arbeitsteilung: historischvergleichende Studien* (Köln: Böhlau, 1992), 149–50.
28. Johannes Huinink and Dirk Konietzka, *Familiensoziologie: Eine Einführung* (Frankfurt: Campus, 2007), 67–71.
29. Huinink and Konietzka, *Familiensoziologie*, 27–29, 56–72; Paul B. Hill and Johannes Kopp, *Familiensoziologie: Grundlagen und theoretische Perspektiven* (Stuttgart: B. G. Teubner, 1995), 12–13, 15–21, 26–33. Among the most often cited anthropological authors are the cultural-materialist Marvin Harris (see for example Rüdiger Peuckert, *Familienformen im sozialen Wandel* [Wiesbaden: VS, 2008]; Hill and Kopp, *Familiensoziologie*) and the conservative cultural ecologist Thomas Bargatzky (for example in Hill und Kopp, *Familiensoziologie*).
30. Franz-Xaver Kaufmann, *Zukunft der Familie im vereinten Deutschland: Gesellschaftliche und politische Bedingungen* (München: C. H. Beck, 1995), 154.
31. Dietzsch, "Geschenkpakete—ein fundamentales Missverständnis."
32. Borneman, *Belonging in the Two Berlins*.
33. For example, Dorett Funcke and Bruno Hildebrand, *Ursprünge und Kontinuität der Kernfamilie: Einführung in die Familiensoziologie* (Wiesbaden: Springer VS Verlag, 2018).

34. Tatjana Thelen and Erdmute Alber, "Reconnecting State and Kinship: Temporalities, Scales, Classifications," in *Reconnecting State and Kinship*, ed. Tatjana Thelen and Erdmute Alber (Philadelphia: University of Pennsylvania Press, 2018).
35. See for example: René König, "Old Problems and New Queries in Family Sociology," in *Families in East and West: Socialization Process and Kinship Ties*, ed. Reuben Hill and René König (Paris: Mouton, 1970); René König, ed., *Familie, Alter: Handbuch zur empirischen Sozialforschung*, vol. 7 (Stuttgart: dtv, 1976).
36. See for example: Deborah Bryceson and Ulla Vuorela, *The Transnational Family: New European Frontiers and Global Networks* (London: Routledge, 2002); Cati Coe, "What Is Love? The Materiality of Care in Ghanaian Transnational Families," *International Migration* 49, no. 6 (2011); Jeffrey H. Cohen, "Migration, Remittances, and Household Strategies," *Annual Review of Anthropology* 40, no. 1 (2011).
37. Tatjana Thelen, "Shortage, Fuzzy Property and Other Dead Ends in Anthropological Analysis of (Post) Socialism," *Critique of Anthropology* 31, no. 1 (2011).
38. Thelen, "Shortage."
39. Thelen, "Shortage."

Bibliography

Borneman, John. *Belonging in the Two Berlins: Kin, State, Nation*. Cambridge: Cambridge University Press, 2000.

Brubaker, Rogers. *Citizenship and Nationhood in France and Germany*. Cambridge, MA: Harvard University Press, 1992.

Bryceson, Deborah, and Ulla Vuorela. *The Transnational Family: New European Frontiers and Global Networks*. London: Routledge, 2002.

Coe, Cati. "What Is Love? The Materiality of Care in Ghanaian Transnational Families." *International Migration* 49, no. 6 (2011): 7–24.

Cohen, Jeffrey H. "Migration, Remittances, and Household Strategies." *Annual Review of Anthropology* 40, no. 1 (2011): 103–14.

Dietzsch, Ina. "Geschenkpakete—ein fundamentales Missverständnis: Zur Bedeutung des Paketaustausches in persönlichen Briefwechseln." In *Das Westpaket: Geschenksendung, keine Handelsware*, edited by Christian Härtel and Petra Kabus, 105–20. Berlin: Links, 2000.

Dietzsch, Ina. *Grenzen überschreiben? Deutsch-deutsche Briefwechsel 1948–1989*. Köln: Böhlau, 2004.

Fassin, Didier. "The Endurance of Critique." *Anthropological Theory* 17, no. 1 (2017): 4–29.

Funcke, Dorett, and Bruno Hildebrand. *Ursprünge und Kontinuität der Kernfamilie: Einführung in die Familiensoziologie*. Wiesbaden: Springer VS Verlag, 2018.

Gladen, Jutta. *"Man lebt sich auseinander": Von der Schwierigkeit, Verwandte drüben zu besuchen*. Sachbeiträge, no. 19. Magdeburg: Die Landesbeauftragte für die Unterlagen des Staatssicherheitsdienstes der ehemaligen DDR in Sachsen-Anhalt, 2001.

Gysi, Jutta, ed. *Familienleben in der DDR: Zum Alltag von Familien mit Kindern*. Berlin: Akademie-Verlag, 1989.

Härtel, Christian, and Petra Kabus, ed. *Das Westpaket: Geschenksendung, keine Handelsware*. Berlin: Links, 2000.

Hill, Paul B., and Johannes Kopp. *Familiensoziologie: Grundlagen und theoretische Perspektiven*. Stuttgart: B. G. Teubner, 1995.
Howard, Marc Alan. "Die Ostdeutschen als ethnische Gruppe? Zum Verständnis der neuen Teilung des geeinten Deutschlands." *Berliner Debatte Initial*, no. 4 (1995): 119–31.
Huinink, Johannes, and Dirk Konietzka. *Familiensoziologie: Eine Einführung*. Frankfurt: Campus, 2007.
Ilgen, Volker. *CARE-Paket & Co. Von der Liebesgabe zum Westpaket*. Darmstadt: Primus, 2008.
Kabus, Petra. "Liebesgaben für die Zone: Paketkampagnen und Kalter Krieg." In *Das Westpaket: Geschenksendung, keine Handelsware*, edited by Christian Härtel and Petra Kabus, 121–39. Berlin: Links, 2000.
Kaufmann, Franz-Xaver. *Zukunft der Familie im vereinten Deutschland: Gesellschaftliche und politische Bedingungen*. München: C. H. Beck, 1995.
König, René. "Old Problems and New Queries in Family Sociology." In *Families in East and West: Socialization Process and Kinship Ties*, edited by Reuben Hill and René König, 504–23. Paris: Mouton, 1970.
⸻, ed. *Familie, Alter: Handbuch zur empirischen Sozialforschung*, vol. 7. Stuttgart: dtv, 1976.
Lindner, Bernd. "'Dein Päckchen nach drüben': Der deutsch-deutsche Paketversand und seine Rahmenbedingungen." In *Das Westpaket: Geschenksendung, keine Handelsware*, edited by Christian Härtel and Petra Kabus, 25–44. Berlin: Links, 2000.
Merkel, Ina. *Utopie und Bedürfnis: Die Geschichte der Konsumkultur in der DDR*. Köln: Böhlau, 1999.
Mitterauer, Michael. *Familie und Arbeitsteilung: Historischvergleichende Studien*. Köln: Böhlau, 1992.
Peuckert, Rüdiger. *Familienformen im sozialen Wandel*. Wiesbaden: VS, 2008.
Roloff, Eckart Klaus. "'Lasst sie nicht allein!' Paketkampagnen zwischen menschlicher Hilfe und politischen Zielen." *DAS ARCHIV*, no. 3 (2009): 6–13.
Schneider, Franka. "Ein Loch im Zaun: Schenken über die Genex Geschenkdienst GmbH." In *Das Westpaket: Geschenksendung, keine Handelsware*, edited by Christian Härtel and Petra Kabus, 193–212. Berlin: Links, 2000.
Schneider, Norbert F. "Familienforschung in der ehemaligen DDR." In *Familie: Soziologie familialer Lebenswelten*, Soziologische Revue, Sonderheft 3, edited by Laszlo A. Vaskovics, 319–25. München: Oldenbourg, 1994.
Segert, Astrid, and Irene Zierke. "Gesellschaft der DDR. Klassen—Schichten—Kollektive, G23." In *DDR-Geschichte in Dokumenten*, edited by Matthias Judt, 165–224. Bonn: Bundeszentrale für politische Bildung, 1998.
Staab, Andreas. *National Identity in Eastern Germany: Inner Unification or Continued Separation?* Westport, CT: Praeger, 1998.
Thelen, Tatjana. "Wege einer relationalen Anthropologie: Ethnographische Einblicke in Verwandtschaft und Staat." *Vienna Working Papers in Ethnography*, no. 4 (2015). Retrieved 8 July 2022 from https://ksa.univie.ac.at/en/research/publications/vienna-working-papers-in-ethnography/details/#c245589.
Thelen, Tatjana. *Care/Sorge: Konstruktion, Reproduktion und Auflösung bedeutsamer Bindungen*. Bielefeld: transcript, 2014.

Thelen, Tatjana. "Shortage, Fuzzy Property and Other Dead Ends in Anthropological Analysis of (Post) Socialism." Critique of Anthropology 31, no. 1 (2011): 43–61.

Thelen, Tatjana. "Partition and Partings: The Paradox of German Kinship Ties." In The Partition Motif in Contemporary Conflicts, edited by Smita Tewari Jassal and Eyal Ben-Ari, 221–42. Thousand Oaks, CA: Sage, 2007.

Thelen, Tatjana, and Erdmute Alber. "Reconnecting State and Kinship: Temporalities, Scales, Classifications." In Reconnecting State and Kinship, edited by Tatjana Thelen and Erdmute Alber, 1–35. Philadelphia: University of Pennsylvania Press, 2018.

Thelen, Tatjana, Cati Coe, and Erdmute Alber. "The Anthropology of Sibling Relations: Explorations in Shared Parentage, Experience, and Exchange." In The Anthropology of Sibling Relations: Shared Parentage, Experience, and Exchange, edited by Erdmute Alber, Cati Coe, and Tatjana Thelen, 1–28. New York: Palgrave Macmillan, 2012.

Part II

Projects

Neoliberal economists during the 1970s and 1980s had a great deal to say about the nature of the private family, and over the following decades they exerted considerable influence on public policies designed to buttress the family as an institution of noncontractual obligation offering free services; these, in turn, were supposed to enable the free-market economy. Melinda Cooper has chronicled the politics of legislation and administrative intervention around issues of welfare reform, fiscal and monetary policy, social spending, healthcare, and education in the United States from the Reagan presidency onward. All of these not only had a profound influence on family relations but also were specifically designed to shape familial life according to what many political actors thought of as traditional but endangered models. Cooper shows, for example, how long-term policies to ensure low interest rates were linked to keeping wages low, encouraging an economy of widespread indebtedness and shifting consumer interest to asset accumulation (for the broad middle classes mostly in homeownership and investments in retirement pensions).[1] A startling example of state planning was to shift the costs of higher education from public expenditure to private "investment," linking generations together in significant long-term indebtedness based on cheap credit. Public policy over five decades was, of course, complex, but it can be summarized around three areas traditionally central to kinship studies: inheritance/property/descent, marriage/alliance/obligation, and childhood/rights/identity. Kinship is still with us in contemporary America, and even neoliberalism, the ideology of the unfettered, free individual, rationally negotiating in the marketplace, was happy to align with the new conservatism in imagining the "primary function of the state as that of sustaining the family, the foundation of all social order."[2]

The chapters in this section deal with projects and models of social and political orders, with ways idioms of families, households, and kinship structures have offered possibilities to think about the state, social hierarchies, and rights and obligations. They move between stereotypes and practices; prescriptions and descriptions. Such idioms were constantly reworked in order to allow for alternative perspectives or contrasting political positions or to imagine new political orders. It made all the difference in the world whether the family was thought of hierarchically, with issues of power, paternal responsibility, and filial obedience at the center, or whether it was thought of as an institution of equality, an alliance of husband and wife and a realm of free consent. In one way or another, the projects and models these chapters consider were concerned with how the family has been understood to generate social and political relations. They circle around issues of filiation and nurture; inheritance, property, and succession; equality and hierarchy; kinship, state, and civil society; patriarchy and spousal alliance. They consider what political theorists, philosophers, journalists, pundits, and critics think the family is supposed to be and how it ought to articulate functionally with law, the political order, and regimes of property, sexual codes, and childhood.

David Sabean argues that political theorists and social scientists developed schemas of modern and traditional familial and kinship forms that were quite different from the social practices within the societies they purported to represent. Indeed, their observations were more likely to be prescriptive than descriptive. Sabean centers his analysis on the German philosopher G. W. F. Hegel, who was instrumental in defining the modern, Western notion of the family as cut off from any encompassing kinship relations. Hegel thought that older notions of descent and forms of property devolution were inimical to familial independence and shifted the analysis of family away from issues of power and hierarchical ordering under a *Hausvater* (paterfamilias, *chef de famille*) to the psychological dimensions of inner-familial relationships and the tie between husband and wife. Anything smacking of descent rules, lineage property holding, or relationships constituted through blood were founded in the unfreedom of nature. The family should be constituted in freedom and consent, not as an alliance between families but as the voluntary engagement of a man and woman liberated from all kinship constraints. For this reason, any form of marriage closely tied to a particular milieu or between cousins or other close relatives violated what he called an "ethical" marriage. Hegel had a particular understanding of state, civil society, and independent bureaucracy in mind when he worked out his theory of the family. Sabean notes that nineteenth-century Germany (and Europe) was, contrary to Hegel's propositions, characterized by forms of social and kin endogamy integral to the production of class relations and the support of political cultures. He looks at Hegel's contemporary, the civil servant and diplomat Basilius von Ramdohr, to work out an empirical description of social and familial relations. He then examines the theory of the "nuclear family" developed by the American sociologist Talcott Parsons to draw parallels with Hegel's notion of the autonomous family cut off from kinship relations and differentiated from traditional and non-Western forms of kinship. Sabean notes the same problem with Parsons as he found with Hegel, namely that social practices among American populations involved kinship relations he failed to recognize.

Julia Heinemann examines political debates about the nature of the monarchy, institutions, and sources of law in sixteenth-century France. At the center of her consideration are the political theories of two important writers: Jean Bodin and François Hotman, both of whom relied on kinship relations to frame political concepts of the monarchy. She demonstrates how specific conceptualizations of kinship and politics were produced and intertwined in the context of the French wars of religion. For Bodin, kinship relations were both a threat and the most important medium to describe the political order. Hotman thought of kinship relations in a less schematic manner than Bodin did and took into consideration a variety of legal customs and social practices. The two theorists worked out their contrasting understandings of power, hierarchies, the nature of law, and the political order through quite contrasting understandings of family and kinship. The nature of kinship had implications for representations of sovereignty, rulership, and resistance as well as for social and gender hierarchies and power relationship between generations and within domestic life. For example, while Bodin referred to Roman and natural law to build a universal family model and argue for natural patrilineality, Hotman relied on customary law to argue for flexible and changeable kinship relations. However, he too arrived at a justification of patrilineal succession, now as a practical and useful solution to property rights. As a tool for thinking about the political order, kinship for these two theorists derived from quite different legal traditions, the one with universalizing tendencies to be found in the natural law tradition and the other with particularizing arguments derived from scholarship on provincial and national customary and statute law.

Susan McKinnon's chapter revolves around issues of egalitarianism. She deals with a series of political representations across the divide of the American Revolution and points out the way analogies were drawn between familial and state forms and relationships. She finds the same organizational ideas in the "big and little commonwealths," the state as a large family and the family as a little polity. Around these forms, political writers worked out issues of hierarchy and equality, nature and choice, kinship and friendship, heredity, and alliance. But it was not just a matter of one institution modeled in terms of the other: the state was very much invested in the constitution of families. As political argument developed in the course of the nineteenth century, three central conflicts arose around issues of marriage and family life: cousin marriage, slavery, and polygamy. In this chapter, McKinnon centers her consideration on political theory and legislation critical of polygamy, which was understood in terms of notions of the family rejected by the Revolution and early Republic. Polygamy was understood to violate ideals of equality, voluntaristic marital union, friendship, and republican liberties. In the eyes of its critics, it restored hierarchical ordering and theocratic despotism. From the late eighteenth century to well after the Civil War, ideas about family, marriage, descent, rank, patriarchy, and reciprocity were integral to notions of the nature and ordering of commonwealths.

Caroline Arni deals with a number of proletarian women writers during the 1830s, together with later feminists who were influenced by their critiques of familial relations. Proceeding from a close reading of texts, Arni pieces together what she designates as a "political economy of the maternal body." Working within a network of Saint-Simonian social theorists, these proletarian writers developed a claim for women's emancipation and political rights on the basis of kinship relationships, challenging nineteenth-century presumptions of right-bearing individuals as devoid of relationships. Their arguments circled around the meaning of filiation, not as a matter of nature but as maternal choice and as a matter of generating social and political relations. They reimagined motherhood as productive work, their labor expropriated by men through a number of mechanisms: property, patronyms, inheritance forms, and genealogical reckoning. They captured their project in the assertion that children should carry the matronymic, which unlike the patronymic did not make claims to either family or offspring as property. Instead, it was embedded in claims to equality. The discourse about motherhood as work opens up different questions about care work, family, and gender from competing conceptions of motherhood as reproduction. Arni draws the conclusion that this discourse about motherhood has informed and can inform anthropologists to put "modern" and "nonmodern" societies on an equal footing around the primacy of matri-centered kinship.

Note

1. Melinda Cooper, *Family Values: Between Neoliberalism and the New Social Conservatism* (Brooklyn, NY, 2019), 22. "Policies to democratize credit markets and inflate asset values sought to revive the tradition of private family responsibility in the idiom of household debt."

Bibliography

Cooper, Melinda. *Family Values: Between Neoliberalism and the New Social Conservatism*. Brooklyn, NY: Zone Books, 2019.

Chapter 6

Making Family and Kinship
Reflections on Hegel and Parsons

David Warren Sabean

While the use of the word "family" to represent domestic relations can be found throughout Western cultures during the several centuries from the Renaissance onward, it took on new meanings toward the end of the eighteenth century and beginning of the nineteenth. Eventually, the term was used by Western social and political observers to rank themselves and others on a scale of "modernity" and thereby enforce assumptions of "fitness" for "modern" life. For many social, political, and cultural scientists in the West, the modern essentially begins in the early nineteenth century (before that, there was "early modern," "premodern," "frühe Moderne," "frühe Neuzeit," "debut de l'ère moderne"). The widespread adoption of "family" and its reconfiguration around that time had something to do with new forms of self-understanding—once conceptualized, the term could become a tool for differentiating contemporary Western society from what once was and from those who lived out their "traditional" or "primitive" lives in other kinds of kinship constellations. It was not until the late nineteenth century that the "modern" term *kinship* was invented to denote earlier and non-Western familial relations.[1] After that, "family" characterized the modern West, and "kinship" (mysterious, convoluted, traditional, primitive, archaic) was found suitable for everyone else. But the semantic slide did not stop there; by the 1940s it was necessary to fit the adjective "nuclear" to the Western family in order to make it very clear that no obligations to kin remained to hold Western societies back from economic and social expansion and democratic political development. And any state or social regime that wanted to fit its population to the exigencies of modern life had to teach it to slough off kin and afix a "nuclear" device to familial relations.[2]

Conceptualizations of family and kinship have always had profound political implications. Here, however, I want to underline a few things at the beginning that they have in common, as well as to open up some problems with the contrast.[3] As far as the state is concerned, issues of property holding and property devolution (how husbands and wives own and administer goods, what claims children have for support, education, and inheritance) and issues of status (genetic vs. birth mother, paternity, nationality, ethnicity) are fundamental political issues. Any analysis of kinship starts here, and in this sense "family," however conceived, offers an ever-shifting mode of kinship, as any history of the family in the West readily shows. A second aspect of kinship or family has to do with marriage rules and alliance strategies. It is easy to see that states have inherent interests in what constitutes a "legitimate" marriage, but, as in contemporary Western states where new forms of cohabitation have developed, states have had to scratch their heads, so to speak, over shifting forms of claims and responsibilities. "Kinship" is in some ways a more supple instrument for examining these kinds of changes than "family," regardless of how observers develop categories to chronicle alterations in familial living. Forms of alliance may seem to be outside the purview of states, but they too are ever shifting and have important implications for class formation (and therefore class-based political expressions); social, occupational, and political networking; and even for health concerns and the expenditure of public monies (for example, cousin marriage being thought to have deleterious consequences for progeny). One of the most remarkable aspects of intervention into alliance formation in the West had to do with the radical rewriting of marriage prohibitions and incest rules at the beginning of the nineteenth century.[4] Alliances that were proscribed in medieval and early modern Europe became all the rage in the nineteenth century. And of course, rapidly changing contemporary issues of who might legitimately form unions, what kinds of unions, and the rights and obligations these imply offer lawgivers, courts, and bureaucracies new arenas for policy decisions and new political practices. A final aspect of kinship and family has to do with how to think about the child: paternal authority, motherhood, child labor, rights to education, genetic identity, consanguinity, claims on family property (see Melhuus and Alber in this volume). The recent demands in all Western states to open up adoption and sperm donor records offer but one example of how to fit the child into a kinship universe.

Taken together, property, alliance, and reproduction are topics that concern anyone who wants to consider the nature of familial relations.

The sharp contrast between "family" for us and "kinship" for others both obscures crucial commonalities and misses the point that both family and kinship are not static institutions but constantly undergoing change, shifting articulations with political regimes, internal contestations, and external interventions. Furthermore, in the West, observers of the *family*—social scientists, moral philosophers, psychotherapists, and social workers—often fail to recognize many of the practices that in fact embed people in webs of kin.[5] When they turn their attention to kinship practices of their archaic past or contemporary "others," they also often fail to give sufficient attention to the small units of parents and children. As the anthropologist Jack Goody puts it, "We know of virtually no society in the history of humanity where the elementary or nuclear family was not important, in the vast majority of cases as a co-residential group."[6]

In this chapter, I want to examine some of the ways "family" was subject to theoretical considerations, how it was shorn of meanings thought to be inherent in "kinship," and how it was fitted as a tool to *imagine* a private, domestic sphere, atomized, with no systemic connections to kin, and mediated primarily through markets or freely entered associations. I want to trace an arc between Hegel, the theoretician of the liberal family at the beginning of the nineteenth century, and Talcott Parsons, who gave the definitive stamp to the notion of the nuclear family in the aftermath of World War II. Both of them tried to differentiate the family from kinship, even though Hegel, at least, did not yet have the actual word "kinship" to use. While Parsons wrote in the style, at least, of an empirical observer, almost everyone read him as an advocate for the stripped-down nuclear family, invested in its future. Hegel was openly a spokesman for a new way of conceiving relationships; differentiating between private and public spheres, domestic and civil society institutions, and the state; and critiquing groups and obligations based on blood beyond the household of parents and children. Neither Hegel nor Parsons got it right, in terms of the complex set of social relations characteristic of their societies. I will look at one contemporary of Hegel, Basilius von Ramdhor—who described an altogether different society from the one Hegel imagined—and sketch how a few of Parsons's critics point toward social relations he could not account for.

Hegel's Family Project

G. W. F. Hegel can be seen as a bellwether among those who formulated the "modern" family. His *Grundlinien der Philosophie des Rechts* certainly was extraordinarily influential, but there were many others moving in the same direction around the same time.[7] The very fact that he talked about the "family" instead of the "house" or "household" reflects a semantic change to be found in England, France, and Germany during the several decades on each side of 1800, not only among publicists, bureaucrats, pastors, and academics but also among villagers and townsfolk as well.[8] It is not my task here to map the shift—in part because the concept of the "house" continued to have resonance and paralleled "family" well into the nineteenth century—but to pry apart the essential meanings of the "family" for Hegel and to examine the series of associated ideas that the philosopher thought important to fix his project. I say "project" because Hegel continuously cautions that he is talking about *ethical* life. While on the one hand he seeks to delineate the actual contours of family life and work out all the implications of this or that aspect to capture the logical coherence of the different parts, on the other he offers critical reflection on kinship structures past and present, judges their strengths and shortcomings, and proposes criteria for ethical action *in the modern era*, which in many instances ultimately comes down to what he calls the "free expression of personality." Given that his understanding of the family resonates with what was later formulated as the "nuclear family," I will look at the Parsonian vision developed in the 1940s in order to draw a few comparisons.

Besides the contrasting concepts of "house" and "family," Hegel was also very much concerned with distinguishing family from kinship. His terms for the latter were *Stamm* (best translated as "lineage," perhaps, but which can mean extended family, clan, house in the sense of a descent group, or tribe) and *Geschlecht* (extended family, lineage, dynasty).[9] And he could use the word "family" for the collectivity of parents and children or in the sense of the extended family, often specified as those with ties of blood. In fact, in one passage he refers to the "nucleus of the family" in order to designate the parent-child unit.[10] Perhaps this foreshadows the 1940s assumption of the "nuclear family," with its radically individualist connotations. Certainly Professor Hegel, the theorist of the bureaucratic state, was championing a familial structure fitted for the intellectual and property-holding middle classes, and the term "bourgeois family," put into circulation somewhat earlier than the Parsonian formulation, would do just as well.[11] The two terms have similar elements. There is another set of opposed concepts at the heart of Hegel's consideration of the family, namely, what he calls the "one" and the "other," man and woman.[12] Here Hegel is working with the idea originating in the last decades of the eighteenth century of universal and opposed—rooted in nature—characteristics of the sexes. In his formulation, the systematic oppositions inherent in the two sexes were: self-conscious conceptual thought vs. feeling, the will to objectivity vs. passive subjectivity, substantial life in the state, learning, work, and struggle vs. vocation in the family and an ethical disposition to piety.[13] Karin Hausen has argued that until late in the eighteenth century gender opposition was figured along social lines (*Hausvater* and *Hausmutter*) and occupation. But gender was reconfigured as embodied differences supporting systematic psychological characteristics in the wake of dangerous Enlightenment notions of "humanity," which offered no obvious defense against claims for equality between the sexes.[14] And both in the general literature of the period and in Hegel, distinctions were made between public and private spheres corresponding with gender polarities. Domestic life characterized both the social and mental life of the female sex, while activity (struggle) in the external world shaped the mental life of men toward objectivity and the consequent ability to generalize.[15]

In contrast, in the early modern period, the starting point for thinking about the family was almost always its male head, with an immediate question of the nature of power in the family or household. Bodin, for example, opens his consideration of the family thus: "Mesnage est un droit gouvernement de plusieurs subiects, sous l'obïssance d'un chef de famille, & de ce qui luy est propre," which the 1606 English translation rendered as "A Familie is the right government of many subiects or persons under the obedience of one and the same head of the family; and of such things as are unto them proper."[16] (See the chapter by Heinemann in this volume.) There are interesting semantic shifts between house/household/householding and family all the way through the original French text and the various contemporary translations, and Bodin even had the French translated into Latin, using the word *familia* for *mesnage* (*ménage*, household). But what held the family or household together was always the authority of the male head or *chef*, conveyed nicely by the German word *Hausvater*, the starting point for all considerations of kinship.

The Family and Subjectivity

Hegel makes a clean break with the tradition of the paterfamilias—at least he begins not with the problem of authority but with a consideration of spousal alliance. His starting point is the married couple, not the head of family: from the beginning, he is unconcerned with the house as a spatial unit, a kind of container needing subjects in order to be conceptualized in juridical terms. In Hegel's analysis, the key thing is the psychological disposition of the marital partners. And that is subject to growth and change in a continuous mutual recognition of each other. At the core of familial relationships is feeling—glossed as "love"—not authority and obedience.[17] But love itself can take on many different forms. There is the "particularism" (*Eigentümlichkeit*) of modern subjectivity, which I take as equivalent to people being attracted to each other, "falling in love," and entering into marriage to fulfill emotional longings or desires.[18] That is too contingent, he finds, to found a stable (ethical) relationship. In fact, inclination—any kind of intimate knowledge of each other before the decision to marry—is not a good sign. Hegel rather likes the idea of parents or friends arranging a marriage in the first place, and what founds the new unity is "free consent," a notion rooted in both Catholic and Lutheran theology but given a novel psychological spin by Hegel.[19] This consent is to constitute a single person and to give up natural individuality for a new kind of individuality, which establishes freedom: self limitation is the foundation for liberation. In his discussion of freedom, Hegel thinks of a break with the family of origin and with kin, on the one hand, and, on the other, of the possibility of becoming fully human, completing the self through the complementary recognition inherent in gender opposition. In Hegel's analysis of identity, the recognition by an *other* is the foundation of self-consciousness. Here in the relationship of husband and wife lies the most intimate and continuous dialectic of other-recognition and consciousness of self. And that is why contingent feeling, which is subject to turning into what he calls "frostiness," should not really be the basis of marriage.[20] There is at the outset an element of decision and commitment to personal unity, and when taken this allows the full flowering of individual personality, something quite different from independence. There is a significant contrast between love as mere feeling and ethical love beyond the "transient, capricious, and purely subjective aspects of love."[21]

Hegel's sense of passionate love is that it is too "contingent," subject to shifts in feeling. Ethical life requires a commitment. But such a commitment has its rewards as, although he does not express it this way, marriage is over time a kind of adventure that offers a full flowering of subjectivity for an individual. In a sense, he argues, the less you know about the person you marry beforehand, the more there is to experience in marriage. That is why establishing connection through the mediation of trusted friends or relatives offers the best guarantee for experiencing ethical love. If this is to be the opposite of mere subjective considerations, then there must be something objective, disciplined about it. But objective cannot be the same as instrumental. In fact, if parents bring property or political connections into consideration, they are violating their obligation, which is to match suitable temperaments with each other. Hegel asserts that thinking of marriage as a mere contract, as did Kant, violates its essence by treating the partners instrumentally. And this also goes for sexuality. There can be no feeling in marriage without it, but on the other hand, sexuality cannot be the foundation of the union, since once again, without subordination to substantial ends, that too violates the mutual and undivided surrender of personality. One partner has to accept the wholeness and identity of the other person in order to develop a suitable consciousness of self.[22] Although Parsons treats the matter differently, as we will see, he too focuses on the psychological dimensions of marriage as fundamentally modern.

The Modern Family Is Founded on Exogamy

Hegel considers nature to be an area of unfreedom. And he thinks of kin relations established by blood as something natural and therefore as a matter of constraint and something to overcome. To marry back into the group with which one is most intimate is an act that violates the liberation that goes together with founding a new family. Marriage is the *free* surrender of their personalities by two people characterized by different sex: "It must not be concluded within the *naturally identical* circle of people who are acquainted and familiar with each other in every detail—a circle in which the individuals do not have a distinct personality of their own in relation to one another—but must take place [between people] from separate families and personalities of different origin."[23] The breadth of his description here goes beyond the incest prohibition. Of course, the circle of close kin—and he does not give a description of just how far the prohibition of kin extends—provides the basis for exogamy rules. But Hegel seems to suggest that any kind of an intimate milieu should be off limits. The wording, "naturally identical," does point to those who are connected through blood, those of the family writ large. It may be that such people are the only ones who are so closely acquainted that their personalities are indistinguishable, but making intimacy the problem suggests that any kind of close knowledge is included. In any event, the incest prohibition is not rooted in divine law prohibition as most early modern discourse would maintain, he argues. Still less does it have any biological foundation. It has to do with the psychological disposition of independent personality. Those who know each other too well are too much alike to offer the proper tension that helps free personality emerge. Marriage between those who are related by blood contradicts marriage as an ethical act of freedom—because it is rooted in nature, which by definition is an area of unfreedom. Founding the incest taboo on "obscure feelings" somehow rooted in nature does not do justice to the essential aspect of free choice in marriage.[24] Freedom has to be associated with reason, and marriage, as a gesture of rationality, therefore breaks with nature. In all of his discussion here, he recognizes that there are two different kinds of kin: those related through blood (nature, unfreedom) and those contracted in alliance (free choice). In this sense, kinship through alliance is quite a different matter from kinship through blood. Nature can characterize blood relations, but alliance formation has to be a fresh start, so to speak. After all this is said, Hegel does think that close marriage is apt to spawn feeble progeny.[25] But he does not handle this at the level of biology, instead approaching it at a more abstract level that suggests that people who know each other too well before marriage are likely to be less actively engaged sexually. Union, he says, can only take place after separation. That is, the spouses have to be fully separate personalities before they can be united. "The power of procreation" is a matter of the "magnitude of opposition."[26]

It may well be that the incest prohibition—the trigger, so to speak, of marrying beyond the family, of exogamy—is in the first instance prompted for Hegel by considerations of blood. But he slips in this passage from blood to friendship, from immediate family to the wider set of kin, from the household to the milieu. "Familiarity, acquaintance, and the habit of shared activity should not be present before marriage: they should be discovered only within it, and the value of the discovery is all the greater the richer it is and the more components it has."[27] There must be a whole *Individuum* being for itself—and an independent unity (*Einzelheit*)—going into marriage. Marriage cannot proceed from something already united (*vereint*), and it also cannot be something that arises from everyday commerce or intimacy, for difference is crucial for the unfolding of a marital relationship over time. "Spiritually felt union arises from sharing," but sharing all those things that are particular or peculiar to two initially complementary personalities.[28] What is already known is uninteresting, and marriage is a matter of continuous discovery, a matter of extended surprise.

Considerations of Exogamy

In Hegel's consideration of the founding of a family, he opposes family to the larger group of kin and to lineages and argues for a thoroughgoing practice of exogamy. And he does not consider the individual family to be a mediating instance between two different kingroups brought together through the particular marriage of a particular husband and wife; rather, he prefers God's commandment to Adam and Eve (Gen.

2:24) to leave father and mother (although they did not seem to have had any) and organize their lives around each other.[29] The whole point of being of age suitable to marriage was to have attained full individual personality and the impulse to leave the strictures of subordination. I will come back to the mechanisms of individual familial identity but want to note that Hegel was quite clearly opposed to some of the most powerful social developments of his age, the age of what in a shorthand manner can be designated as "cousin marriage."[30] From a larger perspective, people were turning toward intimate milieus and close kin to find their marriage partners. And whole families conspired in the pursuit. If indeed parents were to direct the choice of a spouse, their children would be all the more likely to marry those in whose circle they had been brought up. Around the middle of the eighteenth century, all property-holding groups—at least in Western Europe, from Scandinavia to Sicily—began to tentatively search out cousins (often second cousins), closest friends of siblings, relatives of a deceased spouse, sisters- and brothers-in-law, friends of the "house," and members of lineages and clans already attached to their own families.

Given the ecclesiastical, secular, and social exogamy rules and expectations up to the middle of the eighteenth century, marriage had been, at least conceptually, with the "stranger." Modernizing theological, philosophical, and legal pundits chipped away at the older systems of canon and Protestant Church law to free up as many couplings as they could. And by the turn of the century, it was even possible for uncles to marry nieces (although nephews and aunts violated other principles of gender hierarchies). In any event, what started off tentatively at midcentury simply grew exponentially while continuously narrowing the practical field from which kin might be drawn. In short, it seems to me that Hegel, with his thoroughgoing valuation of exogamy, is going against all the tendencies of his age, when people were choosing spouses from the most intimate milieus, from networks of cousins and related kin and from families already in close alliance with each other. Hegel, as we shall see, was trying to create a theoretical perspective on the state, one that made the state independent both of civil society and of the family. Only as an independent instance could it mediate between competing interests, institutions, and social groups, providing rational, noninterested intervention. History, Hegel thought, was proceeding toward ever greater freedom—that is, departing from nature—and its foundation lay in the rational mastery of nature. The independence of individual families and the independence of the state (above kin groups) were two aspects of the same project. The state, of course, could be thought of as an abstraction, but Hegel was concerned with a particular configuration of the state, one that historians conceptualize as the *Beamtenstaat* (loosely translatable as the "bureaucratic state"). Those whose job it was to run the state—the *Beamten*—had to divorce themselves from all private considerations—they could not, at least formally, represent lineages, families, clans, or other kinds of kinship configurations, and implicitly they were also not representatives of class interests. Hegel does not directly say so, but it seems to me that he understood forms of alliance that interwove localities, milieus, classes, or kin to have two fundamental problems. Such networks, on the one hand, could be a threat to the power of the state, especially in their inherent interest to capture state power in one way or another and wield it in their own interests; on the other, these networks would inhibit the ability of any state official to rise above their demands to serve them first and to direct public resources for their own private gain.

A Contemporary Defends Endogamy

There were several bureaucrat-writers around the turn of the century who took up issues eventually worried by Hegel.[31] I want to comment on one of them in order to see how the terms of argument by intellectuals in the first several decades of the nineteenth century were so similar while at the same time able to provide understandings of contemporary social practices much more in keeping with the values of the age. The Hannoverian and Prussian official, Friedrich Wilhelm Basilius von Ramdohr, who was a decade older than Hegel, was one of many commentators trying to rethink the nature of marriage and sexual attraction around 1800.[32] A great deal of what he and other authors had to say had to do with how choices were determined and what constituted desire. After several decades of discussion about the nature of the human as essentially passionate, or rational, or some mixture of the two, together with a secularization of discourse about the ends of human society— geared to happiness or perfectibility—what to do about women or sexual differentiation altogether produced considerable unease. One way to deal with the problem was to think of the truly human as a couple, a union of opposites, a resolution of polarity through emotional attachment. One could go so far as to think—as did Hegel—of male and female as essentially two different kinds of beings, but in any event a consensus was worked out (and embedded in all the major encyclopedias for the next century and a half) that the sexes could best be understood as a series of complementary oppositions. So that was one way to think of same and other.

Like Hegel, von Ramdohr sites the whole matter of familial formation on a psychological plane. In a fashion similar to Hegel's but not quite so well worked out, he thought of the constitution of the self in a dialectical experience of recognition in another. And for this, psychological and temperamental differences ensured the richness of self-formation. Von Ramdohr, for example, thought that love was a matter of approaching another human whose combination of "dispositions" was different from one's own, although he usually spoke of a "he" looking for a complementary "her." Men, tightly wired, exhibited strength, while women were characterized by tenderness and delicacy. And, of course, these were pure types: actual men and women were a mixture of both qualities, and they exhibited sympathy for individuals of the opposite sex who offered the right traits to strengthen or mitigate their own characteristics—which he later called a chemical affinity.[33] Erotic feeling is stimulated by commingling or marriage of male tension (*Spannung*) and female tenderness.[34] "The erotic (*Üppigkeit*), especially of the organs of touch, inherently supports the true character of sexual sympathetic desire (*Wollust*), for we wed here feelings in us," he thought, "which are different in kind but in species the same. They both belong to our [common] sensibility but to their different dispositions."[35] And there is a dialectic: a woman receives strength from a man and then communicates it back to him, augmenting his strength. And the communication of tenderness from a women to her husband works the same way.[36]

For von Ramdohr, sexual dimorphism stimulates the desire for the union of opposite sexes—it is only possible to become a full, complete individual in sexual union of opposite sexes.[37] The heterosexual assumptions here, however, are part of another drive, namely to initiate a newly independent unit and to set up a household. There is no stronger *erotic* drive, he insisted, than domesticity, the impulsion for male and female to become one, to found a family.[38] But there is something about domesticity itself in von Ramdohr's treatment that cannot do without erotic attraction. Even in a family where brother and sister happily dwell together, they have to be seen as a sort of husband and wife.[39] And the man and woman who unite in one person to found a household extend the hand brotherly and sisterly in all their complementary characteristics. Von Ramdohr, here, reflects the widespread assumptions in contemporary literature—not shared by Hegel—of an elemental eroticism between siblings that schools individuals in the aesthetics of marriage choice. A great part of sexual sympathy, therefore, propels people toward domesticity.[40] Sexual polarity, leading to a successful domestic union, also has to have an aspect of friendship to it, which means that there has to have a dimension of similarity as well—they have to have the same tastes and other compatibilities that suggest cultural familiarity.[41] "The Oriental can normally feel no sexual tenderness for his wife. He can love her passionately, but he can not consider her as the trusted, *self selected sister or friend.*"[42] And that is because she does not operate in the same social sphere as he nor share the same amusements. In our socially and morally constructed states today, von Ramdohr argued, the woman participates in the same circles of local society as the man.[43] Clearly, marriage is a search for someone with the same "knowledge, arts, objects of observation, thoughts, judgment."[44] And sexual relations have a significant aspect of friendship to them.[45] What ultimately distinguishes friendship from sexual affection is the erotic, but then between members of a family of different sexes there is an element of sexual attraction even if not passion, itself a longing for an indispensable bliss, a transfer of the whole being into the being of another, indeed an illness, so long as a union does not take place.[46]

Von Ramdohr was very much concerned with the development of class-specific and highly localized milieus. It was in such localities that cultural production took place and where everyday intercourse wove the strands of political cultures. The development of the person, cultivation, education (*Bildung*) is always a local matter for both sexes. And von Ramdohr, like many other writers of the period, considered aesthetics, how one moved, spoke, projected oneself, and displayed manners, to lie at the heart of learning how to negotiate among one's fellows. The analogy von Ramdohr found was choreography. Finding a mate involves a familiar aesthetic expression much like skilled dancing or playing music. It involves social skills and performance before an audience.[47] And the attraction of two souls who desire to please and support each other has to be mediated by aesthetically pleasing bodies.[48] Nonetheless it is the sexual sympathy of souls that unifies humans and knits society together and that can take two forms—perhaps best expressed in English as "liking" and "desiring."[49] In the latter case, even spiritual desire can be expressed in erotic terms. "The tender devotion and loving passion for a person of the other sex cannot be thought of apart from the participation of sexual sympathy of both the body and the soul."[50] And von Ramdohr does not exclude any tender devotion from the participation of sexual sympathy, not brother and sister, father and daughter, mother and son.[51] The "nature [of sexual sympathy] consists of a gentle tension, which happens whenever enhancing tenderness coincides with flexible force, and those persons who live together in domestic intimacy (in itself an erotic idea [*üppige Vorstellung*]) offer the senses erotic impressions through forms, physical expression, and attachment and convey sensuous ideas through thoughts, feelings, expressions, phrases, characters and relations of souls—they should not obey the universal laws of nature? Impossible!"[52]

Von Ramdohr suggests that his reader test himself: if a brother hugs his brother and then his sister he will feel the difference. It is not necessary to think of "coarse symptoms" of what von Ramdohr calls the "nameless drive." "Still the whole power of education and duty is necessary to curb the urgency of desires, even those among parents and children and among siblings."[53] As we shall see, Hegel thought that in an ethical family parents explicitly educate their children to leave, to pursue independence, to not be constrained by eroticized bonds of sentiment. There seems to be no idea, as with von Ramdohr, of a counterpull that needs to be overcome by the substitution of an object as similar as possible to a sister. Whereas we shall see that for Hegel each family is to be thought of as quite independent of all other families, von Ramdohr stresses the intimate interrelationship of family and local society, mediated by what might best be called an eroticized aesthetic. Marriage alliance is oriented not toward independence but toward integration and, when skillfully carried out, makes the couple fit for social roles beyond their individual families and links domestic life to public life.

Von Ramdohr asks, what does one look for in a wife? She has to be a strong personality in her own right so that she will not become boring after a while. And she has to be capable of running a household. For that, she needs to have had an education in all relevant skills as well as in the local customs. Above all, she has to play a role in the social life of her surroundings and to have the necessary social connections and social skills.[54] And this, it seems to me, lies at the heart of von Ramdohr's representation of political life—what links the domestic with the political is a realm of sociality, that site where networks are constructed and cultural assumptions policed. "It is necessary that the wife has become skilled through early education to show herself with propriety in the local society in which she one day will appear on the hand of her loved one as member and promoter of societal amusements."[55] And it is clear that the spouse should come from the same social circles, since without the relevant training, it is very difficult to show oneself apt for everyday intercourse. "It belongs to the independence of a woman that she can maintain her place in the local society as a useful member, useful for social participation."[56] And the husband's standing is inevitably tied to that of his wife. Should he choose a spouse without the same cultivation as himself, he will demonstrate an incongruity with the half of his being and indeed with the rest of society in which he cannot be judged as a single person. "One will not feel the perfection of your union, and for you as for your spouse, the high pleasure will be missing—to know that for her your compound person is also for others the object of agreeable inspection.[57] And a woman can herself only be attracted to a man who is valued in the class they both belong to.[58] The man who sparkles in her social circle has the first claim for her approbation.[59] In many ways, Hegel and von Ramdohr approach political life from quite different directions. Hegel thinks about how to create a strong state capable of rational action and able to attract and retain a set of civil servants who do not act out of class or family interest. Von Ramdohr works out just how class-based politics operates—through the weaving together of socially disciplined families, where marital politics embedded in cultural practices in turn produce and reproduce political expectations.

Von Ramdohr argues that the tone of any society is local—where Hegel talks about the universal and rational and ethical, von Ramdohr puts his money on the particular, the erotic, and the aesthetic. Girls, he thinks, are attracted to the kind of urbanity that makes a man familiar in his surroundings: "How much lies already in the selection of clothes, of furniture, of the apartment, in short, in the actual accessories surrounding the person of the urban man, whereby one can conclude about his taste and for the respect and life he has for himself and others."[60] The point is to be able to see that a person is suited to his class. Whatever interests and capacities couples may have, the area of activity for women is always the local society. It is here that urbanity and the gift of social conversation is displayed and where men perform in front of women.[61] For the woman, it matters what reputation the man has in civil society and how he acts in the local society.[62] Von Ramdohr makes a point here that we will see Hegel take up: civil society is the natural field in which men act, and therefore they are the crucial mediating instance between the family and the outside. "The care for the unity and the pleasure of the larger local society, for the formation of her own mind for conversation in the closer social circle, is again a suitable purpose for her."[63]

Hegel Distinguishes Sharply between Family and Kin

Von Ramdohr clearly sees no sharp break between family and kin. One swims in an ocean of intimates and finds a partner for life among its waves. He does not, however, spend a great deal of time on the nature of kinship as such. During the early modern period, both aristocratic and peasant families were fundamentally concerned with the devolution of property, status, symbolic goods, titles, and offices. Oligarchic tendencies in cities had become ever stronger in the transition from the seventeenth to the eighteenth centuries—in France offices were held as inheritable property, while throughout German states families had come to control tightly regulated patronage systems, in what in South

Germany was called *Vetterleswirtschaft* (nepotism). Hegel criticized the practices in Württemberg in an early essay and noted that these families treated state financial institutions as a "fodder barn," enriching themselves and illegitimately mingling private and public concerns.⁶⁴ As the philosopher of the *Beamtenstaat* (loosely translated, as I have noted, as the bureaucratic—or better, "bureaucrats"—state), characterized by access to tenured careers, regulated promotion, and pensions through an examination system controlled by the officials themselves, he imagined a system where civil servants were at once independent of monarchs, civil society, and kin. In this regard, the model of the extended family as a property-holding association, with the *Stamm* thought of as a conduit of property inherently belonging not to the individual but to the line, violated the principles of bourgeois independence. No bureaucrat would be outside the circle of corruption unless he were free of the private interests of an extended kinship group. In this instance, Hegel's starting point of family formation privileging husband and wife, independent of any obligation to an extended family, actually provides the model for the educated bourgeois (*Bildungsbürger*) or civil servant.⁶⁵

At the outset of Hegel's discussion of the family, he stresses "love" and erotic desire as operations of recognition of the other and self-in-the-other and the other-in-the-self-of-the-other in a constantly mediated dialectic. But the family—the husband and wife in the first instance—needs stability and structure beyond the contingency of feeling, something more substantial and durable to mediate their relationships. The family, for example, will have children—and in some ways it is not yet a real or substantial family in their absence—but the point of marriage is not logically tied to the teleology of reproduction. Rather, it is the other way around: children mediate the relationship between husband and wife.⁶⁶ I will come back to this, which Hegel calls the internal dimension of the independent family. But its external element, the thing that fixes it and offers that independence without which it has no substantial being—or, as he puts it, "personality" (perhaps better translated as "personness," or "personhood," a unity of purpose, a corporation of the whole)—is property. Of course, the kind of property that the couple has (both its quantity and quality) makes a difference. And property as such is not a stable thing over time, since it is used, invested, administered, accrued, depleted. Like love and sex, which mediate the spousal relationship and which change their characters over time, property too is an essential "third" thing, a mediating element, that offers the family "substantial" being. And here Hegel introduces the rare use of "father" in his treatment of the family—the *Familienvater*, not the *Hausvater*—as the representative of this property-holding unit, as manager (but not at all as owner) of its resources.⁶⁷ Without property, there is no proper marriage, for the constitution of a new family with its *independent* resources is not only to offer independence and singularity in the wider society but also to make it independent of the kinship group. As he puts it, property is essentially tied to the marital relationship, not to kin in any immediate sense.⁶⁸ The wife and husband make a completely independent family, but only with their own independent resources. The "new family is more essential than the wider context of blood relations."⁶⁹ Its members compose the "proper nucleus" in opposition to the "family," here understood as a more-or-less extended group of kin.⁷⁰ In this treatment, Hegel essentially introduces the "bourgeois family," although he does not use the term. The stress is on its independence, and the chance use of the term "nucleus" foreshadows the Parsonian formulation that similarly imagines an institution with only contingent ties to relatives, none of whom actively participate in its self-definition or self-conscious understanding. Control over its own property allows the husband-and-wife team to negotiate in civil society without ties of kinship, and it is property that individuates a family and gives it its own character. Hegel would not have thought so much about mobility as Parsons would eventually do, but his own career took him from his Stuttgart origins in a *Beamtenfamilie* (rooted in Württemberg pastoral and official families for many generations on both sides) to the local university in Tübingen and thence to Bern, Jena, Bamberg, Nürnberg (where he found a wife), Heidelberg, and finally, at the age of forty-eight, to Berlin. There is more than a little of both men's own academic careers reflected in their formulations.

Hegel explains how his understanding of the family and its property relations is formulated in explicit opposition to aristocratic rules and practices. The *fideikommissum*, in which property is entailed, not subject to individual ownership, and subject to rules beyond the control of the individual families that follow upon the generations, is one example of a violation of the principle of free property.⁷¹ Here, I think, Hegel is championing a new understanding of property as something that is completely subject to the will of its possessor, grasped in the idea of alienability. Such an idea was being worked out in bourgeois property law around the turn of the century with wide implications for traditional use rights, among other things. The whole point of entails had been not so much to support a particular family (a husband and wife), as innovations in property law would have it, but a lineage or house, a family considered over time and along multiple generations. And in a rather apodictic statement, Hegel denies that the kinship group has any right to recognition.⁷² Freedom is necessary for ethical life—one who is not free has no moral standing, no responsibility for his actions. It is in that context that the freedom to dispose resources is part of the ethical tenor of the family as such. And, I suppose, recognizing his origins in Württemberg, where the law of property devolution specified equality among all the children, male and female, he found partible inheritance much the best system of inheritance for its fairness (treating sons and daughters alike), lack of rigidity (following no prescribed rule that singled out merely contingent phenomena, such as birth order or sex), and freedom from arbitrary sentiment. ("In England, where all kinds of eccentricity are endemic, innumerable foolish notions are associated with wills.")[73] It is, of course, the state, with its promulgation of civil laws and its court system, that determines the rules of the familial estate, ownership and use, and devolution. During the first decades of the nineteenth century, bureaucrats and new state legislatures gave considerable attention to property law—in some ways nothing was more contentious or subject to political debate.[74]

The third fundamental mediating element, after sex and property (and this time internal), is children, introduced from the outset as the "dissolution of the family."[75] The parents love each other through the children, and their own feeling of unity becomes objectively true in the children. Indeed the substantial unity of the parents is only possible in the children.[76] Note that this is all about the husband and wife and not about the children, the more one probes the text, the more one sees that spouses make up the family in the first instance, and Hegel is concerned with how their relationships are mediated. Children are not essential, therefore, for the family, except insofar as they play a role in forming and transforming their parents' relationships. In the child the wife loves the husband, and in the child the husband loves the wife. There may be many aspects in having and parenting children, but Hegel isolates only one moment, namely the teleology of self-sufficiency and freedom of personality. The point of all education is to let the child go. Once again, Hegel brings in the unfreedom/freedom dichotomy. As long as the child remains in the family, he or she is to some degree unfree, and this is intolerable for him, for one thing because until he is a freely deciding, self-motivated being he neither has the independence of adulthood nor a full personality. As soon as the child enters into a new marriage, origins recede, becoming just the point of departure; previous family relationships are renounced; and the field of kin remains just an abstraction for which there is no exchange of rights or obligations.[77]

Hegel is not much interested in the reciprocities or enduring exchanges among kin or within any kind of an extended family. He imagines families as all independent and as not entering into relationships through already prescribed ties of blood or in ascriptively defined fields of inherited relations. The field in which the family satisfies its needs is civil society, which in turn is defined as the set of relations between particular families. Rather than being held together by some sort of clan, families by their very nature disintegrate into "self-sufficient, concrete persons."[78] And just because there are no "natural" relations between families even though they are necessarily connected, civil society logically presupposes the state. Although Hegel does not enlarge upon this point, he is clearly thinking of the Hobbes position that implicitly or explicitly all relations between families-as-persons are of a contractual nature. The state operates as the guarantor of contracts, and therefore civil society cannot be conceptualized without the state, although the state does not in the first instance presuppose civil society. After all, civil society is modern. It is composed of commercial enterprises, businesses, corporations, and voluntary associations—all the things that satisfy personal needs. It is the field in which by satisfying their own particular needs, individuals contribute to the satisfaction of others' needs. As he puts it, "The whole of civil society is the sphere of mediation."[79]

I do not want to develop Hegel's idea on civil society at any length, but I do want to sketch in a few points.[80] His basic framework is to construct two poles of particularity and universality. The particular person in the first instance does not think of the whole but only wishes to satisfy his (expanding) needs through interaction with others. Civil society offers the field, so to speak, where everyone attempts to satisfy their particular needs—it can be thought of as the sphere of universal (*allgemeine*— a word that can also mean "general") concern. Problems arise when individuals see themselves or attempt to act as self-sufficient—and that, he says, is the essence of corruption.[81] His argument here is not all that clear—he cryptically mentions ancient states that fell because of corruption—but I take it that this kind of action involves the use of power to short circuit social interaction by the aggrandizement of particular families coordinating their interests and illegitimately appropriating resources of the state or preventing equal access to other families in the marketplace. He offers the example of the fact that most everyone wishes to avoid taxation as somehow not in their own interests. But the particularity of their own ends is not able to be satisfied without the interests of the whole. Unless civil society is supported by taxation, the interests of the individual cannot be satisfied: "In furthering my end, I further the universal, and this in turn furthers my end."[82] In any event, the contingencies of social interaction lead to such inequalities in wealth that the state has to intervene to restore harmony.

The other point of some interest is his consideration of education, which is the key instrument to induce rationality and thereby overcome nature—that is, education is linked to liberation, learning to view things objectively. Such education is hard work, and anyone who does not take on the task is bound to unfreedom. "Education irons out particularity to make it act in accordance with the nature of the thing."[83] I take it that education in some ways has a similar, although this time internal, effect as the state, which enters into the situation externally through force. Education intervenes in social interaction internally to the particular individual through work. Civil society allows for freedom for the first time (so freedom is quintessentially modern) and is not rooted in the strict necessity of nature. The educated individual is able to see in the interests of society as a whole how not all his own interests might be rationally pursued.

Formulating the Nuclear Family

I want to turn now to the formulation of the "nuclear family" as it was worked out by Talcott Parsons. He too embedded his understanding of the institution in the "modern"—although his modern (now the essential exigencies of industrialization, urbanization, and advanced capitalism) was more so than Hegel's. His family too was independent, and any particular connection to kin was understood to be contingent. One of the things that made it independent was its reliance on male employment, as property in Parsons's understanding was linked to modern forms of income. Crucial to the formulation of the "nuclear family" was its heterosexual basis and clear understanding of sexual dimorphism and polarized space: male outside, female inside; male breadwinner, female domestic servant. At the heart of Parsons's notion of the family, like Hegel's, was the married couple, and indeed he has very little to say about children. The relationship between spouses is mostly reduced to a psychological/erotic dimension. Altogether, they have little use for extended kin, and for the most part the American family is contrasted strongly with systems where kin are integral to social relation. (See Susan McKinnon's article in this volume, which looks at the nineteenth-century American ideologies of family and kinship.)

In 1943, Talcott Parsons addressed the structural features of the American "kinship system."[84] Remarkably, he based his take on the American family on "common sense" and "general experience," and he leaned on the work of Kingsley Davis for much of his profile. His opening gesture was to put the American family into the comparative perspective expected of a grand theorist and a sociologist aware of the categories provided by a half century of anthropological study: "The American family is perhaps best characterized as an 'open, multilineal, conjugal system.'"[85] Like the anthropologist Murdock, down the coast at Yale, Parsons allows for the possibility that the "conjugal family unit of parents and children" was at the foundation of any kinship system, but "we" really only recognize the word "family" to characterize ourselves, and by that we mean that that unit is unconnected to other relatives in any systemic way. He imagines other societies as having solidary "units" that extend the basic family to include specified kin. "Ours then is a 'conjugal' system in that it is 'made up' *exclusively* of interlocking conjugal families" (with no discussion of what "interlocking" might mean, but it sounds like Hegel's account of civil society).[86] Relatives are of no real account in the American system, characterized as it is by small bounded units of parents and children. In the quote above, the term "multilineal" is meant to do considerable work.[87] It means that there are no structural features privileging any particular set of relatives or marking lineages or lines through characteristic patrilateral or matrilateral, agnatic or maternal, lineal or lineage features. And one can marry without reference to any given rules apart from a generalized notion of avoiding ill-defined close relatives. "Preferential mating on a kinship basis, that is, is completely without structural significance, and every marriage in founding a new conjugal family brings together ... two completely unrelated kinship groups which are articulated on a kinship basis *only* in this one particular marriage."[88] Here exogamy is full-blown, and marriage can scarcely be thought of as an alliance. Once again, we see echoes of Hegel's thorough-going project of exogamy.

Throughout Parsons's account, "kinship" was systematically thought of in terms of "group," and with an implicit stage theory of development whereby "family" supplants "kinship," he considered kinship as something residing in "non-literate" cultures.[89] I have no idea whether Parsons read Hegel, but his account of the modern American family offers strong echoes of the philosopher's position, then a project, now thought of as an actuality. The "conjugal family" is isolated, it has its own property and income, it can be described as a household unit (the "normal" one), it is bounded by a home, and it is segregated from both sets of parents. Its social status, which has no intrinsic relationship to the origins of either parent, is exclusively linked to the job of the husband. There is no inherited home, no economic support, and no occupation inherited from father to son.[90] The central message here is the "structural isolation of the individual conjugal family," "the most distinctive feature of the American kinship system."[91] And shades of Hegel once again: "The marriage bond is, in our society, the main structural keystone of the kinship system."[92] But already, Parsons was putting his finger on a source of instability. Although the status of the family and its economic foundation came from the husband's occupation, the physical home was the bailiwick of the wife—which offered a "mother-centered type of family structure" in some instances, and in others a full-blown "matriarchy," especially in the middle-class suburbs.[93] In this instance, the family's basic power structure became distorted and led to an essential fragility. During the decades when Parsons was writing, one of the crucial "political" issues had to do with the undue power mothers were said to have over children. The "attack" on mothers was carried out largely in the psychotherapeutic professions, which, in turn, grew rapidly in numbers with enormous state support as they made claims to being able to "reestablish" paternal authority.[94]

Twelve years after the 1943 article, Parsons revisited the modern American family, this time introducing the full-blown concept of the "nuclear family" and with full emphasis on its psychological dimensions.[95] The family has here lost almost all of its functions, leaving it only with that of "personality," that is, socialization of children and psychological stabilization for adults.[96] He notes that Americans were already experiencing a high divorce rate but dismisses this as largely involving couples who have not yet produced children. In any event, they marry readily again, so that marriage rates were higher than ever.[97] The focus for almost everyone is building a "home," a single-family house, the "preferred residential pattern," divorced from any intense relations with kin.[98] Once again, Parsons is concerned with "units," and the American family/household unit contrasts markedly with non-Western or even early Western units of extended kin, whether or not confined to a single dwelling.[99] A central feature of the American family is the father ("the instrumental leader").[100] He determines the status, and he provides for its economic support through his labor, not through inherited wealth.[101] But father is most essentially husband; it is the marital relationship that counts, for it is in that that the personalities of adults find a necessary balance.[102] Rather than a devolution of resources and responsibilities from father to father, the centering of familial dynamics on the couple weakens ties with the "family of orientation," leaving the "family of procreation" structurally unsupported.[103] In the isolated nuclear family, two generations are thrown together, necessarily in their bounded confinement acting out "residual" eroticism. Parsons calls attention to the quintessential heterosexuality of this constellation, with genital sex "a reenactment of the oedipal mother/child" relationship (that is, the wife and husband, or at least, in this image, the husband acts out "childhood features" with the mother/wife).[104] Parsons reinforces older essentialist notions of the mother of the family: her "expressive role" is rooted in biology, and while the female/mother is always erotic, in the isolated nuclear family, this is supercharged.[105] The complementarity of roles between male and female, husband and wife, father and mother, is accentuated because of the enhanced importance of marriage.[106]

Conclusion

I have argued that Hegel's treatment of the family ought to be seen very much as a project, and the term that tips us off to this is the word "ethical." He does not say that everyone about him is pursuing an ethical life. Indeed, he was well aware of "corruption," which he saw as an illegitimate conflation of public and private concerns through utilizing public goods for the aggrandizement of particular families or networks of kin. And this was no minor matter: his own home country was rife with corruption. Even if Hegel writes in abstractions, his text is a mixture of observation and prescription. Although one should not miss the prescriptive element in Parsons, his essays were couched in the language of empirical observation even if he did no empirical work. Hegel's understanding of the family certainly worked its way into many a nineteenth-century treatise, and yet there was a strong counterreality on the ground of building well-integrated kinship networks through mechanisms of endogamous marriage, both by linking families with each other down the generations and by assortative mating practices by milieu and class. And perhaps it might be useful to pursue how political culture was formed through familial reciprocities, how the familial and the familiar were two sides of the same coin, and how political habitus was formed in the crucible of familial give-and-take.[107] During the nineteenth century, it became increasingly difficult to openly flaunt office for personal and familial aggrandizement (and Hegel's influence, among many others, was important in bringing this about), but access to office was still channeled along less visible but nonetheless real networks of family and friendship. "Careers open to talents" developed in the form of loosely structured kinship networks underwriting the careers of their talented (and not-so-talented) younger members.[108] Those who did arrive at their destinies, struggling all along the way without connections, often bitterly bemoaned the loneliness of really being self-made men.[109]

If I have emphasized the fact that Hegel was "whistling in the dark," so to speak, it is by no means certain that Parsons got it right either. Soon after he formulated the "nuclear family" model, research projects developed to show how much families were indeed embedded in larger neighborly and kin networks.[110] Some of the earliest challenges came from scholars who dealt with rural folk, working-class milieus, and an array of ethnic groups.[111] He may, however, have captured a particular moment of suburban development, which quickly broke down under multiple pressures of high divorce rates, recombined families, working mothers, impoverished single mothers, and the lack of public facilities for the care of children.[112] Coping strategies had to plug family and kin in and out according to the exigencies of life cycles. Perhaps one of the things that links Hegel and Parsons most closely is their parsing "family" in the context of their own self-understanding as academic bureaucrats. Their particular form of mobility posited on more-or-less formal exams is, of course, quite peculiar.[113]

At the heart of both Hegel's and Parsons's formulation of the family is really the couple. And both of them suggest that psychological dimensions of the relationship are primary. And both of them work with strong assumptions of sexual dimorphism. But in Parsons's account there is little sense of anything that mediates the relations between the spouses. Essentially, the wife offers emotional and sexual services, and the husband pays for the whole thing. Whatever complementarity is there, it is purely functional, emotional support on the one hand and financial support on the other. Hegel's sense of complementarity is much deeper, and he spends a great deal of time thinking about the time dimension of familial life in which the partners develop their personalities in a continuing process. And this can only take place by introducing substantial things through which they experience each other. Relations that go places are always mediated. Perhaps at the outset the delight in sexuality provides the necessary mutual recognition and stimulation to emotional attachment. But Hegel was well aware that that is not substantial enough to last very long. Property is, though, and the administration and care for goods that a couple willy-nilly has to deal with offers in a sense a continual dialogue in which care for each other took on concrete form. And perhaps of another order, but still with the same function, children mediate a couple's relationship. So the actual form that any particular family takes over its lifetime is intimately tied up with its own property relations and its own experience in raising and caring for children. Parsons's relative disinterest in processes of meditation may well reflect an implicit recognition of the insubstantiality and fragility of what he formulates as the "nuclear family."

In considering how family/kinship has everything to do with politics, I find it useful to think in terms of political details, the formulation and reformulation of legal prescriptions, and both demands on the part of families for state intervention and state interests in developing policies that impinge on family life. There is a deep paradox in the formulations of Hegel and Parsons that opposed the family to the state. Both of them conceptualized a family that was structurally isolated—from kin, from neighborhood, and from political activity in the public sphere. Hegel's notion of mediation, however, and his sense of historical change, makes the unfolding of any particular family life contingent upon the constant intervention of the state in formulating and imposing regimes of property holding and devolution, sexual codes, and childhood.[114] Hegel tried to formulate a notion of the "family" that broke with older kinship structures, but what he mostly had in mind were forms that kept aristocracies and oligarchies in power. And they were buttressed by property devolution systems that gave particular families only temporary use rights to lineage holdings. His new understanding of property and family set the agenda for state formulation and reformulation of property law for the rest of the century. While he may have observed the corrupt practices of familial alliance in Württemberg during the late decades of the eighteenth century, he does not seem to have taken into account the restructuring of kinship around endogamous alliance throughout his contemporary society. That restructuring had everything to do with class formation and political culture during the nineteenth century. Paradoxically, he had little effect on kinship practices but significant influence in formulating a language of critique. Parsons's attempt to differentiate the nuclear family from all other kinship regimes also had political consequences, among which was an alliance between the new "class" of psychotherapists and the state in efforts to intervene wherever they thought to see a pathology. And he too failed to see the creation and re-creation of kinship networks to buttress strains and stresses of "isolated" family life.[115] Neither Hegel nor Parsons offer guides to understand the actual dynamics of family and kinship among their contemporaries, but both of them were crucial for establishing a language for differentiating the present from the past and their own societies from everywhere else. Both of them thought of the "family" as modern, offering a form that every society had to eventually adopt in order to compete on the plane of political and economic rationality. Extra kin just impeded progress, and lineage structures inhibited individual initiative. Their formulations have become part of state ideologies and tools for political and social intervention, but they often fitted observers with blinders to complex practices of kinship interaction.

David Warren Sabean is Henry J. Bruman Endowed Professor of German History Emeritus. His research interests incude microhistory, social history, and the history of kinship and incest. His publications include: *Power in the Blood: Popular Culture and Village Discourse in Early Modern Germany* (1984); *Property, Production, and Family in Neckarhausen, 1700–1870* (1990); and *Kinship in Neckarhausen, 1700–1870* (1998). He is coeditor of *Kinship in*

Europe: Approaches to Long-Term Development (1300–1900) (2007); *Sibling Relations and the Transformations of European Kinship 1300–1900* (2011); *Transregional and Transnational Families in Europe and Beyond: Experiences Since the Middle Ages* (2011); and *Blood and Kinship: Matter for Metaphor from Ancient Rome to the Present* (2013). During 2016–17, he codirected the interdisciplinary research group on kinship and politics at the Center for Interdiscplinary Research in Bielefeld. He is currently engaged in an extensive study on the history of incest discourse in Europe and America (1600 to the present).

Notes

1. John F. McLennan, *Primitive Marriage: An Inquiry into the Origin of the Form of Capture in Marriage Ceremonies*, ed. and intro. Peter Rivière (Chicago: University of Chicago Press, 1970 [1865]), 4, 48n, 63, seems to have put the modern spin on "kinship." See the *Oxford English Dictionary*, 2nd ed., s.v. "kinship."
2. See William K. Goode, *World Revolution and Family Patterns* (New York: Free Press, 1963) (the conjugal family helped create industrialization and modernization); Marion Levy, *Modernization and the Structure of Societies*, 2 vols. (Princeton, NJ: Princeton University Press, 1966) (the transition from a society based on kinship organization to one that is not is more far-reaching than any other type of changes including the industrial revolution); Alex Inkeles and David H. Smith, *Becoming Modern: Individual Change in Six Countries* (Cambridge, MA: Harvard University Press, 1974) (extended kinship relations cannot be adapted to modern industrial society).
3. For an understanding of the salient aspects of "kinship," see Maurice Godelier, *The Metamorphoses of Kinship*, trans. Nora Scott (London: Verso, 2011), 77–78.
4. See chapter 3, "The Politics of Incest and the Ecology of Alliance Formation," in David Warren Sabean, *Kinship in Neckarhausen, 1700–1870* (Cambridge: Cambridge University Press, 1998), 63–89.
5. For an early overview of debates about the nuclear family and extended kinship relations in the United States, see Bert N. Adams, "Isolation, Function, and Beyond: American Kinship in the 1960's," *Journal of Marriage and Family* 32 (1970).
6. Jack Goody, *The European Family: An Historico-anthropological Essay* (Oxford: Blackwell, 2000), 2–3: "There is no serious sense in which Europe, let alone capitalism, has invented the elementary or nuclear family or even the small household."
7. For the German, I used the text in the "Theorie Werkausgabe," published by Suhrkamp Verlag: G. W. F. Hegel, *Grundlinien der Philosophie des Rechts*, vol. 7, in *Werke in zwanzig Bänden* (Frankfurt a. M.: Suhrkamp, 1970). For the English: G. W. F. Hegel, *Elements of the Philosophy of Right*, trans. H. B. Nisbet, ed. Allen W. Wood (Cambridge: Cambridge University Press, 1991). All citations will be by section and paragraph to enable any reader to use any edition. H refers to notes taken by Hotho and G by Griesheim. The section on the Family is found in part 3, "Ethical Life," section 1, "The Family."
8. For an introduction and overview, see David Warren Sabean, *Property, Production, and Family in Neckarhausen* (Cambridge: Cambridge University Press, 1990), 88–94. See also Joachim Eibach and Inken Schmidt-Voges, eds., *Das Haus in der Geschichte Europas: Ein Handbuch* (Berlin: De Gruyter, 2015).
9. Par. 177 and par. 168, notes (in the German but not the English version). The English word *kinship* has its counterpart in the German *Verwandtschaft*, both important in anthropological texts. Hegel does not contrast *Familie* with *Verwandtschaft*.

10. Par. 172, H.
11. A Google Ngram search suggests that the term *nuclear family* was introduced just after World War II, about five years before *nuclear bomb* entered widespread use. The relative frequency of other terms has varied over the years, but *nuclear family* has remained by far the most common. *Nuclear family* also had a five-year lead on *nuclear bomb* and has remained far more popular. "Google Books Ngram Viewer," Google Books, Google, retrieved 15 April 2020 from https://books. google.com/ngrams.
12. Par. 166.
13. Par. 166.
14. Karin Hausen, "Die Polarisierung der 'Geschlechtscharaktere'—Eine Spiegelung der Dissoziation von Erwerbs- und Familienleben," in *Sozialgeschichte der Familie in der Neuzeit Europas*, ed. Werner Conze (Stuttgart: Ernst Klett Verlag, 1976).
15. Par. 166, H, G. "The difference between man and woman is the difference between animal and plant; the animal is closer in character to man, the plant to woman, for the latter is a more peaceful [process of] unfolding whose principle is the more indeterminate unity of feeling [*Empfindung*]. When women are in charge of government, the state is in danger, for their actions are based not on the demands of universality but on contingent inclination and opinion."
16. The 1592 German version: "Das ist ein Haußhaltung/ da etliche viel/ sampt dem das sie eigens haben/ under einem Haußvatter recht regieret werden."
17. Par. 158.
18. Par. 162.
19. Par. 162.
20. Par. 162.
21. Par. 161, G.
22. Par. 161–63.
23. Par. 168.
24. Par. 168 and 168, H.
25. Par. 168, H.
26. Par. 168, H.
27. Par. 168, H.
28. Addition to the German text, par. 168.
29. Par. 172, and the notes in the German edition.
30. See David Warren Sabean and Simon Teuscher, "Kinship in Europe: A New Approach to Long-Term Development," in *Kinship in Europe: Approaches to Long-Term Developments (1300–1900)*, ed. David Warren Sabean, Simon Teuscher, and Jon Mathieu (New York: Berghahn Books, 2007), 19–22.
31. For example, Karl Friedrich Pockels, *Ueber Gesellschaft, Geselligkeit und Umgang*, 3 vols. (Hannover: Gebrüder Hahn, 1813–17); Ernst Brandes, *Betrachtungen über das weibliche Geschlecht und dessen Ausbildung in dem geselligen Leben*, 3 vols. (Hannover: Gebrüder Hahn, 1802).
32. Friedrich Wilhelm Basilius von Ramdohr, *Venus Urania: Ueber die Natur der Liebe, über ihre Veredlung und Verschönerung*, 3 vols. (Leipzig: Georg Joachim Göschen, 1798).
33. Ramdohr, *Venus Urania*, 1:119, 144, 201. He drew the analogy of chemical affinity eleven years before Goethe did.
34. Ramdohr, *Venus Urania*, 1:127.
35. Ramdohr, *Venus Urania*, 1:135.
36. Ramdohr, *Venus Urania*, 1:155–56.
37. Ramdohr, *Venus Urania*, 1:206, 213.
38. Ramdohr, *Venus Urania*, 1:170.
39. Ramdohr, *Venus Urania*, 1:172.
40. Ramdohr, *Venus Urania*, 1:175.
41. Ramdohr, *Venus Urania*, 1:213.

42. Ramdohr, *Venus Urania*, 1:214, my emphasis.
43. Ramdohr, *Venus Urania*, 1:215.
44. Ramdohr, *Venus Urania*, 1:216.
45. Ramdohr, *Venus Urania*, 1:229.
46. Ramdohr, *Venus Urania*, 1:234, 236, 255–56.
47. Ramdohr, *Venus Urania*, 2:85.
48. Ramdohr, *Venus Urania*, 2:96.
49. Ramdohr, *Venus Urania*, 2:98.
50. Ramdohr, *Venus Urania*, 2:100.
51. Ramdohr, *Venus Urania*, 2:101.
52. Ramdohr, *Venus Urania*, 2:102.
53. Ramdohr, *Venus Urania*, 2:102.
54. Ramdohr, *Venus Urania*, 2:190.
55. Ramdohr, *Venus Urania*, 2:191.
56. Ramdohr, *Venus Urania*, 2:101–2.
57. Ramdohr, *Venus Urania*, 2:192.
58. Ramdohr, *Venus Urania*, 2:205.
59. Ramdohr, *Venus Urania*, 2:206.
60. Ramdohr, *Venus Urania*, 2:228.
61. Ramdohr, *Venus Urania*, 2:238.
62. Ramdohr, *Venus Urania*, 2:239.
63. Ramdohr, *Venus Urania*, 2:354.
64. G. W. F. Hegel, "Ueber die neueste innern Verhältnisse Württembergs besonders über die Gebrechen der Magistratsverfassung" (1798), in *Hegels Schriften zur Politik und Rechtsphilosophie*, in *Sämtliche Werke*, vol. 7, ed. Georg Lasson (Leipzig: F. Meiner, 1913).
65. The sections on bureaucrats are found in par. 277, 288–89, 291, 294.
66. Part C, par. 173.
67. Part B, par. 170.
68. Par. 172.
69. Par. 172, H.
70. Par. 172, H.
71. Par. 180.
72. Par. 180.
73. Par 180, H, G.
74. For one example of a very contentious issue in familial property law dealing with rights of women to ownership, see David Warren Sabean, "Allianzen und Listen: Die Geschlechtsvormundschaft im 18. und 19. Jahrhundert," in *Frauen in der Geschichte des Rechts: Von Frühen Neuzeit bis zur Gegenwart*, ed. Ute Gerhard (München: Verlag C. H. Beck, 1997).
75. Par. 173, 177.
76. Par. 173, H.
77. Par. 174–78.
78. Par. 181.
79. Par. 182.
80. Section 2, "Civil society," par. 182–84.
81. Par. 185.
82. Par. 184, H.
83. Par. 187, H.
84. Talcott Parsons, "The Kinship System of the Contemporary United States," *American Anthropologist*, no. 45 (1943).
85. Parsons, "Kinship System," 24. He was obviously riffing on an earlier piece by Davis and Lloyd Warner: Kingsley Davis and W. Lloyd Warner, "Structural Analysis of Kinship," *American Anthropologist* 39 (1937). The multilineal system meant that neither

spouse had any prescriptive ties to a particular line or lineage, and by that fact the pair was particularized and isolated.
86. Parsons, "Kinship System," 24.
87. Parsons, "Kinship System," 26.
88. Parsons, "Kinship System," 26.
89. Parsons, "Kinship System," 27.
90. Parsons, "Kinship System," 28.
91. Parsons, "Kinship System," 28. Many writers followed the idea of a break between generations, and while some called attention to help and aid from relatives, others emphasized the autonomy of the nuclear family household and thought of connection to "outsiders" as pathological. A case in point is an article by Ruth Albrecht, "The Parental Responsibilities of Grandparents," *Marriage and Family Living* 16 (1954): 201: "Responsibility denotes closeness but grandparents who take this away from the parents of the children may be punishing the second generation, may need personal response and ego-satisfaction, may need power over people, or may need something to do." If the household itself had grandparents in it, that was almost certainly a cause for tension. Marvin R. Koller, "Studies of Three-Generation Households," *Marriage and Family Living* 16 (1954): 205, argued that housing shortages frustrated many couples from founding their own separate households. "The three-generation household was recognized by most of the informants as a hazardous type of family living in which the combined virtues of a diplomat, statesman, and saint are needed," 206. Similar arguments were made for France: Dominique Ceccaldi, "The Family in France," *Marriage and Family Living* 16 (1954): 328. It is also interesting that at least until the end of the 1950s, family sociology focused for the most part on the married pair and neglected the dynamics of the family as a whole: see Winston Ehrmann, "A Review of Family Research in 1957," *Marriage and Family Living* 20 (1958). Ehrmann finds a consistent failure to consider children as fulfilling family roles and to ignore the "whole" family as a focus of research, 389.
92. Parsons, "Kinship System," 30.
93. Parsons, "Kinship System," 28–29.
94. A good example is offered by the writings of Edward Strecker, a practicing psychiatrist, Chairman of the Psychiatry Department of the University of Pennsylvania, consultant to the Surgeons General of the Army and Navy, and advisor to the Secretary of War: *Their Mothers' Sons: The Psychiatrist Examines an American Problem*, new ed. (Philadelphia: Lippincott, 1951). His concern was with young men broken by their war experience, and he blamed their condition on their mothers. He "discovered" a "pathological matriarchy" whereby mothers revel in "the emotional satisfaction, almost repletion, [they] derive ... from keeping [their] children paddling about in a kind of psychological amniotic fluid rather than letting them swim away with bold and decisive strokes of maturing from the emotional maternal womb." Strecker was instrumental for the development of considerable federal funding for the psychological professions.
95. Talcott Parsons, "The American Family: Its Relations to Personality and to the Social Structure," in *Family, Socialization and Interaction Process*, ed. Talcott Parsons and Robert F. Bales (Glencoe, IL: Free Press, 1955). Some thought that the reduction of functions to the personality or social-psychological made relations less binding and the family less stable. Thus the highest rate of divorce was in the United States: M. F. Nimkoff, "The Family in the United States," *Marriage and Family Living* 16 (1954): 395.
96. See also, Sidney E. Goldstein, "The Family as a Dynamic Factor in American Society," *Living* 2 (1940): 8; the family is that institution that meets "emotional and spiritual needs." "The shifting in emphasis from the biological and the economic to the emotional and ethical function of the family is so profound as to mark a new stage in the role of family development," 9. Florian Znaniecki, "The Changing Cultural Ideals of

the Family," *Marriage and Family Living* 3 (1941): 68. "The new family is indeed nothing more than a complex of strictly personal relations ...", 58. There were voices early on advocating against generalizing about *the* American family. M. F. Nimkoff, "The Family in the United States," despite the title of his article remarks on the heterogeneity of the US population and the difficulty in describing family life.

97. Parsons, "American Family," 3.
98. Parsons, "American Family," 7.
99. Parsons, "American Family," 9.
100. Parsons, "American Family," 13.
101. Thomas Piketty, *Capital in the Twenty-First Century*, trans. Arthur Goldhammer (Cambridge, MA: Harvard University Press, Belknap, 2014), characterizes Parsons as depicting "a middle-class society of managers in which inherited wealth played virtually no role. It is still quite popular today among baby boomers," 384. John P. Spiegel, *Marriage and Family Living* 16 (1954) argued that the dominant value orientations of US society are those of the "urban, Protestant, middle class," 10. "The middle class male's role in the occupational subsystem requires a large amount of time and energy away from the home." This role of the middle-class male could not be so well managed outside "a small, detached, nuclear family, living in isolation from other relatives." He goes on to say that almost all "variant families, whether of class, ethnic, religious, or regional origin, are in transition toward the middle-class family," 11.
102. Parsons, "American Family," 19.
103. Parsons, "American Family," 20.
104. Parsons, "American Family," 20–21.
105. Parsons, "American Family," 22–23.
106. Parsons, "American Family," 32–33
107. A good example is offered by Christopher Johnson, *Becoming Bourgeois: Love, Kinship, and Power in Provincial France, 1670–1880* (Ithaca, NY: Cornell University Press, 2015).
108. See Sabean, *Kinship*, 449–65.
109. An example is Adolf Stahr, *Aus der Jugendzeit: Lebenserinnerungen* (Schwerin: A. Hildebrand's Verlag, 1877), 1:10–11. Stahr describes the life of his "homo novus" father, a Prussian regimental chaplain. The fact that he had no kin around during his social climb meant continual humiliation from seeking favors from non-relatives and building obligation on what he considered to be an artificial foundation where he had no kin to aid his career.
110. A great deal of research was instigated by Marvin Sussman and Lee Burchinal, "Kin Family Network: Unheralded Structure in Current Conceptualizations of Family Functioning," *Marriage and Family Living* 24 (1962). A critique looking back over the sociological literature after Parson's formulation of the nuclear family is offered by Karen Hansen, *Not-So-Nuclear Families: Class, Gender, and Networks of Care* (New Brunswick, NJ: Rutgers University Press, 2005).
111. Robert F. Winch, "Permanence and Change in the History of the American Family and Some speculations as to its Future," *Journal of Marriage and Family* 32 (1970), differentiated among different kinds of families by ethnicity, religion, and region. See also Harry K. Schwarzweller, "Parental Family Ties and Social Integration of Rural to Urban Migrants," *Journal of Marriage and Family* 26 (1964). Stephanie Coontz, *The Way We Really Are: Coming to Terms with America's Changing Families* (New York: Basic Books, 1977), 119.
112. Hansen, *Not-So-Nuclear Families*, 1–22, summarizes the trends. Also very useful: Susan Thistle, *From Marriage to the Market: The Transformations of Women's Lives and Work* (Berkeley: University of California Press, 2006).
113. Piketty, *Capital*, 384, has interesting things to say about this kind of mobility and has observations about Parsons in particular.

114. One example might suffice. Early in the nineteenth century, the state of Württemberg imposed new demands on villagers to have children attend school. There were a number of small but significant changes that had implications for family life. Schoolmasters physically disciplined children who were not properly dressed or clean, which in turn put new demands on mothers to present the children according to new expectations. This was only one of a series of new demands on female labor, and it was in the first decades of the century when many husbands and wives fought over the expenditure of time and the use of resources. Indeed such conflicts led to a significant wave of separations and divorce. That was one consequence of novel interventions into familial life through defining the rules of child socialization. Fathers objected to schoolmasters disciplining children, which they saw as an attack on their own prerogatives—indeed their masculinity. And many thought that schooling took away time better spent on work in the family, which brought them into conflict with local state officials. The relationships between husbands and wives might be lived in part through their children, but what children were was never over time the same thing. See Sabean, *Property, Production and Family*, 110, 179–81, 323–24.
115. See Hansen, *Not-So-Nuclear-Family*, for an analysis of changing exigencies of child life and the construction and reconfiguration of kinship networks.

Bibliography

Adams, Bert N. "Isolation, Function, and Beyond: American Kinship in the 1960's." *Journal of Marriage and Family* 32 (1970): 575–95.
Albrecht, Ruth. "The Parental Responsibilities of Grandparents." *Marriage and Family Living* 16 (1954): 201–4.
Brandes, Ernst. *Betrachtungen über das weibliche Geschlecht und dessen Ausbildung in dem geselligen Leben*. 3 vols. Hannover: Gebrüder Hahn, 1802.
Ceccaldi, Dominique. "The Family in France." *Marriage and Family Living* 16 (1954): 326–30.
Coontz, Stephanie. *The Way We Really Are: Coming to Terms with America's Changing Families*. New York: Basic Books, 1977.
Davis, Kingsley, and W. Lloyd Warner. "Structural Analysis of Kinship." *American Anthropologist* 39 (1937): 291–313.
Ehrmann, Winston. "A Review of Family Research in 1957." *Marriage and Family Living* 20 (1958): 384–96.
Eibach, Joachim, and Inken Schmidt-Voges, eds. *Das Haus in der Geschichte Europas: Ein Handbuch*. Berlin: De Gruyter, 2015.
Godelier, Maurice. *The Metamorphoses of Kinship*. Translated by Nora Scott. London: Verso, 2011.
Goldstein, Sidney E. "The Family as a Dynamic Factor in American Society." *Living* 2 (1940): 8–11.
Goode, William K. *World Revolution and Family Patterns*. New York: Free Press, 1963.
Goody, Jack. *The European Family: An Historico-Anthropological Essay*. Oxford: Blackwell, 2000.
"Google Books Ngram Viewer." Google Books, Google. Retrieved 15 April 2020 from https://books.google.com/ngrams.

Hansen, Karen. *Not-So-Nuclear Families: Class, Gender, and Networks of Care.* New Brunswick, NJ: Rutgers University Press, 2005.
Hausen, Karin. "Die Polarisierung der 'Geschlechtscharaktere' — Eine Spiegelung der Dissoziation von Erwerbs- und Familienleben." In *Sozialgeschichte der Familie in der Neuzeit Europas*, edited by Werner Conze, 363–93. Stuttgart: Ernst Klett Verlag, 1976.
Hegel, G. W. F. *Grundlinien der Philosophie des Rechts.* In *Werke in zwanzig Bänden*, vol. 7. Frankfurt a. M.: Suhrkamp, 1970.
Hegel, G. W. F. *Elements of the Philosophy of Right.* Edited by Allen W. Wood. Translated by H. B. Nisbet. Cambridge: Cambridge University Press, 1991.
Hegel, G. W. F. "Ueber die neueste innern Verhältnisse Württembergs besonders über die Gebrechen der Magistratsverfassung." In *Hegels Schriften zur Politik und Rechtsphilosophie*. In *Sämtliche Werke*, vol. 7, 150–54. Edited by Georg Lasson. Leipzig: F. Meiner, 1913 [1798].
Inkeles, Alex, and David H. Smith. *Becoming Modern: Individual Change in Six Countries.* Cambridge, MA: Harvard University Press, 1974.
Johnson, Christopher. *Becoming Bourgeois: Love, Kinship, and Power in Provincial France, 1670–1880.* Ithaca, NY: Cornell University Press, 2015.
Koller, Marvin R. "Studies of Three-Generation Households." *Marriage and Family Living* 16 (1954): 205–6.
Levy, Marion. *Modernization and the Structure of Societies.* 2 vols. Princeton, NJ: Princeton University Press, 1966.
McLennan, John F. *Primitive Marriage: An Inquiry into the Origin of the Form of Capture in Marriage Ceremonies.* Edited and introduced by Peter Rivière. Chicago: University of Chicago Press, 1970 [1865].
Nimkoff, M. F. "The Family in the United States." *Marriage and Family Living* 16 (1954): 390–96.
Parsons, Talcott. "The American Family: Its Relations to Personality and to the Social Structure." In *Family, Socialization and Interaction Process*, edited by Talcott Parsons and Robert F. Bales, 3–33. Glencoe, IL: Free Press, 1955.
Parsons, Talcott. "The Kinship System of the Contemporary United States," *American Anthropologist* 45 (1943): 22–38.
Piketty, Thomas. *Capital in the Twenty-First Century.* Translated by Arthur Goldhammer. Cambridge, MA: Harvard University Press, Belknap, 2014.
Pockels, Karl Friedrich. *Ueber Gesellschaft, Geselligkeit und Umgang.* 3 vols. Hannover: Gebrüder Hahn, 1813–17.
Ramdohr, Friedrich Wilhelm Basilius von. *Venus Urania: Ueber dir Natur der Liebe, über ihre Veredlung und Verschönerung.* 3 vols. Leipzig: Georg Joachim Göschen, 1798.
Sabean, David Warren. *Property, Production, and Family in Neckarhausen.* Cambridge: Cambridge University Press, 1990.
———. "Allianzen und Listen: Die Geschlechtsvormundschaft im 18. und 19. Jahrhundert." In *Frauen in der Geschichte des Rechts: Von Frühen Neuzeit bis zur Gegenwart*, edited by Ute Gerhard, 460–79. Munich: Verlag C. H. Beck, 1997.
———. *Kinship in Neckarhausen, 1700–1870.* Cambridge: Cambridge University Press, 1998.
Sabean, David Warren, and Simon Teuscher. "Kinship in Europe: A New Approach to Long-Term Development." In *Kinship in Europe: Approaches to*

Long-Term Developments (1300–1900), edited by David Warren Sabean, Simon Teuscher, and Jon Mathieu, 1–32. New York: Berghahn Books, 2007.

Schwarzweller, Harry K. "Parental Family Ties and Social Integration of Rural to Urban Migrants." *Journal of Marriage and Family* 26 (1964): 410–16.

Spiegel, John P. "New Perspectives in the Study of the Family." *Marriage and Family Living* 16 (1954): 4–12.

Stahr, Adolf. *Aus der Jugendzeit. Lebenserinnerungen.* 2 vols. Schwerin: A. Hildebrand's Verlag, 1877.

Strecker, Edward. *Their Mothers' Sons: The Psychiatrist Examines an American Problem.* New ed. Philadelphia: Lippincott, 1951.

Sussman, Marvin, and Lee Burchinal. "Kin Family Network: Unheralded Structure in Current Conceptualizations of Family Functioning." *Marriage and Family Living* 24 (1962): 231–40.

Thistle, Susan. *From Marriage to the Market: The Transformations of Women's Lives and Work.* Berkeley: University of California Press, 2006.

Winch, Robert F. "Permanence and Change in the History of the American Family and Some Speculations as to Its Future." *Journal of Marriage and Family* 32 (1970): 6–15.

Znaniecki, Florian. "The Changing Cultural Ideals of the Family." *Marriage and Family Living* 3 (1941): 58–62.

Chapter 7

Conceptualizing Kinship in Sixteenth-Century Political Theories
Bodin's and Hotman's Ideas of Monarchy

Julia Heinemann

In the second half of the sixteenth century, the French monarchy endured eight successive wars that scholars have characterized as civil wars or Wars of Religion. These were violent conflicts between a multitude of different protagonists and factions, both Catholics and Protestants, as well as combinations of both. Religious arguments stemming from the Reformation fueled the conflicts, but they should nevertheless be understood in the context of an ongoing debate about the nature of the monarchy and the roles of the nobility, political institutions, various sources of law, and the king and the royal family. This period is usually described by scholars as the "most serious crisis of the French state and society before the Revolution."[1] At the same time, it is often considered the beginning of absolutism—understood as a strengthening and widening of the king's authority—and thus of the modern state.

Both Catholics and Protestants questioned the foundation of the king's authority, and jurists developed conflicting political theories on the monarchy.[2] Although these debates were not entirely new and had troubled the monarchy since the late Middle Ages, they became increasingly intense during the Wars of Religion. Two central theories from this context remain of particular significance for the history of political thought, both widely received and debated not only within their authors' immediate political and religious circles but also by their adversaries. In 1573, the Calvinist François Hotman published *Francogallia*, in which he argued that sovereignty primarily lay with the people, that the king's authority should be restrained by the institutions and the law, and that a right of resistance existed in cases of tyrannical rule. In 1576, the Catholic

Jean Bodin published *Les Six Livres de la République* (*The Six Books of the Commonwealth*), in which he developed a concept of indivisible royal sovereignty holding the kingdom together and argued for the strong authority of the king and against any kind of right of resistance.[3] Bodin and Hotman are often seen as antagonists and obviously were in many ways.[4] They had different understandings of sovereignty, of rightful rule, and of the ideal form of government. While Hotman favored a mixed state that combined monarchic, aristocratic and democratic elements, Bodin found this idea absurd and advocated a dynastic monarchy. They also argued their cases in different ways: Hotman's work was casuistic and empirical, and he explicitly resolved not to say anything universal about politics while confining himself to the historical origins of the French monarchy, the tradition of "Francogallia"; meanwhile Bodin set out to develop "a universal science of politics."[5] While Hotman was mostly interested in French—or rather "Francogallican"—customary law, Bodin put natural and Roman law at the center of his argument.

Nonetheless, there are also some striking similarities between Hotman's and Bodin's theories, personal backgrounds, biographies, political aims, and even (to a certain point) understandings of law and history. Both authors wanted to put an end to violence and to the religious wars and saw their theories as answers to the current political crisis.[6] Both works might in their own way be considered representative of the legal, religious, and political debate. They must be situated within the context of the intense jurisprudential discussions on Roman law, customary law, and the French constitution that were prevalent at the universities and that strongly influenced political arguments in the sixteenth century.[7] Hotman and Bodin were trained jurists who simultaneously engaged intimately in the political and religious conflicts: for some years both were close to the reformist chancellor Michel de l'Hospital, who shaped French politics in the 1560s.[8] Both were also influenced by the growing skepticism of contemporaries like Michel de Montaigne and many other writers, jurists, and legal humanists who had started to doubt the existence of any universals in human nature, law, and history. They came to consider politics, law, and history subject to almost endless mutability, variability, and particularity.[9] Thus, both Hotman and Bodin acknowledged that reality was constantly changing and often disordered and "detached from the universal principles of divine and natural law,"[10] but they also found different answers to this problem, as their political theories show. And moreover, like most learned men at the time, they were more or less openly misogynistic, arguing (although on somewhat different grounds) for excluding women from politics.[11]

While Bodin is often considered the mastermind of absolutism and the modern state (as in the historiography on absolutism, the concept of sovereignty is central to the building of modern states), modern scholars describe Hotman as "one of the first modern revolutionaries" and a "pre-democratic" architect of constitutionalism.[12] In present-day political theory and history of political thought, both works are thus seen as paving the way for modern understandings of the political, and both writers are seen, in a way, as prophets of modernity. Such characterizations have probably distracted scholars from how much both theorists relied on kinship—which is today often seen as at cross-purposes with public political life—to develop their political arguments. The two authors discussed relationships between parents and children, between husbands and wives, between uncles and nephews, and between the king and his state. They thought of political relations and mechanisms in terms of blood, love, and inheritance. Apparently, notions of kinship and of the family were useful categories for framing ideas of the political in the sixteenth century whether one took a "constitutionalist" or "absolutist" perspective.[13] Focusing on these notions offers new perspectives for political theory about interdependencies of nature, law, and kinship in early modern political thinking. Thus, reading the texts through the lens of kinship can upset some older understandings of political thinking at the beginning of modernity that were based on key terms like sovereignty, absolutism, and constitutionalism that political historians tended to produce and project back.

This chapter explores ways of defining and using kinship relations and family models in order to frame political concepts of the monarchy. By comparing and contextualizing these two important sixteenth-century political theories, I discuss the impact understandings of kinship relations had on political ideas that were central to scholarly debates about absolutism, sovereignty, and state building in the early modern period. In doing so, I highlight the interdependencies of concepts of kinship, law, nature, property, and the political. My aim is to show how concepts of kinship and the family shaped politics not only in the practice—as may be observed in the dynastic state—but also in some influential theories of the period.[14]

I use the term *kinship* here in a broad sense to encompass all the kinds of relationships that people may consider to exist between relatives. Kinship relations may be considered as social practices but also as something to think with, and this second perspective is at the center of my argument.[15] I do not assume that kinship has a universal meaning, whether blood, or alliance, or emotional bonds. The question is what kinship is to different people, how they understand it, and how relatedness is produced.[16] The same goes for the "family"—a concept that we tend to see as a smaller section of a broader kinship network, in the sense of the nuclear family, but which was not self-evident for people in the French monarchy of the sixteenth century.

I first describe Hotman's and Bodin's personal backgrounds and positions in order to situate their works within the context of the French monarchy and the events, factions, and debates of the Wars of Religion. Then, I analyze and compare their writings from three systematic perspectives: how they depicted the relationship between the family and the state, the particular concepts of kinship relations underlying their understandings of the political, and the specific role of property, inheritance, and succession in their theories.

Becoming a Published Author, Balancing Positions: François Hotman and Jean Bodin

François Hotman was born in 1524. His Parisian family of Silesian origin had obtained its position through venal judicial offices (positions aquired by paying a fee to the state).[17] By converting to Calvinism around 1544, Hotman decisively distanced himself from his family. He had begun his law studies at the University of Orléans at the age of fifteen and returned to Paris in 1540, where he met Charles du Moulin, a future Protestant and famous jurist who argued for a uniform French customary law modeled on that of Paris.[18] Hotman, who had studied Roman law, sympathized with the idea of a single French code based on customary law. He became a teacher at the Parisian faculty of canon law in 1546 but in 1548 left for Geneva, where he met John Calvin and Theodore Beza (the latter of whom he already knew from Orléans). For a few months, Hotman worked for Calvin as a secretary and became part of his inner circle.[19] Toward the end of the 1540s, he married Claude Aubelin, a French Calvinist, and published several humanist and legal works. By then, he had entered the transnational Protestant communicative circle, defending Calvinists against accusations of heresy and arguing against canon law and the papacy.[20]

As a jurist, Hotman should be seen as part of a legal humanist school that interpreted law from a historical perspective.[21] He held chairs of law in Strasbourg, Valence, and Bourges in the 1550s and 1560s and published many works on Roman law and history during these years. After the Tumult of Amboise in March 1560, Hotman began to work on Protestant theories of resistance. He served as an intermediary between the Bourbons, defenders of the Protestant cause in France, and the German Protestant princes.[22]

It is not easy to grasp Hotman's positions or to give a systematic account of his publications since he changed his arguments over time. In the 1560s, he was close to Michel de l'Hospital and his ideas for a legal reform of French law. After the St. Bartholomew's Day Massacre in 1572, Hotman again fled to Geneva (and would remain in Switzerland until his death in 1590).[23] The Latin version of the *Francogallia* was published there in 1573, although he probably wrote it in 1567. While the concept of popular sovereignty had already been developed by various writers in the early sixteenth century, the *Francogallia* differed from other Protestant political theory in its emphasis on constitutional custom and a Francogallican past.[24] Hotman argued that contemporary political problems resulted from an attack on the constitution by Louis XI and that they could be solved by turning to the past when the Franks, in his account, "had freed the Gauls from Roman tyranny."[25]

The book immediately was circulated widely, especially among Calvinists.[26] Two revised editions were published in 1576 and 1586, each including new chapters that directly responded to current political changes. The 1576 version expanded the description of the "public council," the "democratic" institution in Francogallia.[27] The 1586 version seems to have been a reaction to Jean Bodin's *République*, as well as to the succession crisis of 1584 when Francis, the king's brother and supposed successor to the throne, died, leaving the Protestant Henry of Navarre the next candidate in line.[28] In 1584, Henry asked Hotman to develop a legal response on the problem of succession since the argument about an elective monarchy that he had developed in the *Francogallia* had quickly been adopted by his Catholic League political opponents who supported a different candidate for the throne, Henry's uncle Charles de Bourbon. Now, therefore, Hotman argued for a hereditary royal succession, even though the rest of the text could be read as an attack on a dynastic, hereditary logic.[29]

While there is still not much historiography on Hotman, a great deal of research has been done on Jean Bodin, although his biography still remains somewhat obscure.[30] He was born in Angers in 1530 into a humbler family than Hotman's: his father was a wealthy tailor. Bodin probably entered the Carmelite order and was educated there, but he left in 1548 (possibly because of accusations of heresy). In 1550, he began the study of law in Toulouse, where he later taught Roman law and published some shorter treatises on law. Like Hotman, Bodin defended the new legal humanist school that interpreted law from a historical perspective. However, he wanted to integrate Roman law into comparative jurisdiction and was interested in universal principles of law.[31]

In 1561, Bodin went to Paris, where he became an *avocat* (advocate) at the Parlement and soon made contact with future leading protagonists of the Wars of Religion, which would begin in 1562.³² Like Hotman, he sympathized with the chancellor Michel de l'Hospital and his ideas of reforming French law during those years. In 1567, he became deputy *procurateur du roi* (prosecutor) in Poitiers. During this time, Bodin seems to have experienced a turbulent period of religious uncertainty and was incarcerated in 1570 *pour fait de religion* (for acts of religion), under suspicion of Protestantism.³³ In 1576, he married a wealthy widow, Françoise Trouillard, whose relatives were associated with the king's younger brother Francis. While Hotman declined an offer of patronage from Francis during this period, Bodin became part of his entourage.³⁴ Francis was considered one of the leaders of the faction of *malcontents*, including both Calvinists and moderate Catholics, who hoped for a pragmatic solution of the religious conflicts. During the Estates General of 1576, Bodin was an elected representative of the Third Estate and spoke openly against any continuation of violence against Huguenots. In the same year, his monumental *Six Books of the Commonwealth* appeared in print and immediately was a great success.³⁵ Unlike Hotman, Bodin wrote his treatise in French. He argued that the family was both the source and the image of the state and based the concept of indivisible sovereignty of the king on the figure of the paterfamilias and his supreme authority.³⁶

In the following years, Bodin was—like many during this period—associated with different factions and protagonists in the Wars of Religion. Although the historiography on Bodin is strongly dominated by his classification as a prophet of absolutism, he can actually be even more difficult to pin down than Hotman. In 1584, Hotman was working on a legal justification for Henry of Navarre, and Bodin became the latter's adviser. In 1587, he became *procureur du roi* in Laôn, but by the late 1580s, when the extreme Catholic League dominated the city, he got into trouble for his supposed association with the Calvinist party and had to openly declare his support for the Catholics.³⁷

This short biographical summary already shows that Bodin and Hotman cannot be reduced to antagonistic figures. The differences and similarities in their theories can be worked out by exploring how they defined and used kinship relations in elaborating their political theories.

Family and State: Defining and Describing Relationships

Due to his understanding of law and of philosophy, Jean Bodin filled the *République* with analogies and often followed a pars pro toto logic.³⁸ The most important relationship was that between the family and the state, which was crucial for Bodin's whole theory.[39] He considered the family the source of, model for, and image of the state. Thus, "the household is a rightful government of several subjects, under the obedience of a head of the family, and of those things which are their property," and, by analogy, "the commonwealth is a rightful government of several households, and of those things which are common to them, with sovereign power."[40] But while families could exist without states, the state could not exist without families[41]: this is why it was so important for Bodin to consider both the family and the state in his attempt to create a universal science of politics.[42]

Bodin used the words *mesnage*, household, and *famille*, family, more or less interchangeably in his theory. He usually called the father *chef de famille*, but also mixed both terms in phrases like "the household cannot bear more than one head … if there were several heads, their commandments would be in conflict and the family in endless trouble."[43] In defining the family in this way, Bodin positioned himself in a tradition of economic literature established by classical authors such as Aristotle and Xenophon, who had already described the household as the foundation of the state and a political microcosm.[44] Anna Becker has recently highlighted this tradition, which has been rather neglected by scholars interested in political ideas and the emergence of a concept of sovereignty.[45] Both late medieval texts on economics and Protestant economic literature contemporary with Bodin followed these perspectives, and Bodin's family model must be seen in this Aristotelian tradition of a household composed of a man and wife, their children, and their servants. It is a restricted version of the family, though, since *famille* was a polysemous term in sixteenth-century French and could also refer to a larger group of relatives.[46]

However, there is a striking difference between Bodin's ideas and these economic texts that can only be seen when the structure of the household, as described by Bodin, is analyzed more closely. As Bodin explained, "I understand by the running of the household the rightful government of the family, and the power of the head of the family over his dependents, and the obedience due to him."[47] This (male) authority inside the family was the crucial element of "Bodin's Universe."[48] It was the key to his concept of sovereignty, which held the state together. He described four forms of domestic government: the power of the husband over his wife, the power of the father over his children, the power of the lord (*seigneur*) over his slaves, and the power of the master (*maistre*) over his servants.[49] The authoritative figure of the *chef de famille* or paterfamilias (the term in the Latin version) actually integrated all four relationships—in a way, the father was also the husband and so on. Thus, the father as paradigm for the sovereign was mostly based on the relationship between husband and wife:[50] Bodin immediately noted that there were no longer slaves in France, and he was not overly concerned about the role of the servants in his following arguments.

However, in late medieval and sixteenth-century political theories on house and household, the structure of the household was more complex, as these had included the mother in the distribution of power.[51] The Protestant *Oeconomia Christiana* (like Justus Menius's) equally considers the household as a microcosm of the political world, characterized by relationships of power and obedience.[52] But while as wife the woman was under the authority of her husband, as mother of the household she had command over her children and over the servants too,[53] a powerful position that conflicted with Bodin's argument of indivisible sovereignty. Therefore, he stressed repeatedly that there should not be more than one head of a household or a commonwealth, carefully avoided writing about mothers in his text, and did not really distinguish between the figures of the father and the husband. From his perspective, wives, children, servants, and slaves were all different elements of the same phenomenon—the governed, or the subjects. Their opposite was the paterfamilias, who had sole and indivisible authority; thus, "the family already bears the structure of sovereignty in it."[54] Sovereignty, according to Bodin, was the foundation of the state and characterized as "the absolute and perpetual power of a commonwealth, which the Latins call 'majestatem,'" and especially as the power to make and unmake law.[55]

Bodin's conceptualization of the family as the source, model, and image of the state thus seems to exemplify a phenomenon that mathematicians would describe as self-similarity: a structure in which every element has the same form and structure as the object as a whole, or in which an object consists of smaller copies of itself.[56] But when looked at more closely, this image cannot fully capture Bodin's *République*. The state included more than just families: magistrates, for example, played an important role for Bodin. When the father left his household, he became a subject and lost his authority as paterfamilias.[57] While the family was the rule of one person over other persons, the state was the rule of one person over several families.[58] Thus, one can usually read Bodin's statements on the family as statements on the order of the state—but one cannot always understand his comments on the state as comments on the family. Nevertheless, close interdepedencies between family models and ideas of the state characterized his argument.

Hotman was not very interested in the analogies and relations between family and state characteristic of Bodin's thought. Indeed, he seems to have carefully avoided precise statements on this topic: his aim was, rather, to show that the kingdom and the king must be seen in relation to each other but are not the same. "For it is so disposed that the king is a unique and individual person in so far as he is the ruler, and he is, as it were, the head of the commonwealth; whereas the kingdom is the very totality of the citizens and subjects, and is, so to speak, the body of the commonwealth."[59] The body metaphor employed here—the king as head and the kingdom as body—was also used several times by Bodin and was a current theme of political literature in the medieval and early modern period that pointed at (hierarchical) forms of belonging and relations between the whole and its parts.[60] Hotman used it as an argument about several equally important elements in the state, of which the king was one, each unable to exist without the others.

In two passages, Hotman made an (implicit) comparison between the king and a husband and father that at first sight resembles Bodin's arguments. First, he compared the king's relationship to the royal domain to that of a husband to his wife's dowry.[61] By this he meant that a king could only have usufruct of the royal domain, just as a husband could never alienate any part of his wife's dowry. While Hotman likewise made use of the relationship between husband and wife, his focus lay on the restrictions it imposed on the husband's authority. The passage concerning the king as father was even more significant in this sense. Hotman explained that

> the king has the same relationship with the kingdom as a father with his family, a tutor with his student, a guardian with his ward, a pilot with the passengers and travelers on a ship, the pastor with a flock, and a commander with his army. Therefore, just as the pupil is not created for his tutor, nor the ship for the pilot, nor the flock for the pastor, nor the army for the commander, but, on the contrary, all these latter are appointed for the former, so the people are not found and procured for the sake of the king, but rather the king for the people.[62]

This is partly the same analogy as Bodin's, but rather than using it to assert the supreme authority of the king (or the father, or the commander, etc.) Hotman's point was that the reason for the latter's existence had to do with those who obeyed him or who were under his protection. Taking up the body metaphor, one could say that Bodin thought from head to toe while Hotman thought from toe to head.

The difference becomes even more nuanced when looking closer at Hotman's use of the word *family*. Neither Bodin nor Hotman used words for *kinship* as an abstract term or as a designation for a social group (like *parentela, parenté, parentelle*)—only expressions for specific kinship figures or positions, like father, agnate, or cousin. However, both used the word *family*. The analogy employed in Hotman's statement above, "The king has the same relationship with the kingdom as a father with his family," points to a possible equation of the kingdom and the family resembling Bodin's analogy. But Hotman left aside the Aristotelian version. His rare mentions of the family were usually in the context of the Francogallican past, as when he stated that there had only been three "dynasties *(familias)* of kings."[63] Hotman's use of the term seems to be consistent with the definition given by Jean Nicot's 1606 French dictionary *Le Thresor de la langue francoyse tant ancienne que moderne*: "race, Familia, Gens."[64] It designated a larger group of relatives and, while it did not necessarily imply patrilineality, it tended to rely on it by mentioning *race*.[65] In the *Francogallia* particular relationships like the one between father and son or between husband and wife thus became part of a broader picture of kinship relations, an integral element of Francogallican history and customs in Hotman's theory. They did not necessarily have anything to do with the state in the sense of a model or an analogy but were sometimes used as metaphors of authority and hierarchies. While analogies were Bodin's main rhetorical tools for *defining* relations, Hotman tended to rely more on *descriptive* metaphors and examples to paint a picture of *Francogallia*.[66]

This initial comparison of Hotman's and Bodin's theories shows that the mere use of family models or kinship relations in political theories does not necessarily lead to the same argument. Furthermore, the same analogy, like that between father and king, can be a way of arguing for or against strong royal authority. Kinship relations and family models are primarily a flexible way of expressing relationships of power or relationships between the whole and its parts. To understand the differences, one needs to take a closer look at how Hotman and Bodin imagined kinship relations and how those understandings shaped their political ideas.

Love, Conflict, Nature: Imagining Kinship Relations

What was Bodin's specific idea of the family? I have already mentioned the four power relationships and the sole authority of the paterfamilias. But Bodin had more to say about the architecture of the family: a family needs at least three members in addition to the paterfamilias and a woman: five persons in total.[67] But Bodin's point was not about an exact number, and a family could in fact even be bigger than a state.[68] It was also not necessary for family members to live under the same roof.[69] Thus, family was not about physical proximity—an understanding that differed from other sixteenth-century economic literature that not only dealt with the hierarchies and ideal of peace within the house but also emphasized common economy in the sense of people working together to obtain what they need to make a living.[70] Instead, Bodin's argument centered on the relationships of power within the family and the interplay of authority and obedience. His description of the father figure was closely based on the patria potestas in Roman law, where he insisted that a father's authority extended to the right of life and death over his children.[71] It turns out that he was not interested in flesh and blood as a medium to designate kinship relations. Relationships within the family model were, rather, a question of power, command, and will, which characterized the family as a political sphere.[72]

Bodin's idea of the family was rather rigid and abstract and aimed to reduce complexity. It was based on divine and natural law, "la loy de Dieu et de nature."[73] This enabled him to understand the family as a universal model whose fundamental task was to create order. Once more, the link to the state was crucial, and Bodin argued that a healthy state can only be founded on healthy families.[74] Following this logic, he explained why he favored monarchic government: The problem with democracies and aristocracies was that they had more than one head, which, like divided authority in a family, only led to conflict. Thus, Bodin's rigid, schematic family model could be used to criticize other forms of government; only in a monarchy with one ruler could real sovereignty exist, just as in a household there could only be one *chef de famille*.[75]

Bodin never argued that this form of *mesnage* already existed: it was an abstract model that was to be the source and image of the commonwealth. So what did his family model not take into consideration? Bodin lived during wartime and was surely aware of the contemporary reality of many households without a mother or a father, but he never mentioned the possibility of single-parent households and whether they played a role in his notion of the state. As I have argued before, he only referred to mothers in the household in a few passages of his work. Other relatives did not occur in Bodin's family model, which was restricted to the married couple and their children and servants. But there was another side to the coin: stories about historical princely families or about the French royal family fill many pages in his work even while remaining strangely unconnected to his family model.[76] In that context, the understanding of kinship relations differed significantly from the family model. This might seem inconsistent at first sight, but I argue that these two understandings validate each other and should be situated in the contemporary context of law and nature: they are due to Bodin's perception of a constantly changing secular world, for which he sought a universal answer. The family model and the stories about kinship relations in princely families were connected to two different concepts of nature found in the *République*.

When Bodin dealt with lived kinship relations (not reduced to the schematic family model) in the *République*, he described murderous mothers, rivalrous brothers, disobedient children, and excessive, irrational parents. For example, parents might kill their children in the heat of passion.[77] The problem of disobedient children was of special importance to Bodin. Filial obedience was to be maintained under all circumstances, even when a father acted against the law and the state itself. Familial order was the only stable element in times of war.[78] Thus, Bodin considered parricide the worst crime imaginable. The same argument was used by contemporary jurists against the right of resistance in comparing parricide to the murder of the king, the father of the kingdom.[79] By writing about disobedient children and parricide, and by stating that insubordination was never justified, Bodin also implicitly positioned himself against the right of resistance, even in the case of a tyrannical king. The sovereign ruler was untouchable, "even if he was an evil and cruel tyrant."[80] But there was another argument against parricide: "although parricide is in itself detestable, it is even more pernicious because of its consequences: if you pay tribute to someone who kills his father for whatever reason, how could anyone be safe from his brothers or his close relatives?"[81] Without punishment, murdering a father could be contagious, spreading like a disease among kin. Notions of contagion in kinship relations were used to argue against the right of resistance and for the untouchable authority of a king. It was only logical that children were obliged to love their parents: as Bodin puts it, in the end it is their love and obedience that guarantees a rightful use of authority by the paterfamilias.[82]

Bodin was well aware that the relationship of love between parents and children carried risks. On the one hand, it ensured that a father never abused his authority—here Bodin took up a contemporary discourse focusing on perfect maternal love and transferred it to the father.[83] The reader was supposed to understand that a sovereign would likewise never be unjust to his subjects because of his love for them. On the other hand, the love that parents have for their children means that they often do not punish them sufficiently. This, Bodin explained, was why it was so important that the father have the right of life and death over his children: to reinstate his power despite the obstacle of love.[84] And there are even more potential conflicts. Bodin noted that everywhere in history there had been murderous mothers, and he mentions sibling rivalry, especially between brothers, several times.[85] Kinship could be a hotbed of envy and jealousy, especially in the case of princely families and their conflicts over inheritance and succession.[86]

What was the purpose of all the stories about kinship and conflict? As Daniel Engster has shown, Bodin agreed with many skeptics of his generation (like Hotman) that human history was characterized by great uncertainty, variability, and mutability—an unsurprising outlook in the context of the Wars of Religion.[87] Accordingly, he doubted that comparisons of human laws and human history could be a source of universal principles of law or natural order.[88] Thus, in the *République* Bodin rarely tried to deduce universal rules from all those different stories. Instead, he acknowledged that "houses" ("*maisons*," used in the sense of dynasties) might have their own particular laws or even, as in the case of the House of Saxony, several *chefs de famille*.[89] And he insisted that "one has to diversify the state of the commonwealth according to the diversity of the localities, following the example of a good architect who adjusts his building to the materials he finds on site."[90] From this perspective, kinship was associated with conflicts and emotions. It was dangerously real. And the historical record made this very clear.[91] This points to Bodin's underlying general understanding of kinship as an area with great potential for conflict.

Despite the variability of actual families and states, unlike many of his contemporaries (like Hotman, as I will show), Bodin did not turn away from universal principles of law, but he did not try to find them in human history and changing reality. Instead, he derived them from divine and natural law, which he considered to be embodied in the family model with its hierarchies.[92] God and nature were universal authorities that could not be questioned. Thus, the family model became an answer to Bodin's fear of disorder, of excessive emotions between parents and children, of murderous dynamics between relatives. By conceptualizing the family as a microcosm with relationships of power and obedience, Bodin offered an alternative and a solution to the current political crisis. In accordance with his methodological approach from general to particular, all the stories of rivalry and conflicts affirmed the necessity of the family model.[93]

Bodin's family model was abstract and universal, based on natural and Roman law, whereas lived kinship relations were chaotic, subject to change, and connected to particular customs and human laws. He did not have a unified concept of kinship underlying his theory: there were at least two kinds at work. Accordingly, two different natures appear in the *République*. One is in the sense of natural law, *loy de nature*, which referred to God and was understood as universal, normative principles standing above all human particularities, showing what ought to be.[94] The family model was the manifestation of this natural order: "the family is a natural community."[95] The other nature, however, was utterly secular: subject to change and an object of observation. Thus, Bodin included a section called "Nurture Goes Beyond Nature" ("La nourriture passe nature"), in which he turned to humoral pathology, to geography, to human customs, and to the social life of animals to show "how much power nurture, the laws, the customs have to change nature."[96] From this perspective, there could be nothing universal about real, particular kinship relations.

Hotman shared Bodin's vision of a constantly changing human history and the particularity of human laws. But he did not turn to natural or Roman law to solve the problem of human disorder and variability.[97] Instead, he explained in the preface of the *Francogallia* that "in reflecting upon these great calamities I have … fixed my attention on what is revealed by all the old French and German historians of our Francogallia, and from their writings I have compiled a summary of its constitution."[98] Thus, looking at customary law and history offered him a way out of political disorder. Given his approach, Hotman had to differentiate neither between an abstract family model and lived, changing kinship relations nor between two natures. When he maintained that "the king has the same relationship with the kingdom as a father with his family," the analogy could imply a variety of kinship relations based on empirical observations and judged on the basis of their regular practice and their capacity for ordering political mechanisms.

In general, Hotman's *Francogallia* was not much concerned with explaining the characteristics and problems of kinship relations. Since he generally argued against hereditary monarchy, he stressed education as more important than birth and filiation in the choice of a king. As he put it, "Just as hunters prefer a dog or a horse that is itself a fine animal to one that is of fine breeding, so those who constitute a commonwealth make a great mistake if they seek birth before quality in a prince."[99] He noted that during the time of the Capetian dynasty, the people elected kings that "were born of royal blood and were instructed and educated in a royal manner."[100] This points to an understanding of lineages and transfers of royalty as being reproduced mainly by education and not (or only secondarily) by filiation: *nourriture* (nurture) was the contemporary term for this, as we have seen in Bodin's writings on this topic. In this context, in fact, Bodin's argument was quite similar. Hotman positioned himself in favor of *nourriture* over birth in the contemporary discussion on the quality of nobility.[101] This conformed to his understanding that it was the role of custom and practice, rather than universal natural law, to shape the political order: if kinship relations could change with *nourriture*, then it was necessary to turn to the past to look for lessons.

In later passages of his work, Hotman found it necessary to argue for a hereditary monarchy. Here, blood played a role in defining patrilineality and succession. His argument resembled that of Bodin, who was generally not interested in blood but turned to it in his discussion of succession, as I will show. Hotman entertained the possibility of adoption (as Bodin had also done), acknowledging that in the past it was quite possible for royal families to adopt strangers.[102] His emphasis on education and the possibility of adoption suggests a rather flexible concept of kinship relations subject to change. Kinship relations in the *Francogallia* were not necessarily concerned with a strict patrilineal structure, nor were they based on laws of nature or universal claims. "Nature" only occasionally appears in the *Francogallia*, and Hotman was not very concerned with this concept. Perhaps he avoided writing about it so as not to weaken his argument. Custom and practice were the key terms in his political theory. Even the exclusion of women from the government was not based on natural law but just a common practice that needed no further explanation.[103] Nonetheless, Hotman did insist that Francogallia ought to return to "its ancient and, so to speak, its natural state."[104] In this respect, nature referred to the past: an ideal and original order that was now lost but could be reinstated by studying this particular past. While Bodin distanced himself from historical realities, Hotman placed himself in the tradition of the "maiores nostri."[105]

When it came to potential conflicts within a family, Hotman saw the problem as with the parents rather than the children, which supported his understanding of popular sovereignty and a necessary restriction of royal authority. Even though royal parents were "moved by ambition for their sons," which normally led them to secure their succession, it was important to make sure that they also could not deprive their children of succession.[106] He was especially concerned in this context with mothers, but he had a problem with ruling women in general.[107] Both Bodin and Hotman concurred in this judgment: it was no coincidence that both wrote during the regencies and rule of the powerful queen mother Catherine de' Medici. When Hotman mentioned mothers, they were usually abusive and greedy for power. The famous thirteenth-century French queen regent Blanche, the mother of Saint Louis, who was usually praised even by learned men, was an ambivalent figure for Hotman since she had provoked armed conflict by asserting her authority against the nobility.[108] There is also a strange passage in the *Francogallia* about another mother, the sixth-century queen Clothild, the mother of the kings Childebert and Lothar and thus of the Merovingian family. Clothild, Hotman states, "favoured with a love akin to madness the sons of another of her sons ... and she caused a very great dispute by trying to exclude her surviving sons and promoting their nephews to royal dignity." The threat of excessive love, against which Bodin also warned, was attributed by Hotman to mothers, not fathers. It had made this particular mother act against the will of the people:

> She took the greatest care to nourish their long hair. When the two royal brothers were informed of her intention [of putting her grandsons on the throne], they at once sent a certain Arcadius to her, who offered her a naked sword and a pair of scissors and made her choose which she preferred to have applied to the heads of her grandsons. "But she, says Gregory of Tours, "was choked by excess of gall, especially when she saw the unsheathed sword and scissors, and in her bitterness replied: 'I should rather see them dead than shorn if they are not to be raised to the throne.'" Thus, each of her grandsons was killed before her eyes.[109]

The ambition and unnatural, excessive love of a mother was dangerous both for the royal family and for the kingdom. In this particular episode, it led to a queen's rage and her grandsons' death. As for Bodin, for Hotman, love was a double-edged sword that could cause both familial conflict and discord in the state. However, he used this understanding as an argument against parental authority as well as female rule, while for Bodin it was an argument for a strong paternal (and thereby royal) authority.

Apart from his concern with ambitious mothers, Hotman understood kinship relations as less conflict ridden than Bodin. He underscored familial alliances with the example of the Gauls and Franks, who came together "as if they had been a twin-born people, and through their intermingling there was one language and one set of institutions and customs."[110] The metaphor of twins was associated with bonding and the unity of the kingdom of Francogallia. Thus, Hotman's conceptualization of kinship relations included both conflict and harmony, allowed for changing customs, and located the greatest threat to stability in parental abuse of authority.

Conceptualizing Transfer, Controlling Authority: Property, Inheritance, and Succession

From the beginning of his treatise, Hotman made clear that from a historical perspective, rulership in Francogallia was not hereditary but elective. "However," regarding the Frankish kings, he wrote that "the sons of deceased kings had prior claims, and, as Tacitus recorded, they were preferred to others." The question of "whether the kingdom of Francogallia was hereditary or elective" was very important to Hotman.[111] Even though there was a tradition of electing the firstborn sons, an election still took place, and there was no right of blood or birth that constituted a clear rule or a natural right. It was crucial for Hotman to emphasize the rights of the people expressed in the elective principle—to repudiate a hereditary, kinship-based logic of rulership was to promote popular sovereignty, which accorded with Calvinist understandings of the right to resistance. In the past, Hotman noted, "the right of the people was supreme." This popular right could even rearrange royal families, eliminate relatives, and integrate new ones by adoption—succession did not follow some kind of natural rule but remained negotiable.[112] His flexible understanding of kinship relations underscored this argument.

In the course of Hotman's book, partly due to changes in the third edition, the picture of an elective monarchy with quasi-hereditary elements shifted focus. Obviously, Hotman had to rethink his concepts of kinship relations as unfit mechanisms for transferring rulership when he was in the course of legitimizing Henry of Navarre's claims to the throne, which was, after all, based on kinship ties and rights of blood and filiation. In *Antitribonian* of 1567, he had already argued that students of law should learn something "of the sovereign right of our Kings, of the power and authority of the estates general, of the rights of the Queen, of the Dauphin, of the King's brothers and their apanages, of the Princes, of the bastards of the King & his brothers, of the Constable, of the Peers, of the Marshalls of France ... ."[113] This implied that the kinship relations of the royal family were part of the French customary "constitution."[114] Accordingly, in the *Francogallia* he explained that

> later, when the custom [of electing the firstborn son] had been clearly established, the crown of Francogallia began to be hereditary, and was passed to a son or to the nearest cousin, and although many of that rank were either sons or cousins, the crown passed to only one such, namely to the eldest.[115]

Here, Hotman was clear that the kingdom was hereditary and that succession passed from father to eldest son—he used the word *agnatus* in the Latin original—by patrilineal filiation. He emphasized, however, that the kings could not choose a successor by testament or prefer a younger or adopted son. He insisted that "ancient custom" and not the king's will determined the transfer of office.[116] But this was still a different form of restriction than the people's choice and departed from the notion of flexible kinship ties he had once praised. There were more inconsistencies: Hotman maintained both that kingship was hereditary and that it was not. He turned to the fifteenth-century jurist Jean de Terre Rouge to explain that

> the right of primogeniture, in so far as it is held to a kingdom of this sort from the law of the kingdom and not from a father, is neither hereditary nor

patrimonial, but rather belongs to the claimant by the mere right of filiation or of blood. Thus the king cannot dispose of the kingdom by testament. ... He holds it only by virtue of that immutable law of the kingdom by which he is called to office.[117]

Hotman insisted that becoming a king was not an inheritance from a father but an office "granted through common law."[118] To avoid clearly endorsing hereditary succession, he differentiated a patrilineal hereditary mechanism based on filiation and blood but granted only by law from the transfer of property and patrimony. In this account, it was perfectly possible for him to note that women were excluded from succession by old practices and customs, even though Hotman did not acknowledge the Salic Law — which was held to exclude females from succession to the French throne — as public law in the kingdom.[119]

Concepts of inheritance and property could be used to define and differentiate political mechanisms, even if the theory in general was not conceived in favor of a dynastic monarchy. Drawing on Roman law, which he normally avoided, Hotman explained that there were four kinds of property: patrimonial property (personal property of the prince), fiscal property (taxes, land, etc., that provided the prince with revenue but was not his true property), public property (courts, markets, etc., under the government of the prince, but not his property), and private property (things that belonged to the heads of households).[120] The crucial point for Hotman was that the king only truly possessed his patrimonial property. He wrote:

> Though by a wider interpretation, one may say of public property that in a sense it belongs to the prince ... it is under his government, not in his domain. It is at his disposal but it is not his property, and it is so in general, not in particular. It is only his by a legal fiction, not in his possession and for his use.[121]

Following this differentiation, Hotman could explain how the kingdom of Francogallia was not hereditary, for only property is hereditary, and a kingdom is not to be mistaken for private property.[122] This argument was to be seen in the context of debates about proprietary notions of the state in the late Middle Ages and the early modern period.[123] The *Francogallia* was a strong voice against such concepts and differentiated between succession based on filiation and blood and the inheritance of property in a monarchy to make its case. In this context, kinship relations became a way of designating the legitimate ruler.

Bodin was less interested in the kinds of differentiations central to Hotman's argument. It is striking, however, that his discussion of succession in the French version of the *République* also supported Henry of

Navarre's claim to the throne. Bodin's preference for a patrilineal hereditary monarchy was unmistakable, and he saw France as the best example of it. Contradicting Hotman, Bodin denied that Frankish kings had been elected, and he also thought an elective monarchy would only have led to more distrust and jealousy.[124] In France, the crown had always gone to the next male relative in line by blood and name.[125] He explained:

> The closest [relative] of the monarch must succeed, I mean [the closest] out of the male relatives, and of his name, that is, strictly speaking, the eldest as the first one originating from him. And the order of nature wants the eldest son to go first after his father and the others to follow each one in the right order, so that he [the oldest] is preferred to the others. And one can say that this is a natural law which has always been common to almost all peoples.[126]

For Bodin, it was the name and the order of birth that determines the succession of relatives by blood, which he understood as patrilineal by nature. He opted for a line of succession not built on the closest degree of kinship but following eldest sons of eldest sons. This argument is not to be read metaphorically, since it clearly supported Henry's claim to the throne over that of his uncle— a closer relative to the king by degree, but not the successor if one followed the line of eldest sons.[127] Bodin even declared that it did not matter if the successor were a coward or deformed, since "the law of God ... does not want the second son to be preferred to the oldest."[128] While for Hotman the question of succession and the concept of patrilineality were customary but subject to historical change, for Bodin they were universal facts connected to nature, blood, and names. This idea of natural patrilineality could be seen as a way to legitimize the dynastic monarchy in the light of Bodin's goal of preventing conflict.

Conclusion

Jean Bodin's and François Hotman's political theories both relied on kinship relations to frame political concepts of the monarchy. By analyzing the ways they defined and used kinship relations to frame political ideas in their works, my aim has been to show how specific conceptualizations of kinship and politics were produced and intertwined in the context of the French Wars of Religion.

Jean Bodin's *République* was conceived as universal political science with the goal of creating order in times of war. Accordingly, he developed an abstract family model that was based on Aristotelian *oikonomia*, which he considered as a statement of natural and divine law and thus as universal. Bodin used analogies as a rhetorical tool to connect the family and the state on various levels. Drawing on Roman law, he defined kinship relations within a family model of power and obedience, not of proximity or blood. In Bodin's observations on lived kinship relations in history, however, there was an underlying perception of kinship as containing a great potential for conflicts, with love as a potentially dangerous bond, disobedient children as constant risk, and murder as a contagious act among relatives. These two ways of thinking about family and kinship were connected to Bodin's perception of the particularity and mutability of human history and human law and his search for a universal answer to secular problems. They implied two different forms of nature. His conceptualizations of kinship and the family offered a legitimatizing force to his argument for a strong authority of the *chef de famille* and accordingly of the sovereign ruler, for a monarchic hereditary government, and against a right of resistance. Following his understanding of natural law and his search for universal principles, monarchical succession had to be both patrilineal by nature and nonnegotiable. In the *République*, Bodin found kinship relations to be both a threat and—in the form of the family model and patrilineal succession—the most important means to assure political order.

François Hotman's *Francogallia* was intended to describe, explain, and settle political order on the basis of history, tradition, and customs subject to change. Accordingly, in the French monarchy "the practices and customs of the nation have acquired the force of written law."[129] His concepts regarding kinship relations were less rigid and abstract and more flexible and lacked the claims to universality found in Bodin's. Hotman relied less on analogies, favoring descriptions and metaphors to integrate kinship relations into his arguments. Consequently, he used the word *family* in the sense of a larger (patrilineal) group of relatives. In his conceptualizations of kinship, there was no universal family model, and patrilineality was a question of tradition and context and not of natural law. Hotman was less interested in conflict than Bodin was and placed emphasis not on the authority of parents but on their potential for transgression and the consequent necessary limits to their authority. For him, the crucial point was the differentiation between patrilineal mechanisms of succession born out of custom and the inheritance of property that followed clear rules. These understandings laid the groundwork for an argument against the sole sovereignty of the king and for a right of resistance and the restriction of royal authority.

Both authors often used the same kinship figures and relations for their arguments—the father-son relation, the love between parents and children, the dangerous mother—but they come to different conclusions.

Kinship relations and family models formed a flexible repertoire for political thinking in the early modern period. Thus, the specific understandings of kinship could differ: it was full of conflict or harmonious, it was universal or negotiable, it was patrilineal by natural law or only by custom. Kinship was not a single uniform concept that could be used as a simple tool to design political order. It was within specific concepts of kinship that differences between the political theories could be located. The authors could make use of their notions of kinship for their specific aims and arguments, whether for or against the indivisible sovereignty of the king or for or against a right of resistance. Here, the interdependencies of understandings of law, nature, and kinship become visible. While Bodin referred to Roman and natural law to build a universal family model and argue for natural patrilineality, Hotman relied on customary law to argue for flexible and changeable kinship relations, but also for patrilineal succession. In other words, kinship produced or looked at through the lens of natural law was not the same as kinship in terms of customary law and historical observation, and this had consequences for the design of political order. I would even argue that confessional divisions were less important—or important only in the sense of providing necessary support for arguments brought up in religious communication circles during the Wars of Religion—than the understanding of law and nature and thereby of the monarchy itself. Neither of the authors can be definitely associated with one group or position in the religious wars, nor was either of them constantly and unambiguously with or against the ruling king. But concepts of kinship, law, nature, and politics were deeply intertwined in their theories and determined the theoretical shaping of sovereignty, absolutism, and the state.

Julia Heinemann is a historian of the early modern period. She received her PhD from the University of Zurich and is currently a postdoctoral researcher at the Department of Economic and Social History at the University of Vienna. Her studies focus on kinship, gender, and the body. She has published several articles and a book, *Verwandtsein und Herrschen: Die Königinmutter Catherine de Médicis und ihre Kinder in Briefen, 1560–1589* (Heidelberg University Publishing, 2020).

Notes

I would like to thank all the discussants of the ZiF Research Group Workshops (March and December 2018), especially Ann-Cathrin Harders for her helpful commentary and the conveners Erdmute Alber, David

Warren Sabean, Simon Teuscher, and Tatjana Thelen for their suggestions for this chapter.

1. Mack P. Holt, *The French Wars of Religion, 1562–1629* (Cambridge: Cambridge University Press, 1995), 3. This especially concerns the time from the beginning of the regency of the queen mother Catherine de' Medici in 1560 (to 1563) to the coronation of King Henry IV in 1594 and his 1598 Edict of Nantes granting the Huguenots partial protection and tolerance. For an overview of the French monarchy in the sixteenth century, see Arlette Jouanna, *La France du XVIᵉ siècle. 1483–1598* (Paris: PUF, 1996).
2. Arlette Jouanna, *Le devoir de révolte: La noblesse française et la gestation de l'Etat moderne (1559–1661)* (Paris: Fayard, 1989).
3. I use the commented, critical edition of the *Francogallia*: François Hotman, *Francogallia*, Latin text by Ralph E. Giesey, trans. John H. M. Salmon (Cambridge: Cambridge University Press, 1972). It includes the versions of 1573, 1576, and 1586 in Latin and English. For Bodin's *République*, there is no complete critical edition in English. I have used the French edition of the 1583 version, Jean Bodin, *Les six livres de la République*, 6 vols., ed. Christiane Frémont, Marie-Dominique Couzinet, and Henri Rochais (Paris: Fayard, 1986). Translations into English are my own.
4. For a concise comparison of Hotman's and Bodin's biographies and works, see John H. M. Salmon, "François Hotman and Jean Bodin: The Dilemma of Sixteenth-Century French Constitutionalism," *History Today* 23, no. 11 (1973): 801–9.
5. This characterization of Bodin's work was recently stressed in Anna Becker, "Jean Bodin on Oeconomics and Politics," *History of European Ideas* 40, no. 2 (2014): 137.
6. Salmon, "Dilemma," 801.
7. For an overview, see Ralph E. Giesey, "The Juristic Basis of Dynastic Right to the French Throne," *Transactions of the American Philosophical Society* 51, no. 5 (1961); Fanny Cosandey and Robert Descimon, *L'absolutisme en France: Histoire et historiographie* (Paris: Seuil, 2002); Roland Mousnier, *Les institutions de la France sous la monarchie absolue: 1598–1789* (Paris: PUF, 1974–80), vol. 2.
8. Michel de l'Hospital was chancellor between 1560 and 1568. He advocated a moderate attitude toward the Protestants and collaborated closely with the queen mother Catherine de' Medici. See Michel de l'Hospital, *Discours pour la majorité de Charles IX et trois autres discours*, ed. Robert Descimon (Paris: Imprimerie nationale, 1993).
9. On the intellectual context of skepticism in the second half of the sixteenth century, with a main focus on Jean Bodin, see the instructive article by Daniel Engster, "Jean Bodin, Scepticism and Absolute Sovereignty," *History of Political Thought* 17, no. 4 (1996): especially 470–72.
10. Engster, "Jean Bodin," 472.
11. For a gendered analysis of Bodin, see Becker, "Bodin," and Claudia Opitz-Belakhal, *Das Universum des Jean Bodin: Staatsbildung, Macht und Geschlecht im 16. Jahrhundert* (Frankfurt a. M.: Campus, 2006).
12. Becker, "Bodin," 135–36, points out that Bodin's writings "are usually analyzed in terms of indivisible sovereignty, and in their significance as the foundational work of absolutism." For the absolutist interpretation, see Quentin Skinner, *Die Drei Körper des Staates* (Göttingen: Wallstein-Verlag, 2012), 17–18; Cosandey and Descimon, *L'absolutisme*, 41. On Hotman see Donald R. Kelley, *François Hotman: A Revolutionary's Ordeal* (Princeton, NJ: Princeton University Press, 1973), vii; Isabelle Bouvignies, "La Francogallia de François Hotman (1524–1590) et l'historiographie française," *Bulletin de la Société de l'Histoire du Protestantisme Français*, no. 152 (2006): 205.
13. This is not restricted to the sixteenth century or even to the early modern period, as shown by several other contributors to this volume: Susan McKinnon for the United States in the eighteenth and nineteenth centuries, David Sabean for Hegel's theories

at the beginning of the nineteenth century, and Jon Mathieu for the ideas of family in contractarian theories.
14. Hanley has convincingly argued that engendered family models strongly influenced the model of political authority and the practice of state building in early modern France. Sarah Hanley, "Engendering the State: Family Formation and State Building in Early Modern France," *French Historical Studies* 16, no. 1 (1989).
15. Pierre Bourdieu, *Sozialer Sinn: Kritik der theoretischen Vernunft* (Frankfurt a. M.: Suhrkamp, 2014), 297.
16. See Janet Carsten, *After Kinship* (Cambridge: Cambridge University Press, 2004); Janet Carsten, *Cultures of Relatedness: New Approaches to the Study of Kinship* (Cambridge: Cambridge University Press, 2000).
17. Salmon, "Dilemma," 802. Hotman's father was a *conseiller* (counselor) at the Parlement of Paris and later a judge of the so-called *chambre ardente*, a special court that investigated suspicions of heresy—that is, Protestantism. One of his brothers became *avocat-général* (advocate general) in the Parlement, another brother was chancellor to Charles, Cardinal of Lorraine, an important figure within the ultra-Catholic party during the Wars of Religion. For Hotman's biography, see Salmon, "Dilemma"; Ralph E. Giesey and John H. M. Salmon, "Editor's Introduction," in Hotman, *Francogallia*, 3–134; Kelley, *François Hotman*.
18. Giesey and Salmon, "Introduction," 11.
19. Kelley, *François Hotman*, 48.
20. Thomas Nicklas, "Repenser la politique: Visions protestantes au lendemain de la Saint-Barthélemy," *Bulletin de la Société de l'Histoire du Protestantisme Français*, no. 153 (2007).
21. Giesey and Salmon, "Introduction," 3.
22. The Bourbons were so-called "princes of the blood," which means that they were considered descendants of French kings in the direct male line and thus potential successors to the throne. They were also sovereigns of the Kingdom of Navarre. Only some of them were Huguenots, including Jeanne d'Albret and the Prince de Condé. During the so-called Tumult of Amboise, a group of Huguenots tried to abduct King Francis II in order to keep him from being influenced by the Catholic Guise family. They were defeated, punished, and killed. In the following months, famous Protestants who had not been present that day (like Louis de Condé) were arrested. Jouanna, *La France*, 350–53.
23. During the Massacre of St. Bartholomew in August of 1572, more than fifty leaders of the Protestant faction were arrested and executed, and thousands of Protestants were killed in massacres all over the kingdom. It is still disputed who was responsible, but modern scholarship tends to argue that the executions had been planned by the royal council while the massacres happened "spontaneously." See Denis Crouzet, "Königliche und religiöse Gewalt im Massaker der Bartholomäusnacht oder der 'Wille' Karls IX.," in *Gewalt in der Frühen Neuzeit: Beiträge zur 5. Tagung der Arbeitsgemeinschaft Frühe Neuzeit im VHD*, ed. Claudia Ulbrich, Claudia Jarzebowski, and Michaela Hohkamp (Berlin: Duncker & Humblot, 2005).
24. Giesey and Salmon, "Introduction," 5, mention Jacques Almain and John Mair on the concept of popular sovereignty. The emphasis on constitutional custom was not a French specialty as the same authors (ibid.) stress that "ancient constitutions were also discovered for Scotland and the Netherlands."
25. Salmon, "Dilemma," 801. See Hotman, *Francogallia*, 446–47.
26. In the sixteenth century, four editions were published in Latin and four in French; see Hotman, *Francogallia*, appendix.
27. For Hotman, the public council corresponded to the contemporary institutions, especially the Estates General. See Hotman, *Francogallia*, 231, 233: "That the kings of

Francogallia were constituted by the authoritative decision and desire of the people, that is, of the orders, or, as we are now accustomed to say, of the estates."
28. See Giesey and Salmon, "Introduction," 95.
29. Giesey and Salmon, "Introduction," 106, argue that in the 1586 version Hotman's theory became, in part, "a kind of patchwork quilt."
30. The following information is from Opitz, *Universum*, and Salmon, "Dilemma."
31. In 1578, Bodin published his text *Juris universi distributio* as an attempt to a synthesis of universal law.
32. Opitz, *Universum*, 23.
33. Quoted by Opitz, *Universum*, 23. Bodin must have had good connections in Paris as he was released with the help of Christophe de Thou, the president of the Parlement of Paris (ibid.).
34. Giesey and Salmon, "Introduction," 91. On the wife see Opitz, *Universum*, 23.
35. From 1576 to 1629, there were fourteen editions in French.
36. In 1586, he published a slightly altered Latin version: Jean Bodin, *De Republica Libri Sex, Latine Ab Autore Redditi Multo Quam Antea Locupletiores* (Paris: Jacques Dupuy, 1586).
37. Salmon, "Dilemma," 809.
38. For example, when he says that individual happiness is the same as happiness of the commonwealth. Bodin, *République*, I.1., 31. See Marie-Dominique Couzinet, "On Bodin's Method," in *The Reception of Bodin*, ed. Howell A. Lloyd (Leiden: Brill, 2013), on "the hierarchy between the whole and the parts," 62.
39. Bodin uses the word *République* in the sense of *res publica* or commonwealth, while he usually employs the word *estat* in the sense of a condition (status) rather than the state in the modern understanding. See Bodin, *République*, I.1., 7: "Jusques ici nous avons touché ce qui concernoit l'estat universel des Republiques" ("Until now we have dealt with what concerns the universal state of commonwealths"). Nevertheless, I also use the word *state* pragmatically here in order to designate the political entity Bodin is referring to with the word *République*.
40. Bodin, *République*, I.2., 39: "Mesnage est un droit gouvernement de plusieurs subjects, sous l'obeïssance d'un chef de famille, et de ce qui leur est propre"; Bodin, *République*, I.1., 27: "Republique est un droit gouvernement de plusieurs mesnages, et de ce qui leur est commun, avec puissance souveraine."
41. Bodin, *République*, I.6., 111.
42. Becker, "Bodin," 146.
43. Bodin, *République*, I.3., 53.
44. On Bodin's general use of Aristotelian concepts, see Couzinet, "On Bodin's Method," 60.
45. Becker, "Bodin."
46. Dieter Schwab, "Familie," *Geschichtliche Grundbegriffe*, vol. 2, ed. Otto Brunner, Werner Coze, and Reinhart Koselleck (Stuttgart: Klett-Cotta, 1975), 266, 268–69. A look at contemporary translations of the *République* into German, Latin, and English shows that the terms were adapted according to particular linguistic and political traditions. Thus, the German translation rendered *mesnage* as both *Haus* and *Haushaltung* and the *chef de famille* as *Hausvater* and was thus oriented toward the Protestant economic literature with its Aristotelian vocabulary. The English and Latin versions used "family" and *familia* for both *mesnage* and *famille* as well as in the phrases "head of family" and "paterfamilias." See Jean Bodin, *Respublica. Das ist: Gründtliche und rechte Underweysung, oder eigentlicher Bericht, in welchem außführlich vermeldet wird, wie nicht allein das Regiment wol zubestellen ... in sechs Bücher verfasset* (Mümpelgard: M. Johann Oswaldt, 1592); Bodin, *De Republica*; Jean Bodin, *The Six Bookes of a Commonweale, Out of the French and Latine Copies, done into English, by Richard Knolles* (London: Impensis G. Bishop, 1606). For the changing meaning of "family" in Hegel's works, see David Sabean's chapter in this volume.

47. Bodin, *République*, I.2., 39: "Or nous entendons par la mesnagerie, le droit gouvernement de la famille, et de la puissance que le chef de la famille a sur les siens, et de l'obeïssance qui lui est due."
48. I refer to the title of Opitz's book *Das Universum des Jean Bodin*.
49. Bodin, *République*, I.3., 51.
50. Here I agree with Becker, "Bodin," who has demonstrated this very convincingly. As Bodin explains, the first relationship of power and obedience was the subjugation of "animal appetite" to "reason." So when God gave the husband authority over his wife, this meant, by analogy, that he had given the soul power over the body and reason over "cupidity." Bodin, *République*, I.3., 52.
51. This is not considered by Becker, "Bodin."
52. Schwab, "Familie."
53. For example, see the sixteenth-century German texts Justus Menius, *Oeconomia Christiana, das ist, von Christlicher haushaltung* (Wittenberg: Hans Lufft, 1529); Paul Rebhun, *Hausfried | Was fur Vrsachen den | Christlichen Eheleuten zube= | dencken, den lieben Haus | fried in der Ehe zu= | erhalten* (Wittenberg, 1546). See Luise Schorn-Schütte, "Kommunikation über Herrschaft. Obrigkeitskritik im 16. Jahrhundert," in *Ideen als gesellschaftliche Gestaltungskraft im Europa der Frühen Neuzeit. Beiträge für eine erneuerte Geistesgeschichte*, ed. Lutz Raphael and Heinz-Elmar Tenorth (München: Oldenbourg, 2006). For late medieval understandings of marriage and household, see Gabriela Signori, *Von der Paradiesehe zur Gütergemeinschaft. Ehe in der mittelalterlichen Lebens- und Vorstellungswelt* (Frankfurt a. M.: Campus, 2011).
54. Becker, "Bodin," 143.
55. Bodin, *République*, I.8., 179: "La souveraineté est la puissance absoluë et perpetuelle d'une Republique, que les Latins appellent majestatem." For Bodin's definition of sovereignty in comparison to other early modern understandings, see Luc Foisneau, "Sovereignty and Reason of State: Bodin, Richelieu and Hobbes," in *The Reception of Bodin*, ed. Howell A. Lloyd (Leiden: Brill, 2013).
56. A famous example in nature is the fractal form of Romanesco broccoli. For an example of self-similarity, see Bodin, *République*, I.2., 39–40: "The second part of the definition of the commonwealth ... concerns the family, which is the real source and origin of all commonwealths, and their principal member. ... So just as the family is well governed, as the real image of the commonwealth, and the domestic power resembles the sovereign power: so is the rightful government of the house the real model of the government of the commonwealth. And just as if each of the members does what he must, the whole body is well: also if the families are governed well, the commonwealth will be well."
57. Bodin, *République*, I.6., 111–12.
58. For this differentiation see Becker, "Bodin," 147.
59. Hotman, *Francogallia*, 398–99. See also 403 on the "clear and observable difference between the king and the kingdom." This statement can only be properly understood in the context of Hotman's reflections on property and inheritance. See the third part of this analysis.
60. For France in the sixteenth century, see Sarah Hanley, "Mapping Rulership in the French Body Politic: Political Identity, Public Law and the King's One Body," *Historical Reflections, Réflexions Historiques* 23, no. 2 (1997); for the Middle Ages, see Jacques Le Goff, "Head or Heart? The Political Use of Body Metaphors in the Middle Ages," in *Fragments for a History of the Human Body: Part Three*, ed. Michael Feher et al. (New York: Zone, 1989); Daisy Delogu, *Allegorical Bodies: Power and Gender in Late Medieval France* (Toronto: University of Toronto Press, 2015).
61. Hotman, *Francogallia*, 257. It is like a fiduciary relationship.
62. Hotman, *Francogallia*, 399, 401.
63. Hotman, *Francogallia*, 218–19. See also 258–259 for the appanages of the "family."

64. Jean Nicot, *Le Thresor de la langue francoyse tant ancienne que moderne* (Paris, 1606).
65. For concepts of "race" in early modern France, see Arlette Jouanna, *L'idée de race en France au XVIème siècle et au début du XVIIème siècle* (Montpellier, 1981), vol. 2. Most writers relied on Aristotle's concept of reproduction in which the father formed the foetus with his sperm from the mother's menstrual blood with the mother being the vessel and the father the active part of reproduction. Thus, it was the father's race that was transmitted to the child.
66. See Michaela Hohkamp's chapter in this volume on the "epistemic practice of writing kinship."
67. In this context, Bodin even calls the wife "mere de famille." Bodin, *République*, I.2., 40. Analogically, a state consists of at least three families, according to Bodin, "because the law wants at least three" ("car la loy veut du moins trois personnes pour faire un college"). The "law" Bodin refers to here is probably Roman law, which says that a group must contain at least three people.
68. Bodin, *République*, I.2., 64: "comme s'il pouvait commander à nature." He found Thomas More's idea of a family having at least ten but not more than sixteen children absurd.
69. Bodin, *République*, I.6., 117: "la maison ne fait pas la famille."
70. This is not to suggest that the early modern household was ever a self-sufficient economic unit either in theory or in practice. For an overview of current research on house and household, see Inken Schmidt-Voges, "Europa—eine Hausgesellschaft? Das Haus in der politischen Kultur Europas vom 15. bis zum 19. Jahrhundert," in *Politische Kultur im frühneuzeitlichen Europa: Festschrift für Olaf Mörke zum 65. Geburtstag*, ed. Dennis Hormuth et al. (Kiel: Verlag Ludwig, 2017).
71. See for example Bodin, *République*, I.4., 66. Bodin was also in favor of adoption. Bodin, *République*, I.4., 78–79.
72. See for example Bodin, *République*, I.3., 51.
73. Bodin, *République*, I.4., 66. This is said in the context of the father's right of life and death over his children.
74. Becker, "Bodin," 144, explains that "the state could not exist unless it was composed of families. Therefore the perfection of the political community was only possible if the family was perfect."
75. Bodin, *République*, I.4., 178–79.
76. Bodin, *République*, I.9.
77. Bodin, *République*, I.4., 65.
78. Bodin, *République*, I.4.
79. Becker, "Bodin," 153.
80. Bodin, *République*, II.5., 80.
81. Bodin, *République*, I.4., 75.
82. Bodin, *République*, I.4.
83. Bodin, *République*, I.4., 65–66. Debates about maternal regency argued based on natural law that a mother's love was supreme and guaranteed altruism toward her children. See Fanny Cosandey, "Puissance maternelle et pouvoir politique: La régence des reines mères," *CLIO: Histoire, femmes et sociétés*, no. 21 (2005).
84. Bodin, *République*, I.4., 65–66.
85. For the mothers and the rivalries, see Bodin, *République*, VI.4., 177: "il s'est veu des meres meurtrieres, et qui ont vendu non seulement l'estat, ains aussi la vie de leurs enfans."
86. Presumably, this statement was influenced by the contemporary conflicts between and within noble families, with the royal brothers Henry III and Francis at war with each other (from September 1575 to May 1576). Francis gathered Protestant troops with Condé. Jouanna, *La France*, 493–510.
87. Engster, "Jean Bodin."

88. Engster, "Jean Bodin," 471. Engster argues that Bodin's opinion on this evolved as in an earlier writing, the *Methodus ad facilem historiarum cognitionem* (Paris, 1566), 479, he contended that history could point to universal principles of political order. In the subsequent Latin version of the *République*, 485, he would stress even more that "there was almost no end to the diversity and variability of human laws."
89. Bodin, *République*, I.2., 47.
90. Bodin, *République*, V.1., 11.
91. Engster, "Jean Bodin," 491.
92. Here, I slightly disagree with Engster's argument that Bodin found the solution in the principle of sovereignty. See Engster, "Jean Bodin," 471. According to Bodin, sovereignty is only imaginable in connection with the family model.
93. Couzinet, "On Bodin's Method," 59. See Bodin, *République*, V.1., 7: "Up to now we have talked about the universal state of commonwealths, let us now say what might be particular to some of them because of the diversities of peoples."
94. In the early modern period, "nature" was not an unambiguous ontological concept. It could be both subject to change and normative. See Lorraine Daston and Fernando Vidal, "Introduction: Doing What Comes Naturally," in *The Moral Authority of Nature*, ed. Lorraine Daston (Chicago: University of Chicago Press, 2004). For the idea of natural law in the République, see Janine Chanteur, "L'idée de Loi Naturelle dans la République de Jean Bodin," in *Jean Bodin: Proceedings of the International Conference on Bodin in Munich*, ed. Horst Denzer (Munich: C. H. Beck, 1973).
95. Bodin, *République*, III.7., 173.
96. Bodin, *République*, V.1., 52.
97. Hotman stated that Roman law had no validity in France; it was only applicable to Roman society. In *Methodus ad facilem historiarum cognitionem*, Bodin still agreed about this with Hotman. Engster, "Jean Bodin," 473.
98. Hotman, *Francogallia*, 142–43.
99. Hotman, *Francogallia*, 220–21.
100. Hotman, *Francogallia*, 406–7.
101. The discussion centered on the question of whether nobility was a matter of virtue or of birth. See Ellery Schalk, *From Valor to Pedigree: Ideas of Nobility in France in the Sixteenth and Seventeenth Century* (Princeton, NJ: Princeton Universtiy Press, 1986).
102. Hotman, *Francogallia*, 229. See the next paragraph for this topic.
103. See Hotman, *Francogallia*, 479: "We shall not discuss the laws of the Romans or those of any other people, but only the practices of this our own Francogallia."
104. Hotman, *Francogallia*, 142–43.
105. Hotman, *Francogallia*, 301, 303, translated by Salmon as "our ancestors."
106. Hotman, *Francogallia*, 242–43. Cf. Hotman, *Francogallia*, 465: "It is unlawful to substitute a younger son for an elder, or to institute any other person as his successor. There is the best of reasons for this, since while parents can deprive their children of anything that originated from the parents themselves, they have no right over their children in anything awarded them either by nature or by the law and customs of their ancestors."
107. For example, see Hotman, *Francogallia*, 469, 483.
108. Hotman, *Francogallia*, 491. See 479–95 for more examples of "bad mothers" as ruling queens. For Blanche see Giesey and Salmon, "Introduction," 56–57.
109. Hotman, *Francogallia*, 482–83. Long hair was understood as a privilege of those belonging to the royal family. See ibid., chap. 9, 276.
110. Hotman, *Francogallia*, 284–85.
111. Hotman, *Francogallia*, 220–21.
112. Hotman, *Francogallia*, 228–29.
113. Quote from *Antitribonian* by Giesey and Salmon, "Introduction," 35.

114. As early as 1547, Hotman had published a commentary on legal problems of kinship relations and succession titled *De gradibus cognationis et affinitatis*. See Kelley, *François Hotman*, 39.
115. Hotman, *Francogallia*, 256–57.
116. Hotman, *Francogallia*, 463, 465.
117. Hotman, *Francogallia*, 466–67.
118. Hotman, *Francogallia*, 465.
119. Hotman, *Francogallia*, 273. He continues: "It is easy to establish the stupidity of those who are bold enough to affirm from the Salic Law, which they have either never read or have failed to understand, that it was a prudent provision to prevent regal power being transferred to women." See also 269–75, 479. Salmon, "Dilemma," 807; Giesey, "Dynastic Right," 32. The Salic Law referred to a law code of the Salian Franks that was used from the fourteenth century to legitimize a strict patrilineal succession to the French throne, excluding both daughters and their male offspring. However, jurists contested its validity. See Craig Taylor, "The Salic Law and the Valois Succession to the French Crown," *French History* 15, no. 4 (2001); Sarah Hanley, "The Family, the State, and the Law in Seventeenth- and Eighteenth-Century France: The Political Ideology of Male Right versus an Early Theory of Natural Rights," *Journal of Modern History* 78, no. 2 (2006).
120. Hotman, *Francogallia*, 247–53.
121. Hotman, *Francogallia*, 252–53.
122. Hotman, *Francogallia*, 247.
123. Lewis argues that, at least up to the fourteenth century, the French royal family conceived of France as their father's estate and that—just like the territories of noble families—the kingdom was "treated as the paternal family holdings." Rowen describes what he calls "the practice of the ownership of the state by the ruling family (dynasty) and the reigning head of that family (the king)" for the sixteenth century. Andrew W. Lewis, *Royal Succession in Capetian France: Studies on Familial Order and the State* (Cambridge, MA: Harvard University Press, 1981), 96; Herbert H. Rowen, *The King's State: Proprietary Dynasticism in Early Modern France* (New Brunswick, NJ: Rutgers University Press, 1980).
124. Bodin, *République*, VI.5., 208–11; Salmon, "Dilemma," 807.
125. Bodin, *République*, VI.5, 212: "le droit de la couronne estoit devolu au proche masle du sang, et du nom."
126. Bodin, *République*, VI.5, 216. However, Bodin stresses that it is possible for other families than the royal family to have their own laws of succession.
127. This has been emphasized by Paul Lawrence Rose, "Bodin and the Bourbon Succession to the French Throne, 1583–1594," *Sixteenth Century Journal* 9, no. 2 (1978). The author argues that Bodin changed his position in the Latin edition *De Republica* of 1586 to argue that "it is seniority of degree rather than ancestry that is the determining factor" (86). The English translation of 1606 then again supported Henry's claim to the throne (87).
128. Bodin, *République*, VI.5., 220.
129. Hotman, *Francogallia*, 274–75. This is articulated in the context of Hotman's discussion of the Salic Law.

Bibliography

Becker, Anna. "Jean Bodin on Oeconomics and Politics." *History of European Ideas* 40, no. 2 (2014): 135–54.

Bodin, Jean. *De Republica Libri Sex, Latine Ab Autore Redditi Multo Quam Antea Locupletiores*. Paris: Jacques Dupuy, 1586.

———. *Respublica. Das ist: Gründtliche und rechte Underweysung, oder eigentlicher Bericht, in welchem außführlich vermeldet wird, wie nicht allein das Regiment wol zubestellen … in sechs Bücher verfasset*. Mümpelgard: M. Johann Oswaldt, 1592.

———. *The Six Bookes of a Commonweale, Out of the French and Latine Copies, done into English, by Richard Knolles*. Impensis G. Bishop, 1606.

———. *Les six livres de la République*. Edited by Christiane Frémont, Marie-Dominique Couzinet, and Henri Rochais. 6 vols. Paris: Fayard, 1986.

Bourdieu, Pierre. *Sozialer Sinn: Kritik der theoretischen Vernunft*. Frankfurt a. M.: Suhrkamp, 2014.

Bouvignies, Isabelle. "La Francogallia de François Hotman (1524–1590) et l'historiographie française." *Bulletin de la Société de l'Histoire du Protestantisme Français*, no. 152 (2006): 199–219.

Carsten, Janet. *Cultures of Relatedness: New Approaches to the Study of Kinship*. Cambridge: Cambridge University Press, 2000.

———. *After Kinship*. Cambridge: Cambridge University Press, 2004.

Chanteur, Janine. "L'idée de Loi Naturelle dans la République de Jean Bodin." In *Jean Bodin: Proceedings of the International Conference on Bodin in Munich*, edited by Horst Denzer, 195–212. Munich: C. H. Beck, 1973.

Couzinet, Marie-Dominique. "On Bodin's Method." In *The Reception of Bodin*, edited by Howell A. Lloyd, 39–65. Leiden: Brill, 2013.

Cosandey, Fanny. "Puissance maternelle et pouvoir politique: La régence des reines mères." *CLIO: Histoire, femmes et sociétés*, no. 21 (2005): 1–15. https://doi.org/10.4000/clio.1447.

Cosandey, Fanny, and Robert Descimon. *L'absolutisme en France: Histoire et historiographie*. Paris: Seuil, 2002.

Crouzet, Denis. "Königliche und religiöse Gewalt im Massaker der Bartholomäusnacht oder der 'Wille' Karls IX." In *Gewalt in der Frühen Neuzeit: Beiträge zur 5. Tagung der Arbeitsgemeinschaft Frühe Neuzeit im VHD*, edited by Claudia Ulbrich, Claudia Jarzebowski, and Michaela Hohkamp, 33–58. Berlin: Duncker & Humblot, 2005.

Daston, Lorraine, and Fernando Vidal. "Introduction: Doing What Comes Naturally." In *The Moral Authority of Nature*, edited by Lorraine Daston and Fernando Vidal, 1–23. Chicago: University of Chicago Press, 2004.

Delogu, Daisy. *Allegorical Bodies: Power and Gender in Late Medieval France*. Toronto: University of Toronto Press, 2015.

Engster, Daniel. "Jean Bodin, Scepticism and Absolute Sovereignty." *History of Political Thought* 17, no. 4 (1996): 469–99.

Foisneau, Luc. "Sovereignty and Reason of State: Bodin, Richelieu and Hobbes." In *The Reception of Bodin*, edited by Howell A. Lloyd, 67–96. Leiden: Brill, 2013.

Giesey, Ralph E. "The Juristic Basis of Dynastic Right to the French Throne." *Transactions of the American Philosophical Society* 51, no. 5 (1961): 3–47.

Hanley, Sarah. "Engendering the State: Family Formation and State Building in Early Modern France." *French Historical Studies* 16, no. 1 (1989): 4–27.

———. "Mapping Rulership in the French Body Politic: Political Identity, Public Law and the King's One Body." *Historical Reflections, Réflexions Historiques* 23, no. 2 (1997): 129–49.

———. "The Family, the State, and the Law in Seventeenth- and Eighteenth-Century France: The Political Ideology of Male Right versus an Early Theory of Natural Rights." *Journal of Modern History* 78, no. 2 (2006): 289–332.

Holt, Mack P. *The French Wars of Religion, 1562–1629*. Cambridge: Cambridge University Press, 1995.

Hotman, François. *Francogallia*. Latin text by Ralph E. Giesey. Translated by J. H. M. Salmon. Cambridge: Cambridge University Press, 1972.

Jouanna, Arlette. *L'idée de race en France au XVIème siècle et au début du XVIIème siècle*. 2 vols. Montpellier, 1981.

———. *Le devoir de révolte: La noblesse française et la gestation de l'Etat moderne (1559–1661)*. Paris: Fayard, 1989.

———. *La France du XVIe siècle: 1483–1598*. Paris: PUF, 2012.

Kelley, Donald R. *François Hotman: A Revolutionary's Ordeal*. Princeton, NJ: Princeton University Press, 1973.

Le Goff, Jacques. "Head or Heart? The Political Use of Body Metaphors in the Middle Ages." In *Fragments for a History of the Human Body: Part Three*, edited by Michael Feher, Nadia Tazi, and Ramona Naddaff, 13–26. New York: Zone, 1989.

Lewis, Andrew W. *Royal Succession in Capetian France: Studies on Familial Order and the State*. Cambridge, MA: Harvard University Press, 1981.

l'Hospital, Michel de. *Discours pour la majorité de Charles IX et trois autres discours*. Edited by Robert Descimon. Paris: Imprimerie nationale, 1993.

Menius, Justus. *Oeconomia Christiana, das ist, von Christlicher haushaltung*. Wittenberg: Hans Lufft, 1529.

Mousnier, Roland. *Les institutions de la France sous la monarchie absolue. 1598–1789*. 2 vols. Paris: PUF, 1974–80.

Nicklas, Thomas. "Repenser la politique: Visions protestantes au lendemain de la Saint-Barthélemy." *Bulletin de la Société de l'Histoire du Protestantisme Français*, no. 153 (2007): 165–78.

Nicot, Jean. *Le Thresor de la langue francoyse tant anciene que modern*. Paris, 1606. Retrieved 20 July 2022 from http://artfl-project.uchicago.edu/node/17.

Opitz-Belakhal, Claudia. *Das Universum des Jean Bodin: Staatsbildung, Macht und Geschlecht im 16. Jahrhundert*. Frankfurt a. M.: Campus, 2006.

Rebhun, Paul. *Hausfried | Was fur Vrsachen den | Christlichen Eheleuten zube= | dencken, den lieben Haus | fried in der Ehe zu= | erhalten*. Wittenberg, 1546.

Rose, Paul Lawrence. "Bodin and the Bourbon Succession to the French Throne, 1583–1594." *Sixteenth Century Journal* 9, no. 2 (1978): 75–98.

Rowen, Herbert H. *The King's State: Proprietary Dynasticism in Early Modern France*. New Brunswick, NJ: Rutgers University Press, 1980.

Salmon, John H. M. "François Hotman and Jean Bodin: The Dilemma of Sixteenth-Century French Constitutionalism." *History Today* 23, no. 11 (1973): 801–9.

Schalk, Ellery. *From Valor to Pedigree: Ideas of Nobility in France in the Sixteenth and Seventeenth Century*. Princeton, NJ: Princeton University Press, 1986.

Schmidt-Voges, Inken. "Europa—eine Hausgesellschaft? Das Haus in der politischen Kultur Europas vom 15. bis zum 19. Jahrhundert." In *Politische Kultur im frühneuzeitlichen Europa: Festschrift für Olaf Mörke zum 65. Geburtstag*, edited by Julia Ellermann, Dennis Hormuth, and Volker Seresse, 237–53. Kiel: Verlag Ludwig, 2017.

Schorn-Schütte, Luise. "Kommunikation über Herrschaft: Obrigkeitskritik im 16. Jahrhundert." In *Ideen als gesellschaftliche Gestaltungskraft im Europa der Frühen Neuzeit: Beiträge für eine erneuerte Geistesgeschichte*, edited by Lutz Raphael and Heinz-Elmar Tenorth, 71–108. München: Oldenbourg, 2006.

Schwab, Dieter. "Familie." In *Geschichtliche Grundbegriffe*, vol. 2, edited by Otto Brunner, Werner Coze, and Reinhart Koselleck, 253–301. Stuttgart: Klett-Cotta, 1975.

Signori, Gabriela. *Von der Paradiesehe zur Gütergemeinschaft: Ehe in der mittelalterlichen Lebens- und Vorstellungswelt*. Frankfurt a. M.: Campus, 2011.

Skinner, Quentin. *Die Drei Körper des Staates*. Göttingen: Wallstein-Verlag, 2012.

Taylor, Craig. "The Salic Law and the Valois Succession to the French Crown." *French History* 15, no. 4 (2001): 358–77.

Chapter 8

Commonwealths of Affection
Kinship, Marriage, and Polity in Eighteenth- and Nineteenth-Century America

Susan McKinnon

Introduction

The idea that familial and political relations were analogues of one another was common currency in the Anglo-American world from the seventeenth through the nineteenth centuries. As the British clergyman and political philosopher George Lawson expressed in 1660, this mutual entwinement could be realized in two ways. Noting that "as a State, or Church, may be said to be a great family; so a family well ordered may be called a little commonwealth," he also argued that the family was the "seminary both of the Church and civil State."[1] That is, not only were the family, church, and state organized in accordance with the same values—such that the family was a little polity and the state a large family—but those values and the form of social relations appropriate to them were also produced in and emanated first and foremost from the family.[2]

This chapter explores what happened when the hierarchical structure of social relations in the big and little commonwealths—and the so-called "ligaments of affection" that bound these relations together—were, over the course of the American Revolution, radically contested in favor of a more egalitarian structure. Since Americans presumed a concordance between the values organizing the big and little commonwealths, their revolution against the British aristocratic and monarchical political order and their attempt to establish the foundations for a more democratic republic not only were articulated in the language of kinship and marriage but also entailed a simultaneous revolution in understandings about the kinds of kinship and marital relations proper to the new republican order.[3]

Because the very notion of aristocracy was based on an ideology that naturalized and sacralized hierarchical differences in social ranks, the revolution required the denaturalization of these ranked differences and it emphasized a more performative understanding of social relations — one based on "doing" rather than essentialized "being," on what had to be created rather than what was given by nature or divine order. In his pamphlet titled "Information to Those Who Would Remove to America," Benjamin Franklin counseled that birth status "is a Commodity that cannot be carried to a worse Market than to that of America, where People do not enquire concerning a Stranger, *What IS He?* but *What can he Do?*"[4]

To probe this transformation, this chapter examines three moments in the reconfiguration of the big and little commonwealths in America between 1700 to 1900. First, during the prerevolutionary period, as Americans debated the grounds that might — or might not — justify rebellion against what they began to perceive as British tyranny, they conceptualized the argument by asking if, and under what conditions, a parent's behavior justified a child's refusal to fulfill his or her duty of subservient obedience. Second, during the revolutionary and postrevolutionary era, as Americans sought to overturn the hierarchical order of British aristocracy and monarchy and to establish the grounds for a democratic republic, they began to imagine their political union in terms of a voluntaristic marital union rather than a naturalized patriarchal hierarchy between parent and child. And, finally, later in the nineteenth century, there was a further specification of the marital forms deemed appropriate to a democratic republic as battles developed around what was understood to be the hierarchical nature and divinely ordained relations of Mormon polygamy and theocracy in contrast to the more egalitarian, voluntaristic ideals deemed critical both to monogamy and to the secular republican experiment.

Throughout this account I want to attend to the ways in which different models of kinship and political formation are conceptualized in terms of one another. How are the specific cultural meanings of descent and/or marriage mobilized to think about different types of polity — specifically hierarchical vs. more egalitarian polities? How are different approaches to political power and status articulated by contrasting patriarchal and marital forms of relationality? How and why are hierarchical as opposed to egalitarian political relations conceptualized in terms of more naturalized or more performative forms of kinship and marriage?[5]

The Patriarchal Commonwealth of Affection

In the seventeenth- and eighteenth-century Anglo-American world, it was widely understood (if also contested) that society was hierarchical—a fact of nature and a divinely ordained order of things. As a hierarchical order, society was a holistic body, one constituted by internal distinctions in rank, wealth, calling, and function.[6] Analogous distinctions were replicated across the different orders of social relations in the big and little commonwealths—including those within the church, the state, and the family. As such, the same patriarchal model of mutual obligations between superior and inferior organized the relations between God and humans, ruler and ruled, husband and wife, parent and child.[7]

This recursive hierarchical ordering not only provided structural unity across different orders of being but also gave prescriptive content to the "ligaments of affections" that tied together superiors and inferiors. In demeanor, word, and deed, inferiors properly displayed an affectionate obedience and subservience—driven by a "loving-feare" or a "fearing-love"[8]—to their earthly superiors as all humans likewise did to God. By contrast, superiors—mirroring the God whose earthly magistrates they were and standing as fathers of their respective earthly commonwealths—properly displayed, in demeanor, word, and deed, the obligations of paternity: authority, benevolence, wisdom, care, and protection.[9]

The patriarchal commonwealth of affections did not stop on the shores of the North Atlantic but extended across the Atlantic to unite Britain and her American colonies in the same recursive order of relational expectations and obligations. Indeed, the very act of colonization was conceptualized in terms of a generative relation between parents and children. Historian Melvin Yazawa notes that in the 1624 volume *A Plaine Path-way to Plantations*, "Richard Elburne described the establishment and growth of colonies as a natural phenomenon, comparing them to 'children,' 'borne and bred up to their father's house,' who eventually leave home for new 'habitations.'"[10] This was more than a simple analogy. The colonial parent-child relation—or what Joseph Reed, in his 1766 volume *Four Dissertations on the Reciprocal Advantages of a Perpetual Union Between Great-Britain and Her American Colonies*, called the "grand FAMILY COMPACT"[11]—entailed a set of behavioral prescriptions that outlined the nature and extent of the political relation. As the parent, England should display the qualities of a faithful and affectionate—if sometimes disciplining—but fundamentally nurturing, protective, and loving parent; in return, the colonies should be "obedient, dutiful, grateful, and properly subservient; attitudinal postures befitting the legitimate offspring of

Mother England."[12] Joseph Reed went on to express the needs of the infant American colony:

> We stand in need of her [Britain's] protection, nurture and care. Exposed by our situation ... and yet in a state of infancy, it would be extremely difficult, if not impossible, to form any Union among ourselves that would be sufficient to repel the attacks of a formidable invader. In this weak, this defenseless, state, therefore, we must look up to our indulgent parent, whose vigorous, salutary aid we have so often already experienced. Upon her we must rely for support, and under her wing shelter ourselves.[13]

As this statement makes clear, just ten years before the 1776 Declaration of Independence, many colonists continued to argue that they were, after all, the legitimate children of Mother England, and, as such, not only required but were due the parental care and nurturance of Great Britain in exchange for their respectful subservience.

Yet, as events unfolded over the 1760s and 1770s, the parental affection of Mother England and King George III increasingly came into question. At the center of the debate was this question: was the parent-child bond fixed by nature and unbreakable, or could failure to perform familial obligations give cause for dissolution?[14] Whatever English popular sentiment might have been about the duties of children to father-tyrants, Sir William Blackstone, in his 1765 *Commentaries on the Laws of England*, made it clear that the natural bonds of paternity held sway in English law, regardless of whether or not the father had actually performed the duties of a nurturing parent. According to Blackstone, a child was obligated to care and provide for "a wicked and unnatural progenitor as for one who has shewn the greatest tenderness and parental piety."[15]

Indeed, from the perspective of the British and the British loyalists in America, such events as the Boston Tea Party in 1773 and the growing resistance to the so-called Intolerable Acts imposed by the British Parliament in 1774 were signs of an unnatural ingratitude of colonial children to Mother England.[16] That the British judged the Americans as derelict in fulfilling what they considered an enduring debt of gratitude, deference, and dependence ultimately became more than a cause for chastisement—it was cause for coercive action.

But from the revolutionaries' perspective, it was precisely the intolerable and coercive acts of the British that proved England's loss of affection for her legitimate children and turned the father-king into a tyrant. Here, the American revolutionaries drew upon earlier debates in England[17] and France (see chapters by Heinemann and Mathieu in this volume) as to whether the power of a king was absolute and uncontestable or whether subjects had the right to overthrow tyrannical kings.

Jonathan Mayhew, a renowned American Congregational minister at the Old West Church in Boston, advocated powerfully in his sermons for the cause of liberty. He gave a highly influential sermon on this topic on 30 January 1750, commemorating the centennial of the execution of Charles I, monarch of the three kingdoms of England, Scotland, and Ireland. Mayhew argued "that those in authority may abuse their trust and power to such a degree, that neither the law of reason, nor of religion, requires, that any obedience or submission should be paid to them; but, on the contrary that they should be totally discarded"; and the conditions for this were met, he claimed, "when from a prince and common father, he exalts himself into a tyrant—when from subjects and children, he degrades them into the class of slaves;—plunders them, makes them his prey, and unnaturally sports himself with their lives and fortunes."[18] Mayhew's sermon was a clear shot across the bow of the imperial familial hierarchy. Indeed, the American patriots turned the Tory accusation of unnatural filial ingratitude on its head and declared that deference to a parent who had lost all affection would itself be unnatural and untenable.

There was, perhaps, no more powerful and persuasive argument for overthrowing the royal parent-turned-tyrant than that written by Thomas Paine in his 1776 pamphlet, *Common Sense*. Paine recounted:

> No man was a warmer wisher for reconciliation than myself, before the fatal nineteenth of April 1775 [the massacre at Lexington], but the moment the event of that day was made known, I rejected the hardened, sullen tempered Pharoah [sic] of England for ever [sic]; and distain the wretch, that with the pretended title of FATHER OF HIS PEOPLE can unfeelingly hear of their slaughter, and composedly sleep with their blood upon his soul.[19]

Paine forcefully argued that Britain had effectively cut the ligaments of parental love and affection and had inflicted unforgivably cruel and unnatural injuries upon her children. When Paine called upon his countrymen and -women to "oppose not only tyranny, but the tyrant" and "let the crown ... be demolished, and scattered among the people whose right it is,"[20] he effectively dismantled—at least for the American revolutionaries who took up the call—the divinely ordained model of patriarchy, hereditary rank, and social hierarchy and gave them the language to envision a radically different social order and to summon the courage to pursue it. Filial gratitude and deference were no longer deemed to flow from the natural relation of paternity itself but rather had to be elicited through the performance of proper paternal nurturance and protection.

The Marital Commonwealth of Affections

Over the course of the Revolution, the American patriots—who contrasted themselves with both the British and the Americans who remained loyal to the British—endeavored to reconfigure the contours of affections that would characterize the big and little commonwealths they undertook to bring into being. As they sought to break apart the vertical, hierarchical, and naturalized bonds between parent and child that held together the imperial family, they imagined the "union" of the Thirteen Colonies in terms of more horizontal, symmetrical, and voluntaristic bonds—conceptualized in terms of a marital "union" (see chapters by Sabean and Heinemann in this volume for analogous uses of the trope of marriage).[21]

In *Common Sense*, Paine observed that "it hath lately been asserted in parliament, that the colonies have no relation to each other but through the parent country, i.e., that Pennsylvania and the Jerseys, and so on for the rest, are sister colonies by the way of England."[22] Countering this assertion, Paine declared that "Independance [sic] is the only BOND that can tye and keep us together."[23] In this way, Paine not only countered the grounds for continued patriarchal authority *over* the American colonies but also disputed the assumption that parental generativity of siblingship should be the only basis for relations *between* the colonies. "The American cause was," Fliegelman asserts, "in the broadest sense of the term, the cause of 'union,' of liberty not as a final autonomy but as the freedom to choose one's bond."[24]

Because of the revolutionaries' rejection of siblingship's link through parental generativity, it was not the bond of siblingship so much as the bond of marriage that could represent the idea of a republican "union," and, in particular, a voluntaristic union—one that, unlike siblingship, was purely a matter of choice. "The point of the Revolution," Fliegelman observes, "would not be simply to dissolve an intolerable union but to establish a more glorious one founded on the most primary of social unions—the voluntary marriage contract."[25]

That the major theorists of the Revolution were concerned with the political lessons of marital unions is plainly evident. For instance, on the eve of the Declaration of Independence during the year and a half between January 1775 and July 1776 when Paine served as the editor of the short-lived *Pennsylvania Magazine; or American Monthly Magazine*—and when he must have also been at work on *Common Sense*—he found time to write several articles on marriage for the magazine, and he included the work of others who likewise reflected on the subject. For instance, under the pseudonym of The Old Bachelor, Paine published an article in *Pennsylvania Magazine* in June 1775 titled "Reflections on Unhappy Marriages." He maintained not only that marriages based on either rash passion or pecuniary interest inevitably ended in unhappiness but also that the divine sanctions provided by church ceremonies that created a supposedly irrevocable bond were likewise no guarantee to happiness. Paine presented an alternative to these unhappy circumstances by addressing this issue from the perspective of a Native American:

> An American savage ... being advised by one of our countrymen to marry according to the ceremonies of the church ... replyed ... "Whereas in [our relationships], which have no other ceremony than mutual affection, and last no longer than they bestow mutual pleasures, we make it our business to oblige the heart we are afraid to lose; and being at liberty to separate, seldom or never feel the inclination. But if any should be found so wretched among us, as to hate where the only commerce ought to be love, we instantly dissolve the band."[26]

Through the words of this "American savage," Paine made two arguments that were relevant to readers in 1775. On the one hand, he provided an argument for separation "if any should be found so wretched among us, as to hate where the only commerce ought to be love" — an argument that was applicable to the political circumstance as much as marital ones (including Paine's own early marriage). On the other hand, he provided the grounds for a new kind of bond forged from the enactment of new world sentiments of love and mutual affection that were born in liberty. Such a bond could not be fixed by divine sanction or "made" to last but lasted only as long as "we make it our business to oblige the heart we are afraid to lose"; and, being freely entered into, it could be freely dissolved should mutual affection and happiness be found wanting. A year before the Declaration of Independence, it was clear that the goals of life, liberty, and the pursuit of happiness threaded their way through both the marital and the political aspirations of the American revolutionaries.

In the years after the Revolution, these sentiments and values coalesced in the concept of "republican matrimonialism," a phrase that, according to Fliegelman, "appears in the popular press in the 1790s."[27] It is a felicitous term that captures the essential merging of marital and political meanings in eighteenth-century political thought.[28] "Marriage," Jan Lewis tells us, "was the very pattern from which the cloth of republican society was to be cut,"[29] and stories about different kinds of marriages were, therefore, simultaneously stories about different kinds of polity.

At the core of republican matrimonialism was a comparative sociology that highlighted the distinctiveness of American marital and political values by setting them in stark contrast to those they assumed to be characteristic of British and European aristocracies and monarchies. One of the most influential works for the founders' conception of the republican order they wished to bring about was *The Spirit of the Laws* by Montesquieu.[30] This volume not only provided them with a characterization of the nature and principles of different forms of governments—despotic, monarchical, and republican (both aristocratic and democratic)—but also schooled them in the concordances between domestic and political forms of governance—in particular, in the contrast between despotic and democratic republican regimes (see Mathieu in this volume). Echoes of Montesquieu's characterization of political types ran through the literature of the revolutionary and postrevolutionary eras.[31] There was the fear-generating tyranny of the despotic state and its harem that—in the absence of virtue, honor, love, or affection—required the coercive subordination and servitude of women in polygamy.[32] There was the monarchical state whose principle of honor demanded preferences and distinctions and made visible its preeminences and hereditary ranks in displays of ostentatious wealth and luxury.[33] There was the aristocratic republic, which, in order to thrive—and resist being undone by a reversion to hereditary distinctions—must display more modesty in manners and dress in order to "blend with the people" so that they "forget their own weaknesses."[34] And, finally, there was the democratic republic, with its virtues of equality and liberty and its leveling sentiments.[35] There is a remarkable passage in Montesquieu that emphasizes not only equality but also modest frugality and public benevolence as core values of a democratic republic.

> Love of the republic in a democracy is love of democracy; love of democracy is love of equality.
>
> Love of democracy is also love of frugality. As each one there should have the same happiness and the same advantages, each should taste the same pleasures and form the same expectations; this is something that can be anticipated only from the common frugality.
>
> Love of equality in a democracy limits ambition to the single desire, the single happiness, of rendering greater services to one's homeland than other citizens. Men cannot render it equal services, but they should equally render it services. ...
>
> ...
>
> Thus by establishing frugality in domestic life, good democracies opened the gate to public expenditures, as happened in Athens and Rome. Magnificence and abundance had their source in frugality itself ... the laws wanted frugal mores so that one could give to one's homeland.[36]

Such qualities set democratic republics apart from their more hierarchical alternatives—particularly monarchical and despotic states, if not also aristocratic republics and their feigned modesty. "In a republic," Montesquieu argued, "the condition of the citizens is limited, equal, gentle, and moderate; the effects of public liberty are felt throughout. Empire over women could not be as well exercised."[37] In this comparative sociology, the idealized qualities and vitality of the republican matrimonial and political order were underscored by its contrast not only with the tyrannical coercion and fear required of despotic states and polygamous harems but also with the ostentatious luxury—the pomp and splendor—necessary for the realization of hereditary distinctions and preferences.

Whether people drew explicitly upon Montesquieu or not, popular novels, magazines, newspapers, and advice books were filled with accounts that echoed some of Montesquieu's contrastive themes as they traced the qualities of good and bad marriages, and thus the qualities that were presumed to support or threaten the fledgling republic. At least three tropes were common in these accountings of republican matrimonialism: the importance of the qualities of equality and friendship and their performative enactment; the centrality of voluntarism and the independence of children free from the coercion of parents or seducers; and the significance of merit and the modesty of republican sociality over against the excessive concern with hereditary rank and luxury associated with European court life.

Central to both the republican political union and marital union, was, first of all, a set of sentiments that revolved around the concept of friendship, and this reverberated with earlier and contemporaneous British feminist and Scottish Enlightenment ideas about the revolutionary value of friendship.[38] Lewis notes:

> Republican characterizations of marriage echoed with the words *equal, mutual,* and *reciprocal,* and marriage was described as a friendship between equals. An essay "Addressed to the Ladies," for example, urged "every young married woman to seek the friend of her heart in the husband of her affection. There, and there only, is that true equality, both of rank and fortune, and cemented by mutual interests, and mutual ... pledges to be found. ... There and there only will she be sure to meet with reciprocal confidence, unfeigned attachment and tender solicitude to sooth every care." Indeed, no word better summarizes republican notions of marriage than *friendship*.[39]

It is significant that the idea of "friendship"—particularly in marriage—is highlighted. Friendship most easily bears the essence of the republican virtues, for it is a relationship that is the most freely chosen, least tied to "natural"—or hierarchical—obligation, and whose mutuality and equality cannot be presupposed, but must be performed through—*created* out of—sentiments and acts of solicitous care.[40]

Second, the values of voluntarism and independence should be central to the marital as much as the political union. As Lewis argues, the stories that filled the popular press featured several stock characters. On the one hand, they "juxtaposed the virtuous, independent child and the oppressive, corrupting parent, and ... found in the union of two virtuous individuals the true end of society and the fit paradigm for political life."[41] On the other hand, they paraded before the public a set of "republicanism's stock villains ... the tyrannical ruler and the designing courtier, ... and—most of all—the vile seducer. The coercive motivations of these figures threatened the consensual union that served as the metaphor of what republicans wanted their society to be."[42]

And third, the republican concern with social merit, modesty of means, and social benevolence was contrasted with the aristocratic and monarchical obsession with rank, wealth, and ostentatious luxury.[43] Lewis observes that both men and women were strenuously warned to stay clear of particular types "associated with the despicable aspects of European court life: flatterers, ... flirts, fops, coxcombs, coquettes, and all persons lacking in honor and virtue. ... [These figures] romp through the pages of republican literature with abandon. Their names are code words that signify luxury, vice, and deceit; ... They promise ruin not only for themselves and their victims but also for the infant nation. ..."[44]

For the American patriots, such qualities were dangerous for the fledgling republic precisely because they presented the specter of everything they had hoped to leave behind in the course of their revolution: divinely ordained hierarchy, hereditary status, patriarchal authority, ostentatious luxury, and the fawning, self-interested attention of inferiors attempting to ingratiate themselves with their superiors. Needless to say, the Revolution did not eradicate aristocratic pretensions and hierarchical values from postrevolutionary America; indeed they remain a strong undercurrent in the inequities of American society to this day. But the revolutionaries maintained that such vice and corruption quashed the innate equality, mutual love and affection, and disinterested benevolence—not to mention the modesty of individual merit—that they deemed critical to the spirit and vitality of a democratic republic.

That the political resonances of such stories were fully evident to readers and that they were noted by many—including leading political figures—is evidenced again in the work of Thomas Paine, who addressed his readers in the April 1775 issue of *Philadelphia Magazine* with a parable on marriage—titled "Cupid and Hymen. An Original"[45]—that contrasted the virtues of marriage for love and affection among social equals over a marriage coerced by parents concerned only with the goal of raising family status and wealth. And it was evidenced by a comment John Adams wrote in the margins of his copy of the 1773 edition of *Eloisa*—the English translation of Rousseau's *La Novelle Heloise*. In it, Fliegelman reports,

> Adams underscored a passage describing the intervention of Julie's cruel parent in the affairs of her heart: "Let rank be determined by merit and the union of hearts by their own choice, this is the proper social order. ... Those who regulate it [the union of hearts] by birth or wealth are the real disturbers of the system." ... Adams adds in agreement: "Peoples, nations, not individuals are guilty of this." ... Adams's comment suggests [that]. ... In a nation ruled by an aristocracy that identifies rank with wealth, marriage will be arranged to perpetuate that order. But in an American republic such as envisioned by Adams, the choice of marriage partners would not only be free but, as it would reward virtue and merit, so it would serve as the foundation of a new order.[46]

Fliegelman goes on to observe that, in the context of his own family, Adams was guided by the principles of "matrimonial republicanism" as he gave his daughter Nabby his consent "to arrange your plans according to your own judgments," despite the fact that her suitor, Royall Tyler, had had a reputation for womanizing in his youth.[47] Nabby eventually broke off the engagement of her own accord.

But Royall Tyler went on to write what Fliegelman bills as "one of the most popular American plays of the eighteenth century," which captured the perceived contrast between American and British marital politics in clear and unmistakable terms.[48] In Tyler's play, pointedly titled *The Contrast*,[49] the authoritarian Mr. Van Rough has betrothed his daughter, Maria, to the British-educated Mr. Dimple solely on account of his fortune; but Maria has perceived that her betrothed is a profligate philanderer (who is actually simultaneously courting two other women—the coquette, Charlotte Manly, and her well-to-do friend, Letitia). When Charlotte's brother, Colonel Manly—a modest, frugal, and virtuous soldier who served in the Revolutionary War—arrives in town, Maria realizes that Colonel Manly is her true love and that she must resist the coercions of her father. Maria is clear in her heart that she could never marry "a depraved wretch, whose only virtue is a polished exterior ... whose heart, insensible to the emotion of patriotism, dilates at the plaudits of every unthinking girl."[50] Luckily her father relieves her of her obligations when he finds out that Mr. Dimple is burdened with massive gambling debts. Fliegelman observes that Tyler skillfully develops a set of "conventional dichotomies into a broader contrast between a corrupt and luxurious England and a virtuous and hearty America. By making one suitor the product of an American education and the other of a British education, Tyler succeeded in unobtrusively having the conventions of the eighteenth-century stage serve a patriotic and antipatriarchal theme."[51]

Here, the political and marital meanings of republican matrimonialism are entirely fused. The revolutionaries sought to imagine and bring into being a union that should be based on voluntarism, not coercion; on the symmetrical sentiments of marital love and friendship, not the asymmetric power of patriarchy; and on the social modesty of means and merit, not the excesses of luxury required to display the distinctions of rank. Yet despite the power of the contrast drawn during the revolutionary and postrevolutionary era, the tension between these contrasting values continued to animate the dynamics of American society into the nineteenth century and well beyond.

Nineteenth-Century Opposition to Political and Marital Hierarchy

By the mid-nineteenth century, the contradictions between the realities of American social relations and the ideals of American equality could no longer be avoided. This was evident at the Republican Party's first national convention in 1856, when delegates adopted a platform that called for the prohibition "in the Territories [of] those twin relics of barbarism—Polygamy, and Slavery."[52] It was also manifest in the opposition to cousin marriage and its association not only with the inherited rank and ostentatious wealth of European aristocracy but also with the rise of a home-grown aristocracy among the emergent urban and plantation elites across the country.

During the second half of the nineteenth century, an extraordinary amount of blood and treasure—not to mention scientific, legislative, judicial, and literary labor—was expended in efforts to eradicate these institutions, which, in different ways, threatened the values of equality, voluntaristic consent, and secular law central to postrevolutionary ideals of the republican marital, political, and economic experiment. The battle against slavery is far beyond the scope of this chapter, and elsewhere I examine the opposition to cousin marriage in the last half of the nineteenth century.[53] Here, I wish to focus on the opposition to Mormon polygamy and theocracy during the same time period and the forging of a strong association between monogamy and democratic republicanism.

It should be noted that the first half of the nineteenth century was a time of particular ferment with regard to the kinds of relations deemed proper to the big and little commonwealths—and to the gendered forms of political, economic, and domestic relations. In the context of the Second Great Awakening religious revival, the social and economic transformations of the industrial revolution, and a series of economic booms and devastating busts, a plethora of utopian societies were founded that experimented with different forms of sexual, gender, and marital relations—ranging from celibacy (the Shakers), group marriage (Oneida), and polygamy (the Mormons), to "free love." And these were generally complemented by differing philosophies of political, economic, and religious organization—from various transcendentalist and perfectionist religious orders to a host of Fourierist phalanxes and socialist utopias (see Arni in this volume).[54] While most of these experiments were short-lived, they nevertheless indicated that neither domestic nor political-economic relations in America were settled matters.

Yet, when the Mormons established an explicitly hierarchical and patriarchal order that united domestic polygamy with a hierarchical priestly theocracy in the Utah Territory, it immediately evoked the specter of Montesquieu's despotic state on American soil—complete with polygamous harems governed by patriarchal coercion and fear. And it precipitated strong and often violent opposition from political theorists, members of the US Congress and judiciary, feminists, and popular writers alike.

It was Francis Lieber—a German immigrant to the United States in 1827 and one of the most influential American political philosophers in the mid- to late nineteenth century[55]—who early on articulated a persuasive case for refusing to grant statehood to the polygamous Mormon theocracy that was being established in the Utah Territory. As a background to his case against polygamy, it is worth knowing that, in his earlier works on political theory, Lieber—not unlike Lewis Henry Morgan a few decades later[56]—had posited that property and marriage were key drivers of the improvement of mankind and the advancement of civilization. Drawing upon Montesquieu[57] and other theorists who had posited a relation between the big and little commonwealths, Lieber argued that "the family, which can exist only where the institution of marriage exists as an exclusive and permanent connexion of the sexes, has been, and will continue to be, through all ages, the true 'nursery of the commonwealth.'"[58]

The existence of the polygamous and theocratic Mormons posed several questions. Constitutionally, should a theocratic state be admitted to the union? If marriage was the "nursery of the commonwealth," did it matter what kinds of marriage formed the nursery of a democratic republic? How were the perceived qualities of different forms of marriage understood to generate different forms of polity?

In the first half of his March 1855 article in *Putnam's Monthly* titled "The Mormons: Shall Utah Be Admitted into the Union?" Lieber addressed the constitutional question regarding statehood and the very foundation of law. He elucidated the logic of the Constitution, which, he pointed out, provided that "Congress *may* [i.e., not shall or must] admit new States"; but that "The United States *shall* [i.e., not may] guarantee to every State in this Union a Republican Form of Government."[59] He went to some length to show that Mormon theocracy could not qualify as a republican form of government (despite its own claims to be a "theodemocracy"), primarily because the Mormons depended upon continual divine inspiration to shape their polity. By "Republic," Lieber argued, the founders meant "a polity founded upon the broad principle that the first source and starting point of power is in the people. Never, even as colonists, have their political convictions been tinctured with the fabled Jus Divinum."[60] He compared the Mormon leaders and their claims to "direct infusion of the Divine Spirit" to the Russian czar, who "considers himself pretty near to the heavenly quarters"; and he compared the hierarchy of Mormon priests to the European hereditary nobility, which he noted had been explicitly prohibited by the Constitution.[61] Here, Lieber insisted that there could be no place in a republican union for a state based on either hereditary nobility or the sacralizing power of divine law as opposed to the power of the people. Lieber's words hark back to Thomas Paine's exhortation that the American polity required a rejection of the divinely sanctioned hereditary power of the Crown, which should be "demolished, and scattered among the people whose right it is."

At the center of the opposition to Mormon marital and political order was the conviction—echoing the association established by Montesquieu—that polygamy required and reflected the coercion and force that was the principle of despotism.[62] Opponents simply could not conceive of the possibility that women under polygamy could exercise individual choice, free will, or the voluntarism that they deemed foundational to Protestant Christian monogamy, religious freedom, and a democratic republic. Women under polygamy were therefore often referred to as "white slaves"—mirroring the "black slaves" that together constituted the "twin relics of barbarism" against which the Republican Party had set itself.[63]

Throughout the second half of his 1855 article, Lieber situated his caustic condemnation of Mormon polygamy and theocracy within the larger evolutionary framework shaped by his deeply ethnocentric and racist contrast between European cultures and those in Asia and Africa. On the one side, he argued, the practice of polygamy among Asian and African "races" is guided by religious superstition and restricts both women and freedom of thought; on the other side, the practice of monogamy among people of the Euro-American Caucasian "race" is guided by Christianity, rational law, Enlightenment social equality, and freedom of thought.[64] For Lieber, polygamy—and the intimate merging of domestic and political forms of governance that Montesquieu had posited for despotic states—tied "Eastern" states to patriarchal despotism, religious dogma, and civilizational stagnation, whereas monogamy was critical to republican liberties (and thus voluntarism and free will) as well as the restless civilizational advance of "Western" states.[65]

But the relation posited between marital and political forms of governance was not always simply an "association": even as the Saints conceptualized polygamy as integral to Mormon theocracy, their opponents equally understood monogamy as the foundation of liberty and even of the Constitution itself. Indeed, both those for and against polygamy agreed upon a central proposition: that there should be an integral and necessary connection between marriage and political forms of governance—that is, in Sarah Barringer Gordon's words, that "commitment to one or the other form of marriage shaped public as well as private life."[66]

In a remarkable passage in his 1855 article "The Mormons," Lieber went further to make a case for monogamy as foundational to law itself and to "all that is called polity."

> Monogamy does not only go with the western Caucasian race, the Europeans and their descendants, beyond Christianity, it goes beyond Common Law. It is one of the primordial elements out of which all law proceeds, or which the law steps in to recognize and to protect. ... Wedlock, or monogamic marriage, is one of the "categories" of our social thoughts and conceptions, and, therefore, of our social existence. It is one of the elementary distinctions—historical and actual—between European and Asiatic humanity. It is one of the frames of our thoughts, and moulds of our feelings; it is a psychological condition of our jural consciousness, of our liberty, of our literature, of our aspirations, of our religious convictions, and of our domestic being and family relation, the foundation of all that is called polity.[67]

For Lieber, monogamy was a primordial element, the font of all law and the foundation of political liberty and the polity itself. Lieber's position on the significance of monogamy and polygamy was echoed by nineteenth-century antipolygamist feminists, politicians, and novelists in the North and East, who saw the hierarchical patriarchal order of Mormon polygamists and theocrats as a stark threat to the egalitarian and voluntaristic qualities that they understood to be vital to monogamy and democracy.[68] In the introduction to her popular 1856 novel *Mormon Wives*, Metta Victor asserted in reference to the corruptive principals of polygamy that "whatever degrades him [man]—whatever corrupts and injures his moral, intellectual, and physical well-being is inimical to the well-being of society, to the State, to the whole country; consequently, to the spirit and intent of that Constitution which is to perpetuate the republic, and render it, in truth, the refuge for the oppressed, the *home* of liberty."[69] By contrast, the antipolygamists, Gordon suggests, "embraced the theory that [monogamous] marriage was not only a component of human happiness but of the *Constitution itself*. The right to emotional and spiritual fulfillment, conceived as the 'spirit and intent of th[e] Constitution,' they argued, was integral to the novelists' claim that polygamy entailed an illegitimate exercise of authority."[70] Authority vested not in patriarchal coercion and tyranny but rather in voluntaristic consent, which was—as the revolutionaries had earlier maintained— essential to both the republican marital and political unions.

Just as they saw monogamy as the "home" of republican liberty, opponents saw Mormon polygamy as the very foundation of tyranny and despotism. Indeed, in *Reynolds v. U.S.*, Chief Justice Morrison R. Waite noted that "Professor Lieber says, polygamy leads to the patriarchal principle, and which, when applied to large communities, fetters the people in stationary despotism, while that principle cannot long exist in connection with monogamy."[71] In this opinion, Justice Waite argued that "Congress was deprived of all legislative power over mere [religious] opinion, but was left free to reach actions [i.e., the acts of polygamy] which were in violation of social duties or subversive of good order," and he went on to declare the decision of the court that "as a law of the organization of society under the exclusive dominion of the United States, it is provided that plural marriages shall not be allowed."[72] That is, the decision was (much to the disappointment of the Mormons) not decided upon the basis of religious freedom itself but rather on the grounds that polygamous acts were "subversive of good order" within the jurisdiction of the United States. Given how threatening the organizing principles of polygamy were to republican ideals, it was inconceivable that polygamous marriage could stand as the foundation or nursery of the republican polity, and it was therefore necessary for it to be prohibited.

With the prohibition of polygamy in the United States, Americans clarified the fact that the "marriage" in "republican matrimonialism" was not just any form of marriage but *monogamous* marriage, and their particularly fierce defensive stance against Mormon polygamy and theocracy reasserted, by contrast, a firm connection between monogamous marriage and democratic republicanism and the acts of consent that were meant to underlie them both.

Conclusion

Eighteenth- and nineteenth-century America is a particularly rich period in which to explore the power that ideas about the relationship between kinship and polity have had not only to shape distinctive forms of social organization but also to radically transform them. I want to make two larger points about this relationship. The first has to do with the different ways in which contemporaneous political and popular theories about the relationship between kinship and polity were configured. On the one hand, the big and little commonwealths were seen to be organized by the same underlying ideas and values and by their recursive application across the different domains. As a result, they were intimate analogues of one another: the political commonwealth was a large family, and the family was a little political commonwealth. A term like "republican matrimonialism" speaks to the ways in which the two were fused, the one unimaginable without the other. On the other hand, often in these texts it appears that the family relations of the little commonwealth—including those of patriarchal power, descent, and marriage—were understood to be the *foundation* of the relations of the big commonwealth. They formed the "nursery" or "seminary" of specific core values which, in turn, created the "foundation" of, or "led to," specific political types. This seems to indicate not simply an analogous concordance between forms of kinship and marriage and different political types but also a generative relation. It is for this reason, for instance, that the eradication of Mormon polygamy was the essential first step in dismantling the Mormon theocratic political order in Utah.

From a "modern" sensibility this is significant, if not also counterintuitive, since most social theory about the development of the "modern" nation-state presupposes the historical subordination of kinship relations to those of politics, making it hard to imagine either their mutual constitution or the generative power of kinship in relation to politics.[73] The material reviewed in this chapter, and throughout this volume, suggests we might reconsider the possibilities.

The second point has to do with the role of more naturalized or more performative ideas about kinship and polity and their relation to hierarchy and equality. Over the past several decades, anthropologists have suggested that kinship systems entail a dynamic relation between those forms of kinship that depend, on the one hand, upon notions of naturalized or essentialized being (for instance, relatedness created out of bodily substances such as blood, bone, or semen) and, on the other hand, those that depend upon notions about doing, performing, and creating kinship (for instance, out of the everyday acts of care, nurturance, labor, and love, etc.). And they have begun to see kinship systems as differentiated by the way they foreground one or the other of these aspects, by the way they presuppose one as foundational and given and the other as something that must be created, as the work of society.[74] It is possible to ask, then, to what extent hierarchical systems tend to foreground—indeed often require—more naturalized and essentialized ideologies of kinship—however that may be embodied or materialized—while systems that strive to be egalitarian tend to foreground more performative ideologies of kinship.[75]

In the American case I have been following in this chapter, it is possible to see how the differential foregrounding of kinship-as-essentialized-being as opposed to kinship-as-created-through-performative-acts-of-doing played out in attempts to transform a hierarchical polity into an egalitarian one.[76] Aristocratic ideas about the hierarchical qualities of kinship and polity foregrounded the notion that differences in rank were natural or divinely given, and transmissible through descent lines.[77] In contesting an aristocratic social order, the American revolutionaries had, in effect, to de-essentialize and denaturalize the notions of hereditary rank, and they did so by arguing that kinship between parents and children—or ruler and ruled—was not natural and unbreakable but could be broken by acts of violence and tyranny and in the absence of performative acts of care, love, and nurturance. Taking a step further, they foregrounded their idea of the voluntaristic marital relation—created through acts of "doing," acts of love, reciprocity, and friendship—as the model for the more egalitarian republican union they wished to bring about.[78]

Although in the fervor of the revolutionary and postrevolutionary era the more performative, egalitarian values of kinship and polity were foregrounded to contest those of an aristocratic naturalized hierarchy, the tension between the two was not then—and has never yet been—finally resolved. Indeed, it continues to animate contemporary controversies in America over how the big and little commonwealths should be constituted and related to one another. Yet, in these contestations, it is possible to see how ideas about descent and marriage—and notions about what is presumed to be given in the nature of things and what must be performed and created—are integral to the ways in which hierarchical and egalitarian commonwealths of affection are imagined and brought into being.

Susan McKinnon is professor emerita in the Department of Anthropology, University of Virginia. Her work has focused on issues relating to kinship, marriage, and gender, including their cross-cultural and historical diversity, their centrality in the structures of hierarchy and equality, and their relation to ideas about nation and modernity. Her books include *From a Shattered Sun: Hierarchy, Gender, and Alliance in the Tanimbar Islands* and *Neo-liberal Genetics: The Myths and Moral Tales of Evolutionary Psychology* (1992), as well as the coedited volumes *Relative Values: Reconfiguring Kinship Studies* (2001); *Complexities: Beyond Nature and Nurture* (2005); and *Vital Relations: Modernity and the Persistent Life of Kinship* (2013).

Notes

1. George Lawson quoted in Gordon J. Schochet, *The Authoritarian Family and Political Attitudes in 17th-Century England: Patriarchalism in Political Thought* (New Brunswick, NJ: Transaction Books, 1988), 181.
2. To the extent that political philosophers agreed with this statement, and not all did, there was nevertheless intense debate from different positions as to the origins, historical development, and nature of familial and political power, the relation between them, and their similarities and differences. See Schochet, *Authoritarian Family*, for a detailed analysis of these differences.
3. In this, I draw upon the work of a number of scholars who, primarily in the 1980s, explored the connections between kinship and politics in the political theory and popular literature of revolutionary and postrevolutionary America. See Winthrop D. Jordan, "Familial Politics: Thomas Paine and the Killing of the King, 1776," *Journal of American History* 60, no. 2 (1973); Jay Fliegelman, *Prodigals and Pilgrims: The American Revolution against Patriarchal Authority, 1750–1800* (Cambridge: Cambridge University Press, 1982); Mary Lyndon Shanley, "Marriage Contract and Social Contract in Seventeenth-Century English Political Thought," in *The Family in Political Thought*, ed. J. B. Elshtain (Amherst: University of Massachusetts Press, 1982); Melvin Yazawa, *From Colonies to Commonwealth: Familial Ideology and the Beginnings of the American Republic* (Baltimore, MD: Johns Hopkins University Press, 1985); Jan Lewis, "The Republican Wife: Virtue and Seduction in the Early Republic," *William and Mary Quarterly* 44, no. 4 (1987); Norma Basch, "From the Bonds of Empire to the Bonds of Matrimony," in *Devising Liberty: Preserving and Creating Freedom in the New American Republic*, ed. D. T. Konig (Stanford, CA: Stanford University Press, 1995); and Nancy F. Cott, *Public Vows: A History of Marriage and the Nation* (Cambridge, MA: Harvard University Press, 2000).
4. Benjamin Franklin, "Information to Those Who Would Remove to America," *Benjamin Franklin: Autobiography, Poor Richard, and Later Writings*, ed. J. A. Leo Lemay (New York: Library Classics of America, 1997), 236-37 (emphases and capitalizations in the original).
5. On the naturalization and denaturalization of hierarchy and power in kinship theory, see Sylvia Yanagisako and Carol Delaney, ed., *Naturalizing Power: Essays in Feminist Cultural Analysis* (New York: Routledge, 1995). On naturalized vs. performative theories of kinship (and their relation to hierarchy), see Susan McKinnon, "Doing and Being: Process, Essence, and Hierarchy in Making Kin," *The Routledge Companion to Contemporary Anthropology*, ed. S. Coleman, S. B. Hyatt, and A. Kingsolver (London: Routledge, 2017).
6. Edmund S. Morgan, ed., *Puritan Political Ideas, 1558–1794* (Indianapolis: Hackett Publishing Co., 1965), xv–xx, 15–59, 143–48.

7. See Robert Filmer, "Patriarcha: The Naturall Power of Kinges Defended against the Unnatural Liberty of the People," in *Sir Robert Filmer: Patriarcha and Other Writings*, ed. J. P. Sommerville (Cambridge: Cambridge University Press, 1991 [1680]), and Peter Clark, *The Rulers [sic] Highest Dignity, and the People's Truest Glory* (Boston: S. Kneeland, Printer to the Honourable House of Representatives, 1739).
8. Yazawa, *From Colonies to Commonwealth*, 20–21.
9. Yazawa, *From Colonies to Commonwealth*, 20–25.
10. Richard Elburne quoted in Yazawa, *From Colonies to Commonwealth*, 87.
11. Joseph Reed quoted in Yazawa, *From Colonies to Commonwealth*, 89, emphasis in original.
12. Yazawa, *From Colonies to Commonwealth*, 89.
13. Joseph Reed quoted in Yazawa, *From Colonies to Commonwealth*, 88–89.
14. A second question, which I do not have the space to detail here, was whether children were bound as subservient to parents for life or could grow to maturity and achieve adult independence. For a consideration of both questions, see Fliegelman, *Prodigals and Pilgrims*, 93–122.
15. Blackstone quoted in Fliegelman, *Prodigals and Pilgrims*, 95.
16. Fliegelman, *Prodigals and Pilgrims*, 95.
17. Most notably, John Locke's *Two Treatises of Government*, ed. P. Laslett (Cambridge: Cambridge University Press, 1988 [1689]) was an explicit refutation of Robert Filmer's robust articulation of the patriarchal model and the absolute power of fathers and kings in his *Patriarcha*. Peter Laslett, "Introduction," in John Locke, *Two Treatises of Government*, ed. P. Laslett (Cambridge: Cambridge University Press, 1988), situates these works in the context of seventeenth-century political philosophy and revolutions in Britain. Locke's works were well-known and highly influential in American revolutionary circles.
18. Jonathan Mayhew, *A Discourse Concerning Unlimited Submission and Non-resistance to the Higher Powers: With Some Reflections on the Resistance Made to King Charles I* (Lincoln: DigitalCommons@University of Nebraska–Lincoln, 1750), 38–39 in footnote, http://digitalcommons.unl.edu/cgi/viewcontent.cgi?article=1044&context=etas. See also Jordan, "Familial Politics," 300. For other American Puritan authors on this subject, see Morgan, *Puritan Political Ideas*.
19. Thomas Paine, *Collected Writings* (New York: Literary Classics of the United States, 1955), 29, emphasis in the original.
20. Paine, *Collected Writings*, 36, 34.
21. For a more extensive exploration of these connections in revolutionary America, see Fliegelman, *Prodigals and Pilgrims*, 123–54; Shanley, "Marriage Contract and Social Contract"; Lewis, "Republican Wife"; and Basch, "From the Bonds of Empire."
22. Paine, *Collected Writings*, 22.
23. Paine, *Collected Writings*, 53, emphasis in the original.
24. Fliegelman, *Prodigals and Pilgrims*, 126.
25. Fliegelman, *Prodigals and Pilgrims*, 127.
26. Thomas Paine (under the pseudonym The Old Bachelor), "Reflections on Unhappy Marriages," *The Pennsylvania Magazine; or, American Monthly Museum* (June 1775), 365.
27. Fliegelman, *Prodigals and Pilgrims*, 295n27.
28. Lewis, "Republican Wife," 691.
29. Lewis, "Republican Wife," 689.
30. Baron de Charles de Secondat Montesquieu, *The Spirit of the Laws*, trans. and ed. A. M. Cohler, B. C. Miller, and H. S. Stone (Cambridge: University of Cambridge Press, 1989 [1748]).
31. Cott, *Public Vows*, 10, 18, 21–22.
32. Montesquieu, *Spirit of the Laws*, 27–29; 59–63. See also Mary Lyndon Shanley and Peter G. Stillman, "Political and Marital Despotism: Montesquieu's Persian Letters," in *The*

Family in Political Thought, ed. J. B. Elshtain (Amherst: University of Massachusetts Press, 1982).
33. Montesquieu, *Spirit of the Laws*, 25–27, 55–58.
34. Montesquieu, *Spirit of the Laws*, 52, see also 24–25, 51–55.
35. Montesquieu, *Spirit of the Laws*, 22–24, 43–50.
36. Montesquieu, *Spirit of the Laws*, 43. One finds an echo of these sentiments in Benjamin Franklin's famous notes on the virtues of frugality and in his equally famous public philanthropy.
37. Montesquieu, *Spirit of the Laws*, 270.
38. I am grateful to Caroline Arni for pointing me to a number of authors who have discussed feminist ideals—primarily from the seventeenth through the nineteenth centuries—of egalitarian marriage and politics imagined in terms of friendship. See, for instance, Mary Lyndon Shanley, "Marital Slavery and Friendship: John Stuart Mill's 'The Subjection of Women,'" in *Feminist Interpretations and Political Theory*, ed. M. L. Shanley and C. Pateman (University Park: Pennsylvania State University Press, 1991); Ruth Abby, "Back to the Future: Marriage as Friendship in the Thought of Mary Wollstonecraft," *Hypatia* 14, no. 3 (1999); Caroline Arni, "Rivalry and Friendship in the Heterosexual Couple: Challenges to Discourses of Society in Late 19th and Early 20th Century Europe," *Occasional Papers from the School of Social Science, Institute for Advanced Study*, paper no. 25 (April 2006); Elizabeth Frazer, "Mary Wollstonecraft on Politics and Friendship," *Political Studies* 56 (2008). For friendship in Scottish Enlightenment ideas about commercial society, see Lisa Hill and Peter McCarthy, "Hume, Smith and Ferguson: Friendship in Commercial Society," *Critical Review of International Social and Political Philosophy*, 2, no. 4 (1999); and for friendship (and "neighboring") in American revolutionary thinking, see Barbara Clark Smith, *The Freedoms We Lost: Consent and Resistance in Revolutionary America* (New York: The New Press, 2010). For a fascinating history of the English use of the term "friendship" to designate the world of kinship relations, see Marilyn Strathern, *Relations: An Anthropological Exposition* (Durham, NC: Duke University Press, 2020), 144–48.
39. Lewis, "Republican Wife," 707, italics in the original.
40. It is critical to note that the "equality" that was referenced here—and also in the debate about polygamy later in the nineteenth century—was meant to highlight a contrast between republican ideals, on the one hand, and the hierarchical distinctions in social rank that were seen as essential to despotic, monarchical, and aristocratic regimes, on the other. As Jan Lewis notes: "True marriage was proportionate; put another way, it was symmetrical. Indeed, the mutuality and reciprocity that republicans so prized were inconceivable in an asymmetrical union—the 'slavery' of so-called barbaric cultures, in which women were thoroughly subordinated to men. That republican marriage was symmetrical does not mean that it was fully egalitarian" (Lewis, "Republican Wife," 707–8). Indeed, although much was changing through the eighteenth and nineteenth centuries with regard to gender in marital relations—see Michael Grossberg, *Governing the Hearth: Law and the Family in Nineteenth-Century America* (Chapel Hill: University of North Carolina Press, 1985), 3–30—the persistence of hierarchical aspects of gendered marital relations (most prominently in the institution of coverture) well into the nineteenth and twentieth centuries is well documented (see, in particular, Cott, *Public Vows*).
41. Lewis, "Republican Wife," 698.
42. Lewis, "Republican Wife," 720.
43. See Clark Smith, *Freedoms We Lost*, 86–133, for the thoroughgoing reorganization of the patriot economy, which, among other things, rejected, as a matter of principle, imported British luxury goods in favor of more modest, American-produced goods, including American "home-spun" cloth, which became a sartorial index of the patriot movement.

44. Lewis, "Republican Wife," 697, 697–98.
45. Thomas Paine (under the pseudonym Esop), "Cupid and Hymen: An Original," *The Pennsylvania Magazine; or, American Monthly Museum* (April 1775).
46. Fliegelman, *Prodigals and Pilgrims*, 133.
47. Fliegelman, *Prodigals and Pilgrims*, 134.
48. Fliegelman, *Prodigals and Pilgrims*, 134.
49. Royall Tyler, *The Contrast: A Comedy in Five Acts* (New York: AMS Press, 1970).
50. Tyler, *Contrast*, 38–39.
51. Fliegelman, *Prodigals and Pilgrims*, 134.
52. The relevant resolution focused on the US government's relation to its territories. It read: "*Resolved:* That the Constitution confers upon Congress sovereign powers over the Territories of the United States for their government; and that in the exercise of this power, it is both the right and the imperative duty of Congress to prohibit in the Territories those twin relics of barbarism — Polygamy, and Slavery" (Independence Hall Association, "Republican Platform of 1856," retrieved 17 December 2020 from http://www.ushistory.org/gop/convention_1856republicanplatform.htm). The Republican Party thereby explicitly opposed both the extension of slavery into the territories and the establishment of Mormon polygamy (and a would-be theocratic state) in the Utah Territory. See Sarah Barringer Gordon, *The Mormon Question: Polygamy and Constitutional Conflict in Nineteenth-Century America* (Chapel Hill: University of North Carolina Press, 2002), 55.
53. Susan McKinnon, "Cousin Marriage, Hierarchy, and Heredity: Contestations over Domestic and National Body Politics in Nineteenth-Century America," *Journal of the British Academy* 7 (2019). This paper explores the ways in which the positive associations of cousin (or "in-and-in") marriage were revalued to link it with the hereditary degeneration and decline of individuals, family lines, and aristocratic/monarchical political regimes, while non-kin "out-marriage" became linked with the constitutional health and vitality of individuals, family lines, and republican polities.
54. See Mark Holloway, *Utopian Communities in America, 1680–1880* (Mineola, NY: Dover Publications, 1966); Lawrence Foster, *Religion and Sexuality: The Shakers, the Mormons, and the Oneida Community* (Urbana: University of Illinois Press, 1984); Lawrence Foster, *Women, Family, and Utopia: Communal Experiments of the Shakers, the Oneida Community, and the Mormons* (Syracuse, NY: Syracuse University Press, 1991); and Donald E. Pitzer, ed., *America's Communal Utopias* (Chapel Hill: University of North Carolina Press, 1997).
55. For an account of Lieber's life and political philosophy, see Frank Freidel, *The Life of Francis Lieber* (Baton Rouge: Louisiana State University Press, 1947); and Dorothy Ross, *The Origins of American Social Science* (Cambridge: University of Cambridge Press, 1991), 37–50.
56. Lewis Henry Morgan, *Ancient Society* (Gloucester, MA: Peter Smith, 1974 [1877]); see also Susan McKinnon, "The Economies of Kinship and the Paternity of Culture: Origin Stories in Kinship Theory," in *Relative Values: Reconfiguring Kinship Studies*, ed. Sarah Franklin and Susan McKinnon (Durham, NC: Duke University Press, 2001).
57. Indeed, Lieber placed himself in the ranks of Montesquieu and de Tocqueville, according to Freidel, *Life of Francis Lieber*, 289.
58. Francis Lieber, *Essay on Property and Labor: As Connected with Natural Law and the Constitution of Society* (New York: Harper and Brothers, 1841), 16.
59. Francis Lieber, "The Mormons: Shall Utah Be Admitted into the Union?" *Putnam's Monthly* 5, no. 27 (1855): 227, emphasis in the original; 229, emphasis added.
60. Lieber, "Mormons," 230.
61. Lieber, "Mormons," 231, 230.
62. Cott, *Public Vows*, 22, reflects on the continued importance through the nineteenth century of Montesquieu's work, which, she argues, "initiated what became a formulaic

Enlightenment association of polygamy with despotism. The harem stood for tyrannical rule, political corruption, coercion, elevation of the passions over reason, selfishness, hypocrisy—all the evils that virtuous republicans and enlightened thinkers wanted to avoid. Monogamy, in contrast, stood for a government of consent, moderation, and political liberty."
63. Gordon, *Mormon Question*, 47–49.
64. Lieber, "Mormons," 235. In *Essay on Property and Labor*, 21–22, Lieber had already set up this contrast: "If we take, from the highest point of view, a survey of the whole history of civilization, we shall find that its two great divisions are Asiatic and European civilization; the one fixing, and often immuring, all knowledge, rights, relations, and even intercourse and exchange among men by means of unalterable religious dogmas; the other characterized by criticism, by boundless, often restless inquiry."
65. Freidel, *Life of Francis Lieber*, 155–56.
66. Gordon, *Mormon Question*, 5; see also Cott, *Public Vows*, 10, 21, 114.
67. Lieber, "Mormons," 234.
68. Indeed, one could say that American monogamous marriage could be characterized as egalitarian and voluntaristic—despite the evident contradictions with coverture and other gender inequalities (which persisted well into the twentieth century)—*precisely because* of the strident contrast drawn between it and the perceived coercion and despotic tyranny of Mormon polygamy.
69. Metta Victoria Fuller Victor, *Mormon Wives: A Narrative of Facts Stranger than Fiction* (New York: Derby & Jackson, 1856), vii–viii, emphasis in the original; see also Gordon, *Mormon Question*, 29.
70. Gordon, *Mormon Question*, 51–52, emphasis added.
71. US Supreme Court, *Reynolds v. United States* 98 U.S. 145 (1878), 166; see also Carol Weisbrod and Pamela Sheingorn, "Reynolds v. United States: Nineteenth-Century Forms of Marriage and the Status of Women," *Connecticut Law Review* 10, no. 4 (1978); Gordon, *Mormon Question*, 81; Cott, *Public Vows*, 114–115.
72. US Supreme Court, *Reynolds v. United States*, 164, 166.
73. For a critique of this argument from various intellectual perspectives, see David Warren Sabean, Simon Teuscher, and Jon Mathieu, ed., *Kinship in Europe: Approaches to Long-Term Development (1300–1900)* (New York: Berghahn, 2007); Susan McKinnon and Fenella Cannell, ed., *Vital Relations: Modernity and the Persistent Life of Kinship* (Santa Fe: School of American Research Press, 2013); and Tatjana Thelen and Erdmute Alber, ed., *Reconnecting State and Kinship* (Philadelphia: University of Pennsylvania Press, 2018).
74. For a review of the significance of these ideas in the history of anthropological kinship theory, see Susan McKinnon, "Doing and Being"; and Susan McKinnon, "Kinship Particularism and the Project of Anthropological Comparison," in *Human Nature and Social Life: Perspectives on Extended Sociality*, ed. J. H. Z. Remme and K. Sillander (Cambridge: Cambridge University Press, 2017).
75. McKinnon, "Doing and Being," 173–75.
76. For an analysis of the ways in which ideas about descent and marriage can be differentially constituted as relations between what is given and created, see Eduardo Viveiros de Castro, "The Gift and the Given: Three Nano-essays on Kinship and Magic," in *Kinship and Beyond: The Genealogical Model Reconsidered*, ed. S. Bamford and J. Leach (New York: Berghahn Books, 2009), 251–60.
77. As Philip K. Wilson notes in "Erasmus Darwin and the 'Noble' Disease (Gout): Conceptualizing Heredity and Disease in Enlightenment England," in *Heredity Produced at the Crossroads of Biology, Politics, and Culture, 1500–1870*, ed. S. Müller-Wille and H.-J. Rheinberger (Cambridge, MA: MIT Press, 2007), 142: "Hereditary aristocracy had long been based on the idea that the essence of nobility was transmissible.

Retaining this essence, so the nobility customarily believed, required a purity of bloodlines without any interference through interclass marriage."
78. One can see an analogous transformation in the process of creating a cultural space for gay and lesbian kinship. David M. Schneider, in *American Kinship: A Cultural Account* (Chicago: University of Chicago Press, 1980), 23–25, argued that in mainstream American kinship, biological/blood relations are assumed to be given, enduring, unbreakable, while marriage or adoption requires an act of choice, must be (legally) created, and can be broken. But Kath Weston, *Families We Choose: Lesbians, Gays, Kinship* (New York: Columbia University Press, 1991), 29 (see also 33–41, 107), pointed to the powerful transformation in this logic created by the innovations of gay and lesbian kinship. She notes that, "while dominant cultural representations have asserted that straight is to gay as family is to no family ... , at a certain point in history gay people began to contend that straight is to gay as blood family is to chosen families"—that is, they contested the dominance—the givenness—of the cultural notion that families can only and necessarily be based upon heterosexual biological procreation and relationships of blood descent and insisted upon the idea that love, choice, and care are the "necessary and the sufficient criterion for defining kinship."

Bibliography

Abby, Ruth. "Back to the Future: Marriage as Friendship in the Thought of Mary Wollstonecraft." *Hypatia* 14, no. 3 (1999): 78–95.
Arni, Caroline. "Rivalry and Friendship in the Heterosexual Couple: Challenges to Discourses of Society in Late 19th and Early 20th Century Europe." *Occasional Papers from the School of Social Science, Institute for Advanced Study*, paper no. 25 (April 2006): 1–21.
Basch, Norma. "From the Bonds of Empire to the Bonds of Matrimony." In *Devising Liberty: Preserving and Creating Freedom in the New American Republic*, edited by D. T. Konig, 217–42. Stanford, CA: Stanford University Press, 1995.
Clark, Peter. *The Rulers [sic] Highest Dignity, and the People's Truest Glory*. Boston: S. Kneeland, Printer to the Honourable House of Representatives, 1739.
Cott, Nancy F. *Public Vows: A History of Marriage and the Nation*. Cambridge, MA: Harvard University Press, 2000.
Filmer, Robert. "Patriarcha: The Naturall Power of Kinges Defended against the Unnatural Liberty of the People." In *Sir Robert Filmer: Patriarcha and Other Writings*, edited by J. P. Sommerville, 1–68. Cambridge: Cambridge University Press, 1991 [1680].
Foster, Lawrence. *Religion and Sexuality: The Shakers, the Mormons, and the Oneida Community*. Urbana: University of Illinois Press, 1984.
———. *Women, Family, and Utopia: Communal Experiments of the Shakers, the Oneida Community, and the Mormons*. Syracuse, NY: Syracuse University Press, 1991.
Fliegelman, Jay. *Prodigals and Pilgrims: The American Revolution against Patriarchal Authority, 1750–1800*. Cambridge: Cambridge University Press, 1982.
Franklin, Benjamin. "Information to Those Who Would Remove to America." In *Benjamin Franklin: Autobiography, Poor Richard, and Later Writings*, ed. J. A. Leo Lemay, 235–43. New York: Library Classics of America, 1997.
Frazer, Elizabeth. "Mary Wollstonecraft on Politics and Friendship." *Political Studies* 56 (2008): 237–56.

Freidel, Frank. *The Life of Francis Lieber*. Baton Rouge: Louisiana State University Press, 1947.
Gordon, Sarah Barringer. *The Mormon Question: Polygamy and Constitutional Conflict in Nineteenth-Century America*. Chapel Hill: University of North Carolina Press, 2002.
Grossberg, Michael. *Governing the Hearth: Law and the Family in Nineteenth-Century America*. Chapel Hill: University of North Carolina Press, 1985.
Hill, Lisa, and Peter McCarthy. "Hume, Smith and Ferguson: Friendship in Commercial Society." *Critical Review of International Social and Political Philosophy* 2, no. 4 (1999): 33–49.
Holloway, Mark. *Utopian Communities in America, 1680–1880*. Mineola, NY: Dover Publications, 1966.
Independence Hall Association. "Republican Platform of 1856." Retrieved 17 December 2020 from http://www.ushistory.org/gop/convention_1856republicanplatform.htm.
Jordan, Winthrop D. "Familial Politics: Thomas Paine and the Killing of the King, 1776." *Journal of American History* 60, no. 2 (1973): 294–308.
Laslett, Peter. "Introduction." In *John Locke: Two Treatises of Government*. Edited by P. Laslett, 3–122. Cambridge: Cambridge University Press, 1988.
Lewis, Jan. "The Republican Wife: Virtue and Seduction in the Early Republic." *William and Mary Quarterly* 44, no. 4 (1987): 689–721.
Lieber, Francis. *Essay on Property and Labor: As Connected with Natural Law and the Constitution of Society*. Reproduced by BiblioLife. New York: Harper and Brothers, 1841.
———. "The Mormons: Shall Utah Be Admitted into the Union?" *Putnam's Monthly* 5, no. 27 (1855): 225–36.
Locke, John. *Two Treatises of Government*. Edited by P. Laslett. Cambridge: Cambridge University Press, 1988 [1698].
Mayhew, Jonathan. *A Discourse Concerning Unlimited Submission and Non-resistance to the Higher Powers: With Some Reflections on the Resistance Made to King Charles I*. Lincoln: DigitalCommons@University of Nebraska–Lincoln, 1750. Retrieved 9 July 2022 from http://digitalcommons.unl.edu/cgi/viewcontent.cgi?article=1044&context=etas.
McKinnon, Susan. "The Economies of Kinship and the Paternity of Culture: Origin Stories in Kinship Theory." In *Relative Values: Reconfiguring Kinship Studies*, edited by Sarah Franklin and Susan McKinnon, 277–301. Durham, NC: Duke University Press, 2001.
———. "Doing and Being: Process, Essence, and Hierarchy in Making Kin." In *The Routledge Companion to Contemporary Anthropology*, edited by S. Coleman, S. B. Hyatt, and A. Kingsolver, 161–82. London: Routledge, 2017.
———. "Kinship Particularism and the Project of Anthropological Comparison." In *Human Nature and Social Life: Perspectives on Extended Sociality*, edited by J. H. Z. Remme and K. Sillander, 150–65. Cambridge: Cambridge University Press, 2017.
———. "Cousin Marriage, Hierarchy, and Heredity: Contestations over Domestic and National Body Politics in Nineteenth-Century America." *Journal of the British Academy* 7 (2019): 61–88.

McKinnon, Susan, and Fenella Cannell, ed. *Vital Relations: Modernity and the Persistent Life of Kinship*. Santa Fe: School of American Research Press, 2013.

Montesquieu, Baron de Charles de Secondat. *The Spirit of the Laws*. Translated and edited by A. M. Cohler, B. C. Miller, and H. S. Stone. Cambridge: Cambridge University Press, 1989 [1748].

Morgan, Edmund S., ed. *Puritan Political Ideas, 1558–1794*. Indianapolis: Hackett Publishing Co., 1965.

Morgan, Lewis Henry. *Ancient Society*. Gloucester, MA: Peter Smith, 1974 [1877].

Paine, Thomas. *Collected Writings*. New York: Literary Classics of the United States, 1955.

―――― (under the pseudonym Esop). "Cupid and Hymen: An Original." *The Pennsylvania Magazine; or, American Monthly Museum* (April 1775): 158–61.

―――― (under the pseudonym The Old Bachelor). "Reflections on Unhappy Marriages." *The Pennsylvania Magazine; or, American Monthly Museum* (June 1775): 263–65.

Pitzer, Donald E., ed. *America's Communal Utopias*. Chapel Hill: University of North Carolina Press, 1997.

Ross, Dorothy. *The Origins of American Social Science*. Cambridge: Cambridge University Press, 1991.

Sabean, David Warren, Simon Teuscher, and Jon Mathieu, ed. *Kinship in Europe: Approaches to Long-Term Developments (1300–1900)*. New York: Berghahn Books, 2007.

Schneider, David M. *American Kinship: A Cultural Account*. 2nd ed. Chicago: University of Chicago Press, 1980.

Schochet, Gordon J. *The Authoritarian Family and Political Attitudes in 17th-Century England: Patriarchalism in Political Thought*. New Brunswick, NJ: Transaction Books, 1988.

Shanley, Mary Lyndon. "Marriage Contract and Social Contract in Seventeenth-Century English Political Thought." In *The Family in Political Thought*, edited by J. B. Elshtain, 80–95. Amherst: University of Massachusetts Press, 1982.

――――. "Marital Slavery and Friendship: John Stuart Mill's 'The Subjection of Women.'" In *Feminist Interpretations and Political Theory*, ed. M. L. Shanley and C. Pateman, 164–80. University Park: Pennsylvania State University Press, 1991.

Shanley, Mary Lyndon, and Peter G. Stillman. "Political and Marital Despotism: Montesquieu's Persian Letters." In *The Family in Political Thought*, edited by J. B. Elshtain, 66–79. Amherst: University of Massachusetts Press, 1982.

Smith, Barbara Clark. *The Freedoms We Lost: Consent and Resistance in Revolutionary America*. New York: The New Press, 2010.

Strathern, Marilyn. *Relations: An Anthropological Exposition*. Durham, NC: Duke University Press, 2020.

Thelen, Tatjana, and Erdmute Alber, ed. *Reconnecting State and Kinship*. Philadelphia: University of Pennsylvania Press, 2018.

Tyler, Royall. *The Contrast: A Comedy in Five Acts*. New York: AMS Press, 1970.

US Supreme Court. *Reynolds v. United States*. 98 U.S. 145, 1878.

Victor, Metta Victoria Fuller. *Mormon Wives: A Narrative of Facts Stranger than Fiction*. New York: Derby & Jackson, 1856.

Viveiros de Castro, Eduardo. "The Gift and the Given: Three Nano-essays on Kinship and Magic." In *Kinship and Beyond: The Genealogical Model Reconsidered*, edited by S. Bamford and J. Leach, 237–68. New York: Berghahn Books, 2009.

Weisbrod, Carol, and Pamela Sheingorn. "Reynolds v. United States: Nineteenth-Century Forms of Marriage and the Status of Women." *Connecticut Law Review* 10, no. 4 (1978): 828–58.

Weston, Kath. *Families We Choose: Lesbians, Gays, Kinship*. New York: Columbia University Press, 1991.

Wilson, Philip K. "Erasmus Darwin and the 'Noble' Disease (Gout): Conceptualizing Heredity and Disease in Enlightenment England." In *Heredity Produced at the Crossroads of Biology, Politics, and Culture, 1500–1870*, edited by S. Müller-Wille and H.-J. Rheinberger, 133–54. Cambridge, MA: MIT Press, 2007.

Yanagisako, Sylvia, and Carol Delaney, ed. *Naturalizing Power: Essays in Feminist Cultural Analysis*. New York: Routledge, 1995.

Yazawa, Melvin. *From Colonies to Commonwealth: Familial Ideology and the Beginnings of the American Republic*. Baltimore, MD: Johns Hopkins University Press, 1985.

Chapter 9

Toward a Political Economy of the Maternal Body
Claiming Maternal Filiation in Nineteenth-Century French Feminism

Caroline Arni

> All men are brothers and sisters united together by our maternity.
>
> —Désirée Gay, 1832
>
> All our political and social institutions may be traced, link by link, to a mother nursing her babe.
>
> —Élie Reclus, 1877
>
> If the child's humanity is mirrored initially in the eyes of its mother, or the maternal function, then we might be able to guess that the social subject grasps the whole dynamic of resemblance and kinship by way of the same source.
>
> —Hortense Spillers, 1987

If social theory were based on the proposition that the mother-child unit is the place to turn to when examining how kinship, society, and politics relate to each other, what would it look like? Judging from the epigraphs above, to raise this question seems plausible. However, it means challenging virtually the entire canon of modern social theory, whose legacy rests on the very conceptual division undermined by that proposition. Within this framework, which sets apart "nonmodern societies" (said to conflate kinship and politics) from "modern society" (credited with safeguarding politics from contamination by kin relations),[1] maternity has been relegated to the sphere of apolitical kinship. While it provides institutions with their "personnel" by bringing forth those who become members of society and citizens, it is not itself perceived as producing relations of social and political relevance.

One obvious way to examine this legacy critically is by historicizing it. First, investigating the emergence of the specific theories that postulate the separation of spheres and that have opposed family and kinship to modern political life provides a vantage point to show that this separation was not descriptive of social relations and practices; rather, it prescribed them and was thus itself a political move. Feminist scholarship has been at the forefront of this examination, providing the historical and theoretical underpinnings of the activist slogan "the personal is political."[2] Second, historicization has proved an effective critical tool in showing how European societies became "kinship hot" societies through practices such as cousin marriages in the very same period that gave birth to the narrative of them having tamed the power of kinship by structuring social relations and political order according to the public/private boundary.[3]

In this chapter, I will take a third path by showing how the conceptual opposition between kinship and politics was challenged at the time of its emergence not only by practices running counter to it but also by alternative concepts that deliberately linked kinship and politics. More precisely, I will examine how in the 1830s and 1840s French feminists of proletarian origin coupled motherhood and emancipation. Drawing on approaches from "symmetrical" or "recursive" anthropology, I will address these women's rather scattered and fragmentary discourses within the same framework as political philosophy and nascent social theory. No less than the canonical master thinkers, they conceptualized social relations by analyzing a given situation. And while this situation was historically and locally specific, their conceptualization of motherhood as a site of emancipation can be used as an analytical concept for examining other localities and time periods.[4] As a matter of fact, by placing maternal filiation in the center of their politics, the authors of these feminist essays and short-lived journals produced nothing less than a political economy of the maternal body.

The maternal body has, according to Karen Middleton, long been "among the most untheorised issues in the study of 'gender' and 'kinship.'"[5] To be sure, Middleton observed this lacuna in social anthropology in 2000, and that field has since witnessed considerable research addressing the issue—most notably concerning egg donation and surrogacy.[6] Also, the maternal body has of course always been a staple of those segments in feminist theory that draw on psychoanalytic perspectives.[7] But much remains to be done about how anthropologists and historians approach the maternal body in history, especially the nineteenth century.[8] This period, during which "life" was conceptualized or reconceptualized in terms of "biology" and the social sciences were founded, is usually considered (by both historians and anthropologists) the origin of those very concepts of kinship and gender that have since been challenged by feminist scholarship and new kinship studies: in its simplest form, the proposition that there is some kind of "natural" kinship or sexual difference that is related (or, for that matter, not related) to some kind of "cultural" kinship or sexual difference.

For my purposes, it is helpful to describe this proposition through the lens of what Philippe Descola calls "naturalism."[9] Not only does it bear the mark of the "great division" between "nature" and "culture" that came to full maturity in the twentieth century but—what is more to the point—it also draws attention to how this framework has constrained inquiries into any phenomenon by the question of what roles "nature" and "culture" have in its composition and how they relate to each other in terms of determination, autonomy, or interaction. It is within this context that notions like "naturalization" or "biologization" have mostly seemed sufficient to describe how the scrutinized concepts of kinship and gender came about in the first place. The nineteenth century has thus become the temporal location of a foil that bestows upon "premodern," "non-Western," and "present-day" concepts of kinship and gender the alterity capable of unmasking the false universalism of their nineteenth-century successors or predecessors.

It is all too easy, then, to miss the fact that in nineteenth-century Europe notions of kinship existed that were equally specific to this time and place but conceptually different from the naturalist paradigm that still informs much feminist theory of the body.[10] Indeed, when socialist feminists of the time turned motherhood into a political issue, they were not dealing with a composite of "the social" and "the biological" or "discursivity" and "materiality." They were not quarreling about how to interpret or represent a "natural" function. They were not being essentialist or constructivist, concerned with what might be "innate" and "unchanging" or "acquired" and "changeable" about motherhood. They were conceptualizing the emancipation of women. And such emancipation was about recognizing the maternal body not as a reproductive body but a productive one that generated social relations.

On Feminism and Motherhood

Feminism might be an unexpected site of making kinship in the nineteenth century. This was, after all, the time when rights-holding individuals were being defined as autonomous subjects, detached from and devoid of relationships that were thought of as distorting their authenticity. To be sure, as Joan W. Scott has shown, this very authenticity itself relied on a relationship.[11] While the rights-holding individual was declared as universal or generically human, authenticity was made concrete as a male capacity. Hence, sexual difference produced a relationship through which men could perceive themselves as being authentic and autonomous subjects as opposed to women, who lacked such qualities. Yet even as it created the modern subject, this very relationality was obscured by the linking of authenticity and individuality. We thus expect feminist critique of the time to articulate, above all, claims for female individuality. Or, in other words, when we look at the nineteenth century, it is claims for female individuality that we usually identify as feminist positions.

This accounts for the challenge historians have faced in understanding those nineteenth-century feminists who based their emancipatory claims upon the notion of women-as-mothers and centered the mother-child unit in their vision of a more just society.[12] This challenge has been even more profound as some of these feminists have had to be acknowledged as articulating among the most radical social critiques of their time. Mostly, historians have addressed their frustration by contextualization. Whether all-pervasive Catholicism, exuberant romanticism, rigid medical theories on women's nature, or the emerging framework of nationalist biopolitics, something else must have accounted for what is seen as an "essentialist idealization" of motherhood, propagated by feminists who (whether consciously or not) "identified" with or strategically "used" ideologies of sexual difference.[13]

Of course, connections have existed between feminist and other contemporary discourses on motherhood while feminist embracement of motherhood did indeed tend to be articulated in effusive, often religious, language. However, such references to "context" all too often serve as shortcuts to pass over what, for feminist historians of the twentieth and twenty-first centuries, is a contradiction in terms or, put more radically, an ontological imposition: emancipatory motherhood. The frustration is justified given the effort with which, from the nineteenth through the twentieth century, social and political theory—as well as the law—have consigned all things maternal to the apolitical realm of "the natural" and thus by association restricted women's agency. But explaining away a frustration limits historical investigation by avoiding a question that could turn out to be very productive: what must motherhood *be* in order to have an emancipatory effect?[14]

The fact that tackling this question takes us from motherhood to maternity, and indeed to (in Margaret Jolly's phrasing) the "corporeal processes of being pregnant, giving birth and nurturing,"[15] does not alleviate the frustration. But it is interesting because it forces the historian to account for historical alterity, and one crucial aspect of such alterity concerns the fact that conceptions of the maternal body might not be about "sexual difference" in the first place.[16] Tackling the question of emancipatory motherhood thus compels us to account for the competence of historical actors: feminists in the past were not simply at the mercy of "sociohistoric forces" or were more or less successful in bending or subverting them.[17] They were critics of their society, and I contend that in articulating this critique they analyzed their situations in a way that might be conceptually useful for others.

Jennifer L. Morgan has recently made a similar argument regarding enslaved women in the English Atlantic during the sixteenth and seventeenth centuries. These women were the ones, she contends, who "navigated the dawning recognition that their reproductive lives would be the evidence of racialized dispossession." More specifically, "enslaved mothers were enmeshed in the foundational metalanguages of early modern Atlantic ideas of slavery, freedom, and racial colonialism."[18] By reconstructing their fights against enslaved maternity construed to transform children into property as no less than a theorization of power, Morgan does more than just identify overlooked contributions to the history of Black radical thought.[19] Although navigating different situations, both her enslaved mothers and my proletarian feminists, through actions or words, exposed oppression as residing in the conditions under which women could be mothers. For me, Morgan's findings thus raise the possibility of imagining a history of the maternal body as theorized through emancipatory struggles—something which is all the more important as the idea of slavery is a recurrent theme in the strand of feminism examined here.[20]

Against this backdrop, I will show in this chapter how a particular instance of French feminist critique of patronymics, coupled with a claiming of maternal filiation, brought forth what must be understood as a political economy of the maternal body. First, I will begin by describing an episode during which motherhood was conceived of as a site of the struggle for equality by being equated with work. Second, I will argue that in rejecting patronymics, feminists conceptualized women's subjugation as maternal labor being incorporated by men. This incorporation, as I will show next, was conceived of as an expropriation from women of the resource that is the maternal body. Fourth, I will examine how the case for maternal filiation, as articulated in the claiming of the matronymic, was not about an alternative genealogical model but about founding relations among equals. In sum, I argue that in French feminism of the 1830s we find a concept of motherhood as the thing that produces children and generates social and political relations out of the inalienable resource and capacity that is the maternal body. Concluding the chapter, I raise the question of whether this concept of motherhood provided political radicals later in the century with the means to address "modern" and "nonmodern" societies in a more symmetrical way than the then-emerging anthropology of kinship.

"The Mother": Embodying Subordination, Claiming Equality

In 1849, the French feminist and socialist Jeanne Deroin (1805–94), in an act quickly condemned as unconstitutional by her friends and ridiculed by her foes, announced her candidacy for a seat in the legislative assembly. She did so "out of a feeling of what is right and just": women were half of humankind and thus men's equals.[21] While limiting her public discourse on her candidacy to this reasoning, in a treatise addressing a female readership she bolstered the claim with another argument: here it was "the woman" as the "mother of humankind" who needed to "raise and speak in the name of humanity."[22] It might seem obvious that this evocation of motherhood was all about "sexual difference"—and all the more so as Deroin's detractors denied women equality on such grounds. However, we should not confound the evocation of "women" with the evocation of "femininity." In mobilizing "the woman," Deroin's appeal to motherhood was all about emancipation, and emancipation was about labor. For "woman," according to her, embodied nothing less than "the sacred type of the ever-suffering, ever-downtrodden, ever-subordinated (*subalternisé*) worker."[23] In the following, I want to show how this linking of "the woman" and "the worker" did not operate as an analogy but an analysis of subjugation.

In the events leading up to the Revolution of 1848, the fight for democracy had taken a pronounced socialist turn when the "right to vote" was infused with the rallying cry for the "right to work." However, this demand was neutralized quite quickly, as Joan W. Scott has shown in her account of Deroin's candidacy.[24] "Work" was redefined as "property" (in the sense of inalienable self-expression) and the "right to work" was accordingly translated into the "right to property and family"—or rather into the right to "property in family," as Scott puts it. Inevitably, a right to work would have brought out social divisions insofar as it questioned the unequal allocation of wealth. Property in family, however, offered unity among men who belonged to different social classes but held the same position with regard to women. "What men had in common was not only this property [of labor], but its objectification in the family, in the wife and child who carried a husband's and father's name and served as the instruments of the transmission of property—the tangible emblem of his person."[25] In other words, even those men who had nothing still had a name to bestow upon others and were thereby confirmed as equally entitled to citizenship.

This shift in the configuration of rights-based demands, which was embraced by most socialist parties, challenged feminist arguments for women's equality with men. A right to work would have included women, who were part of industry in many ways. Women "are producers, too," so much was granted.[26] The right to property in family, however, required another argument than that women were workers just like men. This is where Deroin's reference to "the mother of humankind" as "the sacred type" of the "ever-subordinated worker" comes in. If the patronymic — the transmittable name of the father — served as an emblem of men's entitlement to universal suffrage, motherhood could be mobilized as the complementary emblem of women's equal entitlement. In both cases, political rights were moored in an inalienable aspect of the person: men incorporating their family or mothers birthing humans.[27]

But while sharing the same rationale for political rights, male incorporation of the family and motherhood were not analogous: the figure of the "subordinated mother of mankind" contains an important equivocation. On the one hand, Deroin did tap into the notion of inalienable self-expression that was about to replace work in the discourse of the political parties, but on the other, she conceptualized motherhood as concerning the very work that this replacement relegated to the background, or even *hors politique* (not part of the political sphere). As she would put it several years later, motherhood for her was "the production of the human being" and thus no less than "the most important work of all": "[D]uring gestation, when she gives birth to the child and when she nurtures it, she accomplishes work profitable to all."[28] By thus conceptualizing motherhood as productive work, Deroin insisted that equality was not about property, as represented in the patronymic, but about a person's relationship to their labor, as represented in motherhood. For her, this meant that excluding women from universal suffrage turned them into the very type of all those subordinated.

Scott's analysis of Deroin's strain of French nineteenth-century feminism shows how her conceptualization of motherhood as the foundation of women's equal rights was not complementary to the male right to property in the family but in direct conflict with it. After all, the latter demanded the objectification of the wife and mother as "owned" rather than as someone capable of "owning" herself. I would like to add to this interpretation by arguing that Deroin's stance introduced a distinction in how the relationship to the child articulated the idea that "property in the person" constituted the rights-holding subject. In terms of the patronymic, this was a question of ownership; in terms of motherhood, it became a question of productive labor. In linking the woman and the worker, Deroin thus drew from three propositions in order to conclude on how to address inequality: subordination is about the conditions under which work is performed, work is about a relationship between the laboring person and her labor, and this relationship is at stake in motherhood too. Hence motherhood is a site of the struggle for emancipation.

On How to Not Be Owned: Rejecting the Names of Men

Although my account so far might suggest otherwise, Deroin's concept of motherhood as a productive function was not provoked by the situation within which she mobilized it for legitimizing the insurgent act of her candidacy. Years before, it had been articulated in the writings of a handful of French feminists (including Deroin) engaged with what would later be called "utopian socialism," specifically the Saint-Simonian movement.[29] These women of humble origins, who mostly earned their livings as seamstresses and embroiderers, made themselves heard in the early 1830s when the "woman's question" had come to the foreground of the movement even as women themselves were being shut out of its organizational structure. In 1832, they founded a journal reserved for female authors that, with frequent name changes, would last for two years. The authors chose the title *La femme libre* (The free woman) for the first issues, introducing themselves as "proletarian women" who had set out to fight against the "tyranny" and "exploitation" all women suffered.[30] In other words, their movement was for women's emancipation, ignited by those positioned to understand that the subaltern condition consists in being alienated from one's labor and the wealth it creates—not only, as in their case, through wage labor but also, for women of all social classes, through marriage.

It is within this context that the very patronymic that would come to encode equality among men in the Revolution of 1848 had already been criticized from a feminist perspective. As Deroin herself asked rhetorically in 1831, "[T]his custom that obliges women to carry the name of her husband, is it not the branding iron that imprints on the forehead of the slave the master's initials, for everyone to see that she is his property?"[31] Equating the female condition with that of slaves was a recurrent feature in nineteenth-century feminist discourse.[32] It is important to note that this equation eclipses the question of the enslaved woman—for the very reason that *"the* slave" and *"the* woman" are figurative here. Still, the equation should not be taken as self-evident, whether by reducing it to a simple metaphor or by dismissing it as a misguided obliteration of actual slavery. In equating women with slaves, Deroin was making the specific point that both experienced the same kind of subjugation by having their personhood appropriated by someone else, or—in terms of contemporaneous political theory—by being denied the very property in the person or right to oneself that distinguished the condition of the "slave" from that of the "free man."[33] For Deroin, this was what supported the comparison between women and slaves, even though she was also specific about the particularities: both were "owned," but in the case of non-enslaved women this ownership was comparatively mitigated, to a state of "extreme dependency."[34]

Given this strong criticism of the patronymic, it is not surprising that Saint-Simonian feminists were engaged in what must be understood as a politics of naming and de-naming. Speaking "in one's name as a woman and in the name of all women" was, as Florence Rochefort observes, "an inaugural political act that marked the history of all nineteenth and twentieth-century feminisms."[35] Among the Saint-Simonian feminists of the 1830s, we find a particularly striking realization of this act: to "speak in one's name and the name of all women," for those who wrote in this journal, meant signing their articles with their first names only, often by joining two of them: Marie-Reine, Jeanne-Désirée, Suzanne, Joséphine-Félicité, Christine-Sophie.[36] In doing this, they all rejected the names of men: husbands for those who were married and fathers for the others.

It stands to reason that this practice was about recuperating a female subject position. Accused by male journalists of hiding their names out of fear or shame, the editors of *La femme libre* retorted that the contrary was true: "[W]e want to assume the responsibility for our words and acts ourselves."[37] They met those not capable of comprehending the intricacy of female authorship with sarcasm and kindly offered them prompt assistance with identifying individual authors. Yet this rejection of names passed on from men was not confined to self-presentation in the pages of a journal. It had its correlate in civil life where some of these women—although living with male partners—never accepted their husband's names, and others deliberately had children out of wedlock to prevent them from bearing their father's names.[38] This extension of the practice demands a closer look into the kind of subject position these women assumed by rejecting the name of men, for it does not end with a quest for individuality.

This might seem obvious, considering how concern with social bonds permeated the Saint-Simonian movement. After all, these women adhered to a doctrine that centered its vision of a better society on the idea of "association" as realized through the heterosexual couple, worker's associations, and religious communality.³⁹ Rejecting so-called "family names" could thus be understood as stressing the egalitarian construction of association by women who frequently declared themselves to be "daughters of the people." But male Saint-Simonians, significantly, did not give up their last names. Why did the women? Stefania Ferrando has pointed out that Saint-Simonian feminism should be understood as "relational"—that is, defined by practices through which women related to each other not on the grounds of some supposedly homogenous "femininity" but rather on the grounds of differences among them. Heterogeneity was seen not as an impediment to the movement but as its starting point—the material out of which political communality is made.⁴⁰ By extending this analysis from their literary practices to their practical rejection of the patronymic, I want to argue that shedding the names of men was just as much about redefining kin relations as it was about female individuality. Or, more precisely, it was about female subjectivity that was centered on not individuality but a redefinition of kin relations. And this redefinition, I want to argue, worked by inverting the prescriptions for how women could be mothers, daughters, and lovers.

To be sure, it was perfectly legal not to take on the name of one's husband, and Deroin, who had been studying the French *Code Civil*—or, as she called it, "the book of the law"⁴¹—from 1804, was right in calling the practice of patronymics a "custom." The code neither obliged women to bear their husband's names nor explicitly decreed children of married women to bear the name of the father. However, the former (which derived from administrative practice in the ancien régime) had become customary by the nineteenth century, while the latter was stipulated by the code in various indirect ways. For instance, the most important evidence when someone's affiliation to a family was questioned was that they had always carried the name of the father they claimed.⁴² The omission of any explicit provision mandating the patronymic can thus be interpreted as implicit evidence that it was simply assumed.⁴³ Yet what made it evident was the fact that the code constructed the father as incorporating his family. It was a child's father who reigned over filiation, whether by marriage, recognition, or adoption.⁴⁴ Meanwhile, a child not belonging to a family by paternal filiation—a so-called "natural" child—was devalued by being distinguished from a so-called "legitimate" child. By rejecting the patronymic, Saint-Simonian feminists thus practiced exactly that which was devalued by the code.

Rejecting the patronymic, however, was only one step in realizing an inversion of family relations. What is more, Saint-Simonian feminists anchored this rejection in claiming the matronymic. Reviewing versions of this claim in the history of nineteenth-century French feminism,

Carolyn J. Eichner has deemed it an overarching "linchpin to women's contemporary and historical emancipation."[45] While I do agree with her on this point, I want to revisit her interpretation that such emancipation was about "autonomy," "identity," and "female genealogy" and that these tenets were, in the case of the Saint-Simonians, articulated through the Romantic idea of a "natural supremacy of the maternal over the paternal."[46] Rather, I want to argue that their claiming the matronymic was about who represents the family and why. Exploring the answer to this question will reveal why the matronymic for these feminists was about women's freedom as articulated through relations.

About Expropriation: Claiming the Name of the Mother

The claiming of the matronymic is most strikingly captured in the title of a twenty-four-page booklet by Egérie Casaubon. Little is known about this author except that she published three treatises in dialogue with Saint-Simonian writing.[47] The booklet I want to discuss here appeared in 1834 under the title *La Femme est la famille* (Woman is the family).[48] The wordplay—*est* (is) and *et* (and) are pronounced identically—may or may not have been intended. In any case, the title does instantiate a shift from women being defined by their association with the family *(la femme et la famille)* to them embodying it *(la femme est la famille)*.

In saying that women *are* the family, Casaubon described a concrete situation: that of the numerous women who gave birth to a child out of wedlock and were abandoned by men, left alone with the child and responsible for its livelihood. "It is true to the fact," she contended, that this child "carries the name of the mother." But not content with registering a mother, the registrar recorded something that would stigmatize the child from then on: "father unknown." Yet how could a child be a "bastard," Casaubon exclaimed, a child "that has been cradled in the mother's bosom for nine months! that has received, in the midst of the most awful suffering, her maternal blessing!"[49] To say that women *were* the family thus had a precise rationale. It expressed that the child had to bear the maternal instead of the paternal name because it was the mother's creation. This is how Casaubon presented her case: "WOMAN IS THE FAMILY. *The child has to carry her name. Certainty is where no doubt exists, and the fruit has to carry the name of the tree that gave it life, not the one of the gardener who grafts the bud.*"[50]

Unpacking the argument in this passage begins with taking seriously how in calling the child "the fruit" Casaubon drew not only on the dictum that only maternity is ever certain but moreover on a well-established metaphor for gestation. This theme is recurrent in her text; another passage refers to "the fruit of our womb."[51] An old and common trope—representing the maternal body as a tree bearing fruit[52]—here became, in the context of claiming the matronymic, a means of conceptualizing motherhood as something that can be analogized with authored creation. For the focus here lies on the "giving life," that is, on "bearing a child," which when introduced as an argument for the matronymic indicates the relationship between the one who bears the child and the child itself as what emerges from this activity of bearing.[53] Casaubon underlined this argument—in the same semantic vein but in a striking reversal of a metaphor typically used to reduce women to mere vessels—by likening the mother to "the earth that fertilizes the seed."[54] She was not the passive fertile ground upon which a fertilizing father acts; she was herself the active fertilizing force.[55] A further iteration of the theme reads as follows: "MAY SHE BE THE FAMILY, *since she represents the fecundity of the earth, which fertilizes the germ and gives life to it.*"[56]

The relationship between the bearing mother and the born child makes maternity equivalent to "production" in the domain of labor. This can be seen in how Casaubon mixed a vocabulary referring to natural growth—"tree," "fruit," "earth," "fertilization"—with a language of economics.[57] By imposing his name, the father "seizes" the child, as she put it, claiming it as "his property," even though its coming into existence just "cost" him a short pleasurable moment, while giving birth might well "cost" the mother her life.[58] Conversely, the matronymic then stood as the expression of a mother's investment in making the child, this investment being nothing less than her own life from which the child's life emanates. Seen from this perspective, bearing a child was not some process undergone by a woman that can be decoupled from its outcome. It was a manifestation of the maternal body's productive capacity that is continued through the child's existence, just as "giving life" described a continuum made of everything that makes the child—from conception, gestation, giving birth, and nursing through continued nurturing and caring.[59]

Thus, not just the child but also the maternal body was at stake when the patronymic was analyzed as an act of "seizing." In other words, by denouncing the patronymic as an act of "seizing," Casaubon analyzed the maternal condition as defined by expropriation. To seize is to claim property that belongs to someone else, a change of ownership realized by force, a denial of proprietorship. However, nowhere in her writing do we read that the mother "owns" the child. What is "seized" by the patronym is the productive capacity of the maternal body as that which joins the mother and the child. The act of "seizure," as realized in the patronym, is thus nothing other than a distortion of the relationship truthfully expressed in the matronymic, a relationship not of ownership but of production. And production was understood by both Casaubon and the Saint-Simonians as a creative act, an "oeuvre"—the latter being a key term for the doctrine.[60] By distorting this creative-productive relation between the mother and the child, the act of "seizure" is indeed an expropriation from the mother, not of the child but of that capacity of hers from which the relation emanates.

It is now possible to further examine the equation of the conditions of women and the enslaved, which can also be abundantly found, in Casaubon's writing. I have already argued that with this equation Deroin was making an argument about women being dispossessed of their personhood by the husbands whose names they were supposed to carry. Now, I want to add that the equation defines such ownership, furthermore, as subjugation through expropriation—in the exact sense suggested by political philosopher Nancy Fraser when she defines expropriation as an act of "*confiscating* capacities and resources" realized "outside the wage nexus" that, for its part, constitutes subjugation through exploitation.[61]

Proletarian women were, of course, subject to both expropriation and exploitation. As Casaubon wrote, "For too long have our foreheads withered under slavery, our bodies been stigmatized by labor."[62] But these two are not the same. Significantly, while Casaubon presented maternity as equivalent to production, she did not demand that wages be paid for maternal labor but rather suggested that a "tribute" be offered from the state to the mother in order to "remunerate her for her daily needs": that is, to secure her existence.[63] Such a *"tribute"* would regard maternal labor as inalienable and at the same time acknowledge the creation of wealth through maternity.[64] The state was surely aware of this wealth, since, in a perverse twist of matters, it not only deprived women of their freedom and education but also "taxed" mothers by claiming their sons as soldiers for its pointless wars.[65]

If we read Casaubon's claiming of the matronymic as an analysis of women's condition, the maternal body appears as both the primary site of women's subjugation and the privileged site of their emancipation: women in the current state were subjugated by being expropriated from the capacities and resources of the maternal body and would be liberated by being granted property in this body and its productivity as a source of their livelihood. This is what I want to call a political economy of the maternal body, and Casaubon herself extended her reasoning in that exact vein. In a short postscript to her treatise on women being the family, she announced the further elaboration of "some ideas of political economy as to the realization of the *tribute to the mother.*"[66] These ideas did indeed reappear in a subsequent publication in which Casaubon proposed that the tribute take the form of granting women rights to a piece of land—specifically, "half of the soil's harvest"—on the grounds of their "labor of bearing children."[67]

It is important not to dismiss Casaubon's dictum "woman is the family" as a simple conflation of womanhood with motherhood. In her reasoning, the two are related in the same way that personhood and work are related in liberal political theory: the (fictional) idea of "property in the person" does not conflate a free man's existence with his labor power as he need not sell it in order to be free; what matters is merely that he is free to do so.[68] Likewise, a free woman need not become a mother in order to be free; what matters is that she herself is in possession of her maternal capacity. This, furthermore, must not be confounded with the late twentieth-century notion of "reproductive autonomy." There is, of course, a continuity between the two. But the claim to rights in the capacity of the maternal body as a claim to freedom does not rest upon the individualized notion of the person that informs the concept of autonomy—since this very capacity consists in bringing forth the mother-child relationship. And this is not the only relationship that emanates from the maternal body.

Against Succession: The Case for Maternal Filiation

The most radical engagement with motherhood and parentage came from yet another Saint-Simonian feminist Egérie Casaubon cited quite extensively in one of her publications, Claire Démar (ca. 1800–1833).[69] Although an outlier within the movement, Démar is pertinent to my argument as she took the feminist critique of the patronymic to an extreme conclusion. Indeed, her reasoning ultimately disrupts the political economy of the maternal body I have presented so far. But through this very disruption Démar's position simultaneously puts it into sharper relief by drawing attention to how, within this framework, the question of filiation and succession was addressed.

Démar was controversial among her fellow feminists, who mostly rejected her positions and published her work with an equal measure of reverence and caution after her spectacular suicide in 1833. In a singular and disturbingly resolute way, even for contemporary radicals, Démar called for the absolute freedom from all conventions and interests of amorous feelings and sexual encounters. Such freedom was to be secured by a "right to secrecy" that would protect lovers' encounters from the knowledge of any possible offspring, thus obscuring parentage and filiation to the point of eliminating them altogether. Step by step, her writing advances toward this ever-more-radical conclusion: "against the law of the bloodline, the law of generation" is followed by "no more paternity," which finally leads to "no more maternity, no more law of the bloodline."[70]

This call for the abolition of any kind of parentage and filiation was somewhat in accord with the voluntaristic impetus of the *Code Civil*, which actually did require a formal recognition of the child from not only the father but also the mother.[71] Thus, Démar's rejection of parentage and filiation was a far cry from her fellow feminists' claims for the matronymic. Maternity was not a site of emancipation for her; on the contrary, women's emancipation consisted in freeing mothers from the task of mothering. However, this very position was informed by the same analysis that the current system left women with the choice of either being annihilated through marriage and male lineage or being stigmatized as mothers of illegitimate children. Like Deroin and Casaubon, Démar identified this as the core of women's subjugation. And it is in drawing the exact opposite conclusions from this analysis that her position reveals something significant about the case for maternal filiation as included in claiming the matronymic.

To understand this point, we need to consider that Démar spoke of "the law of the bloodline" when rejecting not only paternal but also maternal filiation, whereas Casaubon, arguing for the latter, spoke of *bearing a child*. Both perspectives refer to paternal filiation as genealogy, but for Casaubon maternal filiation, conceptualized as the productive-creative activity that brings forth the child, can be defined beyond—or rescued from—the genealogical model.[72] Démar, while not commenting on names, actually did share this concept of maternity as an extended work of *bearing*, which she engaged by imagining a division of labor between a *"mother by blood,"* who gives birth to the child, and a *"social* mother" or "professional *nurse,"* who takes care of the child.[73] Like Casaubon's case for the matronymic, Démar's vision of collectivizing care articulated the creative-productive nature of motherhood.

Including Démar's position into my analysis therefore shows that claiming the matronymic was not about replacing male genealogy with female genealogy. Passing on the mother's name to the child was about transmission within a unit of production/creation. Or, more precisely: claiming the matronymic was not about transmission at all but about describing this unit and thus articulating the political economy of the maternal body, which in Démar's argument is a political economy of maternal labor divided between a procreative and a nurturing part.

In rejecting succession, this concept of maternal filiation aligns with the overall political economy developed by the Saint-Simonian school. In opposition to some other strands of socialist thinking, Saint-Simonians did not question—and indeed defended—the right to private property but rejected the inheritance of wealth, as that contradicted their dictum, "To each man according to his capacity, to each capacity according to its works."[74] Démar—again radicalizing the question—explicitly linked this critique of inheritance with her antigenealogical stance. The full passage from which I quoted above reads as follows: "No more paternity, always uncertain and impossible to determine; No more property, no more inheritance; classification according to the capacity, remuneration according to the work. Therefore: no more maternity, no more law of the blood."[75] And Jeanne Deroin, whom I introduced above as a critic of the patronymic, identified two "odious privileges" remaining from "barbarian times": "the enslavement of women and the right to inheritance."[76]

Aligning kinship and the economic here is not just aggregating two domains where succession is at stake: criticism of inheritance and of genealogy both reach their conclusions based on the same concept that productive-creative work consists of a relationship between "producer" and "production." Everyone, Deroin argued in her declaration of adherence to the Saint-Simonian movement, had a right to appropriate some "common ground" *(fond commun)*—the earth and its resources—in order to produce what is needed to satisfy needs and procure pleasure. However, one's right to a share in the common ground expired with one's death, for it was only through working on it that one could lay a claim to it: it simply "ceases to belong to him once he ceases being."[77] This was exactly the argument of Deroin and Casaubon when presenting the maternal body as a resource, labored upon by women, that could not be appropriated by a husband-father who was not the one doing the labor.

In both economic and procreative domains, the concept of productive-creative work thus brought about a rejection of succession. This dovetailed with the radical egalitarianism propagated by Saint-Simonian feminists: what was, in the domain of the economic, equality among all producers was, in the domain of the procreative, equality among all those made by a mother. Maternity, in producing a relation between the child and the mother, was socially expansive: it generated siblinghood among those who came from a mother. As yet another Saint-Simonian feminist, Désirée Gay (1819–ca. 1890), wrote in 1833, "All men are brothers and sisters united together by our maternity; they give birth to doctrines, to systems of thought, and call them by their name; but we, we give birth to men; we should give them our name and have ours from our mothers and from god."[78]

We might be tempted to read Gay's argument on mothers as the origin of social unity and political equality as metaphorical for the simple reason that it carries considerable symbolic weight. In conceiving maternity as the origin of siblinghood, Gay certainly did allude to the social theory of "association" as it was promoted by utopian socialism. Association was the name Saint-Simonians gave to the kind of lateral relatedness that constitutes a just society of equals enacted by addressing each other as "brothers" and "sisters." Furthermore, siblinghood was at the core of the republican struggle in a society that labored under the unfulfilled promise of *fraternité* as proclaimed by the French Revolution of 1789.[79] It was, in short, the model for an egalitarian political bond among equals. However, by reading the argument of motherhood as the foundation for siblinghood metaphorically, we sever it from the concept of the maternal body as a productive resource and capacity and thus miss the "eminent concreteness" of Saint-Simonian feminism.[80] Gay was talking about a corporeal origin: mothers produce children and in doing so generate siblinghood, which was understood as a social and political relation. Furthermore, it was by maternal labor that women were positioned in political society not just as sisters to brothers but—more fundamentally— as the ones from whose labor such society emanated.

In order to underscore this point, let me quote Suzanne Voilquin (1801–76 or 1877) who had her own quite complex analysis of how kinship, society, and politics are related in motherhood. Children born by a woman to different men should, she contended, be treated equally by inheritance law: "[D]o not *all* of them draw on the same well of *life* that is common to them?"[81] And would not this equalizing nature of motherhood furthermore provide continuity over time beyond the "ungodly" transmission of wealth distributed unequally among families that is the "law of succession?"[82] "In the maiden's bosom," wrote Voilquin, "lies the *living link* which ceaselessly ties the generations that succeed to those that pass away."[83]

Conclusion: "Female Kinship" beyond Europe

Throughout this chapter, I have argued that an interrogation of the conceptual split between kinship and politics in nineteenth-century social sciences and political theory must take into account contemporaneous feminist concepts of relatedness and, in particular, the claim to maternal rather than paternal filiation. I have shown how this demand was articulated in the 1830s and 1840s by French feminists who criticized the patronym as a means of expropriating women from their maternal labor. In this critique, they revalued maternity by defining it as the origin of the very siblinghood that served as a template for equal relations among citizens. By coupling the fight for emancipation with questions of kinship, these feminists exposed the latter's inherent political nature. Furthermore, by addressing maternity in terms of a bodily capacity and resource inalienable from the person, they developed what I have presented as a political economy of the maternal body.

I have introduced this chapter by announcing an alternative concept to the opposition between kinship and politics that organized emerging social theory. Interestingly, the claim for maternal filiation as articulated by Saint-Simonian feminists in the 1830s and 1840s can be found in subsequent feminist and radical writing, where it intersects with anthropological curiosity about kinship in "nonmodern" societies. With two final vignettes, I want to glance quickly at how a view of motherhood as political in nature might have provided a framework for addressing "modern" and "nonmodern" societies more symmetrically than did the emerging anthropology of kinship.

In 1877, the anarchist and anthropologist Élie Reclus published a contribution to the debate on the historical primacy of mother-centered kinship.[84] Reclus certainly engaged as a scholar with issues such as how maternal filiation might be considered as "female kinship" without confounding it with "matriarchy." However, as it was characteristic for political radicals, he also examined how "nonmodern" societies might be sources of ideas of alternative systems of social and economic organization.[85] Thus, Reclus, who deplored women's disenfranchisement, was not only interested in what could be learned about female kinship in particular as a bygone point of departure for cultural evolution but also sought to extend the past into the future by stating that "the mother was the first to create the family, and from this fact we may infer that through her will be shaped its final expression."[86]

While Reclus surely did seek to reclaim motherhood as a means to grant women a "fair share in the management of the common property," it was for him (according to the concerns of his time) less a matter of labor than of social bonds: it was only through "maternal instinct" that the human species had evolved from being "among the lowest in the brute creation, more cruel than the tiger, more treacherous than the serpent, more gluttonous than the crocodile."[87] But what interests me most here is that by valuing motherhood as a provision of sociality Reclus placed "nonmodern" and "modern" societies on equal terms when evaluating different organizations of kinship.

A corresponding move regarding contemporaneous societies that social theory considered "nonmodern" can be found in the writing of the feminist Hubertine Auclert. At the very end of the nineteenth century, when French politicians and jurists raised the question about whether the prohibition on investigating the father of an illegitimate child—a notorious peculiarity of the French Civil Code—should be removed, Auclert took a somewhat surprising position. Turning to the trope of the tree and its fruit—which her text specified as the (Algerian) date palm— she argued that holding the father accountable was "not a solution for the woman." Instead, she ("the woman") should "by virile force, claim responsibility for her act and be allowed to herself perform, on the basis of a just remuneration, the social function of maternity."[88]

This statement clearly echoed earlier socialist-feminist conceptualizations of motherhood, but these had not gained political recognition after 1848. However, when Auclert was traveling in the French colonies, she found a society that held dear the very same concept of motherhood: the Saharan Tuareg, who called themselves "Beni-Oummia" (sons of the mother). Auclert explained that they derived their societal organization, which gave women an equal share of political and economic weight, from a belief that it is the womb that "dyes the child." And she contended that it was by being thus "disinterested in paternity" that they—although called "barbarians by those who do not know them"—were more advanced than the French, who, "with regard to feminism, would have a lot to learn from the Tuareg."[89]

We do not know what social theory would look like if it had not banished maternity to the realm of the apolitical, but surely it would have captured the thread that runs through the writings from which I quoted in the epigraphs to this chapter. From Désirée Gay's insistence on maternity being the source of a society of equals, through Élie Reclus's tracing of social institutions back to practices of maternal care, to Hortense Spillers's recognition of the mother's gaze as awakening subjectivity, they challenge us to turn to the mother-child unit when examining how kinship, society, and politics relate to each other.

Caroline Arni is professor of modern history at the University of Basel. She has published widely on the history of feminist critique; on the history of marriage, love, and friendship; and on the history of pregnancy and procreation. Her last book examines conceptualizations of the unborn in the human sciences and will be published in an English translation by Zone Books. She has been a member of the Institute for Advanced Study in Princeton and received fellowships from the Kulturwissenschaftliches Kolleg in Konstanz and the Zentrum für Interdisziplinäre Forschung in Bielefeld.

Notes

1. For this legacy, see Susan McKinnon, "Kinship within and beyond the 'Movement of Progressive Societies,'" in *Vital Relations: Modernity and the Persistent Life of Kinship*, ed. Susan McKinnon and Fenella Cannell (Santa Fe: School for Advanced Research Press, 2013).
2. Among a wide range of classic texts, see, for example, Carole Pateman, *The Disorder of Women: Democracy, Feminism and Political Theory* (Stanford, CA: Stanford University Press, 1989). The phrase "the personal is political" was coined by Carol Hanisch, "*The Personal Is Political*," in *Notes from the Second Year: Women's Liberation*, ed. Shulamith Firestone and Anne Koedt (New York: Radical Feminism, 1970), 76–78. For how the conceptual separation shaped classical social theory, see Barbara L. Marshall and Anne Witz, ed., *Engendering the Social: Feminist Encounters with Sociological Theory* (Maidenhead: Open University Press, 2004).
3. David Warren Sabean, Simon Teuscher, and Jon Mathieu, ed., *Kinship in Europe: Approaches to Long-Term Development (1300–1900)* (New York: Berghahn Books, 2007).
4. This approach draws mainly from the work of Marilyn Strathern and its reception by a variety of authors involved in the so-called "ontological turn," as well as from discussions on "symmetrical anthropology." See Pierre Charbonnier, Gildas Salmon, and Peter Skafish, eds., *Metaphysics: Ontology after Anthropology* (London: Rowman & Littlefield, 2017). For how this discussion can be applied to history writing, see Caroline Arni, "Nach der Kultur: Anthropologische Potentiale für eine rekursive Geschichtsschreibung," *Historische Anthropologie* 26, no. 2 (2018).
5. Karen Middleton, "How Karembola Men Become Mothers," in *Cultures of Relatedness: New Approaches to the Study of Kinship*, ed. Janet Carsten (Cambridge: Cambridge University Press, 2000), 105.
6. For the state of the art, see, for example, *Ethnologie française* 167, no. 3 (2017). See also the chapter by Marit Melhuus in this volume.
7. For instance, see various contributions in Janet Price and Margrit Shildrick, eds., *Feminist Theory and the Body* (Edinburgh: Edinburgh University Press, 1999).
8. Anne Cova, "Où en est l'histoire de la maternité?" *CLIO: Femmes, Genre, Histoire*, no. 21 (2005).
9. Philippe Descola, *Beyond Nature and Culture* (Chicago: University of Chicago Press, 2013).
10. For instance, see Kathleen Lennon, "Feminist Perspectives on the Body," in *The Stanford Encyclopedia of Philosophy*, Fall 2019 ed., ed. Edward N. Zalta, retrieved 25 September 2020 from https://plato.stanford.edu/archives/fall2019/entries/feminist-body/.
11. Joan W. Scott, *Only Paradoxes to Offer: French Feminists and the Rights of Man* (Princeton, NJ: Princeton University Press, 1996).
12. It is indicative of how profound this challenge was (and still is) that political scientist Carole Pateman, when calling for giving attention to how motherhood "is to be understood" in order to grasp its political dimension, proposes to overcome its limitation to "the relation between mother and child." See Carole Pateman, "Equality, Difference, Subordination: The Politics of Motherhood and Women's Citizenship," in *Beyond Equality and Difference: Citizenship, Feminist Politics and Female Subjectivity*, ed. Gisela Bock and Susan James (London: Routledge, 1992), 20–21. The question I want to raise, of course, is about what it would mean if this very relationship between mother and child were itself political.
13. In one variation or the other, this argument can be found in most of the literature on the strand of feminism that I will discuss in this chapter. As a case in point, see the article by Leslie Rabine, "Essentialism and Its Contexts: Saint-Simonian and Post-Structuralist Feminists," *differences*, no. 1 (1989). The idiosyncrasy of the particular

feminist position I examine here has also inspired important discussions on how to address historical alterity within the history of feminism: cf. Geneviève Fraisse, *Les Femmes et leur histoire* (Paris: La Découverte, 1998); see also Geneviève Fraisse, "Des femmes présentes," *Les révoltes logiques,* nos. 8/9 (1979); Jacques Rancière, "Une femme encombrante (à propos de Suzanne Voilquin)," *Les révoltes logiques,* nos. 8/9 (1979).

14. Cf., for turning ontological impositions into research questions, Amiria Henare, Martin Holbraad, and Sari Wastell, "Introduction," in *Thinking through Things: Theorising Artefacts Ethnographically,* ed. Amiria Henare, Martin Holbraad, and Sari Wastell (London: Routledge, 2007); Eduardo Viveiros de Castro, "The Relative Native," *HAU: Journal of Ethnographic Theory* 3, no. 3 (2013). Assuming the heuristic position of not knowing what something—in this case motherhood—is addresses a problem similar to the one Caroline W. Bynum has recently elaborated on in terms of "morphology." Caroline W. Bynum, "Avoiding the Tyranny of Morphology; or, Why Compare?" *History of Religion* 53, no. 4 (2014).

15. Margaret Jolly, "Introduction: Colonial and Postcolonial Plots in Histories of Maternities and Modernities," in *Maternities and Modernities: Colonial and Postcolonial Experiences in Asia and the Pacific,* ed. Kalpana Ram and Margaret Jolly (Cambridge: Cambridge University Press, 1998), 1.

16. Raising this possibility fills a gap in feminist scholarship, which refers the analysis of women's oppression almost completely to an analysis of sexual difference. As a founding text for this move where—not coincidentally—maternity is absent, see Gayle Rubin, "The Traffic in Women: Notes on the 'Political Economy' of Sex," in *Toward an Anthropology of Women,* ed. Rayna R. Reiter (New York: Monthly Review Press, 1975).

17. The quote is from Rabine, "Essentialism," 108. For approaching actors in terms of "competence," see Luc Boltanski, *On Critique: A Sociology of Emancipation* (Cambridge: Polity Press, 2011).

18. Jennifer L. Morgan, "Partus sequitur ventrem: Law, Race, and Reproduction in Colonial Slavery," *Small Axe* 22, no. 1 (55) (2018), 2. For a further elaboration of this take, see also 15–17.

19. Morgan, "Partus sequitur ventrem," 16.

20. I suspect that through the framework of such a history it would be possible to account for the ways in which concepts of nineteenth-century proletarian feminists intersect with those of twentieth-century Black feminism. For the latter, see the classical essay by Hortense Spillers, "Mama's Baby, Papa's Maybe: An American Grammar Book," *Diacritics* 17, no. 2 (1987). For Black feminist concepts of motherhood and emancipation within the analytical framework used here, see Rosalind Pollack Petchesky, "The Body as Property: A Feminist Re-vision," in *Conceiving the New World Order: The Global Politics of Reproduction,* ed. Faye D. Ginsburg and Rayna Rapp (Berkeley: University of California Press, 1995), 397.

21. Jeanne Deroin, *Campagne éléctorale de la citoyenne Jeanne Deroin, et pétition des femmes au peuple* (Paris: Dépot Central de la Propagande Socialiste, 1949). For a comprehensive study of Jeanne Deroin, see Michèle Riot-Sarcey, *La démocratie à l'épreuve des femmes: Trois figures critiques du pouvoir, 1830–1848* (Paris: Albin Michel, 1994). Unless otherwise noted, translations from French are my own.

22. Jeanne Deroin, *Cours de droit social pour les femmes* (Paris: Dépot Central de la Propagande Socialiste, 1848), 8.

23. Déroin, *Cours,* 8. The passage in its entirety reads, "O woman! Mother of humankind, you who contain in your bosom every pain, you who have suffered all martyrdoms, you, the representative of the always-suffering worker, always oppressed, always subordinated (*toujours subalternisé*), arise and speak in the name of humanity!"

24. Scott, *Paradoxes,* 57–89.

25. Scott, *Paradoxes*, 63. For this configuration of the self-owning male individual, see also Carole Pateman, "Self-Ownership and Property in the Person: Democratization and a Tale of Two Concepts," *Journal of Political Philosophy* 10, no. 1 (2002): 34–35.
26. From the journal *La République* (13 April 1848), cited in Riot-Sarcey, *Trois figures*, 247.
27. Both cases rested upon potentiality. Not all women were mothers, just as not all men married or were even meant to: European countries at the time knew a set of religious and economic impediments to marriage, which however—and significantly—were about to be abolished.
28. Jeanne Deroin, "A l'auteur du *'Douaire universel,'*" *Almanach des femmes* (1853), 73–74. The Almanach published its texts in French and English. As the English translation is not precise, the translation here is mine too. As with "motherhood," I do not presuppose any definition of "labor" or "work" external to the conceptualizations at stake. See: Anaïs Albert, Clyde Plumauzille, and Sylvain Ville, "Déplacer les frontières du travail," *Tracés: Revue de Sciences humaines*, no. 32 (2017).
29. On Saint-Simonian feminists, see, among others, Riot-Sarcey, *Trois figures*; Susan K. Grogan, *French Socialism and Sexual Difference: Women and the New Society, 1803–44* (London: Macmillan, 1992); Laure Adler, *A l'Aube du féminisme: Les premières journalistes (1830–1850)* (Paris: Payot, 1979); Claire Goldberg Moses, *French Feminism in the 19th Century* (Albany: State University of New York Press, 1984); Lydia Elhadad, "Femme prénommées: Les prolétaires saint-simoniennes rédactrices de 'La femme libre' 1832–1834," *Révoltes logiques*, no. 4 (1976), no. 5 (1977).
30. *La Femme libre*, no. 1 (1832). The journal appeared from 1832 to 1834. All issues are available in two volumes, from which I will quote here: Anonymous, *Apostolat des femmes* (Paris, 1832–33); Anonymous, *Tribune des femmes* (Paris, 1833–34). Cf. on the journal: Stefania Ferrando and Bérengère Kolly, "Le premier journal féministe: L'écriture comme pratique politique; *La Femme libre* de Jeanne-Désirée et Marie-Reine," in *Quand les socialistes inventaient l'avenir: Presse, théories et expériences, 1825–1860*, ed. Thomas Bouchet et al. (Paris: La Découverte, 2015).
31. Jeanne Deroin, "Profession de foi de Mlle Jenny de Roin (1831)," in *La liberté des femmes: "Lettres de dames" au Globe (1831–1832)*, ed. Michelle Riot-Sarcey (Paris: Coté-femmes édition, 1992), 135.
32. It is usually traced back to Mary Wollstonecraft. Moira Ferguson, "Mary Wollstonecraft and the Problematic of Slavery," *Feminist Review* 42, no. 1 (1992).
33. Pateman, "Self-Ownership," 34–35. Frequently used notions like *annihilation* or *nullité* are apt expressions of this critique of appropriated personhood. For a thoroughgoing exploration on how the usage of "the slave" in the "language of persons, rights, and liberties" fostered a particular conceptualization of liberal individualism, see Saidiya V. Hartman, *Scenes of Subjection: Terror, Slavery, and Self-Making in Nineteenth-Century America* (New York: Oxford University Press, 1997).
34. Deroin, "Profession de foi," 135.
35. Florence Rochefort, "Politiques féministes du nom (France, XIXe–XXIe siècle)," *CLIO: Femmes, Genre, Histoire*, no. 45 (2017): 107. See also on Saint-Simonian feminists' naming practices: Riot-Sarcey, *Trois figures*, 86–90; Carolyn J. Eichner, "In the Name of the Mother: Feminist Opposition to the Patronym in Nineteenth-Century France," *Signs: Journal of Women in Culture and Society* 39, no. 3 (2014).
36. I have not so far encountered a thorough explanation for the coupling of names. It might have been intended to recall historical figures ("Jeanne" for Jeanne d'Arc), to refer to female ancestors or friends, or to indicate sisterhood.
37. S. (Suzanne Voilquin) in Anonymous, *Apostolat des femmes*, 87.
38. Pauline Roland went down in history as the most prominent case in point. On Roland, cf. Edith Thomas, *Pauline Roland: Socialisme et féminisme au XIX siècle* (Paris: Rivière, 1956). For how so-called "natural children," according to custom and civil registration,

went by their mother's name, see Anne Lefebvre-Teillard, *Le Nom: Droit et histoire* (Paris: PUF, 1990), 164–67.
39. For a comprehensive presentation of the Saint-Simonian movement, see Antoine Picon, *Les Saint-simoniens: Raison, imaginaire et utopie* (Paris: Belin, 2002); Nathalie Coilly and Philippe Régnier, eds., *Le siècle des saint-simoniens du Nouveau christianisme au canal de Suez* (Paris: Bibliothèque nationale de France, 2006).
40. Stefania Ferrando traces this mode of feminism back to the writings of Olympe de Gouges while reading it through the lens of the Milan Women's Bookstore Collective from the 1980s and 1990s: "Images de femmes libres: Pour une histoire esthétiques des idées politiques." *Images Re-vues*, Hors-série no. 6 (2018), http://journals.openedition.org/imagesrevues/4284.
41. Deroin, "*Profession de foi*," 129, 135.
42. *Code Civil des Français* (Paris: L'Imprimerie de la République, 1804), Livre Premier, Titre VII, Chapitre II, Article 321.
43. Françoise Dekeuwer-Défossez, "Droit des personnes et de la famille: De 1804 au pacs (et au-delà …)," *Pouvoirs* 107, no. 4 (2003). Anne Lefebvre-Teillard speaks of a "strong" custom that forged the patronym in the image of a "hereditary good" transmitted by men (*Le Nom*, 163).
44. Sylvie Steinberg, "Et le bâtards devinrent citoyens: La privatisation d'une condition d'infamie sous la Révolution française," *Genèses* 108, no. 3 (2017): 18.
45. Eichner, "Name of the Mother," 661.
46. Eichner, "Name of the Mother," 663.
47. Casaubon published her first two treatises by initials (E.A.C.), a third by her first name (Mme Egérie). She has been identified by Geneviève Fraisse, who counts her among the Saint-Simonian feminists, although she might not have been a formal member of the Saint-Simonian school/church: Geneviève Fraisse, *La Raison des femmes* (Paris: Plon, 1992), 100, 104.
48. Egérie Casaubon, *La femme est la famille* (Paris: Gautier, 1834). A subsequent treatise followed up in analyzing the situation of women: *Le nouveau contrat social ou Place à la femme* (Paris: Delaunay, 1834). The third publication—explicitly addressed to the leader of the Saint-Simonian movement—makes the case for the abolition of the death penalty: *Mémoire en faveur de l'abolition de la peine de mort* (Paris: Delaunay, 1836).
49. Casaubon, *Femme*, 7.
50. Casaubon, *Femme*, 8: "Le fruit doit porter le nom de l'arbre qui lui donna la vie, non celui du jardinier qu'y greffa le bourgeon."
51. Casaubon, *Femme*, 4.
52. For the trope see Jacques Gélis, *L'Arbre et le Fruit: La Naissance dans l'Occident moderne (XVIe–XIXe siècle)* (Paris: Fayard, 1984).
53. Casaubon's use of the tree-fruit trope is all the more significant for the fact that she did command the vocabulary that, at the time, transformed the coming-into-being of humans from being an act of procreating parents to being a realization of a biological process: namely by using the term "reproduction of the human species" (Casaubon, *Femme*, 8). For the turn from "*generatio*" to "reproduction," see Ludmilla Jordanova, "Interrogating the Concept of Reproduction in the Eighteenth Century," in *Conceiving the New World Order: The Global Politics of Reproduction*, ed. Faye Ginsburg and Rayna Rapp (Berkeley: University of California Press, 1995).
54. Casaubon, *Femme*, 18. For the history of this ancient trope as classically rendered by Aristotle, see Erna Lesky, *Die Zeugungs- und Vererbungslehren der Antike und ihr Nachleben* (Wiesbaden: Franz Steiner, 1950), 1351.
55. For the trope of women's passive or receptive role in procreation, see Gianna Pomata, "Blood Ties and Semen Ties: Consanguinity and Agnation in Roman Law," in *Gender, Kinship, Power: A Comparative and Interdisciplinary History*, ed. Mary Jo Maynes et al. (New York: Routledge, 1996).

56. Casaubon, *Femme*, 18.
57. This mixture shows traces of how the Saint-Simonian school engaged with the physiocratic tradition, which interpreted natural processes as economic processes. See Michel Bellet, *La critique saint-simonienne de la secte des économistes: Un positionnement original*, working paper, GATE 2014-09, 2014 retrieved 13 March 2019 from https://econpapers.repec.org/paper/gatwpaper/1409.htm.
58. Casaubon, *Femme*, 4, 5.
59. Saint-Simonian feminists usually did not split maternity by setting apart "biological motherhood" from the "social function" of nurturing and educating the child. As an exception, see the case of Claire Démar later in this chapter—although, for her, too, both are subsumed in "motherhood."
60. It would be interesting to explore the links between this concept of motherhood and the idea of the "maternal dominion," as developed in early modern contractarian theory. There, it was argued that mothers had a privileged relationship to the child, the "original dominion over children": Hobbes argued that only maternity is ever certain and the mother is the first to hold the child, while Locke reasoned that she nourishes the child "out of her substance." These were the exact same reasons Saint-Simonian feminists referred to when arguing not for maternal power but maternal productivity. We have no evidence that someone like Casaubon would have read these authors, but she was literate and, like other Saint-Simonian feminists, certainly drew on ideas from earlier periods. For the theory of "maternal dominion," see Anna Becker, "Gender and the State of Nature," in *History, Politics, Law: Thinking through the International*, ed. Annabel Brett and Martti Koskenniemi (Cambridge: Cambridge University Press, 2021).
61. Nancy Fraser, "Expropriation and Exploitation in Racialized Capitalism: A Reply to Michael Dawson," *Critical Historical Studies* 3, no. 1 (2016): 166 (emphasis in original). As examples of such *capacities and resources*, Fraser mentions "labor, land, animals, tools, mineral or energy deposits—but also human beings, their sexual and reproductive capacities, their children and bodily organs."
62. Casaubon, *Femme*, 3.
63. Casaubon, *Femme*, 9, 24. Jeanne Deroin, in the 1850s, spoke of a "dowry" for women who performed maternal labor and deserved to have their livelihood secured by "society." She states this as a "*reward*" for maternal labor and an "inalienable right" of the child (see Deroin, "Auteur," 74).
64. I read the distinction between "wage" and "tribute" as a distinction between alienable and inalienable labor. It should, however, not be forgotten, that wage-mediated labor in the nineteenth century was by some seen as inalienable too. See Pateman, "Self-Ownership."
65. Casaubon, *Femme*, 11.
66. Casaubon, *Femme*, 24 (emphasis in original).
67. Egérie Casaubon, *Le nouveau contrat social ou Place à la femme* (Paris: Delaunay, 1834), 28–29.
68. For the fictionality of the idea, see Pateman, "Self-Ownership." For an explicit elaboration on how women's faculties are "not restrained to maternal obligations," see Deroin, "Douaire," 76.
69. Casaubon, *Contrat*, 52. See for Démar: Christine Planté, "La parole souverainement révoltante de Claire Démar," in *Femmes dans la Cité, 1815–1871*, ed. Alain Corbin, Jacqueline Lalouette, and Michèle Riot-Sarcey (Grâne: Créaphis 1997); Caroline Arni, "'Moi seule,' 1833: Feminist Subjectivity, Temporality, and Historical Interpretation," *History of the Present* 2, no. 2 (2012).
70. Claire Démar, *Ma loi d'avenir: Ouvrage posthume, publié par Suzanne* (Paris: Bureau de la Tribune des Femmes, 1834), 55, 58.

71. In practice, recording the mother in the birth register usually counted as such. See Teillard, *Nom*, 166; for "voluntary motherhood," see also Nadine Lefaucheur, "The French 'Tradition' of Anonymous Birth: The Lines of Argument," *International Journal of Law, Policy and the Family* 18, no. 3 (2004).
72. On the genealogical model, see Sandra Bamford and James Leach, ed., *Kinship and Beyond: The Genealogical Model Reconsidered* (New York: Berghahn Books, 2009). Casaubon as well as Démar referred to James Henry Lawrence, who propagated an antigenealogical framework by harking back to the gnostic tradition in early Christianity. See Astrid Deuber-Mankowsky, *Praktiken der Illusion: Kant, Nietzsche, Cohen, Benjamin bis Donna J. Haraway* (Berlin: vorwerk 8, 2007), 260–64.
73. Démar, *Loi*, 59 (emphasis in original).
74. See Gilles Jacoud, "Droit de propriété et économie politique dans l'analyse saint-simonienne," *Revue Economique* 65, no. 2 (2014).
75. Démar, *Loi*, 58.
76. Deroin, "Profession de foi," 121.
77. Deroin, "Profession de foi," 123. Casaubon also elaborates on the *"fond commun"* in Casaubon, *Contrat*, 30.
78. Jeanne-Désirée (Gay) in Anonymous, *Apostolat des femmes*, 70. Gay here takes a jab at the Saint-Simonian men, who had started excluding women from their organization.
79. For the concept of siblingship in the long nineteenth century, see Lynn Hunt, *The Family Romance of the French Revolution* (London: Routledge, 1992); Stefani Engelstein, *Sibling Action: The Genealogical Structure of Modernity* (New York: Columbia University Press, 2017); Christopher H. Johnson and David Warren Sabean, eds., *Sibling Relations and the Transformations of European Kinship, 1300–1900* (New York: Routledge, 2011).
80. I borrow this description from Fraisse, *Les femmes*, 291.
81. Suzanne (Voilquin), "La justice des hommes," in Anonymous, *Apostolat des femmes* 1, 121–27, 126 (emphasis in original).
82. (Voilquin), "Justice," 126.
83. (Voilquin), "Justice," 127 (emphasis in original). The translation of this quote is taken from Rabine, "Essentialism," 114.
84. Reclus's article was, in fact, a review of Johann Jakob Bachofen's monograph on "Mutterrecht" (1861) and John Ferguson MacLennan's "Primitive Marriage" (first 1865, reprinted 1876): Élie Reclus, "Female Kinship and Maternal Filiation," *Radical Review*, no. 1 (1877). Cf. for these debates: Ann Taylor Allen, "Feminism, Social Science, and the Meanings of Modernity: The Debate on the Origin of the Family in Europe and the United States, 1860–1914," *American Historical Review* 104, no. 4 (1999).
85. See chapter 3 in Kristin Ross, *Communal Luxury: The Political Imaginary of the Paris Commune* (London: Verso, 2015).
86. Reclus, "Female Kinship," 218.
87. Reclus, "Female Kinship," 218. In order to drive home the point on maternal instinct being available to men too, Reclus tells the story of an orphaned child that tamed a "horde of California miners."
88. Hubertine Auclert, "Matriarcat," *Le Radical* (6 July 1897). For Auclert's engagement with the question of the patronym, see Rochefort, "Politiques feministes," and Eichner, "Name of the Mother."
89. Auclert, "Matriarcat."

Bibliography

Anonymous. Apostolat des femmes. Paris, 1832–33.
_____. *Tribune des femmes*. Paris, 1833–34.
Adler, Laure. *A l'Aube du féminisme: Les premières journalistes (1830–1850)*. Paris: Payot, 1979.
Albert, Anaïs, Clyde Plumauzille, and Sylvain Ville. "Déplacer les frontières du travail." *Tracés: Revue de Sciences humaines*, no. 32 (2017): 7–24.
Allen, Ann Taylor. "Feminism, Social Science, and the Meanings of Modernity: The Debate on the Origin of the Family in Europe and the United States, 1860–1914." *American Historical Review* 104, no. 4 (1999): 1085–13.
Arni, Caroline. "'Moi seule,' 1833: Feminist Subjectivity, Temporality, and Historical Interpretation." *History of the Present* 2, no. 2 (2012): 107–21.
_____. "Nach der Kultur: Anthropologische Potentiale für eine rekursive Geschichtsschreibung." *Historische Anthropologie* 26, no. 2 (2018): 200–223.
Auclert, Hubertine. "Le Féminisme: Matriarcat." *Le Radical* (6 July 1897).
Bamford, Sandra, and James Leach, eds. *Kinship and Beyond: The Genealogical Model Reconsidered*. New York: Berghahn Books, 2009.
Becker, Anna. "Gender and the State of Nature." In *History, Politics, Law: Thinking through the International*, edited by Annabel Brett and Martti Koskenniemi, 341–56. Cambridge: Cambridge University Press, 2021.
Bellet, Michel. "La critique saint-simonienne de la secte des économistes: Un positionnement original." Working paper, GATE 2014-09, 2013. Retrieved 13 March 2019 from https://econpapers.repec.org/paper/gatwpaper/1409.htm.
Boltanski, Luc. *On Critique: A Sociology of Emancipation*. Cambridge: Polity Press, 2011.
Bynum, Caroline W. "Avoiding the Tyranny of Morphology; or, Why Compare?" *History of Religion* 53, no. 4 (2014): 341–68.
Casaubon, Egérie. *La femme est la famille*. Paris: Gautier, 1834.
_____. *Le nouveau contrat social ou Place à la femme*. Paris: Delaunay, 1834.
_____. *Mémoire en faveur de l'abolition de la peine de mort*. Paris: Delaunay, 1836.
Charbonnier, Pierre, Gildas Salmon, and Peter Skafish, eds. *Comparative Metaphysics: Ontology after Anthropology*. London: Rowman & Littlefield, 2017.
Code Civil des Français. Paris: L'Imprimerie de la République, 1804.
Coilly, Nathalie, and Philippe Régnier, ed. *Le siècle des saint-simoniens du Nouveau christianisme au canal de Suez*. Paris: Bibliothèque nationale de France, 2006.
Cova, Anne. "Où en est l'histoire de la maternité?" *CLIO: Femmes, Genre, Histoire*, no. 21 (2005): 189–211.
Dekeuwer-Défossez, Françoise. "Droit des personnes et de la famille: De 1804 au pacs (et au-delà …)." *Pouvoirs* 107, no. 4 (2003): 37–53.
Démar, Claire. *Ma loi d'avenir: Ouvrage posthume, publié par Suzanne*. Paris: Bureau de la Tribune des Femmes, 1834.
Deroin, Jeanne. *Cours de droit social pour les femmes*. Paris: Plon, 1848.
_____. "A l'auteur du 'Douaire universel.'" *Almanach des femmes* (1853): 71–78.
_____. *Campagne éléctorale de la citoyenne Jeanne Deroin, et pétition des femmes au peuple*. Paris: Dépot Central de la Propagande Socialiste, 1949.

———. "Profession de foi de Mlle Jenny de Roin (1831)." In *La liberté des femmes: "Lettres de dames" au Globe (1831–1832)*, edited by Michelle Riot-Sarcey, 116–39. Paris: Coté-femmes édition, 1992.

Descola, Philippe. *Beyond Nature and Culture*. Chicago: University of Chicago Press, 2013.

Deuber-Mankowsky, Astrid. *Praktiken der Illusion: Kant, Nietzsche, Cohen, Benjamin bis Donna J. Haraway*. Berlin: vorwerk 8, 2007.

Eichner, Carolyn J. "In the Name of the Mother: Feminist Opposition to the Patronym in Nineteenth-Century France." *Signs: Journal of Women in Culture and Society* 39, no. 3 (2014): 659–83.

Elhadad, Lydia. "Femme prénommées: Les prolétaires saint-simoniennes rédactrices de 'La femme libre' 1832–1834." *Révoltes logiques, no.* 4 (1976): 62–88; no. 5 (1977): 29–60.

Engelstein, Stefani. *Sibling Action: The Genealogical Structure of Modernity*. New York: Columbia University Press, 2017.

Ferguson, Moira. "Mary Wollstonecraft and the Problematic of Slavery." *Feminist Review* 42, no. 1 (1992): 82–102.

Ferrando, Stefania. "Images de femmes libres: Pour une histoire esthétiques des idées politiques." *Images Re-vues*, Hors-série no. 6 (2018). Retrieved 13 March 2019 from http://journals.openedition.org/imagesrevues/4284.

Ferrando, Stefania, and Bérengère Kolly. "Le premier journal féministe: L'écriture comme pratique politique; *La Femme libre* de Jeanne-Désirée et Marie-Reine." In *Quand les socialistes inventaient l'avenir: Presse, théories et expériences, 1825–1860*, edited by Thomas Bouchet et al., 104–12. Paris: La Découverte, 2015.

Fraisse, Geneviève. "Des femmes présentes." *Les révoltes logiques*, nos. 8/9 (1979): 123–25.

———. *Les femmes et leur histoire*. Paris: Gallimard, 1998.

———. *La Raison des femmes*. Paris: Plon, 1992.

Fraser, Nancy. "Expropriation and Exploitation in Racialized Capitalism: A Reply to Michael Dawson." *Critical Historical Studies* 3, no. 1 (2016): 163–78.

Gélis, Jacques. *L'Arbre et le Fruit: La Naissance dans l'Occident moderne, XVIe–XIXe siècle*. Paris: Fayard, 1984.

Goldberg Moses, Claire. *French Feminism in the 19th Century*. Albany: State University of New York Press, 1984.

Grogan, Susan K. *French Socialism and Sexual Difference: Women and the New Society, 1803–44*. London: Macmillan, 1992.

Hanisch, Carol. "The Personal Is Political." In *Notes from the Second Year: Women's Liberation*, edited by Shulamith Firestone and Anne Koedt, 76–78. New York: Radical Feminism, 1970.

Hartman, Saidiya V. *Scenes of Subjection: Terror, Slavery, and Self-Making in Nineteenth-Century America*. New York: Oxford University Press, 1997.

Henare, Amiria, Martin Holbraad, and Sari Wastell. "Introduction." In *Thinking through Things: Theorising Artefacts Ethnographically*, edited by Amiria Henare, Martin Holbraad, and Sari Wastell, 1–31. London: Routledge, 2007.

Hunt, Lynn. *The Family Romance of the French Revolution*. London: Routledge, 1992.

Jacoud, Gilles. "Droit de propriété et économie politique dans l'analyse saint-simonienne." *Revue Economique* 65, no. 2 (2014): 299–315.

Johnson, Christopher H., and David Warren Sabean, ed. *Sibling Relations and the Transformations of European Kinship, 1300–1900*. New York: Berghahn Books, 2011.
Jolly, Margaret. "Introduction: Colonial and Postcolonial Plots in Histories of Maternities and Modernities." In *Maternities and Modernities: Colonial and Postcolonial Experiences in Asia and the Pacific*, edited by Kalpana Ram and Margaret Jolly, 1–25. Cambridge: Cambridge University Press, 1998.
Jordanova, Ludmilla. "Interrogating the Concept of Reproduction in the Eighteenth Century." In *Conceiving the New World Order: The Global Politics of Reproduction*, edited by Faye Ginsburg and Rayna Rapp, 369–86. Berkeley: University of California Press, 1995.
Lefaucheur, Nadine. "The French 'Tradition' of Anonymous Birth: The Lines of Argument." *International Journal of Law, Policy and the Family* 18, no. 3 (2004): 319–42.
Lefebvre-Teillard, Anne. *Le Nom: Droit et histoire*. Paris: PUF, 1990.
Lennon, Kathleen, "Feminist Perspectives on the Body." In *The Stanford Encyclopedia of Philosophy*, Fall 2019 ed., edited by Edward N. Zalta. Retrieved 25 September 2020 from https://plato.stanford.edu/archives/fall2019/entries/feminist-body/.
Lesky, Erna. *Die Zeugungs- und Vererbungslehren der Antike und ihr Nachleben*. Wiesbaden: Franz Steiner, 1950.
Marshall, Barbara L., and Anne Witz, ed. *Engendering the Social: Feminist Encounters with Sociological Theory*. Maidenhead: Open University Press, 2004.
McKinnon, Susan. "Kinship within and beyond the 'Movement of Progressive Societies.'" In *Vital Relations: Modernity and the Persistent Life of Kinship*, edited by Susan McKinnon and Fenella Cannell, 39–62. Santa Fe: School for Advanced Research Press, 2013.
Middleton, Karen. "How Karembola Men Become Mothers." In *Cultures of Relatedness: New Approaches to the Study of Kinship*, edited by Janet Carsten, 104–27. Cambridge: Cambridge University Press, 2000.
Morgan, Jennifer L. "Partus sequitur ventrem: Law, Race, and Reproduction in Colonial Slavery." *Small Axe* 22, no. 1 (55) (2018): 1–17.
Pateman, Carole. *The Disorder of Women: Democracy, Feminism and Political Theory*. Stanford, CA: Stanford University Press, 1989.
———. "Equality, Difference, Subordination: The Politics of Motherhood and Women's Citizenship." In *Beyond Equality and Difference: Citizenship, Feminist Politics and Female Subjectivity*, edited by Gisela Bock and Susan James, 17–31. London: Routledge, 1992.
———. "Self-Ownership and Property in the Person: Democratization and a Tale of Two Concepts." *Journal of Political Philosophy* 10, no. 1 (2002): 20–53.
Petchesky, Rosalind Pollack. "The Body as Property: A Feminist Re-vision." In *Conceiving the New World Order: The Global Politics of Reproduction*, edited by Faye D. Ginsburg and Rayna Rapp, 387–406. Berkeley: University of California Press, 1995.
Picon, Antoine. *Les Saint-simoniens: Raison, imaginaire et utopie*. Paris: Belin, 2002.
Planté, Christine. "La parole souverainement révoltante de Claire Démar." In *Femmes dans la Cité, 1815–1871*, edited by Alain Corbin, Jacqueline Lalouette, and Michèle Riot-Sarcey, 481–94. Grâne: Créaphis, 1997.

Pomata, Gianna. "Blood Ties and Semen Ties: Consanguinity and Agnation in Roman Law." In *Gender, Kinship, Power: A Comparative and Interdisciplinary History*, edited by Mary Jo Maynes et al., 43–64. New York: Routledge, 1996.

Rabine, Leslie. "Essentialism and Its Contexts: Saint-Simonian and Post-Structuralist Feminists." *differences*, no. 1 (1989): 107–23.

Rancière, Jacques. "Une femme encombrante (à propos de Suzanne Voilquin)." *Les révoltes logiques*, nos. 8/9 (1979): 116–22.

Reclus, Élie. "Female Kinship and Maternal Filiation." *Radical Review*, no. 1 (1877): 205–23.

Riot-Sarcey, Michèle. *La démocratie à l'épreuve des femmes: Trois figures critiques du pouvoir, 1830–1848*. Paris: Albin Michel, 1994.

Rochefort, Florence. "Politiques féministes du nom (France, XIXe–XXIe siècle)." *CLIO: Femmes, Genre, Histoire*, no. 45 (2017): 107–27.

Ross, Kristin. *Communal Luxury: The Political Imaginary of the Paris Commune*. London: Verso, 2015.

Rubin, Gayle. "The Traffic in Women: Notes on the 'Political Economy' of Sex." In *Toward an Anthropology of Women*, edited by Rayna R. Reiter, 157–210. New York: Monthly Review Press, 1975.

Sabean, David W., Simon Teuscher, and Jon Mathieu, eds. *Kinship in Europe: Approaches to Long-Term Development (1300–1900)*. New York: Berghahn Books, 2007.

Scott, Joan W. *Only Paradoxes to Offer: French Feminists and the Rights of Man*. Princeton, NJ: Princeton University Press, 1996.

Spillers, Hortense. "Mama's Baby, Papa's Maybe: An American Grammar Book." *Diacritics* 17, no. 2 (1987): 64–81.

Steinberg, Sylvie. "Et le bâtards devinrent citoyens: La privatisation d'une condition d'infamie sous la Révolution française." *Genèses* 108, no. 3 (2017): 9–28.

Thomas, Edith. *Pauline Roland: Socialisme et féminisme au XIX siècle*. Paris: Rivière, 1956.

Viveiros de Castro, Eduardo. "The Relative Native." *HAU: Journal of Ethnographic Theory* 3, no. 3 (2013): 473–502.

Part III

Deployments

Kinship is deployed in a variety of settings: by institutions, in ritual performances, at work, and in hundreds of everyday activities, both formal and informal. These activities are often shaped by implicit assumptions about what kinship is, how it should be, and how relatives should behave and act. In many practical situations, the use of kinship may not be intended to lead to political transformation or a reconfiguration of relationships. And yet even here such transactions may have a dynamic effect. The introduction of a new word from a foreign language can, like the proverbial flapping of a butterfly wing in one part of the world causing a storm in another, produce far-reaching changes with significant implications for how kin relations are understood. But kinship can also be deployed more directly in political negotiations, which in turn have deep and enduring effects on familial relationships. One might consider bureaucratic procedures to acknowledge citizenship or to establish same-sex marriage, movements to establish the rights of children, parents claiming the right to follow their unaccompanied children across borders, or widespread colonial projects of displacing children from their homes and assigning them to schools and orphanages.[1]

While kinship can be transformed through such institutional practices, the effects on kinship relations can follow even when kinship is not directly addressed. Obvious among them are rules about recusal in court proceedings and laws meant to limit patronage, bribery, or outright corruption. Censuses, tax collection, birth registration, or the designation of caregivers can introduce linguistic novelties that in turn can redefine household structures and familial relations. Such practices might also have the effect of excluding someone from being acknowledged as kin. Parenting and marriage are always embedded in and shaped by political, societal, or religious norms, regulations, and laws. Everyday activities such as travel, household conviviality, or care in turn shape these interventions and their effects.

At any one point, kinship may look static and even appear to be based on common understandings or enduring laws, but the effects of political interventions, everyday practices, and institutional organization continuously reconfigure the relationships between families and authorities, relations among families and households, relations within households, lineages, kin-structured networks, and even ad hoc encounters of friends and relatives.

The chapters in this part pay close attention to processes of making kinship through explicit and implicit political interventions. We propose ceasing to think of kinship as a domain on its own or as something that is measurable and instead considering it as immanent in political processes, constantly being remade and constantly subject to linguistic changes. Again, one must guard against the idea of a linear development toward modernity: kinship is always being reconfigured. It is not a matter of the decline or rise of kinship nor of a replacement of this or that function by new or redeployed institutions on its own. As it is always about inclusion and exclusion, the making of kinship is accompanied by processes of hindering, prohibiting, or even unmaking kin as expressed in the concept of "de-kinning"[2] to handle issues of transnational adoption or forced institutionalization or adoption of native children (Australia, Canada, Hawaii).[3] Effective ways of prohibiting the making of kinship can be detected in contexts as different as laws prohibiting egg donation and modalities of excluding those slaves whose procreative relationships were not understood as kinship. Long-term consequences for recognizing and interacting with kin result, for example, from clerics' mapping exercises and legislatures' definitions of who can and cannot marry and how to count what constitutes closeness and distance.

Erdmute Alber looks at translation processes by examining the travel of European, and here explicitly French, notions of kinship and the family to colonial societies in Dahomey (now the Republic of Benin). By tracing how the concept of "the extended family" (*famille* étendue) entered West Africa, she questions the widely shared assumption that "African" societies had been shaped by kinship since times immemorial. There is much to indicate that the colonized societies were far less interested in using kinship as an element of political order than the French colonizers attributed to them. Indeed, the extensive borrowing of

French words to describe many aspects of family and kinship points to the necessity for naming new constellations of relations. French authorities introduced terms to clarify what seemed to them local systems of kinship that stemmed from France's own past. They conducted inquiries to collect unwritten customs and record them in *coutumiers*, a practice the French crown had used in the sixteenth and seventeenth centuries to systematize inheritance rules and make explicit the kinship conceptions of its subjects, thereby inventing what was understood as tradition in the process of collecting and editing. With the redaction of what was then understood as customary law in administrative and jural practices, local societies became familiarized with French understandings of their kinship and sometimes changed their practices accordingly.

Ludolf Kuchenbuch leads us to a historical configuration where kinship was attributed to those who were formerly excluded from it: the manumission of unfree people in the Early Middle Ages. He argues that no kinship vocabulary existed for unfree people and that acquiring kin was an important part of the process of manumission. The kin-making was explicitly expressed in manumission charters that state that formerly unfree persons were henceforth to be treated as if they had free maternal and paternal ancestry. Moreover, manumission opened up new ways to acquire kin through unrestricted marriages and a new role with regard to the church and its system of spiritual kinship. The special importance of the phenomenon rests in the large number of people that were manumitted in this period, a process that was part of a systemic shift toward relaxed forms of domination that extended to both formerly unfree and formerly free segments of the population.

Marit Melhuus focuses on the beginning of life and the related processes of enabling and prohibiting parenting. Observing the intricacies of legal procedures around the making of kinship through technologies of egg donation, she demonstrates that these are interwoven with political ideals of gender equality in Norway. Experts, reviewers, scientists, and journalists—among others who play roles in lawmaking—shape many of the aspects of what is legally accepted as kinship. Using the example of negotiations over the legality of egg donations in Norway, she argues that legislative processes, understood as state practice, may involve the authorization of specific kinship acts and lead to the reconfiguration of notions of kinship in general. Given that egg donation had been prohibited in Norway before 2020, the overall focus of the chapter is on the underlying values that were mobilized to shape the legal provision. More specifically, the chapter examines the differential treatment of egg and sperm cells, following the shifts in arguments articulating this distinction. The chapter demonstrates how the state, through its reproductive policies based on the perspectives of expert commissions, is implicated in the configuration of not only kinship relations but also the entangled notions of gender.

Looking at another time and group of experts, Jon Mathieu examines the extent to which early modern European contractarian theorists dealt with issues related to family and kinship. Their texts had long-term implications not only for how the family was understood in political debate well into the twentieth century but also for an assumed divergence of Western and other traditions and thus the construction of "the West and the Rest." Contrary to others who have claimed that family matters were not important to contractarian theorists, he first shows that about 10 percent of the text of the canon deals with kinship relations. Paying close attention to all the many matters, he shows a large variety of arguments and ways of drawing boundaries between private and public, with issues such as inheritance and devolution of rights, offices, and properties, as well as the construction of others outside Europe thought to come under the purview of the state. His careful delineation of the issues is a contribution to how scientific thought plays a role in deploying kinship in the public realm. Marriage, for example, or the nature of household authority and the relationship between the household and household patriarch and the state were issues that called for considerable analysis. A clearer distinction between public and private would follow on the heels of early contractarian theory, but much of the groundwork had been completed regarding domestic law, political participation, and notions of citizenship.

Claudia Derichs turns in her chapter to the issue of deployment through linguistic translations of kinship in the context of Japan. First, she discusses specific terms related to kinship in order to convey the challenges of how to capture the meanings of concepts and norms when translating between Japanese and English. Tracing how translations of household and family were used in pre- and postwar Japan in relation to political and economic reforms, but also how these shifted and transformed, she illustrates the ambiguous and manifold "faces" of singular words. In prewar Japan, the *ie* system served to support loyalty to the imperial state as family, while after the war the term *ie* helped to install a new stress on the conjugal family and its gendered hierarchies. Given the importance of specific historical contexts that are not conveyed when ideologically laden kinship terms are translated into other languages, the examples illustrate the politics of kinship—here seen either as the Japanese state and household formations or as entanglements between private life and enterprises—as constantly reconfigured and accompanied, but also driven by, the transfer of new kinship terms.

Notes

1. Anthony Simpson: *Half London in Zambia: Contested Identities in a Catholic Mission School* (New York: Columbia University Press, 2003). Elsie Bohr, *Implantation de l'institution scolaire dans l'ancienne colonie de Dahomey: Les écoles des missions chrétiennes (1842–1923)*. *Histoire—Pédagogie—Société* (Strasbourg: Université des sciences humaines, 1982), Thèse de 3e cycle. Marie-France Lange, ed., *Des écoles pour le Sud: Stratégies sociales, politiques étatiques et interventions du Nord* (Bondy: Éditions de l'Aube, 2000).
2. Signe Howell, *The Kinning of Foreigners: Transnational Adoption in a Global Perspective* (New York: Berghahn Books, 2006), 9.
3. Peter Read, *The Stolen Generations: The Removal of Aboriginal Children in New South Wales 1883 to 1969* (Surry Hills: New South Wales Department of Aboriginal Affairs), https://daa.asn.au/wp-content/uploads/2016/07/Reading-7_StolenGenerations.pdf. Judith Modell, "Rights to the Children: Foster Care and Social Reproduction in Hawaii," in *Reproducing Reproduction: Kinship, Power, and Technological Innovation*, ed. Sarah Franklin and Helena Ragoné (Philadelphia: University of Pennsylvania Press, 1998), 156–72.

Bibliography

Bohr, Elsie. *Implantation de l'institution scolaire dans l'ancienne colonie de Dahomey: Les écoles des missions chrétiennes (1842–1923)*. *Histoire—Pédagogie—Société*. Strasbourg: Université des sciences humaines, 1982.

Howell, Signe. *The Kinning of Foreigners: Transnational Adoption in a Global Perspective*. New York: Berghahn Books, 2006.

Lange, Marie-France, ed. *Des écoles pour le Sud: Stratégies sociales, politiques étatiques et interventions du Nord*. Bondy: Éditions de l'Aube, 2000.

Modell, Judith. "Rights to the Children: Foster Care and Social Reproduction in Hawaii." In *Reproducing Reproduction: Kinship, Power, and Technological Innovation*, edited by Sarah Franklin and Helena Ragoné, 156–72. Philadelphia: University of Pennsylvania Press, 1998.

Read, Peter. *The Stolen Generations: The Removal of Aboriginal Children in New South Wales 1883 to 1969*. Surry Hills: New South Wales Department of Aboriginal Affairs, 2006 [1982]. https://daa.asn.au/wp-content/uploads/2016/07/Reading-7_StolenGenerations.pdf.

Simpson, Anthony. *Half London in Zambia: Contested Identities in a Catholic Mission School*. New York: Columbia University Press, 2003.

Chapter 10

Inventing the Extended Family in Colonial Dahomey/Benin

Erdmute Alber

Introduction

During my research on child fostering, I was once talking with Bona, an older woman from the village of Tebo in the north of the Republic of Benin. Bona had never learned French, the former colonial and now national language. Like the majority of those born in her region in the first half of the twentieth century, she was brought up from a young age by a female relative who educated her and whom she refers to as her mother. Seeking to understand the language, norms, and practices of child fostering,[1] I asked her about the widespread practice of children growing up with aunts, uncles, or grandparents. She answered with the following:

> If you go into a marriage with a man, then you will fetch from your *family*, which you have, your own thing, in order to keep it [bring it up]. But even if you bear children for him, you will fetch the child of your brother, the child of your younger sister, and keep it.[2]

This quotation suggests many angles on and possible interpretations of Bona's understanding of child fostering. First and foremost, perhaps, it articulates that a married woman's desire to bring children of her own kin into the household into which she herself has married[3] is the force driving child-fostering practices, not parents' initiative or desire to give children to foster parents. In this chapter, however, I draw attention to something that may appear unimportant at first glance, even though it surprised me when I reread the interview. Here, I mean the word *fami*—the French *famille* (family)—which I was astonished to find in an interview conducted entirely in the local language of Baatonum.[4] This set me off on a line of thought that finally led to this text.

In the middle of a description that embedded fostering in relationships of siblinghood and marriage, Bona used the French term *famille*,[5] even though she repeatedly declared that the practices she talked about had existed forever, or at least for a long time before colonialism. This makes it even more surprising that she borrowed the term *famille* from the colonial language. Superficially, this could be understood as a simple phenomenon of language contact. It is not surprising at all that many words originating in other languages (African as well as European) and reflecting multiple influences have entered local languages in Benin. Loanwords from European languages have entered the region alongside colonial officers, merchants, new technologies, television transmissions, and much more. These words referred, especially, to previously unknown professions, technologies, or things, such as *portable* for mobile phones or *dokotoro* for nurses and medical doctors.

Understanding *famille* as such a loanword would suggest that what Bona referred to here was unknown before colonialism. However, she also made it very clear that practices like child fostering and the related desire to take in children of one's siblings had existed long before the French arrived. Indeed, they are present in tales about the origin of villages or chieftaincies attributed to precolonial times.[6] In some parts of our conversation, Bona even contrasted her understanding with European ideas of parenting and marriage, alluding to how European mothers, like me, would not find it easy to give their children to others to raise. In addition, she mentioned that, in contrast to her own view and lived experience, Europeans understood families as composed of married couples who demonstrated mutual love and closeness to their birth children.

Bona underlined a deep distance between wife and husband in her own society with the phrase "even if you bear children for him" (not "have them with him" or "with your husband"). At the same time, she gave linguistic expression to another distance, that between mother and children. Bona talked about the children "you bear" "for him" quite impersonally, framing childbirth as a duty to or contract with in-laws and using contrasting possessive constructions to express how deeply a woman belonged to her family of origin: to "your brother" or "your sister," and here "your family." Her way of talking about child fostering thus expressed a sharp contrast between her *fami* on one side and her husband on the other.

In this short excerpt from the interview, Bona clearly revealed a strong sense of belonging to what she called *famille*; her ties with it were so close that she would happily take in and rear children from it. One could even say that she understood her *famille* to be those whose children she would always take in and rear. And here she mentioned a small but important detail: when she included both her brother's and sister's children in that category of *famille*, Bona used the term in a wider sense than patrilineage. This is remarkable because when she dissociated herself from the child she bore for "him" and his lineage she did it perfectly in line with the patrilineality that is commonly seen as characteristic of her society. The children a woman bears are not seen or designated as her children but as those of the lineage of her husband.

So, what did *fami* mean in this conversation?[7] It was, first of all, those who belong to another—like brothers and sisters. Bona expressed this with the possessive pronoun "your."[8] Furthermore, it referred to all of those from whom Bona has the right to take in children. This marked the boundary with the in-laws; their children did not belong to Bona at all, not even the child she bore and who could be raised by somebody of her husband's family, or even by hers. In sum, for Bona *famille* means the people she belongs to, including people like her sister's children who were not part of her patrilineage but whom she could easily take in as her foster children.[9] Probably the very best translation for *fami* would thus be *extended kin* in the broad sense of naturalized bilateral social relations: the way the term is widely used in the discipline of anthropology.

While I was at first surprised to hear Bona use the term *fami*, it is not unusual to hear it in everyday conversation all over the country. *Fami* has entered many different local languages in Benin and is frequently used in a broad sense to refer to an unspecified collective category of bilateral kin. Depending on the context, it is sometimes also used to designate a narrower group of "us." A very common part of standard and even obligatory everyday greetings is to ask somebody, "*Et la famille?*" (And [how] is your family?) As it does not require a strongly individualized answer, this greeting is frequently expressed in a mixture of local languages. In Baatonum, for instance, the set phrase would be *wunen fami?* (your family?). An urban middle-class woman might answer that her husband and her children were fine, thus understanding *fami* in the sense of her nuclear family.

In conclusion, *la famille* refers to a sense of belonging in everyday communications that can sometimes mean those one is living with, and sometimes a larger group of kin. Depending on the speaker and the concrete context, sharp boundaries are often drawn between one's family of origin and the in-laws. But *famille* is also quite often used in a more inclusive way. If I had greeted Bona in French, by saying *"Et la famille?"* she would have understood the question (like almost everybody in the country) despite not knowing French. In Benin, talking about *la famille* has become an easy and widespread element of communicating and carrying on meaningful but not completely specified social relations.

In the following, I want to combine my findings from conversations and participations over the years with a historical perspective on the language of kinship asking how the term *famille* was brought into the country and became so matter of course. I argue that it was introduced by French colonial bureaucratic practices with their related language of codifying, judging, counting, and registering. These practices were infused with, and thus organized around, the idea that the extended family (in Anglophone contexts it would probably have been called "extended kin") was the key principle of social organization in precolonial Africa. The term *famille* was thus omnipresent in these documents (and possibly in the spoken everyday colonial communications), used to describe or classify the local population and thereby exert colonial rule.[10]

However, Europeans were not aware that there was no term in the local languages that could easily be translated as *la famille* before the French arrived. This is surprising, because common Euro-American stereotypes of sociability and exchange in the African continent—as well as generally shared anthropological or sociological knowledge—suggest that kinship (in the common language of anthropologists) or the extended family (in the language of sociologists) formed the main element of social and political organization in precolonial Africa.

To mention just a few instances of precolonial African societies being characterized as based on extended kinship over decades, it suffices to remember some important lines and periods of thinking. In the classic *African Political Systems*, as well as in their large-scale research program on kinship and marriage in Africa,[11] the structural functionalists Meyer Fortes and Edward Evans-Pritchard[12] argued that stateless societies in the savanna belt were organized politically around a kinship-based segmentary lineage system. Two decades later and seemingly far from structural- functionalist positions, proponents of modernization theory such as William Goode also attached great importance to the extended family in discussing social formations in Africa. This was framed as an antiquated institution that would be replaced in the process of modernization by the modern nuclear family, but Goode again argued that it would survive longer than elsewhere in Africa, which he considered more traditional or backward than other regions of the world.[13]

But even much later, social science research on what is assumed to be a specifically African manner of exercising power still sees kinship relations and related obligations—such as redistribution of wealth—as a driving force for social and political action.[14] Even in the field of economics, researchers interested in studying what is "specifically African" tend to refer to kinship networks. For instance, a widespread argument holds that African entrepreneurs cannot accumulate wealth because they are constantly obliged to redistribute it among their relatives.[15] Thousands of books and articles could be added to this picture, and in vernacular and intellectual thought in West African countries the importance of the extended family seems to be even more unquestionable. To give just one example, when I presented the arguments of this chapter at the Center for Research on Social Policies (CREPOS) seminar of the German Historical Institute in Dakar in March 2019, the discussion was dominated by statements of colleagues whose personal examples or historical information proved how deeply both everyday life and historical encounters were imprinted with the intensity and importance of family relationships, which the discussion depicted as basic.

The notion of African sociability as fundamentally based on extended kinship or family is omnipresent in the literature, as well as in public discourse. It is often framed in contrast to Western or European politics and sociability, which is imagined to be comparatively free of kinship or family and the related obligations. Of course, such binaries and apparently easy oppositions mirroring the modern/traditional dichotomy have already been deconstructed.[16] While the aim of my chapter is not to do so once again, I want to challenge the shared assumption that African societies have always been based on kinship or the extended family by asking why people would use a loanword from French when speaking in their local language about kinship and family matters.[17] By reconstructing the entrance and consolidation in and expansion of the term *la famille* in Benin, I want to contribute to a temporalizing perspective on the languages of kinship. In order to create a picture of how social relations imagined as kinship/family is mapped out in concrete times and places, I argue that the changing practices and bureaucracies are inextricably entangled with changing languages that shape not only how people interact but also how they imagine, interpret, and understand their relationships and, therewith, their world. Of course, this does not mean at all that I want to dissent the importance and intensity of close social relationships for any historical time and place on the African continent which my colleagues mentioned in the debate in Dakar. Rather, by situating *famille* in the colonial language and imagery, I argue against a seemingly eternal imagery of Africa as the continent of kinship and the related undertones of backwardness, tradition, or, more positively, not affectedness by the coldness of modernization, which seem to me to pop up again and again in the debates.

My first step is to discuss the *Coutumier du Dahomey*, which played a major role in the invention of the *famille* in Dahomey. In the following,

I analyze colonial practices of organizing political succession. I then turn to vernacular concepts connected in some way with ideas of *famille* and show that not all of them existed before colonialism; some, rather, were invented after the arrival of the French. Finally, I present the local concept of *bii nenobu* or child fostering. My arguments are summarized in the conclusion.

The *Coutumier du Dahomey*

As is common knowledge, the colonial project of conquering and colonizing Africa coincided with the establishment of the discipline of anthropology at the end of the nineteenth century.[18] As is also widely acknowledged, the latter was accompanied by the establishment of kinship as a scientific category and an object of research that called upon modes of classification, a process Thomas R. Trautmann has insightfully called the "invention of kinship."[19] This was also a time of broader and sometimes even obsessive interest in kinship, as Michaela Hohkamp (this volume) alludes to in showing how this was already prefigured in academic discourses in the eighteenth century.

The new discipline's tremendous interest in kinship accompanied the stabilization of difference between "civilized" and "primitive" societies[20] — seen either in an evolutionist or a spatial order — and projected divergent sexual practices such as polygamy, levirate marriage, and promiscuity on so-called primitive societies. While defined as systems of consanguinity and affinity, kinship relations were at the same time seen as an innate feature of all branches of the "human family,"[21] one that could be collected and classified through broad comparative research based on linguistic work, genealogies, questionnaires, and typologies. It was exactly this view of kinship — regarded as *the* main principle of social organization in the areas to be colonized — that was brought by colonizers to the African continent at the end of the nineteenth century. Thus, it also arrived in the former colony of Dahomey, which was founded by decree on 10 March 1893 as the "colonie du Dahomey et dépendances" (Colony of Dahomey and Dependencies). A second decree issued on 20 July 1894 removed the colony from the legislative authority of the Conseil d'appel de la Guinée française and made it a separate jurisdiction with a legal code modeled on the "législation civile, commerciale et criminelle du Sénégal" (civil, commercial, and criminal legislation of Senegal), the so-called mother colony of French West Africa.[22]

The establishment of a legal code modeled on the French system went hand in hand with the establishment of two different categories of people, *civilisés* and *indigènes*. Classifying the African population as "indigenous" and distinguishing them from "civilized" Europeans obviously reflected the thought of the times. It enabled a concrete juridical distinction between people ruled under French law and seen as French citizens and others excluded from that. In 1914, the governor general of French West Africa defined who belonged to the category of *indigènes*, namely: "les individus originaires des possessions de l'Afrique Occidentale Française, de l'Afrique Équatoriale Française et des possessions françaises comprises entre ces territoires qui n'ont pas dans leur pays d'origine le statut de nationaux européens" (the individuals originating from the French possessions of French West Africa, French Equatorial Africa, and the French possessions included in those territories who do not have the status of European nationals in their country of origin).[23]

Thus, like other British and French colonies in Africa, Dahomey introduced two legal systems that applied until independence in 1960. One of them, based on the Code Napoleon but applied by the colonial authorities, held for the *civilisés*; the other, *droit indigène* (indigenous law), had jurisdiction over the new category of *indigènes*, imagined as a "peuple sans histoire" (people without history).[24] This *droit indigène* was initially thought of as a continuation of local juridical practices based on orally transmitted knowledge. During the early years of colonial rule, the French commandants asked local authorities, mainly the local chiefs, whom they integrated into the colonial administration as *chefs de canton* (township chiefs)[25] to act as judges. As these steps were being formalized, however, colonial authorities increasingly felt a need for codification. In 1931, therefore, the governor general of French West Africa in Dakar ordered all governors to research and then codify indigenous law in their respective colonies in the form of a *coutumier* (code of customs) for every colony. This term referred to a historical model dating to the French ancien régime: during the sixteenth century, Charles VII had ordered investigations into the oral law in all the provinces of France and the preparation of written *coutumiers* that would help to finally establish and preserve an "eternal law."[26]

It is illuminating to look at the similarities and differences between processes of producing *coutumiers* for each province of early modern France and those in French colonies in twentieth-century colonial West Africa. It is remarkable that a colonial governor would use early modern codification as a model for a similar process in colonial West Africa. In contrast to France, where an assembly of local educated people was nominated in each province and the codes they produced were formally approved by local courts,[27] colonial authorities in West Africa relied on quite centralized and quasi-scientific procedures. A questionnaire was prepared in Dakar and sent to the governors of all the colonies. These were instructed to first organize surveys and then use the material as a basis for codification. Furthermore, the governor general explicitly instructed the governors to supplement local expertise with scientific knowledge, such as that from reports or anthropological publications. Hence, even if the *coutumier* was supposed to be based on the collection of local customs, it was nevertheless influenced by the French colonial interviewers who organized the knowledge production alongside their questionnaires. These reproduced the European concepts—but, importantly, concepts from the European past—into which local customs were then shoehorned. This once more confirmed the paradigm of modernization, according to which the others' present is like our past.

Despite the parallelism assumed, both processes thus differed profoundly: whereas the early modern codifiers aimed at developing a *coutumier* for the whole territory (despite some discussions about whether unfree people should fall under that law),[28] and it was assumed there was no difference in principle between the *coutumier*'s compilers and those whose customs were being codified, French colonial officers in colonial West Africa fixed the customs and the respective laws of the local population, whom they saw as fundamentally different. The codification, then, legally established the making of difference. In early modern France, the provincial experts who did the work of codifying local practices and habits as laws then had to live under those laws, but in colonial West Africa European colonizers codified local laws that would govern those whom they labeled as other and inferior. Nevertheless, both works of codifying customs relied on classifications and led to a process of territorializing law.

Robert Descimon[29] outlines the many disputes over who should participate in the codifying work in the early modern period. Unfortunately, there are no similar sources for the actors and disputes in the case of the West African colonies: we do not know how and to whom the French colonial officers distributed the questionnaires in Dahomey or other colonies. The completed questionnaires are also unfortunately not preserved in the colonial archives. However, the project was nevertheless successfully carried out, at least in the colony of Dahomey where the *Coutumier du Dahomey* was instituted in 1933. This first body of codified customary laws in Dahomey (renamed Benin in 1975) was retained following independence in 1960, despite the immediate abolition of the category of *indigène*. Until 1990, it was used alongside the Code Napoleon for civil law cases. It was not completely replaced until 2004, when the new Code de la famille was adopted following years of intense debate, especially over the issue of polygamy (which was finally officially banned).[30]

The migration of the term *famille* from French into local languages in the colony can be traced back to this *Coutumier du Dahomey* and possibly to the questionnaire that was used in the preceding survey. I will now look at the questionnaire itself, as well as at the body of law derived from it. Both echo the viewpoint that kinship is based on alliance and descent to an extent that rendered the questionnaire incapable of documenting other ways of and were thus excluded from the final *Coutumier*.

Each begins with a section titled *de la famille* (on the family) that establishes *la famille étendue* (the extended family) as the most important unit of social organization, to which all households are subordinated. The *Coutumier du Dahomey* sees this *famille*, with its head, as omnipresent and describes it as being divided into different "subdivisions" or "branches," each with its own *chef* (chief). This account of the structure of the *famille* in Dahomey resembles the lineage system of the Nuer as described in Evans-Pritchard's[31] classic model of a segmentary society.[32] The only difference is that the segments in Dahomey are described as having each their own head. Similarly, segments and subdivisions are depicted in a very orderly and even bureaucratic way. For instance, the *Coutumier du Dahomey* mentions *conseils de famille* (family councils) but also subcouncils, all organized in a clear, hierarchical way.

In sum, the *Coutumier du Dahomey* draws a picture of *famille* that combines elements of *states* with those of *stateless societies* as represented in *African Political Systems*. This image of Dahomean societies as falling between states and stateless societies was later echoed by Jacques Lombard, the most important French ethnographer of the northern parts of the colony. In his classic monograph *Structures de type 'féodal' en Afrique Noire*, Lombard explicitly interpreted the Borgu region as an intermediary type between states and stateless societies and also drew explicit parallels between precolonial West Africa and late medieval and early modern Europe.[33]

Looking at the ways *la famille étendue* is characterized in subsequent parts of the *Coutumier* leads us back to images of kinship in the nineteenth century and specifically to Morgan's "systems of consanguinity and affinity." The second and third parts of the *Coutumier du Dahomey* are concerned with "le mariage" and "filiation et parenté" (descent and kinship relations). The part on marriage recalls another element of nineteenth-century kinship theory: the *Coutumier* maintains that polygamy is slowly giving way to monogamy. It treats the issue of bride price and dowry in great detail, then finally discusses the allegedly weak position of women in marital relationships.[34] Each section comprises several paragraphs that address the various customs of different ethnic groups. Thus, the *Coutumier de Dahomey* systematically reproduces the anthropological knowledge of its time: that kinship (*la famille*) among the *indigènes* was generally shaped by marriage and descent, that different systems of kinship are characteristic of different ethnic groups, and, finally, that these groups could be classified as state and stateless societies, with some intermediate cases. Hence, it not only contributed to establishing and maintaining a view of the extended family as a basic mode of social organization among *indigènes* but also contributed to an image of Africa made up of many ethnic groups, each organized principally on the basis of kinship.

The third part of the *Coutumier*, titled "Filiation et parenté," claims that patrilineality is the central feature of the kinship structures of all of the colony's ethnic groups. However, it also emphasizes that children do not belong exclusively to their patrilineage but are bound in various ways to their mother's line. It is even asserted that *parenté*—here meaning an acknowledged and legal kinship relation between offspring and parents—exists between children and mothers as well as fathers. As in the preceding sections, the descriptions of legal norms of the *famille* are based on European classifications, terms, and assumptions of kinship. As a result, descent is seen as based on biological processes of filiation that adoption can only supplant in exceptional cases. The questionnaire, with its preconceived categories, did not contain any open questions about local concepts that might open space for thinking about children's belonging in other ways, such as questions about the different people they addressed as "father." In consequence, no such practice is even mentioned in the *Coutumier du Dahomey*. This becomes especially evident in the section on adoption, paragraphs 195–99. I will now look at those paragraphs in more detail. The diverse customs are discussed along the classification of different *peuples* or ethnic groups, thus again demonstrating the principle of ethnic classifying:

Adoption

195—L'adoption existe dans les coutumes Nagot, dans le cas où un homme marié est sans enfant ou impuissant; il peut alors recevoir des enfants de ses frères et soeurs.

196—Pédah, où l'adopté ne peut recevoir une part d'héritage de l'adoptant, mais peut recevoir des donations.

197—Pila-pila, où l'adoption n'est tolérée qu'à l'intérieur d'une même famille.

198—Bariba, où elle n'existe que si les époux sont sans enfants. Un cas particulier d'adoption est celle faite par le chef supérieur auquel on a confié des enfants rétifs ou mal conformés qui font partie de sa famille: on les appelle Kiliku.

199 — L'enfant adopté est partout traité comme un enfant légitime.[35]

195 — Adoption exists in the Nagot customs, in the case where a married man is childless or impotent; he can thus receive some of the children of his brothers and sisters.

196 — Pédah, where the one adopted cannot receive a share of the inheritance of the adopter but can receive bequests.

197 — Pila-pila, where adoption is only accepted within the same family.

198 — Bariba, where it only exists if the spouses are childless. A specific case of adoption is that done by the high chief, to whom they have sent rebellious or malformed children who are part of their family: they call them Kiliku.

199 — The adopted child is in every way treated like a legitimate child.

These five paragraphs of the section "Adoption" offer insight into the argumentation of the *Coutumier* and its ways of classifying alongside ethnic groups. Being taken as a seemingly self-evident concept, it was not defined at all. The paragraphs give examples of "customs" of different groups of *indigènes*, such as the "Nagot" (§ 195), "Pédah" (§ 196), "Pila-Pila" (§ 197), or "Bariba" (§ 198) by mentioning in which cases these practiced adoptions, whatever the French or the people thought it was. The Nagots were said to adopt only when the married husband was infertile; the Pèdah were not to give inheritance to their adopted children, but instead could give donations; the Pila-Pila were seen to adopt children of close kin; and finally, the "Bariba" (or Baatombu, see footnote 4) were said to adopt only in case of infertility. But then the *Coutumier* mentions a particular case, called *Kilikou*, of giving children who are seen as (physically or mentally special) to the highest chief as members of his family.

Reading between the lines or from another point of view, the paragraphs that mention cases of children's adoption by close relatives could also be understood as hinting about another different vernacular understanding of parenting practices: that children belong to a group or family and not to their parents as a couple and that, accordingly, childless people may take in their siblings' children since these already belong to them as well. It could also be interpreted as showing that the respective groups do not distinguish between birth parents and their siblings (and indeed both are named with the same term in most of the languages spoken in Benin). However, people's answers when they were asked about adoption obviously confirmed that category and put local customs into that categorical frame.

The last case of "Bariba," i.e., Baatombu, is the most detailed. I want to read it with the background of some ethnographic knowledge. The *Coutumier* mentions that rebellious or malformed children were given to the highest chief of the region as *Kilikou*. My suggestion is to read this as a mix of two different narratives, both present in the region but neither related to each other or even ever combined. One is the narrative of a well-known and still-practiced political or ritual institution that is related to precolonial slavery practices as well. The *sinaboko* in Nikki, who is seen as the highest traditional chief in the Borgu region and was also incorporated into the French colonial administration as a *chéf supérieur*, recruits some young men in the households of his slaves. These are called *kirikou* and act as a special kind of messenger, especially in ritual ceremonies like the Gaani festival or the *sinaboko's* funeral.[36] To the present day, each new *sinaboko* choses some *kirikou* from among those households descended from former slaves. Indeed, the role of *kirikou* is so prestigious that it is still easy to find young adults for it despite a historical link to slavery.[37]

The second narrative concerns the mentioned *enfants rétifs ou mal conformés* (rebellious or malformed children). This refers to a widespread Baatombu practice of giving children who were seen as having dangerous forces of witchcraft to local Fulbe herders to raise. The danger of these children was identified by physical signs such as the eruption of the first teeth eight months after birth. Giving the children to Fulbe herders was seen as removing the danger of these children, especially because the Fulbe are perceived as immune to Baatombu witchcraft. Historically, these children were integrated into groups of slaves working for Fulbe masters. This interethnic giving of children, described decades ago by anthropologists,[38] still seems to continue in modified ways.[39] However, it is not at all seen as a transfer of parental belonging of the kind described as adoption. It is thus important to know that it has never been related to the practice of including some *kirikou* in the court and retinue of the *sinaboko*.

Based on this ethnographic knowledge about the *kirikou* on the one hand and the practice of giving Baatombu children seen as witches to Fulbe on the other, it seems reasonable to understand section 198 of the *Coutumier du Dahomey* as an outcome of the combination of both stories. Probably both were told to colonial officials when they asked about practices of adoption. Obviously, both were practices of circulating children, one about giving children from Baatombu to Fulbe households and the other about giving unfree children to Baatombu chiefs to be messengers. The missing point in the *Coutumier* here is obviously slavery. Multiple and complex forms of enslaving but also of intergenerational maintenance of assumed belonging to groups of unfree families and individuals were present in the region. Part of them were practices of parenting, such as the giving of children to the Fulbe where they were integrated in the groups of slaves. This remained during colonialism even though, at the time of the *Coutumier de Dahomey*, slavery had been officially banned.

However, it escaped the attention of the French that with the *kirikou* and the children given to the Fulbe, some practices related to slavery even entered the codification.[40]

The very broad and widespread phenomenon of *bii nenubu*—the practice of ordinarily giving nearly all children to relatives to be raised, which Bona referred to and which I will come to later in this chapter—is not mentioned at all in the *Coutumier*. This was possibly so ordinary that people did not perceive it as a special custom worth mentioning to be codified in the *Coutumier*. But that again points out that the conceptual lens through which the colonizers investigated practices of non-birth parents raising children was the European concept of adoption. Obviously, this concept was not clear at all, either to those who asked the questions or to those who responded. However, even though the term adoption was not at all well known in the colony, it was also, like *famille*, introduced into local arenas.

To sum up, the *Coutumier du Dahomey* understands *la famille* in terms of the categories within which Europeans imagined sociability in Africa: the extended family (*famille étendue*), clearly divided into subgroups and regarded as a system of marriage and descent, was seen as the most important frame of reference. Other relationships between adults and children that were not based upon genealogical relationships were consequently called adoption, reproducing a European distinction between biological and non-biological kinship. Kinship in this sense was seen as legitimating elements of customary law imagined as typical of "indigenous" or "primitive" societies—including bride service, bride price, and polygamy and the assumption that it would give way to monogamy under the influence of "civilizing" processes.

Succession under Colonialism

The political implications of the invention of the *famille étendue* and its related hierarchies and classifications evoked the idea of an inseparable connection between kinship and politics in the field of local chieftaincy during colonial time. French imageries of chieftaincy influenced decisions over succession after the death of local chiefs. For instance, French colonizers assumed that local chieftaincies passed, like kingdoms in Europe, from fathers to sons. However, chieftainships in northern Dahomey had never passed directly from father to son; first they went to younger brothers or cousins of a chief and only passed to the eldest person from the next generation later, once nobody in the chief's generation remained available.[41]

Historical and anthropological research has shown that the integration of precolonial offices as *chefs* into colonial administration went alongside important and multiple transformations. Many of the political formations that were called *chieftaincies* in the anthropological literature and are today seen as precolonial were created during colonialism, especially in those areas where chieftaincies did not exist before.[42] In Baatombu villages, local chieftaincies had existed before the French arrived. Complex but also flexible succession rules said that chiefs should be succeeded by members of particular lineages, which were said to have the right to the "thrones." In many of these chieftaincies, the right to succeed rotated between some lineages; however sons were never supposed to follow immediately after their birth fathers. Conversations with older Baatombu about local memories on colonialism confirm that some local actors were certainly aware of the French view that sons should succeed their fathers. Therefore, some local chiefs ensured that their office would pass to a nephew or foster son after their death by emphatically describing him as their natural child, which was easily done since there was no linguistic distinction between the two anyway. Thus, they produced an image of local kinship that satisfied the needs of the French and at the same time served their own interests. Stories of clever tricks used to circumvent colonial succession rules are still present in village storytelling.[43] But outwardly they adopted European conceptions and terminology, with the result that the European categories were reproduced willy-nilly and thus gradually accepted.

In general, such practices stabilized the idea of the *famille* as legitimating hereditary rule. Not least, they shaped a political practice of hereditary rule based on European images. It is interesting that this idea of a tribal other who had to be integrated into the colonial structures in order to be kept under control—an idea vitally important to the colonial authorities—was sometimes reinforced by local actors who could not depend on local support and legitimation. This can be illustrated by the story of Yarou Kpaso of the village of Tebo, who was the descendant of a slave and thus destined to work in the fields of his master, the local chief or *chef de village*.

Shortly after the arrival of the French, he went into service with them, which gave him a chance to change his status from that of an unfree man.[44] First, he worked as a private cook for a colonial officer; then became a local policeman. In the 1920s and 1930s, the French became dissatisfied with the local chiefs and sought to "improve" the local chiefdoms, which they described as "traditional," by instituting a policy of filling vacant offices with people who could speak French. As a result of this policy, Yarou Kpaso was appointed the new *chef de village* in Tebo in 1935. He owed his appointment to the fact that (due to his previous status) he had the same name as his former master. Obviously, this contrasted sharply with the local understanding that a former slave could never become the chief. As the status of slavery did not give people the right to claim and live their own familial connectedness, they were often called by the same second name as their masters. Yarou Kpaso's appointment was therefore contrary to existing local rules. It was a scandal that an unfree person who did not even have a different name from his master should be given the local chiefly office, so memories of this scandalous appointment are still vivid today. Moreover, before his death in 1958, Yarou Kpaso made further arrangements (which are also still scandalous in the village) to ensure that his biological son Woru Kpaso would be appointed as his successor.

Stories like this are commonly regarded by historians and anthropologists as evidence of modifications of or innovations in chieftaincy by colonial rulers in West Africa.[45] Up to now, however, little attention has been given to the way they also shaped and maybe even invented notions of kinship. The story of the former slave who worked for the French and founded a dynasty, being succeeded by his son, could be read as such an introduction of kinship for former slaves and, at the same time, a confirmation of European ideas about succession and inheritance.[46] Indeed, the French understanding of *la famille* embraced the idea that every man, even a slave, had a name and with it a *family*, and had the right to pass that name—and possibly associated rights of chieftaincy positions—to his sons or daughters.[47] By using the name of his former master as his own name and then not only passing on the name but also the position of *chef de village* to his son, Yarou Kpaso shows in his story how this new understanding of kinship changed the local political landscape. Locally, this transformation was assured by force, not only directly by colonizers but also through Yarou Kpaso's strategic use of the colonial police he had been part of to accomplish his goals.

In communications with the colonizers, local understandings of relations that anthropologists would call kinship relations, which, more important, led to local rules of succession, were often concealed. This explains why succession rules that privileged nephews and younger brothers as successors remained widely unknown to the French. The fact that Yarou Kpaso actively helped his birth son to become his successor could be read as proof that he had already internalized the French understanding that sons should follow their fathers. It could also be due to the fact that as a former slave Yarou did not belong to an extended group of brothers, cousins, or nephews from which his successor could be chosen. Finding himself newly free, he founded a compound and a *famille* in the village of Tebo and thus also established his family name through bureaucratic procedures. Therefore, he probably did not even have any relative other than his son to suggest as successor. The story thus also shows us that the liberation of former slaves was deeply intertwined with a process of introducing new ways of seeing, understanding, and living kinship or *la famille,* as well as with related emerging understandings of local political rule. Acquiring a family name that could be transferred to the next generation was part of this.

Vernacular Concepts

If it can be accepted that the term *famille* (as Bona used it) was introduced by the French, the question arises as to what local terms were used earlier to denominate significant relations or collectivities. There are older terms, of course, but the first thing that needs to be noted is that knowledge of social relations and the positioning of every person were, and often still are, conceived of in the region as depending on age and status.

Among Baatonum speakers in the Borgu region, knowledge about meaningful relations such as whom to marry or who would follow whom in an important office is attributed to adults, especially to old people and praise singers. They repeat and reproduce this knowledge through storytelling and are especially consulted before a marriage is planned. Children, on the other hand, are generally regarded as having no knowledge about these relations and also as not yet entitled to it. The gradual acquisition of knowledge about how one is situated in complex and hierarchical relations with those who can be married and those who are uncles, aunts, fathers, and mothers is an indispensable task on the way to adulthood. Of particular importance is the acquisition of knowledge about one's position among siblings: which are younger and which are older. Another step is to gain knowledge about the generational order: Baatombu use two generation names, which alternate between fathers and children, so that children have the same generation name as their paternal grandparents.

Eventually, children learn that they belong to a patrilineal clan and thus carry the name of the clan. With that knowledge, they gradually learn to identify hierarchies of respect, as well as joking relationships to some uncles, cousins, or grandparents, but they also start to understand which marriages and burials they have to attend or whom they should not marry. They also learn that the children with whom they grew up belong to different *clans* and attend different rituals or festivities. In this process of gaining knowledge, one important step that is often only achieved when children become teenagers or even adults is to know which person gave birth to oneself and which one was the genitor. These are referred to as *mero* and *baa*, but although both terms are normally translated as "mother" and "father," they are used for many other persons, including the father's brothers or the man with whom children grow up. Many adults who recounted their life histories to me remembered well the moment they learned the identity of the person who gave birth to them.

Adults are commonly seen as people who know—that is, who are aware of their relatedness as well as the relatedness of the people they live with. In consequence, many of the local terms of kinship relations depend on which person speaks and knows. This is quite obvious in the case of the term *sesu*, which is often translated as "sister"; in fact, it only means "sister" when a man uses it and "brother" in the case of a female speaker.

Besides terms that designate individuals, there are also some general terms that denominate collectivities of relatives and overlap with what is today called *famille*. Today, the term most frequently used to denominate a group or collectivity of kin is *mero bisibu*. Literally, *mero bisibu* can be translated as "mother's people." Indeed, I long understood this term to have been the main precolonial expression for kinship or family and only wondered why it referred to the mother in a society that considers itself patrilineal. However, I eventually discovered that the term *mero bisibu* was also invented by Europeans: it was introduced by Christian missionaries who were seeking ways to translate Christian liturgy into the Baatonum language and needed an expression that the pastors or priests could use to address the parishioners. In Christian discourse in Baatonum, *mero bisibu* now signifies "parish" as well as "congregation" or "followers," not only in speech but also in translating the Bible[48]— Jesus always uses it when addressing his disciples. Pastors always use *mero bisibu* when addressing the parish and opening their sermons. From the field of Christianity and discourses of Christian community, the term spread to practitioners in the field of development work and especially into Baatonum texts that draw on discourses of community in development programs. And finally, the term is very frequently used in radio transmissions in Baatonum to address a collectivity or community. Of course, when inventing the term *mero bisibu*, the missionaries had used local material, namely the word *mero*, often translated as "mother," and *bisibu*, a loanword.

Another term, *mannu*, is older than *mero bisibu*. It is derived from *mara*, "to bear," and an easy translation would be "offspring" or "descendants." People say *nen mannu*, "my offspring," to indicate those whom they would call their children or grandchildren, which includes not only the children one procreated but also those of brothers, sisters, and one's spouse's children.

Yet another common term is *bweseru*, which could be and is translated as "species" or "race." If people are asked their *bweseru*, they will respond with (depending on the context) their language, ethnic group, clan, or sometimes nationality. However, *bweseru* is also used to distinguish varieties of maize and millet or breeds of animals.

Finally, another old and frequently used term is *tomaru*. Derived from *toma*, "to praise," *tomaru* refers to the manner in which someone is addressed by praise singers, the specialists and keepers of knowledge about relatedness and political offices in the past. If I ask someone about his or her *tomaru*, I will hear about their ritual name but also their clan name, generational name, important ancestors, and heroic acts in their past, as well as other ways of positioning the person in the web of relations. *Tomaru* and *bweseru* are frequently used to refer to belonging to a collectivity based on common ancestry. Both include an idea of a relatedness through the paternal line that is not only relevant for funeral rites but also access to chieftaincies and other offices. However, since both terms are also used to express national or ethnic belonging, they cannot be translated as lineage alone. For instance, when I was asked about my *bweseru*, I was normally expected to say that I am German.

In my own research, I did the same thing I experienced in everyday communications: I used all these expressions when asking people who they were and to whom they relate to. However, the term that is today most generalized, comprehensive, and independent of location is, in my experience, *famille*. It is also the most appropriate and neutral term for communications about former slaves, who are considered to lack *tomaru* as they were never praised. *Famille*, being free from classifications of free and formerly enslaved, is a seemingly neutral term that can always be used. In particular, it is always used in official documents such as passports or birth certificates, implying that it is natural that everybody today has a *nom de famille* that appears in all official documents and thus that everyone also has a *famille*.

Bii Nenobu

Besides these concepts, which suggest an understanding of kinship that is not purely genealogical, there are also vernacular ideas that diverge from the genealogical thinking of the term *fami*. I am referring here to child fostering or *bii nenobu*, which literally means "holding a child." As far as one can reconstruct today based on local narratives and a few written documents, this local practice affected nearly all peasant children in the Borgu region of Dahomey and beyond during the precolonial period.[49] Well into the twentieth century, a large majority of children were taken in at a very young age by adults who brought them up and whom they addressed as their *baa* (father) and *mero* (mother). However, this practice was so self-evident to the inhabitants of the region that, as I outlined when analyzing adoption in the *Coutumier du Dahomey*, it could not be comprehended with the language and categories Europeans used when talking about social relations in the regions. It was thus widely overlooked by French colonizers, Christian missionaries, and other Europeans. Even today, it is rarely thematized in official documents, not even in the new Code de la famille which succeeded the *Coutumier du Dahomey*.

Practices of taking in children from one's sister or brother to raise are also widely overlooked because there is no linguistic distinction made between the woman who gave birth to a child and the woman with whom it grows up, or between the father who is recognized as the mother's husband and his brother or cousin. This is important because (along with grandparents) it is mainly parents' siblings who are preferred persons for taking in a child. Therefore, there is no essential linguistic difference between the birth parent and the foster parent, and I use the latter term for want of a better one. Locally, the foster parents are seen as the real and rightful parents and are treated accordingly, usually into adulthood.[50]

In the light of the *bii nenobu*, the above conception of knowledge that develops over the time of childhood and youth is important because it helps to solve an apparent paradox: many of my interviewees said only in the course of their youth, or even as adults, did they discover who their birth parents were—and thus to which clan they belonged or which offices they could claim.[51] As children, they had always believed that the people bringing them up were those who gave birth to them.

For a long time, I wondered how it was possible that children could not know that their parents were not their birth parents, especially in a social environment in which it is common knowledge that children are frequently raised by others than their birth parents. Many adults, looking back at their own lives, mentioned that they were surprised to suddenly learn about their birth parents. While it is important to acquire knowledge about one's relations, children are only entitled to acquire this knowledge as part of the process of becoming an adult. Lived parenthood, in the sense of caring for children, bearing responsibility for them, and having rights in their work and duty for their education, is not part of this knowledge: it is taken for granted that the people who care for children and have authority over them are their parents. Thus, it is normal for children not to care about the question of the birth parents at an age when differences of *bweseru* or *tomaru* are not of any importance. This reveals a basic attitude toward the temporalities of relatedness. Knowledge depends on age and status: it changes over a person's lifetime and alters people's understanding of their position within the social networks. This even means that Baatombu people are given new names that reflect their new positions in the web of relations on multiple occasions over their life courses.

Conclusion

In his work on welfare regimes in southern Africa that were built for the relatively small and privileged minority of formal workers, James Ferguson states:

> "Civilization" was not a universal entitlement, but the property of a privileged minority, and the association of "social" rights with this attribute was precisely a principle of restriction, so that social assistance was available only for the "civilized," the "stabilized," the "évolués" — with "the African extended family" the imagined remedy for the less civilized rest.[52]

In this chapter, I reconstructed how the concept of this "imagined remedy for the less civilized rest" — the extended family or *famille étendue* — was invented in colonial Dahomey. Following the compilation of the *Coutumier du Dahomey*, colonizers and locals in the colony used the French term *famille* to express the idea of the extended family as it has continued to be used as a colonial and postcolonial imaginary about relatedness. Even if this is imagined as an ancient part of so-called African culture and projected into a supposed eternal past of people without history, it is a new concept, created by colonial epistemologies, imaginations, and practice. It has become firmly established in the ways colonial officers and Europeans saw and therewith governed the population in the colonies. One could agree with Ferguson that the notion of the extended family allows the state to avoid caring for the whole of its citizens by reserving access to social security to a small minority of people and leaving the large majority to depend on the extended family, but perhaps this is coincidence and not a conspiracy. Nevertheless, it is clear that due to pronounced economic instability and the lack of formal security systems, new imaginations about the extended family are arising. Among other reasons, this is in order to understand how people still survive despite insufficient formal systems of social security. Maybe these new imaginations of the extended family are even more necessary than before.

Introduced by the colonial officers in the colony of Dahomey, *famille* was disseminated through colonial practices of codification and everyday administration. It entered the local languages and became a general term bridging linguistic differences. One could even argue that the dissemination of *famille* has become part of a national language of doing kinship through practices of governing and registering, greeting, and explaining.[53]

In sum, it is obvious that the concept of the extended family is broadly used alongside older terms and concepts, such as *tomaru* or *bweseru*. It is not uncommon for one and the same person to use both these older terms and *famille* to explain social relationships.

In calling this process *invention*, my title of course alludes to reflections on the invention of imagined traditions,[54] as well as to Mudimbe's famous "invention of Africa" and the invention of chieftaincies.[55] These citations are examples of the intense debates during the last two decades of the twentieth century concerning the invented character of institutions in the political arena (such as kingdoms or chieftaincies) and the immense transformations colonial rule effected in local political organization.[56] However, there has still not been a similarly intense debate on the conceptual and linguistic transformations and inventions around relatedness or kinship during colonial rule. This chapter demonstrates, taking the example of the concept of the family, how deep the transformations might have been by shaping the institutional landscapes—and, subsequently, everyday relationships as well as modes of governance. Looking closely at these inventions might also challenge established paths of conceptualizing kinship and politics in African societies. Among the few scholarly works that challenge prevalent concepts in the domain of kinship is Susan McKinnon's rereading of Nuer patrilineality in classical ethnographies.[57] My own methodological approach—mapping and relocating the concept of *famille* based on fieldwork and some written colonial sources—was more ethnographical, but it contributes to the same goal of destabilizing certainties to reconfigure common understandings of what is constructed as Africa.

So far, I have neglected to explain why *famille* has become such a frequently used and well-appropriated term in contemporary Benin. From the establishment of the colony, the French authorities required people to register under a *nom de famille* (surname), whether it was for a passport, a birth certificate, or enrollment in missionary and, later, national schools. This went hand in hand with the process of establishing fixed names during the twentieth century. Even if this seems obvious today and the idea of a *famille* that is represented in the family name and inseparably connected with every person's life and identity has become part of general knowledge, it is worth remembering that this process of establishing, fixing, and thus "eternalizing" family names is still an unfinished and ongoing process in Benin. But together with the bureaucratization of governance, the *nom de famille* has become indispensable for schooling, military service, apprenticeship, formal employment, and social security services.

Today, that wording is attractive for another reason: *famille* is well known among speakers of various languages. So, even if Baatombu are sometimes asked to name their *tomaru* or their *bweseru* (depending on the linguistic proficiency of the inquirer), it has become easier to use the term *famille* throughout the country since it is understood by everyone, not only those who share the same local language. This understanding of *la famille* is useful in everyday communication situations: it is a handy term that will even be understood by somebody like an interviewing anthropologist. In the course of the far-reaching changes that are currently taking place, it is not certain if all the other terms mentioned will survive at all.

Erdmute Alber holds the chair of social anthropology at the University of Bayreuth. Her research, carried out in West Africa and Peru, centers around power and chieftaincy, kinship, childhood, age and intergenerational relations, new illiteracies, and middle classes. Her theoretical work focuses on the interface between kinship, politics, rule, and care. She codirected an interdisciplinary research group on kinship and politics at the Center for Interdisciplinary Research in Bielefeld. She coedited *Reconnecting State and Kinship* (2018), and *Politics and Kinship: A Reader* (2022), and is the author of *Transfers of Belonging: Child Fostering in West Africa in the 20th Century* (2018).

Notes

This chapter is an outcome of intense discussions during my fellowship in the research group "Kinship and Politics" at the Center for Interdisciplinary Research (ZIF) in Bielefeld, 2016/17. Thanks to my coconvenors and the many fellows for wonderful and enriching discussions. I especially want to thank to Jeanette Edwards, Michaela Hohkamp, Jeannett Martin, Susan McKinnon, David Sabean, Judith Schachter, Simon Teuscher, and Tatjana Thelen for valuable comments on former versions. These were also discussed in the frame of a research seminar at the University of Manchester, February 2018, and in the DHI-CREPOS seminar in Dakar, March 2019, with colleagues from West Africa. Thanks to Susann Baller who made that possible.

1. I have published widely on child fostering, especially on its meaning and on historical changes during the twentieth century. See, for instance, Erdmute Alber, "Denying Biological Parenthood—Child Fosterage in Northern Benin," *Ethnos* 68, no. 4 (2003); Erdmute Alber, *Transfers of Belonging: Child Fostering in West Africa in the 20th Century* (Leiden: Brill, 2018), and Erdmute Alber, "Politics of Kinship: Child Fostering in Dahomey/Benin," *Cahiers d'études Africanines*, no. 2 (2019).
2. A n durɔn mi more nɔ wunen *fami* ye a mɔ a ka wunen yam tama wa a n ma neni. Ba a n ka wi bibu maru mɔ yen sɔ ma wunen wɔnon bii ka wunen sesun bii ka be tama a n neni wa.
3. Housing patterns are virilocal. In addition, my research shows that many young men stay in the rural compounds of their patrilineage. Thus, married women are integrated into the often large households of their husbands' kin.
4. Baatonum is one of the languages in the Gur continuum in the West African savanna belt. It is spoken in the Borgu region in northern Benin, as well as in Nigeria, by about one million speakers who call themselves Baatombu. In the anthropological literature, the French name "Bariba" is often used; however, this is not the name they use themselves. For a classic description of the Baatonum language, see Jean-Pierre Grossenbacher, *Abrégé de grammaire de Bariba* (Parakou, 1974); Jean-Pierre Grossenbacher, *Lexiye Baatonum-Français* (Parakou, 1977) and Jean-Pierre Grossenbacher, *Lexique Baatonum-Français: Nouveau tirage avec les tons et des mots* (Parakou, 1989). For the history of the Borgu region and the Baatombu/Bariba, see Jacques Lombard, *Structures de type "feodal" en Afrique Noire: Étude des dynamismes internes et des relations sociales chez les Bariba du Dahomey* (Paris: Imprimerie Nationale, 1965); Richard Kuba, *Wasangari und Wangara: Borgu und seine Nachbarn in historischer Perspektive* (Hamburg: Lit Verlag, 1996); Erdmute Alber, *Im Gewand von Herrschaft: Modalitäten der Macht bei den Baatombu (1895–1995)*, Studien zur Kulturkunde, vol. 116 (Köln: Rüdiger Köppe, 2000).
5. In the following, I will use the French orthography: *famille* instead of *fami*, the way it would be spelled in a text written in Baatonum.
6. See, for instance, Bio Bigou's version of the origin of Parakou, Leon Bio Bigou, *La région de Parakou: Ses chefferies traditionelles et ses rois des origines à nos jours* (Cotonou, 1993).
7. One might also think that Bona used *famille* because she was talking with a European anthropologist; the word might have reflected her expectation about my understanding of the term. However, that would not change the argument since her use of *famille* did not correspond with my (or another European's) use of the word either.
8. On the use of possessive constructions to express both belonging and ownership, see Marilyn Strathern and Jeanette Edwards, "Including Our Own," in *Cultures of Relatedness: New Approaches to the Study of Kinship*, ed. Janet Carsten (Cambridge: Cambridge University Press, 2002).
9. Patrilineage is, of course, a European concept as well. Unlike *famille*, it did not enter the regional vernacular. In contrast, the concept of *clan* has been appropriated and is used, among others, by local intellectuals who talk or publish about their origin or region.
10. On the impact of European categories and categorization of kin and gender relations on colonial rule, see also Ann Stoler, *Carnal Knowledge and Imperial Power: Race and the Intimate in Colonial Rule* (Berkeley: University of California Press, 2002).
11. See among many others Alfred Radcliffe-Brown and Daryl Forde, *African Systems of Kinship and Marriage* (New York: Routledge, 1950); Edward Evans-Pritchard, *Kinship and Marriage among the Nuer* (Oxford: Oxford University Press, 1951).
12. Meyer Fortes and Edward Evans-Pritchard, "Introduction," in *African Political Systems*, ed. Meyer Fortes and Edward Evans-Pritchard (London: Clarendon Press, 1940).
13. William J. Goode, *World Revolution and Family Patterns* (London: The Free Press of Glencoe, 1963), 164–68.
14. For example, see Michael Schatzberg, "Power, Legitimacy and 'Democratisation' in Africa," *Africa* 63, no. 4 (1993).

15. For example, see Marin Trenk, "Dein Reichtum ist dein Ruin. Zum Stand der Forschung über afrikanische Unternehmer und wirtschaftliche Entwicklung," *Anthropos* 86, nos. 4/6 (1991): 508.
16. Among others, Tatjana Thelen and Erdmute Alber, "Reconnecting State and Kinship: Temporalities, Scales, Classifications," in *Reconnecting State and Kinship*, ed. Tatjana Thelen and Erdmute Alber (Philadelphia: University of Pennsylvania Press, 2017), 2–4; and Susan McKinnon and Fenella Canell, "The Difference Kinship Makes," in *Modernity and the Persistence of kinship*, ed. Susan McKinnon and Fenella Canell (Santa Fe: School for Advanced Research Press, 2016), 3–4.
17. Kinship and family are, outside the language of social sciences, often both used in the same or a similar sense. Each concept has its own history and is deeply anchored in Euro-American epistemologies. When, alongside the establishment of anthropology as a new discipline, the "invention of kinship" (Thomas R. Trautmann, *Lewis Henry Morgan and the Invention of Kinship* [Lincoln: University of Nebraska Press, 1987]) took place in the nineteenth century and was established through a set of methods of classifying and counting, kinship came to be understood as a scientific term to denominate genealogical social relations based on descent and marriage all over the globe. In this sense, kinship was seen as universal but most deeply imprinted on societies outside the modern world. *Family*, the older term, then became part of a modernist argument that extended families would, in the process of "civilization," develop into modern nuclear families (Thelen and Alber, "Reconnecting"). Whereas the term *kinship* remained limited to Anglophone usage, Francophone scholars largely use *parenté* in anthropological discourse; however, this term is used much less outside the social sciences; there, as well as in many anthropological and sociological discourses, *famille* is more common. *La famille étendue* could thus be seen as the French equivalent of *extended kinship*.
18. For a summary, see Anna-Maria Brandstetter, "Kolonialismus: Wider die vereinfachenden Dichotomien," in *Geschichte in Afrika: Einführung in Pobleme und Debatten*, ed. Jan Georg Deutsch and Albert Wirtz (Berlin: Das arabische Buch, 1997).
19. Trautmann, *Lewis Henry Morgan*.
20. See also the chapter by Mathieu in this volume.
21. Henry Lewis Morgan, *Systems of Consanguinity and Affinity of the Human Family*, Smithsonian Contributions to Knowledge (Washington, DC: Smithsonian Institution, 1868), 17:vi.
22. Firmin Médénuovo, ed., *Coutumier du Dahomey* (Tillières-sur-Avre: Présence Béninoise, 2004), 7–8; see also in more detailed steps, Robert Cornevin, *Histoire du Dahmomey* (Paris: Berger-Levrault, 1962), 407–10.
23. Médénuovo, "Coutumier du Dahomey," 8.
24. This denomination of "people without history" was frequently used in the colonial documents of the region, as for instance in the *Rapport annuel sur la situation general du cercle pendant l'année 1912*, Archives nationals du Dahomey, Porto Novo, serie 22.
25. A case study of the introducing and modifying rule of the *chefs de canton* in Dahomey can be found in Alber, *Im Gewand von Herrschaft*, 195–98
26. See Martine Grinberg, "La rédaction des coutumes et les droits seigneuriaux: Nommer, classer, exclure," *Annales: Histoire, Sciences Sociales* 52, no. 5 (1997); Martine Grinberg, "Les interprètes et le droit coutumier: Les éditions des coutumes du bailliage d'Amiens," *Les Cahiers du Centre de Recherches Historiques* 26, no. 1 (2001); Robert Descimon, "Quelques réflexions à propos des commissaires du roi dans la rédaction et la réformation des coutumes au XVI e siècle," *Les cahiers du Centre de Recherches Historiques* 26, no. 1 (2001). Thanks to Simon Teuscher to make me aware of these historical practices and parallels.
27. Grinberg, "La rédaction des coutumes"; Descimon, "Quelques réflexions."
28. Grinberg, "La rédaction des coutumes."
29. Descimon, "Quelques réflexions."

30. In the long process of discussing the new Code de la famille (République de Bénin loi 2002–7), which was intensively supported by international and especially German development agencies, monogamy was seen as a sign of progress and women's liberation. A parallel could be drawn to nineteenth-century debates in the United States; see the chapter by Susan McKinnon in this volume.
31. Edward Evans-Pritchard, "The Nuer of the Southern Sudan," in *African Political Sytems*, ed. Meyer Fortes and Edward Evans-Pritchard (London: Oxford University Press, 1940).
32. Regarding different national styles to model African political systems and societies, see also the chapter by Thomas Zitelmann in this volume.
33. Lombard, *Structures*.
34. In the last decades, historians of colonial Africa have criticized the image of the weak position of women in precolonial Africa. Among others, Christian missionary activities are today seen as responsible for processes of weakening the position of women. See, for example, Jean Allman and Victoria Tashjian, *I Will Not Eat Stones: A Womens's History of Colonial Ashante* (Oxford: James Currey, 2000), 169–72.
35. Médénouvo, "Coutumier du Dahomey," 66.
36. See Alber, *Im Gewand von Herrschaft*, 101–3; Lombard, *Structures*, 335–36; Paulo Fernando de Moraes Farias, "For a Non-culturalist Historiography of Bénois Borgu," in *Regards sur le Borgou: Pouvoir et altérité dans une région ouest-africaine*, ed. Elisabeth Boesen et al. (Paris, L'Harmattan: 1998).
37. Concerning slavery and the slow modifications under colonial rule in Northern Benin, see Christine Hardung, *Arbeit, Sklaverei und Erinnerung: Gruppen unfreier Herkunft unter den Fulbe Nordbenins* (Köln: Rüdiger Köppe Verlag, 2006), 89ff.
38. Lombard, *Structures*; Carolyn F. Sargent, "Born to Die: Witchcraft and Infanticide in Bariba Culture," *Ethnology* 27, no. 1 (1988).
39. Jeannett Martin, "Zugehörigkeit: Vorschlag zu einer theoretischen Konzeption und empirische Fallstudien zu Kindheit in Nordbenin" (Unpublished manuscript, 2018), 239.
40. Elsewhere, I have mentioned that the theme of slavery, which had been quite present in the colonial documents, slowly disappeared from 1910 onward. Alber, *Im Gewand von Herrschaft*, 162–64; see also Hardung, *Arbeit, Sklaverei*, 48–52.
41. Lombard, *Structures*, and Alber, *Im Gewand von Herrschaft*.
42. As a classic, see Michael Crowder and Obare Ikime, eds., *West African Chiefs: Their Changing Status under Colonial Rule and Independence* (New York: Africana, 1970). For Northern Dahomey, see, among others, Thomas Bierschenk, "Rituels politique et construction de l'identité ethnique des Peuls du Bénin," *Cahiers des Sciences Humaines*, no. 31 (1995), and Thomas Bierschenk, "Peuls et Etat colonial au Borgou francais," *Nomadic Peoples*, no. 38 (1996). For Baatombu, see Alber, *Im Gewand von Herrschaft*, 153.
43. See as an example Alber, *Transfers of Belonging*, 158.
44. Despite the official end of slavery during colonialism, being a descendant of slaves strongly influenced social relations in the village in the twentieth century. This was still quite noticeable in the second half of the twentieth century. For slavery in the Borgu region, see Hardung, *Arbeit, Sklaverei*.
45. See a case study from northern Ghana, Carola Lentz, "Chieftaincy Has Come to Stay: La chefferie dans les sociétés acéphales du Nord-Ouest Ghana," *Cahier des Études Africaines* 40, no. 159 (2000).
46. This is somewhat comparable to the process of parentalization that Ludolf Kuchenbuch describes in this volume.
47. This was also highly relevant when children were enrolled. Colonial schooling greatly contributed to the stabilization of family names.

48. See for instance UEEB/SIM au Benin, *Bibeli Gusunɔn Gari: The Holy Bible in the Baatonum Language of* Benin, trans. SIM International, 2013, retrieved 18 August 2020 from http://ebible.org/pdf/bba/bba_OBA.pdf.
49. See Alber, "Denying Biological Parenthood," and Martin, "Zugehörigkeit."
50. Forms and practices of *bii nenobu* underwent deep changes during the twentieth century that are the subject of my monograph (Alber, *Transfers of Belonging*). In the frame of this chapter, they cannot be discussed in detail. A condensed summary is found in Alber, "Denying Biological Parenthood," and Alber, "Politics of Kinship."
51. Even if birth parents are often widely ignored in the everyday life in order to demonstrate that the foster parents are the real parents (Alber, "Denying Biological Parenthood"), birth parents are important because belonging to a clan (and thus funeral rites) depends on them, as do rights to chieftaincy.
52. James Ferguson, "What Comes after the Social? Historicizing the Future of Social Assistance and Identity Registration in Africa," in *Registration and Recognition: Documenting the Person in World History*, ed. Keith Breckenridge and Simon Szreter (Oxford: Oxford University Press, 2012), 503.
53. Although I am talking about a national language that enables multilingual communications, this does not mean that it does not extend across national borders.
54. See Eric Hobsbawn and Terence Ranger, ed., *The Invention of Tradition* (Cambridge: Cambridge University Press, 1983).
55. Valentin-Yves Mudimbe, *The Inventions of Africa: Gnosis, Philosophy and the Order of Knowledge* (Bloomington: Indiana University Press, 1988).
56. For a good summary, see, for instance, Thomas Zitelmann, "Formen und Institutionen politischer Herrschaft," in *Geschichte in Afrika: Einführung in Probleme und Debatten*, ed. Jan-Georg Deutsch and Albert Wirz (Berlin: Verlag des arabischen Buches, 1997), or also the chapter by Zitelmann in this volume; on the limits of inventions, see also Carola Lentz and Paul Nugent, eds., *Chieftancy in Ghana: The Limits of Invention* (New York: St. Martin's Press, 2000).
57. See Susan McKinnon, "Domestic Exceptions: Evans-Pritchard and the Creation of Nuer Patrilineality and Equality," *Cultural Anthropology* 15, no. 1 (2008).

Bibliography

Alber, Erdmute. *Im Gewand von Herrschaft: Modalitäten der Macht bei den Baatombu (1895–1995)*. Studien zur Kulturkunde, vol. 116. Köln: Rüdiger Köppe, 2000.

———. "Denying Biological Parenthood—Child Fosterage in Northern Benin." *Ethnos* 68, no. 4 (2003): 487–506.

———. *Transfers of Belonging: Child Fostering in West Africa in the 20th Century*. Leiden: Brill, 2018.

———. "Politics of Kinship: Child Fostering in Dahomey/Benin." *Cahiers d'études Africaines* 2 (2019): 359–75.

Allman, Jean, and Victoria Tashian. *I Will Not Eat Stones: A Women's History of Colonial Ashante*. Oxford: James Currey, 2000.

Archives nationals du Dahomey, Porto Novo. *Rapport annuel sur la situation general du cercle pendant l'année 1912*, serie 22.

Bierschenk, Thomas. "Rituels politiques et construction de l'identité ethnique des Peuls du Bénin." *Cahiers de Sciences Humaines* 31 (1995): 457–84.

———. "Peuls et Etat colonial au Borgou francais." *Nomadic Peoples*, no. 38 (1996): 99–124.

Bio Bigou, Leon. *La région de Parakou: Ses chefferies traditionelles et ses rois des origines a nos jours.* Cotonou, 1993.

Brandstetter, Anna-Maria. "Kolonialismus: Wider die vereinfachenden Dichotomien." In *Geschichte in Afrika: Einführung in Probleme und Debatten,* edited by Jan-Georg Deutsch and Albert Wirz, 75–105. Berlin: Das arabische Buch, 1997.

Cornevin, Robert. *Histoire du Dahomey.* Paris: Berger-Levrault, 1962.

Crowder, Michael, and Obare Ikime, ed. *West African Chiefs: Their Changing Status under Colonial Rule and Independence.* New York: Africana, 1970.

de Moraes Farias, Paulo Fernando. "For a Non-culturalist Historiography of Bénois Borgu." In *Regards sur le Borgou: Pouvoir et altérité dans une région ouest-africaine,* edited by Elisabeth Boesen et al., 39–70. Paris: L'Harmattan, 1998.

Descimon, Robert. "Quelques réflexions à propos des commissaires du roi dans la rédaction et la réformation des coutumes au XVI e siècle." *Les cahiers du Centre de Recherches Historiques* 26, no. 1 (2001): 1–12.

Evans-Pritchard, Edward. *Kinship and Marriage among the Nuer.* Oxford: Clarendon Press, 1951.

———. "The Nuer of the Southern Sudan." In *African Political Systems,* edited by Meyer Fortes and Edward Evans Pritchard, 271–96. London: Oxford University Press, 1940.

Ferguson, James. "What Comes after the Social? Historicizing the Future of Social Assistance and Identity Registration in Africa." In *Registration and Recognition: Documenting the Person in World History,* edited by Keith Breckenridge and Simon Szreter, 495–516. Oxford: Oxford University Press, 2012.

Fortes, Meyer, and Edward Evans-Pritchard. "Introduction." In *African Political Systems,* edited by Meyer Fortes and Edward Evans-Pritchard, 1–24. London: Oxford University Press, 1940.

Goode, William J. *World Revolution and Family Patterns.* London: The Free Press of Glencoe, 1963.

Grinberg, Martine. "La rédaction des coutumes et les droits seigneuriaux: Nommer, classer, exclure." *Annales: Histoire, Sciences Sociales* 52, no. 5 (1997): 1017–38.

———. "Les interprètes et le droit coutumier: Les éditions des coutumes du bailliage d'Amiens." *Les Cahiers du Centre de Recherches Historiques* 26, no. 1 (2001): 1–22.

Grossenbacher, Jean-Pierre. *Abrégé de grammaire de Bariba.* Parakou, 1974.

———. *Lexique Baatonum-Français.* Parakou, 1977.

———. *Lexique Baatonum-Français: Nouveau tirage avec les tons et des mots.* Parakou, 1989.

Hardung, Christine. *Arbeit, Sklaverei und Erinnerung: Gruppen unfreier Herkunft unter den Fulbe Nordbenins.* Köln: Rüdiger Köppe Verlag, 2006.

Hobsbawn, Eric, and Terence Ranger, eds. *The Invention of Tradition.* Cambridge: Cambridge University Press, 1983.

Kuba, Richard. *Wasangari und Wangara: Borgu und seine Nachbarn in historischer Perspektive.* Hamburg: Lit Verlag, 1996.

Lentz, Carola. "Chieftaincy Has Come to Stay: La chefferie dans les sociétés acéphales du Nord-Ouest Ghana." *Cahier des Études Africaines* 40, no. 159 (2000): 593–613.

Lentz, Carola, and Paul Nugent, eds. *Chieftaincy in Ghana: The Limits of Invention.* New York: St. Martin's Press, 2000.

Lombard, Jacques. *Structures de type "féodal" en Afrique Noire: Étude des dynamismes internes et des relations sociales chez les Bariba du Dahomey*. Paris: Imprimerie Nationale, 1965.

Martin, Jeannett. "Zugehörigkeit: Vorschlag zu einer theoretischen Konzeption und empirische Fallstudien zu Kindheit in Nordbenin." Unpublished manuscript, 2018.

McKinnon, Susan. "Domestic Exceptions: Evans-Pritchard and the Creation of Nuer Patrilineality and Equality." *Cultural Anthropology* 15, no. 1 (2008): 35–83.

McKinnon, Susan, and Fenella Canell. "The Difference Kinship Makes." In *Modernity and the Persistence of Kinship*, edited by Susan McKinnon and Fenella Canell, 1–38. Santa Fe: School for Advanced Research Press, 2016.

Médénouvo, Firmin, ed. *Coutumier du Dahomey*. Tillières-sur-Avre: Présence Béninoise, 2004.

Morgan, Henry Lewis. *Systems of Consanguinity and Affinity of the Human Family*. Smithsonian Contributions to Knowledge, vol. 17. Washington, DC: Smithsonian Institution, 1868.

Mudimbe, Valentin-Yves: *The Invention of Africa: Gnosis, Philosophy and the Order of Knowledge*. Bloomington: Indiana University Press, 1988.

Radcliffe-Brown, Alfred, and Daryl Forde, eds. *African Systems of Kinship and Marriage*. New York: Routledge, 1950.

Sargent, Carolyn F. "Born to Die: Witchcraft and Infanticide in Bariba Culture." *Ethnology* 27, no. 1 (1988): 79–95.

Schatzberg, Michael. "Power, Legitimacy and 'Democratisation' in Africa." *Africa* 63, no. 4 (1993): 445–61.

Stoler, Ann. *Carnal Knowledge and Imperial Rule*. Berkeley: University of California Press, 2002.

Strathern, Marilyn, and Jeanette Edwards. "Including Our Own." In *Cultures of Relatedness: New Approaches to the Study of Kinship*, edited by Janet Carsten, 149–66. Cambridge: Cambridge University Press, 2000.

Thelen, Tatjana, and Erdmute Alber. "Reconnecting State and Kinship. Temporalities, Scales, Classifications." In *Reconnecting State and Kinship*, edited by Tatjana Thelen and Erdmute Alber, 1–37. Philadelphia: University of Pennsylvania Press, 2017.

Trautmann, Thomas R. *Lewis Henry Morgan and the Invention of Kinship*. Lincoln: University of Nebraska Press, 1987.

Trenk, Marin. "Dein Reichtum ist dein Ruin: Zum Stand der Forschung über afrikanische Unternehmer und wirtschaftliche Entwicklung." *Anthropos* 86, nos. 4/6 (1991): 501–16.

UEEB/SIM au Benin. *Bibeli Gusunɔn Gari: The Holy Bible in the Baatonum Language of Benin*. Translated by SIM International, 2013. Retrieved 18 August 2020 from http://ebible.org/pdf/bba/bba_OBA.pdf.

Zitelmann, Thomas. "Formen und Institutionen politischer Herrschaft." In *Geschichte in Afrika: Einführung in Probleme und Debatten*, edited by Jan-Georg Deutsch and Albert Wirz, 201–29. Berlin: Verlag des arabischen Buches, 1997.

Chapter 11

"As If Begotten and Born of Freeborn Parents"
Indicators and Considerations on Parentalization of Emancipated Slaves in the Post-Roman Occident

Ludolf Kuchenbuch (translated by Eric Hounshell)

Introduction

Manumission belonged to the repertoire of ideas and actions in the modern West in the long millennium before the worldwide legal abolition of slavery and serfdom.[1] It accompanied and shaped the complex formal transformation of exploitation and dependence, mobility, integration, and distinction. In the process, its economic function, symbolic meaning, spatial purview, and sociopolitical bearing changed constantly. This chapter argues that in the post-Roman Occident the ubiquitous ritual of slave manumission (*manumissio*) can be understood as a basis for legitimization and a point of departure for an implicit "parentalization"—the use and elaboration of natal and affinal kinship relations and other related solidarities that went beyond individual kin-making. So far, this has largely been overlooked.[2] Indeed, in my view the study of kinship relations of the *dominated* in this period is still in its infancy.[3] My thesis implies that we should reconsider not only the tableau of forms of dependency and their long-term transformations (in the sixth through eleventh centuries) but also the influence of relations of dominance (*Herrschaftsbeziehungen*) on the kinship relations of the dominated.

What were manumissions in these centuries about? They were metamorphoses of dependency in which the production and use of kinship played a considerable role. A particularly useful collection of sources pertaining to the Weissenburg Monastery (Alsace) serves as the foundation for this inquiry. On 7 January 797 CE in Ottweiler (Alsace), a certain Rihbald, along with four named witnesses from his regional milieu of lords and Iustolfus, the abbot of Weissenburg Monastery, signed a letter of manumission (*paginola libertatis*) in which he testified that he was conceding freeborn status (*ingenuitas*) to nine named slaves (six *servi* and three *ancillae*).[4]

Over fifty years later, between 861 and 864, a scribe included this piece of writing in a collection of Weissenburg documents consisting mostly of transfers of ownership; exactly why is impossible to determine.[5] He titled this "slaves (*mancipia*) whom [Rihbald] manumitted." My translation is as follows:

> In the name of Christ, [I] Rihbald, in fear of God and for the salvation of my soul and eternal reward, have discharged as freeborn [*relaxavi ingenuous*] my slaves [*servos meos vel ancillas meas*] with the names … [see below]. They themselves should be freeborn [*ingenui*] as if they were born of and procreated by freeborn parents [*ingenui tamquam si ab ingenius parentibus fuissent nati uel procreati*]. None of my inheritors or inheritors' inheritors shall impress them either into service or into obligation from having been freed [*servitium nec libertatis obsequium*]—aside from God alone, to whom all are subject. However, they are to live by the possessions [*peculiare*] that they hold or may obtain in the future [*conlaborare*], to further toil [*laborare*] and possess their yield—this is conceded and indulged [*concessum atque indultum*] to them. You shall seek protection [*mundeburdo*][6] and defense [*defensio*] at the abbey of Saint Peter called Weissenburg and with the stipulation that you are required to give four denari[7] yearly as rent [*census*] at the festival of Saint Martin—and so you will remain freeborn. To defend your freeborn status, as said, and for the illumination [of the abbey church in Weissenburg] you shall deliver [this rent], and if, however, you openly refuse, you shall pay a fine according to law [*legibus*] but remain freeborn—as the undersigned have testified. Negotiated on … day in … year. Signature of Rihbald, who has written this letter of freeborn status [followed by the signatures of the witnesses].

What is the sequence of resolutions? Following the invocation of Christ, the manumitter by way of introduction outlines the reason for his action: his fear of God and the hoped-for effect of his deed on the sanctity of his soul (in the sense of his eternal reward). Then comes the actual protocol statement of his prior action: he declares his slaves, listed by name, freeborn. The referent is an oral ritual—a manumission before witnesses of equal status (when exactly is not specified) and its result a new social status, called freedom (*libertas*) later in the document. Its basic content is that each slave listed by name from now on can refer to the testament of signed witnesses to show that they are considered procreated (*procreatus*) by and born (*natus*) of freeborn parents (*parentes*) by themselves and all "others."

Then come conditions of implementation, in two directions. First, Rihbald addresses his heirs: he forbids them from ever forcing the (henceforth) *ingenui* into their service or into "freedom-specific"duties — that is, from lowering their new status,although notwithstanding the subjection of all under God. This secures the *libertas* of the nine former slaves against claims from or infringement by any of his relatives who might not recognize the status granted by the manumitter or wish to use it to their advantage.

Then, the emancipator changes his addressee and speaks of the status of the manumitted. He sees this as a concession and a grant of a new frame of action and life outside of the lordly manor that had previously sheltered and used them. From now on, they may dispose of their current and future holdings, work with them, and retain future acquisitions — that is, live off them. What is meant here are their holdings of domestic animals and livestock, tools, equipment, and goods for household management and daily survival. Houses and vehicles (still wooden at that time) could also be included, but land (fields, pastures, vineyards, forests) was usually not.

Following these concessions are direct instructions to the nine former slaves. They are to place themselves under the protection (*mundeburdo*) and defense (*defensio*) of Saint Peter's Abbey in Weissenburg. As recompense for their freeborn status (*vestra ingenuitas*), they are to give (*dare, solvere*) a yearly rent of four silver denari on St. Martin's Day to provide for the illumination of the abbey church. This confirms and secures their freeborn status. Thus, after the concessions come the conditions. And if they refuse this rent payment, then the law (the punishment and fines applicable in secular law) takes effect, but this does not change their new status.

With the concluding authentication (the *actum*and *datum*statement) and the manumitter's request of transcription, his signature, and those of the witnesses, the language shifts, now taking the form of a report on everyone involved as witnesses of a true event.

What does this testimonial have to do with becoming related, making related, and being related, in general and in particular? My hypothesis is that it basically means nothing explicitly but a surprising amount implicitly. This will be dealt with later. From this perspective, the connection between my argument and this book's introduction is clear. I am not concerned with discourses on conceptions of kinship but rather with social processes whose kinship-generating role and effect are to be elicited in the first place. This question is indebted to a sort of inversion of an *a priori* in comparative slavery research. Those who become enslaved and who are slavesare deprived not only of their own material milieu and dignity but also their relational embeddedness.[8] What happens regarding the latter when we investigate not the ways *into* slavery and its persistence but the ways *out*? These include manumissions, whether within the manor house or, much more effectively, through a public ritual.

In order to speak adequately to the topic of this book, this investigation must answer the question of whether a period-specific notion of kinship that is suitable for historical and systematic comparisons can be detected in the corpus of early medieval manumissions.[9] Thus, the task is to probe the records of manumissions to see what they reveal about social strategies of kinship formation. Is there a politics of parentalization here?

What Manumissions Were

Before dealing with the details, let us review the basic facts about and the state of scholarship on early medieval manumissions.[10]

Manumissions emerged during these centuries out of the preexisting dichotomizing practice of distinction in Roman law—the polarization of society between free person (*liber/ingenuus*) and slave (*servus/mancipium*). The distinction between freedom (*libertas*) and (*servitus*) serfdom not only remained decisive and widespread in the imperial provinces of Western Rome but was sharpened in the wake of tribal conquests and empire formations. The clergy that became dominant alongside the lay hereditary aristocracy wholeheartedly accepted serfdom, referring to various interpretations by Saint Paul and the Church Fathers that worked around the biblical assumption of equality. In these years, manumissions from serfdom (*servitus*) were conducted through simplifications of complicated forms of manumission in Roman law. Among the things underlying this was that in law slaves were allowed no kin status (*servilis cognatio nulla sit*).[11] Not only did the manumitted'slord change, but the new relationship had a different meaning through the manumitted's connection (comparable to that of the *patrocinium* with a landlord in Ancient Rome) with a church and its protective saint (*patron*), which weredetermined by the manumitter or else chosen by the manumitted. The individual freed from his lord (*dominus*), whom one could also call (following Clausdieter Schott) the newly free, would now become the ward of both a powerful heavenly patron (*patronus*) and a concrete privileged establishment, whether a parish church, abbey, or cathedral, which included its clerical agents (a patronate). For this custodial security (above all in the case of threat, damage, or oppression), an annual rent in money or wax for the illumination of the altar or church was typically required. This is not just evident from normative records of Germanic law codes, lordly edicts, and ecclesiastical decrees from the time but also from records of specific instances of social practices such as manumission.

It is unclear how often manumission occurred and if it was applied to slaves who had been born in the lord's household, to those who had been purchased, or to those who had been reduced to slavery as a result of misdeeds, debt, or penalty. Older persons and (widowed) women, together with their children, seem to have been preferred. It also remains difficult to estimate the relative frequency of manumissions of named individuals as opposed to so-called mass manumissions of groups of unnamed persons.

The latest scholarship emphasizes that early medieval manumission was an instrument *sui generis* that was continually used for social regulation. How manumissions should be periodized—that is, to what extent later ones differed from those in late antiquity and how they contributed to the development of new forms of unfreedom around the twelfth century (*Leibeigenschaft*, serfdom, *servage*)—is controversial.[12] Moreover, there is no agreement over whether duties of memorial service for the deceased manumitter were entailed in manumission, which maintained a second tie alongside that to the new lord.[13]

Further, there is dissent over whether manumissions should be understood as manipulations that led to groups or strata based on legal status among freeborn and slaves or as an open social strategy of solutions situationally appropriate within complex local fields and cases of conflict between lordly and communal claims on material advantage, social security, and ideational prestige. Seen this way, manumission was not the differentiation of a third type of status but a legal argument or instrument for the implementation or negotiation of local interests. Although there is prominent evidence for a tripartite typology of status (*ingenuus, frilaz/lidus, servus*), the various portrayals of the manumitted testify to the vagueness and diversity of the new freedom: they may refer specifically to the ritual, the kind of lordship, the documentary attestation, or the rent payment.

There is, however, scholarly consensus that the broad range of characteristics of a new *libertas* were implemented quite differently in each case.[14]

On the State of Knowledge

Among the types of evidence that report on or deal with manumissions,[15] the most detailed are the few surviving manumission *charters* that name individual slaves, like Rihbald's record introduced above. The collection of Weissenburger records contains five more. These records were without exception created and stylized on a given occasion based on *formularies* in widespread, continual use throughout the Occident. Thus, these formularies, of which a total of twenty from between 600 and 1000 CE survive, constitute an indispensable extended corpus for our questions.

Let us turn back to Rihbald's charter of the manumission of nine slaves. As noted above, it opened with a public ritual, a "release from the lord's hand" (*missio de manu, relaxion/dimissio*). The text, as quoted for a first reading above, consists of a sequence of five conditions that are labeled at the end with the legal term *ingenuitas*.

1. A radically different *status* grounded in the dualistic principle of birth at the time—one was born either free or unfree—was conferred on the named individuals. From then on, they could see themselves as procreated by and born of freeborn parents and refer to this in the course of their activities. The social metamorphosis (from *servus* to *libertus*) by lordly declaration effected, so to speak, a new life condition (*conditio*).
2. The manumitted were henceforth to be free from owing any service to the (future) inheritors and inheritors' inheritors of the manumitter. At the same time, this meant a separation from claims by the relatives of their former lord.
3. The manumitted were granted the right to autonomous disposal of their current and future movable property.
4. It was stipulated that they submit themselves to the protection of a new lord, the abbey of Weissenburg, its holy patrons Peter and Paul, and the abbot. For this patronage they were to remit a four-coin rent on St. Martin's Day.
5. Refusal to pay would be penalized according to the law that was now applicable to them as freeborn and not with the corporal punishment typical for slaves (mutilation, beating). That is, membership in the community of the free would persist even in the case of offense; there was no threat of re-enslavement.

What do the other Weissenburg manumission letters and the contemporary manumission formularies offer when taken together?

The dictum of manumission by the lord, the centerpiece of the ritual— *absolvo te de iugo servitutis* (I absolve you of the yoke of slavery)—was transcribed in the piece of writing. The earlier status was thereby metaphorically devalued and the new *ingenuitas* counterposed to the old *servitus*. Designations such as *vernaculus, famulus,* and *infantulum* indicated indirectly that the manumitted were domestic slaves of the manumitter. The manumission could take place after the transfer to a new ecclesiastical lord—that is, it should be considered the result of the transfer. The emancipation from services to relatives of the manumitter, a genuinely common risk, was emphasized. Justification for the rent obligation could vary—a memorial contribution for the dead, recognition of the patron as new lord, or personal rent as sign of dependence. The manumitted were assigned to particular groups of wards within the social association (*familia*) of the abbey (*censuales, epistolarii*). They could be compelled to resettle in the area (*potestas*) of their new lord. They could bequeath their movable property (*peculium*) beyond their children to further "kin" (*posteritas, generatio, cognatio, proximi*). (In one formulary, this means a comparison of the manumitted with proprietors who held enough farmland for their own subsistence [*mansuarii*] their new life conditions). And, finally, they could be granted the ability to actively take part in the legal monitoring of misdeeds and the settlement of conflicts through participation (*responsio*), testimony (*testimonium*), and oathtaking (*sacramentum*). All of this contributes to extrapolating a general schema from the basic stipulations contained in the Rihbald charter. (Of course, such a schemadid not exist in practice, which varied across cases, implying flexible and situationally applicable decisions).[16]

This concludes the interpretation of the charters and formularies. These remarks on the manumitted's new status, connection to place and space, being investedwith property, and security of existence should suffice for reflections on the kinship effects of manumissions in this period below.

On Parentalizaton: Considerations and Questions

The following considerations are not backed up by unbroken chains of empirical evidence. Instead, they are a further round of interpretations of the material presented thus far, expanded through important details from other evidentiary genres andinterspersed with observations about social-historical aspects, in particular discussions of kinship at the time.

Here I build on Alice Rio's idea that being a slave should not be understood primarily as having the legal status of a social class, stratum, or group but instead as a strategic negotiation of claims made by slave masters. Slavery, she holds, is a form of association in constant variation and modification. In this way it is comparable, as a mode of association, to kinship! Like kinship, being a slave is grounded in intersubjective criteria such as unfree birth; is determined by power relations of variable intensity; delineates social inclusion and exclusion; represents a legal system of rules and obligations, including their emotional, economic, and symbolic baggage; and determines, more or less, the fixing of personal relations of any given individual. Slavery and kinship are thus *each* "inherently promiscuous institutions" involved in every realm of social life.[17] These dicta taken from Michael Mann's theory of power will also guide this discussion.[18] In contrast with Rio, however, I am not concerned with a typologizing *distinction* between the social situation of slaves and the kinship relations of freeborn persons but instead with points of contact, mixtures, re-layerings, and balancings *between* the two.[19] In this way, manumission seems to be a "systemic moment," a threshold that at once represents the distinction and the entanglement of both forms of relation. In the foreground is the question of what role, compared with informal changes, this explicit moment plays for relatedness and in which fields of action it could have an effect.

To what conceptual frameworks of post-Roman kinship can one refer for this purpose? Karl Ubl—convinced like Alice Rio that kinship is to be regarded "not as an institution but a resource for individual strategies and as transmission belt for political and social processes"—has aptly summarized the state of scholarship with three points:[20]

1. From the period of 300–1600, kinship was principally bilateral, i.e., cognatic. Related persons changed with each generation, and every individual had an individual circle of relatives.
2. The nuclear family (*Kernfamilie*)—and not the clan (*Sippe*) was the primary point of reference in the Early Middle Ages. Extended kinship was always only situationally and selectively included but without fixed rules.
3. Kinship was not particularly privileged in comparison with other social forms such as patronage, friendship, and cohabitation but was instead flexibly and dynamically usable owing to its bilaterality.

Ubl's methodological conclusion is indispensable for everything that follows: "Previous scholarship has taught us that neither normative texts nor charters or memorial documents make the structure of kinship 'immediately visible.'" In the wording and isolated facts in the charters and forms presented above, an explicit parental argument is missing (except for one, albeit central, point); which can be found in other written "forums," but not in the practical realm of manumission.[21] This is understandable because the formulation of the acts of manumission focused on individual slaves of course cannot deal in terms of kinship generally,[22] let alone most denotations of concrete relatedness (father, brother, uncle, cousin, grandchild, etc.).

Thus, the charters and formularies examined above are insufficient for making "visible" as many aspects of kin-making and kin-fostering phenomena as possible. Other kinds of sources must lend a hand, such as Germanic law codes, rulers' edicts, property and income registers. Here, however, these will not lead to dense evidence but only allow us to venture hypotheses about practices relevant to kinship. That is to say, we have to consider things the charters and formularies of manumission *did not* deal with because they did not belong to the area regulated by the act of manumission: patronage and godparenthood, weddings and marriage, landed property and inheritance—decisive fields of practice for the manumitted. This was evident in the presence of the manumitted in documents that accounted for persons within a local complex of lordship (the *familia* of a *villa*), along with their goods and obligations of rent and service, and mostly listed them with the status groups *servi* and *ingenui*. This applies, moreover, to people designated in charters or verbal acts as manumitted (*lidi, epistolarii, cartularii*), as protected (*mundilitiones*), or as obligated to pay per capita rent (*censuarii, cerarii,capitalicii*). But what particular form of life are we dealing with here? The manumitted were clearly next-door neighbors—typically as a minority—of farmstead proprietors and cottagers of the manor to which or in which they now belonged. The manumitted shared a local milieu with them, whether it was a large demesne, a dense or dispersed group of farmsteads, a parish, or a preurban settlement near a center of power.[23] As newly free, they had to come to terms with constellations of free- and unfree-born persons—that is with schisms and hierarchies, customs and tensions that resulted from any number of conditions: sexual relations between *servi* and *ingenui*; the distribution of farmsteads and fields; rent and service obligations; usufruct rights to forests, pastures, irrigation, and roads; court rituals of peace and punishment; and the local parish's care of the soul. We know far too little about all of this.[24]

The following points center on these roughly indicated conditions of life in order to be consistent with the perspective of the manumitted. For this reason, they stray from being organized around the structure of testimonies of manumission, their targeting, and their terminological orientation. They are first grounded in considerations of the *ingenuitas* of individuals manumitted. Second, following these, come considerations of the possibilities that ecclesiastical protective lordship could offer the freeborn "dependent" and of his liberty. A third step thinks through the necessary basis of local integration in small-scale kinship: conjugal pairing through weddings and marriage (*matrimonium*). Then the conclusion discusses the ways that the manumitted could actively fill out and secure their existence through work (*labor*)—through possession and management of movable and above all immovable property, along with safeguarding it after death.

Ingenuitas—Free Birth

To recapitulate, the actual practice before all written testimonies of manumission was the rite of passage of the individual slave from *servitus* to *ingenuitas*, taking the form of a public spoken ritual by virtue of his lord's power of definition. This new status of the newly free "person"[25] (*conditio/status/honor*) was anchored in local knowledge and registered, as shown above, as a conglomerate of claims and obligations.

But what did the new social status create? Legal historians speak of a growing unfettering of the slave by the lord's will as a "fiction," a testimony that shaped reality and through which the inborn slave quality was annulled: from now on he "was" born of and engendered by freeborn parents—*ab ingenuis parentibus natus vel procreatus*. This is an evocative formulation. Of course, the emphasis lay on the status-relevant adjective *ingenuus*—*free*born and -engendered. A socially higher birth status was attested for the slave. To some degree, he mutated from *proprius* to *ingenuus homo*. He or she was given a new native quality that, because it was produced in a socially binding way, was "valid" as the basis for a new consciousness and action.

The basis and cause of freedom was henceforth, surprisingly, expressed in two steps—through a general relation and a differential relation. The noun *parentes* can be understood as "parents"—the pair from which the manumitted descended.[26] This is indicated by the two individuations: *natus* and *procreatus*. Perhaps these refer to the mother as the birth-giver and the father as creator. Both attributes are omnipresent, indeed indispensable, throughout the whole body of evidence. Since they alternate in their order, it remains unclear whether the maternal or paternal dimension was seen as decisive for the descent of the newly free. However binding this new dual bond might have been, as a fundamental quality of new freedom it was secondary to the parental relation.

In any case it is clear that the linkage and ordering of the three words expressed fundamental coordinates of kinship at the time: from now on the manumitted derived from an alliance of both maternal and paternal lines of descent, that is, a bilaterally understood lineage community of freeborn. He or she was "equally," that is, freely and cognately, related to father and mother.

But must the analysis end with this parental "resocialization" of the slave as *individual*? Is it not thinkable that his new freeborn status "rubbed off" on his still unfree *consanguini*? Certainly, his parents, their other children (his siblings), and their further descendants were not made freeborn through his manumission. But the status change of their descendants would not be without trace or implications. Without a doubt, a new kind of "mixed" condition emerged in the local fabric, but we simply do not know anything about it.

By way of a detour, however, it can be shown that the manumission that was always minted through singular, nominally identified slaves was not everything. A not-insignificant fraction of the charters (and also the formularies) dealt with variously sized *groups* of manumitted—so-called mass manumissions. Since (according to the personal principle of manumission) all slaves affected were indicated by their *own names*, these can be investigated together as a population. In addition, we can use income registries from the period that list individually named manumitted (with and without landed property) alongside other persons. Such evidence testifies to people's custom at the time of naming their children after themselves or more distant ancestral or affinal relatives by selecting and recombining preferred name parts from the stock of bipartite names (name variation).[27] The enormously varied combinations of names that resulted made it possible to recognize the individual and his individuality by name and at the same time to locate him in a network of kinship relations. In this way, individual identity and social location were to a certain extent created together—a particular way of minting relatedness.[28] This widespread practice of open name-giving,[29] using both lines of descent relatively equally, allows us to speculate that a manumitter set free not only individuals but also groups of slaves who were related consanguineously or by birth, thus granting freeborn consciousness and action to a whole group. Can one see here a tendency of the manumitter to preferentially emancipate servile lineage groups? Did these slave groups intentionally influence the manumitter and negotiate their better status with him? And if so, at what "price"?

A third point: given that female slaves and their children (also individually named) were, evidently, quite often manumitted together,[30] a still deeper parentalizing "attitude" of the manumitter is recognizable that was not limited to the manumitted individual woman but was also connected to her servile motherhood—alone, without a formally acknowledged sexual partner; that is to say, her "marital status." In this way, *ingenui* relatedness was solidified across generations, determining kinship by descent and securing it in the future.

To summarize, the manumitted now "possessed" a corporeal ancestry apart from the encompassing lordly domain that implied new dignity and self-esteem and at the same time encouraged him to adapt to life with the other freeborn, to engage with them "as equals," and this, taken together, ultimately led to the recognition of this corporeal ancestry as a kinship-constituting act for the manumitted. Thus, it modified not only the social consciousness of the manumitted but also his network of near relations by birth. It figured into whom he could appeal to, what could secure him, and what he could use, not only for himself as a newly free individual but as one secured in the circle of his lateral cognates and stabilized through the concession of freeborn status to his existing and future descendants. Altogether, I see a threefold parental "embedding" of ancestry, of the present, and of the future. This is my central thesis.

Libertas—Freedom

If one considers possible parentalization (kin-making) effects of church patronage of the manumitted,[31] then one runs into other, less clearly articulated indications of relatedness that differ markedly from the *ingenuitas* of the manumitted, such as his "first," corporeal birth. In my view, three aspects of the newly free carry implications for his future. First, he is an individual ward of the patron saint (*homo sancti N.*) and member of his social association, his *familia*. Second, he is a free legal associate (*libertus*) within the framework of an ecclesiastic-lordly ministration of peace and law that corresponds in multiple ways with immunity—a legal "exemption" conceded by the king. And finally, he is enmeshed in the fabric of pastoral Christian care of the soul. What could that mean within the perspective of parentalization?

1. Shifting under the protective lordship of the relevant church, the manumitted live within another field of lordship. In place of their previously local and daily present house lord there is the patron, a holy heavenly lord vouched for by his earthly surrogates—abbot, bishop, bailiff, priest. This is thus a change from direct, comprehensive, undivided *dominium* to *patrocinium* (and *defensio, tuition,*or *munboratio*) characterized by distance and mediation—a porous structure of lordship, with multiple levels and instances, which can both offer the manumitted room for their own action and, with insufficiently effective protection, bring uncertainty.

   By annually rendering the agreed-upon payment at the altar harboring the patron's relics, the manumitted was integrated into the imaginative and symbolic world of the church and clerisy shaped by close kinship. While this can be understood as seen from the top—as a paternally regulated house ordered into fraternal communities—subordinates were also qualified through their designation as close kin and set off from the outside by the sacrality of their patrons: they were *family* of the saint. This should not be understood as mere rhetoric but as something that permeated the whole legal discourse. Within the realm of the patron's command and protection—from the monastic or episcopal centers to the local landed estates and parish churches—a climate of order and agreement habituated the manumitted (like all people who belonged) to constructions like the children of God or the saint and to the brotherhood of equals and the paternity of superiors. This encasement and permeation with nuclear kinship could not have failed to influence the actions and thoughts of the manumitted. They existed in a parental climate of lordship and community that was advantageous for them—that is my hypothesis.

2. Occasionally the charters and formularies spoke of *libertas* instead of *ingenuitas*. There is more to this word choice than just using an alternative synonym. Regularly, it was imposed on the manumitted that should they refuse to pay rent they were to be charged and sentenced according to the legal customs applicable to the free, without losing their status as *liberti*. Moreover, there are clear indications that, as legally responsible men, they could also actively participate in dispute resolution in the ecclesiastical court (*mallus ecclesiae*) as witnesses or judges. That meant that they could act with the free use of their senses and with the right of remembering and of witnessing that which was remembered with free ears and eyes and by means of accredited speech. This mental *libertas* empowered them to participate in the resolution of conflicts over descent, marriage, service, and inheritance as well as violent acts. And all of these harbored the most varied kinship references and constellations.[32] Apropos of their *libertas*, the manumitted could be involved not only passively but also actively in such processes. As legal persons like those "born" free, they could join in local activities permeated with kinship as equals.

Even though this can essentially only be inferred here, fragmentary yet striking evidence for *to what extent* the manumitted were or could be kindred is revealed by the consequences of killing them: its expiation through the distribution of the *weregild* (blood money) to the aggrieved kin or (holy) protective lord shows how relatedness and patronage interacted in individual cases. This should absolutely bear further examination.[33]

In sum, alongside his *ingenuitas*, the *libertas* of the manumitted also appears to be a parentally based form of consciousness and means of action within the framework of the local legal life of the freeborn.

3. Sources attest, if only sparsely, that manumissions took place in direct connection with child baptism.[34] Why does this interest us here? It was self-evident for every Christian person to be given a name and to be baptized not as a mature adult but as an immature child; that is, to be spiritually born after the corporeal birth. That said, the shift from

adult to child baptism, however clearly reflected in the written record of dogma and church law, is barely perceptible as a ritual practice. The only clue for child baptism rituals is clerical disputes over delays and competence.[35] It is, however, well documented that the baptism of the child required the participation of adults, chosen by either the child's serf lord (*Leibherr*) or biological parents, in the baptismal ritual, who raised the immature and as yet incapable of confession but now baptized child out of the font following the credo and the Lord's Prayer. They were thereby considered, supplementing the biological, as the child's spiritual parents—the godparents—and thus as ritually created near-kin (*patrini—compater/commater*). In the future, they would be responsible for the child's spiritual well-being.[36] What little we know about control over baptism practice yields only fragmentary evidence of the purpose of this godparentage—the guidance of belief. More important here are the effects of godparent choice on confidential close relationships that also fell under prohibitions to marry kin.[37]

Thus, questions about the influence of baptism on the parental relations of those who were bound in serfdom were urgent. Were unfree baptized "differently" from those who were free? Was namegiving connected with birth or with baptism? Did baptized slaves have their "own" godparents chosen by their parents, or did their *dominus* alone advocate for their spiritual existence? What degree of flexibility did they have in the baptism of newborns?

For the manumitted, unfortunately, evidence is similarly lacking, and therefore so is scholarship. Thus, answers can only be inferred when asking what happened with respect to their spiritual kinship in the wake of a change of lordship to the care of the church. Those in the guardian roles mentioned in the manumission charters took the place, as explained above, of their own lord's control of the Christian life of the slave: but who were these and how was this accomplished? The holy heavenly patron, the distant abbot, or the local priest who served them—who became the *patrinus* (godfather)? And who determined the choice of godparent? This concerns not only manumitted adults but also their children. Which spiritual kinship relations could be "initiated" with their baptisms? For the newly free, to have or obtain spiritual kin offered another opportunity of additional local integration in the local milieu of the freeborn.

In sum, the new ecclesiastically protected *libertas* opened up three possibilities that it offered to the manumitted allowing them to use their new social position for making kin. They could function and feel secure as the saint's people within the social frame of the patronate. They could both integrate themselves as equally empowered (and equally subject) in *secular* legal practice (such as participating in the court as jurors) and create new ties in *ecclesiastical* social life (as a brother/sister within the parish). From their perspective, their new social status thus offered two new ways of using their *libertas* in kinship—the patronal and the pastoral.[38]

Matrimomium—Marriage

What the corpus of formularies of manumission charters lacks, as already noted, are determinations of weddings and marriage: neither requirements nor prohibitions are found. Such sexual companionship, dedicated to both procreation and work for survival, did not inherently belong to the act of manumission.[39] Accordingly, a link between a wedding and the manumission of a male slave and a female slave *as* a pair is also missing. And yet, asking about the meaning of manumission for wedding and marriage is justified for two reasons.

That female slaves were manumitted with their children indicates the effects of sexual relations that took place *before* manumission.[40] This is also evinced by manumissions of slave groups whose cognatic relatedness shines through their densely interwoven names. Even if only perceptible in the background, relatedness founded in servile marriage—not only in their lord's will to manumit—could be a motive for manumission.

Second, and more important, is the perspective of *future* sexual ties. What conditions determining wedding behavior and marital relations do manumitted men and women come across in their milieu? How can they refer to the situation there as newly free? How can they make use of it?

Understanding the complexity of the situation requires a few words on the state of scholarship, which is anything but clear or unanimous. We are concerned here with "marriage" forms: with monogamy, marriage consensus, marital lineage relations, and connubiality internal and external to lordship (*Herrschaft*). In general, despite all efforts, there is disagreement over what counts as "legitimate marriage" (*matrimonia legitima*) among and between those under lordly domination, whether freeborn (*ingenui, coloni*), unfree (*servi/ancillae, mancipia*), or manumitted (*cartularii, censualis, lidi, epistularii*, etc.). How were they socially arranged, administered, conducted, ended, and renewed after widowing?

The descriptions of legitimate but above all reprehensible sexual relations (along with their sanctioning) found, in all their casuistic richness, in Germanic legal codes, penitential books, ecclesiastical and royal regulations, and charters and formulary records give us no clear picture, even when they, as recently noted, refer equally to men and women.[41]

In this way, the marriage forms long assumed by positivist legal history, above all so-called *Friedelehe* (sexual relations with others besides the legitimate wife), are fully deconstructed. But we are also no longer so sure of the universal success of the ecclesiastical campaign for monogamy: it is seldom clear which form of relation is subsumed under the standard formula of traditional records and registers, men named individually "with wife and child": formless *conjunctio, contubernium* decreed or tolerated by the lord, *matrimonium* arranged by the authorized close male kin of the bride and groom, or *conjugium* determined through a bilateral agreement. One must thus be more careful and assume a practice of wedding and marriage of dependents that is formally less rigid regarding the influence of the church on incest prohibitions, the form and location of the wedding ritual, and remarriage after widowing as well.

The meaning of the lordly rights regarding the wedding and marriage of members of the *familia* is also controversial: decree, permission, concession, accordance, agreement—what are the forms of lordly consent?[42] We know too little about their influence through negotiation, gifts, and license "prices"/costs. The emergence of wedding fees (*Heiratszins*) for manumitted in the ninth century indicates the difficulty of regulating local marital affairs. This commutation to a cash fee, likely due to the lord's absence, for his "participation" in the wedding had a future: it would spread not only among the free peasantry (*censuarii*) but also later as a head tax to symbolize a new *servitus*, serfdom.[43]

There is also no scholarly consensus on the relationship between husband and wife. Were the *coniugati* primarily a labor-sharing "pair"?[44] In what sense and with what consequences were they, and thereby also their consanguines, considered kin? Or did a husband govern "his" dependents even when he was unfree (*servus*) and his wife manumitted (*epistolaria*) or even freeborn (*ingenua*)?

The least clear of all are the forms and consequences of connubium between people of different birth status and their place within and among ecclesiastical and lay constellations of lordship that were often interlaced. However, frequent and detailed normative documents emerged in the sixth to eighth centuries that handled disreputable sexual relations of the freeborn and slaves, and in fact there was no marriage taboo between them. The practical implications of the numerous written "updates" on incestuous suspicions, transgressions, and sanctions thereof are unclear. Written norms probably only provided a general framework for various decisions from case to case. The means were lacking to control and punish them, even if these norms were taken literally.

The registers of estates that recorded not only landed property but also people who had to pay dues or do services make it possible to "observe" the marriage behavior of the manumitted indirectly. Every now and then, they included freeborn *coloni* who had an *ancilla* or *epistularia* as *uxor*, as well as descendants. *Cartularii* and *lidi* were connected with their kind or with *ancillae*. Likewise, *servi* led a farmstead (*mansus*) together with *ingenuae*. This rapprochement and even mixing of status groups through marriages between categories such as free and unfree was indeed common in many places. And it could lead to conflict in the courts over what one "was," genealogically, by birth—more free or more unfree? And to what *conditio* did the children belong? Customary designations say one or the other. Manumission, one can infer, helped to improve one's position on the marriage circuit of the domain.

But such socially ambiguous relations in which manumitted could quickly establish themselves are by no means ubiquitous. In many places the servile and ingenuile groups lived sharply separated from each other, and the manumitted who lived "only" under the protection of the lords and lacked farmsteads were accounted for differently. And yet, one still can perceive the socially leveling effect of manumission.

Altogether, one gets the impression that connubium among slaves, free, and manumitted played into the hands of lords' and their local agents' aim of keeping the balance between the sexes (and the labor stability based upon it) and local revenues simultaneously reliable and flexible. Whether it fit into theological ideas of marriage and ecclesiastical sexual morality was scarcely relevant. The freeborn could use these open constellations to establish and expand lateral kinship through marriage. Connubium within relations of domination (*Herrschaft*) fostered marriage behavior, including that of the manumitted.

Finally, inmarriage and outmarriage between neighboring domains belong here as well. The evident frequency of such ceaselessly denounced practices leads one to infer how precarious the endogamous potential for expansion of a domain, a group of domains, or a manor was in comparison with the actual sex ratio. Rigid marriage prohibitions or decrees were of little use here. What remained to lords in the face of the evasions found by members of their *familia*, including the manumitted, was taxation as a concession to the marriage—the marriage payment (*Heiratszins*)—and an endless struggle over whom the children (as a labor pool) "belonged" to. The kinship implications of such "mixed" marriages—"intradomain" and "interdomain" alike—could only foster or inhibit neighboring domains through licenses or fees.

In sum, forms of marriage, lordly license, the position of the husband, gender relations, and connubium without a doubt contributed to the modeling of becoming and being kin among dependents in the domain milieu, despite lords' attempts at control. And the manumitted, in using the strategic advantage of their freeborn status for the purpose of marriage, played their part.

Labor—Labor and Inheritance

Finally, the standard documented concession of movable property (*peculium*), the conduct of life allowed through autonomous work (*labor*), and their intergenerational disposal (*hereditas*) can also be understood as stimuli for the structuring and elaboration of kin ties and protections, even when, as in the case of death or at the beginning of a new household cycle, they included fees for inheritance or loans.[45] Or put differently, a *present* livelihood was opened up for the manumitted and his dependents, in connection with those of equal status nearby. On the other hand, the chance was given for a *future* continuity beyond his own death through the bequest of property to a descendant regardless of his or her parental position.

However—and in both respects—it was not just *mobile* property in play. It was certainly a precondition for the manumitted to have access to arable land, including the attached use rights (to pasture, forest, bodies of water, roads). These rights would, on the one hand, make him into both a freeborn "peasant" among his equals *and* the possessor of a *mansus* within the domain, while on the other hand, it would anchor him as "resident obliged" (*mansuarius*) on the grounds of the *villa* and bind him to unceasing service within the framework of the domain. While such agricultural work made the manumitted economically "freer" than his movable property alone, it also bound him into a clearly different relationship of domination (*Herrschaftsverhältnis*) based in land and soil (*domaniales Seniorat*).

That this took place and *how* it did are captured once again in the registers of property and income from the time. Even if only fragmentarily, various stages or constellations are recognizable. Here are some clues. The relationships in the eighteen domains of the abbey of Saint Remi (*Reims*) in the mid-ninth century are clearest: in more than half of them the *cartularii* or *epistolarii* proportion of farmstead proprietors varied from 7 to 38 percent. According to their service and rent obligations, they were much closer to that of the freeborn than to that of the unfree. In the register of the Paris abbey of Saint-Germain-des-Prés (ca. 830), multiple *lidi* with a status-specific rent (*lindimonium*) are mentioned, which also follow the farmsteads of the *ingenui*. Equally sporadic are the *mansi lediles* in the registers of the abbeys of Prüm, Lobbes, Werden, and Fulda (all ninth century). The rents and services typical of these characterize them as enterprises that go back to the freeborn status of their prior possessor, again in contrast with the slave farmstead.

All of this indicates that in many cases the manumitted succeeded in establishing themselves alongside the freeborn as near equals within the domain *familia* and—in clear distinction from the slaves and their farmsteads—in claiming this status in the long term. How many farmsteads are "hidden" among the thousands in these registers that may have been held by manumitted or their heirs, not indicated as such because they did not fit into the descriptive schema or because their status as manumitted had entirely faded away and they (like other status groups) were only categorized as "people" (*homines*) or as the *familia* of a lord?

Moreover, one must distinguish between the ways that these manumitted came to hold land, without which they would have only been able to realize the status and property conceded to them in a very limited way. Two practices were possible. One was for the lord or his local agent to allocate land, either a settlement on fallow or uncleared terrain (collocation) or an abandoned farmstead. The other was marriage into a farmstead, within or outside the domain, as a male head of household or as wife of an heir.

In both cases, the manumitted was fully localized within the framework of the domain and became joint proprietor of a work-"residence" (*manens*) that secured his subsistence. From this base beyond the conjugal residence group ("household family"), integration into cooperation with other freeborn *familia* of the lord could best succeed.[46] This meant cooperation with his equals—his *socii* or *commarcani*—in the use of communal forests, pastures, roads, and bodies of water. Further, he had to adjust to the local opportunities, to adapt his plot of land to the ratio of those who worked to those who ate, which changed with the household cycle, and that necessitated the purchase, barter, or borrowing of extra land. Every residence group had to strive to anchor itself as an ally (*socius*)—to connect itself most advantageously through marriage, alliance, godparenthood, and the absorption of (younger) singles from other farmsteads into their own through local rotation of farmhands. Whether acquired through birth, marriage, baptism, or inheritance, every personal detail could function as a wildcard. Even the agrarian *Frondes* on lordly lands—who arranged services such as transportation, protection, and repairs—contributed to the consolidation and distinction of relationships among familiars of a domain. What did it mean, for example, for a *litus* (a dependent with restricted status) to occasionally have to load manure from the domain farm and transport it to the fields, when the arduous work of spreading it over the fields was left to the slave?

To all of this, as is well documented, belonged the partitioning of farmsteads and their lands according to household cycles and inheritance strategies in households of parents and their descendants. What the manumitted could benefit from here was, as mentioned above, their freely disposable movable property. One could call this a "dowry" with which they "entered into" the local business of survival and which, when possible, they used in a parentalizing (kin-making) way: he who possesses his holdings (rent) free is good for close relationships—as a neighbor, friend, or even relative (or all of these at once). Finally, is not the attestation in the formula of the *proximi* as possible heirs in the case of the manumitted dying childless implicit evidence of their parentalizing activity? The consequence was that work, beginning with one's own movable property and on the basis of autonomous household management, including agricultural equipment, "forced" domain-oriented relatedness *beyond* descent, one's status in legal life, and the lineage community.

Conclusion

The Profile of Manumissions within a Periodized Context

In the course of this investigation, the impression may have arisen that manumissions in the post-Roman West constituted a significant portion of the restructuring of kinship relations in general. In the lordly descriptions of local social associations (*familiae*) that have been transmitted, manumitted tend to be absent, and even where present they constitute a minority alongside unfree and free persons. Nevertheless, the use of formularies into the tenth century indicates a constant need to carry out manumissions in a recorded form through the tenth and eleventh centuries.

Both social processes brought up earlier were probably more important. On the one hand was the often-violent binding of autonomous freeborn peasants into domination that consisted mostly of rents and services and was accompanied, with very diverse limitations, by their self-organization through neighbors and kin. On the other was the (large or small and chronologically highly varied) gradual transformation of (house) slaves, born or otherwise attained into members of the lordly *familia*, who farmed on their own and were subject to corvee. This transformation proceeded through settlement, farm and land allocation, tolerance of or support for relations between the sexes, and other custodial concessions. Both processes are known under the name of *seigneurialization*, which was proposed by Marc Bloch (1941) and remains plausible in its broad contours.[47]

What did manumissions contribute to this framework? Many aristocrats, spurred by benevolent morality and their aspirations for salvation, contributed to the decimation of domestic slavery between the sixth and eleventh centuries through their manumissions. (One could also speak of de-servilization.[48]) These also served as a building block in the epochal process of a far-reaching ecclesiasticization, both through the expansion of the ecclesiastical administration of salvation (through parishes) and the control of belief and morality (through church law) and through countless transfers of "land and persons" to ecclesiastical institutions. The *patronage* of wards expanded this material, personal, and symbolic permeation with the help of a new instrument that, compared with other forms of domination at the time, offered the wards advantageous opportunities for action and in exchange only asked for minimal rent contributions in a way that unified heavenly and secular life, was socially flexible, and was oriented toward the central location with the holy altar. In this framework, a free-related ancestry anda new form of existence open to the future were simultaneously initiated. The manumitted entered close relationships that they could use to make kin for themselves and their dependents (*villa*),-internal or -external marriage among the free, earning a living, assigning their property and its inheritance a new legal quality (e.g., as *mansus ledilis*), agricultural neighborly cooperation, participation in legal life (oaths), and networking through godparenthood. All of these fostered their integration, their status-specific socio-synthesis on location. In this way they could constitute a considerable social group within the domain milieu as "the saint's people"—those under his special protection and with particular ties to him.

The manumitted dissolved into the melting pot of the domain or associations of seigneurial subjects (the *familia*) that reconstituted themselves over the very long term into locally anchored village communities.[49] Or they preserved their mobile "landless" point of origin, where they were increasingly joined by freeborn who gave their land and themselves up to patronal protection—the so-called *censuarii*.[50] In this way, "their" history passes over into another—that of high medieval serfdom (*servage*).[51]

Change of Lordship and Kinship

Manumissions and their written records from the post-Roman centuries indeed have much to offer regarding this book's basic question of how self-evidently, consciously, deliberately, programmatically—or how casually, implicitly, unarticulatedly, and "repressedly"—kinship was dealt with and accordingly written about, and what active or passive role it played in the elaboration of power relations.[52]

According to everything that could be exposed here from multiple angles, manumissions served at that time as a veritable escape valve for social transformation. Or, to represent it visually, they constituted a passageway between two forms and spaces of domination. Their documentary inscription makes it possible to raise the curtain in front of the oral ritual of this passage, a passage tantamount to an elementary social metamorphosis. How can it be grasped conceptually?

The act of transformation from a state of comprehensive and undivided serfdom (*servitus*) to freedom (*ingenuitas/libertas*) concerns the manumitted in two senses—as a change of his basic relationship from the *dominus* to the *patronus* and as a change of his milieu of domination from the manor (*curtis*) to the shrine (*altare*). This change is therefore dissolution and reconstruction alike. With it, the powerlessness of the slave (*servus/ancilla*) is converted into the capacity for action of the man (*homo*) dependent on an ecclesiastical lord. It opens up a flexible course of life for him, from which it is possible to trace which parental relations can be generated.

What obtains after the moment of manumission? If I see it correctly, then this state can be distinguished as follows. Being manumitted "begins" with the status enhancement pertaining to birth, which makes him "socially capable" among the freeborn. However, this took place within the framework of a new, loosened, and distant form of domination whose language of relations and style of domination was shaped by close kin. In this framework, the manumitted could organize his own survival together with his dependents and also implement his personality as a legal associate. Temporally and structurally secondary consequences could be added to these, including the elaboration of social integration through marital affiliation, acquiring new relatives through baptism, and taking over a farmstead.

One can, finally, capture these processes more narrowly from the perspective of the newly free: the "leap" from their origin of servile (non) relatedness determined by the domain into patronal-domination-created-space for the structuring and elaboration of kinship ties for the manumitted through birth, marriage, inheritance, and baptism. Along with these ties came opportunities reflecting the ecclesiastical climate of lordship, landholding, protection of peace, and pastoral life. Perhaps it does not go too far to speak of a special position of the manumitted, however limited, within the unstable conglomerate of *manorial kinship*.

Early Medieval Manumissions as Politics of Parentalization?

If one follows the approach of the inquiry presented here, then the kinship dynamics of manumissions belong to the local exertion of power.

And given their quantity and distribution, then, this relationship certainly counts among the "problems of the time."

An explicit concept of comprehensive parentalization based on freeborn status cannot be proven. That said, the combination of "recourse" to freeborn status and transformation into a relaxed form of domination is absolutely "systemic." This weakened the Germanic legal principle of freeborn status by fostering overlapping patronage, jurisdictional mediation, and attempts to regulate connubium, and perhaps also through a pastoral expansion of marriage restrictions. We cannot rule out seeing this as a deliberate attempt by churches to expand their patronal power through a "symbolism" of relatedness.

The fact that the whole vocabulary of kinship of the manumitted is missing indicates how indirectly this took place. The manumitted is called neither *ingenuus* nor *liber* but *libertus*. This designation obscures more than it reveals. Other classifications—*censuarius, lidus, mundilio*— also lack a sense of relatedness. But manumission can absolutely be seen as *one* pattern *among others* of the extension of power. Macropolitically, it is a significant variation on the gigantic aristocratic exchange of real goods (including slaves) for holy goods offered by churchmen (nominally not related through marriage) from their hegemonial position—a basic process of the primitive accumulation of the feudal regime.

Manumission, aside from its initial impetus, was *in the end* about incremental displacements—gradual, unarticulated developments. One can certainly recognize that movements or their precursors in the lower social orders—again aside from manumission from the height of lordship—are not to be understood in the absence of the ideological and institutional frameworks that, whether through direct mediation or filtering, regulated the action of the manumitted in the milieu of the domain. The yearly offering of rent to the patron's altar shows this alone just as much as the emerging taxes upon marriage and inheritance. But at the same time, they indicate the limitation of power from above.

Ludolf Kuchenbuch is professor emeritus of premodern history at the Fern Universität in Hagen since 2004. He has published widely on discourses on European feudalism, medieval work, peasantry and seignorial administration, anthropology of literacy/orality/text, and waste. His last book examines the use of silver currency in the early medieval period. He was a coeditor of *Historische Anthropology, CAMPUS Historische Studien,* and *Historische Semantik*. He was a visiting professor at the Collège de France (Paris).

Notes

Heartfelt thanks for encouragement and for listening go to David Kuchenbuch, Ylva Eriksson-Kuchenbuch, Simon Teuscher, Marcel Müllerburg, Michaela Hohkamp, and Stefan Esders. English renderings of authors quoted are the responsibility of the translator.

1. This chapter concerns at least three forms of kin-making: birth, baptism, and marriage. In German, *Parentalization* is an overarching term that encompasses all three forms. In English, this is not a natural use: "parental" is too suggestive of "parent." One potential translation, "kinning," has other misleading connotations. We have chosen to borrow the German term here, even where it does not refer to the English "parent."
2. Most recently Karl Ubl, "Zur Einführung: Verwandtschaft als Ressource sozialer Integration im frühen Mittelalter," in *Verwandtschaft, Name und soziale Ordnung (300–1000)*, ed. S. Patzold and K. Ubl (Berlin: De Gruyter, 2014), 14–18.
3. For an exploration of this, see Ludolf Kuchenbuch, "'...mit Weib und Kind und...': Die Familien der Mediävistik zwischen den Verheirateten und ihren Verwandten in Alteuropa," in *Die Familie in der Gesellschaft des Mittelalters*, ed. K.-H. Spieß (Ostfildern: Thorbecke, 2009), 345–76. The time is ripe for a comprehensive inquiry into *servile* and *domainal* kinship.
4. Anton Doll, ed., *Traditiones Wizenburgenses: Die Urkunden des Klosters Weißenburg 601–864* (Darmstadt: Selbstverlag der Hessischen Historischen Kommission, 1979), 267–68.
5. Here, the assumption that the abbot preserved the documents as evidence against potential entitled heirs of the manumitter is reasonable. We know from other cases that the manumitted also received a copy of the document. No copies survive.
6. Relationship between patron and client.
7. Silver coins of about one and a half grams, the currency unit at the time.
8. Egon Flaig, *Weltgeschichte der Sklaverei* (Munich: Beck, 2009), 20–22, in critical engagement with Patterson, *Slavery and Social Death*, and Meillassoux, *Anthropology of Slavery*.
9. My focus on compiling a register of the components and aspects of manumission that is as comprehensive as possible offers a clearly structured basis for detailed considerations on the parentalization thesis. In this way it is methodologically orthogonal to the genuine task of studying each manumission as a singular case, or in other words it is upstream of the latter.
10. For a comprehensive treatment with regional differentiation and attention to legal practice, see Alice Rio, *Slavery after Rome, 500–1100* (Cambridge: Cambridge University Press, 2017), 75–131. For excellent sources with greater regional depth, see Clausdieter Schott, "Freigelassene und Minderfreie in den alemannischen Rechtsquellen," in *Beiträge zum frühalemannischen Recht*, ed. H. Schott (Freiburg: Konkordia, 1978); Carl L. Hammer, *A Large-Scale Slave Society: Slaves and Their Families in Early Medieval Bavaria* (Aldershot: Ashgate, 2002), 57–62; Gabriele von Olberg, "Freigelassene," in *Reallexikon der Germanischen Altertumskunde* (RGA) 9, ed. H. Jankuhn and H. Beck (Berlin: de Gruyter, 1995); for a foundational study on development out of the ecclesiasticization of late-Roman patronage, see Stefan Esders, *Die Formierung der Zensualität: Zur kirchlichen Transformation des spätrömischen Patronatswesens im früheren Mittelalter* (Ostfildern: Thorbecke, 2010); on the history of the body, see Ludolf Kuchenbuch, "Vom *caput* zum *corpus*: Basisthesen und hominologische Hypothesen zur *servitus* im mittelalterlichen Millennium," in *Pars pro toto: Historische Miniaturen zum 75. Geburtstag von Heide Wunder*, ed. A. Jendorff and A. Pühringer (Neustadt a.d. Aisch: Ph. C. W. Schmidt, 2014); for a very useful spatial and diachronic comparison after the thirteenth century,

see Tore Iversen, *Knechtschaft im mitteralterlichen Norwegen* (Ebelsbach: Aktiv Druck, 2004).
11. Elisabeth Herrmann-Otto, *Sklaverei und Freilassung in der griechisch-römischen Welt* (Hildesheim: Olms, 2009), 125–77, esp. 169–72.
12. P. Freedman and M. Bourin, eds., *Forms of Servitude in Northern and Central Europe: Decline, Resistance, and Wexpansion* (Turnhout: Brepols, 2005).
13. Michael Borgolte, "Freigelassene im Dienst der Memoria: Kulttradition und Kultwandel im Übergang von der Antike zum Mittelalter," *Frühmittelalterliche Studien*, no. 17 (1983); Ingrid Heidrich, "Freilassungen als Sicherung des Totengedächtnisses im frühen Mittelalter," in *Nomen et Fraternitas: Festschrift für Dieter Geuenich zum 65. Geburtstag*, ed. U. Ludwig and T. Schilp (Berlin: de Gruyter, 2008); for a recent in-depth study see Rio, *Slavery after Rome*.
14. One should keep in mind for all cases that post-Roman slavery/unfreedom was not made and kept visible (such as through tonsure, bodily signs, chains). See Kuchenbuch, "Vom *caput* zum *corpus*," 16–17.
15. Testaments, land and rent books, reports of wonders, hagiographies, provisions of ecclesiastical law, royal edicts, and systematic collections of both secular and ecclesiastical infractions along with their punishments.
16. For further cases, see the excellent regional studies by Schott, "Freigelassene und Minderfreie"; Hammer, *Large-Scale Slave Society*; Guy Halsall, *Settlement and Social Organization: The Merovingian Region of Metz* (Cambridge: Cambridge University Press, 1995).
17. Rio, *Slavery after Rome*, 11–13.
18. Rio, *Slavery after Rome*, 12, in reference to Mann, *Sources of Social Power*, 1:18.
19. Alice Rio uncovers the promiscuous character of slavery (as distinct social field) by breaking it down to the practical meaning of evocative cases. On this basis, she then compares and generalizes by region and period.
20. Ubl, "Verwandtschaft als Ressource," 18–19. Important supplementation and differentiation in Bernhard Jussen, "Verwandtschaftliche Ordnungen," in *Enzyklopädie des Mittelalters*, ed. G. Melville and M. Staub (Darmstadt: Wissenschaftliche Buchgesellschaft, 2008). My own skeptical reflections are in Kuchenbuch, "Familien der Mediävistik," 345–76.
21. Gerhard Lubich, *Verwandtsein: Lesarten einer politisch-sozialen Beziehung im Frühmittelalter (6.–11. Jahrhundert)* (Köln: Böhlau, 2008); Karl Ubl, *Inzestverbot und Gesetzgebung: Die Konstruktion eines Verbrechens (300–1100)* (Berlin: De Gruyter, 2008).
22. *Consanguinitas, parentela, proximitas, cognatio, affinitas*. On this, see the impressive Anita Guerreau-Jalabert, "Kinship Structures," in *Encyclopedia of the Middle Ages*, ed. A. Vauchez (Cambridge: Clarke, 1997); Lubich, *Verwandtsein*, and the epoch-spanning Michael Mitterauer, *Historische Verwandtschaftsforschung* (Vienna: Böhlau, 2013), 27–85.
23. Local studies of such local constellations (*Gemengelagen*) are plentiful but too seldom compared and synthesized into regional profiles. For the eighth and ninth centuries, see Jean-Pierre Devroey, *Puissants et misérables: Système social et monde paysan dans l'Europe des Francs (VIe–IXe siècles)* (Brussels: Académie Royale de Belgique, 2006). On the tenth century, see Ludolf Kuchenbuch, "Abschied von der Grundherrschaft: Ein Prüfgang durch das ostfränkisch-deutsche Reich 950–1050." *Zeitschrift d. Savigny Stiftung f. Rechtsgeschichte. Germanist. Abt.*, no. 121 (2004); Thomas Kohl, *Lokale Gesellschaften:Formen der Gemeinschaft in Bayern vom 8. bis zum 10. Jahrhundert* (Ostfildern: Thorbecke, 2010).
24. The best, richly detailed overview is Devroey, *Puissants et misérables*. The exemplary analysis of household structures in the domains of the lordship of Saint-Germain-des-Prés abbey by David Herlihy, *Medieval Households* (Cambridge, MA: Harvard University Press, 1985), 56–77, is still indispensable. For the secular and ecclesiastical legal witnesses of the marital relations of the free and unfree in the early Middle

Ages, see Ines Weber, *Ein Gesetz für Männer und Frauen: Die frühmittelalterliche Ehe zwischen Religion, Gesellschaft und Kultur* (Ostfildern: Thorbecke, 2008). On patronage, see Esders, *Formierung der Zensualität*.

25. On *homo*-ization of "personae," see Kuchenbuch, "Vom *caput* zum *corpus*," 5–12.
26. For a historical overview, see Andreas Gestrich, "Eltern," in *Enzyklopädie der Neuzeit* 3, ed. F. Jaeger (Darmstadt: WBG, 2006).
27. Michael Mitterauer, "Mittelalter," in *Geschichte der Familie*, ed. A. Gestrich, J.-U. Krause, and M. Mitterauer (Stuttgart: Kröner, 2003), 209–11.
28. One case for clarification: in an 886 conveyance document by the abbot of Prüm (Eifel), two individually named rent-obligated groups, who belonged to two neighboring domains, were transferred. Among the total of thirty-four bipartite names, seven elements are repeated from one to eight times: *atalsuint, otbrat, ... sigibrat, ... folebrat et uothilbrat, meginbrat et uuinibrath, engildrut, helmdrut, regindrut*, etc. See Ludolf Kuchenbuch, ed. *Grundherrschaft im früheren Mittelalter* (Idstein: Schulz-Kirchner, 1991), 163–67.
29. For a foundational treatment of this topic, see Monique Bourin and Patrice Chareille, eds. *Serfs et dépendants au Moyen Âge (VIIIe–XIIe)* (*Genèse médiévale de l'anthroponymie moderne*, vol. V-1) (Tours: Presse Universitaire *François*-Rabelais, 2002).
30. Men with (their) children do not appear. On the clearly closer bond of children to their mothers, see Ludolf Kuchenbuch, "Opus feminile: Das Geschlechterverhältnis im Spiegel von Frauenarbeiten im früheren Mittelalter," in *Reflexive Mediävistik. Textus—Opus—Feudalismus* (Frankfurt a. M.: Campus, 2012).
31. On this matter with respect to the Middle Rhein region, see Ludolf Kuchenbuch, *Bäuerliche Gesellschaft und Klosterherrschaft im 9. Jahrhundert. Studien zur Sozialstruktur der Familia der Abtei Prüm* (Wiesbaden: Steiner, 1978), 260–68; for a recent and almost exhaustive treatment, see Esders, *Formierung der Zensualität*, 37–61.
32. There is not the space to go into detail here. Much is covered in Weber, *Gesetz für Männer und Frauen*; Schott, "Freigelassene und Minderfreie"; and Hammer, *Large-Scale Slave Society*.
33. Esders, *Formierung der Zensualität*, 58; Stefan Esders, "Wergeld und soziale Netzwerke im Frankenreich," in *Verwandtschaft, Name und soziale Ordnung (300–1000)*, ed. S. Patzold and K. Ubl (Berlin: De Gruyter, 2014).
34. Heidrich, "Freilassungen," 229.
35. Edward J. Yarnold, "Taufe III," in *Theologische Realenzyklopädie* 32, ed. G. Müller (Berlin: De Gruyter, 2001); Arnold Angenendt, "Der Taufritus im frühen Mittelalter," in *Segni e riti nella chiesa altomedievale occidentale* (Spoleto: Centro, 1987).
36. On the emergence and dissemination of godparenthood, see the pathbreaking Joseph H. Lynch, *Godparents and Kinship in Early Medieval Europe* (Princeton, NJ: Princeton University Press, 1986); the indispensable historical-anthropological analysis by Anita Guerreau-Jalabert, "*Spiritus* et *caritas*: Le baptême dans la société médiévale," in *La parenté spirituelle*, ed. F. Héritier-Auge and E. Copet-Rougier (Paris: Édition des archives contemporaines, 1996); for a typology of kinship, see Mitterauer, *Historische Verwandtschaftsforschung*; for new categorization and weighting, see Jussen, "Verwandtschaftliche Ordnungen."
37. Scattered details in the first visitation handbook of the time: Winfried Hartmann, ed., *Das Sendhandbuch des Regino von Prüm* (Darmstadt: Wissenschaftliche Buchgesellschaft, 2004). Godparenthood is not even mentioned in the sixty baptismal tracts on correct liturgical instruction of priests from Carolingian times, which have been meticulously edited and studied by Susan Keefe and compiled in *Water and the Word: Baptism and the Education of the Clergy in the Carolingian Empire* (Notre Dame, IN: Notre Dame University Press, 2002), because the book deals exclusively with adult baptism.
38. Because, as suggested above, manumitted were compelled to pay a prayer and wax rent at the annual commemorative ceremony for their manumitter (memorial service),

the question arises over evidence of group-specific conduct of the manumitted upon the death, burial, funeral, and annual commemoration. The answer: in the ecclesiastical control of parish clergy, death rites (*ordo defunctorum*) and the behavior of the parishioners absolutely had their place; however, *who* exactly within the parish community (*parrochiani, ignobile vulgus,* or *populus et fratres*) was included remains obscure. On this, see the regional study by Nikolaus Kyll, *Tod, Grab, Begräbnisplatz, Totenfeier: Zur Geschichte ihres Brauchtums im Trierer Lande und in Luxemburg unter besonderer Berücksichtigung des Visitationshand-buches des Regino von Prüm (+915)* (Bonn: Rohrscheid, 1972).

39. The classic position on the (successful) valorization and implementation of monogamy in the early Middle Ages is Pierre Toubert, *L'Europe dans sa première Croissance: De Charlemagne à l'an mil* (Paris: Fayard, 2004), 249–356. One cannot do without the excellent recent collection of materials (secular and ecclesiastical legal evidence) and exegesis on the marriage of free and unfree from the perspective of their negotiated occurrence (marriage) by Weber, *Gesetz für Männer und Frauen*. On the marriage of slaves, see al Rio, *Slavery*, 218–44. Also useful are the rich pages on slave marriages in Hammer, *Large-Scale Slave Society*, 26–34. Skeptical arguments upon which the following is based are found in Kuchenbuch, "Familien der Mediävistik," 357–65.
40. In many accounts of people and their traditions from the time, slaves (*ancillae*) also appear along with their children.
41. This is the thesis of Weber, *Gesetz für Männer und Frauen*.
42. Scholarly consensus holds that *ius primae noctis* is a trope of the rhetoric of lordship.
43. Esders, *Formierung der Zensualität*.
44. Kuchenbuch, "Opus feminile."
45. The most differentiated overview is Devroey, *Puissants et misérables*, 377–441. In addition, see Kuchenbuch, "Bauern"; Ludolf Kuchenbuch and Joseph Morsel, "Ländliche Räume," in *Enzyklopädie des Mittelalters*, ed. G. Melville and M. Staub (Darmstadt: Wissenschaftliche Buchgesellschaft, 2008).
46. Mitterauer, *Familie*, writes—in this sense—of the household family as opposed to the kinship family: an insightful categorization! For a period-specific refinement and critical distance to the reach of his historical conceptualization of the family in the Middle Ages, it could be more appropriate to speak here of a "matrimonial residence."
47. Ludolf Kuchenbuch, "'Seigneurialisation'—Marc Blochs Lehre im Lichte heutiger Forschung und Diskussion," in *Marc Bloch aujourd'hui: Histoire comparée & Sciences sociales*, ed.H. Atsma and A. Burgière (Paris: Éditions de l'École des Hautes Études en Sciences Sociales, 1990).The current definitive accounts are Chris Wickham, *Framing the Early Middle Ages, Europe and the Mediterranean, 400–800* (Oxford: Oxford University Press, 2006), 519–88; and Devroey, *Puissants et misérables*, 265–351.
48. Kuchenbuch, "Vom *caput* zum *corpus*," 10–12.
49. Joseph Morsel, ed., *Communautés d'habitants au Moyen Âge (XIe–XVe siècles)* (Paris: Éditions de la Sorbonne, 2018); Joseph Morsel, "Die Ausbildung der Einwohnerschaften im Mittelalter: Die Verräumlichung des Sozialen als Grundmerkmal der historischen Entwicklung im Mittelalter." *Historische Anthropologie*, no. 17 (2009): 202–21.
50. Esders, *Formierung der Zensualität*, 73–83.
51. Ludolf Kuchenbuch, "*Servitus* im mittelalterlichen Okzident—Formen und Trends (7.–13. Jahrhundert)," in *Penser la Paysannerie Médiévale, un Défi impossible? Recueil d'études offert à Jean-Pierre Devroey*, ed. A. Dierkens, N. Schroeder, and A. Wilkin (Paris: Publ. Sorbonne, 2017).
52. Ubl, *Inzestverbot und Gesetzgebung*.

Bibliography

Angenendt, Arnold. "Der Taufritus im frühen Mittelalter." In *Segni e riti nella chiesa altomedievale occidentale*, 275–336. Settimane di studio sull'altro medievo 33, no. 1. Spoleto:Centro, 1987.

Borgolte, Michael. "Freigelassene im Dienst der Memoria: Kulttradition und Kultwandel im Übergang von der Antike zum Mittelalter." *Frühmittelalterliche Studien*, no. 17 (1983): 234–50.

Bourin, Monique, and Patrice Chareille, eds. *Serfs et dépendants au Moyen Âge (VIIIe–XIIe) (Genèse médiévale de l'anthroponymie moderne*, vol. V-1). Tours: Presse Universitaire François-Rabelais, 1992.

Devroey, Jean-Pierre. *Puissants et misérables: Système social et monde paysan dans l'Europe des Francs (VIe-IXe siècles)*. Brussels: Académie Royale de Belgique, 2006.

Doll, Anton, ed. *Traditiones Wizenburgenses: Die Urkunden des Klosters Weißenburg 601–864*. Darmstadt: Selbstverlag der Hessischen Historischen Kommission, 1979.

Esders, Stefan. *Die Formierung der Zensualität: Zur kirchlichen Transformation des spätrömischen Patronatswesens im früheren Mittelalter*. Ostfildern: Thorbecke, 2010.

———. "Wergeld und soziale Netzwerke im Frankenreich." In *Verwandtschaft, Name und soziale Ordnung (300–1000)*, edited by S. Patzold and K. Ubl, 141–60. Berlin: De Gruyter, 2014.

Flaig, Egon. *Weltgeschichte der Sklaverei*. Munich: Beck, 2009.

Freedman, P., and M. Bourin, eds. *Forms of Servitude in Northern and Central Europe: Decline, Resistance, and Wexpansion*. Turnhout: Brepols, 2005.

Gestrich, Andreas. "Eltern." In *Enzyklopädie der Neuzeit* 3, edited by F. Jaeger, 222–30. Darmstadt: WBG, 2006.

Guerreau-Jalabert, Anita. "*Spiritus* et *caritas*: Le baptême dans la société médiévale." In *La parenté spirituelle*, edited by F. Héritier-Auge and E. Copet-Rougier, 133–203. Paris: Édition des archives contemporaines, 1996.

———. "Kinship Structures." In *Encyclopedia of the Middle Ages*, edited by A. Vauchez, 1:804–5, Cambridge: Clarke, 1997.

Halsall, Guy. *Settlement and Social Organization: The Merovingian Region of Metz*. Cambridge: Cambridge University Press, 1995.

Hammer, Carl L. *A Large-Scale Slave Society: Slaves and Their Families in Early Medieval Bavaria*. Aldershot: Ashgate, 2002.

Hartmann, Winfried,ed. *Das Sendhandbuch des Regino von Prüm*. Darmstadt: Wissenschaftliche Buchgesellschaft, 2004.

Heidrich, Ingrid. "Freilassungen als Sicherung des Totengedächtnisses im frühen Mittelalter." In *Nomen et Fraternitas: Festschrift für Dieter Geuenich zum 65. Geburtstag*, edited by U. Ludwig and T. Schilp, 221–33. Berlin: De Gruyter, 2008.

Herlihy, David. *Medieval Households*. Cambridge, MA: Harvard University Press, 1985.

Herrmann-Otto, Elisabeth. *Sklaverei und Freilassung in der griechisch-römischen Welt*. Hildesheim: Olms, 2009.

Iversen, Tore. *Knechtschaft im mittelalterlichen Norwegen*. Ebelsbach: Aktiv Druck, 2004.
Jussen, Bernhard. "Verwandtschaftliche Ordnungen." In *Enzyklopädie des Mittelalters*, edited by G. Melville and M. Staub,1:163–71. Darmstadt: Wissenschaftliche Buchgesellschaft, 2008.
Keefe, Susan A. *Water and the Word: Baptism and the Education of the Clergy in the Carolingian Empire*, 2 vols. Notre Dame, IN: Notre Dame University Press, 2002.
Kohl, Thomas. *Lokale Gesellschaften: Formen der Gemeinschaft in Bayern vom 8. bis zum 10. Jahrhundert*. Ostfildern: Thorbecke, 2010.
Kuchenbuch, Ludolf. *Bäuerliche Gesellschaft und Klosterherrschaft im 9. Jahrhundert: Studien zur Sozialstruktur der Familia der Abtei Prüm*. Wiesbaden: Steiner, 1978.
———. "'Seigneurialisation' — Marc Blochs Lehre im Lichte heutiger Forschung und Diskussion." In *Marc Bloch aujourd'hui: Histoire comparée & Sciences sociales*, edited by H. Atsma and A. Burgière, 349–61. Paris: Éditions de l'École des Hautes Études en Sciences Sociales, 1990.
———, ed. *Grundherrschaft im früheren Mittelalter*. Idstein: Schulz-Kirchner, 1991.
———. "Abschied von der Grundherrschaft: Ein Prüfgang durch das ostfränkisch-deutsche Reich 950–1050." *Zeitschrift d. Savigny Stiftung f. Rechtsgeschichte. Germanist. Abt.*, no. 121(2004): 1–99.
———. "'…mit Weib und Kind…': Die Familien der Mediävistik zwischen den Verheirateten und ihren Verwandten in Alteuropa." In *Die Familie in der Gesellschaft des Mittelalters*, edited by K.-H. Spieß, 325–76. Ostfildern: Thorbecke, 2009.
———. "Opus feminile: Das Geschlechterverhältnis im Spiegel von Frauenarbeiten im früheren Mittelalter." In *Reflexive Mediävistik: Textus — Opus — Feudalismus*, 279–315. Frankfurt a. M.: Campus, 2012.
———. "Vom *caput* zum *corpus*. Basisthesen und hominologische Hypothesen zur *servitus* im mittelalterlichen Millennium." In *Pars pro toto. Historische Miniaturen zum 75. Geburtstag von Heide Wunder*, edited by A. Jendorff and A. Pühringer, 3–25. Neustadt a.d. Aisch: Ph. C. W. Schmidt, 2014.
———. "*Servitus* im mittelalterlichen Okzident — Formen und Trends (7.–13. Jahrhundert)." In *Penser la Paysannerie Médiévale, un Défi impossible? Recueil d'études offert à Jean-Pierre Devroey*, edited by A. Dierkens, N. Schroeder, and A. Wilkin, 235–74. Paris: Publ. Sorbonne, 2017.
Kuchenbuch, Ludolf, and Joseph Morsel. "Ländliche Räume." In *Enzyklopädie des Mittelalters*, edited by G. Melville and M. Staub, 2:249–56. Darmstadt: Wissenschaftliche Buchgesellschaft, 2008.
Kyll, Nikolaus. *Tod, Grab, Begräbnisplatz, Totenfeier: Zur Geschichte ihres Brauchtums im Trierer Lande und in Luxemburg unter besonderer Berücksichtigung des Visitationshand-buches des Regino von Prüm (+915)*. Bonn: Rohrscheid, 1972.
Lubich, Gerhard. *Verwandtsein: Lesarten einer politisch-sozialen Beziehung im Frühmittelalter (6.–11. Jahrhundert)*. Cologne: Böhlau, 2008.
Lynch, Joseph H. *Godparents and Kinship in Early Medieval Europe*. Princeton, NJ: Princeton University Press, 1986.
Mitterauer, Michael. "Mittelalter." In *Geschichte der Familie*, edited by A. Gestrich, J.-U. Krause, and M. Mitterauer, 160–363. Stuttgart: Kröner, 2003.
———. *Historische Verwandtschaftsforschung*. Vienna: Böhlau, 2013.

Morsel, Joseph, ed. *Communautés d'habitants au Moyen Âge (XIe–XVe siècles)*. Paris: Éditions de la Sorbonne, 2018.

———. "Die Ausbildung der Einwohnerschaften im Mittelalter: Die Verräumlichung des Sozialen als Grundmerkmal der historischen Entwicklung im Mittelalter." *Historische Anthropologie*, no. 17 (2009): 202–21.

v. Olberg, Gabriele. "Freigelassene." In *Reallexikon der Germanischen Altertumskunde* (RGA) 9, edited by H. Jankuhn and H. Beck, 537–42. Berlin: De Gruyter, 1995.

Rio, Alice. *Slavery after Rome, 500–1100*. Cambridge: Cambridge University Press, 2017.

Schott, Clausdieter. "Freigelassene und Minderfreie in den alemannischen Rechtsquellen." In *Beiträge zum frühalemannischen Recht*, edited by H. Schott, 51–72. Freiburg: Konkordia, 1978.

Toubert, Pierre. *L'Europe dans sa première Croissance: De Charlemagne à l'an mil*. Paris: Fayard, 2004.

Ubl, Karl. *Inzestverbot und Gesetzgebung: Die Konstruktion eines Verbrechens (300–1100)*. Berlin: De Gruyter, 2008.

———. "Zur Einführung: Verwandtschaft als Ressource sozialer Integration im frühen Mittelalter." In *Verwandtschaft, Name und soziale Ordnung (300–1000)*, edited by S. Patzold and K. Ubl, 1–28. Berlin: De Gruyter, 2014.

Weber, Ines. *Ein Gesetz für Männer und Frauen: Die frühmittelalterliche Ehe zwischen Religion, Gesellschaft und Kultur*. 2 vols. Ostfildern: Thorbecke, 2008.

Wickham, Chris. *Framing the Early Middle Ages: Europe and the Mediterranean, 400–800*. Oxford: Oxford University Press, 2006.

Yarnold, Edward J. "Taufe III." In *Theologische Realenzyklopädie 32*, edited by G. Müller, 681–94. Berlin: De Gruyter, 2001.

Chapter 12

From Natural Difference to Equal Value
The Case of Egg Donation in Norway

Marit Melhuus

In 2017, the Norwegian Ministry of Health and Care issued an evaluation of the Norwegian Biotechnology Act.[1] One of the contested issues it addressed was permitting egg donation, which Norway has prohibited since passing its first law regulating assisted conception in 1987.[2] Until 2020, Norway was one of the few countries in Europe (along with Italy, Germany, Austria, and Switzerland) that did not permit egg donation. With a shift in the coalition government, the opposition gained a majority that supported significant changes in the Biotechnology Act, including a provision to permit egg donation.[3]

Although prominent voices have argued through the years for permitting egg donation in Norway, they had not previously won sufficient support to sway the vote in Parliament. This situation has markedly changed. Among other things, this is connected to a discursive shift regarding the properties of egg and sperm. Whereas in the past the dominant discourse regarding egg and sperm donation was grounded in a differential treatment of sperm and eggs attributed to a natural difference between men and women, this position has been challenged over the last few years based on egalitarian principles of sameness and equality. One thought-provoking argument here is that male and female sex cells have the same "ethical value."

This argument about the equality of gametes was first made in 2003 in connection with the revision of the Biotechnology Act[4] and reiterated in 2011 by the Norwegian Biotechnology Advisory Board in a statement on egg donation to the Ministry of Health and Care.[5] This document pointed out that in connection with the earlier revision (in 2003) of the Biotechnology Act, a majority of the parliamentary hearings had expressed the ideas that male and female sex cells should be granted the same ethical value, that the prohibition against egg donation was biased and discriminated between infertile men and infertile women, and that it was difficult to see a morally relevant difference between sperm and egg donation.[6] This statement is, in my view, perhaps the most telling example of a discursive shift: it displaces arguments based on the difference between men and women with arguments based on some notion of equality between sperm and eggs and between men and women. I will return to this later.

Summarizing the statement, the majority of the Biotechnology Advisory Board declared:

> They wish that men and women, and sperm and egg cells, should be treated as similarly as possible in the law. ... The majority does not find it any more problematic that egg donation introduces a distinction between genetic and biological/social mother than that the use of sperm donation already has established between biological and social father. The majority, therefore, does not find that there are good enough reasons to maintain the prohibition on egg donation.[7]

This declaration represented a significant move toward a change in the regulation of egg donation in Norway. It did so by explicitly repeating an equality argument—between men and women as well as between sperm and eggs—while simultaneously addressing counterarguments against egg donation. Importantly, the Biotechnology Advisory Board reaffirmed this position in 2015 in an evaluation of chapter 2 of the Biotechnology Act, which concerns egg donation.[8] Nevertheless, it is worth noting that although the majority (nine of fifteen members) supported a move to allow egg donation, a minority wished to uphold the existing regulation that forbade it. In the following, I trace this shift in the public legal discourse, paying particular attention to the progressive displacement of reproductive horizons for men and women. I do so with an eye to the significance of exposing the political underpinnings implied in the very acts of legally shaping and enabling and thus making kinship. Moreover, I do so with the fundamental recognition that gender and kinship are mutually imbricated.[9]

The politics in this case have to do with legal regulations and the various policy deliberations that undergird them. What is fundamentally at stake here are notions of maternity, paternity, and filiation (kinship), on the one hand, and equal opportunity for infertile men and women (gender), on the other. With kinship and gender placed squarely within the realm of politics, the question turns on how these categories are inscribed in the very acts that inform public legal considerations. The eventual results of such deliberations are animated by broader social processes and practices, to which they, in turn, contribute.[10]

Legislating Kinship and Gender

My overall focus, then, is on the state and its legal regulations. More specifically, I am interested in legislative (broadly understood) processes as state practices and also in the values mobilized to underpin a particular legal provision—such as egg donation. Such mobilizations may be attempts to stabilize kinship and/or gender or (on the contrary) efforts to effect significant changes. The state is implicated through its policies in both configuring and reconfiguring kinship and gender relations. As the basic materials of gender—sperm and eggs—are simultaneously seen as vital essences of kinship, it can be difficult to keep gender and kinship separate—it depends on what you wish to keep in view—so one might ask how the reconfiguration of kinship implies a reconfiguration of gender and vice versa. Moreover, the foundations on which such configurations are made will necessarily vary over time, so a historical dimension is necessary to capture the shifts that occur. While keeping in mind the gendered character of kinship, I examine state-produced and authorized acts of kinship and the grounds upon which such authorizations are based.[11]

In focusing on how the state authorizes kinship (and by implication gender), I also recognize that such authorizations will necessarily vary cross-culturally, not only around the world but also within Europe. Moreover, and significantly, this position implies that so-called Western or Euro-American kinship must also be addressed in its diversity—and even more, in its historicity—and hence not assumed to be already known or of a certain kind. Thus, it is important to keep in mind the differences between various North American and European state regulations and norms. Such differences have significant historical legacies, which the historical chapters in this volume ably demonstrate.[12] In other words, we must avoid a certain reductionism regarding kinship and direct our endeavors at documenting complexities and changes—in Euro-America as well as around the globe—as is exemplified in various chapters of this book (Alber, Thelen, Zitelmann).[13] Hence, I follow Edwards's argument, concerning "diblings," that we must interrogate the peculiarities of Euro-American kinship and thus broaden European kinship's ethnographic record regarding understandings, practices, and performances.[14] Such interrogations should include comparative investigations into the processes of the political character of kinship-making through legal regulations, such as documenting variations in the United States and Europe in how they have incorporated reproductive technologies.[15] My earlier work exploring legislative processes concerning assisted conception in Norway serves as a backdrop for my present discussion of the discursive shift regarding egg donation and this discourse's particular emphasis on equality.[16]

As I have suggested, one obvious site where such state-authorized acts of kinship can be localized is precisely in laws or legislative processes, especially in those laws that (directly or indirectly) concern acts of procreation and birth—for example, regulations that concern marriage, birth certificates, naming, inheritance, and establishing paternity and maternity. These issues are regulated through different legislative and bureaucratic practices that impinge on each other but are not all of one piece. (For an example from Africa, see the chapter by Alber in this volume.) Nonetheless, they should ideally cohere, and kinship is thus regulated by various acts that in different ways identify persons and relations. The one that concerns me at the moment is the Biotechnology Act. Among other things, this act regulates who will have access to assisted conception, what forms of assistance are permitted, and which technologies are appropriate.[17] It is directly engaged with vital matters and instrumental in producing persons and relationships. Although not framed explicitly in terms of kinship, the act itself—and many of the practices it regulates—can be viewed as making kinship by authorizing the means through which people can procreate and be related. This is especially the case with regulations on assisted conception. What draws my attention here is the way in which these acts of kinship are gendered and how particular notions of gender surface and are intentionally mobilized either to maintain or to potentially shift the very ground upon which assisted conception has been based.

Distinctions

Returning to the summary statement on egg donation issued by the Biotechnology Advisory Board, I will now quote the minority:

> The minority maintains that to introduce a distinction between genetic and biological/social mother is more problematic than the already-established distinction between biological and social father. They claim that it is not correct to juxtapose sperm and egg donation because egg donation is technologically more demanding and invasive than is sperm donation. Egg donation objectifies [both] reproduction and the children more than sperm donation does. If

egg donation is permitted and it becomes common to move egg cells from one woman to another, this will lower the barrier for surrogacy. The minority holds that technological development alone cannot decide what reproductive technologies are to be permitted in Norway. They insist that there are so many ethical problems surrounding egg donation ... that it should not be permitted as a medical procedure to overcome infertility in Norway.[18]

This quote articulates some of the main issues, often framed as ethical, that recur in the debate in Norway about egg donation (see also below). Most significantly, it turns on the question of who is considered the mother, since egg donation represents a fragmentation of motherhood. The minority also points to the fact that egg donation is a more invasive procedure than sperm donation as it requires both hormone treatment and a surgical extraction of the egg and is viewed potentially burdensome for the women donating the eggs. Bringing up "objectification" (although the question is not spelled out) suggests that the very use of advanced technology is inherently objectifying. Moreover, it may also refer to the potential commodification of eggs and the commercialization of reproduction, which is intensified by the practice of surrogacy. This is a situation that both Norwegian legislators and the public in general want to avoid at all costs. This is partially prevented by assisted reproduction being part of the public healthcare system (although over the years many women and couples have traveled abroad for egg donations and paid for the treatment themselves). Moreover, the minority claims that the very possibility of moving eggs between women is a step toward permitting surrogacy, a contested practice that is prohibited in Norway.

What is interesting about the two main positions contained in the statement issued by the Biotechnology Advisory Board is that they quite succinctly sum up the historical trajectory of egg and sperm donation in Norway, albeit without providing any historical context. In fact, the persistence of certain arguments is striking, as they can be traced back to the 1980s. Both positions address the issue of technological development, reproducing the tension between optimists who view reproductive technologies as potentially liberating and those with a firm conviction that it is the duty of legislators to control the technologies and not let the technologies set the pace, so to speak. As mentioned, the minority also addresses the degree of technological invasiveness and the objectification of reproduction, concerns not so prevalent among the majority. Both positions, albeit with different perspectives, address the problem of the identity of the "donor child." Most significantly, however, they also both address the issue of differences between maternity and paternity and of social and biological/genetic relatedness in procreation and reproduction.

As is evident in the two quotes, both the majority and the minority of the advisory board emphasize precisely this aspect: the distinction between the genetic and biological/social mother and the genetic and social father. And it is this distinction that captures the different treatment of sperm and eggs, which has to do with how these substances, as detachable parts of the body, are perceived as related to the whole from which they emanate.[19]

Let me briefly present the arguments against egg donation. I here condense a set of arguments that have been reiterated over time in public documents, legal debates, and media.[20] These have often been framed in conjunction with sperm donation and turn on the difference between men and women's reproductive functions, differences that are articulated locally in terms of nature (*natur*) and, not least, in terms of what is perceived as natural (*naturlig*). Whereas sperm donation is considered an extension of natural reproduction, egg donation is seen as radical interference. The point that sperm is accessible outside the body (and hence more easily exchangeable) is often made, underscoring that this form of detachment implies, ipso facto, paternal uncertainty and a potential discrepancy between biological and legal/social paternity. Thus, sperm donation has been viewed as not very different from what occurs naturally. However, eggs are situated differently. Their availability is limited in terms of quantity and access, as well as time. They are seen as intrinsic to a natural whole of which they are a part. This is framed in terms of a unified process from conception, through gestation and birth, which was (and still is by some) seen as invoking the notion of inviolable "unified motherhood" (*enhetlig morskap*). Egg donation is said to upset natural procreation because the uterus and egg constitute a natural unity. Introducing a foreign (*fremmed*) egg would not only destroy this unity but also undermine the most fundamental emotion—the feeling of "mother belonging" (*morstilhørighet*). Hence, in splitting this unity, egg donation would also cause insecurity about who was the real mother and thereby threaten the identity of the child.

The legal status of egg donation was determined by two moves. First, egg donation was implicitly forbidden (in 1987 and 1994), as the law stipulated that fertilized eggs had to be returned to the woman from whom the egg cells were taken. It was explicitly banned in 2003 with the addition of §2-18, "Prohibition against Egg Donation and Transplantation of Gamete-Producing Organs."[21] Moreover, as a consequence of reproductive technologies, Norway had amended the Children's Act in 1997 to define the mother as the one who gives birth. (Until then, it had been deemed unnecessary to have a legal definition of *mother* as its meaning was considered obvious). Hence, eggs are inalienable and birth is privileged, upholding the notion of a unitary motherhood by underscoring both biological and genetic relatedness.[22]

In 2003, Norway repealed its anonymity clause with regard to sperm donation and required the use of a known donor. The decision was based on a child's right to know its biogenetic origin, which was seen as fundamental to its identity. A donor register was established to ensure that the identity of the biological father was recorded with the state and made available to the child on demand from the age of eighteen. Through donor disclosure, sperm is not only made to identify the "real" father but also reattached to its source and restored to its "proper" (biological) relation. From the perspective of the state, this is a matter of getting the facts right and of distinguishing between the biogenetic and the social/legal father. However, for the child this knowledge is conditional, as the parents are not obliged to reveal the facts of conception.[23] In my understanding, this repeal of the anonymity clause is fundamental because it is a statement about the significance attributed to genetics in establishing filiation and identity.

I read this to mean that in Norway, a child can de facto have two fathers (legal/social and genetic) but never more than one mother. For maternity, however, the distinction between social/legal and biological/genetic is not made relevant. In effect, eggs and sperm have been subjects of inegalitarian practices. These practices rest on established notions of maternity and paternity, reflecting a point of Marilyn Strathern's about the different kinds of proof needed to establish the fact of procreation in what she terms pre-technology Europe: motherhood was established through birth; fatherhood through presumed coitus with the mother.[24] With the advent of new technologies, such as assisted conception and DNA testing, as well as specific legal changes (see below), the issue of "proof" took a different turn.

From Difference to Sameness

I have claimed that this shift in the public legal discourse articulates a displacement of the reproductive horizons of men and women. This displacement converges on a renegotiation of the cultural value placed on eggs and sperm. Earlier, the differential treatment of eggs and sperm (in law) had followed (naturally) from the differences between men's and women's reproductive bodies and hence from the difference ascribed to motherhood and fatherhood. Present efforts have been directed at creating some form of equality. However, this is not an easy argument to make.

The Biotechnology Advisory Board states that equal treatment (*likebehandling*) of infertile men and women has been an important premise for their consideration of egg donation. While recognizing the importance of granting equal opportunity to men and women in this matter, it simultaneously acknowledges that there are significant differences between sperm and egg cells and between women's and men's reproductive roles that cannot be disregarded.[25] Thus, the question is how to reconcile equal opportunity with what are considered significant differences—that is, how to fit sperm and egg cells, men and women, and the distinction between biological and social/legal parenthood into the same frame.[26]

This conundrum is precisely what Kristin Spilker and Merete Lie address in an article concerning the question of gender equality in the context of assisted reproduction in Norway.[27] More specifically, they focus on egg donation and ask (drawing on feminist discussions of gender) what is to be equalized here—women and men or eggs and sperm.[28] They suggest that the debate on egg donation in Norway "contains an implicit 'sex war' combined with an explicit emphasis on equal opportunities."[29] Basing their discussion on the debates in Parliament in 2003, Spilker and Lie make an interesting observation about what kinds of claims can be made for equality. Drawing on Marianne Gullestad's argument that Norwegians are obsessed with a quest for equality understood as sameness, they suggest that in Norway it is easier to justify a claim based on social inequality (equal opportunity) than it is to justify a claim based on a natural difference (such as between men and women).[30] However, in the case of assisted conception these two dimensions of the debates on gender come together because claims for both equal opportunity and reproductive difference are raised. As these authors note, the Labor Party sustains an equality argument (not recognizing the difference between sperm and egg donation for infertile men and women by insisting on equal treatment in the law and not favoring those who can pay for their treatment abroad).[31] The conservative Høyre (Norwegian for "right") Party insists that not everything can be equal—nor should it be. This party rejected egg donation (at that time) on the grounds of biological difference. (This difference, according to Spilker and Lie, was that women gave birth and there should be no doubt about biological motherhood.) The Christian Democrats (then part of a conservative coalition government) also represented a significant voice in these debates and framed their objections in terms of human dignity and the danger of creating a "sorting society" or confusion about motherhood.[32]

Spilker and Lie's argument is that the Labor Party transferred a principle of equal opportunity from the area of social policy to the area of reproductive policy by conjoining a gender equality argument with one tied to economic means. In other words, issues of economic opportunity (concerning, e.g., who had the means to travel abroad and pay for treatment) were conjoined with questions of gender equality. As they point out, however, the conservative coalition emphasized the ultimate difference between men and women and also made a clear distinction between reproductive policy and other policy fields. These authors ask whether the debate on egg donation represents the limits for negotiating gender equality, as arguments based on equal opportunity collapse when the debate shifts to issues of reproductive policy. Hence, the debate about sperm and egg donation oscillates between the possibility of equalizing sperm and eggs and that of equalizing men and women. Spilker and Lie's concluding point is that the argument based on gender equality is valid within a general political debate (about equal opportunity, for example) but its validity is contested in the context of egg donation as that articulates a biological difference between men and women's reproductive roles that cannot be subsumed into a claim for equal opportunity.[33]

Spilker and Lie do not address the argument that sperm and eggs should be granted the same ethical value. Moreover, it is noteworthy that this claim is not elaborated in the Biotechnology Advisory Board's statement, even though other arguments are framed in ethical terms. For example, the board points out that

> egg donation has a positive *ethical* aspect that sperm donation lacks: with sperm donation the social father has no genetic or biological connection to the child, only a social one. With the use of egg donation, the social [sic] mother will not be the child's genetic mother, but will have a biological relation to the child through pregnancy. ... Therefore, one could claim that in the case of a child conceived by egg donation, mother and father would be more equal in their relation to the child than is the case for families that make use of sperm donation.[34]

Moreover, the board claimed in 2011 that from a gender equality perspective egg donation would potentially offset the biological differences between men's and women's reproductive ages since women's fertility declines after the age of thirty-five and can end by around forty-five.[35]

In trying to work around the issue of biological differences, the board concluded that it did not see "modern biotechnology's role as one that should aim to equalize all differences that are grounded in such fundamental biological differences."[36] It is in this context that the advisory board makes its statement concerning the equal ethical value of male and female sex cells. However, it does not spell out what exactly that ethical value is explicitly, so this must be inferred. My interpretation is that the claim of equal ethical value refers to the genetic properties of eggs and sperm. As material substances, eggs and sperm share a fundamental characteristic: they are both necessary for and contribute equally to the formation of a child. It is this shared property that they grant the same ethical value. In other words, sperm and egg cells' equivalent genetic contribution to the human embryo should be recognized. They have the same constitutive role in creating persons and identities and hence also kinship relations. As of yet, this same constitutive property has not translated into an equal treatment of sperm and eggs.

Whereas in earlier debates, sperm and eggs were configured as different by nature, they are now being reconfigured as equal in one essential natural/factual aspect. Each contributes equally to the creation of the embryo and (presumably) this implies that they have the same ethical value. This argument's force comes from placing motherhood and fatherhood on the same level, so to speak. Thus, a child may have two mothers—one genetic and one social/legal (who is also presumed to gestate the child)—and this is considered no different from a child having both a genetic and a social/legal father.

By not differentiating between sperm and eggs based on natural differences between men and women, the board's statement opens a space for a similar classification of the ethical value of sperm and eggs, which I understand to be based on their equal genetic contribution to procreation. Hence, although sperm and egg cells are still understood as biologically different (due to the difference between men's and women's reproductive bodies), this difference is superseded by an overarching (and perhaps more significant) value of ethical sameness.[37]

Insofar as one can make a convincing argument regarding the same or shared properties of sperm and egg cells, it should be possible to position biological and reproductive arguments within the same frame as social inequality and gender discrimination. Moreover, it is not as if the genetic element with regard to motherhood has not been recognized. The fact that some have seen the introduction of a donated ("foreign") egg as implying the introduction of an unknown mother suggests the salience of the egg cells in constituting a child's identity and hence admits to the unique contribution of the egg cells. And finally, recognizing the genetic relation between a woman and a child does not undermine a legal definition of mother as the one who gives birth; it only makes explicitly visible the distinction between biological, genetic, and social/legal motherhood, thus upsetting a notion of unified motherhood. However, an explicit recognition of the genetic relationship between mother and child has potential ramifications for claims to motherhood in cases such as surrogacy, where the intending social/legal mother contributes her own egg but does not bear the child.[38]

Gender and Kinship Intertwined

I have framed my argument in terms of the state and of state-produced or state-authorized acts of kinship while always insisting on the mutual implication of kinship and gender. I have explored some of the specifics of this entanglement in the case of egg donation in Norway. Since it is difficult to keep kinship and gender separate, I asked how a reconfiguration of kinship implies a reconfiguration of gender and vice versa. In the case of egg donation, this is difficult to determine: as we have seen, gender equality arguments have been mobilized to both support and oppose its legalization (that men and women should have equal access to infertility treatments, for example). Although egg donation will (at a certain level) affect the perception of kinship relations, I am not sure whether it will meaningfully transform gender relations. Those who claim the significance of gender difference in reproductive policies will continue to do so. Those who see egg donation as a viable way to motherhood and parenthood will avail themselves of the option—elsewhere, if necessary. Up to now, eggs have been the discursive glue of a unitary motherhood. Their reconfiguration has demanded a different discursive formation, one based on equality and, hence, a refusal of discrimination. The recent amendments to the Biotechnology Act and the enactment of the new legislation indicate that values of equality and nondiscrimination override ones grounded in ideas of a natural difference between men and women. Nevertheless, it is apparent that those regulations pertaining to gender and those pertaining to acts of procreation do not necessarily work in tandem.

I turn now to one recent twist in the configuration of gender and kinship and the authorization of kinship/gender acts through legislation. The example moves beyond the discursive shift with regard to eggs and sperm and perhaps only indirectly addresses the question of sameness and difference. Rather, it turns on the mutual entanglement of gender and kinship. Adding a layered complexity, the example illustrates how difficult it can be to tease these apart. The nexus of this example is the gendered body.

In 2016, the Norwegian government passed a law regarding legal gender recognition and specifically changing one's legal gender.[39] This law represents a significant step for persons who do not identify with what the law refers to as their "bodily gender." It grants any person over the age of sixteen the right to declare their own legal gender by simply filling out a form; no medical or other evidence is required. Moreover, it follows that such a declaration may be revoked.

This law affected the Biotechnology Act, and the amendments suggested in response are worth noting. First, it was recommended that all gendered terms be replaced with gender-neutral terms such as *person*. For example: "Fertilized eggs cannot be inserted into the uterus of another *person* than the one from whom the egg cells originated."[40] More significant, in this context, is the paragraph (§2-1) about providing assisted conception to persons who have changed their legal gender. In these cases, the person's "birth gender"[41] is the basis for the authorization to initiate treatment. In other words, a person assigned female gender at birth who subsequently declared male legal gender would be offered the assisted conception procedures available to women. Moreover, persons who have changed their legal gender from male to female and who seek assisted conception would still be able to use their own sperm. It is the gendered body that determines whether treatment can be pursued.

In its comment to the proposed law on legal gender change and its impact on the Biotechnology Act, the Biotechnology Advisory Board observes:

> From nature, the human body is so constituted that it is women who can become pregnant and give birth. The law proposal ... challenges the traditional understanding of gender and pregnancy by introducing a distinction between bodily and legal gender. When neither orchiectomy nor sterilization is required in order to change legal gender, a person who is legally a man can become pregnant and give birth.[42]

It adds that "if the amendments [to the biotechnology law] are passed, it would then make it possible for men and women to use their own gender cells (the Norwegian word for "gamete," *kjønnscelle*, literally means "gender cells") to procreate children independent of their legal gender."[43]

This is not just an example of the efforts involved in harmonizing different laws by substituting gendered terms for gender-neutral ones. More significantly, this example addresses the question of whether a reconfiguration of gender implies a reconfiguration of kinship. By introducing a distinction between birth gender and legal gender, a legally male person with a body that was designated female at birth may become a mother (through giving birth) while legally being the child's father. Although this is a far cry from the situation Edith Clarke (1979) describes in her monograph *My Mother Who Fathered Me* (which is about Jamaican family systems), it does potentially give that title a different twist.[44] A law that addresses fundamental issues of gender discrimination, acknowledging the significance of gender plurality, potentially authorizes a simultaneous continuity and a radical shift in the kinds of proof needed to establish motherhood and fatherhood. The continuity rests in upholding the gendered "nature" of the body (as given by birth) when it comes to assisted conception and procreative practice. The radical shift is that mother and father are in a certain sense conflated. The distinction between mother and father is now articulated in one and the same person, albeit with different legal connotations: "mother" due to giving birth; "father" due to a change in legal gender.[45] Both "proofs" rest on one embodied relationship and have a definitive impact on the way persons are related and on perceived kinship relationships.

If the Biotechnology Act were to be amended in line with these proposed changes (that is to give "birth gender" precedence over legal gender with regard to procreation), kinship would be reconfigured as a consequence of the reconfiguration of gender. The mother/father distinction gains new meaning. Nevertheless, this very privileging of birth gender indicates the sway that biological criteria hold. At one and the same time, the proposed amendments to the law recognize reproductive differences between women and men while acknowledging that gender identity is self-determined. The current coalition government decided in 2018 that it will "continue the basic principle that [a person's] legal gender is to be the basis with regard to consideration of other laws ... also including regulations regarding assisted conception."[46] In other words, the government insists that it is a person's legal gender (and not that assigned at birth) that should form the basis for accessing assisted conception. This is in line with the act regulating legal gender change. However, the government also states that persons who are undergoing gender-confirming medical intervention may store sperm for later use in assisted conception.[47]

With the current legal situation, it remains an open question how privileging of legal gender over birth gender will reconfigure kinship. The government states that persons who declare their gender as male are male despite their female "birth gender." This then has implications for their rights regarding, for example, assisted conception or priority for a position allocated according to a gender quota (*kjønnskvotering*). Significantly, however, the act regulating legal gender change—while recognizing the primacy of legal gender regarding other laws and regulations—nevertheless makes an exception regarding the ascription of parenthood and parental responsibility. In cases where parental responsibility needs to be assigned, it is the person's "birth gender" that constitutes the premise for such ascription, in accordance with the Children's

Act. Thus, a person who has legally changed gender from female to male will, when giving birth, be granted the rights and obligations that follow from being a mother.[48] In other words, it is a person's birth gender that will determine that person's rights and obligations (such as pregnancy leave) as a parent. Hence, the rules that apply to a woman giving birth apply in the same way to a person giving birth after having changed legal gender (from female to male).

There is another interesting point to be made. This has to do with the assignment of the terms *mother* and *father*. The law itself does not regulate how parenthood is to be registered. Rather, there is a specification of which rules apply to establish parenthood in these cases. The provision does not prevent a legally registered man, who is designated a parent according to the regulations on motherhood in the Norwegian Children's Act, from calling himself "father." The same holds for a woman who has been designated a parent according to the rules of paternity, who may choose to call herself "mother." The National Population Register only records whether a person has children. It does so without employing the terms *mother* or *father*.[49] This policy, then, avoids the ascription of motherhood (or fatherhood), instead employing the terms parenthood, parent, or parental responsibility. Nevertheless, avoiding traditional terms (presumably in a spirit of gender equity) does not mirror the situation on the ground. Rather it circumvents it, leaving it to the parents' discretion to find suitable terms of address. It is too early to say how this will work out in practice. However, this terminological tangle is perhaps a sign of how gender can still reconfigure kinship. It is also an interesting contrast to the debates regarding egg donation, where it is precisely the category of mother that has been at stake. The act on legal gender change definitely complicates the procreative landscape.[50]

This last twist on the impact of law and legal regulations for kinship indicates the extent to which politics are profoundly embedded in the very making of kinship relations and the extent to which kinship is core to grasping the complexities of contemporary biopolitical processes.[51] Moreover, these cases draw attention to the kinds of distinctions that may be mobilized (legally, politically, and socially) to address the mutual entanglement of gender and kinship and the concomitant reproductive horizons of men and women. What seems evident, at least in Norway, is that when it comes to issues of procreation there is no way around the gendered body. Perhaps, the examples I have presented may also challenge us to recast the relation between gender, kinship, and notions of the body—and make us rethink the ways these are engrained in state policies.

Marit Melhuus is professor emerita in the Department of Social Anthropology, University of Olso. She has previously worked in Latin America and conducted long-term fieldwork in Argentina and Mexico addressing themes such as economy, peasantry, social change, morality, and gender. In recent years, she has been researching questions of kinship, biotechnology, and law in Norway and publishing widely on these interlinked themes, including the monograph *Problems of Conception: Issues of Law, Biotechnology, Individuals and Kinship* (2012). She is a member of the Norwegian Academy of Science and Letters.

Notes

This chapter is a somewhat revised version of an article titled "De la difference de nature à l'égalité de valuer: La question du don d'ovules en Norvège," previously published in "Le corps reproductif," special issue, *Ethnologie française* 37, no. 3 (2017). I want to thank Nicolas Adell, the current editor of *Ethnologie française*, for kindly authorizing the use of the English version of this article in the present volume. The revisions include an update on the legal situation in Norway since the article was initially written, indicating the ongoing character of legislative processes. The revisions are also a response to critical comments received from collaborators on this volume, for which I am grateful. I especially want to thank David Warren Sabean for his incisive and critical queries, not all of which I have been able to address adequately, as well as Simon Teuscher and Tatjana Thelen for their careful reading and helpful comments. I am grateful to Daniel Flaumenhaft for his astute language editing and suggestions regarding transgender issues. Finally, I wish to thank Erdmute Alber, David Warren Sabean, Simon Teuscher, and Tatjana Thelen for generously inviting me to participate in their project "Kinship and Politics: Rethinking a Conceptual Split and its Epistemic Implications in the Social Sciences," for warmly hosting me at the Center for Interdisciplinary Research in Bielefeld, and for the opportunity to contribute to this volume.

1. Helse- og omsorgsdepartementet, *Meld.St.39 (2016–2017), Evaluering av bioteknologiloven* (Oslo, 2017).
2. Lov 1987-06-12-68: Lov om kunstig befruktning [Artificial Procreation Act].
3. The amendments to the Biotechnology Act were proposed after this chapter was submitted for publication but before its final publication. See Lov-2020-06-17-98: Lov om endringer i bioteknologiloven. However, the fact that egg donation will now be permitted does not alter the thrust of my arguments.
4. See Bioteknologinemda, *Bioteknologinemdas uttalelse om eggdonasjon* (Oslo, 2011), 12. It is in this statement that the Biotechnology Council quotes an earlier parliamentary

document (Ot.prp.nr 64 [2002–3], 60–61) regarding the ethical sameness of sperm and eggs.
5. The English website gives the following description of the board: "The Norwegian Biotechnology Advisory Board is an independent body consisting of 15 members appointed by the Norwegian government. Each member has a background and/or education that makes him/her competent to discuss questions regarding modern biotechnology. The main task of the Norwegian Biotechnology Advisory Board is to evaluate the social and ethical consequences of modern biotechnology and to discuss usage which promotes sustainable development" (http://www.bioteknologiradet. no.english, accessed 2.12.2016). The members of the board are appointed individually on the basis of their professional expertise and do not necessarily reflect the political composition of Parliament. Hence the varying minority/majority constellations cannot be read directly onto the political landscape or along party lines. The Biotechnology Advisory Board deliberates on central issues regarding the use of biotechnologies, issuing statements and discussion papers as well as organizing public conferences. The board is actively present in the Norwegian *offentlighet* (public sphere). Often setting a public agenda, it represents an important sounding board for the various positions on contentious issues, such as egg donation.
6. Bioteknologinemda, *Uttalelse om eggdonasjon*, 12. All translations are mine unless otherwise indicated. Bioteknologinemda (Biotechnology Council) changed its name to Bioteknologirådet (Biotechnology Advisory Board) in 2014. I use the latter term throughout, except when reference is made to the former name.
7. Bioteknologinemda, *Uttalelse om eggdonasjon*, 1.
8. Bioteknologirådet, *Bioteknologirådets uttalelse om eggdonasjon. Evaluering av bioteknologiloven, kapittel 2* (Oslo, 2015).
9. Susan McKinnon and Fenella Cannel, "The Difference Kinship Makes," in *Vital Relations: Modernity and the Persistent Life of Kinship*, ed. Susan McKinnon and Fenella Cannel (Santa Fe: SAR Press, 2013); Janet Carsten, *After Kinship* (Cambridge: Cambridge University Press, 2004); Signe Howell and Marit Melhuus, "The Study of Kinship; The Study of Person: A Study of Gender?" in *Gendered Anthropology*, ed. Teresa de Valle (London: Routledge, 1993); Sylvia Yanagisako and Jane Collier, "Toward a Unified Analysis of Kinship and Gender," in *Gender and Kinship: Essays toward a Unified Analysis*, ed. Jane Collier and Sylvia Yanagisako (Stanford, CA: Stanford University Press, 1987); Gayle Rubin, "The Traffic in Women: Notes on the 'Political Economy' of Sex," in *Toward an Anthropology of Women*, ed. Rayna R. Reiter (New York: Monthly Review Press, 1975).
10. For the details of how this plays out in everyday life, see Marit Melhuus, "Ønske om et eget barn: Muligheter, forestillinger og forhandlinger," in *Reproduksjon, kjønn og likestilling i dagens Norge*, ed. Malin Noem Ravn, Guro Korsnes Kristensen and Siri Øystebø Sørensen (Bergen: Fagbokforlaget, 2016); Marit Melhuus, *Problems of Conception: Issues of Law, Biotechnology, Individuals and Kinship* (New York: Berghahn Books, 2012); Marit Melhuus, "Cyber-Stork Children and the Norwegian Biotechnology Act: Regulating Procreative Practice," in *From Transnational Relations to Transnational Laws*, ed Anne Hellum, Shaheen Sardar Ali and Anne Griffiths (Surrey: Ashgate, 2011).
11. Michael Lambek, "Kinship, Modernity and the Immodern," in *Vital Relations: Modernity and the Persistent Life of Kinhsip*, ed. Susan McKinnon and Fenella Cannel (Santa Fe: SAR Press, 2013).
12. See also Bob Simpson, "Scrambling Parenthood: English Kinship and the Prohibited Degrees of Affinity," *Anthropology Today* 22, no. 3 (2006); Enric Porqueres i Gené, *Individu, personne et parenté en Europe* (Paris: Éditions de la Maison des sciences de l'homme, 2015).

13. See also Susan McKinnon and Sydel Silverman, "Introduction," in *Complexities: Beyond Nature and Nurture*, ed. Susan McKinnon and Sydel Silverman (Chicago: University of Chicago Press, 2005).
14. Jeanette Edwards, "Donor Siblings: Participating in Each Other's Conception," *HAU Journal of Ethnographic Theory* 3, no. 2 (2013). "Dibling" is the term she uses to connote the emerging kin figure of "donor siblings," capturing the relationship between donor-conceived children who share the same donor. In an article from 2015, Edwards discusses the issue of donor disclosure and is concerned with what cannot be included in national legislation and policies, much in a similar vein to what Lambek (2013) denotes as the superfluity and excess of kinship. See Jeanette Edwards, "Donor Conception and (Dis)closure in the UK: Siblingship, Friendship and Kinship," *Sociologus: Journal for Social Anthropology* 65, no. 1 (2015); and Michael Lambek, "Kinship, Modernity," 255.
15. See for example Janet Dolgin, *Defining the Family. Law Technology and Reproduction in an Uneasy Age* (New York: New York University Press, 1997); Gay Becker, *The Elusive Embryo: How Women and Men Approach New Reproductive Technologies* (Berkeley: University of California Press, 2000); Charis Thompson, *Making Parents: The Ontological Choreography of Reproductive Technologies* (Cambridge, MA: MIT Press, 2005); also Marilyn Strathern, *After Nature: English Kinship in the Late Twentieth Century* (Cambridge: Cambridge University Press, 1992); Joan Bestard Camps, Gemma Orobitg Canal, Julia Ribot Bellabriga, and Carles Salazar Carrasco eds., *Parentesco y reproducción asistida: Cuerpo, persona y relaciones* (Barcelona: Estudios d'antropologia social y cultural, 2003); Enric Porqueres i Gené *Individu*; Enric Porqueres i Gené ed., *Défis contemproains de la parenté*, (Paris: Editions de l'École des Hautes Études en Sciences Sociales, 2009); Jeanette Edwards and Carles Salazar, ed., *European Kinship in the Age of Biotechnology* (New York: Berghahn Books, 2009), and Merete Lie and Nina Lykke, ed., *Assisted Reproduction across Borders: Feminist Perspectives on Normalizations, Disruptions and Transitions* (New York: Routledge, 2017). For a broader perspective, see Tatjana Thelen and Erdmute Alber, "Reconnecting State and Kinship: Temporalities, Scales, Classifications," in *Reconnecting State and Kinship*, ed. Tatjana Thelen and Erdmute Alber (Philadelphia: University of Pennsylvania Press, 2018).
16. Melhuus, *Problems*.
17. Lov 2003-12-05-100. For example, both preimplantation diagnosis (PGD) and prenatal diagnosis (PND) and research on embryos are regulated in the Biotechnology Act.
18. Bioteknologinemda, *Uttalelse om eggdonasjon*, 2. It is not coincidental that the question of surrogacy is raised in this connection. Although cross-border surrogacy is a practice that persons and couples increasingly make use of also in Norway, it is, nevertheless, a practice that is highly contested. See Marit Melhuus and Aslak Syse, "Gestational Surrogacy in Norway," in *Handbook of Gestational Surrogacy: International Clinical and Policy Issues*, ed. E. Scott Sills (Cambridge: Cambridge University Press, 2016).
19. Marit Melhuus, "Sperm, Eggs and Wombs: The Fabrication of Vital Matters through Legislative Acts," in *Anthropos and the Material: Anthropological Reflections on Emerging Political Formations*, ed. Penny Harvey, Christian Krohn-Hansen, and Knut Nustad (Durham, NC: Duke University Press, 2019).
20. Melhuus, *Problems*.
21. This is taken from an English version of the Act of 5 December 2003 No. 100 relating to the application of biotechnology in human medicine, etc. See Lov 2003-12-05-100: Lov om humanmedisinsk bruk av bioteknologi m.m. (bioteknologiloven) [Act Relating to the Application of Biotechnology in Medicine etc./Biotechnology Act], retrieved 12 September 2011 from www.ub.uio.no/ujur/ulovdata/lov-20031205-100-eng.pdf, 1515.
22. Marit Melhuus, "L'inviolabilité de la maternité: Pourquois le don d'ovocytes n'est-il-pas autorisé en Norvège?" in *Défis contemporains de la parenté*, ed. Enric Porqueres i Gené (Paris: Editions de l'École des Hautes Études en Sciences Sociales, 2009).

23. As mentioned in note 3, Parliament voted on amendments to the Biotechnology Act on 15 May 2018. One amendment approved by a majority vote obligates parents to tell children when they had been conceived with donor sperm. This amendment will be implemented by the current coalition government (Bioteknologirådet 28.01.2019: Regjeringsplattformen og bioteknologi, retrieved 11 February 2019 from http://www.bioteknologiradet.no/2019/01/regjeringsplattformen-og-bioteknologi/, 1415).
24. Marilyn Strathern, *Property, Substance and Effect: Anthropological Essays on Persons and Things* (London: Athlone Press, 1999), 78.
25. Bioteknologinemda, *Uttalelse om eggdonasjon*, 1. The way this is expressed in the document ties it to an understanding that a child's relation to its mother (through gestation and birth) is different from its relation to its father.
26. This situation reflects a recurrent tension, pointing to a gender paradox in European egalitarianism: a gender configuration based on a double discourse of ontological difference and equality (Christine M. Jacobsen, "The (In)egalitarian Dynamics of Gender Equality and Homotolerance in Contemprorary Norway," in *Egalitarianism in Scandinavia: Historical and Contemporary Perspectives*, ed. Synnøve Bendixsen, Mary Bente Bringslid, and Halvard Vike (New York: Palgrave Macmillan, 2018); Jorun Solheim, *Kjønn og Modernitet* (Oslo: Pax, 2007).
27. Kristin Spilker and Merete Lie, "Gender and Bioethics Intertwined: Egg Donation within the Context of Equal Opportunity," *European Journal of Women's Studies* 14, no. 4 (2007).
28. Spilker and Lie, "Gender and Bioethics," 328.
29. Spilker and Lie, "Gender and Bioethics," 329.
30. Marianne Gullestad, *The Art of Social Relations: Essays on Culture, Social Action and Everyday Life in Modern Norway* (Oslo: Scandinavian University Press, 1992). In Norwegian discourse, the term *likhet* conveys both equality (in the sense of being of equal value) and sameness (in the sense of being identical or culturally similar). These two meanings of the term are easily conflated. See Marianne E. Lien and Marit Melhuus, "La Norvège: Vues de l'intérieur," *Ethnologie française* 39, no. 2 (2009): 199. The point here is that men and women are seen as "naturally different," and the question is whether this also applies to sperm and eggs.
31. Norway grants infertility treatment (within certain limits) as part of the public health services.
32. "Sorting society" (my literal translation of the Norwegian term *sorteringssamfunn*) is a particular Norwegian term that has had much political salience in these debates. The term suggests selection, discrimination, and, more bluntly, eugenics. It refers to a society that allows selection of fetuses—that is, selective abortion (as, for example, following a prenatal diagnosis)—and/or selection among fertilized eggs for desired qualities (through preimplantation screening) and makes an ethical claim that Norway should avoid becoming a sorting society—that is, a society that allows for the potential elimination of undesirable embryos/fetuses or a sorting of individuals according to specific criteria. For a discussion of the notion of "sorting society," see Marit Melhuus, "Qui a peur de la 'societé de tri? Les biotechnologies, L'individu et l'État," *Ethnologie française* 39, no. 2 (2009); and Marit Melhuus, *Problems*, 89–108.
33. Spilker and Lie, "Gender and Bioethics," 337.
34. Bioteknologirådet, *Bioteknologirådets uttalelse om eggdonasjon*, 6, my emphasis. This claim is based on the assumption that the sperm used is the husband's/father's (and not donated). This observation is one that I made early on in my research, based on my conversation with the involuntary childless (see Marit Melhuus, "Procreative Imaginations: When Experts Disagree on the Meanings of Kinship," in *Holding Worlds Together: Ethnographies of Knowing and Belonging*, ed. Marianne Elisabeth Lien and Marit Melhuus [New York: Berghahn Books, 2007]; Melhuus, *Problems*).
35. Bioteknologinemda, *Uttalelse om eggdonasjon*, 11.

36. Bioteknologinemda, *Uttalelse om eggdonasjon*, 12.
37. Bioteknologinemda, *Uttalelse om eggdonasjon*, 12.
38. In Norway, citizenship is primarily based on jus sanguinis; hence, if the father or mother is Norwegian, the child is also Norwegian. However, maternity and paternity are differently ascribed, with implications that become amply evident in cases of surrogacy. As long as the mother is defined as the one who gives birth, a woman who makes use of cross-border surrogacy using her own eggs has no way to claim legal motherhood. Legal motherhood can only be transferred by adoption. However, men who make use of surrogacy using their own sperm can claim fatherhood and thus bring the child to Norway. Here, also, we see how sperm and eggs are subject to inegalitarian practices. See Melhuus and Syse, "Gestational"; Marit Melhuus, "Bringing It All Back Home: Cross-Border Procreative Practices. Examples from Norway," in *Assisted Reproduction across Borders: Feminist Perspectives on Normalizations, Disruptions and Transmissions*, ed. Merete Lie and Nina Lykke (New York: Routledge, 2017).
39. Lov-2016-06-17-46: Lov om endring av juridisk kjønn. This act follows in the wake of a previous legal move, the law that forbids discrimination due to sexual orientation, gender identity, and gender expression in general (Lov-2013-06-21-58).
40. My emphasis. This is expressed in a brief (*Høringsnotat*) submitted by the Ministry of Health and Care during the hearing process regarding the proposed law of changing legal gender. See Helse- og omsorgsdepartmentet, *Høringsnotat. Forslag til lov om endring av juridisk kjønn* (Oslo, 2015), section 10.3, section 13 (no page numbers given).
41. The terms *bodily gender* and *birth gender* seem to be used interchangeably in different public documents. The text of the "Act on Changing Legal Gender" uses the term *birth gender* and not *bodily gender*: §6 states that it is a person's legal gender that should be applied in relation to other laws but that "birth gender" shall nevertheless apply when there is a question of establishing parenthood. Following the legal text, I will use *birth gender*, the gender a person is assigned at birth.
42. Bioteknologirådet, *Høringssvar: Forslag til lov om endring av juridisk kjønn* (Oslo, 2015), 6.
43. Bioteknologirådet, *Høringssvar*, 6.
44. Edith Clarke, *My Mother Who Fathered Me: A Study of the Family in Three Communities in Jamaica* (London: George Allen & Unwin, 1979).
45. On the question of gender embodiment and gender of kin positions, see Ramberg's compelling monograph on the *devadasis*; Lucinda Ramberg, *Given to the Goddess: South Indian Devadasis and the Sexuality of Religion* (Durham, NC: Duke University Press, 2014), 196–200.
46. Helse- og omsorgsdepartementet 2015–2016 (Oslo, 2015–16), section 4.14, box 4.7.
47. Helse- og omsorgsdepartementet, section 4.14, box 4.7.
48. Lov-2016-06-17-46 §6.
49. Helse- og omsorgsdepartementet, *Prop. 74 L (2015–2016) Proposisjon til Stortinget: Lov om endring av juridisk skjønn* (Oslo, 2015–16), section 8.5, 31–32.
50. For a further discussion of the legal implications—especially the changes in the legal categories of male and female—as well as the categories of motherhood and fatherhood, see Anniken Sørlie, "Rettighetssubjekter i endring: Den fødende mannen," in *Rettigheter i velferdsstaten: Begreper, trender, teorier*, ed. Ingunn Ikdahl and Vibeke Blaker Strand (Oslo: Gyldendal, 2016).
51. I do, however, recognize that there are some unresolved issues. I have limited my discussion on the "gendered body" and kinship to mainly apply to those persons who self-declare a legal gender without medically transitioning and who did not have intersex traits at birth. In the latter case, that person's "birth gender" might never have matched the person's reproductive capacities. Thus, even if the terms *birth gender* and *bodily gender* once coincided, they no longer necessarily do. This potentially raises other questions regarding kinship that I cannot address at present but may be worth further consideration. I thank Daniel Flaumenhaft for alerting me to these possibilities.

Bibliography

Becker, Gay. *The Elusive Embryo: How Women and Men Approach New Reproductive Technologies*. Berkeley: University of California Press, 2000.
Bestard, Joan Camps, Gemma Ortobitg Canal, Julia Ribot Ballabriga, and Carles Salazar Carrasco, eds. *Parentesco y reproducción asistida: Cuerpo, persona y relaciones* [Kinship and assisted reproduction: Body, person and relations]. Barcelona: Estudios d'antropologia social y cultural, 2003.
Bioteknologinemda. *Bioteknologinemdas uttalelse om egg donasjon* [The Biotechnology Advisory Board, statement on egg donation]. Oslo, 2011.
Bioteknologirådet. *Bioteknologirådets uttalelse om eggdonasjon: Evaluering av bioteknologiloven, kapittel 2* [Biotechnology Advisory Board, statement on egg donation: Evaluation of the Biotechnology Act, chapter 2]. Oslo, 2015.
———. *Høringssvar: Forslag til lov om endring av juridisk kjønn* [The Biotechnology Advisory Board: Hearing statement; Law proposal regarding changing of legal gender]. Oslo, 2015.
Carsten, Janet. *After Kinship*. Cambridge: Cambridge University Press, 2004.
Clarke, Edith. *My Mother Who Fathered Me: A Study of the Family in Three Communities in Jamaica*. London: George Allen & Unwin, 1979 [1957].
Dolgin, Janet. *Defining the Family: Law, Technology and Reproduction in an Uneasy Age*. New York: New York University Press, 1997.
Edwards, Jeanette. "Donor Siblings: Participating in Each Other's Conception." *HAU: Journal of Ethnographic Theory* 3, no. 2 (2013): 285–92.
———. "Donor Conception and (Dis)closure in the UK: Siblingship, Friendship and Kinship." *Sociologus. Journal for Social Anthropology* 65, no. 1 (2015): 101–22.
Edwards, Jeanette, and Carles Salazar, eds. *European Kinship in the Age of Biotechnology*. New York: Berghahn Books, 2009.
Gullestad, Marianne. *The Art of Social Relations: Essays on Culture, Social Action and Everyday Life in Modern Norway*. Oslo: Scandinavian University Press, 1992.
Helsedirektoratet. *Rett til rett kjønn—helse til alle kjønn: Utredning av vilkår for endring av juridisk kjønn og organisering av helsetjenester for personer som opplever kjønnsincongruens og kjønnsdysfori* [Directorate of Health: Right to correct gender—health to all genders; Report on the conditions for changing legal gender and the organization of health services for persons who experience gender incongruence or gender dysphoria]. Oslo, 2015.
Helse- og omsorgsdepartementet. *Høringsnotat: Forslag til lov om endring av juridisk kjønn* [Ministry of Health and Care: Consultation paper. Proposal regarding the law on changing legal gender]. Oslo, 2015.
———. *Prop.74L (2015–2016). Proposisjon til Stortinget. Lov om endring av juridisk skjønn* [Ministry of Health and Care. Proposition to Parliament. Act relating to change of legal gender]. Oslo, 2015–16.
———. *Meld.St. 39 (2016–2017): Evaluering av bioteknologiloven* [Ministry of Health and Care: Report to Parliament 39 (2016–17); Evaluation of the Biotechnology Act]. Oslo, 2017.
Howell, Signe, and Marit Melhuus. "The Study of Kinship; The Study of Person; A Study of Gender?" In *Gendered Anthropology*, edited by T. del Valle, 38–53. London: Routledge, 1993.

Jacobsen, Christine M. "The (In)egalitarian Dynamics of Gender Equality and Homotolerance in Contemporary Norway." In *Egalitarianism in Scandinavia: Historical and Contemporary Perspectives*, edited by Synnøve Bendixsen, Mary Bente Bringslid, and Halvard Vike, 313–35. New York: Palgrave Macmillan, 2018.

Lambek, Michael. "Kinship, Modernity, and the Immodern." In *Vital Relations: Modernity and the Persistent Life of Kinship*, edited by Susan McKinnon and Fenella Cannel, 241–60. Santa Fe: SAR (School for Advanced Research) Press, 2013.

Lie, Merete, and Nina Lykke, ed. *Assisted Reproduction across Borders: Feminist Perspectives on Normalizations, Disruptions and Transitions*. New York: Routledge, 2017.

Lien, Marianne, and Marit Melhuus. "La Norvège: Vues de l'intérieur." *Ethnologie francaise* 39, no. 2 (2009): 197–206.

Lov-2020-06-17-98. Lov om endringer i bioteknologiloven mv [Act relating to amendments in the biotechnology law]. 2020.

Lov-2016-06-17-46. Lov om endring av juridisk kjønn [Act relating to the changing of legal gender]. 2016.

Lov-2013-06-21-58. Lov om forbud mot diskriminering på grunn av seksuell orientering, kjønnsidentitet og kjønnsuttrykk (diskrimineringsloven om seksuell orientering) [Act relating to prohibition of discrimination due to sexual orientation, gender identity and gender expression.] 2013.

Lov 2003-12-05-100. Lov om humanmedisinsk bruk av bioteknologi m.m. (bioteknologiloven) [Act Relating to the Application of Biotechnology in Medicine etc/Biotechnology Act]. 2003.

Lov 1987-06-12-68. Lov om kunstig befruktning [Artificial Procreation Act]. 1987.

Lov 1981-04-08-7. Lov om barn og foreldre (barneloven) [Children's Act]. 1981.

McKinnon, Susan, and Fenella Cannell. "The Difference Kinship Makes." In *Vital Relations: Modernity and the Persistent Life of Kinship*, edited by Susan McKinnon and Fenella Cannell, 3–38. Santa Fe: SAR Press (School for Advanced Research Press), 2013.

McKinnon, Susan, and Sydel Silverman. "Introduction." In *Complexities: Beyond Nature and Nurture*, edited by Susan McKinnon and Sydel Silverman, 1–22. Chicago: University of Chicago Press, 2005.

Melhuus, Marit. "Procreative Imaginations: When Experts Disagree on the Meanings of Kinship." In *Holding Worlds Together: Ethnographies of Knowing and Belonging*, edited by Marianne Elisabeth Lien and Marit Melhuus, 37–56. New York: Berghahn Books, 2007.

———. "L'inviolabilité de la maternité: Pourquoi le don d'ovocytes n'est-il pas autorisé en Norvège?" In *Défis contemporains de la parenté*, edited by Enric Porqueres i Gené, 35–58. Paris: Editions de l'École des Hautes Études en Sciences Sociales, 2009.

———. "Qui a peur de la 'societé de tri'? Les biotechnologies, l'individu et l'État." *Ethnologie francaise* 39, no. 2 (2009): 253–64.

———. "Cyber-Stork Children and the Norwegian Biotechnology Act: Regulating Procreative Practice; Law and its Effects." In *From Transnational Relations to Transnational Laws*, edited by Anne Hellum, Shaheen Sardar Ali, and Anne Griffiths, 51–70. Surrey: Ashgate, 2011.

———. *Problems of Conception. Issues of Law, Biotechnology, Individuals and Kinship.* New York: Berghahn Books, 2012.

———. "Ønske om et eget barn: Muligheter, forestillinger og forhandlinger i etablering av foreldreskap" [The desire for a child of one's own: Possibilities, imaginations and negotiations in establishing parenthood]. In *Reproduksjon, kjønn og likestilling i dagens Norge* [Reproduction, gender and equality in contemporary Norway], edited by Malin Noem Ravn, Guro Korsnes Kristensen, and Siri Øystebø Sørensen, 65–86. Bergen: Fagbokforlaget, 2016.

———. "Bringing It All Back Home: Cross-Border Procreative Practices. Examples from Norway." In *Assisted Reproduction across Borders: Feminist Perspectives on Normalization, Disruptions and Transmissions*, edited by Merete Lie and Nina Lykke, 112–23. New York: Routledge, 2017.

———. "Sperm, Eggs and Wombs: The Fabrication of Vital Matters through Legislative Acts." In *Anthropos and the Material: Anthropological Reflections on Emerging Political Formations*, edited by Penny Harvey, Christian Krohn-Hansen, and Knut Nustad, 122–42. Durham, NC: Duke University Press, 2019.

Melhuus, Marit, and Aslak Syse. "Gestational Surrogacy in Norway." In *Handbook of Gestational Surrogacy. International Clinical Practice and Policy Issues*, edited by E. Scott Sills, 217–224. Cambridge, UK: Cambridge University Press, 2016.

Ot.prp. nr 64. *Om lov om medisinsk bruk av bioteknologi m.m. (bioteknologiloven).* Proposition to Parliament. Regarding the act of medical use of biotechnology (the Biotechnology Act). 2002–3.

Porqueres i Gené, Enric. *Individu, personne et parenté en Europe* [Individual, person and kinship in Europe]. Paris: Éditions de la Maison des sciences de l'homme, 2015.

———, ed. *Défis contemporains de la parenté* [Contemporary challenges to kinship]. Paris: Editions de l'École des Hautes Études en Sciences Sociales, 2009.

Ramberg, Lucinda. *Given to the Goddess: South Indian Devadasis and the Sexuality of Religion.* Durham, NC: Duke University Press, 2014.

Rubin, Gayle. "The Traffic in Women: Notes on the 'Political Economy' of Sex." In *Toward an Anthropology of Women*, edited by R. R. Reiter, 157–210. New York: Monthly Review Press, 1975.

Simpson, Bob. "Scrambling Parenthood: English Kinship and the Prohibited Degrees of Affinity." *Anthropology Today* 22, no. 3 (2006): 3–6.

Solheim, Jorun. *Kjønn og modernitet.* Oslo: Pax, 2007.

Spilker, Kristen, and Merete Lie. 2007. "Gender and Bioethics Intertwined: Egg Donation within the Context of Equal Opportunity." *European Journal of Women's Studies* 14, no. 4 (2007): 327–40.

Strathern, Marilyn. *Property, Substance and Effect: Anthropological Essays on Persons and Things.* London: Athlone Press, 1999.

Strathern, Marilyn. *After Nature: English Kinship in the Late Twentieth Century.* Cambridge: Cambridge University Press, 1992.

Sørlie, Anniken. "Rettighetssubjekter i endring: Den fødende mannen" [Subject rights under change: The birthing man]. In *Rettigheter i velferdsstaten: Begreper, trender, teorier* [Rights in the welfare state: Concepts, trends, theories], edited by Ingunn Ikdahl and Vibeke Blaker Strand, 227–48. Oslo: Gyldendal, 2016.

Thelen, Tatjana, and Erdmute Alber. "Reconnecting State and Kinship: Temporalities, Scales, Classifications." In *Reconnecting State and Kinship*, edited by Tatjana Thelen and Erdmute Alber, 1–35. Philadelphia: University of Pennsylvania Press, 2018.

Thompson, Charis. *Making Parents: The Ontological Choreography of Reproductive Technologies*. Cambridge, MA: MIT Press, 2005.

Yanagisako, Sylvia, and Jane Collier. "Toward a Unified Analysis of Kinship and Gender." In *Gender and Kinship: Essays towards a Unified Analysis*, edited by Jane Collier and Sylvia Yanagisako, 14–52. Stanford, CA: Stanford University Press,

Chapter 13

Family and Kinship in Early Modern Contractarian State Theories

Jon Mathieu

In a recent Marc Bloch lecture, the US social theorist Andrew Abbott called for problematizing the common European heritage of contractarian political theory and its consequences for the modern social sciences. "The normative ontology of contractarian liberalism," he asserts, "did not include intermediate institutions between individual and society. Even the family was for most contractarians not an important part of liberal society, but only a sort of primitive model or microcosm of that society. As for the other intermediate institutions there was an open hostility to them. It was after all the point of the French Revolution to destroy such things, and the authors of the Federalist Papers condemned any association among political actors as 'faction.'" In theory, according to Abbott, all intermediate institutions were relegated to private matters with a sharp split between the public and the private realms. But in spite of their universal claims, the contractarians, and later the social scientists, had a quite particular historical background. In today's world their attempts contribute to the divergence of Western and other traditions and form an obstacle to a truly global theoretical understanding.[1]

This chapter aims to problematize ideas about that contractarian tradition regarding to family matters and their standing. What points, especially, were taken up by early modern scholars, and how did they value them? To what degree is it realistic to generalize about their work, like Andrew Abbott did? There are some valuable family studies of single political authors, but relatively little work in this respect appears to have been done for a more comprehensive group of theories.[2] In addition, the canon of the contractarian tradition is usually taken for granted—with currently famous names in philosophy and political science—and not reconstructed in a historically satisfactory way. In this chapter, I will employ an earlier list of texts that has not been reshaped by changing scholarly trends during the nineteenth and twentieth centuries. The first two sections present that list and sketch the variety it displays, while the following ones use the testimony of contractarian theories to give selected information about five topics: family inheritance and succession, marriage, household rule and citizenship, public and private, and social relations beyond Europe. Following the language of the sources, I usually speak of "family," not of "kinship." Quotations from Latin, French, and German texts are given in English. When available, standard early translations are used; otherwise I provide my own versions.

Which Contractarians?

For discursive and motivational reasons, the early modern contractarians were more readily considered a group by their adversaries than by their intellectual allies. One of the most vehement of these adversaries was Karl Ludwig von Haller (1768–1854), a Bernese aristocrat and the grandson of Albrecht von Haller, a celebrated naturalist and poet in his time. While Albrecht had been politically conservative and ostentatiously religious, his grandson Karl Ludwig far surpassed him in both respects—and by far. He was a fierce enemy of the French Revolution and, starting from his experiences in the 1790s, fought a lifelong intellectual battle against its ideas. His major work bore a combative title later used to label the entire historical period after 1815: *Restauration der Staats-Wissenschaft oder Theorie des natürlich-geselligen Zustands; der Chimäre des künstlich-bürgerlichen entgegengesezt* (Restoration of the science of the state or theory of the natural-social condition; opposed to the chimera of the artificial-bourgeois one). The work was published between 1816 and 1834 in six volumes and provoked heated debate in many political milieus in post-Napoleonic Europe.[3]

In *Restauration der Staats-Wissenschaft*, Haller wanted to develop a fundamental political theory to counter the philosophical idea of a social contract. According to him, this idea of the seventeenth and eighteenth centuries was responsible for the misguided politics that culminated in the French Revolution. The contractarians, he explained, started from the wrong assumption that mankind originally lived in a natural, lawless state, either at war or in peace, and later had to conclude a social contract to organize and protect themselves. The political point of the accounts aimed at the legitimacy of power. In theory, the organized "civil association" (*Bürger-Verein*) could, for example, delegate its authority to a monarch, and thus the monarch ruled neither by the grace of God nor in his own name by virtue of family heritage but by assignment from the sovereign people. In order to refute this notion, Haller reviewed numerous texts of public and private law. He was hostile to the idea of a public space, and the passages about private relations seemed unsatisfactory to him as well: He considered them "extremely meager and poor." It was not Haller's aim to enumerate all the contractarian publications. He restricted himself to authors that, for personal qualities or accidental circumstances, had become so well-known and influential that other authors could be considered their followers.[4] His review started with Hugo Grotius's *De jure belli ac pacis libri tres* (The rights of war and peace, 1625) and finished with Immanuel Kant's *Metaphysische Anfangsgründe der Rechtslehre* (Metaphysical foundations of law, 1797). I have listed the fourteen authors and seventeen treatises with more than twenty volumes in table 13.1.

During and after the French Revolution, militant writings of this genre were rather common. Still famous is a treatise of 1794–96 by the strong-minded Savoyard royalist Joseph de Maistre. Also known as *anti-contrat-social*, it deals with the problem of people's sovereignty. However, Maistre opposed "*Rousseau and his cronies*" as a group and did not list and review individual authors; his manifesto is thus less useful for our purpose.[5] Later views of the contractarian tradition were often influenced by particular philosophical ideas and by the evolving canon of great philosophers in history. Patrick Riley, one of the foremost experts of the last academic generation, focused on the notion of "willing" and identified the tradition with five celebrated thinkers: Hobbes, Locke, Rousseau, Kant, and Hegel. The last name is not included in our list, and modern scholarship mostly puts Hegel into other categories.[6] This is also the view of political scientist Carole Pateman in her pathbreaking study *The Sexual Contract*, first published in 1988. She discusses the contractarians from a feminist perspective, using gender as the basic category. Pateman is broader than Riley but like him takes the canon for granted, and frankly she declares herself not to be primarily interested in the historical texts but in the light they shed on present-day society.[7]

As we have seen, contractarian authors have a reputation for marginalizing family and kinship in their political thought. With the goal of a more comprehensive assessment, I reviewed all the works listed in table 13.1 and marked the passages where such issues were clearly dealt with. In order to follow Haller and his comments more closely, I took care to use the same edition of the works investigated whenever possible. Family topics are not always easy to demarcate in the texts. Nevertheless it seems possible to get a rough idea of the extent of attention paid to the topic.[8] The chapter has no ambition of offering a close reading of the

Table 13.1. Haller's 1816 Sample of Contractarian State Theories. Number, author, *title of publication*, year of first edition (edition used by Haller, number of pages).

1.	Hugo Grotius, *De jure belli ac pacis libri tres*, 1625 (Amsterdam, 1720, 979 pp.)
2.	Thomas Hobbes, A *Elementa philosophica de cive*, 1642 (? Amsterdam, 1657, 403 pp.); B *Leviathan, or The Matter, Forme, & Power of a Common-Wealth Ecclesiasticall and Civill*, 1651 (London, 1651, 396 pp.)
3.	Algernon Sidney, *Discourses Concerning Government*, 1698 (London, 1704, 424 pp.)
4.	John Locke, *Two Treatises on Government*, 1690 (London, 1690, 467 pp.)
5.	Samuel Pufendorf, *De jure naturae et gentium libri octo*, 1672 (Frankfurt, 1744, 2 vols., 1226 pp.)
6.	Justus Henning Böhmer, *Introductio in ius publicum universale*, 1710 (Halle, 1726, 656 pp.)
7.	Baron de Montesquieu, *De l'esprit des loix*, 1748 (? Geneva, 1751, 3 vols., 1483 pp.)
8.	Jean-Jacques Rousseau, *Du contrat social; ou Principes du droit politique*, 1762 (Amsterdam, 1762, 376 pp.)
9.	Karl Anton von Martini, *Positiones de jure civitatis*, 1768 (Vienna, 1773, 386 pp.)
10.	Joseph von Sonnenfels, *Grundsätze der Polizey, Handlung und Finanzwissenschaft*, 1765–1769 (? 1770–76, Vienna, 3 vols., 1296 pp.)
11.	Heinrich Gottfried Scheidemantel, *Das Staatsrecht nach der Vernunft und den Sitten der vornehmsten Völker betrachtet*, 1770–73 (Vienna, 1770–73, 3 vols., 1274 pp.)
12.	Emmanuel Joseph de Sieyès, A *Vues sur les moyens d'exécution dont les Représentans de la France pourront disposer en 1789* (? s. l., 1789, 168 pp.); B *Qu'est ce que le tiers état?* 1789 (s. l., 1789, 130 pp.); C *Reconnoissance et exposition raisonnée des droits de l'homme et du Citoyen*, 1789 (Paris, 1789, 32 pp.)
13.	August Ludwig von Schlözer, *StatsGelartheit nach ihren HauptTheilen, im Auszug und Zusammenhang*, 1793 (Göttingen, 1793, 202 pp.)
14.	Immanuel Kant, *Metaphysische Anfangsgründe der Rechtslehre*, 1797 (Frankfurt, 1797, 235 pp.)

Source: Haller, *Restauration der Staats-Wissenschaft*, vol. 1, 1816, 36–75. The titles of the treatises are according to the edition used by Haller and for this chapter. Where Haller's edition seems particularly uncertain, a nearby edition is given (marked by "?"). For two authors (Hobbes and Sieyès), Haller indicates more than one text; these are distinguished here with letters. Non-English titles are translated in the bibliography at the end of this chapter.

contractarians. My principal intention is to identify and sort out family topics in the corpus in order to observe some general outlines. Therefore, I consistently confine myself to the seventeen texts listed and do not consider other works by the same authors that might distort the test.[9]

A Variety of Theories

Let us first have a look at the format of the treatises. Most of them are several hundred pages long. The record is held by the Baron de Montesquieu's celebrated essay *De l'esprit des loix* (*The Spirit of Laws*, no. 7), first published anonymously in Geneva in 1748. The 1751 edition, used in the present chapter, has three volumes and amounts to 1483 pages according to the Arabic pagination; including the preface and the three tables of contents, given in Roman numerals, the publication exceeds 1550 pages. Much shorter is the Abbé Sieyès's piece on the *Droits de l'homme et du Citoyen* (*Rights of Man and Citizens*, no. 12 C) with thirty-two pages (the only one of less than one hundred). This is a printed version of a speech delivered in July 1789 to the Comité de Constitution in Paris in order to prepare the revolutionary declaration.[10] Of course, the pages in the treatises have very different formats. Some are small and have few annotations. The clearest example of this type is Rousseau's 1762 literary-style essay on the *Contrat social* (*Social Contract*, no. 8). Other treatises abound with learned annotations, such as Justus Henning Böhmer's *Ius publicum universale* (*Universal Public Law*, no. 6), which gives the general statements in the text and supports them by explanations in the footnotes. The footnotes are so long and detailed that the main text from time to time vanishes and the reader has to skip ahead to follow the argument through the book.

Just as varied as the formats of the treatises under study are their contents. The "contractarian" idea is mostly visible but used in different ways and political directions. Still, in the eighteenth century it became quite common to see the beginning of a new tradition with Grotius and Hobbes, the first authors of our sample.[11] Famously, these beginnings were quite dramatic: the Dutch lawyer Hugo Grotius started writing his *De jure belli et pacis* (no. 1) in prison and proceeded to publish it from exile in Paris in the 1620s. The British tutor and scholar Thomas Hobbes was also living in the French capital when he wrote his works *De cive* and *Leviathan* (no. 2 A and B): the civil war in his country had driven him away during the 1640s. Algernon Sidney, the nobleman next in our list, was beheaded in London in 1683, not least because he had dared to write *Discourses Concerning Government*, published posthumously in 1698 (no. 3). However, the eighteenth century turned out to be calmer in this respect. Joseph von Sonnenfels, for example, found no textbook to accompany his lectures: existing ones were all either too long or too limited. So he published his own three-volume *Grundsätze der Polizey, Handlung und Finanzwissenschaft* in Vienna during the 1760s (*Principles of Governance, Commerce and Financial Science,* no. 10). This work seems to have been just the right size (1296 pages): it went through many editions and became a standard handbook in the Austrian lands.

Taken together, the treatises of our sample total slightly over ten thousand pages. The pages touching family issues add up to a bit less than a thousand pages. Thus one can maintain that nearly 10 percent of the contractarian sample is dedicated to the family. The figure indicates that the focus of the theories was not on family matters but on general power relations and regulations in the early modern states. Nevertheless, a body of nearly one thousand pages of text about the family does carry weight. Interestingly, that amount was distributed in a very uneven manner and ranged from 1 percent to more than 40 percent depending on the work. At the top of the list are Locke (no. 4, 43 percent), Sidney (no. 3, 20 percent) and Pufendorf (no. 5, 15 percent). Both Locke and Sidney wrote their work in opposition to Robert Filmer's *Patriarcha, or the Natural Power of Kings*. The British gentleman author had supported absolute monarchical rule against the parliamentary party. The posthumous publication of his book in London in 1680 provoked a strong reaction from the other side.[12] Since Filmer asserted that the King's power derived from the natural authority of parents, and that Adam was the first King on Earth so that monarchical rule had been there right from the start, the argument was framed in family and religious terms. While Sidney reacted with perceptible emotion, Locke methodically dismantled the arguments of his adversary, step by step. One of the problems he identified was the missing rules of Filmer's royal lines since the times of Adam.[13]

If we take the roughly one thousand family-related pages from the sample together, it is hard to imagine any family issue that is *not* touched upon in this collective document. Of course, the individual treatments are highly varied. In what follows, I shall use them to give selected information about family inheritance and succession, marriage, household rule and citizenship, public and private, and social relations beyond Europe. These topics represent central questions of historical and anthropological research and are roughly ordered in sequence, from inside to outside.

Family Inheritance and Succession

Contractarians were interested in the underlying principles structuring civil society, whether they were based on natural law, divine law, or (later) "metaphysical foundations" (Kant 1797). In elaborating their treatises, they had to switch between descriptive and prescriptive, empirical and normative observations and considerations. The issue of family inheritance and succession was often addressed but not easy to deal with when trying to uncover general truths. Grotius (1625/1720), after having screened a few social attitudes against the backdrop of older and newer authors, stressed the variability of family rules:

> But what we have here advanced, tho' highly agreeable to a natural Conjecture, yet is it not of any absolute Necessity from the Law of Nature; and therefore very frequently altered, according to the various Humours of People, either by Compacts, by Laws, or by Customs. In certain Degrees they admit the Right of Representation, in other Degrees they do not; in some Places they consider from whence the Estates came, and in others they mind no such Thing; in some Countries the Eldest has a larger Share than the Younger, as among the antient Jews, and in others the Children have all alike; with some, Preference is shewn to the Relations on the Father's Side; with others those of the Mother's Side are upon a Level with them; some have a particular Regard to the Sex, and others have none at all; with some the nearest Degrees of Relation only are allowed of, with others the most remote ones are not excluded. But to enter into a Detail of all these, as it would be extreamly tedious, so would it be far from agreeable to our present Purpose.[14]

The right of representation mentioned in this passage concerned the discussion of whether (for example) a grandson or a granddaughter could inherit in lieu of their deceased parents. The question was much debated in the transition from the Middle Ages to the early modern period. Other factors producing variability, according to Grotius, concerned the matrimonial property regime (whether the goods should return to the families from which they had come), the distribution among the siblings (between elder and younger brothers and whether or not to include daughters), and the range of kin admitted to inheritance.

If the contemporary situation in Europe was ill-suited to providing a unitary vision, one could go back in time and seek support from remote ancestors. Montesquieu was particularly active in that field. In his essay on *The Spirit of the Laws*, he included a lengthy chapter about Roman inheritance and succession maintaining that he was the first to go back to the very beginning. The Roman laws, according to Montesquieu, started when Romulus distributed the lands of his small state among the citizens:

> The law of the division of lands made it necessary that the property of one family should not pass into another: from hence it followed, that there were but two orders of heirs established by law, the children and all the descendants that lived under the power of the father, whom they called his direct heirs; and in their default, the nearest male relations, whom they called *Agnati*. It followed likewise, that the relations by the wife, whom they called *Cognati*, ought not to succeed; they would have conveyed the estate into another family, which was not allowed.[15]

A survey of regional law in early modern Europe was easier, if restricted to royal families. On this subject, we find not only general but quite specific information in the sample of contractarian state theories. Algernon Sidney, previously mentioned as an adversary of absolute monarchy, was most prolific in this regard. He displayed his rich knowledge about royal succession past and present, and from time to time he offered general views. Sidney distinguished two exclusively male regimes: in one, the crown passed to the next man in the straight eldest line; the other privileged the eldest man in the entire reigning family rather than the eldest line. France and Turkey were prominent examples of the first regime, as females there were "thought naturally uncapable of commanding Men, or performing the Functions of a Magistrate." Other countries, such as England, extended the advantages of proximity to both sexes, "by which means our Crown has bin transported to several Familys and Nations." In some cases, female royal succession was admitted only under the condition that the sovereign not marry a foreigner or without the consent of the estates, "according to which Law, now in force among the Swedes, Charles Gustavus was chosen King upon the resignation of Queen Christina."[16]

Later treatises appear more rigorous and systematic. Karl Anton von Martini, one of the founders of the Josephinian reforms in Austria, writing a few generations after Sidney, explained to the readers that the succession depended either on individual or lineal degrees of proximity. The lineal systems could be classified according to the rigidity of the exclusion of women into three systems: the Castilian, the Salic, and the Narbonic (or Austrian).[17]

Marriage

A good introduction to the wide range of issues raised by marriage is provided by Samuel Pufendorf. The sixth of his eight books, *The Law of Nature and Nations*, first published in 1672 and later supplemented with many scholarly annotations, was dedicated to domestic matters.

Pufendorf had the habit of giving a summary preview of the chapters by means of section titles. The chapter on matrimony comprised not less than thirty-six items:

> I. The Coherence. II. Matrimony the Propagation of Mankind. III. Whether there be an Obligation to marry. IV. A wandring Lust opposite to the Law of Nature. V. Mankind not to be propagated but by Marriage. VI. What Obligation may be laid on Men to marry by the Laws of Nations. VIII. What it is by the Law of Nature. VIII. How far the Laws of Nations may order concerning Marriage. IX. The disorderly Marriages of the Amazons. X. The Laws and Rights of a regular Marriage. XI. Whence arises the Man's Power over the Wife. XII. Whether it be bestowed immediately by God. XIII. Whether it necessarily implies a Power of Life and Death. XIV. Whether Consent, not Bedding, makes the Marriage. XV. No Woman may marry more than one Husband. XVI. Polygamy in use among many People. XVII. XVIII. Whether it be repugnant to the Law of Nature. XIX. The true nature of Marriage is for one Man and one Woman to be joined together. ....[18]

And so it continued: the remaining sections dealt with divorce, the physical and legal conditions of marriage (sexual intercourse, contractual transparency, incest prohibitions), nakedness, and secondary wives. Three sections were needed in this chapter to discuss the power relationship between husband and wife. According to Pufendorf, marriage was not only an unequal alliance but an outright dominion (*imperium*) of men over women, imposed most immediately by the civil contract between the sexes and ordained by divine command. This might have been expected in an early modern treatise: after all, the authors in the sample were invariably male. But some of them raised their voices in favor of the other sex.

In his *Elementa philosophica de cive*, Hobbes maintained that originally all human beings of a certain age were both equal and in a state of war and that according to natural law the conqueror was the lord of the conquered: "By the right therefore of nature, the dominion over the infant first belongs to him who first hath him in his power." As it was obvious that the "newly born is in the mothers [sic] power before any others," it was the woman who rightly decided the child's fate. By bearing the child, she could impose the condition that her descendant, once fully grown, would not become her enemy but would instead obey her. "And thus in the state of nature, every woman that bears children, becomes both a mother, and a lord." Hobbes dismissed the opinions of authors who pointed to paternal rights by reason of the preeminence of sex, adding the further argument that in the state of nature the father could not be known except by the testimony of the mother. "Wherefore original dominion over children belongs to the mother: and among men no less than other creatures, the birth follows the belly."[19]

Another advocate of maternal rights was Locke. According to his *Two Treatises on Government*, no one could deny that the woman had "an equal share, if not the greater, as nourishing the Child a long time in her own Body out of her own substance." Maternal rights supported his arguments against Filmer's *Patriarcha*. Backed by the childbearing capacity, he could deconstruct royalist "paternal power" and replace it with republican "parental power."[20] Ironically, out of all the authors and texts in our sample, it was a German professor usually supporting monarchical rule who made a true plea for mothers at the height of the French Revolution. Schlözer's *StatsGelartheit* (*State Learnedness*, no. 13) described the original association of man and woman as an equal relationship.

> Beyond comprehension, how mankind, since thousands of years, misconceives in practice of this undisputable truth. One entire half of the human family is therefore deprived of a primordial right. The parental rights which are older and mostly better founded than the rights of the husband, are grossly violated. It is a blasphemy that even the beautiful Christian religion, a persistent defender of natural law, has been turned into a complice of this tyranny. Still some litanies holler the inhuman "He shall be your master"![21]

Household Rule and Citizenship

Schlözer, a Göttingen professor, continued in this vein when describing other domestic relations: the father, already tyrant over the wife, also seized all rights over the control of education of the children, while it was hard to understand how servants could give up their original liberty.[22] His colleague Heinrich Gottfried Scheidemantel, a Jena professor who, like Schlözer, had been born in the 1730s, held quite different views about household rule. The master of the house needed to have the right to punish servants physically and the police the duty to help him keep them under control. But fining servants money was unwise as they would try to recover the amount at the expense of the master of the house. Jailing them would not be a good idea either: then they could not carry out their daily duties for the household. He also had to watch the manners of his wife and children, an unavoidable measure "against the disgraceful fashions." Printed extracts from law books and police regulations, provided by the state, would also do much good.[23]

But of whom was that state really comprised? The question was posed from the very beginning. Grotius in his treatise on war and peace maintained that no commonwealth was "ever found so popular" as to admit the very poor, the strangers, women, and young folks in public councils.[24]

Pufendorf, writing half a century later, also noted that the designation of "citizen" (*civium nomen*) applied particularly to the masters of families and that women, children, and servants were already comprehended within their name and will.[25] Alongside an increase in state organization, the question gained in importance in the second part of the eighteenth century. The Austrian reformer Martini explicitly asked, "Who is a citizen [*Bürger*]?"

> The members of the state or citizens have to be free humans and their own masters, i.e. not subject to lordly or parental power. It is not necessary for everybody to have a family. Sons and servants therefore are no citizens although they live in a district and state territory inhabited by citizens.[26]

In the unfolding French Revolution, the question was much debated. Abbé Sieyès, one of the chief political strategists, wanted to bypass the problems. In his *Views of the Executive Means Available to National Representatives in 1789*, he imagined humankind in the state of nature at the very moment when the individuals wanted to form a civil association:

> Here relations internal to the family can be set aside. In a subject like this it is necessary to simplify as much as possible. Even if the basic elements of the association were not simple individuals but the heads of families, this, for the time being, is perfectly admissible. This is not the place to discuss this question now. Here what matters are those members of the union who can be taken to be its integral parts—namely, those admissible as contracting parties—and what has to be said here is that there cannot be any other relationship between them than one based upon a free act of each individual's will.[27]

Soon after, the facts of life intervened, and the "simplification" ceased to be a methodological device. It became clear that women were, "for better or worse" (*bien ou mal*), everywhere excluded from political rights. According to the Abbé, the same fate was shared by vagabonds and beggars, servants and foreigners, who could not be true *citoyens* (citizens). The members of the French nation were mostly composed of male *chefs de famille* (heads of the family), while the female half of the population still had a long time to wait (until World War II) before they would get voting rights.[28]

Public and Private

A sense of the public-private distinction is palpable in even the earliest texts in the early modern sample. Grotius's treatise includes a lengthy chapter about the difference between private, public, and "mixed" wars, and in Hobbes's *Leviathan*, written in France while he was exiled during the English Civil War, he makes some sharp observations about figures turning up in a foreign country. Are persons sent by a private party in a troubled state or persons sent by a prince for purely celebratory occasions to be called public, even if they are received at court? And what about a man sent by legitimate authorities—but on a secret mission and without being noticed by other rulers? Hobbes classifies all these cases as private.[29]

In the eighteenth century, the reflection about the public-private distinction became more explicit and general. The author who stands out in our sample is Justus Henning Böhmer. In *Ius publicum universale*, originally published in 1710 and revised in 1726, he tried to analyze the public-private issue methodically by pointing both to the distinctive elements and to their entanglement. When civil society replaces the natural state, he wrote, activities begin to change, and a new distinction between public and private is introduced:

> Those acts are called "public" that concern the relations between rulers and subjects and the civil government, as well as the preservation and administration of the civil estate, and that belong particularly to the republic as such, and do not exist outside of the state.[30]

Böhmer added detailed annotations to the single notions of this definition and continued to distinguish core activities of public administration (such as lawmaking, the judiciary, and internal security) from activities a bit distant from that core (such as the care for the poor, the weak, and orphans; schools; and the arts). The latter were to be categorized as public if they were approved and supervised by the prince. In still another sense, "public" was also opposed to "hidden": a marriage agreement between two persons becomes known as betrothal; there were taverns and workshops open to everybody; one could make a public performance and sell something on the marketplace. Goods common to several people, such as water resources, were often called "public." Yet all these activities and items should be distinguished from the aforementioned core of public administration. Even the activities of the prince are not always public. When he happens to buy or lease something, he may "be considered as a pater familias, and one says that he has engaged in a private activity."[31]

The figure of the prince acting as a private person seems to open a new chapter in early modern "princely society."[32] Nonetheless, I do not think that the characterization of Andrew Abbott, quoted in the introduction to this chapter, passes the test of our sample. In reality, the separation of public and private was a less fundamental distinction than he seems to assume, and there were serious attempts to develop a theory of intermediate institutions. We have seen that the German professors Scheidemantel and Schlözer held different views about household rule, but they both had conceptions of a "domestic society" (*häusliche Gesellschaft*). Scheidemantel distinguished "state law," relating ruler to subjects, from "private law," concerning relationships among subjects, and pointed to the difficulties of separating the two juridical realms strictly one from the other. He dealt extensively with a group of social entities called "societes" or "associations" (*Gesellschaften* or *Verbindungen*). There were private and public, simple and composite societies. Families were named both under the simple category (regarding the single relationships) and under the composite category (family as a whole, like corporations of craftsmen or artists). To be sure, the domestic societies were on the private side of the associations, but they were of particular importance:

> Domestic societies and their kinds form the biggest and best part of associations. They keep the order of the family. Through procreation and education, they produce the future citizens and link private interest even more precisely to the wellbeing of the state. Therefore, they merit the special attention of the ruler. In spite of their being numerous, it is both very easy and necessary to prescribe laws and domestic regulations to them. And it is no small mistake in a government to leave the families on their own, for they have the strongest influence on the interest of the whole.[33]

Thus, Scheidemantel. His colleague Schlözer began the *StatsGelartheit* with a politicohistorical course and proceeded to a politicophilosophical course. Domestic society is found in the first section of this philosophical part, dedicated to the natural state of humankind, before the formation of civil society. In the beginning there was the "solitary man" (*homo solitarius*); then came the "social man" (*homo socius*), followed by "domestic society" (*häusliche Gesellschaft*), which was composed of three relationships: husband and wife (*homo coniux*), parents and children (*homo parens*), and master and servants (*homo herus*).[34] This tripartite structure was, of course, a traditional way of dealing with families. In our sample, it is especially explicit in Pufendorf, who occasionally used the term *society* in relation to domestic authority (*societas herilis*) but spoke more often of "paternal power" (*potestas patria*) or "the master's power" (*potestas herili*).[35]

In his *Metaphysische Anfangsgründe der Rechtslehre* (1797), Kant still employs similar categories. What is new in Kant, compared to the other texts of the sample, is the basic structure of his work. This consists of two parts: private law, which is characterized as "quintessence of the laws not requiring an exterior proclamation," and public law, which requires a general proclamation. The domestic society is put in the middle of the private part; the public part consists of state law, international law, and world-citizen law.³⁶ In all the earlier works of our sample, the main structure of the presentation followed different lines: in Grotius, for example, the family mostly appears not under the heading of general private law but in the chapter "Of the Original Acquisition of a Right over Persons."³⁷

Beyond Europe

With a few exceptions, the treatises under study offered observations about the character and customs of non-European peoples. The authors reflected on their own societies also in relation to this large "other" world. Symbolic for the expansionist move stands the appendix added to Grotius's *De jure belli ac pacis* in the 1720 Amsterdam edition used in this chapter. This is a tract called *Mare liberum* (The free sea), commissioned by the Dutch East India Company and first published in 1609. In the pamphlet, the Dutch scholar defended the right of his country to free trade with this eastern part of the world. Its original occasion was the seizure of a Portuguese vessel off Singapore in 1603 by Company ships. Their prize consisted of extremely valuable goods from China and Japan and greatly pleased most shareholders. However, the case was questionable even under Dutch law, and Mennonite shareholders had moral objections to the use of force in the seizure. Thus, Grotius had to mobilize his impressive scholarship to support the case in the public debate.³⁸

"Freedom" of course not only was an effective token when dealing with the sea but also served as a distinctive element of political self-description. China and Japan, from which the Dutch riches came, were said to be despotically ruled countries; according to Montesquieu, this part of the world had always known large empires. As Asian geography featured great plains and was not fragmented by snowy mountains and swollen rivers, state power always had to be despotic: otherwise nature would have led to partition. The topography of Europe, on the other hand, produced medium-sized countries where the rule of law was not incompatible with the preservation of the state. It was this that shaped a genius for liberty, rendering it very difficult for each part to be subdued by foreigners.³⁹

Professor Scheidemantel, writing a generation after the French baron, did not agree with his theories about environment and freedom. "Liberty! A word that single persons and entire nations proclaim so readily," he grumbled. The ideas associated with the word, however, were extremely diverse, and although the republicans claimed to be the greatest proponents of liberty, this Saxon royalist had all sorts of objections to their arguments.⁴⁰ He was more receptive to other elements of Montesquieu's ethnographic accounts, for instance to the uxorilocal marriage customs on the isle of Formosa (Taiwan). These customs contrasted with the European model, where the bride more often moved into the house of the bridegroom. Montesquieu described them in quite a value-neutral way as producing no difficulties. Like the female warriors of the Amazons, and other exotic phenomena of the "other world," the uxorilocality of Formosa propogated through the early modern treatises.⁴¹

This is not the place to discuss all the evaluations of relationships between European peoples and peoples abroad. But we should still ask what particular terms were used to designate the social structures of non-European peoples. "Despotism" was one, "savagery" another. In *Leviathan*, Hobbes tried to dispel doubts about war as the state of nature:

> It may peradventure be thought, there was never such a time, nor condition of warre as this; and I believe it was never generally so, over all the world: but there are many places, where they live so now. For the savage people in many places of America, except the government of small Families, the concord whereof dependeth on naturall lust, have no government at all; and live at this day in that brutish manner as I said before.⁴²

The idea that families were the focal point and the only political or "governmental" structure in an early stage of humankind was widespread in the contractarian tradition. We have seen, for example, that Professor Schlözer classed "domestic society" not with civil society but in its natural precursor. In his famous *Contrat social*, Rousseau stated: "The most ancient of all societies, and the only natural one, is that of a family." Otherwise he had little to say about the subject. Still in the chapter about aristocracy he added that in the first societies the heads of families used to discuss public affairs, the young accepting their authority unquestioningly. "The savages of North America are governed in the same manner to this day, and are extremely well governed."⁴³

Whether Native Americans lived in a "brutish manner" (Hobbes) or were "extremely well governed" (Rousseau), their basic social structure was designated by the word *family*, not *kinship*. This corresponded to the general linguistic conventions in the treatises under study. In contrast to usages of the late nineteenth and the twentieth centuries, no scholarly distinction was made between "civilized" family and "savage" kinship. The central expression was "family," usually designating a social group. "Kinship" (in the form of "kindred," "kinsmen," "Blutsfreunde," "Verwandte," etc.) was much more rarely used and mainly for the designation of personal or collective relationships.⁴⁴ Although kin-related clientelism was seldom discussed in early modern contractarian theories, it had a bad reputation when it was. Royalists sometimes claimed that clientelism and favoritism were more widespread in democratic states, and vice versa republicans in monarchies.[45]

Conclusions

The early modern period was an era of unprecedented growth in scholarship in Europe: there had never been so many universities, libraries, and printed books. Numerous attempts were made at reordering and stabilizing political thought in a systematic, learned manner. For later observers, Grotius and Hobbes opened up a new tradition of political thinking with the idea that state and society were the result of a general contract, leading mankind from a natural to a civil phase. In this chapter, I examined a sample of fourteen authors and seventeen contractarian treatises that was compiled and criticized in 1816 by Karl Ludwig von Haller, a fierce adversary of contractualism. Six of these treatises were first published in the seventeenth century, eleven in the eighteenth century. Together, they include nearly a thousand pages on family issues — roughly 10 percent of the total text. However, the proportion dealing with the family in each individual single text is extremely variable: in the first part of the sample, it is inflated (relative to the second) by the treatises of Locke, Sidney, and Pufendorf, as Haller's comments also reflect.[46]

The chapter has looked at how contractarian texts represented family inheritance and succession, marriage, household rule and citizenship, public and private, and social relations beyond Europe. It has become clear that the state-family nexus had a complex character. Families were considered political entities in all these texts by the very fact that they were discussed in an entirely political context. Yet not all authors linked their views of family and state in the same manner. Locke, for instance, opposed both absolute monarchy and paternal power, while Schlözer supported monarchical rule against republican attack while showing much more radicalism in his assault on domestic tyranny. Indeed, one conspicuous characteristic of the texts is their variability in format and contents.

It seems difficult, therefore, to generalize about contractualism as Andrew Abbott does. He maintains that these early modern treatises made a sharp split between the public and private realms and obliterated the intermediate institutions. Through their influence on modern scholarship, they contributed to the divergence of Western and non-Western ways of social reasoning in today's world. However, as we have seen, some of the treatises clearly perceived the family as a significant part of civil society and made serious attempts at a theory of intermediate institutions between public and private. By describing contractualism in his restricted way, Abbott paradoxically widens the distance between "the West and the rest" that he wants to overcome. He seems to be under the spell of Rousseau's *Contrat social*, the most famous but certainly not a typical text of the contractarian legacy. It is important to recover also other parts of the history of European political thought.[47]

Jon Mathieu is editor in chief of the journal *Histories* and professor emeritus of history at the University of Lucerne, Switzerland. He has widely published about family and kinship in the early modern period and about the history of mountain regions. His recent articles in the former field include "Temporalities and Transitions of Family History in Europe: Competing Accounts" (2019) and "Domestic Terminologies: House, Household, Family" (2020).

Notes

I would like to thank the commentators at the Bielefeld conference (March 2018) and the reviewers of the first version of this chapter; Latinist Bärbel Schnegg who helped with my readings and checked my translations; and the commentators at family history conferences in Stockholm and Paris (June 2018, December 2020).

1. Andrew Abbott, "The Future of Social Sciences," Marc Bloch Lecture 2015 (online), *Annales HSS* 71, no. 3 (2016): 10.
2. For Bodin, see Claudia Opitz-Belakhal, *Das Universum des Jean Bodin: Staatsbildung, Macht und Geschlecht* (Frankfurt a. M.: Campus, 2006), and Anna Becker, "Der Haushalt in der politischen Theorie der Frühen Neuzeit," in *Das Haus in der Geschichte Europas: Ein Handbuch*, ed. Joachim Eibach and Inken Schmidt-Voges (Berlin: De Gruyter, 2015); see also the chapters by Julia Heinemann (on Bodin and Hotman) and David W. Sabean (on Hegel) in this volume; for a more collective approach, see Carole Pateman quoted below.
3. Kurt Guggisberg, *Carl Ludwig von Haller* (Frauenfeld: Huber Verlag, 1938); Ronald Roggen, *"Restauration"—Kampfruf und Schimpfwort: Eine Kommunikationsanalyse des Hauptwerks des Staatstheoretikers Karl Ludwig von Haller (1768–1854)* (Freiburg: Universitätsverlag, 1999).
4. Carl Ludwig von Haller, *Restauration der Staats-Wissenschaft oder Theorie des natürlich-geselligen Zustand; der Chimäre des künstlich-bürgerlichen entgegengesezt*, vol. 1, *Darstellung, Geschichte und Critik der bisherigen falschen Systeme* (Winterthur: Steinersche Buchhandlung, 1816), xxvii, 16–25, 35–36.
5. Joseph de Maistre, "Étude sur la souveraineté," in *Oeuvres complètes de Joseph de Maistre* (Paris: Librairie catholique, 1924).
6. Michael Rosen and Jonathan Wolff, eds., *Political Theory* (Oxford: Oxford University Press, 1999), 70–71, put Hegel in the chapter "Against the Social Contract"; Patrick Riley, "How Coherent Is the Social Contract Theory?" *Journal of the History of Ideas* 34,

no. 4 (1975); Patrick Riley, "Social Contract Theory and its Critics," in *The Cambridge History of Eighteenth-Century Political Thought*, ed. Mark Goldie and Robert Wokler (Cambridge: Cambridge University Press, 2006).
7. Carole Pateman, *The Sexual Contract* (Oxford: Polity Press, 1988), 4.
8. Criteria for including a page in the count of those dealing with the topic of family are chapter titles that refer to family issues or relevant statements of at least a few continuous lines. Sometimes the implicit framework matters: if "women and children" are referred to in a family context, the page would be included; if the mention only indicates a social category in a more abstract sense, the page would be excluded. Regarding the problematic of family definitions, see Jon Mathieu, "Domestic Terminologies: House, Household, Family," in *The Routledge History of the Domestic Sphere in Europe, 16th to 19th Century*, edited by Joachim Eibach and Margareth Lanzinger (London: Routledge, 2020).
9. I am aware that some of these authors wrote other works in which family issues loomed larger than in the publications listed and also works less concerned with issues of the family.
10. Emmanuel Joseph Sieyès, *Reconnoissance et exposition raisonnée des droits de l'homme et du Citoyen* (Paris: Baudouin, 1789), article XXXI, 32 (no. 12 C).
11. Böhmer divides the scholarly literature into periods before and after Grotius and Hobbes: according to him, they solidified the study of public law. Justus Henning Böhmer, *Introductio in ius publicum universale* (Halle: Impensis, 1726), 105–25 (no. 6).
12. Johann P. Sommerville, "Absolutism and Royalism," in *The Cambridge History of Political Thought 1450–1700*, ed. J. H. Burns (Cambridge, UK: Cambridge University Press, 1991).
13. John Locke, *Two Treatises on Government* (London: Avnsham Churchill, 1690), 157–58 (no. 4).
14. Hugo Grotius, *The Rights of War and Peace*, ed. Richard Tuck (Indianapolis: Liberty Fund, 2005), 600; Latin original: *De jure belli ac pacis libri tres* (Amsterdam: Jansson Waesberg, 1720), 293 (no. 1).
15. Baron de Montesquieu, *The Spirit of Laws* (London: J. Nourse and P. Vaillant, 1750), 2:222–223; French original: *De l'esprit des loix* (Geneva: Barillot & Fils, 1751), 3:121 (no. 7).
16. Algernon Sidney, *Discourses Concerning Government* (London: J. Darby, 1704), 78–79, 167 (no. 3).
17. Karl Anton von Martini, *Positiones de jure civitatis* (Wien: Johann Thomas Trattner, 1773), 213–14 (no. 9).
18. Samuel Pufendorf, *Of the Law of Nature and Nations: Eight Books* (London: J. Walthoe, 1729), 559; Latin original: *De jure naturae et gentium libri octo* (Frankfurt: Officina Knochiana, 1744), 2:3 (no. 5).
19. Thomas Hobbes, *De Cive or The Citizen*, ed. Sterling P. Lamprecht (New York: Appleton-Century-Crofts, 1949), 106–7; Latin original: *Elementa philosophica de cive* (Amsterdam: L. et D. Elzevir, 1657), 148–49 (no. 2); see also Pateman, *Sexual Contract*, 44–47.
20. Locke, *Two Treatises*, 70 (no. 4); see also Pateman, *Sexual Contract*, 21–25, 85–96.
21. August Ludwig von Schlözer, *StatsGelartheit nach ihren HauptTheilen, im Auszug und Zusammenhang* (Göttingen, 1789), 54–55 (no. 13).
22. Schlözer, *StatsGelartheit*, 56–63 (no. 13).
23. Heinrich Gottfried Scheidemantel, *Das Staatsrecht nach der Vernunft und den Sitten der vornehmsten Völker betrachtet* (Wien: Johann Rudolph Cröcker, 1771, 2:169–70 (no. 11).
24. Grotius, *Rights of War and Peace*, 265–66; Latin original: *De jure belli*, 89 (no. 1)
25. Pufendorf, *Law of Nature*, 651; Latin original: *De jure naturae*, 2:153 (no. 5).
26. Martini, *Positiones*, 6 (no. 9).
27. Emmanuel Joseph Sieyès, "Views of the Executive Means Available to the Representatives of France in 1789," in *Emmanuel Joseph Sieyès, Political Writings*, ed. Michael Sonenscher (Indianapolis: Hackett Publishing Company, 2003), 10; French

original: *Vues sur les moyens d'exécution dont les Représentans de la France pourront disposer en 1789* (n.p., 1789), 15 (no. 12 A).
28. Emmanuel Joseph Sieyès, *Qu'est ce que le tiers état?* (n.p., 1789), 29 (no. 12 B); Sieyès, *Reconoissance*, 21–22 (no. 12 C). For family politics in the Revolution, see Lynn Hunt, *The Family Romance of the French Revolution* (London: Routledge, 1992).
29. Grotius, *Rights of War and Peace*, 240–335; Hobbes, *Leviathan*, 126 (no. 2 B).
30. Böhmer, *Ius publicum universale*, 55 (no. 6).
31. Böhmer, *Ius publicum universale*, 54–57 (no. 6).
32. On the concept of «Fürstengesellschaft' see Christian Windler, "Symbolische Kommunikation und diplomatische Praxis. Erträge neuer Forschungen," in *Alles nur symbolisch? Bilanz und Perspektiven der Erforschung symbolischer Kommunikation*, ed. Barbara Stollberg-Rilinger, Tim Neu, and Christina Brauner (Cologne: Böhlau, 2013), 161–85.
33. Scheidemantel, *Staatsrecht*, 1:9–10; 2:63; 3:244–50, 294–97, quote 294 (no. 11).
34. Schlözer, *StatsGelartheit*, 32–63 (no. 13).
35. Pufendorf, *Law of Nature*, 598, 614; Latin original: *De jure naturae*, 2:69, 92 (no. 5).
36. Immanuel Kant, *Metaphysische Anfangsgründe der Rechtslehre* (Frankfurt, 1797) (no. 14).
37. Grotius, *Rights of War and Peace*, 508; Latin original: *De jure belli*, 237 (no. 1).
38. Grotius, *De jure belli*, after page 936 (no. 1); see also Hugo Grotius, *The Free Sea*, ed. David Armitage (Indianapolis: Liberty Fund, 2004).
39. Montesquieu, *Esprit des loix*, 2:104–5 (no. 7).
40. Scheidemantel, *Staatsrecht*, 1:182–85; 3:187–205, quote 187 (no. 11).
41. Montesquieu, *Esprit des loix*, 2:373 (no. 7); Scheidemantel, *Staatsrecht*, 3:296 (no. 11).
42. Hobbes, *Leviathan*, 63 (no. 2 B).
43. Jean-Jacques Rousseau, *A Treatise on the Social Compact; or The Principles of Political Law* (London: T. Becket and P.A. De Hondt, 1764), 3, 114; French original: *Du contrat social; ou Principes du droit politique* (Amsterdam: Marc-Michel Rey, 1762), 5, 170 (no. 8).
44. Significant examples in Grotius, *De jure belli*, 111, 159, 916 (no. 1); Pufendorf, *De jure naturae*, 1:352, 629 (no. 5); Martini, *Positiones*, 126 (no. 9).
45. Hobbes, *De Cive*, 167 (no. 2 A); Montesquieu, *Esprit des loix*, 1:132, 413 (no. 7).
46. Haller comments on family issues in the first part of the sample up to Böhmer (no. 6), but not in the second part from Montesquieu (no. 7) to Kant (no. 14). His general judgment about the poorness of family treatment in contractarian treatises was evidently also influenced by his own approach to state theory: in the second volume of *Restauration der Staats-Wissenschaft* (Winterthur: Steinersche Buchhandlung, 1817), he develops his ideas about "patrimonial states" growing out of family relations.
47. *The Cambridge History of Political Thought* discusses family issues only up to the fifteenth century but not in the early modern period—not even Filmer's royal patriarchalism, which so much irritated Sidney and Locke, is taken up in family terms. See Anthony Grafton, "Humanism and Political Theory," in *The Cambridge History of Political Thought 1450–1700*, ed. J. H. Burns and Mark Goldie (Cambridge: Cambridge University Press, 1991); Riley, "Social Contract Theory and Its Critics"; Sommerville, "Absolutism and Royalism."

Bibliography

Abbott, Andrew. "The Future of Social Sciences." Marc Bloch Lecture 2015 (online), published in French in *Annales HSS* 71, no. 3 (2016): 577–96.
Becker, Anna. "Der Haushalt in der politischen Theorie der Frühen Neuzeit." In *Das Haus in der Geschichte Europas: Ein Handbuch*, edited by Joachim Eibach and Inken Schmidt-Voges, 667–83. Berlin: De Gruyter, 2015.
Böhmer, Justus Henning. *Introductio in ius publicum universale*. 1710. 2nd ed. Halle: Impensis Orphanotrophei, 1726.
Grafton, Anthony. "Humanism and Political Theory." In *The Cambridge History of Political Thought 1450–1700*, edited by J. H. Burns, with Mark Goldie, 9–29. Cambridge: Cambridge University Press, 1991.
Grotius, Hugo. *De jure belli ac pacis libri tres*. 1625. Amsterdam: Jansson Waesberg, 1720. [English edition: *The Rights of War and Peace*. Edited by Richard Tuck after the 1738 English edition. Indianapolis: Liberty Fund, 2005.].
———. *The Free Sea*. Edited by David Armitage. Indianapolis: Liberty Fund, 2004.
Guggisberg, Kurt. *Carl Ludwig von Haller*. Frauenfeld: Huber Verlag, 1938.
Haller, Carl Ludwig von. *Restauration der Staats-Wissenschaft oder Theorie des natürlich-geselligen Zustand; der Chimäre des künstlich-bürgerlichen entgegengesezt*. 6 vols. Winterthur: Steinersche Buchhandlung, 1816–34.
Hobbes, Thomas. *Elementa philosophica de cive*. 1657. Amsterdam: L. et D. Elzevir, 1657. [English edition: *De Cive or The Citizen*. Edited by Sterling P. Lamprecht after the 1651 English version. New York: Appleton-Century-Crofts, 1949.]
Hobbes, Thomas. *Leviathan, or The Matter, Forme, & Power of a Common-Wealth Ecclesiasticall and Civill*. London: Andrew Crooke, 1651.
Hunt, Lynn. *The Family Romance of the French Revolution*. London: Routledge, 1992.
Kant, Immanuel. *Metaphysische Anfangsgründe der Rechtslehre*. Frankfurt, 1797.
Locke, John. *Two Treatises on Government*. London: Avnsham Churchill, 1690.
Maistre, Joseph de. "Étude sur la souveraineté." In *Oeuvres complètes de Joseph de Maistre*, 309–553. Paris: Librairie catholique Emmanuel Vitte, 1924.
Martini, Karl Anton von. *Positiones de jure civitatis*. 1768. Wien: Johann Thomas Trattner, 1773.
Mathieu, Jon. "Domestic Terminologies: House, Household, Family." In *The Routledge History of the Domestic Sphere in Europe, 16th to 19th Century*, edited by Joachim Eibach and Margareth Lanzinger, 25–42. London: Routledge, 2020.
Montesquieu, Baron de. *De l'esprit des loix*. 3 vols. 1748. Geneva: Barrillot & Fils, 1751. [English edition: *The Spirit of Laws*. 2 vols. London: J. Nourse and P. Vaillant, 1750.]
Opitz-Belakhal, Claudia. *Das Universum des Jean Bodin: Staatsbildung, Macht und Geschlecht*. Frankfurt: Campus Verlag, 2006.
Pateman, Carole. *The Sexual Contract*. Oxford: Polity Press, 1988.
Pufendorf, Samuel. *De jure naturae et gentium libri octo*. 2 vols. 1672. Frankfurt: Officina Knochiana, 1744. [English edition: *Of the Law of Nature and Nations: Eight Books*. London: J. Walthoe, 1729.]
Riley, Patrick. "How Coherent Is the Social Contract Theory?" *Journal of the History of Ideas* 34, no. 4 (1975): 543–62.

———. "Social Contract Theory and Its Critics." In *The Cambridge History of Eighteenth-Century Political Thought*, edited by Mark Goldie and Robert Wokler, 347–75. Cambridge: Cambridge University Press, 2006.

Roggen, Ronald. *"Restauration"—Kampfruf und Schimpfwort: Eine Kommunikationsanalyse des Hauptwerks des Staatstheoretikers Karl Ludwig von Haller (1768–1854)*. Freiburg: Universitätsverlag, 1999.

Rosen, Michael, and Jonathan Wolff, ed. *Political Theory*. Oxford: Oxford University Press, 1999.

Rousseau, Jean-Jacques. *Du contrat social; ou Principes du droit politique*. Amsterdam: Marc-Michel Rey, 1762. [English edition: *A Treatise on the Social Compact; or The Principles of Political Law*. London: T. Becket and P.A. De Hondt, 1764.]

Scheidemantel, Heinrich Gottfried. *Das Staatsrecht nach der Vernunft und den Sitten der vornehmsten Völker betrachtet*. 3 vols. Wien: Johann Rudolph Cröcker, 1770–73.

Schlözer, August Ludwig von. *StatsGelartheit nach ihren HauptTheilen, im Auszug und Zusammenhang*. Göttingen: Vandenhoek und Ruprecht, 1789.

Sidney, Algernon. *Discourses Concerning Government*. 1698. London: J. Darby, 1704.

Sieyès, Emmanuel Joseph. *Vues sur les moyens d'exécution dont les Représentans de la France pourront disposer en 1789*. N.p., 1789. [English edition: "Views of the Executive Means Available to the Representatives of France in 1789." In *Emmanuel Joseph Sieyès, Political Writings*, edited by Michael Sonenscher, 1–67. Indianapolis: Hackett Publishing Company, 2003.]

———. *Qu'est ce que le tiers état?* N.p., 1789. [English Edition: "What Is the Third Estate?" In *Emmanuel Joseph Sieyès, Political Writings*, edited by Michael Sonenscher, 92–162. Indianapolis: Hackett Publishing Company, 2003].

Sieyès, Emmanuel Joseph. *Reconnoissance et exposition raisonnée des droits de l'homme et du Citoyen*. Paris: Baudouin, 1789.

Sommerville, Johann P. "Absolutism and Royalism." In *The Cambridge History of Political Thought 1450–1700*, edited by J. H. Burns, with Mark Goldie, 347–73. Cambridge: Cambridge University Press, 1991.

Sonnenfels, Joseph von. *Grundsätze der Polizey, Handlung und Finanzwissenschaft*. 3 vols. 1765–69. Wien: Joseph Kurzböck, 1770–76.

Windler, Christian. "Symbolische Kommunikation und diplomatische Praxis: Erträge neuer Forschungen." In *Alles nur symbolisch? Bilanz und Perspektiven der Erforschung symbolischer Kommunikation*, edited by Barbara Stollberg-Rilinger, Tim Neu, and Christina Brauner, 161–85. Cologne: Böhlau, 2013.

Chapter 14

Translating the Family

Claudia Derichs

> How realistic is it to expect translation to render the world intelligible in a context shaped by different historical trajectories and experiences? Can we rely on human universals to translate through the unique and specific webs of meaning that languages represent?
>
> —Mamadou Diawara, Elísio S. Macamo, and Jean-Bernard Ouédraogo,
> *Translation Revisited*[1]

Language shapes and reflects social orders in both its written and spoken forms. Words considered synonyms in one language may not be in another. And even when they are, it is not guaranteed that each term will have the same connotations for all people. Before reflecting on and interpreting conceptual terms such as *kinship* and *family*, then, we must first become aware of the boundedness of the words and terms we are so "at ease" with in everyday academic life. We might ask whether definitions would help in reducing the number of interpretations of "words" around the globe. Definitions do have some merit: they help to hold authors and speakers accountable to their readers and audiences and to provide orientation, but they can also narrow the semantic scope. Because translating a term or concept requires clarity about its meaning and history, the practice of definition may be reconsidered during attempts at translation. However, translations may also become challenging tasks. In this chapter, I will discuss the advantages of and difficulties with getting to know the meanings of ideas, concepts, norms, and the like by looking at what some terms—specifically, *household* and *family*—imply in the field of society and kinship and how translating them into other languages might restrict our own understanding of them. In the case of Japanese, the characters for *household*, *family*, and *society*, as well as the concepts represented by compounds that include these characters, show that the conceptual split between kinship and politics is not as deep as social science theories of the "modern state" would suggest. The examples I use to demonstrate this refer to spectrums of meaning of a particularly contested concept in Japanese anthropology, 家 *ie*. (For now, we may simply take this as a term for a family-type "household".) I contrast its semantic content in prewar Japan (the second half of the nineteenth century to the beginning of World War II) with that it had in postwar Japan (the 1950s to 1980s). In both those periods, the concept had a significant impact on Japanese social organization—an impact that not only was not always embraced but also received formidable criticism.

First, however, I have to make a disclaimer: while I immerse myself in these times and discourses as traceable through literature and lived experiences (fieldwork, research, and study visits), the literature from and on Japan that I use is predominantly authored by Japanologists and/or written in Japanese script. This means that certain terms, notions, expressions, and concepts mentioned below are embedded in their own local, temporal, and discursive context. *Modern* and *traditional* and *modernization* and *tradition*, for instance, should be understood as terms used by the authors and speakers I cite, not as terms that I have chosen. The same goes for notions of Japanese otherness or uniqueness, as well as for the question of performance or performativity. My task is not to judge certain ascriptions that are disputed today; I am interested in discussing how certain terms and concepts seem to have shaped certain discursive currents in Japan, especially various applications of the character 家 *ie*, the core character for illustrating the relationship between household/kinship/family and politics.

In Japanese, 家 *ie* denotes the family in agrarian villages of the nineteenth and twentieth centuries, but the concept is "not directly based on descent."[2] According to the anthropologist Akitoshi Shimizu, 家 *ie* is not even a kinship system "if the latter is defined as a system of marriage and filiation." However, it could be considered a kinship system due to its place in the cultural and structural dimensions of social organization. "In this sense," Shimizu says, "the whole structure of the *ie* is a medium for kinship phenomena."[3] The complexity of the relation between kinship and 家 *ie* would fill a book,[4] but my intent is not to draw dichotomies between the West versus Japan, the one versus the other, or anything of that sort. I simply want to look at what contextual information is missing when we deal with translations between Japanese idiographic characters and English words in a phonetic alphabet.

Translations and Dictionary Entries

The easiest and laziest—though a highly pragmatic—way to get an idea of how certain terms have been translated in different languages is to look them up in generally accepted dictionaries. While this does not guarantee an exhaustive result that encompasses the full semantic scope of a term, it gives us a rough first idea of what linguists and translators were thinking about when composing the definitions. Dictionary entries also become revealing when looked at diachronically: they teach us how a particular term has been translated at different points in time, over decades and centuries. How understandings and, even more, moral judgments of terms, ideas, and concepts change over time has been examined intensively by Reinhart Koselleck and other scholars of the history of ideas.[5] For instance, to political scientists working on the concept and the theory of democracy, the early typology of Plato is interesting because he designated it as a "bad" political system. However, Plato is still a comparatively easy example to look at because he did not have to translate the term *democracy* from a foreign language; he only evaluated its meaning in the political reality of his time. It becomes more difficult when terms are translated across language families or when meanings of a term have to be introduced to societies in which there was no previous concept, idea, or object of reference corresponding to that particular term. And the difficulties multiply when the act of written translation means converting the meaning(s) of words in alphabetic letters into idiographic characters. Employing the example of "democracy" once again, what character should be chosen to transmit the notion of demos inherent in democracy when the concept of demos is alien to the target society? Difficulties like this came along with many European political and juridical terms that were translated into Japanese during the late nineteenth and early twentieth centuries. As a case in point, the word *society* saw a number of Japanese translations during the decades after 1853, when the country was pressured to increase its foreign and diplomatic relations after several centuries of relative isolation. Translating the English term *society* and its equivalents in other European languages (such as German *Gesellschaft*) during this period meant introducing various and changing comprehensions into Japanese even though the alphabetic spelling of the word of origin (*society*; *Gesellschaft*) did not change. Accordingly, we can trace a whole series of Japanese renderings of different understandings of what remained "society" in English.[6] Translating words like *society* introduced a constellation of theoretical and juridical semantic fields that had not been known in Japan before—among them, individual rights. In order to convey the meaning of new terms in this era, a common practice was to choose two Chinese characters as "translation words"[7] for foreign terms.

Of the various translation words for *society* in a social science understanding, only the composite 社会 *shakai* has continued to be used in scholarly discourses (social sciences) as well as by the general public today. But as Akira Yanabu points out, the choice of these two characters (社 *sha* and 会 *kai*) did not mean that the initial Western meaning was likewise transported into Japanese.[8]

> In comparison, *shakai* amounts essentially to a neologism coined as translation for *society*. It may have had a history as a Chinese compound, but examples of its use in Japan had been exceedingly rare; the translation word *shakai* lacks the original sense of both *sha* and *kai*, and should rather be thought of as a recombination of these characters into a new word. Certainly, there is no obvious gap in meaning between *society* and the newly invented *shakai*, but neither do they actually share anything in common.[9]

Is this not the case with basically all languages? Accordingly, Yanabu argues that translations quickly reach their limits when they are supposed to convey the meaning of "words that belong to a different world."[10] Kin'ya Abe argues along a similar line, stating that it took considerable time and effort to translate the term *society* into Japanese in the second half of the nineteenth century. The idea of an individual simply did not exist, making it even more difficult to convey that a "society" is something composed of "individuals."[11] The same goes for the theoretical-contextual notions that are incorporated in conceptual terms. "Translation, the great equalizer of historically distinct political movements," Andre Haag writes, "allowed these theories [i.e., Western theories of social and political organization of the late nineteenth century] to be introduced almost as soon as they were written, but long before the social and economic conditions that they described had come into being in Japan."[12] In this light, we may ask about terms that apparently *did* have a meaning in Japan and were among those used in common conversation. Did their meaning change because of Western influences entering the country? I will discuss this using the example of the word *family*, for which Japanese terms did exist. However, these, unlike *shakai*, were laden with ideologized semantics in Japanese—semantics that the translation word *family* (and its French and German equivalents) simply did not convey. In what follows, I will show examples of how the Japanese character 家 *ie*, which is commonly translated as "household" and "family," has been discussed and described in the literature; this may give an idea of how *ie* was perceived *in* Japan during different time periods.

I will first reflect on the relationships between language, nation, and ethnonationalism on a general level. I will then look at the Japanese character 家 *ie* and the ideological underpinnings inherent in this concept, beginning with its translation as "household" in Meiji Japan[13] (1868–1912) and its connection with other conceptual terms. Then, switching to postwar Japan, I sketch out how the character 家 *ie* was combined with other characters to designate the "modern family" and how the family concept diffused into corporate ethics—that is, how companies became perceived of as families. In the subsequent section, I introduce an example of the criticism directed at the morally influential concept of 家 *ie* and the family in postwar decades. Here, feminist thought gives an idea of what the ideological baggage of 家 *ie* and the term *family* meant for segregating and regulating men's and women's lifeworlds—and with them the nation's social organization—from the 1950s to 1980s. I end with a summary of what requires particular attention when discussing kinship and politics across cultures and using terms such as *family* that seemingly denote the same thing everywhere.

Language, Nation, Ethnonationalism

Language occupied an important role in the framing of eighteenth- and nineteenth-century theories in which language, nation, and state were conceptually bound together. In order to administer a state and create a sense of a national identity, these theories claimed that a language shared by "the nation" formed an indispensable element of a unified nation-state. This led to what Rachel Leow calls a normative isomorphism.

> The isomorphism of language, nation and state has become normative. Many scholars trace this back to the writings of Johann Gottfried Herder (1744–1803), who defined language as a fundamental marker of ethnic groups and ethnic nations, and posited most famously that language is an authentic product of an ancestral, innate culture, predating all political reason: one which expresses the soul or sentiments of a people.[14]

J. G. Herder's reflections were subsequently elaborated on by German romantics such as August Wilhelm Schlegel (1767–1845) and Johann Gottlieb Fichte (1762–1814).[15] Fichte's famous *Address to the German Nation* (1807/8) takes this way of isomorphic thinking to a height that must have driven translators in Asian countries mad in its unclear distinction between *Volk*, *Staat*, and *Nation* and frequent use of them as synonyms, presumably a deliberate choice to underline the unity of all three.[16] According to Leow, Herder's long shadow is discernible today in the slogans of ethnolinguistic movements. "'Who speaks?'" she states, "is always contingent on 'Who is spoken to?' Between the speaker and the spoken-to lies a field of power relations enacted through language."[17] The late nineteenth century distrusted the idea that nations with more than one language could to survive. In Susan Gal's words: "Multilingualism was seen as dangerous ... raising the possibility that speakers had loyalty to more than one state."[18]

A massive influx of terms from European languages was translated into Japanese in order to achieve "modernization" (*kindaika*) and administer a unified nation-state in the nineteenth century. Modernization then designated a process of "moving forward" toward a particular end, often associated with standards and notions of dominant Western nations of the time.[19] Nearly in parallel to the state-endorsed exercise of modernization, the orientation toward the West made a number of Japanese intellectuals feel uneasy. The equation of "Western," "modern," and "setting the standard for civilization" was not entirely convincing to them.[20] This unease gradually developed into a conservative reaffirmation of what was understood as tradition-compliant indigenous Japanese values.

With regard to the role of language, this was most visible in the treatment of the Ryukyuan languages spoken in the southernmost prefecture, Okinawa.[21] The Ryukyuan languages were disparaged as "dialects" of Japanese, and local children who dared to speak their native tongue at school were forced to wear a wooden badge with the inscription *hōgen fuda* or "dialect tag."[22] This badge served to stigmatize the children wearing it. The linguist Patrick Heinrich states that "standard Japanese became a key measure for the transformation of Ryukyuans into Japanese nationals."[23] The government needed a single language in order to address "the people" as a whole—as a coherent entity—and thus used "family" to frame the notion of national belonging. Heinrich points out how, even in twentieth-century Japan, the attempt by the government to forge loyalty to a single state was codified in slogans that the Ryukyu people were meant to internalize. These slogans described using the standard language (standard Japanese) as *the* vehicle for consolidating national unity. "The Movement for Enforcement of the Standard Language (active from 1939) created slogans exhorting people to use the standard language for the sake of national unity, progress and development"[24] through connecting nation, language, and family. Slogans "such as 'One family altogether—standard language' (*Ikka kozotte hyōjungo*)" or "'Particularly in familiar relationships—standard language' (*Shita-shiki naka koso hyōjungo*)"[25] were common. The character 家 *ie* became a component of the translation word for nation-state (国家 *kokka*), thus underlining the association of the nation with one family or household.[26]

The modern polity thus relied on a single language for a range of purposes, including administrative, bureaucratic and/or executive needs for implementing government policies and running the state.[27] In this regard, the Japanese state was no exception: it not only endorsed the idea of one language for the entire nation but a whole range of other policies to render Japan a unified and "one of a kind" state. Efforts to restore "Japanism" led to the construction in the 1930s of the *kokutai* or "national polity," which denoted "Japan's unique structure of state and society which was based upon a divine emperor."[28] In a compilation of sources of Japanese tradition, one of the fundamental texts on the unique structure of the Japanese state and society propagated this national polity. One of the *kokutai*'s fundamental principles was the notion of filial piety, which in turn had the family as its basis.[29] Here, the explanation of filial piety rooted in the family as a link between the past and the future was extended and connected to the principle of loyalty (see also Susan McKinnon's chapter in this volume). It is revealing to quote this paragraph because it succinctly asserted the inseparable relationship between the emperor and the people as one family: "Filial piety in our country has its true characteristics in its perfect conformity with our national polity by heightening still further the relationship between morality and nature. Our country is a great family nation,[30] and the Imperial Household is the head family of the subjects and the nucleus of national life.[31]"

The 家 *ie* was one of the core institutions to foster the idea of the Japanese as a unique nation that formed a family with the emperor at its head. The deconstructed character 家 *ie* shows a pig (豕) under a roof (宀): a symbol of an economic unit, of sharing residence and of domestic belonging, and strongly associated with the notion of lineage and persistence. Connecting the household/family (家 *ie*) and the emperor gave the concept a "religious character" that became explicit in the Civil Rights Code of 1898. The system of 家 *ie* in those days, as the sociologist Shingo Shimada explains, revealed a normative power through its ideological embeddedness, and its institutionalization served to create an "imagined community" (in Benedict Anderson's sense), the nation.[32] In former centuries, *ie* in the sense of household had "usually formed around an elementary family as its nucleus" but often included "other relatives and even nonrelatives. Once established, a household [was] expected to exist through generations."[33]

The triad of language, ethnonational identity, and the nation-state survived well into postwar times. The ideological notion of *kokutai*, for instance, had strong repercussions in this period for Japan's defense of "Japanese uniqueness," in which the concept of family played a crucial role. The Japanese language came to underpin notions highlighted by those who cultivated the idea of Japanese uniqueness in order to prove exactly that. In postwar times, this discourse was commonly referred to as *nihonjinron* or the "discourse on Japanese-ness." "The *nihonjinron* [proponents]," writes Peter Dale in a highly critical assessment of this discourse, "in their attempt to define the specificity of Japanese identity, range over the whole complex of Japanese historical culture, choosing their illustrative material from classical records, folklore materials, historical chronicles, contemporary news, dictionaries of Japanese usage etc."[34] *Ie* is among the terms of the discourse on Japanese-ness that are said to signify the essence of being Japanese.[35] I highlight a few of the many connotations of *ie* that are described in the literature on *nihonjinron* that I used to read during my studies of Japan and Japanese language in the 1980s.

Ideologies of Family in Postwar Japan

While the terms *ie* and the English term *house(hold)* are used to refer to the primary unit of Japanese social organization in prewar times, a two-character translation for the term *family* was preferred in post–World War II decades, since the laws on personal status and family were changed. The (new) concept of family became more closely connected to the lifeworld of the time, but most of all it followed economic requirements. The postwar notion of family was explicitly differentiated from the ideologized *ie* of prewar times, and the *ie* system was "pejoratively connoted."[36] Even so, the character for *ie* still forms a component of the words *kazoku* (家族) and *katei* (家庭), which were both established to denote the concept of family in postwar times. (*Kazoku* is the composite most commonly used to designate the nuclear family.) Initially, the reasons for giving up the single character 家 *ie* were primarily legal and political. Discrediting the prewar *ie* system that had declared the Japanese people to be a family with the emperor at its head required the introduction of a "fresh" and ideologically less contaminated concept of family after 1945. The new—and legally consolidated—understanding of family, as conveyed in *kazoku* and *katei*, was meant to refer to a new image of the family as an entity comprising two individuals (a man and a woman)—as well as their children—enjoying a relationship based on partnership and civil rights for both of them. However, 家 *ie* and its connotations persisted, partly in the new terms for family but also, according to family sociologists, in the moral framework of the postwar family concept. In Japanese, only a single character is read differently than it was in the prewar system: 家 is read as *ka* instead of *ie* (i.e., 家族 has become *kazoku* and 家庭 *katei*).[37] Translating both of these with the English word *family* obscures this character, even though it remains visible in the Japanese compound. Nonetheless, it is an important component of the concept of family, not least because of the legacy of the premodern *ie* (家) system. As Shimada relates, the prewar *ie* was preserved in postwar times as a cultural-societal reality, despite its abolition as a legal system. *Kazoku* and *katei* were "products of a translation effort, in which the legal system was adopted as an outer frame."[38] "There is ample reason," Shimada writes, "to assume that the *ie* phenomenon is on the one hand accepted in a transformed version, but on the other hand still plays a crucial role in deeper layers of reality in social life" — in the moral notion of venerating ancestors and parents, for instance.[39] In the twentieth century, rules and mores associated with the traditional meaning of *ie*, such as inheritance laws, changed considerably. But even in the 1990s, "despite the decline of the *ie* system as a family institution, the basic concept has in fact survived as a structural basis for contemporary Japanese groups."[40] How, then, did the moral conceptual elements of *ie* get transformed and yet survive in postwar Japan?

The intense prewar tradition of serving the nation as a family or *ie* spread into postwar politics and economics, instilling an image of the corporate world as a family system in post–World War II Japanese society. Okumura Hiroshi coined the term "corporate capitalism" (*hōjin shihon shugi*) for this particular kind of corporate domination over a whole nation (cf. the chapter by Zitelmann in this volume) — or, put the other way around, for a nation concentrating solely on the well-being of its companies and business corporations as if these were part of a family.[41] What could be described as a politically induced consensus about caring for Japan's (by which we can read the nation's) economy was based on three pillars, which Okumura describes as follows:

1. The idea of a company's employees as a community.
2. The idea of the eternal existence of a company.
3. The idea of a company as an educational institution.[42]

It is a short step from forming an idea of a company based on these features to characterizing the "company man" in Japan as someone who *belongs* to the company until retirement as opposed to a Western employee *employed* by a company with a formal contract serving as the central reference framework regulating the relationship between employer and employee. The feeling of family-type belonging is accompanied by that of moral and mental instruction provided by the company's leader, fostering the loyalty of the company man to his company. I observed this many times in the late 1980s, when Japan's economy was still thriving and the so-called economic bubble had not yet burst.[43] One of the most intensive impressions of how ultimate loyalty to the company was performed in interaction with a guest and foreigner was when an employee who happened to practice karate was summoned to the home of his supervisor, the company boss, on a Sunday afternoon in order to demonstrate some karate techniques for me. I felt ashamed: I was causing somebody to use up his precious free time from work solely in order to please his boss and an unknown guest. However, the employee himself told me he was proud of having been chosen by his boss to share his hobby (*shumi*) with me. References to the company were always accompanied by the ingroup signifier for "my" or "our," *uchi no*. *Uchi no* is not grammatically classified as a personal pronoun but is rather a signifier of belonging to an in-group and usually contrasted with *soto* (outside).[44] *Uchi no* is also used when referring to one's father or mother, or simply to somebody who belongs to one's group.

The renowned Kodansha Encyclopedia, a two-volume reference work for students of Japan, interprets this corporate culture as follows: "Each company's leader seeks to create a distinct ideology and company spirit; yet in fact company ideologies vary little. They portray the company as a big family, or in terms that underline common interest, comradeship and long-term relationships.[45"]

During my studies in Tokyo in the 1990s, it was not unusual for company leaders to seek advice and spiritual guidance from priests and monks or other religious scholars. I was sometimes invited to accompany one company manager on his visits to a highly revered spiritual authority both to seek personal advice and to attend group sessions to inspire managers and corporate executives spiritually and help them become good leaders. Books and other publications by spiritual authorities were also in high demand. All this underlines what the abovementioned encyclopedia refers to as a "distinct ideology and company spirit." Moreover, "The company's work is seen as contributing to the glory and prosperity of Japan. Company ideologies of this type encourage a Confucian rather than a utilitarian sense of productive organization in Japan. The money, the people, the company's history, and the results of business are all seen as merged into one organic social entity.[46"]

Part of the nation-focused ideology of prewar times was thus sustained after World War II when (as Okumura notes) it was not the Japanese state but the Japanese company that took on the role of the *ie* and the notion of "corporate capitalism." During the postwar decades and Japan's stunning economic rise, companies were considered *ie*, signifying that all employees were members of a household with the employer as its head. "The company envelops the employee's personal family, taking social and economic responsibility for it, and the employee's family in turn considers the company its primary concern. In this sense the *ie* institution is now played by the company, or any unit of work organization, and the concept of the *ie* persists in group identity as the basis of Japanese social structure.⁴⁷"

Simply put, during much of the postwar period the company resembled a family-like community that consisted, like the household of the premodern era, of relatives and nonrelatives. The legacy of this premodern concept of household was crucial for the normative power of the economized family idea in the decades of Japan's high growth (the 1950s through the 1980s). The postwar conceptual triad, we might therefore say, consisted of the family (ideology), the (nation-)state and the company. The ideological underpinnings of the *ie* system not only survived the war and the defeat but were transplanted into postwar Japan's new image of an economically successful and peaceful nation. Unsurprisingly though, harsh criticism was also directed toward the family notion's vulnerability to being captured, and this ultimately exposed the government's alliance with big business in the pursuit of economic progress at all costs.[48] In the wake of the New Left movement of the late 1960s and early 1970s, radical feminists depicted the concept of the family as the cornerstone of a system that continued to adhere to the patriarchy of the *ie*.

Criticizing Family

The preservation of the *ie* concept as a latent cultural-societal reality received a remarkable level of criticism in postwar Japan. In the late 1960s, the country experienced a vibrant student movement in which New Left groups were hugely prominent, not unlike the situation in many Western democracies of that decade. Similarly, the formation of a "new" or "second-wave" women's movement in Japan resembled developments in other countries in the late 1960s and early 1970s. But these are almost all the similarities that can be discerned because Japanese feminists' perception of what aspects of the status quo required criticism differed significantly from those of their counterparts in Europe or the United States. Among the most intriguing concerns of the Japanese new women's movement in this era is the strong attention devoted to other Asian women. As Vera Mackie puts it, "they wanted to locate their own struggle in the broader context of their location in Asia."[49] This included reflecting on Japan's past as an aggressor in World War II, the forced prostitution of thousands of (mostly) Asian women by the Japanese military during that war, the increase in sex tourism by Japanese (company) men to other Asian destinations after the war, and discrimination against Asian immigrant women in Japan.[50] Food and consumer goods produced by exploited labor in Asian countries and then imported to Japan were a serious issue to deal with, because low-paid women produced such goods and in many cases Japanese middle-class women bought them. In 1977, an organization called the Asian Women's Association (Ajia no onnatachi no kai) formed. Mackie explains some of the group's concerns: "These women attempted to close the temporal gap which separated them from their mothers who had experienced the militarized state of the 1930s, the age of imperialism and colonialism in Asia, and the Pacific War. In documenting women's complicity with the militarist state, they implicitly and explicitly questioned the workings of the postwar Japanese political system, and the roles women should play in this system."[51]

The political system and the role political and economic authorities expected women to play in it were ongoing issues for Japanese second-wave feminists. As early as 1970, another organization had formed under the name of the Conference of Asian Women Fighting against Discrimination (Shinryaku sabetsu to tatakau Ajia fujin kaigi).[52] As well as problematizing the relationship between Japanese men and women and women from other Asian countries, the conference discussed "the 'household' system and the links between familial ideology and imperialist ideology."[53] Here, "household" refers to the 家 ie concept described above and "familial ideology" to the continuation of this concept in postwar times.

One movement that addressed the ideologically loaded notions of household and family in a very radical way was the ūman ribu movement—ūman being the transcription for the English word woman and ribu the abbreviated transcription for the term liberation. The movement emerged in the early 1970s and is usually referred to as ribu. Ribu activists considered Japan's postwar transformation "from a wartime belligerent to a demilitarized and peaceful nation" to have been a "highly gendered process."[54] The postwar system restored the prewar gender ideology of "good wife, wise mother" (ryōsai kenbo). The democratic promises of the equality-oriented postwar Constitution, underscored by new laws and policies, remained mere promises, ribu argued. While "the postwar state produced a new modern family system," it "continued to regulate proper gender roles through legal and bureaucratic means" at the same time.[55] The trend toward regulation had a precedent: "The governmental regulation of the Japanese family began in the twentieth century through the establishment of the Civil Code that enforced family law based on a patriarchal (ie) household."[56] While the postwar Civil Code had been meant to implant ideas of gender equality and an emancipation from the social order of the nineteenth century, *ribu* women exposed several reasons why it had failed to do so.⁵⁷

> The Civil Code and the legal regulation of the family unit through the family registration system (*koseki seido*) functioned as a key mechanism in the biopolitics of the modern nation-state. The family registration system, established in 1872, continued to function as the key bureaucratic and regulatory device through which the state documented the population's birth, movement, and reproduction since the end of the nineteenth century. The family registration (*koseki*) has served as the official document that provides proof of one's birth and records one's place of residence, marital status, and death. Despite the postwar reforms of the Civil Code and family registration system, legal scholars have documented how a patriarchal family model underlies the family registration system and have argued that it serves to maintain hierarchy and discrimination in modern Japanese society.⁵⁸

It is no surprise that the legacies described in the quote above included the promotion of an idealized image of women as wise managers of the house and good mothers to their children. The official state-endorsed national and regional women's associations in postwar Japan were, accordingly, "Housewives' Federations," which were called *Shufuren* at the national level and *Chifuren* at the regional level. Several million women were organized in these federations. Welfare and education policies, employment schemes, and reproductive health laws all catered to a gendered division of labor and a gender ideology that portrayed Japanese women as idealized housewives. "The close ties [of the Housewives Federations] to the government and investment in women's roles as good wives and wise mothers formed the basis of the interlocking relationship between the Japanese family and state capitalism."⁵⁹

During my fieldwork with radical-left activist organizations in Tokyo in the 1990s, the normative power of the "good wife and wise mother" notion and the family as a signifier for a unity of husband, wife and children made an impression on me. The women of the groups I worked with lived in shared apartments as communities (called "cells," gender-segregated groups of male and female fellow activists). Their way of residing in such communities was considered "strange" by members of mainstream society because they did not live up to the expectations of a housewife. Single mothers were particularly discriminated against. For a woman's main occupation to be political activism transgressed the model of role assignment in "corporate capitalism."

In linking Okumura's "corporate capitalism" with the feminist critique of a housewife-centered family ideology, it becomes quite obvious that the idea of family means different things to different people in Japan. The basically bilateral pattern of kinship might help explain the relative success with which political and economic elites in pre- and postwar Japan respectively managed to let the idea of the nation(-state) family and the company family take root in many citizens' minds. "Both the paternal and maternal sides are symmetrically referred to and addressed by the same terms."[60] No difference is made between relatives by blood and relatives by marriage. Spouses are addressed with the same terms as cognates. Conceptually—and unsurprisingly—this again goes back to the *ie* system. "A set of relatives called *shinseki* [親戚, the Japanese term for kinship] is conceptualized in terms of households rather than individuals."[61] The woman who marries the son of a family (in English, the daughter-in-law) is the one who "moves into the house." This is expressed in Japanese by one character 嫁 that is composed of the component for "woman" (女) and "house" (家) and read *yome*. In the field of kinship, translating 家 as "household" hardly covers the conceptual range of meanings that goes along with this character. As mentioned above, the term for nation-state also contains the character 家, suggesting that the nation-state is one big "house" that is home to the people. In the prewar term *family state/family nation* (家族国家 *kazoku kokka*), 家 even appears twice, illustrating not only how the nation-state was perceived to "house" or be home to its people but also that it was understood as an organic family entity with the emperor as head. Moreover, the character 家 signifies a professional or expert in a certain field (here pronounced *ka*: for example a *judoka* is a person who practices judo). All these combinations and composites suggest that we can look up the translation words for *kinship* and *family* and arrive at 親戚 *shinseki* and 家族 *kazoku*, but then we would miss most of the relevant context for the concept of family by veiling them in non-Japanese semantics.

Conclusion

Looking up the terms *ie* (household) and *kazoku* (family) in the dictionary gives us a rough idea of what these words refer to in Japan. Such "translation words" do not produce a "gap in meaning"[62] between Japanese and English. But at the same time, Yanabu's judgment that "neither do they have anything in common" is true as well for the Japanese term on the one hand and the English term on the other hand. The ways in which concepts of household and family were utilized in pre- and postwar Japan to form normative frameworks for social and economic organization speaks to the many "faces" of the concept of family that the "translation words" do not immediately convey. In the prewar framework of the *kokutai* (national polity), the *ie* system served to instill a sense of loyalty to the imperial state as family in the form of filial piety. In postwar Japan, the normative legacy of the *ie* system helped foster a particular gender ideology in accordance with the ideas of the company as family and the woman as housewife—"corporate capitalism." The postwar period, in particular, saw harsh criticism of the "mainstream" concept of family, as the example of the *ribu* feminists shows. Although the reflection presented here merely skims the surface of the deep, many-layered discourse of *ie* and family in Japan and its numerous currents, it makes it clear that translation words are hardly capable of conveying the contextual notions around specific terms—particularly when these original terms are ideologically and normatively loaded. In the case of *ie* and family, however, putting the various facets of meaning into perspective can reveal the close relationship and connectivity between kinship terms and politics.

Claudia Derichs is professor of Transregional Southeast Asian studies at Humboldt Universität zu Berlin (HU), Germany. She studied Japanese and Arabic in Bonn, Tokyo, and Cairo and holds a PhD in Japanology (1994). Her habilitation thesis (2004) addressed the topic of nation-building in Malaysia. Her current research focuses on transregional studies in Asia and the Middle East, including a critical assessment of academic knowledge production. Her most recent monograph, co-authored with Kevin Coogan, is *Tracing Japanese Leftist Political Activism* (2023).

Notes

1. Mamadou Diawara, Elísio S. Macamo, and Jean-Bernard Ouédraogo, eds., *Translation Revisited: Contesting the Sense of African Social Realities* (Newcastle upon Tyne: Cambridge Scholars Publishing, 2018), back cover.
2. Akitoshi Shimizu, "*Ie* and *Dōzoku*. Family and Descent in Japan," *Current Anthropology* 28, no. 4 (1987): 88.
3. Shimizu, "*Ie* and *Dōzoku*," 88.
4. Shimizu, "*Ie* and *Dōzoku*," 88, devotes a short paragraph to the question, "Is the *Ie* a kinship system?" Very roughly, the study of domestic affairs in Japanese anthropology concentrates on *ie* while the study of societies other than (ethnic) Japan uses kinship as an analytical category. Research on contemporary Japan may not retain this division, but it is quite apparent for work on the time period discussed here.
5. Cf. Reinhart Koselleck and Todd Samuel Presner, *The Practice of Conceptual History: Timing History, Spacing Concepts* (Stanford, CA: Stanford University Press, 2002).
6. See Akira Yanabu, "Shakai—The Translation of a People Who Had No Society," in *Translation in Modern Japan*, ed. Indra Levy (New York: Routledge, 2011), 51–52, for a chronological list of translations of "society" and its various Western equivalents into Japanese.
7. The expression "translation words" goes back to the Japanese scholar Akira Yanabu, who "problematized between what he calls "Translation words" … and the everyday

language of Japanese spoken at home and in the workplace." Cf. Indra Levy, "Selections by Yanabu Akira: Editor's Introduction," in *Translation in Modern Japan*, ed. Indra Levy (New York: Routledge, 2011), 44.
8. Yanabu, "Shakai," 61.
9. Yanabu, "Skakai," 61, emphasis in original.
10. Levy, "Yanabu Akira Introduction," 44.
11. Abe Kin'ya, "Was bedeutet seken (öffentliche Sphäre) für Japaner? (1992)," trans. Robin Weichert, in *Geschichtsdenken im modernen Japan: Eine kommentierte Quellensammlung*, ed. Ken'ichi Mishima and Wolfgang Schwentker et al. (München: Iudicium, 2015), 93.
12. Andre Haag, "Maruyama Masao and Katō Shūichi on Translation and Japanese Modernity," in *Translation in Modern Japan*, ed. Indra Levy (New York: Routledge, 2011), 33.
13. Meiji Japan is the period from 1868 to 1912. Historians refer to this period as "modern Japan," which differs from the more popular understanding of the postwar period (1945ff.) as "modern Japan."
14. Rachel Leow, *Taming Babel: Language in the Making of Malaysia* (Cambridge: Cambridge University Press, 2016), 2.
15. For Herder's work, see Johann Gottfried Herder, *Abhandlung über den Ursprung der Sprache* [Treatise on the Origin of Language] (Berlin: Christian Friedrich Voß, 1772).
16. Katsuo Nawa, "Triangulating the Nation-State through Translation: Some Reflections on 'Nation,' 'Ethnicity,' 'Religion,' and 'Language' in Modern Japan, Germany, and Nepal," *Internationales Asienforum/International Quarterly on Asian Studies* 47, nos. 1–2 (2016).
17. Leow, *Taming Babel*, 2.
18. Susan Gal, "Polyglot Nationalism: Alternative Perspectives on Language in 19th Century Hungary," *Language et société* 136, no. 2 (2011): 33, cited in Leow, *Taming Babel*, 17–18.
19. The tremendous difficulty with and resulting variety of translations for the terms *modern* and *modernity* is traced in Wolfgang Schamoni, "Wie übersetzt man 近代 *kindai*? Anmerkungen zum Begriffsfeld 'Moderne' im Japanischen" [How to translate 近代 *kindai*? Remarks on the conceptual field of "modernity" in Japanese], in *Begriffsgeschichten aus den Ostasienwissenschaften. Fallstudien zur Begriffsprägung im Japanischen, Chinesischen und Koreanischen* [Conceptual histories from East Asian Studies: Case studies on conceptualization in Japanese, Chinese and Korean], ed. Harald Meyer (München: Iudicium, 2014).
20. For a compilation of primary sources debating Japan's status within the region (such as in relation to China) and in an international context of "modernity" see Ken'ichi Mishima and Wolfgang Schwentker, eds., *Geschichtsdenken im modernen Japan* (München: Iudicium, 2015).
21. The Ryukyu Islands, which comprise today's Okinawa Prefecture, were annexed by the Japanese nation-state in 1879.
22. Cf. Patrick Heinrich, "Language Planning and Language Ideology in the Ryūkyū Islands," *Language Policy* 3, no. 2 (2004).
23. Heinrich, "Language Planning," 157.
24. K. Kondō, "Kokka sōdōin taisei-ka no Okinawa ni okeru hyōjungo reikō undo" [The movement to enforce the standard language in Okinawa through the national mobilization (campaign)], *Nantō shigaku* [Historical Studies of the Southern Islands], no. 49 (1997): 32.
25. Heinrich, "Language Planning," 160, emphasis in original.
26. In Chinese translation, the same characters were chosen.
27. Leow, *Taming Babel*, 2.

28. Ryusaku W. Tsunoda et al., "Fundamentals of Our National Polity," in *Sources of Japanese Tradition*, compiled by Ryusaku W. Tsunoda et al. (New York: Columbia University Press, 1958), 2:278.
29. Ryusaku et al., "Fundamentals," 282. See also Klaus Antoni, *Der himmlische Herrscher und sein Staat: Essays zur Stellung des Tennō im modernen Japan* (München: Iudicium, 1991).
30. The term *great family nation* is a translation of the Japanese 一大家族国家 *ichidai kazoku kokka*; it is a literal translation of the Japanese characters. The term for family (*kazoku*) is in the middle.
31. Tsunoda et al., "Fundamentals," 282.
32. Shingo Shimada, *Grenzgänge—Fremdgänge: Japan und Europa im Kulturvergleich* [Border crossing—straying: Japan and Europe in cultural comparison] (Frankfurt: Campus Verlag, 1994), 140.
33. Naoki Arakawa, ed., *Japan: An Illustrated Encyclopedia* (Tokyo: Kodansha, 1993), 1:583.
34. Peter N. Dale, *The Myth of Japanese Uniqueness* (London: Taylor & Francis, 1986), 1. See also Aoki Tamotsu, *Der Japandiskurs im historischen Wandel: Zur Kultur und Identität einer Nation* [Theories on Japan in historic change: On culture and identity of a nation] (München: Iudicium, 1996).
35. Cf. Dale, *Japanese Uniqueness*, 57.
36. Shimada, *Grenzgänge—Fremdgänge*, 140.
37. The characters for nation-state (国家*kokka*) were not changed after 1945.
38. Shimada, *Grenzgänge—Fremdgänge*, 143.
39. Shimada, *Grenzgänge—Fremdgänge*, 143.
40. Arakawa, *Encyclopedia*, 583.
41. Hiroshi Okumura, *Kaisha hon'i-shugi wa kuzureru ka* [Is the enterprise-based system collapsing?] (Tokyo: Iwanami shoten, 1992).
42. Cf. Okumura, *Kaisha hon'i-shugi wa kuzureru ka*, 71–95.
43. The Japanese economy of the 1980s was called a "bubble economy" because equity and land prices increased rapidly and to an unprecedented extent in what economists call an "asset bubble." By 1990, this bubble burst. For details, see Thomas F. Cargill and Takayuki Sakamoto, *Japan Since 1980* (New York: Cambridge University Press, 2008), 83–100.
44. For a detailed discussion of *uchi* and *soto* see Takeshi Ishida, "Conflict and Its Accommodation: Omote-Ura and Uchi-Soto Relations," in *Conflict in Japan*, ed. E. S. Krauss, T. P. Rohlen, and P. G. Steinhoff (Honolulu: University of Hawaii Press, 1984).
45. Arakawa, *Encyclopedia*, 246.
46. Arakawa, *Encyclopedia*, 246.
47. Arakawa, *Encyclopedia*, 246.
48. For the close association of the ruling party, big business, and the ministerial bureaucracy in postwar Japan, the term *iron triangle* was coined.
49. Vera Mackie, "Dialogue, Difference and Distance: Feminism in Contemporary Japan," *Women's Studies International Forum* 21, no. 6 (1999): 601.
50. Cf. Mackie, "Dialogue, Difference and Distance."
51. Mackie, "Dialogue, Difference and Distance," 602.
52. Mackie, "Dialogue, Difference and Distance," 601.
53. Mackie, "Dialogue, Difference and Distance," 602.
54. Setsu Shigematsu, *Scream from the Shadows: The Women's Liberation Movement in Japan* (Minneapolis: University of Minnesota Press, 2012), 4.
55. Shigematsu, *Scream from the Shadows*, 6.
56. Shigematsu, *Scream from the Shadows*, 4–5.; cf. Shimada, *Grenzgänge—Fremdgänge*, 134–43.
57. See also Shimada, *Grenzgänge—Fremdgänge*.
58. Shigematsu, *Scream from the Shadows*, 6.

59. Shigematsu, *Scream from the Shadows*, 10.
60. Arakawa, *Encyclopedia*, 787.
61. Arakawa, *Encyclopedia*, 787.
62. Yanabu, "Shakai," 61.

Bibliography

Abe, Kin'ya. "Was bedeutet seken (öffentliche Sphäre) für Japaner? (1992)" [What means seken (public sphere) for Japanese people?]. Translated by Robin Weichert. In *Geschichtsdenken im modernen Japan: Eine kommentierte Quellensammlung* [History thinking in modern Japan: A commented collection of sources], edited by Ken'ichi Mishima and Wolfgang Schwentker et al., 90–96. München: Iudicium, 2015.

Antoni, Klaus. *Der himmlische Herrscher und sein Staat: Essays zur Stellung des Tennō im modernen Japan*. München: Iudicium, 1991.

Arakawa, Naoki, ed. *Japan: An Illustrated Encyclopedia*. 2 vols. Tokyo: Kodansha, 1993.

Cargill, Thomas F., and Takayuki Sakamoto. *Japan Since 1980*. New York: Cambridge University Press, 2008.

Dale, Peter N. *The Myth of Japanese Uniqueness*. London: Taylor & Francis, 1986.

Diawara, Mamadou, Elísio S. Macamo, and Jean-Bernard Ouédraogo, eds. *Translation Revisited: Contesting the Sense of African Social Realities*. Newcastle upon Tyne: Cambridge Scholars Publishing, 2018.

Gal, Susan. "Polyglot Nationalism: Alternative Perspectives on Language in 19th Century Hungary." *Language et société* 136, no. 2 (2011): 31–54.

Haag, Andre. "Maruyama Masao and Katō Shūichi on Translation and Japanese Modernity." In *Translation in Modern Japan*, edited by Indra Levy, 15–43. New York: Routledge, 2011.

Heinrich, Patrick. "Language Planning and Language Ideology in the Ryūkyū Islands." *Language Policy* 3, no. 2 (2004): 153–79.

Herder, Johann Gottfried. *Abhandlung über den Ursprung der Sprache* [Treatise on the origin of language]. Berlin: Christian Friedrich Voß, 1772.

Ishida, Takeshi. "Conflict and Its Accommodation: Omote-Ura and Uchi-Soto Relations." In *Conflict in Japan*, edited by Ellis S. Krauss, Thomas P. Rohlen, and Patricia G. Steinhoff, 16–38. Honolulu: University of Hawaii Press, 1984.

Kondō, K. "Kokka sōdōin taisei-ka no Okinawa ni okeru hyōjungo reikō undō" [The movement to enforce the standard language in Okinawa in its correlation with the national mobilization (campaign)]. *Nant_o shigaku* [Historical Studies of the Southern Islands], no. 49 (1997): 28–47.

Koselleck, Reinhart, and Todd Samuel Presner. *The Practice of Conceptual History: Timing History, Spacing Concepts*. Stanford, CA: Stanford University Press, 2002.

Leow, Rachel. *Taming Babel: Language in the Making of Malaysia*. Cambridge: Cambridge University Press, 2016.

Levy, Indra. "Selections by Yanabu Akira: Editor's Introduction." In *Translation in Modern Japan*, edited by Levy Indra, 44–50. New York: Routledge, 2011.

Mackie, Vera. "Dialogue, Difference and Distance: Feminism in Contemporary Japan." *Women's Studies International Forum* 21, no. 6 (1999): 599–615.

Mishima, Ken'ichi, and Wolfgang Schwentker et al., eds. *Geschichtsdenken im modernen Japan: Eine kommentierte Quellensammlung* [History thinking in modern Japan: A commented collection of sources]. München: Iudicium, 2015.

Nawa, Katsuo. "Triangulating the Nation-State through Translation: Some Reflections on 'Nation,' 'Ethnicity,' 'Religion,' and 'Language' in Modern Japan, Germany, and Nepal." *Internationales Asienforum/International Quarterly on Asian Studies* 47, nos. 1–2 (2016): 11–31.

Okumura, Hiroshi. *Kaisha hon'i-shugi wa kuzureru ka* [Is the enterprise-based system collapsing?]. Tokyo: Iwanami shoten, 1992.

Schamoni, Wolfgang. "Wie übersetzt man 近代 *kindai*? Anmerkungen zum Begriffsfeld 'Moderne' im Japanischen" [How to translate 近代 *kindai*? Remarks on the conceptual field of 'modernity' in Japanese]. In *Begriffsgeschichten aus den Ostasienwissenschaften: Fallstudien zur Begriffsprägung im Japanischen, Chinesischen und Koreanischen* [Conceptual histories from East Asian Studies: Case studies on conceptualization in Japanese, Chinese and Korean], edited by Harald Meyer, 208–46. München: Iudicium, 2014.

Shigematsu, Setsu. *Scream from the Shadows. The Women's Liberation Movement in Japan*. Minneapolis: University of Minnesota Press, 2012.

Shimada, Shingo. *Grenzgänge—Fremdgänge: Japan und Europa im Kulturvergleich.* [Border crossing—straying: Japan and Europe in cultural comparison]. Frankfurt: Campus Verlag, 1994.

Shimizu, Akitoshi. "*Ie* and *Dōzoku*: Family and Descent in Japan." *Current Anthropology* 28, no. 4 (1987): 85–90.

Tamotsu, Aoki. *Der Japandiskurs im historischen Wandel: Zur Kultur und Identität einer Nation* [Theories on Japan in historic change: On culture and identity of a nation]. München: Iudicium, 1996.

Tsunoda, Ryusaku W., William T. de Bary, and Donald Keene. "Fundamentals of Our National Polity." In *Sources of Japanese Tradition*, compiled by Ryusaku W. Tsunoda, William T. de Bary, and Donald Keene, 278–88. New York: Columbia University Press, 1958.

Yanabu, Akira. "Shakai—The Translation of a People Who Had No Society." In *Translation in Modern Japan*, edited by Indra Levy, 51–61. New York: Routledge, 2011.

Index

A
Abbott, Andrew, 377, 388, 392–93
Abe, Kin'ya, 401, 413
Abraham, 41
Adam, 179, 382
Addis Abeba, 119
administration, 10, 23, 68, 82, 116, 118–20, 122, 128–30, 194, 302, 307, 309, 316, 344, 346, 388
administrator, 2, 14, 30, 63, 118, 122, 132
adoption, 7, 14, 105n6, 120, 172–73, 218, 220, 258, 271, 292, 305–8, 314
affiliation, 25, 98–99, 271, 345
affinity, 5, 18, 26, 36, 79, 80–81, 85, 88, 94, 105, 182, 197, 301, 304
affinal, 36, 83, 117, 149, 151, 153, 324, 334
affine, 87, 93–94
affinitas, 38; *generis*, 38
affinitatis, 93, 95; *affinitatis vincula*, 40
Africa, 5, 121–22, 128–29, 153, 248, 299, 301–2, 305, 308, 315–16, 320, 357; West, 101, 292, 300–4, 310, 317
agency, 119, 133, 265
agnate, 34, 95, 213; agnatic, 107, 116–17, 191
agnatio, 35, 40; *agnatus*, 384
Agnes, sister of Berthold V, 62
Ahnenprobe, 46
Alexander II, Pope, 31–32, 36–37, 41, 43–44
alliance, 2, 94, 116, 119–20, 167–68, 170, 173, 179–81, 184, 191, 195, 206, 219, 304, 333, 342, 385, 408; formation, 173, 179; strategies, 173; spousal, 168, 176
Alsace, 324–25
Amboise, 207, 226n22
America, 91, 96, 167, 196, 236, 238, 244–45, 247, 251–54, 268, 391; North, 85, 91, 391; Americas, 46
amity, 131, 133
Amsterdam, 390
ancestor, 10, 33, 35–36, 38–39, 45–46, 49, 61–63, 69, 93–94, 106, 116, 230, 283, 313, 383, 406; ancestral, 11, 40, 69, 93, 334, 402
ancestry, 24, 57, 60–61, 82, 90, 98–99, 231, 293, 313, 335, 344; corporeal, 334; fictive, 127
Anderson, Benedict, 404
Angers, 208
Anna Amalia, Saxon duchess, 68
Anna, Sister of Berthold V, 62
anthropology, 3–9, 25, 26–27, 29, 69, 79, 82–83, 87, 96, 102–3, 104n4, 127–28, 145, 157–58, 298, 301, 319n17, 399, 412n4; critical, 133; French, 126; functionalist, 128; modern political, 115; of kinship, 5, 96, 267, 279; physical, 96, 100–101; racial, 26; social, 5, 26, 93, 114–15, 120, 122–23, 126, 130, 132–34; "symmetrical" or "recursive", 263, 281n4
anthropometry, 83, 96, 99–100

Aquinas, Thomas, 42
arbores consanguinitatis and *affinitatis*, 93–95
Aristotle, 210, 229n65, 284n54
Asad, Talal, 126
Asia, 85, 87, 248, 408–9, 412
association, 9, 87, 124, 126, 174, 186, 189, 209, 246, 248–49, 265, 270–72, 278, 315, 330, 335, 343, 386–87, 89, 403, 409–10, 414n48; fraternal (*Genossenschaft*), 121–22, 124
Aubelin, Claude, 207
Auclert, Hubertine, 280
Augustine, Saint, 30, 41
aunt, 81, 88, 149, 151–52, 154, 180, 296, 311
Austria, 121, 354, 382, 384
authenticity, 53, 264–65; authentication, 4, 326
authority, 10, 14, 37, 53, 99, 118, 123–24, 173, 176–77, 192, 204, 209–15, 218–20, 223, 226n14, 228n50, 237, 239–40, 244, 250, 294, 301, 314, 378, 382, 389, 391
autonomy, 147, 199n91, 240, 264, 272, 275

B
Baden, 60–62
Bamberg, 187
baptism, 336–37, 342, 345, 347n1, 349n37
Basilius von Ramdohr, Friedrich Wilhelm, 169, 181–85
bastard, 220, 272
Beamte, 181, 187; -*nstaat*, 181, 186
Becker, Anna, 210, 228n50, 285n60
belonging, 58, 93, 97, 145, 147–48, 161, 186, 212, 271, 297–98, 305, 307, 313, 318n8, 321n51, 359, 403–4, 406–7
Benin (republic), 292, 296–300, 303, 306, 316–17
Berlin, 99–100, 130, 138n90, 148, 187
Bern, 61, 187
Berthold V, last Duke of Zähringen, 62
Beza, Theodore, 207

bilateral, 35, 122, 298, 331, 333, 339, 410; bilaterality, 331
biogenetic origin, 360
biological, 6, 80–81, 83, 91, 101, 103, 178, 258n78, 264, 284n53, 285n59, 305, 308, 310, 337, 355, 357–63, 366; knowledge, 91; biologization, 264; biology, 7, 23, 25–26, 69, 102, 179, 192, 263
biopolitical, 81, 367; instrument, 82, 103; dispositive, 103
biopolitics, 13, 103, 265
biotechnology, 354–55, 357–58, 361–62, 364–65, 369nn5–6, 370n21; act, 354–55, 357, 364–65, 366, 368n3, 370n17, 371n23
birth, 3, 59, 63, 83, 91, 102, 133, 150, 156, 173, 188, 217, 219, 222, 230n101, 236, 245, 286n71, 291, 297, 306–10, 314–15, 321n51, 329–30, 333, 334–35, 337, 339–40, 342, 345, 347n1, 357, 359–60, 365–67, 371n25, 372n38, 372n41, 372n51, 385, 410; certificate, 313, 316, 357; corporeal, 335–36; giving, 265, 268, 272–73, 276–77, 312, 314, 333, 359, 361, 363, 365–67, 372n38
Bizzocchi, Roberto, 53
Blackstone, William, 94–95, 238
Bloch, Marc, 343, 377
blood, 26, 35, 38–45, 46, 60–63, 65, 68–69, 80, 88, 92–94, 98–99, 102, 148, 150, 174, 178–79, 206, 214, 217–23, 226n22, 229n65, 239, 246, 251, 258n78; Christian, 31; community of, 126, 131; French, 98; impure, 46; Indian, 99; *mélange du sang*, 92; mixed, 46, 48n29, 99; mixture of, 92; metaphor of blood, 80, 93; metaphor of shared, 26, 80–81; money, 117; Negro, 98; purity of, 46, 100, 257–58n77; relations, 81, 187; relationship, 101, 104n6; relationships constituted through, 168, 258n78; shared, 26, 35, 45–46, 80–81; ties of, 175, 188; white, 92, 98. See also *limpieza de sangre*

bloodline, 57, 61–63, 68, 222, 258n77, 276
Boas, Franz, 26, 82, 96–101, 103
Bodin, Jean, 169, 176, 204–19, 221–24
body, 26, 36, 39, 45–46, 114, 183, 212, 237, 264, 274, 359, 364–67, 372n51, 386; gendered, 364–65, 367, 372n51; human, 37, 39–40, 45, 365; maternal, 170, 262–64, 266, 273–79, 386; productive, 265, 268, 273, 278; reproductive, 264, 266, 359–60, 362–63; productivity, 274, 285n60
Böhmer, Justus Henning, 380–81, 388, 394n11, 395n46
Bologna, 32
bolshevism, black, 128
Bona, 296–98, 308, 311, 318n7
Borgu region, 304, 307, 311, 314, 318n4
Borneman, John, 156
Bouquet, Mary, 6, 17n18, 94
bourgeois, 175, 186–87, 378;
    Bildungsbürger, 186
Bourges, 207
branch, 38–40, 56, 61, 94, 301, 304
bride price, 304, 308
British Columbia, 101
brother, 33, 40, 49n45, 87–88, 97, 104, 148–49, 160, 180, 182–84, 208–9, 215, 219, 220, 226n17, 229n86, 245, 262, 277–78, 296–98, 308, 310, 312–14, 331, 338, 383
brotherhood/*fraternité*, 126, 278, 336
Brunswick-Lüneburg (family), 62
Buchanan, Richard T., 97–98
bureaucracy, 2, 12, 103, 169, 173, 300; bureaucrat, 1, 175, 186, 188, 194; -writers, 181; bureaucratic, 181, 186, 291, 299, 304, 311, 357, 404, 409, 410; state, 1, 175, 181
Burma, 120

C
Calvin, John, 207; Calvinism/Calvinist, 204, 207–9, 220
canones, 37–38. *See also* law
capitalism/capitalist, 27, 123, 126, 145–46, 149, 152–53, 158, 190, 410;
    hōjin shihon shugi ("corporate capitalism"), 406–7, 410, 412
care, 2, 4, 9, 24, 144, 148, 153, 159–60, 167, 170, 185, 194, 219, 237–38, 243–44, 251–52, 276, 280, 291–92, 314, 332, 335, 337, 354, 358, 388; across German-German border, 146, 149
Casaubon, Egérie, 272–77, 284n47, 284n53, 285n60, 286n72
casta, 46, 92–93; *castas*, 92, 106n37; *caste*, 79–80, 99
Catholic Church, 10, 23, 25, 30, 32, 36, 43
censuarius, 332, 339, 344, 346
Champeaux, Ernest, 35
Charles I (king), 239
Charles VII (king), 302
Charles Albert II, Prince of Hohenlohe-Schillingsfürst, 65
Charles de Bourbon, 208
Charles Frederick, Margrave of Baden, 61
Charles Gustavus (king), 384
Chicago, 96, 122
Chickasaw (tribe), 97–98
child/childhood, 9, 14, 33, 41, 44, 83, 92, 97–98, 105n14, 133, 149, 152–53, 156, 167–68, 170, 173–75, 180, 184, 186, 188, 190–92, 194–95, 201n114, 206, 210–11, 214–15, 218, 223, 229n68, 229n83, 236–40, 243–44, 252, 254n14, 262, 265–68, 270–78, 280, 281n12, 283n38, 285n59–61, 285n63, 286n87, 291–92, 296–98, 305–9, 311–15, 320n47, 328, 330, 334, 336–40, 343, 349n30, 350n40, 357–60, 362–67, 370n14, 371n23, 371n25, 372n38, 383–87, 389, 394n8, 403, 405, 410. *See also* grandchild
child fostering, 296–97, 301, 313–14, 321n51; *bii nenobu/bii nenubu*, 301, 308, 313–14, 321n50; *enfants rétifs ou mal conformés*, 305, 307; foster children, 298, 309
Childebert (king), 218
China, 125, 390, 413n20

Choctaw (tribe), 97–98
Christ (Jesus), 41, 325
Christianity, 249, 286n72, 312; Christian/Christian community, 44, 46, 312, 336
Christina, Queen of Sweden, 384
cieng, 116, 117, 120, 135n28
citizen, 44, 63–67, 69, 145, 148–49, 155, 158, 162n7, 162n12, 212, 242–43, 262, 279, 302, 315, 383, 387, 389–90, 411; *Bürger/Staatsbürger*, 63–64, 67, 186, 378, 387; *citoyen*, 387; *civium nomen*, 387
citizenship, 4, 13, 24, 103, 120, 148, 150, 155, 268, 291, 294, 372n38, 378, 382, 386, 392
civilisé/civilized, 301–2, 308, 315, 391; civilization, 16–17n11, 247, 249, 315, 319n17, 403
clan, 79, 98, 102, 113, 116, 127, 130–31, 175, 180–81, 189, 311, 313–14, 318n9, 321n51, 331; *diel*, 116–17; *Sippe*, 125, 331
Clarke, Edith, 365
class, 6, 7, 12–13, 16n4, 34, 58, 68, 81, 119, 131, 167, 169, 173, 175, 181, 183, 185, 192–93, 195, 239, 267, 269, 298, 317, 330, 391, 409
classification, 6, 46, 85, 87, 127, 129, 133, 277, 301, 303, 305, 308, 313, 346, 363; classify, 5, 10, 23, 27, 82, 87–88, 99, 121, 299, 301–2, 305–6, 384, 388, 407
clientelism, 119, 391–92
closeness, 23, 25, 29–30, 32, 34, 36, 41–44, 93, 292, 297; emotional, 145–46, 151–52, 154–55, 159
Clothild (queen), 218
Code Napoleon, 93, 125, 302–3
cognate, 83, 90, 94, 335, 411; cognately, 333; *cognatio/cognatus*, 38, 42, 327, 330, 348, 384; cognatic, 331, 338
cohabitation, 173, 331
cohesion, 9, 130
collateral, 38–40, 85, 87, 94–95, 105n22
collectivism, 26–27, 114, 131
colonus, 338, 340

colonial, 2, 5–6, 8, 17n19, 27, 31, 46, 80, 118–19, 121–22, 128–29, 132, 237–38, 291, 296–97, 299–300, 302–3, 307–10, 315–16, 318n10, 319n24, 320n34, 320n37, 320n40, 320n47; administration, 82, 116, 118, 120, 128–29, 302, 307, 309; language, 297, 300; societies, 92, 292
colonialism, 266, 297, 300, 307–9, 320n44, 409; colonize/colonizer, 132–33, 161n3, 237, 292, 300, 303, 308, 310, 314–15; colony, 128, 237, 240, 248, 280, 302–3, 315
commater, 337
community, 26, 46, 54, 82–83, 116–17, 12–22, 125–26, 130–31, 133, 139n103, 156–57, 216, 250, 312, 329, 333, 335–36, 343, 350n38, 404, 406, 408, 410; *Gemeinschaft*, 130–31, 139n103
company, 390, 406–8, 411, 412
compater, 337
conception (becoming pregnant), 35, 133, 273, 359–60; assisted, 354, 357, 360–61, 365–66
Congo, 122
conjugal, 332; family, 27, 149, 155–56, 160, 190, 196n2, 294; system, 190–91
conjugium, 339
conjunctio, 339
connubium, 339–40, 346; connubiality, 338
consanguine, 30, 36, 38, 41–42, 93, 117, 149, 334, 339; *consanguineus/ consanguinus*, 37–38, 333; consanguinity, 5, 26, 30, 36, 41–42, 80–81, 85, 94, 104–5n6, 173, 301, 304, 334, 348n22
contractualism, 392–93; contractarian theories, 225–26n15, 285n60, 294, 377–78, 380–81, 384, 391–93
contubernium, 339
cooperative, 130–31
corporate, 114, 116–17, 120–27, 130–34, 136n31, 402, 406–7, 410, 412; group,

26, 115–16, 120–24, 126, 131–32, 134, 139n103; *Verband*, 123–25
corporative, 123, 124–26, 130–32, 134; corporation, 27, 115, 121–22, 124–26, 134, 186, 189, 389, 406; corporatism, 26, 122, 126, 133–34
corporeal, 37, 265, 278, 334–36
corruption, 2, 186, 189, 193, 244, 291
cousin, 10–11, 33, 36, 81, 87, 90, 98, 149, 151–53, 168, 170, 173, 180, 213, 220, 246, 256n53, 263, 308, 310–11, 314, 331
Coutumier du Dahomey, 300–1, 303–5, 307–8, 314–15
culture, 1, 8, 45, 81, 102, 108n71, 132–33, 157, 169, 172, 183, 191, 193, 195, 248, 264, 315, 402, 405, 407

D

Dahomey, 293, 296, 300–5, 307–8, 314–16
Dakar, 300, 302–3, 317
Dale, Peter, 405
Damian, Peter, 25, 29–37, 39–46, 48n26
Darwin, Charles, 80, 91
daughter, 11, 49n45, 62, 81, 87, 97, 100, 183, 188, 231n119, 245, 271, 310, 383, 411. *See also* granddaughter
David, 41
Davis, Kingsley, 190
degree, 8–9, 11, 14, 16–17n11, 25, 30, 33–35, 37–42, 46, 49n45, 85–88, 90–91, 93–94, 102, 106n28, 117, 125, 153, 188, 222, 231n127, 239, 333, 337, 358, 369n12, 377, 383–84
Démar, Claire, 275–77, 285n59
democracy, 13, 243, 249–50, 400
demos, 400
dependency, 270, 324
Deroin, Jeanne, 267–71, 274, 276–77, 283n28, 285n63
descendant, 33, 38–39, 45, 61, 87, 94, 226n22, 249, 309, 320n44, 333, 335, 340–41, 343, 384–85
descent, 2–3, 7, 10, 13, 15, 24–25, 33, 37, 41, 46, 57–60, 62, 65, 80–81, 83, 88, 93–94, 99, 107n46, 122–23, 127, 146, 148–50, 161, 167–68, 170, 236, 251–52, 257n76, 258n78, 304–5, 308, 319n17, 333–34, 336, 343, 399; descent group, 175
Descola, Philippe, 264
diagram, 14, 24–25, 37–39, 45, 89–90, 93–96, 101–3, 108n70; genealogical, 90, 94, 95, 102
dibling, 356, 370n14
diffusionist, 127, 131
discursivity, 264
DNA testing, 24, 360
document, 53, 58–63, 65; documentation, 4
domestic, 2, 7, 169, 172, 174, 176, 182–84, 190, 210, 228n56, 242, 247, 249, 256n53, 294, 329, 344, 384, 386, 389, 391–93, 405, 412n4; domesticity, 182. *See also* house
dominion, 57–58, 250, 285n60, 385; maternal, 285n60
dominus, 327, 337, 345
donor, 173, 360, 370n14, 371n23; child, 358, 370n14; register, 360. *See also* reproduction
Dörflis, 69
Dow, James, 123
dowry, 212, 285n63, 304, 343
Duchesne, André, 59, 70n1, 73n32
Durkheim, Émile, 114, 121–22, 125–27, 130, 133–34, 156
dynastic, 10–11, 205–8, 221–22; histories, 58–60, 64; *Geschlechterhistorien*, 58; dynasty, 11, 58, 175, 217, 231n123, 310

E

economy, 1–2, 12, 16n4, 27, 79, 99, 118, 123–25, 128, 145–46, 148, 150–51, 154–60, 162n7, 168, 170, 172, 191–92, 195, 199, 210–11, 214, 224, 228n53, 246–47, 255n43, 262–63, 266, 273–74, 276–77, 279–80, 283n27, 285n57, 294, 299, 315, 324, 330, 341, 362, 368, 401, 404–9, 411, 414n43
Edwards, Jeanette, 356, 370n14

egg, 354–56, 360, 364, 372n38; cells, 355, 358–59, 363, 365, 369n4, 371nn30–31; commodification of, 358; donation, 263, 292–93, 354–59, 362–63, 367, 368n3, 369n5; donated, 363, 371n34; fertilized, 365, 371n32; foreign, 359, 363; *fremmed*, 359
Eichner, Carolyn J., 272
emancipation, 25, 98, 263–64, 267, 269, 272, 274, 276, 279, 330, 409
embryo, 363, 371n32
endogamy, 81, 104n4, 127, 169, 181
endowment, 13, 124–25; *Stiftung*, 124
Engels, Friedrich, 80, 155
England, 63, 94, 175, 188, 237–40, 245, 384
Enlightenment, 2, 57–59, 64, 176, 243, 249
Ephraim, 41
epistemology, 14–15, 23, 30, 315, 319; ethno –, 81; epistemological, 2, 8, 24–27, 95, 129, 160
equality, 125, 145–50, 153–54, 157, 159, 168, 170, 188, 242–44, 246, 249, 251, 253, 255n40, 266–69, 277–78, 293, 327, 354–55, 357, 360–64, 409
Ethiopia, 118–20, 135
ethnic, 24, 26, 30, 69, 147, 162n3, 173, 200n101, 307, 311, 412n4; classifying, 305–6; groups, 157, 194, 304–6, 313, 402. *See also* identity
ethnicity, 26, 29, 147, 173, 200n111; *peoples*, 305
eugenicists, 80, 101, 104n4
Euro-America, 249, 299, 319n17, 357
Europe, 2, 4, 6–7, 9–13, 17n18, 26, 29, 55, 62, 79–81, 91–92, 98–100, 115, 121–26, 131, 134, 158, 169, 173, 180, 196, 242–44, 246, 248–49, 257n64, 263–64, 278, 283n27, 292, 294, 297, 299–300, 302–5, 308–10, 312, 314–15, 318n7, 318nn9–10, 346, 354, 356–57, 360, 371n26, 377–78, 382–84, 390–93, 400, 403, 408
Evans-Pritchard, Edward E., 5, 7, 114–20, 122, 129–30, 132, 299, 304
Eve, 179

evidence, 25–26, 35, 58–60, 62, 64–66, 68–70, 72n21, 98, 100, 126, 244–45, 266, 271, 285n60, 310, 328, 330, 332–34, 336–37, 343, 347n5, 350n38, 365
evolutionist, 79, 96, 301
exogamy, 10, 80, 99, 104n4, 127, 131, 178–80, 192
exploitation, 270, 274, 324

F
familia, 176, 213, 227n46, 330, 332, 335, 339–40, 342–44
familial, 14, 95, 167–70, 172–73, 175, 177, 182, 192–95, 198n74, 201n114, 215, 219, 235, 238–39, 253n2, 291–92, 310, 409; estate, 188; identity, 180
famille, 210, 227n46, 272, 297, 298–301, 303–5, 308–17, 318n5, 319n17, 320n30; *chef de*, 168, 176, 210, 214, 216, 223, 227n46, 387; *etendue*, 292, 304, 308, 315, 319n17; *fami*, 297–98, 313, 318n5
family, 2–3, 7, 9, 11, 14, 16n4, 17n12, 26–27, 44, 56, 58, 64–67, 80, 85, 91, 94–95, 100–1, 103, 115, 121, 123, 125–31, 134, 144, 149, 151, 153, 155–57, 167–70, 172–80, 182–88, 190–95, 199n91, 199n95, 200n96, 201n114, 204, 206–20, 222–24, 226n14, 227n46, 229n68, 230n92, 231n123, 231n126, 235, 237, 240, 245, 247, 249, 251, 256n53, 263, 267–68, 271–75, 279, 292–94, 296–98, 300–1, 304, 306, 310–12, 316–17, 319n17, 320n47, 335, 342, 350n46, 365, 377–79, 381–84, 386–87, 389–93, 394nn8–9, 395n46, 398–99, 401–12, 414n30; American, 190–92; bilateral, 122; company, 411; conjugal, 27, 155, 160, 191, 196n2, 294; extended, 131, 156, 175, 186, 188, 292, 296, 299–300, 304–5, 308, 315–16; *katei* (家庭), 405–6; *kazoku* (家族), 405–6, 411, 414n30; modern, 131, 156, 174, 178, 195, 402; nuclear/ *Kernfamilie*, 3, 9, 149, 160,

169, 174–75, 190, 192–95, 196nn6–7, 197n11, 199n91, 200n101, 200n110, 207, 298–9, 331, 405; tree, 58, 60, 67, 94–95
fascism/fascist, 27, 114, 123, 126, 133–34
Fassin, Didier, 147
father/*baa*, 11, 67, 83, 87–88, 90–91, 97–8, 100–1, 104, 119–20, 126, 180, 183, 186, 191–93, 200n109, 201n114, 208, 210, 211–15, 217, 219–23, 226n17, 229n65, 231n123, 237–39, 245, 254n17, 267–68, 270–73, 276–77, 280, 305, 308–12, 314, 327, 331, 333, 360, 362, 365–67, 371n25, 371n34, 372n38, 383–86, 407; biological, 360; social/legal, 355, 357, 359–60, 362–63; fatherhood, 24, 360, 363, 366–67, 372n38, 372n50; *Familienvater*, 186; *Hausvater*, 168, 176, 186, 227n46
Federal Republic of Germany *or* FRG, 147, 148–9, 162n7; West German side, 145, 156
feminism/feminist, 170, 243, 247, 249, 255n38, 262–72, 275–80, 281–2n13, 282n16, 282n20, 284n40, 284n47, 285n59–60, 361, 379, 402, 408–10, 412; proletarian, 266, 282n20; theory, 263–64
Ferguson, James, 315
Ferrando, Stefania, 271, 284n40
fertility, 306, 358, 362 371n31
Fichte, Johann Gottlieb, 402
filiation/filial relation, 14, 36, 38, 41, 82–83, 87, 91, 93, 95, 101, 105n14, 168, 170, 217, 220–21, 262, 275–76; maternal, 263, 266, 275, 276–77, 279, 304–5, 355, 360, 399; paternal, 271, 276, 278
Filmer, Robert, 382, 386, 395n47
Fischer, Eugen, 101
Florence, 33
Fortes, Meyer, 5, 114–15, 122–23, 129, 131, 133–34, 299
Foucault, Michel, 103
France, 9, 11, 64, 66, 75n59, 125, 169, 185, 199n91, 208, 211, 220, 222, 228n60, 229n65, 230n97, 231n123, 238, 293, 302–3, 384, 388
Francis II, Emperor, 64, 226n22
Francis, Duke of Anjou and Alençon, 208–9, 229n86
Franklin, Benjamin, 236
Fraser, Nancy, 274
Frederick Wilhelm III, King, 65, 75n61
free/*liber*/*libertus*, 44, 66, 121, 175, 178–80, 186–87, 243, 245, 247–50, 269–70, 275, 293, 300, 313, 327, 329, 332–38; -born, 324–26, 328–29, 331–38; *ingenuus*, 325–29, 333–34, 336, 338–41, 345–46; freedom/*libertas*, 126, 130, 134, 156, 167–68, 174–75, 177–80, 187–88, 190, 240, 248–50, 266, 272, 274–75, 325–8, 333, 335; unfreedom/freedom dichotomy, 188. See also *censuarius*, *colonus*
french colonies, 280, 302
Friedelehe, 339
Friedrich, Duke of Saxe-Hildburghausen, 68
friend, 66, 130, 177, 180, 183, 243, 245, 267, 283n36, 292, 343; friendship, 16n6, 131, 133, 170, 179, 182–83, 193, 243, 246, 252, 255n38, 280, 331
Fulda, 68, 341
Fulda, Daniel, 72
functionalism/functionalist, 80, 122, 127–28, 145, 158, 299

G

Galton, Francis, 26, 81–82, 88, 89, 90, 91, 93, 94, 99
Gambella, 119
gamete, 354, 359, 365
Gardner, Helen, 103
Gatterer, Johann Christoph, 25, 54–56, 58–61, 63–66, 69
Gay, Désirée, 262, 277, 280
gender, 2, 26, 68–70, 88, 99, 121, 169–70, 176–77, 180, 225, 226n14, 247, 252, 255n40, 257n68, 263–64, 294, 318n10, 333, 340, 355–57, 361, 363–68, 371n26, 372nn40–41, 372n51, 379, 409–10, 412; birth, 365–67,

372n41; bodily, 364, 372n41, 372n51; cells, 365; difference, 364; equality, 293, 361–62, 364, 409; identity; legal, 364–67, 372n41, 372n51; reconfiguration of, 356, 364
gene, 31; genetic, 17n15, 24, 80, 100, 103, 173, 355, 357–60, 362–63; genetics, 24, 29, 46, 103, 360
genealogical, 6, 8, 10, 25–26, 41, 53–54, 56–57, 59–61, 64–65, 67, 69–70, 73n34, 88, 96–97, 100, 101, 103–4, 116, 170, 313, 340; analysis, 82, 94–95, 102–103; anti- stance, 277, 286n72; data, 96, 127; diagrams, 90, 94–95, 102; grid, 80, 83, 102; history, 26, 54, 63–68, 70; history (*genealogische Historien*), 54, 56–57, 59, 69, 72n19; method, 6, 8, 26, 81–83, 87–88, 96–97, 101–3; model, 266, 276, 286n72; relation/relationship, 80, 97, 105n14, 308, 319n17; representation, 58, 83; thinking, 313; work, 53, 57–59, 62, 65
généalogies fabuleuses, 53, 69
genealogy, 17n15, 17n18, 25–26, 42, 53–54, 58, 60, 62, 66, 68–70, 72n20, 72n23, 80, 82–85, 87, 97, 101, 114, 276–77, 301; female, 272, 276; male, 276; of Christ, 41
generation, 2, 6–7, 9–11, 23, 29, 33, 35–37, 40–42, 44, 46, 61, 81–82, 85, 90–93, 95, 97–99, 106n32, 106n37, 114, 151–52, 155, 167, 169, 187, 192–93, 199n91, 276, 278, 308, 311, 331, 334, 341, 404
Geneva, 207–8, 380–81
Georg, Prince of Saxe-Hildburghausen, 68
German Democratic Republic *or* GDR, 147–56, 162n8, 162nn11–12; *Neue Länder* (new states), 150
German states (the two German states/ GDR and FRG), 147, 150–51, 156–59; German states (Holy Roman Empire), 185
Germany, 27, 65, 146–50, 155, 157, 159–60, 162n8, 169, 175, 354; eastern, 144, 149, 153, 158; South, 185–6; East-West, 150; West, 149, 155, 159
Geschlecht (dynasty), 11, 175
gestation, 268, 273, 359, 371n25. *See also* reproduction
Gierke, Otto, 27, 115, 121–22, 124–25, 134, 139n103
gift, 149, 151–52, 154, 163n18, 185, 329
Gliddon, George R., 93
Global North, 157; Global South, 157
Gluckman, Max, 5, 120, 132
God, 61, 216, 222, 237, 277, 325–26, 336, 378, 385
godparent, 337; godparenthood, 332, 342, 344, 349nn36–37
Goode, William, 299
Goody, Jack, 6, 9–10, 174
Göttingen, 54, 59, 386
Gouges, Olympe de, 284n40
Grabfeld, 65, 68
grandchild, 39–42, 312, 331
granddaughter, 33, 37, 40, 49n45, 383; great-, 39, 42
grandparent, 33, 98, 149, 199n91, 296, 311, 314; great-grandparent, 33, 36
grandson, 33, 88, 219, 378, 383; great-, 33, 39, 42
Gratian, 31
Grotius, Hugo, 379–81, 383, 386–87, 390, 392, 394n11
Guerreau, Anita, 35–36
Gullestad, Marianne, 361

H
Haag, Andre, 401
Habsburg (family), 61–62
Haeckel, Ernst, 94
Halle (Saale), 144
Haller, Albrecht von, 378
Haller, Karl Ludwig von, 378–80, 392, 395n46
Hardenberg, Karl August von, 121
Hausen, Karin, 176
Hegel, Georg Friedrich, 27, 115, 121, 123, 134, 168–69, 172, 174–82, 184–91, 193–95, 225–26n13, 379
Heidelberg, 74n46, 187

Heinrich, Patrick, 403
Helwig, daughter of Anna (sister of Berthold V), 62
Henderson, A. M., 123
Henry of Navarre, 208–9, 220–22, 225n1, 231n127
Herder, Johann Gottfried, 402
hereditary, 3, 26, 65, 68, 88–90, 99, 107n44, 208, 217, 219–21, 223, 243, 248, 256n53, 257–8n77, 284n43, 309; status, 29, 223, 239, 242–4, 248, 252, 256n53; heredity, 23, 31, 80, 83, 88, 91, 101, 104, 170, 256n53; social and biological, 88–90, 99, 107n44, 239
Herrschaft, 124–25, 338, 340; *-sverband*, 125
Herwig, Johann Justus, 63–67
heterosexuality, 155, 182, 190, 192, 258n78, 270
Hildburghausen, 66
Hiroshi, Okumura, 406
historiography, 3, 9, 25–26, 53–59, 66, 69–70, 80, 109, 206, 208–9
Hobbes, Thomas, 189, 285n60, 379–81, 385, 388, 391–92, 394n11
Hohenlohe (family), 63–65, 67, 74n52, 75n53
Hohenzollern (family), 65
Holy Roman Empire, 61
Holzschuher (family), 64
hormone, 358
Hotman, François, 169, 204–9, 211–13, 216–24, 226n17, 227n29, 228n59, 230n97, 230n101, 230n106
house, 7, 11, 61–65, 67, 75n54, 120, 128–29, 132, 154, 175–76, 180, 187, 192, 211, 214, 216, 228n56, 229n70, 237, 327, 335, 343, 391, 410–11; *bet*, 120; concepts of, 7, 175, 211; master of the, 386; *Hausmutter*, 176; *Hausvater*, 176; *société à maison*, 6–7, 11, 36. See also domestic
household, 3, 97, 125–27, 171n1, 174–76, 179, 182, 184, 191–92, 198n6, 199n91, 210–11, 214, 229n70, 292, 294, 296, 326, 328, 341–42, 350n46, 378, 382, 386, 389, 392, 398–99,
401–2, 404, 407–9, 411; economy, 125; *mesnage*, 176, 210, 214, 227n40, 227n46; householding, 176
human, 5–7, 11, 16–7n11, 17n19, 24, 37–40, 43–5, 67, 79–81, 85, 91, 93, 101–2, 104, 126–7, 148, 151, 153, 177, 181–3, 205, 216–7, 223, 230n88, 237, 250, 265–8, 279–80, 282n23, 284n53, 285n61, 301, 361, 363, 365, 385–7, 389, 391, 399; humanist, 207–8; humanitarian, 150, 153, 160; humanity, 6, 54, 63, 91, 174, 176, 249, 262, 267, 282n23
Humboldt, Alexander von, 92, 106n37
Hungary, 144, 148
husband, 83, 87, 101, 151, 168, 173, 177, 179, 182, 184, 186–88, 191–93, 201n114, 206, 210–13, 228n50, 237, 243, 267, 269–71, 274, 277, 297–98, 306, 314, 318n3, 339–40, 371n34, 385–86, 389, 410

I
identity, 59, 67, 68, 103, 167, 177–78, 180, 272, 312, 316, 334, 358–60, 363, 366, 372n39, 402, 408; ethnonational, 404; genetic, 173; Japanese, 405
ideology, 26, 79–80, 167, 190, 195, 236, 252, 265, 405, 407–10, 412
in-laws, 10, 11, 30, 36, 149, 297–98, 411; sisters- and brothers-in-law, 81, 149, 151, 180
incest, 34, 80, 128, 178, 195–96, 339; legislation, 31; prohibition, 23, 34–35, 93, 178–79, 339, 385; rule, 35, 173
independence, 168, 177, 180, 184, 186–88, 238, 240–41, 243–44, 254n14, 256n52, 302–3
India, 46, 92, 97, 121, 125, 390
indigenous, 302, 403; *indigènes*, 302–3, 305–6; category of *indigene*, 302–3
individualism, 9, 283n33; liberal, 122
individuality, 177, 265, 270–71; natural, 177
Individuum, 179

industrialization, 126, 190, 196
infertile, 306, 355, 361; infertility, 306, 358, 371n31
inheritance, 10, 16n4, 24, 37, 40, 43, 79–80, 82–83, 88, 90–91, 93–95, 144, 163n21, 167–68, 170, 173, 188, 206–7, 215, 219, 221, 223, 277, 293–94, 306, 310, 332, 336, 341–42, 344–46, 357, 378, 383; critique of, 277; family, 215, 382–83, 392; human, 80, 93; law, 14, 24, 99, 278; Mendelian patterns of, 101; Roman inheritance law, 24, 36–38, 40, 43–44
institution, 16n4, 85, 115, 124, 128, 167–68, 170, 187, 190, 200–1n96, 209, 247, 299, 306, 331, 406, 408; *Anstalt*, 124
Institutiones, 33
Isidor of Seville, 44
islands of Mabuiag and Badu, 83
Italy, 354
Iustolfus, 325

J

Jantz, Richard L., 96
Japan, 294, 390, 399–412, 412n4, 414n48
Jena, 65, 75n61, 187, 386
Jerome, Saint, 41
Jesus. *See* Christ
Johnson, Douglas, 118
Jolly, Margaret, 265
Joseph, 41
Joseph, prince of Saxe-Hildburghausen, 68
jus sanguinis, 148, 150, 372n38
Justinian, 32–33, 37, 42–43

K

Kant, Immanuel, 177, 379–80, 383, 389
Kaufmann, Franz-Xaver, 156
kin, 2–3, 9–13, 23, 30, 33, 36–38, 40, 44–45, 63, 67, 80, 82–83, 87–8, 90, 93–95, 99, 117, 120, 144–6, 148–55, 157–60, 169, 172–74, 177–81, 185–88, 190–95, 200n109, 215, 256n53, 292–93, 296, 298–99, 306, 312, 318n3, 327, 330–31, 335–37, 339–41, 343–45, 347n1, 370n14, 372n45, 383, 391; ascendent, 94; consanguineous, 30, 36, 38; prohibited, 30, 38, 42, 178; relation, 10, 12, 23–24, 29, 32, 38, 40–42, 80–82, 87, 90–91, 97, 100, 102, 105n6, 145, 147, 155, 157, 159, 178, 192, 262, 271, 291; spiritual, 337; term, 85, 87, 101–2, 162n11; terminology, 6, 81, 90; vocabulary, 85
kinning, 151, 347n1; de-kinning, 150, 152–54, 158, 292
kinship, 3–15, 16n6, 17n14, 24–27, 29, 31–32, 35–38, 40, 42–46, 53, 57, 61–62, 67–70, 79–81, 83, 85, 87–88, 90–97, 102–3, 104–5n6, 114–15, 117–20, 122–23, 125–30, 132–34, 139n103, 144–51, 153, 155–61, 167–76, 179, 181, 185–87, 189–91, 193–95, 196n2, 196n5, 196n9, 199n91, 206, 209, 211, 213–24, 231n14, 235–36, 251–52, 253n3, 258n78, 263, 267, 277–80, 291–94, 299–301, 304–5, 308–13, 316, 319n17, 324, 326–27, 330–36, 340, 343–45, 347n3, 350n46, 355–57, 363–67, 370n14, 372n51, 377–79, 391, 398–99, 402, 410–12, 412n4; *shinseki* [親戚], 411; *Verwandtschaft*, 113; affinal kinship relations, 93, 324; American kinship system, 191; artificial, 119, 126; biological, 308; body of, 45–6; calculating, 25, 30, 34, 48n26, 82, 90, 94, 319n17; conceptualization of, 3–4, 14, 16n6, 23–24, 27, 30, 32, 34, 36, 38, 43–45, 169, 204, 206–7, 216, 219, 223, 264, 293, 316; cultural, 264; decline of, 10, 13, 29, 146; dissolution of, 144; Euro-American, 356; extended, 131–32, 146, 150–51, 153–54, 156–57, 159–60, 186, 196n2, 299–300, 319n17, 331, 356; German-German, 154–55, 159–60; idiom of, 1, 168; interpretation of, 148; mapping, 24; network, 3, 154, 195, 207, 300, 334; new kinship studies, 264;

nonbiological, 308; nuclear, 336; practice, 62, 195, 229n66, 316; quantification of, 30–31; spiritual, 293, 337; term, 37, 42, 85–86, 104–5n6, 113, 119, 126, 131, 156, 162n11, 172, 206, 211, 224, 312, 319n17, 331, 357, 391, 398, 411; terminology, 37, 42, 85, 87, 116–17, 120, 293, 299–300, 346
Koller, Marvin R., 199n91
Königsberg, 66, 75n65
Koppers, Wilhelm, 131
Kornai, Janos, 157
Koselleck, Reinhart, 400
Kpaso, Woru, 310
Kpaso, Yarou, 309–10
Krader, Lawrence, 123
Kuklick, Henrika, 88
Kuper, Adam, 122
Kurka *or* Arthur, 82
Kyburg (family), 62

L
L'Hospital, Michel de, 205, 208–9
labor, 9, 85, 126, 128–29, 132–33, 156, 170, 173, 192, 201n114, 246, 251, 267–69, 273–75, 277–79, 283n28, 285n64, 339–41, 409; alienable and inalienable, 285n64; division of, 126–27, 276, 410; labor-sharing pair, 339. *See also* maternal *and* work
Labouret, Henri, 128–29
Landauer, Carl, 123
language, 7, 11, 17n14, 45, 54, 64, 82, 85–88, 90, 99, 115–17, 128, 133, 147–48, 161n3, 193, 195, 219, 235, 239, 265–66, 273, 283n33, 291, 294, 296–300, 304, 306, 312–14, 316–17, 318n4, 319n17, 321n53, 326, 345, 378, 398, 400–5, 413n7, 413n24
law, 1, 12, 14, 23, 25, 30, 38, 83, 99–101, 115, 120, 122, 124, 129, 150, 156, 168–69, 187–88, 195, 198n74, 205–8, 211, 214–17, 220–21, 224, 229n67, 231n119, 238–39, 242, 246, 248–50, 265, 271, 276–77, 291–4, 302–4, 325–27, 329, 332, 335, 348n15, 354–55, 357, 359–61, 364–68; canon, 23–24, 31, 35, 44, 93, 207, 372n39, 372n41, 378, 383–86, 388–90, 405, 409–10; *canones*, 37–38; church, 23, 31, 180, 337, 344; civil, 33, 35, 93, 125, 188, 302–3; family, 2; *Institutiones*, 33; Code Napoleon, 93, 125, 302–3; *Code Civil, 271, 275, 280; Coutumier du Dahomey*, 300–5, 307–8, 314–15, 319n26; customary, 169, 205, 207, 217, 224, 293, 303, 308; divine, 37, 178, 222, 248; inheritance, 14, 23, 38, 40, 99, 278, 406; marriage, 32; natural, 205, 214, 216–18, 222–24, 229n83, 383, 385–86; of nature, 183, 218, 384; of succession, 231n26, 278; international, 390; private, 379, 389; Roman, 32–34, 36, 40–41, 43–44, 58, 93, 205, 207–8, 214, 216–17, 221, 223–24, 229n67, 230n97, 327, 383; Roman civil, 33, 35, 37–38, 40–41, 44; Roman inheritance, 36, 38, 44; world-citizen, 390; legal regulations, 355–57, 367
Le Play, Frédéric, 9
Leach, Edmund, 120, 123
Leclerc, Georges-Louis, Comte de Buffon, 92
Legendre, Pierre, 38–39
legislation, 30, 100, 167, 170, 301, 364, 370n14; legislative practices, 257; legislative process, 293, 356–57, 368
Leibniz, Gottfried Wilhelm, 62–63
Leow, Rachel, 402
Lessing, Gotthold Ephraim, 55
Lévi-Strauss, Claude, 6–7, 11, 17n19, 36, 81, 109n80
liberty, 239–43, 249, 250, 332, 386, 390
Lie, Merete, 361–62
life, 3–4, 23, 27, 38, 68, 85, 91, 103, 117, 123, 127, 130, 132, 155, 162n11, 167, 170, 175–76, 180, 184–85, 194–95, 200n96, 200n109, 201nn114–15, 206, 214–15, 217, 229n73, 239, 241, 243–44, 249, 254n14, 263, 266, 270, 272–73, 278, 293–94, 300,

314–16, 321n51, 326, 329–32, 334, 336–38, 341, 343–45, 369, 385, 404, 406; domestic, 169, 176, 184, 242; ethical, 175, 177, 187, 193, 196n7; modern, 1–2, 172–73, 263; primitive, 172; traditional, 172
limpieza de sangre, 46. See also blood
line, 2, 10, 13, 33, 39–41, 45, 61, 81, 94–95, 98, 100–2, 176, 186, 191, 199n85, 208, 222, 252, 256n53, 305, 313, 333–34, 382, 384; collateral, 38–40; direct, 11, 42; female, 62; filial, 94; male, 53, 61, 226n22
lineage, 7, 13, 26, 60, 93, 115–17, 119–22, 135n28, 168, 175, 179–81, 187, 191, 195, 198–99n85, 217, 292, 298, 309, 313, 333–34, 343, 404; male, 94, 276; marital, 338; system, 119, 122, 299, 304. See also *cieng*, *Geschlecht*, patrilineage and *Stamm*
lineal, 40, 94, 191, 384; multi-, 190–91; multi- system, 198n85
Lobbes, 341
Locke, John, 16n6, 254n17, 285n60, 379–80, 382, 386, 392, 395n47
Lombard, Jacques, 304, 318n4
London, 115, 128, 381–82
lordship, 328, 332, 335–39, 344–46, 348n24, 350n42. See also *Herrschaft*
Lothar (king), 218
love, 29–30, 46, 177, 182, 186, 206, 213, 215, 218–19, 223, 229n83, 237, 239, 241–42, 244–47, 251–52, 258n78, 271, 275, 297; passionate, 177, 183
Lugard, Lord Frederick, 128–29

M
Mackie, Vera, 408–9
Mahir, 41
Maine, Henry, 27, 115, 121–22, 134
Maistre, Joseph de, 379
Maitland, F. W., 122, 137n60
Malinowski, Bronisław, 102, 115, 127–29, 133
man, 26, 46, 80, 92, 94, 116, 168, 170, 175–76, 182–85, 193, 199n94, 205, 210, 218, 242, 244, 250, 255n40, 262, 265–72, 277–78, 283n27, 284n43, 286n78, 286n87, 296, 306–7, 309–10, 312, 318n3, 336, 338–39, 345, 349n30, 354–55, 359–67, 371n30, 372n38, 381, 384–86, 388–89, 405–6, 408–9; masculinity, 2, 201n114
Manasseh, 41
Mann, Michael, 331
manumission, 293, 324–25, 327–34, 336–38, 340, 343–46, 347n9; *manumissio*, 324; manumitter, 325–30, 334, 347n5, 349n38; manumitted, 293, 325–27, 329–30, 332–46, 347n5, 349n38
market, 12, 92, 131, 156, 167–68, 174, 189, 221, 236, 388
marriage, 2, 6, 10–14, 38, 41, 43–45, 48n22, 59, 62, 80, 83, 94, 102, 104n6, 116–17, 127, 131, 149, 156, 167–68, 170, 177–84, 186–88, 191–93, 228n53, 236, 240–41, 243–45, 247, 249, 250–52, 255n38, 257n68, 257n76, 258n78, 269, 271, 276, 283n27, 291–94, 296–97, 299, 304–5, 308, 311, 319n17, 332, 336, 338–42, 345–46, 347n1, 350n39, 357, 378, 382, 384–85, 388, 391–92, 399, 411; consensus, 338; cousin, 98, 170, 173, 180, 246, 256n53, 263; in-, 340; legitimate/*matrimonia legitima*, 173, 338; levirate, 301; mixed, 92, 340; law, 32; out-, 256n53, 340; payment (*Heiratszins*), 340; prohibitions, 23, 25, 30–31, 33, 35–37, 40, 44, 46, 173, 340; prohibitions against marrying kin, 30; Catholic/ecclesiastic marriage prohibitions, 10, 24, 35, 44; rule, 116, 173; psychological dimensions of, 178; re-, 339; married couple, 176, 190, 214, 297; wedding, 149, 332, 338–39; wedding fees (*Heiratszins*), 339
Martini, Karl Anton von, 380, 384, 387
Mary, the Virgin, 41
materiality, 264
maternal, the, 272; maternal, 46, 60, 88, 90, 94–95, 98, 191, 215, 229n83, 262,

Index

265, 272–73, 275, 279–80, 285n60, 286n87; body, 170, 263–64, 266, 273–79, 293, 333, 386, 411; filiation, 263, 266, 275–79; labor, 266, 273, 276, 278, 285n63; productivity, 285n60

maternity, 262, 265, 272–74, 276–80, 282n16, 285nn59–60, 355, 357–58, 360, 372n38; biological/genetic, 360; enslaved, 266; social/legal, 360

matriarchy, 192, 279; pathological, 199n94

matrilineal, 98, 101

matrimonium, 332, 338–39; matrimonial property regime, 383; matrimony, 385

matronymic, 170, 266, 271–74, 276

Mauss, Marcel, 126, 134

Mazzolini, Renato, 80, 106n37

McKinnon, Susan, 256n53, 316

Melanesia, 128

Melhuus, Marit, 371n32

memoria, 37, 38

Menius, Justus, 211

meritocratic, 13

method, 6, 8, 23–26, 30, 32–33, 36–37, 40–43, 46, 49, 54, 58, 61–63, 67, 80, 96, 108n71, 118, 129, 133; Du Chesne, 59; genealogical, 6, 8, 26, 81–83, 85, 87–88, 96–97, 101–103; method of measuring/calculating kinship, 23, 25, 29, 31–36, 40, 42–46, 48n26, 82, 319n17

Mexico, 92

Middle Ages, 9–11, 13, 23–24, 30, 35, 44–45, 48n29, 63, 65, 93, 123, 204, 221, 228n60, 293, 331, 350n38, 350n46, 383

Middleton, Karen, 263

migration, 4, 13, 83, 100, 119, 129, 150, 157, 304

missionary, 2, 85, 128, 312, 314, 316, 320n34

Mitterauer, Michael, 349n36, 350n46

mixture, 45, 92, 101, 181–82, 298, 331; *mestizaje*, 92

modern, 1–5, 8–9, 12–14, 24–27, 31, 37, 46, 71n12, 80, 102–3, 109n82, 115, 146, 149, 155, 157–61, 168, 170, 172–75, 177–78, 189–92, 195, 196nn1–2, 204, 206, 213, 226n23, 227n39, 251, 253, 262–63, 265, 267, 279, 292, 299–300, 319n17, 324, 362, 369n5, 377, 379, 392, 399, 403–4, 410, 413n13, 413nn19–20; family, 131, 156, 174, 178, 402, 409; subjectivity, 177; early modern, 2, 9, 12–13, 23, 31, 53, 57–58, 62, 67, 69, 72n21, 82, 92, 93, 172–73, 176, 178, 185, 206, 212, 221, 224, 225n13, 226n14, 228n55, 229n65, 229n70, 230n94, 266, 285n60, 294, 302–4, 377–78, 382–85, 387–88, 391–92, 395n47; premodern, 1–3, 9, 12, 172, 264, 406, 408; frühe Moderne, 172; frühe Neuzeit, 172; debut de l'ère modern, 172

modernization, 2–3, 6, 9, 12, 29, 123, 155–57, 196n2, 299–300, 303, 399, 403; *kindaika*, 403; ideas of, 159–60; theory, 8–9, 159, 299

monarchy, 169, 204–8, 214, 217, 220–24, 225n1, 236; absolute, 384, 392

monogamy, 236, 246, 248–50, 304, 308, 320n30, 338–39, 350n39

Montaigne, Michel de, 205

Montesquieu, Baron de, 242–43, 247–49, 256n57, 256n62, 380–81, 383, 390–91, 395n46

Morgan, Jennifer L., 266

Morgan, Lewis Henry, 5, 17n12, 26, 81–82, 85–88, 90–91, 93–94, 101–2, 105n15, 105n17, 105n23, 107n40, 107n43, 108n71, 109n80, 247, 304

Moses, 32, 40–41

mother, 81, 83, 87–88, 90–91, 97–98, 100, 107n46, 126, 132, 151, 173, 180, 183, 192–94, 199n94, 201n114, 211, 214–15, 218–19, 223, 225n1, 225n8, 229n65, 229n83, 229n85, 230n108, 238, 262, 265–66, 268, 271–80, 283n27, 284n38, 285n60, 286n71, 296–97, 301, 305, 311–12, 314,

333, 349n30, 358–60, 363, 365–67, 371n25, 372n38, 383, 385–86, 407, 409, 410; *mero/mero bisibu*, 312, 314; biological/social, 355, 357, 359; by blood, 276; genetic, 362, 363; *social, 276, 362*; social/legal, 363, 364; mother belonging (*morstilhørighet*), 359; mother-child unit, 262, 265, 280; mother-child relationship, 192, 275, 281n12; of humankind, 267–68
motherhood, 170, 173, 263–69, 273, 275–76, 278–80, 281n12, 282n14, 282n20, 283n28, 285nn59–60, 286n71, 344, 358, 360–61, 363–64, 366–67, 372n38, 372n50; biological, 361, 363; emancipatory, 265–66; genetic, 363; social/legal, 363; unified (*enhetlig morskap*), 359; unitary, 360, 364; voluntary, 286n71
Moulin, Charles du, 207
Müller-Wille, Staffan, 31

N
Nadel, Siegfried, 121, 130–31, 133
name, 10–11, 41, 62, 79, 97, 116, 222, 244, 268–73, 276–77, 283n36, 284n38, 310–11, 313, 315–17, 318n4, 320n47, 325, 334, 336, 338, 349n28, 379, 387; father's, 267, 270–71, 273; husband's, 267, 269–71, 274; name-giving, 334, 337; naming, 10, 13, 270, 357
Naples, 32
nation, 4, 6, 54, 56, 66–67, 85–86, 88, 103, 146, 148–50, 160, 161n3, 223, 244–45, 384–85, 387, 390, 402–4, 406–9; *Nation*, 402; state, 80, 102–3, 251, 402, 404, 408, 410–11, 413n21; 国家 *kokka* (nation-state), 403, 414n37; -building, 121; idea of the nation(-state) family, 411; family state/family nation (家族国家 *kazoku kokka*), 411, 414n30
national, 8, 26–27, 68–69, 82, 122, 124, 128, 133, 147, 169, 246, 296, 302, 313, 316, 320n32, 321n53, 367, 370n14, 387, 402–4, 410; polity (*kokutai*), 404, 411; unity, 403
nationality, 26, 173, 313
natural, the, 265; natural, 16, 67, 80, 87–88, 92, 96, 117, 127, 133, 146–48, 159, 169, 177–78, 185, 189, 205, 214, 216–18, 220, 222–24, 229n83, 230n94, 237–39, 244, 252, 264, 271–73, 283n38, 285n57, 309, 313, 347n1, 354, 359, 361, 363–64, 378, 382–83, 385–86, 388–89, 391–92; *naturlig*, 359; sciences, 31; naturally, 160, 178, 359–60, 371n30, 384
naturalism/naturalist, 85, 264, 378; naturalization/naturalized, 8, 26, 102, 146–47, 159, 236, 240, 251–52, 253n5, 264, 298
nature, 1, 15, 31, 37, 43, 81, 87, 90, 102, 148, 167–69, 170, 173, 175–76, 178–81, 183, 189–90, 204–6, 213–14, 216–18, 222–24, 228n56, 230n94, 236–38, 252, 253n2, 264–65, 276, 278–79, 294, 359, 363, 365–66, 380, 383–85, 387, 390–91, 404; *natur*, 359; concept of, 215; of kinship, 42–43, 45, 145, 159, 169, 185; of reproduction, 31
natus, 325, 333
Needham, Rodney, 6
neighborhood, 3, 125, 131, 133, 195
nephew, 42, 88, 107n44, 126, 149, 180, 206, 218, 309–10
New York (city), 96
New York (state), 85
Nicot, Jean, 213
niece, 81, 149, 151, 180
Nietzsche, Friedrich, 70
nobility, 10, 44, 62, 204, 217–18, 230n101, 248
notation, 88, 90; system, 88–90
Nott, Josiah C., 93
Nuer, 5, 7, 114–16, 118–20, 125, 129–30, 132, 304, 316
Nürnberg, 187
nursing, 262, 273
nurturing, 237–38, 265, 273, 276, 285n59

O

Occident, 114, 302, 324, 329
Oertzen, Christine von, 99
Okinawa, 403, 413n21
Oklahoma, 97
Oldham, Joseph, 128
organization, 1, 3–5, 7, 10–11, 16n6, 79, 85, 101, 124–27, 132–33, 153, 196n2, 247, 250–51, 279–80, 286n78, 292, 299, 301, 304–5, 316, 387, 399, 401–2, 405, 407–11; ruling, 125
origin, 6, 24–25, 46, 63–69, 81, 91, 178, 187–88, 191, 205, 207, 263, 269, 278–79, 297, 302, 318n6, 318n9, 344–45, 360; history of, 67; family of, 80, 177, 297–98
Orléans, 207
other, the, 3–4, 9, 131, 148, 154–55, 157, 175, 177, 181, 186, 303, 309, 390–91; othering, 27, 153, 155, 158; otherness, 145, 151, 161, 399
Ottweiler, 325

P

Paine, Thomas, 239–41, 244, 248
parent, 33, 41, 44, 83, 90, 92–93, 97–98, 103, 133, 149, 174–75, 177, 180, 184, 188, 191, 206, 214–16, 218, 223, 237–40, 243–45, 252, 254n14, 284n53, 291, 296, 305–6, 314, 321n51, 333, 336–37, 343, 347n1, 360, 367, 371n23, 382–83, 389, 406; biological, 337; birth, 306, 314–15, 321n51; foster, 314, 321n51; freeborn, 325, 329, 333; non-birth, 308; spiritual, 337
parentage, 275–76; shared, 61, 103
parental, 98–99, 219, 238–40, 307, 331, 333, 335–36, 341, 347n1, 386; power, 386–387; relation, 97, 333, 337, 345; responsibility, 366–67
parentalization, 320n46, 324, 327, 335, 345–46, 347n9; *Parentalization*, 347n1
parenthood, 133, 314, 364, 366–67, 372n41; biological, 361; social/legal, 361; parenting, 188, 292–93, 297; parenting practices, 306, 307
Paris, 207, 209, 226n17, 227n33, 341, 381
Parsons, Talcott, 27, 123–24, 169, 174, 178, 187, 190–95, 200n101, 200n113
Pateman, Carole, 281n12, 283n25, 285n68, 379
pater, 35; *familias*, 168, 176, 209–11, 213, 215, 227n46, 388
paternal, the, 272; paternal, 10, 46, 88, 90, 94–95, 159, 168, 231n123, 239, 271–72, 276, 278, 293, 311, 313, 333, 335, 359, 385, 411; authority, 123, 173, 192, 219; power/*potestas patria*, 386, 389, 392
paternity, 35, 173, 237–39, 276–77, 280, 336, 355, 357–58, 360, 367, 372n38; biological, 359; legal/social, 359
patriarchal, 119, 125, 131, 236–37, 240, 244, 247, 249–51, 254n17, 409–10; regime, 127
patrilineage, 298, 305, 318n3, 318n9; patrilineal, 7, 9, 62, 101, 115, 169, 218, 220–24, 231, 311–12; patrilineality, 169, 213, 217, 222–24, 298, 305, 316
patron (*patronus*), 327, 330, 335, 337; patron-client relationship, 119, 347n6; patronage, 13, 209, 291, 329, 331–32, 335–36, 344, 346, 347n10, 349n24; patronage systems, 185
Paul, Saint, 37, 45, 327, 329
Paulus Prudentissimus, 34
pedigree, 6, 82–84, 87, 89, 94–95, 101
Perham, Margery, 122
Peter, Saint, 329
Philadelphia, 96
philosophy, political, 254n17, 256n55, 263
Piketty, Thomas, 2, 200n101, 200n113
plant, 67
Plato, 400
Poitiers, 209
political, 1–14, 23–27, 30, 44, 54, 60–61, 64–70, 91, 100, 114–19, 122–23, 129, 132, 144–48, 150, 154–55, 157–61, 163n21, 167–74, 177, 183–85, 188,

192–95, 204–7, 210–14, 216–17, 221–22, 224, 226n14, 227n39, 227n46, 235–37, 240–44, 246–51, 253n1, 254n17, 256n53, 256n55, 257n62, 262–64, 266–68, 270–71, 274–80, 281n2, 281n12, 291–94, 299, 301, 307–11, 313, 316, 331, 355, 357, 362, 369n5, 371n32, 377–79, 381, 387, 390–93, 400–2, 405, 410–12; order, 2, 11–12, 26, 126, 168–69, 217, 223–24, 230n88, 235, 243, 248, 251, 263, 292; participation, 2, 294; projects, 1, 14, 146; reform, 294; support, 150; system, 114, 120, 153, 299, 304, 320n32, 400, 409; theory, 2, 14, 168–70, 204–6, 208–9, 211, 213, 218, 222, 224, 247, 251, 253n3, 265, 270, 275, 278, 377, 378; transformation, 13, 291; vision, 14, 158

politics, 1–2, 4–5, 8, 12–15, 16n4, 17n19, 25–27, 29–30, 114–16, 120, 122, 124, 133, 145–46, 150, 155, 159–61, 162n7, 167, 169, 185, 194, 205–6, 210, 222, 224, 245, 251, 253n3, 255n38, 262–63, 270, 278–80, 294, 300, 308, 316, 327, 345, 355, 367, 378, 395n28, 399, 402, 406, 412; of making kinship, 146, 148, 158–61

polygamy, 170, 236, 242, 246–51, 255n40, 256n51, 257n68, 301, 303–4, 308, 385

population, 17n19, 44, 82–83, 88, 91, 95–97, 99–102, 126, 169, 172, 200n96, 293, 299, 302–3, 315, 334, 367, 387, 410

power, 3, 11–13, 24–25, 30, 57–58, 60–61, 63, 90, 124, 126, 147, 168–69, 176, 179, 181, 184, 189, 192, 195, 210–11, 213–18, 220, 223, 228n50, 238–39, 246, 248, 250–51, 253n2, 253n5, 254n17, 263, 266, 275, 285, 299, 330–33, 344–46, 378, 380, 382, 384–85, 389–90, 403–4, 408, 410; parental, 386–87; paternal, 386, 389, 392; political, 61, 67, 119, 236

practice, 4, 9, 10, 13, 27, 31, 53, 57, 62, 67–69, 80, 82, 91, 103, 108n71, 114, 123–25, 127, 131–33, 145–46, 148, 149–51, 155, 157, 159–60, 168–69, 173–74, 179, 181, 185–87, 193, 195, 206, 217–18, 221, 223, 226n14, 229n70, 248–49, 263, 270–71, 280, 283n35, 291–93, 296–97, 299, 300–3, 305–9, 314–16, 319n26, 321n50, 327–28, 330, 332–34, 337–40, 342, 347n10, 356–58, 360, 366–67, 370n18, 372n38, 386, 398, 400

pregnancy, 91, 362, 365, 367

premodern, 1–3, 9, 12, 172, 264, 406, 408

private, 1–3, 134, 167, 174, 176, 181, 186, 193, 221, 249, 277, 294, 309, 377–79, 382, 387–90, 392–93; interest, 127, 186, 389. *See also* public *and* property

procreation, 5, 91, 192, 284n55, 338, 357–58, 360, 363–64, 366–67, 389; human, 80; natural, 359; power of, 179; procreative, 276–77, 292; practice, 366–67

progenitor, 45

progeny, 61, 173, 179, 238

proof, 46, 60, 67, 101, 145, 310, 360, 366, 410

property, 2, 6, 10–11, 17n12, 36, 40–41, 44–46, 63, 66, 79, 83, 124, 127, 167–70, 173, 177, 185–87, 190–91, 194–95, 198n74, 206–7, 210, 219, 221, 223, 228n59, 247, 266–67, 269, 273–74, 277, 294, 315, 329–30, 332, 334, 341–42, 344, 384; bourgeois property law, 187; common, 279; devolution, 13, 35, 44, 168, 173, 185, 188, 195; *fideikommissum*, 187; free, 187; holding, 173, 175, 180, 186, 195; in family, 267–68; in the person, 268, 270, 275; landed, 332, 334, 339; matrimonial property regime, 383; movable/*peculium*, 332, 341, 343; private/privatized, 3, 221, 277; relations, 157, 187, 194

Prüm, 341, 349n28

Prussia (territory), 65

Prussia (the Royal House of), 65, 67

psychological, 79, 88, 130, 168, 176–78, 182, 190, 192, 194, 199nn94–95, 249; psychotherapist, 174, 192, 195
public, 1–3, 117, 124, 134, 150, 152, 167, 173, 181, 184, 193–95, 206, 208, 221, 226, 242–43, 255n36, 267, 294, 300, 327, 329, 333, 355–56, 358–59, 360, 369n5, 371n31, 372n41, 381, 386–91, 394n11; and private, 127, 186, 193, 249, 378–79, 382, 389, 392; -private distinction, 1, 174, 176, 294, 377, 387–88, 393; –/private boundary, 263, 294; space, 379
Pufendorf, Samuel, 380, 382, 384–85, 387, 389, 392
Putnam, Frederic Ward, 96

R

race, 79–82, 92–93, 99–100, 103, 147, 213, 229n65, 249, 313; concept, 29, 46, 100, 229n65; mixture, 92, 101; "purity of", 101, 104n4; *bweseru* (race), 313, 315–17
racial, 8, 25–26, 31, 80–82, 92, 98–100, 266; categories, 81, 108n65; hygienists, 80; defining status, 82; types, 100; racism, 46, 80
Radcliffe-Brown, Reginald, 115–16, 122, 128–29, 130, 133
Raum, Johannes, 122
Ravenna, 31–34, 36–37
Reclus, Elie, 262, 279, 286n84, 286n87
Reims, 341
relatedness, 23, 36, 44, 46, 145, 206, 251, 312–13, 315–16, 331, 334–36, 338, 343, 345–46; biological, 358, 360; feminist concepts of, 278; genetic, 358, 360; lateral, 278
relation, 3, 10–13, 16n6, 23–24, 26, 29, 32, 38, 40–42, 80–83, 85, 87–88, 90–91, 93, 95, 97–98, 100, 102, 105n6, 105n14, 120, 125–26, 128–29, 131, 133, 144–47, 150, 155–60, 162n5, 163n21, 168–70, 174, 178–79, 183, 187–90, 192, 194, 196n2, 196n5, 199n95, 206–7, 209, 211–24, 231n114, 235–37, 239–40, 246–47, 249, 251–52, 255n38, 255n40, 256n52, 257n76, 258n78, 26–64, 266, 271–72, 274, 277–79, 291–94, 298–301, 304–5, 310–15, 318n10, 319n17, 320n44, 324, 330–35, 337–40, 343–45, 348n24, 356–57, 360, 362–64, 367, 371n25, 378–79, 382–84, 387–88, 392, 400, 403; domestic, 2, 172, 247, 386; familial, 44, 167, 169, 170, 172–73, 235, 249, 251, 271, 292, 395n46
relative, 61, 85, 87–88, 94–95, 107n46, 149, 151–55, 157, 159–60, 163n21, 168, 177, 180, 187, 191, 199n91, 200n109, 206, 209–10, 213–16, 220, 222–23, 291–92, 296, 300, 306, 308, 311–12, 326, 329–30, 334, 343, 345, 404, 408, 411; circle of relatives, 151, 331
reproduction, 4, 6, 30, 91, 93, 101, 170, 173, 186, 229n65, 284n53, 357–58, 410; assisted, 358, 361; natural, 358; sexual, 4, 80, 91, 103; commercialization of, 358; reproductive processes, 80, 95; reproductive technologies, 7, 80, 357–59
republic, 54, 170, 235–36, 242–45, 247–48, 250, 388
revolution, 54, 99–100, 125, 169, 170, 196n2, 204, 235–36, 240–41, 244, 247, 254n17, 267, 269, 278, 377–79, 386–87, 395
Rheinberger, Hans-Jörg, 23, 31
Richards, Audrey, 130
Riehl, Wilhelm, 9
right, 3, 7, 13, 24, 63, 117, 119, 121, 124–25, 146, 167–70, 173, 187–88, 195, 198n74, 204–5, 214–15, 219–21, 223–24, 229n73, 238–39, 250, 264–65, 267–68, 270, 275, 277, 285n63, 291, 294, 298, 309–10, 314–15, 321n51, 329, 332, 336, 339, 341, 360, 365–67, 379, 381, 383, 385–86, 390, 400, 404–5; political -s, 170, 268, 387
Rihbald, 325–26, 328–330
Riley, Patrick, 379

Rio, Alice, 331, 348n19
Rivers, William Halse Rivers, 6, 17n15, 82–83, 85, 87–88, 94–96, 101–2
Rochefort, Florence, 270
Romania, 148
Rome, 24, 242, 327; Western, 327
Roth, Guenther, 124
Rousseau, Jean-Jacques, 379–80, 391
Rudolf of Habsburg, king, 62
Russia, 125, 148

S

Sartre, Jean-Paul, 17n19
Scandinavia, 180
Scheidemantel, Heinrich Gottfried, 380, 386, 389–90
Schlegel, August Wilhelm, 402
Schlözer, August Ludwig von, 380, 386, 389, 391–92
Schneider, David Murray, 6, 80, 102, 258n78
Schöpflin, Johann Daniel, 25, 54, 60–62, 64
Schott, Clausdieter, 327
Scott, Joan W., 264, 267
Selassie, Haile, 119
Senegal, 301
service, 157, 167, 194, 242, 308, 317, 325–26, 328–30, 332, 336, 339, 341–43, 349n38
sex, 14, 97, 178, 182–83, 186, 188, 340, 361, 383, 385, 408; female, 176, 354–55, 362; genital, 192; male, 60, 354–55, 362; sexual, 4, 80–81, 91, 102–3, 168, 181–83, 190, 194–95, 247, 275, 301, 334, 338, 340, 372n39, 379, 385; sexual difference, 264–67, 282n16, 291; sexual relation, 331, 338–39
sexes, 175–76, 181–83, 247, 340, 343, 384–85; sexually, 45, 179; sexuality, 14, 178, 194. *See also* heterosexuality
Shimada, Shingo, 404, 406
Shimizu, Akitoshi, 399
sibling, 33, 37, 87, 97, 103, 133, 149, 151, 180, 182, 184, 215, 297, 306, 311, 333, 370n14, 383; siblinghood, 71n12, 148, 277–79, 297; siblingship, 148, 154, 160, 161n4, 240, 286n79
Sicily, 180
Sidney, Algernon, 380–81, 384
Sieyès, Emmanuel Joseph de, 380, 387
Simpson, Audra, 4
Singapore, 390
sister, 33, 54–55, 62, 87–88, 97, 148, 151, 160, 182–84, 262, 277–78, 296–98, 306, 312–13; full, 62; -in-law, 81, 149, 151, 180
slave, 44, 98, 120, 210–11, 239, 248, 269–70, 283n33, 292, 307, 309–11, 313, 320n44, 324, 327–31, 333–34, 337–40, 342–43, 345–46, 350nn39–40; slavery, 170, 246, 256n52, 266, 270, 274, 307–8, 310, 320n37, 320n40, 320n44, 324–31, 344, 348n19; post-Roman slavery/unfreedom, 348n14. *See also* unfreedom
Smith, Michael Garfield, 123
social, the, 264; social, 1, 3, 5, 9, 12, 14, 17n19, 24, 26–27, 29, 59, 68–69, 80, 85, 91, 93, 101–3, 114–15, 120, 122–28, 130–34, 139n103, 167–69, 172–74, 176, 180–81, 183–85, 189–90, 206, 217, 236, 239–40, 244–47, 249–50, 262–63, 265, 267, 269–70, 276, 278–80, 285n59, 299–300, 314–15, 317, 326–31, 334–35, 337–38, 343, 345, 348n19, 355–64, 369n5, 378–81, 383, 389, 392–93, 394n8, 401, 406–7; cohesion (*soziale Bindung*), 130; group, 10, 44, 130, 132, 180, 212, 344, 391; intervention, 123, 195; order, 14, 79–80, 127, 168, 239, 245, 252, 346, 398, 410; organization, 1, 7, 11, 101, 132–33, 251, 279, 299, 301, 304–5, 399, 401–2, 405, 411; regime, 172; relations/relationships, 6, 83, 131, 168–70, 174, 190, 235–37, 246, 263–64, 266, 278, 298–300, 311, 314, 316, 319n17, 320n44, 358, 378, 382, 392; sciences/scientists, 1–3, 14, 27,

131, 145, 147, 155–57, 159–60, 168, 172, 174, 263, 278, 299, 319n17, 377, 399, 401; structure, 116, 119–20, 133, 139n103, 391, 408; theory, 123, 146, 155, 159, 170, 251, 262–63, 265, 278–80, 281n2, 377. *See also* status (social)
socialism, 138n90, 153, 155, 158; utopian, 269, 278
society, 2, 3, 5–9, 12–13, 27, 46, 69–70, 79–80, 85, 95, 122, 127, 146, 158, 160, 168, 172, 174, 181, 183–85, 187, 190–91, 195, 196n2, 200n101, 204, 230n97, 237, 241, 244, 246–47, 250, 252, 255n38, 262–63, 265–66, 270, 278–80, 285n63, 292–93, 297–300, 304, 312, 316, 319n17, 327, 377, 379, 388–92, 398–401, 404, 406, 410, 412n4, 412n6; capitalist, 123; civil, 2, 115, 121, 169, 174, 180, 185–87, 189–91, 383, 388–89, 391, 393; "civilized", 301; colonial, 92, 292; democratic, 117; domestic (*häusliche Gesellschaft*), 389, 391; industrialized, 126; matrilineal, 101; modern, 1, 3–4, 8, 146, 157, 159, 161, 170, 196n2, 262, 267, 279; "nonmodern"/"premodern" 1–2, 12, 170, 262, 267, 279; native, 130; patrilineal, 7, 101; "primitive", 2, 301, 308; segmentary, 10, 26, 114, 304; *société à maison*/house society, 6–7, 11, 36, 120, 135n28; sorting, 361, 371n32; stateless, 115–16, 299, 304; totalitarian state-, 126; traditional, 3–4, 9, 29; tribal, 132; *Gesellschaft*, 400
solidarity, 9, 12, 125, 132, 148
Sonnenfels, Joseph von, 380, 382
Sorel, Georges, 126
South Africa, 147
sovereignty, 169, 204–6, 208, 210–11, 214, 218, 220, 223–24, 226n24, 228n55, 230n92, 379; indivisible, 209, 211, 224
Spain, 46

sperm, 229, 293, 354–56, 359–66, 369n4, 371n23, 371n30, 371n34, 372n38; donation, 355, 357–62; donor records, 173. *See also* seed
Spiegel, John P., 200n101
Spilker, Kristin, 361–62
Spillers, Hortense, 262
spouse, 33, 60, 179–80, 184, 188, 190, 194, 198n85, 306, 313, 411
Stahr, Adolf, 200n109
Stamm, 58, 61, 94, 175, 186
state, 2–5, 8, 9, 12, 14, 26, 115, 119, 121, 124, 126, 134, 148, 155, 160–61, 162n8, 162n15, 167–68, 170, 172–74, 176, 180–81, 185, 188–90, 192, 194–95, 201n114, 205–7, 209–16, 219, 221, 223–24, 227n39, 229n67, 235, 237, 242, 247–48, 250, 256n52, 274, 293–95, 305, 356, 357, 360, 364, 367, 378, 383, 386–90, 392, 402–4, 407, 409, 410, 412; building, 12–13, 226n14; bureaucratic, 175, 181, 186; capitalist, 410; contemporary Western, 2, 150, 173; democratic, 392; early modern, 382; "family state/family nation" (家族国家 *kazoku kokka*), 411; ideologies, 195; modern, 1, 3–4, 14, 204, 206, 399; nation, 161n3, 251, 403–4, 408, 410–11, 413n21, 414n37; natural, 385, 387–89, 391; practices, 293, 356; socialist, 149, 158–59; theories, 378, 380, 384, 395n46; statehood, 120, 123, 247–48; *Staat*, 378, 402. *See also Beamte*
stateless, 3; societies, 115–16, 299, 304–5
status (social), 12, 25, 29, 44, 46, 59, 65, 68, 79, 82, 117, 123, 157, 173, 185, 191–92, 236, 244–45, 309–11, 315, 325–30, 332–36, 338–46, 405, 410; *Stand*, 121
Stein, Karl Freiherr vom, 121
Stieda, Wilhelm, 99
Stieglitz, Christian Ludwig von, 67
Stocking, George, 80
Stonewall, 97
Strasbourg, 60, 207

Strathern, Marilyn, 16n6, 102, 255n38, 281n4, 318n8, 360
Strecker, Edward, 203
structure, 5–6, 8–11, 14, 27, 79, 81, 90, 95, 97, 116–21, 124, 129, 133, 139n103, 168, 175, 186, 192, 195, 210–11, 218, 235, 253, 269, 292, 304–5, 309, 331–32, 335, 348n24, 389–91, 399, 404, 408
succession, 3, 11, 13–14, 24, 46, 93, 95, 107n46, 168–69, 207–8, 215, 218–24, 231n114, 231n119, 231n126, 275, 277–78, 301, 308–10, 383–84; family, 378, 382–83, 392; successor, 11, 61, 65, 208, 220, 222, 226n22 264, 310–11
Sudan, 115, 118–21, 129–30, 134
surrogacy, 14, 263, 358, 364, 370n18, 372n38
Switzerland, 208, 354

T
Tebo, 296, 309, 311
temporality, 9, 24, 315
terminology, 37, 42, 85, 93–94, 125, 147–48, 309
Tishomingo, 97
Tönnies, Ferdinand, 130–31
Torres Straits, 83, 85
Toulouse, 208
Trautmann, Thomas R., 87, 301
tree, 63, 67, 69, 81, 94, 272–73, 280, 284n53; family, 58, 60, 67, 94–95
tribe, 67, 79, 97–101, 103, 116–17, 175; tribal, 25, 85, 98–100, 117, 129, 132, 309, 327. See also *cieng*
Trouillard, Françoise, 209
Turkey, 384
Tut, Koryum, 119–20, 135n24
tyranny, 208, 236, 239, 242, 250, 252, 257n68, 269, 386; domestic, 392

U
Ubl, Karl, 35, 331
uncle, 42, 88, 149, 152, 180, 206, 208, 222, 296, 311, 331

unfree, 44, 188, 293, 303, 307, 309–10, 329–30, 332–41, 343, 348n24, 350n39; *mancipium*, 325, 327, 338; *servus/ancilla*, 325, 327–29, 332, 338–40, 345, 350n40; unfreedom, 168, 178–79, 190, 328, 348n14
union, 81, 92, 102, 124, 170, 173, 178–79, 18–84, 236, 238, 240, 243–48, 250, 252, 387
United States of America, 4
urbanization, 190

V
Valence, 207
Vansina, Jan, 122
Varo, 34
Verdery, Katherine, 157
Vetterleswirtschaft (nepotism), 186
Vierkandt, Alfred, 130–31, 138n90
Virchow, Rudolf, 100
visualization, 14, 17n15, 25
Voilquin, Suzanne, 278

W
Walther, Gottlieb, 57
war, 32, 57, 115–17, 121, 138n90, 151, 162n5, 162n8, 169–70, 174, 197n11, 199n94, 204–5, 207, 209, 215–16, 222, 224, 226n17, 229n86, 245, 274, 294, 378–79, 381, 385–88, 391, 399, 405–9; Cold, 27, 159
wealth, 2, 14, 25, 91, 153, 189, 192, 237, 242, 244–46, 267, 269, 274, 277–78, 299–300
Weber, Max, 114, 121, 123–27, 133–34
Weissenburg, 324–26, 329
Welf (family), 65, 67
Werden, 341
West, 1–3, 7–9, 12, 16n6, 29, 146–47, 149–50, 152–55, 160, 162n21, 163n24, 172–74, 294, 324, 343, 393, 399, 403; non-Western, 5, 8, 12, 157, 169, 172, 192, 264, 392; Western, 1–3, 5, 8, 10, 13, 17n19, 23, 81, 90, 125, 133, 144–45, 147, 150, 152–56, 158–59, 168, 172–73, 180, 192, 249, 294, 300, 356, 377, 392, 401, 403,

406, 408, 412n6; *Westpaket*, 149, 152, 153, 156. *See also* modern
Westermann, Dietrich, 115, 121, 128–30, 138n90
Weston, Kath, 258n78
White, Hayden, 121
wife, 81, 83, 87, 101, 116, 168, 173, 177, 179, 182, 184, 186–88, 192–94, 201n114, 206, 210–13, 227n34, 228n50, 229n67, 237, 268, 297, 339, 342, 385–86, 389, 409–410
Wittich, Claus, 124
Wollstonecraft, Mary, 283n32
woman, 2, 12–13, 98, 151, 168, 170, 177, 181–85, 198n74, 205, 211, 213, 218, 221, 244, 248–49, 263–80, 282n16, 283n27, 284n48, 284n55, 285n63, 285n68, 286n78, 296–98, 304, 314, 318n3, 320n30, 320n34, 328, 334, 338, 354–55, 358–67, 371n30, 372n38, 384–87, 394n8, 402, 405, 408–12; enslaved, 266, 269; proletarian, 170, 269, 274; -'s question, 269; -'s subjugation/subordination, 242, 266, 274, 276
work, 176, 190, 194, 201n114, 266–69, 275–77, 283n28, 341–43; *labor*, 332, 341; productive-creative, 170, 268, 276–77; right to, 267–68
Worms, 35
Württemberg, 186–88, 195, 201n114

X
Xenophon, 210

Y
Yanabu, Akira, 401, 411, 412nn6–7

Z
Zähringer (family), 60–62, 74n46

www.ingramcontent.com/pod-product-compliance
Lightning Source LLC
Chambersburg PA
CBHW051522020426
42333CB00016B/1742